THE ODYSSEY

Also by R. L. Eickhoff

THE ULSTER CYCLE (Translations)
The Raid
The Feast
The Sorrows
The Destruction of the Inn

NOVELS
Return to Ithaca
The Fourth Horseman
Bowie (with Leonard C. Lewis)
Fallon's Wake
The Gombeen Man
A Hand to Execute

NONFICTION
Exiled

THE ODYSSEY

❖ ❖ ❖ ❖ ❖ ❖ ❖ ❖ ❖ ❖ ❖ ❖ ❖ ❖ ❖ ❖

A MODERN TRANSLATION
OF HOMER'S CLASSIC TALE

BY

R. L. EICKHOFF, Ph.D.

A TOM DOHERTY ASSOCIATES BOOK
NEW YORK

A Forge Book
Published by Tom Doherty Associates, LLC
175 Fifth Avenue
New York, NY 10010

www.tor.com

Forge® is a registered trademark of Tom Doherty Associates, LLC.

Library of Congress Cataloging-in-Publication Data

Homer.
  [Odyssey. English]
  The odyssey : a modern translation of Homer's classic tale / by R.L. Eickhoff.—1st ed.
    p. cm.
  "A Tom Doherty Associates book."
  ISBN 0-312-86669-0 (acid-free paper)
    1. Epic poetry, Greek—Translations into English. 2. Odysseus (Greek mythology)—Poetry.
I. Eickhoff, R. L. II. Title.

PA4025.A5 E38 2001
883'.01—dc 21
                                                                    2001041819

First Edition: November 2001

Printed in the United States of America

0 9 8 7 6 5 4 3 2 1

To
Robert Gleason, my editor,
for his brilliant guidance,

and Tom Doherty, my publisher,
for his patience and understanding,

and to both for their friendship.

gratias vobis ago

ACKNOWLEDGMENTS

First of all, I would like to thank my wife, Dianne, for putting up with so much over the past "odyssey" of our own, as I was writing this translation during my lengthy illness.

And I would like to thank Dr. Ron Stroud for his constant and cheerful help in preparing this work and for loaning me his copies of *Ομηρου Οδυσσδια (The Odyssey of Homer),* edited with general and grammatical introduction, commentary, and indexes by W. B. Stanford, Litt.D., vols. I and II., 2 ed. (New York: St. Martin's Press, 1967), from which this translation was prepared. I am grateful, as always, for my agent, Jacques de Spoelberch, whose patient ear was often bent with my whining and whose patient year was interrupted by my constant telephone calls. *Il faut une volonté, une seule volonté.* Merci. Robert Cloud, this book's production editor, deserves many thanks for his queries and painstaking editing.

CONTENTS

CONTENTS

To follow knowledge, like a sinking star,
Beyond the utmost bound of human thought.
—Tennyson

❖ ❖ ❖

My soul, your voyages have been your native land!
—Kazantzakis

❖ ❖ ❖

L'homme n'est ni bon ni méchant,
il naît avec des instincts et des apitudes.

—Balzac

On First Looking into Chapman's Homer

John Keats

Much have I travell'd in the realms of gold;
    And many goodly states and kingdoms seen;
    Round many western islands have I been
Which bards in fealty to Apollo hold.
Oft of one wide expanse had I been told
    That deep-brow'd Homer ruled as his demesne;
    Yet did I never breathe its pure serene
Till I heard Chapman speak out loud and bold:
Then felt I like some watcher of the skies
    When a new planet swims into his ken;
Or like stout Cortez when with eagle eyes
    He star'd at the Pacific—and all his men
Look'd at each other with a wild surmise—
    Silent, upon a peak in Darien.

October 1816

INTRODUCTION

My fascination with Homer's *Odyssey* has filled my life since the summer of 1954 when I read it in the Carnegie Library in Pierre, South Dakota, in between asthma attacks. I remember being enthralled by the descriptions of battles and wars and wondering how it would feel to be away from home for twenty years. Just trying to comprehend what the world would look like in 1974 buffaloed me. This was pre-Sputnik, pre-Internet, and the rapid acceleration in science and changes in culture and society seem now, as I look back, to give complete credence to the chaos theory. That summer was like other summers in the fifties: hot, humid, no air-conditioning; nights spent in the park in front of the band shell listening to Sousa marches, picnics, ball games (although I could seldom play because of my asthma), impromptu music soirées at my grandparents' home across the Missouri River in Fort Pierre, where family members congregated on Saturday nights after the stores closed, and performed songs in a whimsical manner upon a concertina, piano, and guitar. Somehow, I couldn't comprehend that a person could be away from home for twenty years and then return to it. What would it be like? I was filled with romantic awe at the possibilities of the unknown.

We read *The Odyssey* in the sixth grade. That sounds a little odd, today, given that few high school curriculums include the work in its entirety, satisfying themselves with a few snippets culled from the work (if that) in the sophomore year. Somehow, I can't help thinking that education is working its way forward into oblivion. In a few more decades, will our high school seniors have to pass a test on a simplistic canon that substitutes mediocrity for classics? I shudder at the possibility and am grateful to Mrs. Welch, a crabby, blue-haired teacher, who insisted that not only should we understand the *Iliad* and *Odyssey,* but who also introduced us to the Invocation in the original Greek to give us "a taste of what it feels like." We read the rest of the work in a prose translation, but I no longer remember whose translation was used.

I encountered a poetic translation of *The Odyssey* in college and was fascinated. Again, I thrilled to the tale and eagerly read a paperback version of it over and over again, slowly coming to the conclusion that this had to be the second greatest work ever written, taking a backseat only to the Bible. When I went to Vietnam in early 1965, I had three books with me: a Bible (King James version), Kahlil Gibran's *The Prophet,* and Homer's *Odyssey.* I packed those three books all over Vietnam, into Cambodia, Burma, and some places better left unmentioned. I never tired of reading any of the three and slowly came to feel a certain mystical camaraderie with Odysseus. I was married at this time and had been away from my wife and newborn son for nearly a year. While I wasn't exactly lost (although sometimes I wondered, given the archaic French maps we were using that had flat plains where mountains stood and mountains where plains were indicated), I experienced a feeling of being lost. In a certain sense, I was lost culturally and socially, for when I finally managed to return to the United States, I stepped into a world I no longer recognized.

I returned to the university to pursue my studies, and this time stumbled upon a classics course being taught by Dr. Franz Blahak from Heidelberg University. To say that he unlocked doors I thought I had already opened is to understate the impact he had upon me. I was older, I was for all practical purposes a modern Odysseus, and now I found myself eager to step into the world of antiquity. An M.A. came, and then a Ph.D. I had long come to the conclusion that all adventure novels have at their secret hearts a link to Homer. I began to write novels of my own, and then, one day, an offer was made that I couldn't refuse: Would I be willing to make a prose translation of Homer's *Odyssey*? I took a couple of minutes to think it over, then eagerly agreed.

I do not know how it happened, but the deeper I delved into the original, searching out nuances, grasping for meaningful allusions that would not leave modern readers scratching their heads in puzzlement, the more I regained the feeling of kinship with Odysseus that I had discovered thirty-some years before in Vietnam. The romantic in me would like to envision that this revelation came beside a lonely fire, high in the mountains of Southeast Asia. Perhaps it did. I no longer remember the precise moment when I felt Odysseus to be, if not my former life, at least a kindred one. I think it occurred in Laos—that, somehow, seems right—but it could as easily have been anywhere. We did a lot of reading in those days—we didn't have radios or televisions to distract us—even though reading material was scarce and valued greatly. I missed my wife and child, and although no supernatural beings were keeping me away from them, the political gods were, and the more I read, the more I resented not only being in Southeast Asia, but being isolated in places where even maps were vague. I was angry for being taken away from my new family by fanatic politicians to fight a war, then angry at myself for becoming maudlin and reflective, for feeling that I had been singled out for this ordeal by the "gods" that were, and angry again at myself for thinking that way, which I knew was logically unsound.

But I began to realize the depth of the agony that Odysseus might have felt while, at the same time, he must have felt the excitement of the adventures he encountered as he tried to make his way home. I felt the same excitement at various times when thoughts of home were pushed away by the excitement of the moment. Was this, then, part of the human condition that Homer recognized in the warrior? Yes, I concluded, and felt the bond between the ancient warrior and myself grow even stronger.

When I began to translate *The Odyssey,* I experienced the déjà vu of Vietnam again. Dreams that I didn't want came at night, and yet the days seemed to grow boringly longer and longer when I was away from the work. I began to immerse myself in lexicons and grammars, going deeper and deeper into the text, looking for those small idiosyncrasies that would help to define Odysseus and perhaps myself as well. But that fierce quest for knowledge becomes a personal matter and, like most idiosyncrasies of writers, meaningless to his readers.

The Language

Today when we refer to the Greek language of the Homeric period, we are usually thinking of the Attic dialect that was spoken in Athens and its surrounding territory. However, there was no standard Greek language at that time, and all of the city-states had variant forms of speech. Although most of these dialects were mutually intelligible, enough differences existed to provide for confusion in certain situations. Yet the Greeks thought of themselves as speaking a common language. Herodotus considered Greek culture to be based on shared blood, customs, religion, *and* language.

Literary Greek seems to start with Homer, although we don't know whether Homer was a strict adherent of the bards' oral tradition or whether he set down his works in written form. There was a poetic language that was remote from normal conversation, but epic poetry, because of its cultural importance, did provide a common linguistic ground. Yet we cannot even be certain if what we read today as the language of Homer was indeed the language Homer used in the eighth century B.C., since the Alexandrian editors five hundred years later, whose recensions are the earliest "Homeric works" that exist, may have reworked his verse in the Greek idiom of their time.

The Paradox of Translation

There is much to justify a new translation of Homer's *Odyssey,* though some readers might question *if* there is a need for a new one, given the many excellent translations and versions that have preceded this one. A few might be tempted to answer quickly and emphatically, "No!" I beg to differ. Each generation has a need for a new translation of *The Odyssey* since each has a different lexicon reflecting its experiences and representing them by major or minor changes in the meanings, both connotative and denotative, of its vocabulary.

Let us take a pithy example from the history of the word *blackguard,* which, at the time of its inception, was an honorable word designating men who worked in an honorable profession, namely, those who polished the high boots of the king's musketeers. Today, however, that word has an offensive and provocative connotation that has, in some cases, led to blows between two individuals careless with their choice of words.

No, it's clear that there is a need for a new translation, especially now with a new millennium upon us. The question to ask is, what *type* should the translation be? Should one attempt Homer's dactylic hexameter construction for 12,109 lines or abandon verse for a modern prose rendition? That provides a fairly complex situation for debate, one I do not intend to get into here. Suffice it to say that the English language does not lend itself well to dactylic hexameters, and rather than try a stilted approach such as that, I have elected to focus mainly on a modern prose rendition, not only narrating the story but also explaining particular events as they occur in the story itself.

We must remember, however, that the modern reader *is* a modern reader and not a time-transplanted Hellene. Today's reader responds in a far different way to the stimuli of the written word than did Homer's listeners, accustomed to the oral tradition of Greek bards, or the readers unrolling the scrolls of the Alexandrian editors who were the first to put a pen to the story of Odysseus. Indeed, the current problems facing today's reader stem, more than likely, from the attempt of those Alexandrian editors to formalize what Homer *may* have intended to be an adventure story. We have no way of knowing just what his intent was, and speculation is useless, even frivolous, since there will be no consensus by scholars on this point. Even during Homer's time the question was moot, and, later, no less a scholar than Plato argued that Homer should be severely censured for his lackadaisical dealings with the gods. Plato contended that Homer did not pay proper respect to the gods when he portrayed them with values and foibles similar to those of humans. But then, what generation or civilization hasn't portrayed its god or gods in a similar fashion? Even in Christianity we see temper tantrums thrown by a god whose one monumental tirade almost destroys his own creation, and we hear his own admission that he has learned a lesson from this close call, and will never do that again as he places a rainbow in the sky as a

mark of his covenant with man. Consequently, I have decided to do away
with the formulaic interpretation and concept of gods that has marked other
translations and show them as I believe Homer meant them.

Other problems exist as well, from interpreting Homeric epithets to the
very meanings of certain words. For example, let us consider the intended
meaning of Agamemnon in the Eleventh Book when he explains to
Odysseus the manner of his death. Agamemnon says that he was butchered
like swine (one can assume he was bitter about this). A swine is butchered by
having its throat cut. Consequently, one can assume that Agamemnon meant
that his throat was cut which is, if we remember the commentary by Jose-
phus on the deaths of the Jews at Masada, a most humane way of dealing
death. But later, Agamemnon says

τμν κτινε Κλυτθρμνωοτωη δολομητιζ
άήφ έμοι, αυταρ έγώ ποτι γαίηχειρθζ άείρων
βάλλον άψ;θνήσκων περι φαδγάνω (426–28)

which has proved to be a highly controversial passage among scholars.

George Chapman, Homer's first English translator (1615), rendered these
lines as

". . . But that which most I ru'd
Flew from the heavie voice that Priam's seed,
Cassandra,[1] breath'd, whom she that wit doth feed
With banefull crafts, false Clytemnestra, slew,
Close sitting by me; up my hands I threw
From earth to heaven, and tumbling on my sword,
Gave wretched life up—when the most abhord
By all her sexe's shame forsooke the roome,
Nor daind (though then so neare this heavie home)
To shut my lips, or close my broken eies." (554–63)

And Alexander Pope, in 1725, translated them as

"Her breast all gore, with lamentable cries,
The bleeding innocent Cassandra dies!
Then though pale death froze cold in every vein,
My sword I strive to wield, but strive in vain;
Nor did my traitress wife these eyelids close,
Or decently in death my limbs compose.

O woman, woman, when to ill thy mind
Is bent, all hell contains no fouler fiend:
And such was mine! who basely plunged her sword
Through the fond bosom where she reign'd adored!" (528–37)

While E. V. Rieu, in his mid-twentieth-century translation, rendered the
scene in prose:

"Yet the most pitiable thing of all was the cry I heard from Cassan-
dra, daughter of Priam, whom that treacherous schemer
Clytaemnestra murdered at my side. I raised my hands, but then
beat them on the ground, dying, thrust through by a sword."
(421–24)

Robert Fitzgerald translates these lines as Kassandra

". . . piteously crying
as the traitress Klytaimnéstra made to kill her
along with me. I heaved up from the ground
and got my hands around the blade, but she
eluded me, that whore. . . ." (424–28)

and Richmond Lattimore renders them as

". . . and most pitiful was the voice I heard of Priam's
daughter Kassandra, killed by treacherous Klytaimnestra
over me; but I lifted my hands and with them beat on
the ground as I died upon the sword, but the sluttish woman
turned away from me. . . ." (421–25)

while Allen Mandelbaum translates the same passage as

"I heard Cassandra, Priam's daughter, wail
even as—clinging to me—she was killed
by Clytemnéstra, mistress of dark guile.
Face down, along the ground, my chest pierced through,
lifting my fists, dying, I beat the earth,
and my bitch-wife moved off. . . ." (498–510)

and Robert Fagles translates it as

"But the death-shriek of Cassandra, Priam's daughter—
most pitiful thing I heard! My treacherous queen,
Clytemnestra, killed her over my body, yes, and I,
lifting my fists, beat them down on the ground.
dying, dying, writhing around the sword." (476–80)

Each shows a different way of working Homer's passage. Which is correct? Who can tell? Chapman even has Agamemnon dying on his own sword! Some have Agamemnon claim he was killed like a swine while others have him killed like an ox. The differences are probably negligible and only academic squabbling. The fact remains that Agamemnon was killed by his wife and her lover, as was Cassandra.

I elected the following:

"But the most terrible of all was the cry I heard from Cassandra, Priam's daughter, murdered by my treacherous wife, that whore Clytemnestra. I threw up my hands, trying to help her, but another sword stroke felled me, and that bitch laughed to see me lying there, taunting with her naked body, her breasts and white belly splattered with my blood, while my soul seeped from me and began its journey to Hades. . . ."

The difficulty lies in determining what action Homer was trying to convey to his listeners. If we consider the original word for word (and even in *that* we have a problem), we can literally translate: "but I, lying upon (against?) the ground, lifted my hands / and threw (drew? closed?) them [while dying?] around the sword blade [while dying]."

We could assume that βάλλον άψ;θνήσκων περι φαδγάνω refers to "dying with the sword blade in my body" or "dying around the sword blade," which is contrary to the method usually used to kill swine. (In the case of Chapman, who has Agamemnon falling upon his own sword blade, we can only suppose that Chapman was recalling the incident of Ajax from *The Iliad*.) The question then becomes why Agamemnon is throwing up his hands. We could assume that Agamemnon is trying to block another sword stroke, trying to aid his concubine Cassandra (my interpretation), or literally beating his hands on the ground. A severe stomach wound would explain the latter behavior, as individuals who suffer such a wound often react in this manner—although usually the limbs beating against the ground are the legs. Perhaps Agamemnon is simply trying to retaliate against Clytemnestra or, in the reflexive act of a dying man, trying to wrench the sword from his stomach.

Which translation or interpretation one elects depends on the dramatic sense one takes toward the scene described, and that depends on the dramatic view one has in regard to the character of Agamemnon. Is Agamemnon to be seen as a hero? A male chauvinist? A man caught up in his own pain? There is even the possibility of interpreting Agamemnon as a vain and arrogant man being brought low by his wife in retaliation for bringing home his "whore" or for having sacrificed his daughter Iphegenia ten years previously to propitiate the gods and so enable the Greek fleet to sail to Troy.

Consequently, a translation depends not only on the literal (if that is indeed possible) definition of words but on one's sense of dramatic unity as well. A translator has to be fluent in the language in which he is working and also must have a solid grounding in the historical events of that period, the customs and attitudes of the people involved (insofar as they can be determined), a dramatic vision, and a "feel" for the reason of the work itself. Working with ancient texts is more difficult than translating modern works as the translator doesn't have the convenience of the "now" to fall back on in order to verify an interpretation. We know that the language of Homer is not a language that anyone spoke. It is an artificial language, poetic though it may be, filled with archaisms, incongruities, and idioms that are difficult if not impossible to explain. The interpreter or translator must be aware of this as he must also be aware of the time between Homer and the present. One cannot entirely isolate time in that respect. There was Homer's time, there is our time, and there is time in between the two that weathers our understanding of Homer.

Ultimately, we must consider the poet himself. What type of individual was Homer? What was his reason for writing *The Odyssey* in the first place? Was it to create epic literature? I doubt it. We must keep in mind that although writers may have a high purpose or vision in mind, their ideals are tempered by function. In short, the work must be supportive to the writer in addition to carrying his vision. Although all writers would like to be dramatically pure, they must also eat. Therefore, there must be a practical side to their work. Was Homer different from today's writers in this respect? Perhaps. He may have had a patron or two who supported him and provided the opportunity to create "great literature." But even patrons like to have egos stroked. Perhaps this is one reason why so many lineages are given in Homer's works. We can almost imagine Homer inserting into his poem the lineage of his patron of the moment to stroke that ego and enjoy that patronage a bit longer. Although some may look askance at this hypothesis and claim that it would have compromised his creation, it is highly possible (even probable) that Homer did practice this form of flattery. Yet we can't be sure since we simply do not know the circumstances under which *The Odyssey* was written.

Several of my peers have accused me of being irreverent in my approach to the ancient gods and goddesses, most notably Athene. In the first place, we must try to realize how the ancient Greeks viewed their gods and goddesses. Yes, they were a part of the religious doctrine of the day, but exactly what was that religious doctrine? We must be very careful not to confuse the ancient Greek attitude toward religion with our own. In short, the degree of reverence, or even the *type* of reverence, that was paid to the Olympians by the ancient Greeks is not simply an early version of our own attitude(s) toward our god(s). Indeed, we can see the problem in modern times, if we consider the Christian god and the attitudes of various sects toward Him (or Her, for that matter). The Baptists take a totally different line from the Methodists, who take a totally different line from the Catholics. So how is God to be observed? Let us take a similar approach to the ancient Greek gods. How was Ares seen by Athenians, and how did their concept of the war god compare to that of the Spartans? How was Achilles viewed in comparison to Odysseus by the Athenians as compared to the Spartans, or to the Macedonians during the time of Alexander the Great, who admired Achilles more than he did Odysseus? (An interesting anecdote here: Perhaps Alexander, a bisexual like many Greeks of that time, knew the verse fragment by Aeschylus that suggests Achilles and Patroclus were lovers.) We must also remember that the Spartans had far more admiration for Hercules than did the Athenians, who viewed Theseus in a far more favorable light. Even within one Greek city-state, Athens, for example, we can see a great difference in schools of thought between Aristotle and Plato regarding the worth of Homer and his works. Which, therefore, is accurate? And how were the gods and goddesses viewed? Was Athene such an icon of reverence that she did not have "feet of clay"? Even her origin is questionable since her traditional epithet, *Tritogeneia,* a word of unknown meaning, suggests that Athene was born beside a lake or stream, instead of being hewn from Zeus's head with an ax blow by Hephaestus. Is she the goddess of wisdom or the goddess of cunning intelligence, and which did Homer mean when he composed his work? And how is Athene's name "Pallas" to be explained? Did she take it from the giant Pallas whom she slew in the battle between the Giants and the gods? Or did she take it in remorse after accidentally killing a playmate called "Pallas"? Or is "Pallas" the appellation of the warrior goddess in Mycenaean times who was Athene's predecessor? This last explanation might have some likelihood since the presumed date of the Trojan war falls in the thirteenth century B.C. at the end of the Mycenaean age.

Debate on these subjects is endless and topical, depending on the whim of the times. Frankly, I have my doubts that the ancient Greeks saw their gods and goddesses as theosophic icons above reproach; rather, I think they saw their Olympians as extensions of themselves, sharing the values and foibles that the Greeks knew from their everyday experiences. Evidence abounds to support this interpretation, from the petty tirades of Poseidon, who hated Odysseus, to Ares's vainglorious boasting and bullying ways. Who can forget the war god's blubbering and bawling when he is wounded by Diomedes in *The Iliad* or Zeus's comment that he "hates" (detests?) Ares but will cure him of his hurt because Ares is his son? In fact, one must remember that the whole *Iliad* and *Odyssey* hinge on nothing more than a beauty pageant among three vain goddesses—Hera, Athene, and Aphrodite—vying for the title of most beautiful among the gods.

Above all, we must not become too engrossed in academic argument and must not forget that Homer's epic is one man's interpretation of a time long past, made accessible to modern readers by another man (the translator). In the end, I believe that we must look at *The Odyssey* as a romance and adventure tale that offers readers a window through which they can look into the past and understand an ancient world.

The Religion

The Greeks were not familiar with the concept of religion as a set of beliefs and practices espoused by adherents until late antiquity, when some thinkers, under pressure from Christianity, sought to formulate age-old traditions. In the classical period, Greek religion appears to have been more a public ritual than an individual devotion, but during the Homeric period, religious practices were deeply rooted in the daily life of the community, or *polis,* which formed the most conspicuous aspect of the city-states. The polis organized its identity around a common ground of deities and cults, and the Greek pantheon supplied recognizable figures—Zeus, Demeter, and Hermes, for example—for worship. Their stories were known throughout the Greek world, but a city-state might single out one god or goddess for special worship when the deity had played a role in founding or protecting the city, as Athens did with Athene.

These early cultic practices seem to have been formed around the concept of animal sacrifice, although the exact significance of the need for this is unclear. The sacrifice probably related both to human-divine relations and to the bonding of the community that shared in the sacrificial meal following the ritual offering of the animal to the deity being honored.

The anthropomorphizing of the gods as we see in Homer indicates that the boundaries of divine individuality can be altered in context and circumstances, depending on group interpretation. But we again must try and explain the rationale for the relationship between Odysseus and Athene. The picture of Athene in *The Odyssey* is an individual interpretation of a goddess by Odysseus—although we are constantly reminded of the presence of Homer even in the syntax of Odysseus. We must remember, however, that we are looking at Odysseus's picture of Athene not only through the first-person narration of Odysseus, but through the interpretation of Homer in regard to how he perceived Odysseus's relationship with Athene. Inevitably, however, we always come back to the realization that the gods and the goddesses were generally seen as superhuman beings and not aesthetic manifestations of thought and air. The interpretations of the gods and goddesses were often personifications of philosophical ideas and the reasons for natural forces that were not explainable through scientific inquiry at the time. Thunder and lightning, for example, were not understood by the ancients except as manifestations by superhuman individuals or gods.

The soul, or *psyche*, is what leaves the body at death, but it is also a shade or a recognizable being. The concept of the transmigrational being was really not a part of the Homeric period but rather came much later, as is seen in the writings of Plato.

THE PARADOX OF ATHENE

Probably no other member of the Greek pantheon is as complex an individual as the goddess Athene. In *The Iliad* 5.73–77, Homer describes how Athene strips off the finely wrought robe "which she had woven with her own hands" and dresses herself for war. This suggests that Athene is not only skilled in the weaving of cloth but also fearless in battle, uniting in her person the two major characteristics of the sexes: the traditional view of woman maintaining the home and the traditional view of man as a warrior.

As the patron of crafts, however, she symbolizes the womanly arts as well as carpentry and metalworking, those crafts that were generally held to be male professions. At Athens, she shared a temple and a festival with Hephaestus, the smith god, and is seen on vases seated in full armor. Myths celebrate her love of battle, which is epitomized as well in those cults that celebrated Athene Victory (as Nike) in which statuary shows her poised with one leg advanced, wearing on her breast the terrible *aegis* that threw terror into the hearts of all who opposed her.

Although the traditional tale of Athene's birth has her leaping from Zeus's head fully armored after Zeus, complaining of a headache, has Hephaestus take a bronze ax and cleave his head open, the epithet *Tritogeneia* at times attached to her name suggests she was born beside a lake or stream called Trito or Tritonis, or that she was raised by the sea god Triton.

She is closely associated with the masculine world in her role as a helper of male heroes. This is apparent throughout *The Odyssey* as she befriends Odysseus, in other tales where she helps Hercules, and in *The Iliad* when she befriends Diomedes. Although her virginity provides a metaphoric bridge between the two sides of her nature, she was highly desirable sexually, attracting the males in tales such as the one where Hephaestus tries to rape her. The goddess narrowly avoids this, and the seed of Hephaestus fertilizes the ground, giving birth to Erichthonius.

Although the owl, which symbolizes wisdom, is her symbol, she is also the goddess of "cunning intelligence," which endears Odysseus to her. Consequently, she represents intelligence, wisdom, and strategy.

The Question of Death

The Greek attitude toward Hades, the god of the Underworld, is best summed up by Achilles in *The Odyssey:*

> "I would rather be the most common slave in the fields for some landless peasant than rule these lifeless dead as their king." (XI: 489–91)

The dead are pathetic in their helplessness and seem to be deprived of their wits (*phrenes*) as they flit around drafty halls, giving out little batlike squeaks. The judges of the dead seem to think that once an individual is dead, all sense leaves the body/spirit as well, reducing them almost to senseless children, doomed to wander pathetically until given basic direction. Yet the precise relationship between the dead and the living is unclear. If a body is not buried with the appropriate rites, it appears that the living as well as the dead are insulted. A belief in a dualistic afterlife, however, seems to be absent from the Greek eschatology.

Although there appears to be a popular and continuous belief in the Halls of Hades as a place for the dead, other concepts of the afterlife are indicated in legends, such as a person's likeness being transformed into a constellation, the body/soul/spirit being etherized, and, to certain initiates, a life in the Mysteries of Eleusis.

AGRICULTURE

Greek life was generally sustained by barley and wheat planted in the fall to take advantage of the rainy season. Hulled barley (two- and six-row) and hulled wheat (*emmer* and *einkorn*) were introduced to the region during the Neolithic period. Other strains, including tetraploid, durum wheat, and hexaploid bread wheat, came later. Crops were cultivated with a crude wooden plow that was, on occasion, tipped with iron (especially in the stony regions such as Ithaca). But this rare use of iron occurred only in areas where the soil was fertile enough to grow food to support not only a family but the oxen needed to pull the plow as well.

Other crops included broad beans, olives, grapes, and vegetables. Fruits, notably apricots, apples, figs, and pears, were grown in orchards in extremely fertile areas where the farmland was more plentiful. Potatoes, tomatoes, and most citrus fruits (with the exception of oranges) were not available in antiquity.

THE GREEK DIET

The ancient diet relied primarily on cereals and grains, legumes (field beans, peas, chickpeas, lentils, lupines), oil, and wine. Wheat and barley were the staple food and were eaten in porridge and bread. Athenaeus describes many different breads and cakes, but even the cakes of antiquity were much coarser than the modern diner would find palatable, having a consistency of sand due to the grain being rough ground.

Olive oil was the main source of fats. Butter was not popular and was considered to be barbarous, as was the drinking of beer. Milk was used primarily for making cheese. Wine was the preferred drink and was usually sweetened with honey for young children.

Fish also was a mainstay of the diet and was eaten fresh, dried, or pickled, but the absence of large expanses of continental shelf limited the fisherman's catch to those species that were readily obtained close to shore. Lobster and crab were not common items in the Greek diet.

Red meat was a luxury and usually limited to major feasts. Pork was a staple, as was poultry. But the ordinary people usually lived on vegetables such as onions, garlic, turnips, radishes, lettuce, artichokes, cabbages, leeks, celery, and cucumber. The rude behavior of Penelope's suitors is highlighted by their daily diet of meat that results in the slaughter of the animals of Odysseus.

THE PROBLEM OF WINE

The best Greek wines came, in order of quality, from Cos, Chios, Thasos, Lesbos, and Rhodes, where they were allowed to age three to four years. (The Romans believed that the best wines came from vines that grew on trees, a horticultural practice that they may have copied, like much of their civilization, from the Greeks.) However, the fermentation process was never stopped. The must was usually cut with seawater to improve its smoothness and to give it "life," although some hosts cut their wine with fresh water. The reason for using seawater is not clear; perhaps the saltwater reduced the wine's acidity, or it may have honored Poseidon.

The ancient Greeks were probably not aware of the connection between drinking in excess and alcoholism, but they were well aware of wine drinkers' propensity toward self-destruction. They considered it uncivilized or an act of drunkenness to drink wine that had not been heavily diluted with water. On the island of Thasos, according to Jean Pouilloux's *Recherches sur l'histoire et les cultes de Thasos* (1954), laws were even passed governing the drinking of wine.

In *The Odyssey,* Homer notes that wine causes great problems for those who do not use it in moderation. Elpenor informs Odysseus in the Eleventh Book that immoderate drinking brought about his death, when in a drunken stupor he rolled off Circe's roof and broke his neck. Here and elsewhere allegations of intemperance were used to draw attention to an individual's weakness. Abstainers, however, were rare in ancient Greece despite Athenaeus's near deification of water drinkers in *The Deipnosophistae*.

THE HOMES

Private houses opened onto one or more sides of a rectangular courtyard, as did a doorway that led through a passageway to the street. Windows were few and small (presumably to discourage thieves), and the living areas of the house were not visible from the street. Stairways were not common, and upper stories were generally reached by ladders (except in the homes of the wealthy). The walls were of a mud-brick composition over stone socles, while the interior walls were usually plastered and painted red or white. The floors were mostly beaten earth. Cooking took place on simple hearths or on portable braziers that could be carried from room to room as the situation warranted.

There was usually one elaborate room to receive guests (predominately for men), which would be paved and filled with dining couches. The portion of the room closest to the door would be decorated with pebble mosaics. Although most literature traditionally locates the women's rooms in the upper stories, this cannot be ascertained through architectural studies. Scholars now believe that the entire house was probably the woman's domain apart from the room maintained for male visitors.

MARRIAGE

Marriage in Greece was a transfer in which the *kyrios* (lord) of a woman, usually her father, gave her away to another man for the procreation of children. This was usually a private agreement, although laws did exist regulating marriage in order to provide a definition for legitimacy.

In Athens, a marriage was legal only if it began with a formal statement by the father (or his representative) granting the woman to a husband. The woman's own consent was not legally required. She could not, however, be married to a direct ascendant or descendant, nor to her brother or half-brother by the same mother (although marriage to a half-brother by the same father or to an uncle or a cousin was permitted). Bigamy was not allowed, although a man could have a concubine if he wished. A man could divorce his wife by sending her back to her father.

Usually, marriage was accompanied by gifts, but in Homer's time they tended to be gifts from the husband to the father.

THE PROBLEM OF ADULTERY

A law in Athens generally attributed to Draco allowed a man to kill another if he discovered that man in sexual congress with his wife, mother, sister, daughter, or concubine. This was considered justifiable homicide. Generally speaking, one assumes as well that there was also a *graphē* (judgment) that could be brought against adulterers, or that they could even be brought before the eleven "judges" for trial and execution.

Adulterous wives *had* to be divorced and, because of their adultery, were excluded from all public sacrifices—an ostracism that had profound impact within the religious world of the time. In the case of unmarried women, the law provided a kyrios the right to sell his daughters or sisters into slavery if they were discovered not to be virgins. Of course, this was extremely rare, and husbands generally preferred to not to press charges against their wives to avoid public dishonor. In some cases, the situation was settled out of court with the adulterers paying reparations (and, one presumes, their honor) in order to avoid public humiliation.

THE WOMEN IN *THE ODYSSEY*

Although the Greek philosopher Aristotle wrote in his *Poetics* in the fourth century B.C. his version of *The Odyssey* plot—"A certain man has been abroad many years; he is alone, and the god Poseidon keeps a hostile eye on him. At home the situation is that suitors for his wife's hand are draining his resources and plotting to kill his son. Then, after suffering storm and ship-wreck, he comes home, makes himself known, attacks the suitors: he sur-vives and they are destroyed"—there is much more to the tale, of course, than that simple dismissal. We are aware, however, that Plato, too, summar-ily dismissed Homer's work, claiming that the story should be banned as Odysseus's habit of lying and using trickery and cunning to succeed would teach the youth of Athens that it was acceptable to lie. Besides, Plato was per-turbed at Homer's casual treatment of the gods, for the poet gave them human qualities that Plato thought sacrilegious. Yet the Greeks saw their gods as being "larger than life" extensions and manifestations of themselves. They too could lie, hate, steal, cheat, as well as love, procreate, play politics— exhibiting every trait that man has but on a grander scale.

True, *The Odyssey* explores man's affirmation of the heroic code, but it is the presence of the women in the story that elevates the epic from a mere adventure tale of posturing men thumping hairy chests in macho rivalry. The women in *The Odyssey* give the story hope and a sense of the possibility of peace, although some of the women, notably Scylla, Charybdis, and the wife of the Laestrygonian king, present us with horrid monsters that cannot be defeated through arms and man. They represent women in man's night-mares, the fear that he may be devoured by women, passivity suddenly become demonic. When Odysseus encounters these monsters, he is hard pressed to escape with his life. To make his escape, he must finally realize the place of women within his world.

Both Paris and Odysseus must undergo an initiation into the world of woman before entering into a stately sense of well-being and peace. Paris has his peace before the Trojan War and suffers, of course, when the Greeks manage to invade his homeland, signifying that although he had peace, he was not complete. Odysseus undergoes the same trial when he returns home and finds the suitors have invaded his home. The difference between the two is the difference between those who are beloved of the gods and those who aren't. Odysseus is "better regarded" than Paris, for he is capable of trickery. Even Odysseus's name suggests that he was the "victim of enmity" (Greek *odyssesthai:* "to hate" or "to be angry").

The fact that Hera and Athene oppose Paris indicates the triumph of mother love and wisdom over sensual love. The love between Paris and Helen is an *imitation* of the manifold aspects of love, whereas Odysseus and Penelope's love embodies all of the four aspects. That is, Paris and Helen embody only that love symbolized by lust and wifely love combined. There is no wisdom to it, no motherly love. The love between Penelope and Odysseus, however, is a combination of the four loves: lust (suggested by the anger Odysseus demonstrates when he thinks someone has tampered with the secret of his bed), wisdom (demonstrated by the "tricks" Odysseus plays upon Circe and by the "trick" Penelope plays upon the suitors with her weaving), maternal love (demonstrated by Odysseus's yearning for home when Calypso holds him captive and by Penelope's entreaties to Telemachus), and wifely love (shown by the determination of Odysseus to reach home and Penelope's determination to remain faithful to him until he does *and* by the combined trickery inherent in the challenge of Odysseus's bow to the suitors and the husband and wifely bedding after Odysseus has eliminated the suitors).

Odysseus must undergo several challenges not only to atone for angering the gods with his enormous pride, but also to demonstrate that he has matured from the warrior who left Ithaca ten years before to wage war at Troy. Although Odysseus knows all there is to know about warfare, he understands little about love. Consequently, his voyage is not only a search for home, but a voyage of awareness, a rite of passage, in which he discovers the deep power of love. It is love that keeps Penelope true to him all the years that he is away; it is love that causes some of the problems of Odysseus as well. For our purposes here, let us consider love as being divided into four categories: philia, storge, eros, and agape.

Philia is that great love in friendship between two individuals who are equal or as nearly equal as time and station allow. We can also see that love as the happiest and most fully human of all loves. Aristotle classified philia among the virtues he considered most needed by man, and no less a person than Cicero wrote a book on what he called *Amicitia,* but philia has taken on less importance over the years, as it is not needed for procreation and does not depend upon a biological uniting of two individuals. We can live and breed without friendship, but friendship is a valuable asset to man. For a modern example, we could cite that love, based on close intellectual ties between Alfred Tennyson and Arthur Hallam, that was immortalized in Tennyson's poem, *In Memoriam.*

We can see philia embodied in the figure of Arete, who convinces her husband, Alcinous, the king of the Phaeacians, to befriend Odysseus and give him a ship to reach his home despite a warning that the king's constant assistance to strangers will one day bring Poseidon's wrath upon his people—a threat that becomes reality when the ship that takes Odysseus to his home is turned into a rock upon reentering the Phaeacian harbor, thus blocking it from future use.

It is philia that proves to be most important to Odysseus, for it is the love he has for members of his crew that keeps them from open mutiny (we regard the bag of winds episode as a momentary lapse only), and it is that love that keeps Athene fighting for Odysseus in the councils of the gods when Poseidon wants to destroy Odysseus for having blinded Poseidon's son Polyphemous.

Athene represents the thoughtful virgin who does not have to resort to sexuality in order to maintain an equal position in the company of men. She is not, however, above utilizing men's susceptibility to women as sexual objects, as knowing how to get around men is also a part of her cunning. The fact that she sprang from Zeus's head fully armed, signifying that she was born ready to participate vigorously in a man's world, indicates that she is by far the most significant of the goddesses. The point here is that she leaps from a *man's* mind, which suggests that although she does represent wisdom, it is a cognate and didactic wisdom that is built upon man's principles and awareness. Consequently, Athene represents philia in *The Odyssey.*

Storge is that love which is mainly affection—the love parents have for their children or the love Hera demonstrates as the matriarch of the family, the mother. She is a bit cranky in *The Iliad,* as she is being put aside by men much as the goddess was treated as the abomination in Canaan. When man suddenly takes an interest in his surroundings, in the earth, the female goddess is pushed aside. Yet she is also seen as the goddess who is needed early in life, the one who possesses the mystery of life. Of all the goddesses, she is the one who is most difficult for man to understand. Part of the reason for Hera's anger is that she sees herself being put aside by man in favor of "the pretty face" represented by Aphrodite. This shunting off of the mother goddess in favor of momentary sexual gratification is a sign of the weakness within man. There is sexuality within philios, but it is a comforting sexuality that comes from friendship as well as lust. We could almost see it as a "marriage debt," in that it is the discharging of the husbandly and wifely duty to engage in sexual relations. Yet this love does not depend solely upon sexual gratification. This love goes much deeper in that it also embodies the family, for the sexual love predicated within philios is that sexual love which is not simple gratification (although that is certainly implied within the sexual act) but is also the desire to build and maintain a family.

The abomination of Canaan is also seen as the Rapture of the Cannanites. Here the love of the goddess is needed to propagate the species. Earth as the bountiful mother, the plowing and seeding of the fields as the sexual act, the reaping of the fields representing the birth of a child, are metaphors needed to ensure the continuance of life.

Other women in *The Odyssey* represent aspects of storge as well, most notably Nausicaa, who represents the innocence of youth, a daughterly innocence, a virtuous innocence. Although in the *Naustoids* we are aware of her attachment to Odysseus, it is the attachment of a young girl who mistakes physical attachment and love for the love for a father. Her mother, Arete, demonstrates matronly awareness of this love by advising her husband to give Odysseus the means to make his voyage home. We could make a case for including another mother, Clytemnestra, as she is angry at Agamemnon's sacrifice of their daughter Iphigenia. But it is her anger also that drives her away from her husband and into the embrace of Aegisthus, making Clytemnestra more a figure of eros than storge.

Calypso, on the other hand, does fit this category, because it is her great love for Odysseus that drives her to help Odysseus prepare a raft to sail away from her island to his home. In addition to the gentle shoving of Zeus, who demands that she "give up" Odysseus, Calypso knows that she cannot ever have the "whole man" and, sadly, lets him go.

Eros is the easiest of all loves to explain and see in *The Odyssey*, as sexuality is the primary function of this love. The sexual experience can occur without eros, but eros cannot operate without sexuality. Although eros is sometimes merely the state of "being in love," it is sexual attraction that initiates eros. Among the women in *The Odyssey*, that sexual attraction is best seen in Aphrodite, who represents woman as sexual desire, that love which is physical in nature.

Eros, that soaring and iridescent love which reduces thought to minor consideration, is typified by Circe, who tries to keep Odysseus and his men prisoners on her island. When Circe transforms Odysseus's men into swine and places them in a pigsty, we are reminded of the swinish behavior of men who regard women merely as sexual objects. This action is paralleled by what is happening to Penelope, who does not have the sorcery of Circe and must depend upon her wits to keep the suitors at a distance. Circe also uses charm to keep Odysseus on her island, but she lacks the innocence of Penelope, who represents the whole woman—wife, mother, lover, worthy opponent. Circe may hold Odysseus for a short while with her sexual allure, but that is not enough to detain the warrior/husband/father from his voyage to Ithaca and home.

Circe is perhaps the most unusual woman/goddess that Odysseus comes in contact with on his voyage. It is Circe who punishes man for his role in eros, suggesting that woman can be a creature who exacts vengeance on man for his thoughtless actions and for the lust that drives him to see women only as passive beings to satisfy his desires. Circe is the witch-whore, that woman who is an extension of Aphrodite, but that woman who is not intrigued by men. Instead, she is the manipulator, the one who uses men for her own whims, then discards them when she is finished. Love to Circe is only a game, but it is a game that Odysseus must learn how to play, and he must learn how to emerge from the contest as the victor instead of the victim. Fortunately, in a gesture of comradery, Hermes, at the urging of Zeus, delivers a secret herb to Odysseus (*moly*) and information on how Odysseus can win Circe over to his cause. Although she represents lustful love, lust proves to be Circe's undoing, for she temporarily wins the love of Odysseus, but loses him to the memory of Penelope.

Eros in its negative aspect is that love which may constitute mindless desire, adultery, betrayal, and desertion. In Homer's *Iliad,* Briseis is the object of mindless desire. She is the "blonde," who brings about the downfall of men in *The Iliad,* which is not so much a psychological portrait of Achilles despite what Homer tells us in his introduction. No, *The Iliad* is primarily a story about who gets the blonde. We can see Clytemnestra in this negative role as she engages in adulterous loves as revenge while Agamemnon is away in the Trojan War. We can also see Helen in this negative role in Homer's *Iliad*—but we cannot see Penelope in this role.

It is *agape,* spiritual love, that Odysseus needs the most. It is this love, perhaps, that is most indicative of his feelings for Penelope. Yet we note the disdain of Odysseus for the gods other than Athene, a disdain that is most evident in the scene where he taunts Polyphemus after blinding him, taunting both the son of Poseidon and the god of the oceans himself. Indeed, there are many other examples in *The Odyssey* where Odysseus dismisses the gods. Although he does make sacrifices, those sacrifices suggest a social obligation rather than a need to beseech the gods. His sacrifices are made for the benefit of his men, not for himself. Odysseus in modern times might be that shop-keeper who makes a point of being seen in church on Sundays because it is good for business.

The concept of spiritual love, however, is not relegated only to the gods. Arete's compassion is also spiritual, and Odysseus is made aware of this before entering the palace of Alcinous when he is told to approach Arete first instead of her husband. The suggestion here is that Arete's compassion is more of a governing force in Alcinous's household than the ruler himself. Although she is a minor character in the story, it is her compassion (agape), demonstrated by her entreaty to her husband, that provides Odysseus with a ship to take him on the final leg of his voyage to Ithaca.

There are other women who aid Odysseus through agape, such as Ino, the sea-nymph who gives Odysseus her girdle to protect him in the raging seas stirred up by Poseidon, and Eurycleia, who nursed Odysseus as a boy and helps him in his final battle to rid his home of the unwanted suitors.

Of all the women in *The Odyssey,* the most important is Penelope, who represents all the loves, philia, storge, eros, and agape. She is the perfect woman and is what man dreams of in a woman: the witch-mother-whore-goddess, or the one who is capable of being all things to man. It is she who faithfully keeps the hearth while Odysseus is away, who rejects the suitors when they come clamoring for her hand, who raises Telemachus, and yet she is the one who greets Odysseus with love and affection (eros and philia and agape combined) when he returns home. Odysseus is not only her husband but her mortal god as well, and she does not waver in paying her devotion to his memory, although she does, on occasion, express her frustration at being kept to a barren marriage bed for twenty years.

Here, then, is one of the problems that Odysseus must overcome before he arrives home: He must return a better man than when he left. Although we would like to see him return home with the riches he earned while away at war, when he does reappear at his palace in Ithaca, it is only as a beggar in a beggar's rags, signifying that all he has to bring to Penelope is himself and his love. He has lost everything in the sea, and it is only through the good graces of Alcinous that he does not arrive empty-handed. But Odysseus is forced to hide those riches in a cave before he makes the last lap of his journey, thus signifying that wealth must remain secondary to love.

The Judgment of Paris:
The Beginning of *The Odyssey*

A number of classical texts relate the legendary events that began when Paris awarded the golden apple to Aphrodite and ran off with Helen, which led to the Trojan War and the wanderings of Odysseus.

Odysseus is mooning about Calypso's island and bemoaning the fate that has marooned him there, when we first encounter him in Homer's *Odyssey*. Poseidon is preventing him from returning home to Ithaca because Odysseus has angered the sea god by his presumption and pride. In fact, Poseidon would have destroyed the Greek hero long before had not Athene cleverly interceded on his behalf. Yet it is not simply a set of random circumstances that has resulted in the wanderings of Odysseus. Rather, a series of events was set in motion by what was probably the world's first beauty contest, which took place at a party thrown by Zeus and Hera. The story goes as follows:

One day, Zeus and Hera decide that they will entertain the gods and goddesses of Olympus and issue a grand invitation to all, with the exception of Eris, the goddess of discord. We can understand this, for Eris is one of those quarrelsome wenches whose acid tongues drip constant vituperation. So Zeus and Hera neglect to send her an invitation.

Unfortunately, Eris learns about the party, and when her invitation doesn't arrive, a great feeling of bitterness creeps over her. She bides her time, and when the party is in full swing, she collects a beautiful golden apple and attaches a message to it—"For the Fairest of Them All"—and tosses it into the middle of the party.

Immediately each goddess lays claim to the golden apple, and a great furor develops among them. Eventually, however, the contest comes down to three goddesses—Athene, Hera, and Aphrodite—who each claim to be the most beautiful of all. Unable to resolve the matter, the goddesses turn to the gods, demanding that they decide who deserves the golden apple. The gods, however, did not become gods by being stupid, so they refuse the goddesses. When the three turn to Zeus, he wisely tells them to decide for themselves. Zeus is married to Hera and wishes to keep his home life untroubled. We can imagine the tempest that would rage on Olympus if Zeus proclaimed either Aphrodite or Athene more beautiful than Hera.

"Now, what do we do?" asks Hera.

Aphrodite simpers and tosses her golden mane back from her forehead. "Well, I don't know what the fuss is all about. Surely *everyone* is aware that I am the most beautiful."

"Humph," scoffs Athene. "Your beauty is only temporal while mine is forever."

A tiny frown pricks its way between Aphrodite's eyes. "My beauty temporary? I have been around far longer than you, warrior maiden, and my beauty is still more than enough to make men weak in their knees."

"Stuff and nonsense!" scoffs Athene. "What are you but a bit of a tumble in a meadow, a dalliance along a rose-scented path, a quick slap-and-tickle in the stable?" Aphrodite's eyes narrow, but Athene ignores her. "I, on the other hand, offer wisdom—"

"And I," interrupts Hera, eyes glinting dangerously, "offer peace and contentment that can come only from a good family life."

"Would that were true," sighs Zeus, whose notorious roving eye has made him the recipient of many of Hera's barbs over the years.

"What's that? What's that?" says Hera, looking sternly at her husband.

"Nothing, nothing," he says hastily, then pretends to examine a callus on the bottom of his foot.

"Hmm. Something, I think, but we'll get to that later." Zeus sighs and rolls his eyes as she turns back to the others. "And as for you"—she looks sternly at Athene and Aphrodite—"it's obvious that the golden apple was meant for me."

"A disputable point," says Athene loftily. "If a man has knowledge, why, then he will select the right mate for himself and earn a happy life with his wisdom."

"And what would that life be without love?" Aphrodite puts in.

"Carnality does not mean happiness," Hera says crossly.

"Well," Athene says, musingly, "it's obvious that we're getting nowhere here. Someone who is not one of us is going to have to decide."

Aphrodite, meanwhile, bored with the bantering of the other two, has been staring down on earth at a handsome, golden-haired youth sprawled under an olive tree. She knows him well—Paris, Priam's son, who is renowned for his skill in lovemaking. Countless women have gazed upon (or enjoyed) his beauty, their hearts pitter-pattering hard enough to cause an ache behind the breastbone.

"What are you staring at?" Athene asks.

"Me? Oh, nothing," Aphrodite answers coyly.

Athene comes up to her shoulder and looks down, seeing that the love goddess has been studying the manly form of Paris. "Not bad," she says grudgingly, "but I don't sense much between the ears."

"I'm not interested in what is between the *ears*," Aphrodite says pointedly, smirking.

"Now, that's enough of that," enjoins Hera, who has joined them. "Why don't we let him decide?"

The other two exchange glances and give a nod. The goddesses disappear in a wink and a whistle and suddenly reappear in front of the youth who is resting from a night of overindulgence in rich resin wine.

"Well, what have we here?" Paris asks on the goddesses' sudden appearance. He brightens at their beauty and sits up, wincing from a sudden stab of pain behind his eyes. "Ahem. Well. And where do you three come from?"

"Enough," Hera says snappishly. She waves a white hand at the other two. "We have decided to let you choose which of us is the most beautiful. Select carefully. You will be rewarded for your decision."

Paris's eyes dart among the three, noticing the perfection of their figures, the way their breasts mold to their chitons, the regal jut of chin, the locks flowing over their shoulders in careful curls. And then strange thoughts begin nudging at his mind.

Yes, you will be rewarded if you choose wisely. I am Athene, the goddess of wisdom. Choose me and I will give you the wisdom of the world.

Choose me, and I will give you the best woman for a wife, wise children, and a friendly hearth to warm you. I am Hera, the protector of the family.

But if you choose me, I will give you the most beautiful woman in the world for your wife. I am Aphrodite, the love goddess.

Paris rubs his forehead as the thoughts crowd in, one upon the other. He sighs and stares at the three goddesses. His eyes linger on Aphrodite as she leans forward to give him a look at her breasts. He swallows hard, feeling his lust come upon him. He points a finger at her and says, "You. I pick you."

A clap of thunder resounds, and his eyes burn from the rapid departure of the other two. Aphrodite laughs and pats her hair. "Jealous trollops," she says. She smiles seductively at Paris. "Thank you, Paris. You shall have my gift."

She blows him a kiss and gently departs. He stares at the empty space where just now the three lovely apparitions stood. He rubs his eyes. "I've gotta cut back," he mutters to himself. But he remembers the promise of Aphrodite and hopes that it will come true.

Now, the problem is that the most beautiful of mortal women is Helen, the wife of Menelaus, the king of Sparta. Legend tells us that when Helen was twelve years old, word of her beauty spread far and wide. Legions of heroes began showing up on her doorstep, clamoring to wed her. Tyndareus, her mortal father (Zeus was her immortal father with Leda, which made Clytemnestra her sister and . . . but we can go on and on in the matter and get nowhere), worried that those he rejected would cause trouble for him. One day he was wringing his hands in despair when Helen approached him, asking what the problem was. (Another legend claims it was Odysseus who gave Tyndareus the answer to his predicament.)

"Woe, oh, woe!" he cried, tugging hard at his hair. "If I choose one, the others will kill me for not choosing them." He glared bitterly at Helen. "Why couldn't you be born as ugly as a crone?"

"Because the gods decided otherwise," the minx said, tossing her golden curls over her shoulders. "But if choosing a husband for me distresses you so, why then, let me choose."

"Might as well be hung for a sheep as a goat," he muttered. "Go ahead."

The next day, Helen, dressed in a diaphanous chiton that revealed her charms to all, appeared in front of the assembled kings and heroes. She paused for a moment to let all there enjoy the sight of her, then told them that her father had decided to let her make the choice of a husband. "But," she added, "I will only choose from among those who agree to befriend the one I select. As for the rest of you"—she shrugged—"why, I will not consider you among my choices."

A brief flurry of bantering words met her announcement, but Helen remained firm in her resolve and every hero reluctantly agreed to her demands.

"Good," the wily vixen said, simpering. "Now, for my choice." She carefully studied each one, then pointed to Menelaus, the king of Sparta, saying, "You shall be my husband."

The others left, disappointed at not being chosen, but they remained true to their word, and although tempers occasionally flared among themselves, they carefully refrained from bringing Menelaus into the fray.

One day Paris was moping around Priam's palace at Troy, complaining bitterly about having nothing to do. Exasperated, Priam told his son to put together a ship for a trading voyage along the Greek coast. Paris was reluctant to leave the palace, but the king's order could not be disobeyed and Paris soon left on his voyage, much to the relief of several husbands at court who suspected him of playing fly in the butter churn.

Eventually, Paris came to the court of Menelaus and, dressing himself in his finery, paid a call on the palace. Menelaus greeted him with open arms.

"Welcome, my boy! Welcome!" he cried, coming forth to greet Paris. "I trust your voyage has gone well?"

"As well as can be expected," Paris said, stifling a yawn. Then he froze, staring open-mouthed as Helen appeared at the head of the stairs. Menelaus turned to see what had drawn his attention. Then he beamed.

"Ah, my wife! Come, my dear, let me introduce you to Paris, newly arrived from Troy."

At that moment, Aphrodite, remembering her promise to Paris, turned to her precocious son Eros, and ordered him to shoot golden arrows into the hearts of Helen and Paris so they would fall in love with each other.

"What? Absolutely not!" he said. "She is already married to Menelaus, and one of the laws of hospitality is, thou shalt not diddle thy host's wife! If I make them fall in love with each other, Zeus will banish me to the land of Hades. There's no slap-and-tickle among those shades! No!"

"If you don't," Aphrodite said edgily, "I will tell your wife, Psyche, I saw you dallying with Artemis's Nymphs in a forest pool. I might even tell Artemis!"

Eros glared at his mother, then sighed and, taking his bow, carefully sent golden shafts into the hearts of Helen and Paris. Instantly, they fell in love. But they also knew the impossibility of enjoying that love, and so, as the days passed, they grew more and more unhappy.

One day, while they were walking along the beach, Paris lamented their situation.

"Helen," he said, "I don't know what to do. You love me and I love you but"—he gestured helplessly—"you're married to Menelaus."

At that moment, Helen looked up and saw Paris's boat pulled up to the beach. His men were casting lots on the beach beside its prow. The glimmer of an idea came to her.

"Paris," she said slowly, "I have an idea. Why don't you throw me over your shoulder and run for your ship, and your men will row, row, row. We'll be safely away before Menelaus finds out we are missing. After all, he has been called away to Crete to arrange the funeral for his grandfather Catreus."

Now, Athene had pegged Paris correctly when she questioned his intelligence. "Helen," he said, "I know you mean well, and I love you deeply, but you're married to Menelaus—"

"Paris," she said patiently, "why don't you throw me over your shoulder, run for your ship, and have your men row, row, row us to your homeland? We'll be away before Menelaus knows we're missing."

But Paris shook his head, saying, "Helen, you know I love you, but—awk!" He squawked as Helen seized his ear, twisting it.

"Paris," she snarled, "why don't you throw me over your shoulder—"

"Hey!" Paris yelped. "I have an idea! I'll throw you over my shoulder and run for my ship, and my men will row, row, row, and we'll be safely away before Menelaus even knows we are gone."

"Why didn't I think of that?" Helen muttered as Paris put action to his words.

Menelaus was very angry when he discovered that Paris had left with Helen. He took the matter up with his brother Agamemnon, king of Mycenae, the most powerful of the Greek kings.

"Well," Agamemnon said, "there's nothing for it but to fetch her home." He put out a call to all those who had promised to befriend Menelaus, and soon a thousand ships lay anchored in the harbor ready to sail to Troy. But the wind was against them and they could not set sail. Agamemnon called a council of the heroes and kings.

"Why have the gods forsaken us?" Agamemnon asked the others.

"Well," Calchas said (he was a bit of a prophet), "I can tell you, but you have to promise to protect me."

"Speak," Agamemnon said. "You are under my protection."

"All right," Calchas said, making himself comfortable. "Well, it seems that you have offended Artemis and Poseidon. Artemis, because you bragged once that you were a better hunter than she; Poseidon, because you forgot to sacrifice a bull to him before the voyage."

"A bull?" Agamemnon said, brightening. "That's easy. I have a lot of bulls in my herds." He made to summon a servant, but Calchas held up his hand.

"No, too late for that. Now you must make a supreme sacrifice to appease both. You must sacrifice a virgin."

"A virgin?" Agamemnon said, exasperated. "Now, where am I going to find a virgin. You know how it is when you have an army ready to go to war and such. Besides, in this day of free love and all—wait a minute! I have an idea! My daughter Iphigenia!"

And so Agamemnon sent word to Clytemnestra, his wife, to prepare Iphigenia to be married. He said proudly that he had arranged the marriage of the century to none other than Achilles, who was the dream of all maidens.

Clytemnestra was ecstatic at the news and quickly dressed Iphigenia in her best garments and jewels and rushed her down to the harbor before the mercurial Achilles could change his mind.

"I don't know how you did it," she exclaimed to her husband as she brought their daughter to him.

"I didn't," Agamemnon said. He gestured, and warriors rushed forward, seized Iphigenia, and took her to the waiting altar and sacrificed her. The winds changed and the fleet sailed away for Troy.

However, the Trojans stubbornly refused to return Helen to her husband. After ten years of fighting, the Greeks were ready to give up when Athene gave Odysseus a plan by which he tricked the Trojans into hauling a huge wooden horse within the thick walls of their city. The Trojans, believing the war was finally over, held a huge celebration that lasted until the wee small hours of the morning. Then, while everyone was sleeping off the effects of the party, Odysseus and his hand-picked men crept out from the belly of the horse and threw open the city gates. The Greek army entered the city and ravaged it. In the fighting, however, Aias raped Cassandra in front of Athene's statue while the Trojan princess clung to it for sanctuary. To avenge herself, Athene sent a storm to scatter and sink the Greek ships as they were trying to sail for home, but Odysseus's ships were spared.

Eventually, Odysseus landed on the island of the Cyclopes, where he blinded Polyphemus, who happened to be the son of Poseidon. Angry, Poseidon said that Odysseus would never reach home, and so Odysseus was forced to wander the seas, searching for Ithaca and his home, where Penelope waited patiently for him.

Thus begins *The Odyssey*.

THE ODYSSEY

THE FIRST BOOK

The Council of the Gods

❖ ❖ ❖ ❖ ❖ ❖ ❖ ❖ ❖ ❖ ❖

The Invocation to the Muse, greeting
Her and the gods' meeting.
Athene ordered to start Odysseus
Homeward and the visit
Of the goddess to Telemachus.

❖ ❖ ❖ ❖ ❖ ❖ ❖ ❖ ❖ ❖ ❖

Sing, Muse,[1] of that wanderer who sundered
The sacred walls of Troy and traveled
Many sea-lanes while struggling for his
Life and his men's return. His men, who
In their folly slew and consumed the holy
Cattle of the Sun, Hyperion,[2] who
Therefore spurned their journey home.
Now, Muse, begin the tale of that man
Of many masquerades. Sing to us how he,
Bereft of hearth and home, pined for his wife
In hallowed Calypso's cave, the divine Nymph,
Eager him to wed and bed, but when
The circling seasons ran their wheel, they spun
The thread for his return to Ithaca.
Yet the gods determined that he would not
Find his peace at home until all the gods
Took pity upon him. At last all did,
Save Poseidon, who grimly blocked the noble
Wanderer until the man of masquerades
Finally reached his native land, there to
Find grim designs waiting for his return.

1–24*

*All line references are to the Greek text in the W. B. Stanford edition.

Sing, Muse, of that man of men and tell me
The story of the man whose own wisdom
And trickery wounded him and caused him
To languish far from the loving arms of
His wife. Sing to me the story of that
Wanderer who sacked Troy and sundered her
Heaven-built walls, only to be forced to roam
Uncharted seas and visit strange lands
Where he faced many grueling trials.
Sing to me of his great adventures among nations
Of all manners, minds, fashions, and traditions.
Sing to me of a man, abandoned by the gods
After his men slew the sun god's sacred cattle,
Who still proves himself worthy of song and story.
Sing, O Muse, of him in his glory. How after ten
Long years at Troy trying to storm the many-
Towered city of Ilium, the gods
Denied Odysseus³ return passage
Home to his loving wife while other
Comrades were led to safe haven where
They sleep free from the horror of war and
The sea. Tell me how the Nymph Calypso,
Yearning for his love, trapped him by magic
In her caves, making him her lord and spouse.
Sing, Muse, why Poseidon, the god of the sea—
Despite destiny—blocks his passage home.
Explain why Poseidon spurned Zeus's council
Determining Odysseus's fate and
Sped to Ethiopia at the end
Of the earth, feasting at his festival
While the other gods obeyed the summons
Of mighty Zeus. Let us listen to Zeus's words:

25-52 "Vain, petulant men! Yes, that's what they are! All of them! Look at them playing their games, misusing their freedom, and blaming their sins on wicked fate. Fate! And blaming us for their crimes! I tell you that I will not tolerate these floundering fools for long! Look! Look there! Do you see what I mean? Adulterous Aegisthus making love to Agamemnon's wife and scheming that king's slaughter!⁴ Listen to the cry of Agamemnon, 'Oh, I am killed by a mortal blow!' Why does man sin knowing he will suffer? I even sent Hermes (who slaughtered Argus—but enough of that waggling tale) to Aegisthus before he struck the mortal blow, telling him to beware of desecrating the marriage bed. Yet he ignored my warning. Orestes, the son of Agamemnon, wreaks vengeance on Aegisthus now. Blood war ensues! Oh, these mortal fools! Oh! My head, my head!" moaned Zeus, rubbing the heels of his hands hard against his temples.

Athene rose, her graceful form and azure eyes drawing covetous glances from the others, and said, "Now, Father, son of the Titan Cronus,[5] king of kings, the well of power upon the earth—"

"Yes, yes. Out with it," Zeus growled, glowering from beneath heavily beetled brows. "Nuts and nails! I know you! Wandering words where one will do! Speak!"

"All right." Athene drew herself up, her bold beauty hammering pulses. She shrugged. "All right. Aegisthus is fate past. Nothing can be done, and Agamemnon's land is a blood ground. So be it! Why wail over its fate? The die is cast: Aegisthus deserves his death. But my heart aches for Odysseus's sorrows. Why should he suffer because proud Poseidon pouts, refusing to lift his yoke and forgive Odysseus for the innocent insult he flung at the sea god? Now Odysseus suffers in Calypso's arms,[6] daughter of Atlas,[7] upon her sylvan island, where she has entrapped him with sorcery and beauty—"

"Aye, we should all suffer such pains!" one god broke in. The others roared in mirth while Athene cast a disapproving eye upon the author of the ribald jest.

"Now," she said softly, "Calypso's wizard father, the author of many jests *53–79* himself, shoulders the colossal columns that separate heaven and earth." The offender averted his eyes, reddened, gulping nectar to conceal his chagrin. "Yes, great Odysseus languishes on a rocky isle amid the thunder of great Poseidon's roaring waves. A lesser man—thrall to Calypso's charms—would be content, but Odysseus remembers his chimney smoke, the bleat of his sheep, and the warmth of Penelope's arms.[8] For seven years Calypso has sought to soothe his troubled mind, vanquish memory, and smother in his breast all thoughts of Ithaca. For seven years he is lost to hearth and home because he has angered one of us. Yet many times in Troy he honored you, Father, with burnt sacrifices. Still, he is denied Ithaca."

The cloud-trembler glowered, but she boldly stared him down. He sighed and said, "All right. What words fly so boldly from your lips! Pale daughter, how can I not recall Odysseus? No more resourceful man treads the earth or has so enriched the Immortals enthroned on high. His gifts are vast, but remember he is bold. It is he who stole the Cyclops's glaring eye. This same Polyphemus, I might add, who is the son of Poseidon from the sea Nymph

Thoosa, daughter to the sea king Phorcys, who lay with Poseidon in his hollow caves and bore this wheel-eyed Cyclops to the god of storms. This is why Poseidon torments the great Odysseus. But"—he raised his hands, stifling Athene's lips—"let us reason and seek to ease the torment of Odysseus since no one god can prevail against a man despite his vaunted powers."

80–110   The gray-eyed maid laughed and cried, "Father and adored king! Let all who reside on Olympus make the wandering Greek their public care and succor his misery. Let Hermes carry our message to the golden-tressed Nymph on Ogygia that it is our will that she no longer hold him fast. I will travel to Ithaca and seek out his son who, despite his green, unpracticed years, shows spirit—although he is hot-blooded and headstrong when caution should work its way through his words. I will advise him to assemble Ithaca's Greeks and denounce his mother's suitors who devour their sheep and oxen and desire her for their pride." She gave a short, ugly laugh. "The suitors will, of course, like foxes whose noses are filled with a vixen's scent, scorn the words of Telemachus.[9] I will counsel him to sail to Sparta and to Pylos to gather news of his wandering father. His search for his father far from Ithaca will draw its people to him. This I will do! You do your part!"[10]

And she placed her glittering golden sandals upon her alabaster feet, those sandals fledged with ambrosial plumes with which she flies like the wind, and wielding her army-slaughtering spear, she soared from the halls of Olympus to the rocky shores of Ithaca. There, close at Odysseus's gates, she shape-shifted her lovely form into the lumpy muscled form of Anchialus's son Mentes, the king of Taphia. She leaned upon her spear, disdaining the suitors lounging on oxhides. They slew those beasts before the gates, diced, drank, roared, and laughed. Serving wenches moved about them, sponging tables, dodging the drunken hands that groped for their breasts and buttocks.

111–136   Amid all this sat Telemachus, scorning their drunkenness. His heart ached for his father's return to scourge these beasts from his palace door. Now, in his mind, he imagines that violent return of Odysseus and hears the thunder of heaven. But in the middle of his daydreams, he sees Athene, disguised, standing alone at the gate and, rising, hastens to her.

"I beg your pardon," he said hastily. "Whoever you are, please forgive this . . . this . . ." He cast about him for words and at a loss shook his head. "Enter. Please. You are most welcome. Join our feasting and tell us why you have come to my home."

Saying so, he took her spear and placed it against a column where stood many of Odysseus's spears, dusty with disuse. He led her to a richly embroidered seat far from the boasting suitors. Placing a footstool for her feet, he signaled a maidservant to bring them water in a gorgeous golden pitcher. He took the pitcher from the maidservant and filled a silver basin for her to wash her hands. Another servant brought fresh bread and clear wine for them, and the meat carver sliced the meat free from fat and placed it on a platter before them.[11]

Some of the rude suitors saw how this newcomer was being treated and sauntered over to take their places on rough-hewn oaken benches near to them, sprawled, legs akimbo, and eyed the newcomer blearily while dribbling wine through gnarled and twisted beards.   *137–165*

With a gesture of distaste, Telemachus motioned for them to be served too, and serving wenches swinging saucy hips hastily brought in baskets filled with coarse-ground bread and set them before the bold wooers, who quickly stuffed their mouths with rich and greasy meat, wiping their hands and fingers on soiled tunics.

"Bring more wine!" one bawled drunkenly and closed one eye in an obscene wink. "And bring in the girls and let us have a bit of wiggle and giggle, eh, boys? What do you say?"

Shouts of agreement followed his words, and a servant brought a harp finely tuned and thrust it into the hands of Phemius. Reluctantly, the famed singer touched his fingers lightly to the warbling wires and began to sing.

"Blustering braggarts!" Telemachus growled, then quickly apologized to Athene. "Forgive me. That was most unmannerly. I am afraid that I have behaved most boorishly." He could not help but cast a disapproving eye at the revels beginning before them. "But I hope that you will not be offended by these . . . others," he finished lamely. "I'm afraid that singing comes cheaply enough for those who do not have to pay the harpist. They forget that this feast has been paid for by one whose white bones lie wasting in some unknown land. And," he muttered beneath his breath, "if he were here, he would put their fat buttocks to flight sorely enough." Then, raising his voice and forcing a smile to his young lips, he said, "But enough of my troubles. Please tell me where you are from and what brings you to Ithaca. Are you a stranger to my father's house or have you been here before?" Then a thought dabbed at him. His eyes narrowed. "You are not a would-be contender for my mother's hand, are you?"

Athene smiled and dabbled her fingers daintily in the silver finger bowl   *166–193*
placed before her and carefully cleaned them with a white damask cloth. "I am Mentes, son of Anchialus, king of the Taphians. I have come with my ship and men across the wine-dark seas on a voyage bound for Temesa with a cargo of iron I wish to trade for copper. My ship rests at anchor in the harbor of Rheithron under Neius's wooded slopes. Our fathers were friends, as

old Laertes, your grandfather, will tell you if you should seek him out. But I understand he seldom comes to town these days, preferring to live by himself in the country with only an old woman to care for him when he comes in from the day's heat after pottering around in his vineyard. I came because I was told your father had returned home, but"—she looked around the hall with contempt—"I can see that was only the scuttlebutt of wayward rowers more limber with tongue than hands. Mind"—she raised her hands warningly—"I am no prophet, but I have heard from the tongues of those who are that he languishes in some wood somewhere, bearing the inflictions of the gods. I thought he might have made his way here, but he has not. That doesn't mean he won't. No iron fetters have been forged that could keep him away! Mark my words upon that, my young friend! Patience! Patience!"

194-222   Telemachus blinked away bright tears and said, "I thank you for your words, Mentes. But I wonder about my father and think that he must be dead, or else why has he not returned?"

"Stuff and nonsense!" Athene said hotly. "Dead? Your father?" She frowned. "You are Telemachus, the son of Odysseus, correct?"

"Yes," Telemachus sighed. "So my mother tells me. I am the son of that star-crossed man."

"Well, then," Athene beamed and clapped him on the shoulder so heartily that he caught himself upon the edge of the table to keep from landing face first in the meat sauce. "Fear not your line's demise while Penelope has a fine lad like you, what? Now, what"—she gestured disdainfully at the drunken disorder about them—"is this chaos about? Hm? Do you celebrate some feast? A wedding in the family? A banquet? No one seems to have brought any food of his own. Most unseemly even for the poorest of guests. And"— she leaned close to the ear of Telemachus—"I must say that they behave like pigs."

223-249   Telemachus sighed and shook his head. "Ah, well! I am afraid, sir, that bad times have fallen upon us. The gods in their displeasure have hidden my father from us, and so these . . . these 'fellows' have come to woo my mother into believing he is dead and to accept one of them in his place. I almost wish my father had fallen gloriously upon the field of Troy, for then the Greeks would have built a mound over his ashes and I would have inherited his fame. But the storm winds have blown that away from me, and now I inherit nothing but shame and this drunken revelry. If this wasn't enough, the gods have caused me further grief and headache with my father's absence, for all the chiefs of our islands—Dulichium, Samos, and the forested island of Zacynthus—along with certain headmen from Ithaca itself are eating up our flocks and herds while pretending to court my mother."

"And your mother?" Athene asked delicately. Telemachus shrugged and spread his hands in dismay.

"What can she do? She does not offer her hand. Night after night these suitors take what they will. Soon I'm afraid, there will be nothing left. And then"—he shrugged—"I'm afraid they will kill me as well."

Athene sighed and shook her head, sipping from her wine. "I can see that   *250–276* you do need your father about. Give Odysseus a helmet, sword, spear, and shield, and he'd quickly set these oafs on their ears, mark my words! I remember when I saw him in our house. He was coming from Ephyra where he had traveled to visit Ilus, son of the Centaur Mermerus,[12] to learn the art of poison for his arrows. Ilus wouldn't give him any because he feared the wrath of the gods—even then, we knew he had angered the gods somehow, Odysseus, I mean—but my father liked Odysseus and gave him some poison to help him out in his troubles. Now, if Odysseus is half the man he was then, the dust would quickly fly from the heels of these would-be wooers." She sighed again. "But such is in the hands of the gods." She pursed her lips and smiled at Telemachus. "A word of advice, my young friend! Call a council tomorrow and lay your case before them. Tell this rabble to shake the dust from your threshold and be away. Then tell your mother that if she is thinking about marrying again, to go back to her royal father who will attend to all the proprieties and find her a worthy gentleman with rich gifts to sustain her.

"After you have done this, take a good ship and trusty men with you and   *277–305* travel first to Pylos where your father's friend Nestor rules and then to Sparta where golden-haired Menelaus, the last to sail away from the shores of Troy, rules. See if any of them has any word of your father. If you hear he is dead, then return home here and prepare the proper funeral games and feast and erect a mighty tomb in his memory—it doesn't matter if it harbors only dust and not his bones; it is the thought that counts." She leaned closer, seeking his ear and whispering gently into it. "Then—and only then, mark you!—make your plans—foul or fair, it doesn't matter, these rogues haven't earned any better—how to rid your house of this vermin. You are old enough to be done with the sniveling and whining of youth. Why, haven't you heard how the people are singing the praises of Orestes who, fired with revenge, killed his father's murderer, Aegisthus? You have a finely muscled and finely balanced frame. Could you do no less than Orestes? But"—she winked solemnly and held a forefinger in caution against her lips—"mind what I say. Mum's the word until you make the plan right."

Telemachus smiled and said, "Thank you for your advice, my friend. I   *306–333* can sense the heart of a friend in your speech, and I can see the soundness of your words. Now, let me call my manservant and have your bath prepared, and while you bathe, I shall select a present for you in gratitude—a keepsake, if you will, of the sort that one friend would give to another."

Athene shook her head. "Don't keep me from my trip. As for any present you would wish to give me, why, keep it until I return this way again. I will accept it then and bear it home with me at that time. I will do likewise and leave you with one as worthy as the gift you would have selected for me."

And like a lark mounting to the sky, she flew away, leaving Telemachus to ponder her words. Strengthened and emboldened, he considered his father's life and courage. After which his thoughts returned to his guest, and he stood, amazed, wondering if it had not been one of the gods who had traveled from Olympus to bring him the courage to do what needed to be done.

He strode bravely to where Phemius was still singing his sad tale of Odysseus's return from Troy. His song traveled up the stairs to the room of Penelope who, hearing the sweet trilling of his voice, descended the stairs winding to the courtyard, attended by only two handmaidens. And when the queen entered and stood by a column, holding a veil across her face and weeping bitter tears, all grew silent, waiting for her words.

334–363 "Phemius," she cried, "you have a great many stories about the deeds of the gods and men. Stop this sad song and sing a tale of arms and men. I don't need to be reminded about my wandering husband even though his fame has spread throughout Greece and Argos."

Inspired by her bold words, Telemachus said, "Mother, let the poet sing what he wishes, for he isn't responsible for the song. Music is conjured by mighty Zeus who imparts it to men to make them sad. This man means us no harm by singing of the Danaans' ill-fated return. It's the latest of many, and everyone wants to hear the latest song. It's only human, you know."

"But—" Penelope began, but her son interrupted her.

"But, nothing. Odysseus isn't the only one who didn't return home. Many another wife and mother cries over her losses as well. Go back to your room and your loom and other business. Making speeches is the job for men, and I number among them. Go, now, for I am master here and have a thing or two to say to these jackals."

She stood for a moment, wondering at her son's sudden spirit, then turned soundlessly and slipped like a shade back into the house and into her room where she cried and wept her loneliness until Athene took pity upon her and dusted her eyelids with the sands of sleep.

364–387 "Ah, now!" cried one suitor drunkenly. "Let one of us come with you and comfort you in your bed. Gods' balls, but we can make you forget your husband. Our spear is as stiff as his!"

Laughter followed his words. Telemachus turned slowly to the feasters and stared until their laughter broke into hiccoughs and chuckles, then spoke, saying, "You drunken scum! It's a rare thing to hear a voice as sweet as Phemius has, and I wouldn't deny you this. So enjoy it for the rest of the night. But in the morning, when the rosy fingers of Dawn[13] flicker from the east, be awake and in full assembly, for I intend to give you formal notice at that time to leave my house immediately. You bear yourselves too proudly to suit me. If you wish to continue your feasting, then do it at somebody else's house, not mine. If you refuse this warning of mine, I'll add your name to my list, and then you will suffer all that your pride brings upon you."

The revelers bit their lips to keep from smiling at the youth's rash words (although some did secretly admire the fire in them), then Antinous, the son of Eupeithes, cried out, "Telemachus! The gods have given you courage, I see. You speak most bravely, although I think there is a bit of cream to your words. May Zeus never give you the throne of Ithaca as he did your father!"

Telemachus eyed him coolly, then answered, "Antinous, don't be offended when I say that I will be king here, god willing, and it would be no shame to be a king as my father before me. Is that the worst you can wish upon me? If so, your words are written upon water and not the pages of time. Mark me well, loudmouth! I will be king in my own house and will rule those chosen for me to rule."

388–414

"Ah, now, Telemachus! What are these words?" asked Eurymachus, the son of Polybus. "Don't don the garland before it is draped around you. Only Zeus can decide if you are to be the king here. You may be master in your house and of your possessions. None of us will take them from you. Now, where is this stranger who walked among us? Did he bring word of your father that makes you speak so bravely now?" He chuckled wickedly at his taunt, and others near him snickered in reply.

"My father," Telemachus said slowly, "is dead and gone, and should rude fame send a flattering messenger with words of his safe return, I wouldn't give a fig for them. Sometimes my mother sends for a prophet, and I listen to his stories with half an ear, for I no longer believe in divine reckoning. As for the stranger who was among us, he was Mentes, son of Anchialus, king of the Taphians, an old friend of my father." But, he added silently to himself, also the goddess his father held most highly.

The suitors laughed at his words, commented rudely, gestured obscenely, and returned to their drinking and their brawling. Slapping the serving wenches upon their saucy hips, they pawed their full breasts bouncing bountifully beneath their loose blouses. And when they had drunk enough, they staggered off to their own homes and their own beds.

415–440

Telemachus slowly climbed the stairs to his own room high in the tower facing the inner courtyard, thinking weighty thoughts over the words of Antinous and Eurymachus. Eurycleia, daughter of Ops, the son of Peisenor, an old woman who had nursed him through his youth, went before him, bearing a blazing torch in each hand to light the way. Laertes had bought her when she was young, paying twenty oxen for her rare beauty, although he did not bed her, out of respect for his wife.

441-444   Telemachus opened the door to his room and sat upon the bed to remove his sandals and tunic. He handed the tunic to her, and she folded it carefully for him and placed it over a beam pin near the bed. She left, pulling the door to with a silver catch, and drew the iron bolt firmly home. Long after her footsteps had faded upon the stairs, Telemachus lay, covered by a blanket of woolen fleece, thinking about his voyage and the counsel that Athene had designed for him.

Here ends the First Book of Homer's **Odyssey.**

THE SECOND BOOK

The Council of the Ithacan Elders

❖ ❖ ❖ ❖ ❖ ❖ ❖ ❖ ❖ ❖ ❖

Telemachus complains to the elders
About the behavior of the suitors.
He borrows a ship to secretly
Travel to Pylos across the sea.

❖ ❖ ❖ ❖ ❖ ❖ ❖ ❖ ❖ ❖ ❖

When Dawn's pink fingers peeped shyly on the eastern sky   1–30
And politely plucked the eyelids of Telemachus,
Odysseus's son blinked sleep from his eyes, and
Rose and quickly dressed, transversing the shoulder strap
Of his sharp sword across his broad chest, and
Bent to the rawhide sandals around his shapely feet.
Then he took olive oil from a goat sack and
Rubbed it through his hair until it gleamed as black
As a raven's wing in early sunlight, before stepping across
The threshold and into the Great Hall of Odysseus.
Two swift dogs slipped down at his heels and followed
The young man with a god's brilliance upon him.
He found the clarion-voiced criers and ordered them
To bring the unshorn and unwashed Greeks to him
In full assembly, and obediently the criers sang out
His demands and the wondering men filled
The great assembly grounds where Telemachus waited,
Spear in hand, the swift hounds at his feet.
And then Athene washed him with golden sunlight,
And the multitude fell quiet and gave way
As the youth made his way to his father's chair.

A low mumbling followed his brave action, for none would have dared to sit in Odysseus's seat in the council room while the mighty warrior lived.

"I don't believe it," muttered one of the ancients under his breath. He hawked and turned to spit but noticed the youth's steady eyes upon him and swallowed instead. His gnarled fingers combed their way through his tangled beard, wincing as stubborn knots refused to unravel. "Does this mean what I think it does?"

"I don't know," his friend answered. He pretended to hack, hiding his lips behind his hand. "But I think we are going to discover thorns in his words now." He motioned over to where a few of the suitors for Penelope's fair hand lazed on stone benches, sipping wine to dispel the fog from the previous night's tippling. "I think we'll have an accounting of their actions now. And high time, I says. Had himself been here, they would have been sent packing a long time ago, tails between their legs and haunches smarting from a well-earned kick."

"The laws of Zeus," the other murmured quietly. "The laws of hospitality, now. Let's not be forgetting them. Remember Tantalus?[1] One has to be careful how one abuses his obligations."

The other snorted in derision and hawked again and spat, forgetting himself in his indignation. "Damn me if I can see how the gods would punish a man for kicking the loafers and recreants out of his house. Look at the bloated boasters! Tunics spotted with wine and grease! To Hades with them! They are behaving in a foul manner, eating the fat goats and sheep from the herds of Odysseus and drinking the rich wines from his cellar as if they were already the chatelain in bed with Penelope, the chatelaine, and chatting up the bold-breasted chattels in their chambers! They go too far, I tell you! Too far!"

"Hush," the other said, alarmed at the other's angry words. "You'll have a knife to your throat if you're not careful. And mine, too, for all your prattle. Enough! Listen! Aegyptius speaks."

They turned to watch the humpbacked figure step forward, trembling fingers grasping for the speaker's rod held by Peisenor, the herald. All deferred to the aged one whose words and wiles—wise in the ways of life— had spared many a catastrophe. All remembered his son, Antiphus, the lance—the good and faithful companion of Odysseus—who had sailed in the hollow ships to Ilium,[2] where many fine horses grazed in thick, green pastures, and guarded his king's back many times in the ten-year battle before the walls of Troy, twice keeping swords from falling on his defenseless back during the sacking of that mighty city, only to fall in the cave of the cruel cannibal Cyclops who chose him for his final feast.

Ever since word came from the sea traders about the fate of Antiphus, Aegyptius had donned black, grieving greatly his great loss.[3] Three other sons had been spawned by that wise sire—two who plowed their father's fields faithfully and husbanded his herds wisely; the other, Eurynomos, had found hard toil not to his liking and had joined Penelope's suitors sporting for her hand, for his eye lusted after the radiant queen despite the differences in their ages, and his belly rumbled when he ruminated on the vast herds of Odysseus over which he soon might rule.

And now Aegyptius stepped forward, his trembling hand firm upon the speaker's rod, tears running like rheum from his eyes, his reedy voice thinly lifting above the rumbling mutterings of the others.

"Listen to me, Ithaca! Listen, I say!" He paused as the others obeyed him, falling silent. Their sandaled feet scuffed the stone as they turned to face the wise speaker. "That's better. Yes, much better. We meet today for the first time since hollow ships bore bright Odysseus away to his fate (whatever that is), and now I ask: Who among you brought this council together? What is the need? A private complaint that would be better dealt with by a judge? Is there news of an armed fleet sailing toward Ithaca's shores with rape and rapine in the minds of its stern warriors? Or is it of some public concern? Come! Let us hear from the one who called this assembly instead of standing in the shade of the fig trees and lime trees and passing gossip like fishmongers and old women! Whoever called this was bold enough to disturb us, and for that I ask mighty Zeus to fill his heart with his greatest desires."

Snuffling, he handed the speaker's rod to Peisenor, its keeper, wiped his 31–57 eyes on the sleeve of his robe, and sighed a sigh so deep it rattled in his chest. He looked pointedly around the courtyard, his pale eyes peering at blurry shapes. He had not long to wait, however. Telemachus, pleased at the words of Aegyptius, stood up before the council. Peisenor handed the speaker's rod to him, and Telemachus turned respectfully to the old councilor and spoke to him, though his words were meant for all.

"Respectfully, sir, the man you call for stands before you now. I called this meeting, for I am greatly troubled by what has been happening in my own house. There may not be a great fleet approaching Ithaca's shores with mischief in mind, but great mischief has already been done to my house. Normally I would not bother this august body with such pithy patterings, but the troubles that infest my house might well infect Ithaca herself. I speak of my father's loss, the man who once ruled wisely and well over you, the man who treated all of you as if you were his offspring. Yes, that would be bad enough for any house, but an even greater plague has cursed my house and if unchecked will soon despoil my father's fortunes. (And need I tell you that as the king's house goes, so goes the nation?) My mother, faithful Penelope, who patiently waits for my father's return, is beset and besieged by many suitors, some the sons of those who stand here"—several men flushed and exchanged sheepish looks—"none of whom dare to approach her father's house for they are afraid that Icarius will demand great bridal gifts for his daughter's hand before choosing the one who would best suit her. No!" he said, his voice dripping with sarcasm. "No, they do not dare do that! Instead, they plague our house like locusts, waste our oxen and rams and fat goats and guzzle our rich wine, while they praise Penelope with pompous platitudes pretending love for her and love for Ithaca! These are sorry suitors indeed, for they know that no Odysseus shall boot their backsides from the house. But we cannot strike ourselves, as we are few and they are many. You, too, should abhor the scorn of these swine and dread the wrath of Zeus and Themis[4] for allowing them to wreak their wicked ways.

58–83   "I don't ask for much—just to be left alone. That is all. Let me mourn my father and my mother's loss. It is a bitter enough load to bear without the burden of pretending friendship for fools who abuse the rites of hospitality, exploiting the disappearance of Odysseus. Why, I ask, do you, whom my father trusted and assisted in your times of need, why do you treat me and my mother thus? Did my father step on your toes a time or two? Insult your houses? Why do you encourage scum to press their presence on my house?

"Far better for you to eat my stores of grain, my flocks, my herds, drink my wine. Then I might claim redress from you. I could have a herald trumpet my case throughout the town, proclaiming how you plundered my goods, deriding you as cheats and thieves until you requited me in full. But now, your silence weighs heavily upon me and I must silently suffer these humiliations because your silence insists that I suffer your betrayal of my father and his house!"

With that, he cast the speaker's rod on the ground and fell back onto his father's chair, bitter tears burning his cheeks. The men looked away—staring at the stone floor beneath their sandals—and glanced embarrassed at each other. They knew the truth of Telemachus's words. The arrogant ones who sought to supersede Odysseus upon his throne and usurp his bed had long abused the laws of hospitality as laid down by Zeus the lawgiver. No one dared to scorn Telemachus with harsh words. None reminded him of his place and the youth of his years that had not yet won him a seat in the council of the elders.

Then from the back of the crowd came a mocking, steady clap. Heads swiveled to stare at Antinous, the leader of the suitors, lounging against a young fig tree, an apple held between strong white teeth, his eyes sardonically sarcastic as they stared across the hall at the youth.

He took the apple from his mouth and tossed it to another, wiping his hands across the front of his tunic as he swaggered forward. The others drew back, leaving a corridor between him and Telemachus.

"Oh, this is well-spoken, Telemachus! But your words are angry words *84–115* designed to move friends and defame us. We do not stay here because we desire to deceive you." He spread his arms wide and gazed mockingly on those assembled. He picked up the speaker's rod, studying it. "No, it is not our fault that we reside here so long, but your mother's. Ah, ah!" He held up the rod and waggled it as Telemachus sprang to his feet, rage upon his lips. "Remember the rule!"[5] Telemachus dropped back down, his lips a sharp white line. Antinous mocked him with a half bow and turned to the elders. "Yes, this is the fault of Penelope, who could have driven us all away had she but chosen one of us. But she didn't. Hasn't"—he corrected himself—"and she conjures conniving games, teasing each of us with hope." He turned and pointed the rod at Telemachus. "You cannot blame us for courting her. For three years, she plays us off. We dream of pomegranates, while she gives us air, and Ithaca languishes without a man to take command.

"At first, we recognized her grief. We did not restrain her from setting up that massive loom in her room to weave a shroud against the day when Laertes is struck down by dark death. None of us denied her when she said, 'Ah, young men! Please forgive me if I do not marry one of you until I have finished this cloth which is prone to unravel if I cease. Without a winding sheet, Laertes—who has won such honors—is dishonored. At least in the eyes of Ithaca's women.' And so we stood by as she laid a great warp up and down her loom and wove throughout the day, but"—and here his voice dropped ominously—"during the night by torchlight she unraveled the shroud she wove by day, halving, then halving again her work so that it proceeded painfully slow. Yes! This your mother did while we waited upon her pleasure, while *Ithaca* waited upon her pleasure. For three whole years she plied her woman's wiles against us—mocking us, if you will.[6] But then, in the fourth year, through a servant sick of her deceit, we learned of her deception. So." He took a breath and grinned insolently at the youth, who ground his teeth in anger. "We have no fear of her father's choice. Send her away, if you will. You are the man of the house now, aren't you?" His eyes twinkled with laughter. "Let her father choose the suitor he favors and who is pleasing to her.[7] Now, we do not say that she should spurn Athene's gifts— nay, how could I speak against the goddess of wisdom who imbued her handiwork, her weaving, with such subtle craftiness? Not even famous Mycene of the lovely tresses or Alcmene or Tyro can equal her wit[8]—and we do not say her gambit wasn't clever, but she should never have deceived us or Ithaca with this wickedness. So that is why we devour your herds, your bread, and drink your wine. Now, I hope you understand the plainness of my words. We now have no intention of leaving. Although," he added carelessly, "we might have earlier had you approached us as a man instead of with these playground posturings of youth. No, we will not leave until she weds one of us. Or," he grinned, "you force her into wedlock."[9]

116–140

The suitors who lounged around the perimeter of the elders growled their assent. Antinous looked at the elders, who chewed thoughtfully on their beards and nodded at each other and scraped their sandals against the stone like barnyard cocks scratching earth, waggling their eyebrows as if to say that the suitors' woes within the house of Odysseus were brought by its mistress who played wicked matchmaking games with the youth of Ithaca.

"By the gods," muttered one sneeringly to his mate, "perhaps we should think on this instead of jumping in headfirst? Perhaps the queen has deceived these guests with promises of honey from the hive."

"Ah, yes," another said, lewdly pumping his arm. He burped, reeking of sour wine and onions. "Every ewe needs a ram and often 'fore she dries up and forgets—What? What?" he said, glowering at one near him who dug an elbow into his side. The other looked away embarrassed. "All I meant was a woman needs a man about to think for her. That's the way of things and all. What woman . . ."

Antinous grinned and looked back at Telemachus. He shrugged and tossed the speaker's rod at Peisenor's feet and swaggered off, a grin splitting his saturnine face as the elders shushed the fat one in their midst who sputtered into pouting silence.

Telemachus rose and seized the rod from the startled Peisenor as he retrieved it from the stone floor. His eyes widened in surprise at the fire blazing in Telemachus's eyes. He quickly backed up against the wall. Those in the front shifted nervously from foot to foot at the youth's rage, their eyes widening with dismay as Telemachus drew a deep breath. But his lips pursed in thought and his face became serenely calm before he spoke. No longer vehement, he chose his words judiciously, in the manner of a seasoned speaker.

"Antinous," he said, waiting until the suitor faced him, raising an eyebrow. He smiled at the older man. "Your remarks are measured, and there may be some truth to them—although I must wonder about a man or men so easily led down the primrose path by a woman, hm?" Antinous's face darkened at Telemachus's words. "But you know well I cannot drive my mother from this house. Nor would I on the flimsy evidence you offer here. Who would dare challenge Ithaca's queen on the word of a serving wench? Be realistic!" Antinous's eyes narrowed watchfully at him. "My father—alive or dead, I do not know, although I think the former—is"—he gestured vaguely—"somewhere on this vast earth, watched over by the gods. If I sent my mother away, then the bitter cost of repaying Icarius her dowry would descend on me. And, as you have stated so eloquently, Antinous, you and your friends have severely depleted those, ah, stores that I would need to cover that debt. You mentioned earlier, Antinous, that you admired my father's feats, and I assume you would not wish to face my father's wrath. Can you blame me if I too shrink from that possibility? Think how severe would be my father's wrath if upon returning he discovered that I had betrayed his trust, the very blood in my veins. Imagine then his bloody revenge. How would the gods respond to my betrayal if I surrender my mother to fate and she calls upon the dread Avengers to requite me for my cruelty to her? Then"—he gestured toward the elders before him—"there is the matter of the men of Ithaca. How would they feel if I surrendered their queen to the seafaring wanderers who plunder undefended shores, or put her out into the country to wander with the lepers?"

He shook his head and sighed. "No, Antinous, this I cannot do. I cannot *141–169* send my mother packing. Never. No. This is not an option. But"—he raised a commanding finger—"if you feel some sense of sorrow for me and my mother, a twinge of conscience—as most men of reason would—then I ask you simply to leave my halls. Take this rabble and hold your drunken debaucheries in another's house. Or, better yet, go home and glut yourselves on your own food and wine. Invite each other to your homes and slaughter your own bulls and swill your own casks of wine. If you think I shall not beseech the gods to intercede on my behalf, you are wrong. You will not gnaw your way through my wealth like a rat chewing through a wheel of cheese. I will ask Zeus—after making the proper sacrifices, of course; I am no piker to ask favors and not expect to honor the lawgiver in return—to absolve me from the laws of hospitality, and then, you drunken fools, all of you will perish unavenged within these halls. There will be no blood payment for your deaths; there will be no avengers sailing to Ithaca's shores."[10]

And after Telemachus had spoken, Zeus, whose mighty voice roars amid thunder and whose justice blazes in his flashing bolts, sent a pair of eagles to soar on high winds above the courtyard, spiraling and spiraling in an ever-widening gyre, until they reached the zenith; then they wheeled and folded their wings, swooping like thunderbolts toward the earth, their yellow eyes staring at the suitors with a promise of death. They opened their wings at the last moment and glided to the right over the peaks of the roofs and across the city. No one needed a priest to divine this augury. Yet, aged Halitherses, the son of Mastor, read it all.

" 'Tis an ill omen indeed and one that cannot be ignored. Of course, you will do what you will—that is your right (although it would behoove you to pay a little more attention to the proof of your eyes instead of belching sour wine and onions and scratching your piles)—and you can choose to ignore what will become a gloomy sea of troubles that Odysseus will bring with him when he comes. He's near—mark my words—and he has already sown the seeds of death and slaughter for those who clamor after Penelope's hand. And"—he turned to the assembly, his eyes burning beneath grizzled brows—"all those who side with the foreigners against the wishes of their young prince will journey to the end of night that will cover Ithaca's bright sun. Oh, yes. It is time for choice, I say. Choice. Now, which is it to be? Do we end the drunken revels of these men—unless, of course, they choose wisely to end their own drinking and whoring—or let the gods ravage our land as they will?" Someone sniggered, and Halitherses stared angrily in his direction. "Don't mock me! These aren't the ravings of an aged fool. I am no beginner at reading auguries and omens! Odysseus is coming. It's just a matter of when. No one but the gods knows the time and day of what will happen." He hawked and spat, and his red-rimmed rheumy eyes glared around at his townsmen. He raised a thick-knuckled forefinger and pointed at the suitors. "You all remember my prophecy when our lord sailed away to join the others on their journey to Troy. I told you he would return but only after he had suffered much at the hands of angry gods. I told you he would return alone, while the others who sailed with him would be lost, their names already written in the Books of Fate. And I told you twenty years would pass before we would see our king again! Well," he said with satisfaction, "those twenty years have passed, and now an angry man returns. You have seen his wrath before, but it will be nothing compared to the destruction he will bring with him this time! Zeus will send the Furies to back him! I would not want to be the one who stands in his way when blood-red anger clouds his vision!"

170–198   Eurymachus, the son of Polybus, laughed scornfully. "Old men should warm their ancient bones by their fires, not play cat's cradle with their betters! Play the prophet for your sons—perhaps they will heed your foolish warnings!" He thumped himself on his chest with a splayed thumb. "As for me, well, I'm the seer here. Birds are meant to fly and all kinds of birds fly back and forth in the heat of the sun. Would you foretell a nightingale twittering at twilight or a lark warbling at dawn? Posh! Better to pluck a tune from a stringless harp!" The suitors sniggered and nudged each other with elbows. Eurymachus grinned and idly scratched his chest through his tunic. "Now, we all are aware of your wishes and pompous postulating, predicting that the godly wrath will be penultimate upon our pates (ah! sheer alliteration, eh?), but I promise you Odyssesus is food for worms in some far-off land. Otherwise, would he not be here? And even if he isn't, why, what kind of husband and father would forsake his wife and son in this unseemly way? Would any of you be led by this procrastinator? Eh? Perhaps it would be better if you had sailed off and died with him instead of babbling omens and stoking the fire of Telemachus's anger. I know you want to see the wrath of Odysseus descend upon us, and pander to generous Telemachus in the hopes he will reward you with a fine gift for your convenient prophecies. But"—he glowered at the old man—"I'm warning you, now: We have had enough of this prophecy peddling! If you pretend to know so many of the ancient works and ways of the gods and continue to lead that boy astray with your dream accounts, we will exact a heavy due for your bitter folly." He craned his heavy head and stared with bloodshot eyes from the pouchy folds of his cheeks. "And as for you, Telemachus"—he drawled out the name insolently, bringing a flush to the youth's face—"my advice for your 'predicament' is to take your mother to your grandfather's house and have him prepare a wedding feast"—he grinned, exposing mossy teeth like tombstones—"replete with lavish gifts. The kind a gentleman deserves for relieving dotards of expensive daughters.

"But until Penelope weds again, these well-born Greeks will continue their courting ways." He laughed and gestured expansively. "Who here will drive us from this house? You?" He pointed at Halitherses. "No. You?" He pointed at Aegyptius. "No. You, Telemachus?" He laughed. "I think not. No, no, and no. There is no one for us to fear, despite your pompous bluster and wounded pride, Telemachus. All these empty auguries amount to only air rattling in empty throats of old men long past their grave day. If your mother continues her games denying us her wedding day, that long will we avail ourselves of your hospitality. We have no intention of repaying you for your, er, 'generosity.' Don't blame us! Blame your mother! She teases and leads us on day by day, flirting with one or the other. But the prize is well worth it, we think, right, men?" He winked coarsely and they roared with laughter.[11]

Telemachus flushed red, but he held rash words from his lips, carefully *199-223* forming a prudent reply. But all there could see his anger in the tiny white knots at his jaw. "What more could I ask from you, Eurymachus, and the rest of this"—he gave a tiny smile—" 'august' body? But give me twenty men and a seaworthy ship—swiftly cut and tall-masted for a quick voyage out and back—and I will go to sandy Pylos and Sparta and ask of Nestor and Menelaus what they know of my father.[12] All sea roads lead to their courts at one time or the other. Harp singers journey there too for the money—'tis a blessing and a curse, that—and there I shall surely discover if my father lives or lies dead on foreign soil. Perhaps I will even discover when he is coming home. That would be interesting news, I should think, even for you, Eurymachus! But no matter. Surely one mortal will share a cup of wine with me and recite the tales he's heard. Or," he mused, "maybe Zeus will speak to me. I have heard that he occasionally speaks to mortals outside of the priestly ranks when he tires of their meandering prayers and demands.

"If I hear that Odysseus lives, then I shall wait one more year, regardless how my patience is tried. But if I hear that he is dead, then when I return to this hall, I shall order a death mound raised to his memory and offer the richest funeral games ever recorded. And"—he hesitated, then lifted his chin, and bright lights sparkled angrily in his eyes—"I will give my mother in marriage to another husband."

224–252 He abruptly left the floor and sat on his father's chair, placing his hands on his knees as if ready to fling himself at an enemy. The Ithacans stared curiously at him, seeing the man inside the youth for the first time. Aegyptius cleared his throat and shuffled his feet, wanting to relieve the heavy tension in the air, feeling his age as his intent weighed heavily upon his shoulders. But Mentor rose, and many briefly pondered the faith their absent king had shown in entrusting his household to Mentor, who was to defer only to aged Laertes. And now they leaned forward, each eagerly awaiting Mentor's wisdom.

"Fellow citizens," he said, smiling benevolently at the gathering, "a man can no longer be a kind and benevolent king. Times have changed. Men no longer listen to the words of righteous rulers. In truth, a man must be cruel and corrupt to succeed today in bending people to his will. Yes, it is true! I can see that here." Suddenly the Ithacans knew that Mentor's words were directed to their faults, and they milled uneasily, guiltily glancing at each other. "No, don't look at others and pretend that I am not talking about you. When godlike Odysseus ruled this sceptered isle, none here thought to challenge his word or the will of his household. His rule was so kind and gentle that even the guilty found his judgments fair. And now you stand idly by and watch while his lands are plundered by jackals gathered beneath his roof under the pretense of hospitality, seeking even to steal his wife. Surely there is a new breed of men in Ithaca. These are not the men who in years past pledged themselves to Odysseus." Disdainfully, he shook his head. "No, lift your heads. I do not judge you or even the plots and violence these 'guests' hatch like hens sitting on old eggs. They waste Odysseus's wealth and desolate his estate in the hope that he is gone forever." He shrugged. "That's their choice and right insofar as Zeus gave all men the right to choose their path in life—down to the very wine they drink. No, I am not angry with them. A man makes his way in this world and they have selected theirs. The Furies will call them to account in their own time. No, it is you who sit in silence and with your silence give your sanction to their misdeeds who rankle me. You are many. You could drive these jackals from this house of Odysseus if you desired. But you sit contentedly in the sun and sip your wine and arrogantly nod at one another's words that Odysseus is surely dead. A man's honor lives on whether his mortal flesh does or not—in case you have forgotten!" He spat on the floor at his feet. "I see no man here worth as much as a grubworm!"

Up leaped hot-blooded Leocritus, son of Evenor, shouting, "And you, Mentor, are nothing more than a rabble-rousing oaf! A bag of wind! By what right do you stand before us, condemning us to the Ithacans and demanding that they block our suit?" He turned and faced the Ithacans and, placing his hands on his hips, said, "Who among you is willing to take up arms and go to war over a *meal*? Well? Who is willing to try and drive us from this house? Eh? Speak! Not one? Not one word? I thought not." He gestured contemptuously at Telemachus. "If that one's sire did come back, his wife would only grieve his loss again, and a dismal end that would be, fighting alone against all of us, for surely none of you would be willing to stand at his side and wield a sword or pluck a bowstring! Your words are only"—he gestured limply—"air. Be off with you now! Go snap at some dog's heels and pretend that you are still man enough to speak to men. Go on! Leave! Let Mentor and Halitherses, old friends of Odysseus—or so they have often told us—hurry Telemachus on his sea voyage. Although," he added, casting an eye on the latter, "I think that one will sit on the sands of Ithaca at wave's end and wait for word to come to him. From the look of him, he's not much for journeying!"

The suitors laughed as the elders took his advice and stumbled over each *253–283* other as they hurried away, glad to be free from the assembly. The suitors smirked at Telemachus and his friends and sauntered to the great hall, where they called to the servants to bring wine and cups and fondled the breasts of the serving wenches as they scurried around among them, filling cups with the rich, red, resinous wine of Ithaca.

Telemachus gritted his teeth and left the palace, making his way down the dusty streets to the shore. People stepped aside at his approach, averting their eyes and pretending a sudden interest in the roof of a building, a neighbor's ring or cloth. They lowered their voices as he hurried by. When he reached the gray surf and knelt upon the wet sand, he washed his hands and splashed the seawater upon his face. He raised his eyes to the heavens in prayer to Athene, saying, "Hear me, please! I followed your advice when you came to my house yesterday and told me that I must cross the misty seas to learn if my long-lost father will ever return to the warmth of his hearth and the arms of his wife, my mother. But those brutal and arrogant men who plot to take my mother to a new marriage bed stop me at every point."

And as his voice lifted in prayer, Athene, now in the guise of Mentor, spoke to him with winged words. "Telemachus, I said that you would prove to be neither a fool nor a coward in the future if you assumed your father's mantle and put your words to deeds as did he many times. Your journey will not be a waste if you follow his lead. This I promise you! But if you beat your chest and wail how badly you've been treated, why, then you are not the son of Odysseus and Penelope, and your plans will scatter like dust motes in the air. Few sons are mirrored images of their fathers—most are worse, a few better. Pay no attention to the word bandy of the posturing, preening fools whose pompous words are but saltwater gargle! Ignore them! They don't know the darkness that waits for them as fate stalks them. All will be struck down in a single day. Now think about your journey. You have your father's wily ways. One true spirit lives in your father's house who will gladly lend you a hand. Go and show yourself among the suitors and act courteously for the moment. Bear their taunting words and dismiss them as they are spoken. I will select those few Ithacans whose spirits have not been broken by those drunken swillers and who will serve you faithfully as crew. I will also select a ship, the best one that swings at anchor at this sea-girted island, and have her rigged in no time and ready to launch upon the open sea when you are ready. You find the one who is still loyal to your father and yourself and have provisions readied and stored, the barley meal in strong skins and the wine in jars."

284-314   Telemachus rose with Athene's words ringing in his mind and hurried back to his house, smoothing his tunic as he went and running his hand across his curly locks. He took a deep breath as he neared his gate and let it out slowly as he steeled himself to face the suitors. He smelled the spitted and roasting hogs when he stepped in through the gate. His lip curled in distaste at wanton wooers, elbow deep in blood and guts from skinning goats and flinging the offal at each other while roaring with laughter.[13]

Antinous came up to him, chuckling, and clasped his hand with a greasy paw, saying, "Well, now, my fiery orator! Are you done now with your childish words and ways? No harm meant or done! Come, put these hard words and warlike thoughts behind you. Eat and drink with us as usual. We'll pretend that nothing happened. Meanwhile, I'll send some of the men down to make, ah, arrangements for your sailing and speed you away to old Nestor's land."

Telemachus remembered the winged words of Athene. He smiled at Antinous as he gently pulled his hand from the other's grasp and wiped it fastidiously upon Antinous's tunic as he pretended to grip the man's shoulder in friendship. The suitor's eyes narrowed fractionally, then he laughed.

"You constantly surprise me, Telemachus," he said. "Sometimes I wonder if you aren't playing fox and geese with me."

"Now, Antinous," Telemachus answered, "is that any way for a possible foster father to talk to his son? Still, you aren't my father yet, and there's many a slip between the cup and the lip. Ha. Ha." He gave Antinous's shoulder a sharp shake, then stepped back. "I do thank you for your offer, but it is simply out of the question to expect a humble person such as myself to dine in such august company. Perhaps you are right to ransack my riches—as long as my goods don't become your grave."

He spread his hands and smiled innocently as an angry look hooded Antinous's eyes. "Mind you, I don't mean to be insolent—as you reminded me, that would be foolish, since you are so powerful, and I am not a foolish person—but you really can't think that I should share the meal that these rogues have stolen from me, do you? Hm?" Then his eyes sharpened and he threw his head back, his chin jutting toward the man like the bold prow of his father's ship. "I have set my own course for Pylos. Whether I get a ship and men is immaterial: I will go as a passenger aboard a trading vessel if nothing else is available—and I have a feeling that you would feel better if I was not given my own ship to command in my search for my father."

He shrugged, smiled disarmingly, and stepped back, waiting for the other 315-338 to speak. The suitors roared with laughter at his words and shouted a storm of insults. One young man swaggered up to him, saying scornfully, "Hm. Bless me if I do not think he means to murder us! Cut our throats in our sleep, eh, boys? What? He sails to sandy Pylos all right, but it's not to seek news about his father. He plots to hire avengers (there are a lot of roving mercenaries out there since the war, you know) and bring them back to avenge himself upon our bawdy ways. Heh, heh. Or"—he added as an afterthought, rolling his eyes and wagging his eyebrows in mock derision—"maybe he's off to Sparta to beg warriors from Menelaus (and sneak a look at that wanton queen whose lusting loins sent a thousand Greek ships to Trojan shores) to help him in his obsession. Or again, maybe he's off to Ephyra's loamy soil to purchase rare poisons from there to drop in our wine cups while we enjoy our evening sups and watch as we writhe in agony, gasping our death rattle in our throats." He gripped his throat and pretended to gag as he staggered, wide-eyed, around the courtyard to the roaring laughter of the others.

Another leaped to his feet and said, "Aye, who knows? Perhaps if he sails too far in one of those hollow ships Poseidon may drive him off course like his father and leave him to roam unknown seas until time turns his beard hoary and his loins limp." He shook his head. "But then he would make another problem for us, eh, mates? Why, we would have to figure out how to divvy up his wealth among us. Of course, we'd let his mother keep this palace—and whichever one of us crawls into bed with her!"

They roared with jest and shouted among themselves while Telemachus made his way through them and in disgust climbed the stairs to the store-room built by his father—a big and high-ceilinged room with thick oak tim-bers and a door of oak strapped in iron. Here, in teak and cedar chests, lay rich robes spun with gold threads, stacks of gold and bronze won in coastal raids by his father before seagoing Odysseus married Penelope and traded his seaways for landways. Huge amphorae of rare oils,[14] heady with scent, and tuns of sweet old wine still aging in burnt pne lined the walls: mellow, vintage wine waiting unblended for the day Odysseus returned. This room had defeated the hands of the suitors, its strong locks and closely fitted planks defying the drunken advances of the suitors as did its housekeeper, watchful Eurycleia, daughter of Ops, Peisenor's son, who, with the guidance of Athene, kept the key hidden, locking the doors behind her when her duties took her into the room.

339–367 And now Telemachus entered the storeroom, calling to her. "My dear nurse! Pull a flagon of the sweetest wine you have kept away from our drunken guests against the return of my father. Then fill twelve flagons and stopper them well. And pour out twenty measures of mill-crushed barley into our sturdiest leather bags. I sail to Sparta tonight by way of sandy Pylos to discover what I will about my father. And," he added hastily, "keep this to yourself. No need to worry my mother with my plans. I won't leave until she climbs to her rooms for the night."

Tears sprang to her eyes as Eurycleia cried and said, "What on earth has put this idea into your mind, dear son? Why do you feel you have to go wan-dering around the world in search of your father? Is it not enough that he is lost that you will lose yourself and doom the rest of Ithaca to those beasts below? Think! What will happen the moment you turn your back on sunny Ithaca? Why, those wooers will plot great mischief, devise some plan for your death. Then they will divide your wealth among themselves while they plot to plunder your mother's bed. And"—she waved her age-spotted hands around the room—"all of this as well. They know what is in here, thanks to some of those nervy wenches who wave wanton legs at the ceiling when the horned moon rises. No, better for you to stay home where you have strength—such as it is—among the Ithacans outside these walls. As long as you are here and your mother hasn't taken one for a new husband, they do not dare to make a move against you. But if you go over the barren seas, wandering through wayless wilderness, who knows what will happen?"

"Now, don't weary yourself about that," Telemachus said carefully. "A 368-396 god's hand moves me to make this journey. I'll be safe with that hand upon my shoulder. Well enough, at any rate. But say nothing about my trip to my mother for at least eleven or twelve days or until she misses me and discovers I'm gone. We don't want her pretty eyes red with tears or her shoulders stooped with woe. Come, now: swear. Please?"

Grumbling, the old woman swore by the gods that she would keep his secret, then shuffled off to fill flagons with wine and pour barley into sacks for him. Telemachus slipped away to rejoin the revelers in the courtyard before he was missed, pretending that he had simply been relieving himself.

Meanwhile, gray-eyed Athene, disguised now as Telemachus, slipped quietly through the city, selecting the twenty bravest and most loyal men she could find, warning each to meet at the docks when the silver moon slipped up from the horizon and cast soft light upon the gentle sea. She found Noemon, the son of faithful Phronius, who had his father's loyalty, and asked him for the loan of a ship, which he gave willingly, spitting in contempt at the mention of the suitors.

The sun fell and sable shadows slid through every street. Athene stocked the good ship and moored it in a dark part of the harbor, leaving it swinging by a stern anchor. Then she waited in the shadows of a tavern while the men she had selected gathered quietly around her. She filled their hearts with a quiet fire.

Then another idea came to the goddess, and she hastened through the streets to godlike Odysseus's palace. There she drugged the wine of the suitors, and soon the wine cups fell from their drink-laden fingers and they staggered off through the town in search of their beds and bawds to lie with. Only then did Athene, again assuming Mentor's shape, call Telemachus, already wearing his armor and carrying his weapons, from the palace.

"Telemachus," she said, "your well-armored companions sit at their oar- 397-428 locks, waiting for your command to row away from Ithaca's shores. Come, now. Don't dawdle. Let's begin the journey."

With those words, Athene turned her back upon the palace walls and led him quickly to the harbor. Telemachus hurried behind her, wondering how a man of Mentor's age could pass so swiftly through the streets. When they reached the dock where the sea waves lapped gently against the pilings, they found the soldiers Athene had chosen waiting for them, long hair clubbed, eyes gleaming with anticipation.

"Come, my friends!" Telemachus said. "Let us get the stores aboard. All are stacked and waiting at the palace. But be careful," he cautioned. "Do not let anyone see you bringing them down or word will slip out about our plan and we shall have a fight on our hands!"

Together, they brought the stores to the harbor and stowed them aboard the ship. Then Telemachus followed Athene aboard, and the men cast away the hawsers. Telemachus took his place in the stern with Athene and ordered the sail raised upon the beechwood mast. Athene called a steady wind to come from the west, and the wind filled the sail and sent the vessel singing over the deep dark main. The purple waves spilled from each side of the bow, and Telemachus called to the crew to secure the mast in its hollow box and fasten it securely with oxhide ropes. The black ship gathered itself and leaped forward, eager to begin its journey.

429–434 When all was made fast against the rugged wine-dark seas, the men took a sip of wine each in his cup and offered it to the immortal gods who live forever and took again a cup each and offered it to the divine daughter of Zeus, the lady of the gleaming eyes.

And all night long, the black ship's keel plowed through the dark and endless seas.

Here ends the Second Book of Homer's Odyssey.

THE THIRD BOOK
A Visit to the Lord of Pylos

❖ ❖ ❖ ❖ ❖ ❖ ❖ ❖ ❖ ❖ ❖

At Pylos, Nestor receives Telemachus
And tells the tale of Troy and Odysseus.
Telemachus sent to Menelaus.

❖ ❖ ❖ ❖ ❖ ❖ ❖ ❖ ❖ ❖ ❖

From the splendid morning waters, Helios's chariot rose
And climbed high into brilliant azure heaven. Brazen rays
Brightened upon Immortals and mortals who gratefully rose
To tend their grain fields. On Pylos's sandy shore, priests blessed
Jet-black bulls to blue-haired Poseidon who shakes the earth.
Nine companies—each five hundred strong—sat and waited
For the moment when they would taste the entrails and
Offer burnt thighbones to the god watching from his place
Beside the flames of his bone fire. The sea rovers anchored
Their ship with Athene's face painted upon its sail in the bay
And set out with a quick pace with Athene leading the way.
She paused and looked irritably over her shoulder to where
Telemachus lingered tentatively at the column rear
And said sharply, "Come now, put your shyness aside.
You sailed the briny deep on evening's tide
And now is not the time to play the blushing boy!
Step up to Nestor, the breaker of horses,[1] and ask where
The great earth hides your father and what has befallen
Him that he tarries so long from home! Be courteous,
For Nestor is wise and will tell you history and no lies."
And Telemachus took her words for great wisdom and went
To where Nestor sat, dressed in his kingly clothes.

27-52 And Pallas Athene stepped swiftly ahead of Telemachus, leaving him to fol-
low in her footsteps. They walked to the center of the sacred feast where
Nestor sat with his sons, surrounded by his people. A few held long skewers
filled with chunks of meat dripping fat into the flames; others had spitted
huge quarters and straightened them over the coals to turn and roast slowly.
But when they saw the strangers approaching, all the men of Pylos rushed to
meet them, welcoming them with outstretched hands, begging them to join
in their celebration.

Nestor's son Peisistratus came first, grasping their hands and begging
them to sit on pads of soft fleece that had been newly sheared from young
sheep and spread out across the sand for his father and his brother
Thrasymedes. As they sat, Peisistratus scurried away to bring them the
choice cut of meat, pausing only to pour the richest wine into golden cups for
the newfound guests. He welcomed them with warm words and lifted his
own cup, pledging them by invoking the goddess Athene, the aegis-bearing
daughter of Zeus.[2]

"Welcome!" he cried, offering a chalice to Athene, whom he saw in the
guise of Mentor. "Welcome to our lands! Join us, now, in prayers to Lord
Poseidon, strangers! We honor him with this festivity, and after you have
poured libations to him and invoked him with your prayers—as is only right
in accordance with the commandments given us by the gods—pass this cup
of sweet wine to your companion that he may share in our celebration too. I
can see he is a brave fellow who would honor the Immortals with his prayers.
But since he is of my own age, it is only right that you should sip first from
this golden cup!"

With that, he placed his golden chalice into her hand and stepped back,
beaming at her with happiness and honesty. Athene heard the honesty
behind his words and the glad tidings that he felt at their coming, and she
was pleased with his courtesy and tact in handing the cup to her first. At
once, the gray-eyed goddess raised the chalice over her head and cried,
"Hear me, Poseidon, earthshaker, whose embrace holds the earth together
and keeps it from flying to the heavens, and look favorably upon what we are
about to do here. Do not prevent us from hearing the words from Nestor
that we would hear after sailing so far from the shores of Ithaca. Grant glory
and honor to Nestor and his sons and to the other men of Pylos. Honor their
requests as they have honored you with this sacrifice of one hundred fine cat-
tle. And let Telemachus and me sail back home across smooth waters once
we have received what we have traveled so long to attain."

53-77 She took a long draught from the beautiful two-handled cup, then passed
the chalice to Telemachus. He took it in his own hands and, standing, raised

it high and prayed fervently to Poseidon that the sea god grant Odysseus's son the words that he needed to hear and a safe journey back home. He spilled a small amount of the rich wine onto the sand for the god, then sealed his invocation with a long drink before passing the cup back to Peisistratus.

By now, fat ran freely along the backs and flanks and rump roasts above the flames and coals, and the men of Pylos hurried to strip them from the spits, handing each person a generous share of the abundant feast. They ate with relish and drank deeply of the dark, resinous wine, laughing and telling stories politely for the benefit of their visitors to make them feel welcome indeed to the shores of sandy Pylos.

When they had finished, Nestor puddled his greasy fingers in a small bowl of rose-petaled water and wiped them upon a cloth. Then he spoke, saying, "Now, then. Surely it is time now, after we have eaten, to properly inquire of our guests to tell us who they are and what they want. So, without further ado, who are you, strangers, and from what land have you sailed across the seaways to these sands? I hope you are not raiders, although my hospitality is yours just the same in accordance with the rules given us by Zeus. Perhaps you are traders, with goods to barter: fine silks, kohl, rare Ephesian wine? Tell me, please, that you are not a rabble of prowling crew forced to wander and risk your lives to plunder and loot others' riches."

Telemachus cleared his throat, wondering what he would answer, then felt the words move strongly in his heart, and he spoke, sure and confident, his words sharp and wise, as he questioned the horseman about his long-lost father. His words were bold but honest and respectful.

"Thank you for your greeting and food and drink, Nestor, son of Neleus, 78–108 pride of the Greeks. You wonder where we have sailed from. All right. My words are true. We come from Ithaca, the sunlit city beneath Mount Neion whose haughty head rises high above the island and is our seamark. But we are not traders. We seek only words—your words—about my father, Odysseus, the man with the bold step. Some say that it was he who fought at your side as you destroyed the great citadel of Troy whose topless towers kept the Greek army at bay for ten years. I have heard many of these stories about how other kings were killed in that war against the Trojans, but no one knows what happened to my father. The son of Cronus has kept that knowledge from us. No one has been able to tell us if he was killed by enemies upon dry land or if he was lost at sea during a fierce storm when strong winds struck the waves of Amphitrite.

"Therefore, I come to sit by your knees and listen to the words of wisdom from your own lips. Tell me, please, about my father's sad death (if, indeed, he has died or been killed). Were you there at his side when he came to grief?

Or do you know what has become of this doomed man? The woman who bore him gave birth also to grief and sadness and so he was named Odysseus, the man of pain and agony. And because of his name, I have come to expect the worst. Please don't play pittering word games with me. I don't need honeyed words of grief. Speak plainly, please, and tell how with words and deeds mighty Odysseus fulfilled his promises with you and the other kings in that miserable land ruled by Troy."

109–138   Nestor pulled at his beard as he regarded the youth standing confidently in front of him for a long moment before he spoke. Then he sighed and said, "Well, my friend, you have certainly reminded me of things I thought I would keep buried. We suffered greatly, those of us who traveled to that godforsaken land to fight continuously without much rest. Aye, I can recall the many miseries we suffered as we roamed the misty seas in our bold ships in search of booty behind the brave Achilles. I remember our long struggle for the citadel of Priam. The best and brightest of our brave warriors fell on those bloody plains, let me tell you! There fell mighty Ajax[3] whose shield was so large that two ordinary men had a hard time carrying it! And Achilles, whose bloodlust over the death of his friend, Patroclus[4]—whose wisdom matched the gods'—angered the river god, who rose in fury when blood poured from the battlefield into his waters, choking him. There fell, too, Antilochus, my own son"[5]—his throat clicked and his eyes misted at memory—"a dear lad, brave, unflinching, strong, fast of foot, and bold in battle. Ah, by the gods, how I miss him! And it is of these you want me to speak? What mortal man could tell the full tale of that war? Of all the battles, the skirmishes, the councils? Even if you stayed here for some five or six long years, I could not tell you everything you want to hear about that dark and dreary story. No, I couldn't tell you everything. You would grow weary of an old man's memories and make your way back to your own country. Yes, you would! But let me think, let me think."

His eyes turned inward upon his memory, and he sipped the cool wine in his cup for a moment before setting it aside. Then he pursed his lips and began again. "For nine long years we tried constantly to breach the walls of Troy and pull its mighty towers down to the plain. We tried trick after trick but got nowhere. We were about to give up and return home and leave Troy to the taunting Trojans who knew we could not breach those strong walls, that bronze-sheathed gate. Then the son of Cronus helped us with our plotting.

"The smartest one among us was wily Odysseus. No one could compare with his cunning. (Indeed, if you are his son—and now that I take a close look at you I can see much of his ways in yours, hear his words in your words. Unusual in one so young! Where was I? Oh, yes.) And yet divine Odysseus and I never argued. We were of one mind in council with the others. Together, our wisdom and shrewdness constantly gave the Greeks the best of an impossible situation time and time again. Ah, how I remember those violent times, the great arguments, the posturing and preening of pampered heroes frustrated from their futile efforts to break through the ranks of the Trojan army and breach the walls of Troy. Those were the times, lad! Those were the times!"

He paused to take another sip of wine and ease his dry throat. He hawked and spat. Then his features darkened. "But after we sacked Troy, the heart of Zeus turned against us, for some of us had not behaved in an honorable manner. The mighty god plotted a poor voyage home for us, and many came to grief through the anger of gray-eyed Athene.

"At the time, I wondered about this sudden change in our fortunes, but *139–168* then I thought about all that had happened and I remembered that not all of the Greeks had been just and wise in their dealings with the gods. Many of them met sorry deaths when the gray-eyed goddess struck them with her anger. Aye, Athene! That is the one! The daughter of so powerful a father brought a quarrel between the two sons of Atreus,[6] and that proved a ruination upon many.

"You see, the two had asked the Greeks to assemble at sunset (which we should have ignored, but when that summons came we were woolly-headed with wine). When they tried to justify interrupting our drinking, loud arguments broke out. Menelaus begged everyone to use a bit of horse sense and think about how they had to return across the wide, wine-dark sea. But they did not listen to him and continued to shout insults back and forth between them.

"Then Agamemnon came into the fray and told everyone that the Greeks should not leave, and rather than think about sailing away from the Trojan shore after going through nine years of war and returning to their shores empty-handed, sporting only their wounded pride, they should present a sacrifice to the goddess who had turned her back on them and try to soothe her terrifying anger by sacrificing several hundred cattle."

He snorted with derision and shook his head. "What a fool!" he said scornfully. "To think that a mere burnt offering could ease the anger of Athene! An idiot's plea, that is. The minds of gods don't easily forget slights and are not prone to sudden shifts like wind-whims."

He sighed. "So, being the fools mortals be, the two brothers took up arms and the night rang with the clash of swords on shields. The others heard this warring clatter and rose with relish, brawling bitterly among themselves. All night long plots were hatched and blows struck as hot tempers flared from the grapes of wrath. I could see that this was all part of a dark design by great-browed Zeus[7] and determined at daybreak to launch my ship and leave the blood-soaked shores of Troy. Some of the others who kept a cool head when drunken riot roiled through our camps followed me down to launch ships upon the glowing sea. We moved our goods down into the ships along with the low-girdled Trojan women we had taken as slaves, half naked from the sacking of their city.

"But half of the Greeks remained behind with Agamemnon, once a worthy shepherd of our people but now arrogant with his triumph. We said our farewells and launched our ships upon the tranquil sea, determined to reach our homes. But Zeus was not yet done with us. Again, violent argument rose among us when we reached Tenedos. Some turned their vessels back to join with Agamemnon's plans." He paused for a moment, reflecting. "Yet all of our troubles might have been averted had it not been for Aias, the son of Oileus,[8] who caught Cassandra[9] when she tried to hide in Athene's temple. He found her clinging to the sacred image of the gray-eyed goddess and yanked her away from her sanctuary. His blood boiled with desire, for the unbelieved prophetess was a beautiful woman. He tore her clothes from her and raped her there on the spot in front of Athene's eyes. That, I think, may be why Athene killed many of our men as they made their way home after the war. Your father, mighty Odysseus, the wise and crafty king, decided to join them in their return to the son of Atreus.

169–192 "I tried to warn your father about the sinister plan plotted against him, but Odysseus laughed at my fears and commanded his sail be raised and ordered his helmsman to steer away from the fleet I led. I ordered my helmsman to set the quickest line home. Warlike Diomedes[10] followed my lead, as did blond Menelaus with his wife Helen (that witch caused the death of many brave men with her lust), and overtook us at Lesbos where we swung at anchor in a safe harbor while plotting our course. Our paths forked there, and we debated whether to sail north of the rugged Chios coast and strike out across the sea, keeping Psyra on our left, or to sail boldly south of Chios past the windswept cliffs of Mimas.

"We prayed for a sign, and a large gull flew out west across the sea in answer to our prayer. I ordered the course to be set for Euboea, chilled by the omen that we should risk the open sea to get out of harm's way as quickly as possible. A whistling wind wailed from our stern, and our ships rode swiftly across the seaway led by dolphins. So fast did we fly across those waves that we reached Geraestus late that night. There, we built an altar and a huge fire and offered the thighbones of many bulls to Poseidon for allowing us to safely cross the open sea!

"You look startled, lad. Aye, we crossed the open sea instead of hugging close to the coast as did many ships behind us, and such was the wind from the gods that many ships were carried by the waves into the rocky shoals beside the dangerous shores we had left behind.

"Four days out, Diomedes, the brave son of Tydeus, the tamer of horses, brought his fine craft to anchor in Argos. But I ordered our course to be set straight for Pylos, for the god was making the breeze favorable for the moment and I knew that the wind was only a temporal force. Still, the god never let the wind ease until I ordered the lowering of the sail as we rowed into Pylos's safe harbor.

"And that, dear young one, is why I arrived without any knowledge of what happened to those who stayed behind at Troy or rowed out onto the wine-dark sea with mighty Odysseus. I have no idea who escaped the wrath of the goddess and her father or who fell to their fury." He shrugged and spread his hands in apology.

"But I have heard things." His eyes clouded for a moment, and he sucked at a piece of meat caught in his teeth. He spat it free. "Yes, I have heard things. And these I will cheerfully give to you. It is your right to know what I know (or rather what I know from the words of others)." He cleared his throat and took a sip of wine, smacking his lips with relish. "Now, then! Let's see. Yes. The Myrmidons,[11] those marvelous spearmen, made it safely to their home thanks to the seamanship of Achilles's brave son. The brilliant son of Poias, Philoctetes,[12] made a safe return, too, as did Idomeneus,[13] who brought his men safely to their home in Crete. The sea claimed none of them.

"As for Agamemnon"—he shook his head—"now that, you've probably *193–220* heard about, even in Ithaca's far-flung shores. The bards and poets have become quite fond of singing how Agamemnon was greeted by that whore of a wife, Clytemnestra, Helen's sister, who killed his concubine, Cassandra. A wretched fate for any man, slain in his wife's bed by his wife's lover, Aegisthus! (Some say he was slain in his bath, but I don't think that is so. Even then, Aegisthus would have been hard-pressed to kill Agamemnon, naked and defenseless as he might be. Others say that Aegisthus killed him after inviting him to a feast. But I don't believe that, either. No, it had to be while he rocked in his wife's love embrace and did not guard his back. Where was I?) But a grim reckoning awaited that man, Aegisthus! It is good for a man to have a son who will wreak vengeance upon his father's slayer, and Agamemnon had such a son in Orestes. When that young man returned home, his mother and her lover were soon dealt with, I hear! Of course the young man is now being pursued by the Furies[14] for slaying his mother—or so the singers sing—but his father's shade must rest easier now, knowing that his murderers have met the judgment of Zeus.

"So, my young friend—and a strong and handsome young man you have become!—follow the lead of Orestes,[15] I say, and ensure that your name will be sung with praise by men still unborn."

He reached for his cup and drained it. A servant immediately sprang forward to refill it from a dark-red pitcher. The servant motioned to refill the cup of Telemachus, but the youth set it aside. He chose his words carefully, saying, "King Nestor, son of Neleus, great glory of the Greeks, Orestes wreaked great revenge upon the murderers of his father! I am sure that his fame will travel throughout the Greek lands and the islands of the vast sea! I can only hope that the gods might grant me the same strength that I might crush the insolent suitors who infest my house like fleas! I would pay them back for their arrogant ways! But"—he sighed heavily—"now I must stay my hand and bear their insults. I have little choice in the matter."

The Gerenian charioteer pursed his lips, considering the youth across from him. "Now I remember! Yes, of course, of course! I have heard stories about how many suitors have swept down upon your house like locusts. Tell me," he said, leaning forward, "do you accept this freely, or have your own people been listening to some god who has his heart set against you and your mother? No, I see by the expression upon your face that you stand alone against them. Perhaps the gods will give you strength on your voyage back, and upon your return you will be able to drive them from your house or strike them down and leave them in the dust of the street. I do wish that Athene, that gray-eyed goddess, would show you some of that loving care and attention that she gave to your father! But I have never seen the gods bestow that much love upon a human being. Too bad. If she did love you as she did your father, those men would soon forget all their marriage plans in the face of that goddess's wrath!"

221–247 "Hm," Telemachus ventured cautiously. "I am amazed at your bluntness," he said delicately in order not to offend the elder statesman. "But I don't think Athene listens with a full ear. No, no, I don't think what you say will ever happen. Although," he added, "I do hope that I am wrong. The gods don't seem to want to let it happen."

"Tch. Tch," the burning-eyed goddess said, frowning. "Now, Telemachus, your words escape your lips before you've done with thinking! If a god wishes to bring a man safely home without minding the distance, then that god can easily do so. If I were such a man, I think that I would rather face the hardest tests as I traveled before I arrived at my safe harbor than find death disguised, as did Agamemnon behind the masks of Aegisthus and his own wife. Yet," she mused, "even gods have their limits. Not even the Immortals can free a man from the dark clutches of death. That belongs to man alone, and no god can share it with him."

"There is much truth behind your words, Mentor," Telemachus said. "But let us not muse on matters like these. My father will not return. The gods have already launched their decree upon his soul: Dark death has already destroyed what lived in him. Now pardon me while I put another question to wise Nestor." He turned to the horseman. "Now, Nestor, brave son of Neleus, tell me how the ruler of such vast holdings as the son of Atreus, Agamemnon, was killed. I have heard many stories and wonder about the truth. I do not understand how a man like Aegisthus—brave, perhaps, but more a dolt than a planner—could launch such a plan by himself. And Menelaus. What about that brave king? Did his absences from Argos give Aegisthus enough sand to plan death for his king? There are inconsistencies in the stories, wise sir, and a man is hard-pressed to find the truth among them."

Nestor raised his wine cup and swallowed a long draught, placing it in 248-273 front of him before speaking. He ran his hand along the frosty rime of his beard, then said, "Well, then, my son, I'll tell you what you wish to know. You may have heard many things—doubtless this, for even I have heard many things about what I have seen from prattlers and fools who do not know their words from air—but I doubt that you have heard everything. Now, let's see: You know that if blond Menelaus, Agamemnon's brother, had found Aegisthus riding the saddle of Agamemnon's mare, there would have been no burial mound built for that horseman. His body would have been cast into the dusty street by the docks for the dogs and birds to feast upon. No, not even there: Aegisthus would have been thrown upon the plains outside the city so that not even his bones would have found comfort in the dust of the streets and not a woman would be found in all of Achaea to mourn his soul and shed a tear over his bones. No, not one.

"We had been long at Troy's walls, trying to smash through that fortress, living in tents amid dust, blood, and death while Aegisthus lolled in Argos, raising horses and trying to seduce Agamemnon's wife with his charming words. I must give the wench her due—she didn't tumble into bed with him at his first words. Now, I don't know, mind you, if that was by her choice or because Agamemnon had left a poet-singer to watch over her, but there came a time when she could have said no and said yes instead. A day or two after that, Aegisthus tricked the poet-singer into going with him to a deserted island on the pretext of finding Artemis bathing (all know the story of Actaeon who saw the divine form naked at her bath on Mount Cithaeron, but despite the dangers, who wouldn't risk his life to see such perfection?) and killed him, leaving his body to be picked over by vultures and ravens. Then he returned and carried Clytemnestra—by now a fond lover, willing to wrap her shapely legs around his lean waist—to his house. There, Aegisthus heaped thighbones upon the altars of the gods—he didn't miss a one—and on the ones he thought would protect him if Agamemnon should return, he left finely woven cloaks and tunics with gold thread spun through their hems and golden toys and trifles of the sort that would appeal to the vain gods. He was careful there, he was, but the gods knew they were bribes to them to look the other way for the success he had in luring Clytemnestra to his bed. She may not have been as good in Aphrodite's ways as her rosy-breasted sister, Helen, but I remember listening to the pleasure cries coming from her apartment one night before we sailed. At the time I envied Agamemnon's luck, but now, hm, I wonder if the cries weren't deliberate, calculated.

"The gods, however, are fickle about the bribes they take—as you undoubtedly know—so they beguiled Aegisthus with Clytemnestra's naked-ness, and his thoughts daily twirled around her naked thighs, gleaming alabaster. Meanwhile, Menelaus and I were sailing over the choppy seas from Troy. We had, by now, become the best of friends and kept our fleets close together as we made our run for the mainland.

274–301   "But the gods had other plans for us. When we were just off the cape of sacred Sunium, Athene's town, Apollo killed the helmsman of Menelaus with an arrow." He belched, and the scent of onions and sour wine carried to Telemachus's nose. The youth leaned back away from it, pretending to sip from the cup of wine in order to not give offense. "Unfortunately, the helms-man had not been relieved and the tiller was still in his hand when he keeled over dead. What was his name?" He screwed his eyes tight shut, thinking, then snapped his fingers. "Phrontis, son of Onetor. The world's best helms-man he was, especially in a gale. Hands thickly callused from the tiller and a strength to match the strongest wave of Poseidon. No tempest could drive him from the tiller. But Menelaus, despite his desire to return home, was forced to lay over at Sunium until proper burial could be made for Phrontis. 'Twas only right, I suppose, given all that man had done for his king.

"When Menelaus finally put back out to sea, he called for all sails to be raised and stretched tight to run as fast as possible over the wine-dark seas. He made it as far as the steep mountains and cliffs of Malea before he made a poor choice of words and offended mighty Zeus! Aye"—he sighed and ran his gnarled hand over his gray locks—"that was an unfortunate act! Zeus sent him a howling gale to reward him! The giant waves split the fleet in two, driving one-half toward Crete where the Cydonians live on the Jardanus River. That's a treacherous coast, you know—or maybe you don't know; it doesn't matter; remember it well if you ever journey there—where a craggy cliff falls straight to the water. It was a southwesterly wind that blew, it was, driving great rollers in toward Phaestus's Strand.[16] There is a reef there that helps provide a shaky harbor, but the angry sea waves poured over that reef without giving it a thought.

"Those ships driven there made it by the breadth of a goat's hair, although their ships were sorely battered and beaten. A few planks stove in by the reef but not enough to send them to the bottom. Menelaus, with the rest of his five blue-prowed ships, tried to turn in, but the waves rose up against him and carried him speedily across the sea to Egypt's shore.

"Of course, he didn't know where he was for a while—five years, I think—and he sailed around over there building a good fortune in gold and spices, rich balms, fine cloths, so much in fact that his ships nearly became overloaded with the weight of his wealth. Messengers made it to the house of Aegisthus and told him that the war was over, and not one to dilly-dally, knowing that Agamemnon had to be on his way home, Aegisthus began to weave a web around Clytemnestra, sating her lust well, and lay his wicked plans. After he killed Agamemnon and mounted the throne, he ruled for seven years. But on the eighth, divine Orestes came home from Athens where he had been studying and killed the usurper. Foul death given is foul death received. Mind you! This isn't something to be passed off lightly! One reaps what one sows. *302–328*

"Well, Orestes held a fine funeral to celebrate the death of his mother and her lover, and at the grave feast who should stride through the doorway but Menelaus of the loud war cry! Servants brought in chest after chest of the treasures he had gained in his wanderings.

"Now, there is a lesson in this, Telemachus! Don't stay too long from your house lest those bold suitors consume everything and divide that which they can't eat among them. You might return home to nothing but ruin. But since you've come this far, I think you should visit Menelaus up in Sparta. He's just returned home (or so I'm told) from a filthy land so far removed that a bird couldn't fly across the sea to it in a year! Take your ship and crew and sail to Sparta. Or," he reflected, "if you'd rather travel by land, I'll have a chariot and horse readied for you. My own son can guide you"—he winked bawdily— "and there's a fair maiden in that court who draws Peisistratus." The youth blushed furiously at his father's words, much to the laughter of those present. "There you will be able to ask Menelaus for news of your father. That amber-locked man will tell you the truth, for he is a wise man and wise men know that what lies are told come back tenfold to haunt them."

329-357 As Nestor drank thirstily from his wine cup, the sun fell below the dark sea and shadows came. Athene's eyes glowed as she said, "Good father, your tale was well told! But now it is time to divide up the tongues of the sacrifices and mix the wine to pour out in offering to the sea god Poseidon and the other Immortals before sleep overtakes us. The sun god's chariot has ridden the sky and dusk has fallen in its trail. It is not seemly for us to remain any longer without giving the gods their due. We must not sit too late telling tales, you know."

Her words sparked the heralds to action. They poured water into clean bowls and brought them to the feasters so that they might wash their hands before pouring libations for the gods. Servants filled bowls brimming with wine and carried them around, filling each man's cup with a few drops that were promptly poured onto the ground for the gods, then the cups were refilled for the final toast. The tongues were cut up and thrown onto the flames of the fires, and each man stood and offered his prayers and drank his fill.

Athene and Telemachus turned to go, but Nestor stayed them, protesting loudly, "God forbid that you should return to your ships and sleep in those cramped holds. I haven't drunk of poor Penia's whip—that is to say, I'm no pauper! You'll find my house much more comfortable. I assure you that there's room enough there for all of you and myself—rugs and blankets galore to warm you from the night's frosty air. No son of my friend Odysseus will sleep on the hard deck of a rocking ship as long as I—or my sons— survive to entertain any visitor who comes to my door. I insist, now!"

"Well said," cried Athene. "And it is right that Telemachus should go with you to your house and accept your invitation. But I must return to the black ship and reassure our men that we haven't come to mischief. That is my duty. We've been gone long enough, and you know how men's tongues get to wagging. I'm the oldest one of the party. All the rest are friends of great-souled Telemachus who would follow him everywhere. I will sleep there aboard our black ship and on the morrow set out to visit the Cauconi- ans. Some there have owed me a large debt for quite a while. In the morning, give Telemachus a chariot drawn by the fastest and strongest horses and one of your sons as a guide and send him on his way."

358-384 She raised her arms, and the form of Mentor gave way to Ossifrage, the Vulture, and with a mighty flap of her wings rose into the air and disap- peared. Nestor's jaw dropped open, then he closed it with a snap and shook his head. "Strong wine," he mumbled. He rose and stood in front of Telemachus.

"Well, my boy," he said, seizing his hand and shaking it vigorously. "You can walk boldly now for certain! Any man can who has his guardian attending him! This surely was the daughter of Zeus, Tritogenia herself, who honored your brave father more than any other Greek. Oh, my! Athene! Here at my feast, eating my meat, drinking my wine!" He gave a slow wink and shook his head, hawked and spat. He lifted his eyes and peered into the darkness, vainly seeking her shape against the stars. "Favor me and mine, Athene, and I'll sacrifice a broad-browed ox to you. A yearling, yoke-free and unbroken. I'll cover his horns with gold!" he shouted to the dark.

And Athene heard his prayer and promises. Then Nestor led his sons and 385-416 relatives to his house and sat them on high-back chairs as elegant as thrones. With his own hands, he mixed each a bowl of sweet wine that had aged ten years in a burnt-oak cask before being poured into a jar and sealed in leather by his servant. He prayed long and fervently to the aegis-bearing daughter of Zeus as he handed round a cup to each guest, then led them in drinking her health. Cup after cup was refilled again and again until all had drunk their fill and staggered off to their homes and beds, their minds reeling delightfully from the heady wine.

Telemachus was shown to a royal bed, the wood richly carved, the blankets embroidered by skillful fingers into works of art. Peisistratus, the fine spearman among Nestor's sons—and the only one unwed—slept beside him, sharing his bed joyfully. Nestor, however, climbed unsteadily to his room high up among the rafters where his lovelorn queen, his beloved wife, waited in anticipation for the arms of her loving husband.

When rosy-fingered Dawn cast a fingertip of light into his bedroom, Nestor rose, splashed water over his face, and dabbed a finger in a small bowl of salt and rubbed it across his teeth before hurrying down to sit upon a white-stone bench that had been carefully polished with oil. Other benches stood around each side, curving away from Nestor's as the king imagined the seats of the Immortals curved away from the seat of Zeus. The old man's sons staggered out of their rooms, Perseus, godlike Thrasymedes, Aretus, Echephron, Stratius, and last Peisistratus with Telemachus. They took their seats and waited for Nestor to speak.

"Now, my boys, attend to me well and don't dawdle about my words. Last 417-441 night, Athene blessed us with her presence and I've promised her an ox for her gift to us and I mean to keep that promise. One of you go to my fields and from my herds select a yearling unbroken to the yoke and have a herdsman bring it here. Let another of you go to our guest's black ship and fetch his crew to our court. Leave two to stand watch against pirates. One of you needs to find Laertius, the goldsmith, and tell him to bring his hammer and anvil to form a coat of gold to fit around each of the ox's horns. The rest of you round up the maids and tell them to prepare a feast in the great hall. Bring in the groundskeepers and have them set seats around the altar and wash everything with pure water. Attend, now!"

His sons rose and rushed to do his bidding. The herdsman brought in an ox just as Telemachus's friends arrived. The goldsmith arrived with his anvil, hammers, and tongs, while Athene watched secretly as Nestor brought a generous supply of gold to the smith. The smith thinned it down and began to pound it into shape to fit the horns of the ox. Athene watched with delight as Echephron and Stratius held the horns while blossom-freshed water was poured over the head and neck of the ox, purifying it. A scantily clad virgin, bouncing breasts boldly displaying ruby nipples, brought a basket of barley bread to the room and stood by, her cheeks rosy from the eyes of the men. A fire was lit in a great bronze bowl upon a tripod. Thrasymedes stood by with his sharp ax, ready to cut the ox while Perseus held a large basin to catch the purple blood as it spilled from the wound.

442–467   Nestor checked that all was ready, then carefully washed his hands and broke the bread, praying to the goddess. He pulled hairs from the bawling ox's head and cast them into the flame. Then stout Thrasymedes carefully spread his legs, measured the distance to the nape of the ox, and with one blow of the ceremonial ax severed the spinal column. The ox dropped nerveless as the daughters and wives of Nestor's sons and his own wife, Eurydice, gave a shout of glee. Peisistratus stepped forward, placed the bowl beneath the neck of the ox, drew its head back, and cleanly sliced the great vein there. Black blood splashed into the bowl, and when life had left the flesh, they instantly cut him up, hacked out the thighs and, wrapping them in a thick layer of fat, laid them upon the burning logs. The brisket was then sliced and, along with the sweetbreads, carefully placed upon the fire, where Nestor splashed them with wine. The young maids stood by with five-tined forks, and when the fire had burnt Athene's offering, pulled the sweetbreads from the fire and served them to all waiting. Then chunks of meat were carved and spitted and roasted in the fire.

468–494   While the meat was roasting, Polycaste, the youngest daughter of Nestor, bathed Telemachus, washing him carefully before anointing him with rose-scented oils and wrapping him in a tunic and rich cloak. When he was thoroughly cleaned and sated from Polycaste's nubile charms, Telemachus took his place beside Nestor, shepherd of his people, and all ate and drank their fill.[17]

At last, Nestor rose, commanding, "Yoke the handsome, high-maned horses and bring them in a chariot for our guest. It is time for the journey to begin."

Inside the chariot, the maids placed bread and wine fit for Zeus to last the youths on their journey. Then Telemachus stepped into the chariot, followed by Peisistratus—captain of men—who took the reins carefully in hand and uncoiled his whip over the backs of the horses. They leaped forward and galloped out of the courtyard, the wheels rattling over the cobblestones as they flew down the streets and out onto the dusty road leading to Sparta and the palace of Menelaus.

All day the horses raced tirelessly, and when the sun sank and the road darkened with purple shadows, they came to Pherae where they stayed in the house of Diocles as guests. He, whose father was Ortilochus, Alpheus's son, received them, honoring them with every courtesy possible.

When Dawn's rose fingers graced the sky, again the team was yoked and 495-497 the two climbed aboard their many-colored chariot and galloped out and across the roads that led through fertile fields of grain, the flying steeds running effortlessly across the dusty highway, their journey ending just as the sun dropped below the horizon and purple shadows were thrown across the earth.

Here ends the Third Book of Homer's Odyssey.

THE FOURTH BOOK

A Visit to Menelaus and Helen

❖ ❖ ❖ ❖ ❖ ❖ ❖ ❖ ❖ ❖

Menelaus receives Telemachus
And tells what he knows of Odysseus,
Which he received from Proteus.

❖ ❖ ❖ ❖ ❖ ❖ ❖ ❖ ❖ ❖

Telemachus spat dust from his mouth and wiped the grime   *1–28*
From his face with his cloak as the weary horses climbed
The rise leading to the Lacedaemon valley ringed by hills.
Olive trees, twisted by time, clung tenaciously to the rocky slopes.
Vines, well cropped in the fall, now bore plump purple grapes.
For a moment, he wished that he could sip the blood of the grapes,
But then he saw the tiny fields of onions, garlic, cucumbers,
Artichokes, carrots, and pumpkins and wished he could number
His hours instead on the cool heights of Ithaca's mountains,
Lying upon the dappled earth beneath the trees. The mountains,
He decided, closing his eyes and smelling the sweet apricot
Blossoms, where he could eat Ithaca's sweet dates any old time
With a fine, saucy wench by his shoulder. He sighed, wishing.

Peisistratus clucked to the wheel horse and guided the horses down the narrow, twisting trail past the village's olive press, past orchards of apples and pears, plums and figs, to Menelaus's house. The sound of great merriment came to them as they pulled to a stop at the gate.

"Do you think they are waiting for us?" Peisistratus grinned, spitting.

"No one knows we are coming," Telemachus said. "Unless, of course, our ships rounded the point before we could make our way overland."

"Impossible," grunted Peisistratus, wrapping the reins around the chariot rail. He took care that the horses had slack enough to droop their heads and nuzzle the water at a trough. "You may have mighty warriors at the oars, but no one can pull against the tide with that speed."

A beefy servant appeared at the gate, brow wrinkled quizzically. "Aye, and what brings you to our doors on this happy day, strangers?"

"Happy day?" Telemachus asked.

"Aye, a happy day," the gatekeeper said. "So lift the sour look from your face. Gods' balls but you look as if you have eaten a bushel of sour cherries without a maid to take the tartness from your lips with a sweet kiss." His eyes rolled merrily. " 'Tis not seemly to take such a face into a wedding hall. Especially one that is doubly so."

"A double wedding?" Telemachus said.

"My master's son and faultless daughter will find themselves well mated by this day's end," the gatekeeper said, then amended himself. "Well, his son, Megapenthes,[1] basely born but loved the same as a father would any of his children nevertheless, will bed boldly by night." He waggled his bushy eyebrows. "But the daughter has a long journey to the Myrmidons' fair city before she can share her bed (and more's the shame, for her white breast and thighs have caused many a man a restless night in Morpheus's arms). 'Tis the end of a promise that Menelaus made in Troy years past. Hermione is to wed Neoptolemus, the valiant son of brave Achilles, who broke the back of the Trojan army after his friend, Patroclus, had been killed by Hector when he borrowed Achilles's fine armor from his tentmate and charged the Trojan ranks."

"Megapenthes was born to a slave woman?" Peisistratus asked, wrinkling his brow.

"Aye." The gatekeeper looked around him, then lowered his voice and moved closer. He belched softly, and a small cloud of sour wine billowed over them. "The gods—well, you know those fickle ones—allowed Helen no more children after Hermione's birth—one to challenge Aphrodite, that one."[2]

"Sounds like great times," Peisistratus said, looking pointedly over the gatekeeper's shoulder.

"Oh, 'tis," the gatekeeper said, ignoring the hint. "We got a singer whose godlike voice graces the beauty of the ladies." He kissed his fingertips airily. "And acrobats—"

"A very good time," Peisistratus added emphatically.

"Aye," the gatekeeper said. "Oh. Yes. Pardon me."

He turned and raised his voice, shouting for Eteoneus, the frustrated chamberlain of Menelaus. "Tell Menelaus that a couple of dusty friends from the south crave his audience."

Eteoneus waved his hand as he bustled past, hurrying into the huge andron,[3] the dining room, where the people's shepherd held court amid the wedding feast. Men dressed in himations,[4] long cloaks wrapped around the body and draped over the shoulder, sprawled upon couches. Hetaerae, wearing loose chitons, moved laughingly from couch to couch, dodging the playful hands of the men who played cottabos, a wine-flicking game. Servants moved quietly among them with pitchers of wine drawn from huge kraters at either end of the room.[5] A poet sang and played softly on a kithara, a small harp, from his seat on a diphros, a low stool placed to the side of the room. His apprentice sat on the floor beside him, blowing softly on panpipes.

The chamberlain came to the auburn-haired king seated upon a marble thronos,[6] saying with winged words, "My king, two strangers wait without the gate for audience with you. They seem like men descended from Zeus, who guided you during your wanderings. Broad-shouldered and decidedly handsome. Should I order their horses unhitched in your stables, or send them on into the town and direct them to a tavern where they will find someone who is not so, um"—he indicated the feast—"occupied with the amenities that he—" 29-63

Menelaus lowered a cup of wine and stared contemptuously at him. "Now, why would you want to do a thing like that? You babble like a blithering idiot, Boethus's son. Think! Use your noodle! Remember how we begged Zeus to guide us to a man with hospitality when the two of us plodded our way across those wastelands to the south? By Hephaestus's hammer![7] Have the gatekeeper take their horses to the stable lads and have them unhitched and groomed, and lead our new guests into our house to share our feast. How do you know this isn't a test by Zeus the trickster to see if we valued his help in the past? Hurry, man! You don't want to give offense to someone you don't know. This could be disastrous!"

"Oh my," Eteoneus squeaked and, turning, hustled through the hall shouting to other servants to lend a hand. They took the sweating horses from Telemachus and Peisistratus and led them to the stables. There, they unhitched them and brought them into stalls where fresh straw had been strewn. They poured out wheat mixed with white barley and lightly touched with honey. Then they propped the chariot against the gleaming wall and directed a youth to wash it carefully.

Meanwhile, Eteoneus took the young men to the bathhouse, where servants took their dirt-stained chlamyses[8] from them. Peisistratus and Telemachus stripped off their tunics and lowered themselves into the water, washing hurriedly as handmaidens scraped the dirt from them with strigils. When they emerged from the baths, slaves quickly toweled them and smoothed their glowing skin with oils taken from aryballoess. Then the slaves helped the young men dress in long tunics with gold thread at the hem, fastening the wool at the shoulder with gold brooches. They slipped soft leather sandals on their feet and followed the chamberlain from the bathhouse to the house. They paused, touching the base of the herm, the protective god chosen by Menelaus, standing in front of the door, then stepped in to join the feast.

64–91   "Welcome!" Menelaus called from his seat. He gestured at two chairs with curved arms and stools that had been placed beside his thronos. "Join us. Eat with us. When we've finished, then we will know who you are. There's no need of early introductions for 'tis certain that you are from sceptered kings sired by Zeus. No commoner could claim such sons sprang from their loins."

They took their seats, and a servant poured fresh water from a cleverly engraved golden ewer into a silver basin for them to puddle their fingers before eating. The old housekeeper directed large platters heaped with fat flanks carved from well-fed ox, the choicest parts reserved for high-ranking men and guests, to be placed before them. Fresh-cut melons were placed beside them, and they ate heartily. Then, with their appetites sated, Telemachus leaned close to Nestor's son and said, "Look well around you, Peisistratus. These glorious halls are well decorated with gleaming bronze and gold, silver, ivory, and amber.[9] The walls are as richly decorated as the walls of Zeus's hallowed home. Such wealth is amazing!"

And although he spoke low and for Peisistratus's ear alone, Menelaus overheard him through a lull in the conversation and answered with winged words, "Ah, now, sons, no mortal man's home can match that of Zeus. All this"—he waved his arm around—"is only temporal. The halls of Zeus will last forever. And as for my wealth among mortal men"—he shrugged— "there may be others whose trappings will match mine. I don't know. But I can tell you that what I have came from many wanderings and cost me many men and griefs. I traveled seven long years to bring these treasures home. Through Cyprus, Phoenicia, Egypt, and other lands too numerous to name, I roamed, seeking a way back to my home. I roamed the barren sands of Egypt, saw Sidonians, Erembians, and Ethiopians, crossed the lands of Libya where lambs grow horns as soon as they are born and ewes give birth three times a year. A blessed land, that, for no shepherd or master can complain that they lack sweet milk or meat or cheese." He paused to take a drink and grinned. "Why, the entire year is one long milking season!" A low titter ran among the guests who were listening. Menelaus's face grew somber. "But despite all my sightseeing, gathering treasures, I suffered greatly. A traitor killed my brother, surprising him in the arms of his faithless wife. All this wealth is not worth the loss of one's brother.

92–119   "But surely you know all this! Your fathers surely told you about the trials

I endured and how, while I was away, my house and fields fell into ruins. Nothing could be saved on my return. I wish that it could. I would give two-thirds of my wealth to have that house back and the friends who died on the dark plains of Troy, so far from Argos. Often, late at night when I drink wine, I grow maudlin and my heart aches for those Greeks who lost their lives. My eyes fill with tears and I feel the lonely chill of sadness. Yes, I mourn them still. All of them. Yet none more than Odysseus. When I think of him, food turns foul in my mouth, and my sweetest wine becomes bitter bile. I will never forget his trials, his tribulations."

He shook his head and stared off into the fire of a brazier standing by his elbow. "No," he said softly. "No, I will remember him and wonder where he is and if he is well. Does he walk with bold strides in Stygian gloom? I mourn his memory and mourn even more that I do not know what lies past my memory. I'm sure that I'm not alone in that; certainly old Laertes and wise Penelope, yes, she, too, must shed many tears over the fate of her long-lost husband, and the newborn son he left behind, Telemachus, mourns him as well."

And overcome by drink and memory, Menelaus wept bitter tears that streamed down his leathery cheeks into his gray beard. And seeing this, Telemachus wept too, hiding his tears in his purple-edged cloak. But when Menelaus saw his tears, he sat back, frowning on his thronos, contemplating the youth who struggled manly to hide his grief. By the gods, he thought, this youth does bear a semblance to mighty Odysseus.

But before he could voice his thoughts to his young guest, Helen entered 120–151 the room from her high-roofed and perfumed chamber. Her hair shone with a bright brilliance, a soft halo circling her white brow. She wore a white chiton embroidered at the hem and pinned at the hip and shoulder with two golden serpents. Her creamy breasts—snowcapped mountains exposed to the very halos of her nipples—dried men's mouths and they reached for their wine cups, burying their noses in the depths to hide their desire. Her handmaidens hastened to serve her. Adraste brought a chair for her while Alcippe[10] draped a soft cloak woven from fine wool over the chair. Phylo brought a silver basket, a gift from Alcandre, the wife of Polybus who lived in Thebes in Egypt, where the houses are richly furnished. There Polybus[11] had given Menelaus two silver bathtubs, two tripods, and ten red-gold talents to welcome his guest on his wanderings to that land. The wife of Polybus had given Helen a golden spindle and a silver-wheeled basket with gold rims.[12] Phylo placed the basket, heaped with fine wool, next to Helen's elbow as she sat, placing her dainty feet upon a footstool. She looked boldly at Telemachus and his companion, then raised her eyes to her lord.

"Menelaus, who are these two? If I didn't know better, I would swear that one is so like Odysseus that he must be Telemachus, the son of that great warrior. Now, tell me, am I right or wrong? I am truly lost in admiration," she said sultrily, looking back boldly upon the youths. Telemachus blushed furiously at her bold stare. "Yes, I am sure that this must be the son great-hearted Odysseus left behind when he came with you Greeks to Troy, to avenge your honor that I stained with my charms."

Menelaus coughed and pulled his fingers through his beard. "Well, my lady, you do point out a certain resemblance that I can see—although I must swear that the thought never crossed my mind 'til now—for his gestures are the same as are his feet. Hm. Yes, that same nobility lies upon his brow, and the shape of his head and the way his hair falls in ringlets over his shoulders does remind me of Odysseus. Zounds! Only minutes ago I was reminiscing on bold Odysseus and explaining to this young man and his friend all that that wily man had done for me when tears began to stream down his cheeks and he covered his face with that purple cloak."

152-178 Nestor's son Peisistratus said, "Menelaus, great pastor of the people, this is Odysseus's son, my friend. You must forgive his modesty, for he is not used to speaking forthrightly on first visits." He grinned. "You must invite him to speak, and then you will find his words as musical as a poet's words. My father, Nestor, sent me as his companion since Telemachus was most anxious to seek your advice. He has had many difficulties at home with no one to help him fight the injustice being done to him."

"By the gods," Menelaus exclaimed, leaning forward. His elbow knocked over a cup of wine, and servants hastened to sop up the spilled grape before it could stain. Menelaus fidgeted and frowned impatiently. "Who would have thought it? I loved Odysseus as a brother! Why, I could do little else after he performed all those arduous and wondrous tasks for me. My, my! And now his son comes to my house! You know," he said, winking conspiratorily at them, "I did promise Zeus that I would honor Odysseus above all else if the mighty thunderer ever deigned to grant my wishes. I even promised to build a palace and a city in his honor and bring him and his blushing bride from Ithaca to Sparta so that we could be neighbors and take pleasure in each other's company until Death's veils draped over each of us. But"—he sighed—"a jealous god must have taken issue with my intentions and ensured that Odysseus would never reach his beloved Ithaca."[13]

179-208 The words of Menelaus brought tears to the eyes of everyone there. Helen cried openly, using a cloth hastily provided her to dab kohl from her eyes to keep her cheeks from appearing bruised. Telemachus and Menelaus, feeling the maudlin wine within them, cried as well, heeling their tears from their eyes. Even Nestor's brave son who had shared the bed of Telemachus wailed as he thought of how bright Dawn had killed his brother, the handsome Antilochus. He harrumphed and coughed, sniffled, then drank deeply from his wine cup. He cleared his throat and said:

"Menelaus, son of Atreus, old Nestor claims that you are the wisest of men. As such, please hold your sorrow—if, indeed, that is possible, for it is most disheartening to one trying to dine when his guest sobs rivers of tears— for it is almost morning. Now, I'm not saying that it's wrong for a man to cry over the loss of a friend. What else can one do but shed tears and cut a lock of hair from a loved one? I know what you are feeling. I have my own dead to mourn as well. My brother wasn't the worst one to wear armor in the Greek camp before the walls of Troy. Perhaps you knew him? Antilochus? I never saw him myself, but I have heard that he was a great runner and fighter and could hold the reins of a chariot with the best of them."

Menelaus wiped his tearing eyes on his robe and stared blearily at Nestor's son. "My friend, you are wiser than your years. Those are the tactful words of a far older man. It's easy to see that Nestor is your father—you have his way with circling words. But that's breeding. After all, what can one expect when Zeus blesses one's marriage bed before the romping and rutting? Nestor had the fatherly eye of Zeus on him all the time and now ages peace- fully at his home with good sons about him who have proved themselves good spearmen and wise. Well spoken! And now"—he raised his newly replenished wine cup—"let's forget our sorrows and woes and maudlin maunderings and drink and be merry. Here, here!" He clapped his hands and motioned to a servant to bring a basin of water. "Bring us some water to puddle our fingers in and remove the grease. Telemachus! I commend myself to you! Come morning, I'll meet and discuss these important matters with you!"

Asphalion hastened to his master's side and poured a thin stream of water 209–235 over his hands. When Menelaus had finished, he did the same with the oth- ers and all reached for the feast laid out before them. Telemachus nodded at a servant holding a wine pitcher as he reached for a chunk of meat.

Helen, however, had an idea and slipped a powder into the pitcher of wine, a drug that stilled anger and cares, banishing painful memories. No one who drank that wine would be able to shed a single tear, even if his mother or father, brother or son, were put to the sword before him. It was a drug that Helen had received from Polydamna, the wife of Thon, ground from petals plucked from the rich soil of Egypt by wise physicians who are the true sons of Paeon the Healer.[14]

Helen watched with guarded eyes until she saw that wine poured into 236–264 cups and drunk. Then she spoke. "Menelaus, favorite of the gods, husband, my young and noble guests, we all have had our good times and bad times—wise Zeus sees to that," she hastened to add when the bushy brows of Menelaus drew together in a frown. "So I propose that we enjoy our dinner now and content ourselves with each other's stories as we make merry. I have just the one to start with, and it is one that our young guest here"—she fluttered delicate fingers at Telemachus—"might enjoy. I cannot, being a woman, of course"—here she batted kohled eyes at Telemachus, who blushed furiously—"adequately describe all the daring feats of dauntless Odysseus—that would more properly belong to a singer than a mere woman—but I do have a little snippet that I think might entertain you."

She raised a delicate eyebrow to her husband who, feeling the pleasant melancholy of the drug, nodded his permission for her to proceed. "Now, then. Let me think how best to begin." She pretended to frown prettily, allowing her fingers to slide absently over the crowns of her white breasts.

"He cut himself with many wounds and then, casting the vile, manure-smelling clothes of a slave over his royal shoulders, he crept through the broad streets of high-towered Troy disguised as a beggar. Anyone who looked on that filthy figure slinking the streets—save I, who immediately saw through his disguise—would not have taken that broken and beaten figure to be the brave Odysseus! But even when I tried to question him, he cleverly kept from giving straight answers. But when I ordered him to be bathed and anointed with Persian perfumes, and gave him clean clothes to cover his body with military purple, and solemnly pledged my word not to disclose his presence to the taunting Trojans before he returned to the Greek camp near the ships, he relented and gave me the Greek plans.

"Before he returned to the ships with the information he gathered as a spy, however, he had to kill many Trojans with his sword. The women of Troy were loud with their lamentations after his visit inside the city, I tell you! I pretended to grieve with them—after all, what could I, a prisoner of sorts, do? But I secretly rejoiced, for by now the veils of lust cast over my eyes by Aphrodite—I was a gift, you know, to Paris for having chosen her as the most beautiful over Athene and Hera—had fallen and I felt a great bitterness toward that fair goddess who had brought me to Troy with her wily ways, blinding me to my own husband—who lacks nothing, as you can see, in manly grace and mind"—Menelaus preened at this flattery—"and my bridal chamber and Hermione, my own daughter."[15]

265–295   "My dear," auburn-haired Menelaus said, reaching over to pat her hand. He belched lightly. "All that you say is true! By my life, I swear it! I have traveled far over this broad world and heard many stories of great men and would-be great men, but I have never seen anyone with as much will and skill as Odysseus! I have seen many things done by that man, but what he did inside that wooden nag we built to trick the Trojans was a remarkable feat. Here we were"—he leaned back and fixed bleary eyes upon his guests—"sitting inside that wooden horse[16] with the best and the bravest and the brightest of all our army, waiting to release the dogs of war upon the Trojans inside their walls, when you, my wife, along with Prince Deiphobus, came up to the horse and, laying your hands upon it, circled it three times, and each time you circled, you called out to the men inside it, disguising your voice like their wives. My wife"—he turned to explain to his guests—"is an excellent mimic. Almost as skilled at pretending as Odysseus himself. I don't know why you did that," he admonished, "but I can only presume it was some god's prompting. Both Diomedes and I, sitting in the middle with good Odysseus, heard your moanings and soft promises. Both of us were tempted to leap up and come out or shout an answer from inside, but Odysseus held us back with his wise words. Still," he mused, "there was a minute there when Anticlus tried to shout out, but Odysseus clamped his great paw over the man's mouth and held him quiet until Athene called you off."

A sudden drowsiness fell over the company and, stifling a yawn, Telemachus said, "Menelaus, these stories are good, but now I feel sadder for knowing that not even his wiliness or iron heart could shield him from disaster. Enough, I beg of you. Can you show us to our rooms, now, where we might sleep and rest?"

Then Helen of Argos ordered her handmaidens to spread two beds in the 296–326 portico and cover them with warm, purple fleece and spread heavy blankets over this with thick coverlets. The maids took burning torches and led the yawning youths to their beds, giggling among themselves while boldly eyeing the men's broad shoulders. There, the youths disrobed and fell exhausted in their beds while the maidens stripped their chitons from their bodies, exposing bouncing brown breasts rosy-tipped, and snuggled in beside them.

Meanwhile Menelaus took Helen, wearing a long dress, by her hand and led the stately woman to his room at the back of the palace. His fingers slipped the golden serpents from her dress, and the chiton fell in folds at her dainty feet. She laughed throatily and fell into his bed with him, as Eros shot golden arrows of desire and lust into the hearts of each.

When Dawn gently pressed rosy fingers against his eyes, Menelaus awoke, fully sated and vigorous. He yawned and stretched, then giving his war cry, leaped from his bed. Startled, Helen snarled and burrowed deeper into the bedclothes, muttering matterings about men rethinking their youth.

Menelaus ignored her cross words and slipped into a short tunic, slinging a sharp sword over his broad shoulders. He tied a pair of fine, soft leather sandals around his callused feet and ran his fingers through his long hair. He strode from the room, his heels slapping hard against the floor.

"Men," growled Helen, burrowing even deeper into the bedclothes until only a few strands of her long blond hair could be seen.

"Telemachus!" Menelaus roared, as he walked like a god through his palace. Servants scurried out of his path. "Telemachus!"

The youths heard him and rolled out of their beds, much to the disappointment of the maids, who protested the early hour. Hurriedly, the young men slipped into their clothes and stepped out of the portico to encounter their kingly host. He clapped each on the shoulder, then took a seat and called for breakfast to be brought. He grinned at the tousle-haired youths and said, "Well, then! Tell me, Telemachus, my royal youth, what brings you over the wide seas to the pleasant land of Sparta? Public business? Or"—he eyed them slyly and nodded at the door behind them where their bed partners were dressing—"private? Eh? Come, now. Speak the truth. Either way, you are welcome, whether you want wise words or wanton wenches. Speak!"

"Menelaus, god's favorite, I came to see if any word had come to you about my father," Telemachus replied. He shook his head sorrowfully. "We have fallen on hard times in Ithaca. My house has been infested with a lawless people—vermin all—seeking my mother's hand, saying that surely my father has died or been killed since he has not returned home ten years after the war. Although my mother has rejected them, they still persist in their attentions to her. Meanwhile, they have sacked my house, paupered my stores, and killed my sheep and oxen for their own pleasures. Now, I'm not saying that I begrudge them food and shelter, but they have abused the laws of hospitality, even by the most generous interpretation, that Zeus has laid upon us. Lately, their suit to my mother has become most obnoxious, most inhumane, insulting even though they are not guests. Because of this, I have come to your court to see what you might have learned about the sad and wretched end of my wandering father, whether you witnessed his death with your own eyes or have heard rumblings and stories about his demise from sea traders and poets. If ever my father gave you his word at Troy and kept it, tell me what you know."

327-355   Menelaus sighed and scratched his head. He leaned back on his seat and studied the youth before him. "Tch. Tch. Disgraceful." He shook his leonine head. "I have heard rumblings about the difficulties in Ithaca, but to think that such a thing has gone this far—humph! This is the way of the youth, apparently. Why, in my day we would never think about doing such a thing!" He leaned forward, shaking his finger. "I blame the times for this, boy. The times! The sense of honor is gone when a woman and her son would be treated thusly by men pretending to be gentlemen. So. These cowards, these milksop recreants, these jackanapes want to crawl into a brave man's bed and romp with his wife, do they? Unthinkable! Might as well have a deer put her unweaned fawns in the lion's den for safekeeping while she ranges the high hills for sweet grass. Back comes the lion to his den and *wfffft!* He finds his dinner waiting. A grisly fate for the fawns. Your mother's suitors will suffer the same fate at the hand of Odysseus. Mark my words!"

He fell back against his chair, his face red with anger. His fingers clawed his beard. He seized a cup of wine, drained it, and set it aside, taking deep breaths to compose himself. "I hope when he does return that he comes with that same strength I saw years ago when we put in at the pleasant island Lesbos and saw him take on Philomeleides in a wrestling match. Ah, there was a man! He fetched that muscle-bound oaf such a blow that Philomeleides staggered around on the sand like someone had poured a skin of wine down his gullet. Then your father seized him and threw him with a hiplock, slamming him to the earth with such force that for a moment we thought Poseidon had thrust his trident into the bowels of the earth! A great cheer rose at that from all the Greeks who had watched this same ruffian beat all contenders before your father. By the beard of Zeus and Apollo! That was a day. And if those would-be suitors, those men whose wispy beards are little more than fuzz, are still around when that man returns, why, it would be a swift death and sorry wedding they would be attending, I tell you that!

"But"—he sighed—"I have no wish to deceive you or raise false hopes. On the contrary, I'll let you know what I have heard from the Old Man of the Sea himself about your father. Let's see." He closed his eyes in great thought for a moment, then nodded as memory crept back in. "Yes, it was in Egypt where I had been wandering for some time, anxious to get back home. But"—he gave an expansive wave of his hand—"the gods detained me, for I had not given them the proper offerings, the proper sacrifices—a paltry offering of one scabby calf instead of the perfect hundred—and the gods do not forget those who ignore their commandments. Well, there was this island called Pharos, guarded well with high seawalls from the mouth of the Nile, that lies a day's sail with a roaring wind off the coast of Egypt. There's a sheltered cove there where seafarers can put in for fresh water from its deep wells before returning to the sea-lanes. We put in there. A bad mistake, that, for the gods kept us there for twenty days. We were dangerously low on supplies when Eidothea, the daughter of Proteus,[17] the Old Man of the Sea himself, visited me. Low on supplies? Better to say that my men spent their days casting barbed hooks into the surf to catch fish, and when was the last time you saw warriors stoop to such a thing? Never. So, I tell you the sight of

356-385

her touched me deeply when I met her while walking along that rock-strewn coast, racking my brains for a way off that cursed isle. Lord, she was a beautiful creature, and I admit I had hunger pains lower than my belly when I saw her high-breasted form appear!" He chuckled and shook his head. "But she unleashed her tongue on me, nearly flaying my skin from my shoulders, she did! 'Sir,' she said. 'Are you plainly stupid or just a total fool?' Her words took me back a step or two, I tell you. 'What kind of a slacker are you that you would stay on this stony isle by choice? Do you like to suffer? Is that the kind of man you are? Or are you a sadist and like to watch your men grow weaker by the day? Eh?' she says.

³⁸⁶⁻⁴¹⁶ "And I says back to her, 'Well, I don't know what goddess you may be, but I tell you that I'm not hanging around here by choice! The only thing I can think of is that I have offended one of the gods—or maybe all of them, for that matter—of the broad heavens, for they are keeping me landlocked. Now, you gods seem to know everything long before we mortals, so tell me how I can return home across that raging sea.'

"And that day the sea was raging! Huge, gray waves licked with dirty foam as tall as the mast of my ships rushed inward to crash upon the land. Sea wrack draped the rocks. The spray was like sleet stinging the flesh. But that lovely goddess answered me without hesitation.

" 'Stranger,' said she, 'I'll tell you what you need to know, or at least how to find out what you need to know. Not far from here lives an old seadog quite adept at scrying the secrets of the sea—immortal Proteus, the Egyptian seer, the Old Man of the Sea, as some call him—who will tell you what you want to know even though he serves Poseidon. Some say he fathered me. But that's beside the point. Lie up and wait for him, and if you catch him by and by, he will tell you about your journey, how far you will have to travel to reach your home, and give you directions that will carry you across these teeming seas. He'll also tell you what has happened in your palace while you've been journeying hither and thither without plan or purpose.'[18]

" 'Thank you,' I said to her. 'Now, if you'll do me one more favor, I'll be forever in your debt. How would you suggest that I waylay this ancient god? Sounds to me a bit dangerous, you know. He might see me first or hear about my plans, and then where would I be? 'Tis not as easy as you make it seem for a mortal to beat a god at any game. Especially this one.'

" 'All right,' she sighed. 'I'll give you a plan. Clean the wax from your ears, now, and pay attention. When the sun climbs to its meridian height and the West Wind ripples the dark waves, the old sea god slips from his salty lair and goes to his cave where he sleeps, guarded by the sea calves, lovely Halosydnes's children. They sleep in herds around him, snoring and snorting pungent odors from the sea. Take three men you trust from your crew and meet me here at daybreak. I'll lead you to a place where you can lie in wait. The old god has a way about him that is predictable. First he makes his rounds and counts each of the sea calves like a shepherd does his flock. When he is satisfied that all are there, he will settle down with them. When you see him make his bed, screw your courage to the sticking place and drop down upon him. Be brave! Be strong! You must hold him no matter how hard he struggles and no matter how many promises he makes! Remember that gods are tricky, and although they must make their promises good, they can find ways of meandering about the truth. He'll try all sorts of things and change himself into every beastie and creature you can see on earth, in water, or in fire. He's a wily shape-shifter, you know. But each time he changes, you must hold him all the tighter and press him hard to keep him from passing from your hands. But when he tires, he'll shift back into himself, and when he does that, relax your grip on him and ask him then which of the gods is keeping you from your hearth and home and how you can navigate over the shifting waves of the sea.'

" 'Thank you,' I said politely. 'And what can I do for you?' For the truth be told, I sort of hoped for a tumble with her on the sands, you know, but she only smiled and dived into the wavy seas. I sighed and trudged back to where my ships waited on the sands. My men had been lucky with their hook casting, and we had a fine meal of fish fried in a little olive oil. Then the ambrosian shade of night fell on us and we slept at the water's edge.

"When Hyperion's daughter Eos stepped saffron-robed from her bed, I set out with the three men I had chosen who had more than once guarded my back in our travels. I didn't take any chances; I offered many prayers to the heavens and Zeus and poured out a fine bottle of currant wine to him as an offering before we trekked our way to that cove where I had met Eidothea. I had no idea about her plan, but we sat and waited for her and soon she emerged from the gray waves with four freshly flayed sea calf skins. She dug a hole in the sand for each of us and made us lie in the holes, covered by the skins." He wrinkled his nose and scrubbed it vigorously with the heel of his hand. "I still smell the sour odor of those fish-fed brutes and at the time had a hard time holding down my gorge, as did my mates, and who could blame us? It isn't everyone who can lie with those creatures, and I wonder about those who can and do. But the good goddess came to our rescue even there, for she had some sweet ambrosia that she smeared on our nostrils that killed the stench of the sea calves.

"And so we waited through the morning's hot sun, and when the sun reached its meridian height, huge herds of sea calves came up and lay down

417–447

448–479

in rows to snooze on the sandy beach. Not long after, here came the old man, walking dripping from the hoary waves of the sea. He found his fat calves there and counted them slowly, and painstakingly, and when he had finished, counting the four of us among his herd, he too lay down to sleep. When his eyes slitted shut, I gave a signal to my men and we leaped up, shouting, and fell upon him. That old forger's skill had not left him, and he shape-shifted first into a mighty-maned lion, then a dragon with rancid breath, then a panther and a great boar. Finally he slipped into running water and a great-leafed tree. But we hardened our hearts and grips and held him firmly.

"At last, the old one grew weary and spoke to me. 'Menelaus,' he said, 'tell me which of the gods gave you the gift to waylay and capture me. And why do you feel you have to treat me in this disrespectful manner?'

" 'Old man,' I said, 'I have been kept here on this island long enough. And don't lie to me: You are fully aware that I have been held here against my will due to the tricks you have played with the shifting winds. We are starving, growing weaker day by day. What god has commanded you to keep my ships here?'

" 'Your fault! Your fault! Not the gods!' he yelped. 'You never made a proper sacrifice to Zeus and the other gods before you set sail over the wine-dark seas. Your fault! Not the gods! And you never will reach your homes until you once again sail the heaven-fed waters of the Egyptian flood and perform the proper rites. You know,' he said, blinking his own eyes furiously at me, 'you must needs pay your respects before traipsing off on a voyage. When you have done that,' he added primly, 'then the gods will lift the bans against you. Don't know what you were thinking,' he muttered. 'Typical mortal, forgetting his duty to the gods yet wanting everything from them. No give-and-take in a respectable manner. No, sir!'

480–508 "My heart broke when I heard those words, I tell you!" Menelaus said to the youths. "Now I had to make my way back across those misty waters to Egypt and burn a bull on the beaches there. A good lesson there, I suppose, but a costly one. But we must not presume our own importance at the sacrifice of the gods, and occasionally the gods must tweak our noses to remind us of our places in the scheme of things. Excuse the ramblings of an old fool. That's not what you wanted to hear. I decided that I would take advantage of the situation, holding the Old Man of the Sea as I did, and put to him other questions.

" 'Old man,' I said, 'I'll follow your advice—not much else I can do about it—but tell me about the other seafarers, all countrymen of mine, that Nestor and I left on Troy's shores when we first raised sail for home. Did any of them die at sea or in an accident or in the arms of their friends?'

" 'By the bull's blood, why do you ask me these questions?' he complained. 'You don't need to know any of this stuff and nonsense! A man's life and a man's death matter little to the gods. Men's knowledge has proper limits set to it. A man's not given to know everything about the gods' plans. It's all how he lives. Yes, that's it! How a man lives! The rest is all spiderwebs and dust balls! But,' he added hastily, when I raised my fist, 'there's no reason to get violent about the affair! I'll tell you! You'll be sorry that you pressed yourself into the mind of Zeus, but you want to know, why then, I'll heap the sorrows upon your head and let your tears help fill the salty seas.

" 'Many were killed, but some were spared. Only two of your fellow kings—give a man a house and he calls himself a king'—he grumbled, hawked, and spat—'but man always wants to appear better than he is, fooling himself more than the others, wants to be a god, I expect—where was I? Oh, yes, as I was saying, two of your kings'—*snicker*—'lost their lives while homeward bound. You know about the fighting, for you were there, so I don't have to speak about it unless your pate has been properly muddled somewhere along the line and if so, so much the better for you. There can be wisdom in madness. But there is a third, a prisoner somewhere in the wide sea. Although,' he muttered to himself, looking with watery eyes out to the broad horizon, 'a man could do worse than to find himself a prisoner in those white arms and thighs. Ah me!' he sighed. 'Let's see: Aias went first, losing the light in the wreck of his long-oared ship when Poseidon drove him upon the great cliff at Gyrae. No, I'm mistaken. Poseidon pulled him from that wreckage, but the pompous fool moaned on about his own importance despite Athene's warnings to keep his words to himself and not dally in human folly by speaking arrogantly to the gods and boasting that his prowess as a swimmer in that mighty surf brought him safely to land. Words may be temporal at best and often lost in air, but gods hear them—especially when they have little toadies willing to carry snippets to their ears. Poseidon became enraged at this pompous boasting and jabbed his trident into the Gyraean rock, splitting it in half. Half stood firmly landlocked, and the other half that Aias had been resting on fell into the sea, taking that boaster with it. He drank a lot of water there to remind him of his sin before he drowned.

" 'Now, your brother Agamemnon is another story,' he said, laying watery eyes upon me. He grinned nastily. 'Somehow that fellow managed to evade his fate and slipped away in his great ships'—he cast a quick look around, then leaned forward conspiratorially, winking and thumbing his nose—   *509–535* 'some say it was Hera herself, mighty Zeus's wife, who took a hankering for his curly locks and broad shoulders—but this, you understand, is only shipboard twaddle—and helped him slip willy-nilly over the waves. Still, when he reached the steep cliff of Cape Malea, a most tempestuous blow drove him over the fishy world to the borders of the land that Thyestes called home in the old days and where now his son Aegisthus lives. Agamemnon bided his time well there, and eventually the gods relented and turned the winds to let him sail for home.

" 'When your brother set foot on the land of his fathers, he fell to his knees and kissed it and cried and cried for joy. But there was a watcher placed in a watchtower there with many pandering promises of two golden talents by crafty Aegisthus to keep a-spying for Agamemnon's landing. He had kept watch for a year, and when he saw the king fall upon his native shore, he promptly set out for the palace and informed Aegisthus, the usurper of Agamemnon's bed and crown.

" 'Now, Aegisthus had no desire to give up the warm arms and lusty loins of Clytemnestra'—he winked lewdly—'a fine wench whose bed skills draw many dreams—besides, Aegisthus was the brother of Tantalus, the man your brother killed so he could share your sister-in-law's bed. Anyway—long story needing to be short and all that—Aegisthus devised a rather elaborate trap. He took twenty of his best men and left them in an ambush in one part of the palace and ordered a feast be laid to welcome home the king. Heh, heh'—he chuckled—'Agamemnon had no idea that his wife had taken a lover—although, truth be known, she had worked her way through the ranks of the palace guard until she found the one to satisfy her. Then Aegisthus called up his fanciest chariot and went out along the highway to bring Agamemnon home in right proper pomp and splendor. Agamemnon, thinking this was all a great celebration in his honor—ah, the arrogance of it all, beautiful!—came rushing up the coast to the palace. There, Aegisthus feasted him, then killed him like an ox in its own manger when he rocked in his wife's saddle. A bloody battle broke out in that house, I tell you, until the halls ran with a blood tide! Not a single one of the king's men or of Aegisthus's came out the door alive. All were killed.'

536–565　　"My soul shrank with grief from his words, and I fell to my knees upon that sandy shore and wept. I thought my heart would break, for Agamemnon and I had made long plans to stop warring and live the rest of our lives in peace. And now"—he shook his head—"well, that was gone. When I had cried enough and stopped rolling on the sands, gnashing my teeth and swearing vengeance on Aegisthus, the old sea prophet jabbed me with a horny finger and said, 'Menelaus, you've cried enough! Nothing comes of grief but more grief, and you keep on doing this you'll get nowhere. Far better to spend your time getting back to your home. It's all out of your hands, anyway: You'll either find Aegisthus still living and cut his belly and let a dog drag his insides out and eat them before his eyes, or Orestes may have saved you the effort and cut his throat. You might even get there in time for his funeral feast if you hoist anchor and shake the salt from your sails now.'

"Well, these words cheered me, I tell you. I started to leave, but then I remembered there was a third one who was still a prisoner. I turned back to him and asked who this one was that I might properly mourn him. He answered, 'Odysseus, Laertes's son, who is kept a love captive in the palace of the Nymph Calypso. There he cries when he's not making love to her because he knows his country, grand Ithaca, lies just over the horizon from the island's shore, yet far enough that he can't make it without a ship and men to sail it.

" 'And now, Menelaus,' he said, spitting and eyeing me balefully, 'hear your own fate: You will not die in Argos despite your willingness to end your days watching fine horses graze in grassy meadows. The gods will send you to the Elysian Fields at the ends of the earth where you will join auburn-haired Rhadamanthys[19] in the land he rules where living is easy: no snow falls there, no rain, and the winds are not gales. There, where Zephyr's breath[20] blows gently from the west to refresh its people, there you will retire with Helen by your side. After all, you are the son-in-law to Zeus, even if you do forget to give him proper respect and all.'

"With this, the old man slipped away from me and dropped beneath the 566–626 heaving waters of the sea. Well, my men and I returned to our ships, my heart and mind churning with the thoughts planted there. Solemn Night had fallen by the time we arrived. We made a hasty supper and lay down to sleep on that sandy shore.

"When Dawn stretched forth her rosy fingers, touching the waves and turning them gold, we ran our ships down into the foaming ocean, raised our sails, and trimmed our ships. The men climbed aboard and found their oarlocks and beat the heavy waves with their paddles. We made our way to where the heaven-falling flood of Egypt ran into the land. I lowered anchor there and made the proper sacrifices to appease those gods with burnt offerings of a hundred cattle. Then I built a funeral mound for the glory of Agamemnon. And, finally, set out for home. The gods sent me a favorable wind for a change, and I sailed quickly back to my homeland."

He paused and thirstily drained a bowl of wine, belched, and eyed them, slapping his hands on his knees. A dog whimpered and rose, laying its head upon his hands to be fondled. He scratched its ears and the dog grunted with pleasure. "Well, my friend, that's all that I can tell you. Stay here for a while and visit. It would be a gladsome change from the gossip of the sea traders. In twelve days, I'll send you off in royal style. I'll give you the gifts that a man should give in hospitality: chariot, three horses, and a finely made chalice wrought in gold to remind you of me every day when the sun fills your skies and you drink your morning toast to the immortal gods."

Telemachus cleared his throat, saying tactfully, "Please do not ask me to stay here too long. I am delighted with your stories and would willingly sit and listen to them for a good year and never feel homesick for my parents. But I have friends waiting for me in sacred Pylos. I value your generous offer but ask, instead, if you wish to give me a gift, give me one that I can carry. I would not care to take any of your horses to Ithaca, for they are quite accustomed to the rich meadows filled with clover and galingale. Indeed, your kingdom is better suited for horses. It is a broad plain filled with wheat and rye and white, broad-bearded barley. In Ithaca, we have mountains. There is no vast plain for horses to run nor any meadows. It is a place for goats, not horses and chariots. Most of the Greek isles are this way, you know, Ithaca most of all."

Menelaus grinned at the youth's words. "Well spoken, young man. You have a good eye for the world and, I can see, the right blood flowing through your veins. Of course I will change my plans for you. Instead of the horses and chariot, I'll open the doors of my treasure house and give you the best there. I'll give you a serving bowl richly engraved in solid silver with a gold rim. It was made by Hephaestus himself and the only thing that Phaedimus, Sidon's grand king, gave to me when I stayed at his palace on my journey home. But it is the gift of gifts and I will gladly give it to you. Perhaps it will bring you luck."

He patted him on the shoulder and rose. Together, they left for the great hall, where guests had arrived while they spoke, bringing with them sheep and resin-flavored wine. Their wives wore filmy chitons slit to the hip to expose long thighs and finely turned calves and cast saucy eyes at the youths who grinned and shared flirtatious looks with the prettiest.

627–651 **W**hile Telemachus and his friend enjoyed themselves in the palace of Menelaus, back in Ithaca the suitors amused themselves with idle games, throwing the javelin and tossing the stone in the courtyard of the house of Odysseus. Antinous and Eurymachus, who had by now emerged as the leaders of the suitors, sat in the shade of an olive tree, propping their sandaled feet upon a stool as they lolled on wooden chairs. They sipped wine, swatted flies, and chatted idly, pausing when Noemon, the son of Phronius, came up with a question for Antinous.

"Antinous," he said, "have we heard anything about when that upstart Telemachus is due to return from sandy Pylos? He borrowed my ship for his trip and now I need it myself to make a trip over to Elis. I have a farm over there with large fields where I keep twelve delicate mares and each has a sturdy mule sucking a teat. None have yet to know the yoke or plow a field. I want to fetch one here so I can tame him."

Antinous and Eurymachus exchanged quick looks and frowned. Antinous cleared his throat, looked at Noemon, and said quietly, "This is extremely important, my friend. How long has he been gone and which young men went with him? Townspeople, or did he make up a crew from his own serfs and servants? And did he steal the ship, take it from you with force, or," he added dangerously, "did you give it willingly when he asked for it?"

"I let him take it when he asked for it," Noemon answered boldly. "Why not? When a man like him who has many troubles asks for a favor, only a churl would refuse him! As for the young men, he took the best of our youth from the town—present company excluded. The captain was Mentor. At least I think it was him or a god masked in his likeness," he added, "because I think I saw Mentor here yesterday morning. Yet," he said, scratching his head in puzzlement, "I know I saw him board that ship for Pylos. Ah, well! I can see this is all news for you."

He nodded at each pleasantly and ambled back through the heat of the day to his father's house.   *652–679*

Antinous and Eurymachus exchanged furious looks. Antinous threw his cup against the wall. Shards of pottery flew through the air. The others paused in their game playing and looked over at them. Antinous leaned forward, eyes flaming, heart seething with black passion, and said, "Damn it, this Telemachus has outreached himself this time! A boy, a child, outwitting us! And we thought nothing would come of it when we taunted him to try and take it. So here we are, sitting here and swilling wine while that . . . that pup of a mongrel bitch calmly picks his men, gets a ship, and slips off without a single farewell. Well, I'll see that nothing good comes of this insolence! I hope Zeus lops his balls off before he learns what they're about! Get me a fast ship with a twenty-man crew and I'll lie up in wait for him by the cliffs of Samos when he tries to run the straits for Ithaca's seas. I'll make a grim ending of this voyage of his," he said.

The others applauded and hurried to ready a ship for his leave-taking, not noticing the herald, Medon, who had been eavesdropping in the shadows and heard their plotting. He sped off to find Penelope, climbing the stairs to her room, his arthritic joints popping and making his progress painful. She looked up from her loom as he limped into her room.

"Well, my herald! You seem out of breath from your climb. What do our guests want of us now? To tell Odysseus's maids that they must stop working and prepare their banquets? How I wish they would leave us and stop swarming around like flies and dogging my every footstep! They would never feast here again, if I could stop them. They never meet but to decide what they will have to eat and to reap the benefits of our people and our fields and orchards. Always taking from us what we have gained with our own honest effort. How dare they treat us in this fashion? Odysseus never gave their fathers a harsh word when these suitors were children and never took anything from them. And where are those fathers now? Skulking in the shadows, hoping to benefit from the spoils of their sons. It's easy to see that good acts are often forgotten when greed rears its ugly head."

"My queen," said fair-minded Medon, "I wish that their behavior toward you was the worst that they could do, but it seems that they are planning something much more deadly. I have no doubt that Zeus will not grant them success in this, but still, well . . ."

"Say it, good Medon," Penelope said, her face blanching white at the hesitation in the herald's speech.

"They are planning even now to assassinate Telemachus as he returns home from sandy Pylos, where he has traveled to learn news about his father."

When Penelope heard this, her knees trembled, and a great hammering seemed to come from her heart. For a moment, she didn't trust her voice as tears filled her eyes. Then she said, "Why has my son left? Why did he leave safe shore and put to sea? There was no need for him to venture across the vast sea. Does he wish his name to disappear completely from this world?"

"I do not know," wise Medon replied. "Perhaps some god urged him to journey to Pylos; perhaps it was his own need to satisfy his feelings. But travel he did to discover what has happened to his father, to learn when he will return, or"—he hesitated—"to learn of his father's death."

Saying this, Medon turned and left, making his way down the long stairs to where he had left the suitors. Overwhelmed with her anguish, Penelope started for one of the many chairs in the room, but her legs failed her and, turning, she sat on the raised threshold of the room. She covered her eyes with her hands, weeping bitterly while her handmaidens stood helplessly around her.

"The gods have deserted me," she moaned between her sobs. "Tell me, my friends, has any woman ever been so sorely treated by Zeus? I had a husband many years ago who was the best and the bravest among the Greeks, a man with the heart of a lion whose fame stretched from Hellas to the heart of Argos. That man I have lost. And now I am near to losing my son who has been led from the household by the gods. I was not even told that he had left. And not one of you came to tell me his plans. Unhappy wenches! How dare you stand here and wail with me when none of you thought well enough of my feelings to rouse me from my sleep to tell me that he had left in his hollow black ship? Had I known about this journey ahead of time, I swear by the gods that I would have forced him to stay.

"Stop!" She held up her hands as they began to stammer their innocence. "The harm has already been done. One of you call my old servant Dolius,[21] the slave my father gave me who attends my orchard. Tell him to go to Laertes and tell him the whole story. Perhaps Laertes will be able to figure out a plan and come from his seclusion and appeal to these men who would wipe out his and Odysseus's royal line."

Her nurse, Eurycleia, said, "Dear lady, let me die by the cruel knife or cast me out. But I'll not keep one word of what I know from you. I knew the plan that Telemachus had made. I helped him supply his ship by giving him the bread and wine he needed for his travel. It was all he asked for, except for my promise that I would not tell you for at least a dozen days after his ship had slipped away into the night. He didn't want tears to spoil your lovely cheeks or let the suitors know that he had left.

"Now," she continued, "go and wash and dress yourself with fresh clothes. Then go to your room with your maids and pray to Athene to preserve your son. She will save him. The old king who you hope will save your son with his grave words to the suitors has enough of his own troubles without hearing any of yours. I don't think that the happy gods will destroy the lineage of Arceisius. No, these lofty halls and fertile fields will survive."

And so Eurycleia hushed Penelope's woes, and the good queen used the sleeve of her chiton to wipe the tears from her eyes. Obediently, she washed and changed her clothes and, cleansed, went upstairs to her room with her maids. There, she filled a sacrificial basket with cakes of barley and grains of salt and prayed to Athene, saying, "Hear me, great virgin! If ever Odysseus sacrificed the fat thighs of sheep and oxen to you from his great halls to show his devotion to you, hear me! Do not forget these sacrifices he made to you and show your appreciation by safely guiding my son on his journey. Guard him against the brutal hands of these would-be wooers who have passed all limits of hospitality with their insolence and bearing and who daily insult us with their continued presence."

As she finished her prayer, her heart broke and she raised her voice in a great wail of grief. Athene heard her prayer, and great pity came from her. But in the halls, the suitors roared with laughter as they heard Penelope's shriek. One of the callous youths cried out, "It appears that the much-courted

739–765

766–792

queen will finally rid herself of her spleen and take one of us as a husband. I wonder if she knows that her son's death has already been arranged?"

Antinous, however, rose up among them, scattering them with a great oath, saying, "Hold these brave speeches. What's the matter with you? Anyone could have heard these words and that would be not in our best interests. Now, keep your flapping lips shut and go away. All of you know our plan; that's enough. Let's get on with it!"

He stepped among them, slapping the shoulders of the twenty men he wanted to sail with him, and they left for the seashore where they launched their black-prowed ship and raised the mast, setting sails. They fixed oars in heavy leather slings and rubbed their shoulders with heated oil to loosen them for rowing as servants brought down their weapons and armor. Then, mooring the ship in deep water, they came back to shore, where they ate and waited patiently for night to fall.

Meanwhile, Penelope lay awake in her upper room, touching no food or drink and wondering if her rash son would meet his death or escape the ambush being readied by the suitors. She tossed and turned upon her couch, then lay still, terror for her son filling her mind as a lion will stand trembling when beaters close stealthily upon it. At last, however, Morpheus touched her eyelids, and she fell into a heavy sleep.

793–820 Athene, hearing Penelope's plea, came up with another plan. King Icarius, the father of Penelope, had yet another daughter called Iphthime who was now the wife of Eumelus and lived in Pherae. Carefully she made herself into a shadow of Penelope's sister and sent it to Penelope's room to keep the unhappy queen from languishing in even more sorrow. In her dreams, Penelope heard Athene's words coming from the shadow of her sister, saying, "Do you sleep, now, Penelope, worn out from your grief? Don't worry. The gods don't bear you any malice. Your son shall return home safely. The gods promise this to you, for the boy has never wronged any of them."

Penelope stirred restlessly at the Gate of Dreams, saying, "Dear sister, why do you travel to me in this fashion so far from your household? You have never come here before at this hour and now you come and give me cheer, telling me to forget my anxieties and sorrows. This is difficult to do as I have lost not only the best and the brightest of the Greeks whose fame spread across Greece to the very heart of Argos. Now I have lost my son to whom I have given all of my love. He is a mere child, untrained for war. I worry so much when I think what might happen to him at sea. He has so many enemies who thirst after his blood and yet he is still a child."

"Be brave," the shadow said. "He isn't alone on his journey. Pallas Athene *821–847* travels with him and holds him safely within her power. It is she who heard your prayers and felt your pain and sent me to you to bring this message and comfort you in your grief."

"If you are truly from the goddess and heard wise Athene tell you these things, then perhaps you can answer another question for me? Please tell me about my husband. Does he still live and see the bright rays of morning and day, or has darksome earth covered his head and does he now live deep in the House of Hades among the dead?"

"I will not tell you this. Whether he lives or dies is of no consequence at this time. These would be only empty words that escape into air."

She transformed herself into a fog and disappeared through the keyhole of the door, vanishing like a breath of wind. Penelope awoke with a start, then remembered her dream that had flown to her in the dark of the night and lay back again, slowly, taking comfort in the dark.

The suitors slipped their ship from its mooring and, rowing quietly, sailed out of the harbor and onto the dark seas, their hearts heavy with malice and plotting murder for Telemachus. They rowed hard until they reached the open strait between rocky Samos and rough Ithaca, and there they hid among the shadows of a great cliff near the rocky isle of Asteris, where they lay in wait, hoping to make their massacre.

Here ends the Fourth Book of Homer's **Odyssey.**

THE FIFTH BOOK

The Loving Nymph and the Open Sea

❖ ❖ ❖ ❖ ❖ ❖ ❖ ❖ ❖ ❖ ❖

The Gods send Hermes to Calypso
And order her to help Odysseus to
Build a raft and sail across the sea.
But Poseidon's anger nearly
Drowns Odysseus, saved by Ino.

❖ ❖ ❖ ❖ ❖ ❖ ❖ ❖ ❖ ❖ ❖

*D*awn rose from her sleeping bed beside bright Tithonus[1] to bring   *1–27*
Day to Immortals and mortals. The gods stretched and yawned
As they made their way to the called council. The dawn
Was not made for celestial pleasure, but for man, and that,
Athene reflected, was enough to make them as irascible as bats.
But she determined to confirm the fate of Odysseus
And had little time for twittering twits and ruffled feelings.
It was time for mighty Zeus to forbid angry-eyed Poseidon
His vengeful ways and free Odysseus from Calypso's arms.
She waited impatiently for the Immortals to settle, then spoke.

"Father Zeus," she began formally. She cleared her throat and waited until the grumbling and whispering quieted among the other Immortals. "Father Zeus," she began again, "and all this magnificent assembly of Immortals whose generosity and sense of justice are fairly pronounced upon the mortals and who"—she nodded at Zeus—"holds the scepter as king of us all and needs, by right, to be benign and cordial in his dealings among all—"

"Great balls," sighed Ares to Aphrodite. "Here we go again! You know what she needs?" And he leaned forward to whisper in Aphrodite's ear. She giggled, then hid her smile behind her shapely hand as the wisdom goddess glared at her.

"As I was saying," Athene said, snapping each word like a bean. "Anyone who does not deal fairly with the misfortunes of others might as well toss the reins of his rule to anarchy and lawless deeds. Consider how Odysseus ruled with a gentle but firm hand among the people of Ithaca. A father could not have been more protective of his children and home than Odysseus was with his people and island kingdom. But few of those people even give his name a passing thought, and when they encounter his name now, furrow their brows in puzzlement before realizing that he was once their king. Now he languishes, a miserable mortal mired in the enchantments of the Nymph Calypso,[2] who keeps him captive there to satisfy her own lust and love."

"And a lustful wench she is, too," Ares mumbled, drawing another glare from Athene. Apollo grinned while Hermes[3] waggled his heavy eyebrows, drawing a few laughs from the coarse-minded among them.

"Well," Athene said, gesturing in dismissal, as she turned to face Zeus. "It's all a matter of wishes and wants, I suppose. Poor Odysseus hasn't the means to do anything about it even if no magic spell had been placed upon him. He hasn't either ships or oars, and even if he had, there's not one man with a broad back to man them. No one to help him cross the wide seas. And now"—she glared at Ares slyly running his hand along Aphrodite's shapely leg while Hephaestus, her husband, frowned his thick brow in heavy concentration at Athene's words—"those would-be seducers of his wife Penelope plot ways to murder his dear son, Telemachus, who has sailed to sacred Pylos and blessed Sparta to seek words of his father, when the youth turns the prow of his ship back toward Ithaca."

28-56 "Ahem," Zeus cloud-gatherer said, clearing his throat and frowning. "What's this? What's this you're saying? Daughter, I believe this is all part of your plan, isn't it? This delay to keep Odysseus far from his sceptered isle until the time ripened for him to take revenge upon the suitors was your scheme, not the result of any of Calypso's love potions and spells. At least, not entirely," he amended. "Of course, if you place a man in Calypso's path, you surely can't begrudge her a little dalliance with him. It's a matter of thistles and thorns as I see it." He held up his hand as argument sprang to her lips. "Hear me. It is my wish, my command." She clamped her lips shut tightly, her gray eyes narrowing. "And don't give me that look. I get enough of that from Hera," he added under his breath, glancing at the stern visage of his wife seated next to him. He coughed and said, "You have the skill and power to bring Telemachus back to Ithaca's port safe and sound. Give him a safe sea-lane to travel and let those baffled fools who lie in wait for him return with empty hands."

He turned on his seat, grimacing as a cramp knotted his kingly thigh. He rubbed a thick forefinger over his grizzled eyebrow and said to Hermes, his beloved son, "I know you have served us well on many missions—even if you have taken a few liberties in doing them—and now I have another for you. Take my words to Calypso. Tell that lovely-haired Nymph that I have decreed she free Odysseus from the love chains that bind him to her bed. He is to be allowed to return home. But," he emphasized, holding up his palm, "he is to sail alone without gods or men to help him. Make certain that she understands she is expressly forbidden to sail with him. I don't want his mind confused anymore with her ruby-tipped breasts and white thighs. He is to build his vessel himself with his own hands so that he learns again what it is to be a man instead of a love slave. His raft shall be rude planks hewn by him and crosstied with leather thongs brine-soaked and dried. I further decree"—he raised his eyes to include all in his company—"that although his crossing may be difficult that he will, upon the twentieth day of his sailing, reach Scherie's fertile soil in the land of the Phaeacians who are close to the hearts of all here. There, he will be honored as they would honor a god who came into their midst and eventually be taken by ship to his own land. They will give him more gifts in bronze and gold and finely made clothes than he had when he sailed from Troy. This is his destiny, that he shall return to his own land, his friends, and his high-beamed house with treasure that should have rightfully been his. The rest, well, let us say it is a form of compensation for what he has been through."

He nodded at Hermes, and the bold messenger and Giant-killer hurried to obey. First, he fastened a pair of golden sandals over his feet to carry him like the wind over land and sea. Then he picked up his wand that charmed the eyes of men in either sleep or awakening and stepped down from Olympus in flight. He soared past Pieria's proud peaks and swooped down on the sea, skimming the rolling waves like a seagull bathing its wings in briny rollers as it searches the unharvested waters of the dreaded abyss for food, riding crest after crest in joyful merriment until he reached the remote island home of Calypso. There, he left the blue sea and made his way to the fair Nymph's cave.

He paused outside the entrance to the cave, then crept forward on stealthy 57–89 toes like a thief, hoping to catch an unguarded glimpse of the beautiful Nymph. She was at home before a splendid fire that cast its warmth into the darkest corners of the cave. The fragrant scent of burning logs—juniper and cedar—filled the cavern. Calypso sat in front of her loom, weaving with a golden shuttle. Her lilting voice rose in song, soaring out from the grotto into the rich forest that surrounded it, the notes flitting in and out among the alders and fragrant cypress where wide-winged birds, horned owls, falcons, and long-tongued cormorants, seabirds, built nests. Vines heavy with clusters of purple grapes ringed the entrance while four springs bubbled with crystal waters running in rivulets to soft meadows filled with iris and violets and wild celery and parsley.

Hermes paused to drink in the beauty of its surroundings before he entered the cave. Calypso heard his magical heels shuffle on the air above the stone floor and raised her eyes to his face, recognizing him instantly. All gods know each other, despite the disguises each takes when plotting mischief, even if they live far apart. Hermes looked quickly around the cave, but Odysseus was sitting alone along the shore in a distant cove, sighing and crying, grieving as he stared with aching heart across the barren sea. Hermes shrugged and dropped into a polished chair of cypress, slouching carelessly as he eyed the clad Calypso with disappointment.

The Nymph read his thoughts in his eyes and smiled faintly at him, saying, "Well, Hermes of the golden wand, what brings you to my home? Hm? It's been quite a while since you visited me—I believe last when I was bathing in the sea—so tell me what's on your mind. Tell me what you want. I'll do anything—within reason, of course—that I can to make your stay a happy one. But first, let me offer you something to eat and drink."

90–122 She rose from her loom, conscious of his eyes upon her breasts, and brought a bowl of ambrosia to him and a cup of red nectar. Hermes grinned and ate and drank, and when he was fully sated, he leaned back, belched, and said, "As one god to another—and that was very good"—he indicated the remains of his lunch—"you ask me what brings me here. I cannot lie to one so beautiful. Zeus sent me here—this wasn't my idea, you understand?" he added hastily as she frowned prettily at his words. "No one would cross that endless briny water on his own. By the bull, I didn't think I would ever arrive here! Not a single city along the way or a mortal soul to offer a bit of beef or mutton to a god." He gave her a mournful look, but she remained silent. He sighed. "Well, on with it then. No one would cross that wide span unless aegis-bearing Zeus[4] had ordered him. You know how he is when he gets his mind set—easier to change the wind than that. Anyway"—he cleared his throat—"it seems that you have a miserable mortal here with whom you play at husband and wife. Now, I don't know about that and I don't care—although why you would prefer a mortal's company to that of the gods seems silly to me—but Zeus has determined that you have dallied with this man long enough, and it is time that he return to his home and his family."

He frowned as she raised an eyebrow in pretended perplexity. "Don't give me that look, Calypso! Your bizarre bed preferences are well-known among the gods. I am talking about the man who fought with his warriors and friends for nine years, trying to crack Priam's citadel, finally sacking that stronghold in the tenth thanks to his trickery. I'm talking about the man whose comrades sinned against Athene—not wise, that—and she sent gales and tempests against them for punishment. I'm talking about the one who lost all his noble companions to the wind and waves and who managed to make it to this isle of yours. He is not fated to die here in your arms— although I admit it would be a pleasant dalliance—away from all his friends. No, no." He shook his head regretfully. "I am sorry, but you must let him go back to his friends, his family, and his high-roofed home on Ithaca's sunny shores."

The divine goddess shuddered at his words. She bit her lip, looking away, *123-153* then straightened her shoulders as she faced him, milk-white breasts rising passionately with her indignation. "This is more than a simple matter of man's fate," she began. She held up her hand as he tried to speak. "No, no. It is. You hard-hearted gods are jealous because I have chosen to take a mortal to bed and play with him as a wife will her husband. No, it is not his fate that you are concerned with, but the fact that I have chosen a mortal over one of you. No, don't deny it. It is true. It is all right for you and the other gods to dally with mortal women—how many sons and daughters has Zeus sired away from the watchful eye of Hera?—but when a goddess takes a mortal man as her lover, why then, suddenly we hear pompous postulations that we are degrading our standing in the godlike community.

"I know what you gods are like. You punished rosy-fingered Dawn when she embraced Orion.[5] You were outraged when she chose him as her hus-band. In the end, you had Artemis of the golden throne hunt him down in Delos and kill him with her arrows. She prefers women to men, anyway. And when blond-haired Demeter[6] gave way to her passion and made love to Iasion[7] in the three-furrowed field during the seeding ceremony,[8] Zeus quickly punished him with a fiery thunderbolt. You gods have always denied the goose what the gander likes.

"And now you come here and tell me that Zeus has determined that Odysseus's fate is not to remain in my bed. Yet when Zeus sent his terrible thunderbolts and smashed his ship on the wine-dark sea and Odysseus rode the heavy seas with his arms wrapped around the mast-spar of his ship, the favorable winds blew him up on my coast. There I found him, half drowned and, in accordance with the hospitality rules laid down by Zeus himself, I welcomed him. I fed him. I took him in and comforted him against the loss of his comrades. I even offered to make him immortal and ageless." A lone tear curved down her lovely cheek. "But now, now Zeus tells me that I can no longer care for this man who must again face his fate on the restless seas. Very well. I cannot defy aegis-bearing Zeus. I will let him leave and travel across the barren water. I cannot help him leave, however. I do not have a ship, no oars, no crew. I will advise him so that he may safely make his way back to his own land. This I will do. But do not come and pretend that it is fate that has dictated this to me! It is not fate! It is the double standard of you gods who live one way and insist the goddesses live another. Hypocrites!"

Hermes moved uneasily at her words, twisting on his chair. "Apples and oranges are not alike and neither are gods and goddesses," he said. "But I'm not here to debate. Send the mortal off at once before Zeus's wrath descends on you. Think what you will about the gods. Zeus is not an enemy you want to make."

The Giant-killer stepped to the cave opening and leaped gracefully into the air, flying away from Calypso's island. Calypso watched him leave, then rose from her seat and went down to the beach to where brave Odysseus, the man of masquerades, sat wet-eyed, staring across the empty sea. For a moment, she lingered, studying his bold profile, the heavy muscles along his shoulders, then she felt the ache in his heart, the loneliness of his spirit yearning to be united with another's, and realized with a pang that the mighty god was right. It was time for Odysseus to leave. At night they would still lie together and lust would drive thought temporarily from their minds, but when day rolled night's covers away, he would sit once again on the rocks and sands, staring out across boundless seas, his eyes set unfocused on the watery wilderness.

154–184 The goddess moved up to stand beside him. She dropped her hand upon his head, her fingers moving through his thick hair. She tugged gently on it until he turned his face up to her. "Oh, my unhappy friend," she said. "It is time that you leave. What life would you have here with me if tears clouded your days? I have loved you, and because I still love you, I must let you go. Come! Bring your heavy ax and I will show you the trees to cut, stout trees that will serve you well on your voyage across the seas. You must build a broad-beamed raft, cross-planked, with half decks fitted well on top. Within that I will store much bread and water and red wine so that you will not become weak with hunger and thirst during your voyage. I shall clothe you warmly against the cold nights and command fair winds to carry you safe and sound to your own country." Her voice became grave. "Of course, that depends upon the gods of the seas and sky, who are far more powerful. Even I must obey their will and way."

Odysseus shuddered at her ominous warning, but he smiled gratefully at her. "I don't think it is my safety that you are really thinking about, Calypso. I think you are hinting at something far more dark and dangerous. This sea"—he gestured toward its vast rolling waves—"is so formidable that even the fastest sailing ships do not cross the dreadful deep, this dismal and dour abyss of Poseidon's." He shook his head. "No, I won't build such a craft as you have described unless I have your solemn promise that this isn't another trick of yours to bring me to your bidding."

Calypso smiled gently at him and caressed him, saying, "Odysseus, what a fellow you are even to suggest such a thing. No wonder you are the man of masquerades. Trickster, you have my word that I plan no mischief on you. Let earth be my witness and the vast canopy of heaven and the fearful River Styx—there is no oath more solemn that I can swear by except my own immortality, and that too I will swear by—that I plan no harm to your body or soul. My heart is not made of iron, and I know the meaning of pity even if others of my race pay only lip service to it."

She turned and left, moving swiftly inland along a path. Odysseus rose *185–215* and followed her to the cave, seating himself on the polished chair recently vacated by Hermes. Calypso brought him the food and drink that mortal men can enjoy and sat, waiting, as her servants brought her ambrosia and red nectar. Together they ate, and when they had finished, the beautiful goddess spoke first.

"Well, Odysseus, man of many masquerades, my favorite trickster, Laertes's son. So you are keen to leave immediately for Ithaca's shores? I do wish you a safe journey." Her face grew solemn. "But I must warn you that if you were only to know the trials that still lie ahead of you, you would choose to stay here with me and become one of the Immortals. Although you despair for your wife, I know that I am not inferior to her in shape or beauty." Her face clouded. "No. I know what I have promised. But it isn't right that an immortal woman should have to compete with a mortal woman for a man's love."

Odysseus, the man of many masquerades, looked lovingly at her, skillfully *216–244* masking his feelings. "Calypso, don't be angry at what I'm about to say. Please understand that you are far more beautiful than my Penelope, and your lovemaking, well, that is more skillful than any mortal woman could ever achieve. Your youth will last forever, while Penelope and other mortal women will grow lined and gray. A man would be a fool to want something other than what you offer. But that is what I am: a man. I was meant to be a man and to have a woman for a wife, not to become one of the Immortals. That is my destiny. If I am to find my fate at the bottom of the wine-dark sea, that is what I must do. I have seen many terrible things, and this has hardened my heart so much that now, to keep from becoming a bitter and vexed man, I must follow my destiny. I have fought wars and seen much bitterness. If another disaster is to come my way, let it come. That is only one more thing I must suffer to reach my home. You see, dear goddess, that although I value your love and devotion, I cannot accept your gifts. A man is only a man, not a god, and I long to see once again my home and my wife and my son. These are the pleasures of the mortal. We cannot be what we are not."

As he spoke, the sun sank and darkness filtered its way into the reaches of the cave. His words touched the goddess in a part of her immortal soul where no words had touched before. She rose and took his hand and silently led him to her bed where they found pleasure in making love once again, and this time there was a different fever to their lovemaking, for each knew that the end was near and in that knowledge there came greater passion.

When Dawn pushed night away and stretched rosy fingers into the far reaches of the cavern, Odysseus rose and donned his tunic and cloak. Calypso rose, her flesh showing the blush of lovemaking, breasts high and rosy-tipped, and slipped into a long chiton, silver-colored, and girdled around her narrow waist a gold belt. She draped a shawl over her head and led him from her cave.

She handed Odysseus a broad-bladed, double-headed ax, both edges ground to hair-splitting sharpness, the olive-wood haft firmly fixed to the head. He swung the ax, then nodded, pleased at its balance. The goddess smiled faintly and handed him a highly polished adze for smoothing the planks that he would cut, then led him to the farthest reaches of the island where poplar and alder shook golden leaves gently in the light breeze and tall pines lifted fragrant needles to the heavens.

Odysseus moved slowly among the trees, carefully selecting those of the driest matter, the oldest whose grain was firm and settled. He smiled at Calypso and slipped his tunic from his shoulders, freeing the large and knotted muscles. The sun's warmth came down upon them, warming them. He lifted the ax, testing its heft, finding the balance, then spread his feet and sank the blade into the first tree. Soon he fell into the rhythm of the ax, the twin-edged blade lifting and falling, his muscles moving smoothly under the skin covered with a light sheen of perspiration.

245–276   Calypso watched sadly as Odysseus moved steadily, purposefully, from tree to tree, then turned and left for her cave. Odysseus gave little attention to her leaving, carefully setting the blade on each cut. When he had dropped the twenty trees he had chosen, he trimmed the branches from the thick trunks with his ax, then split the trunks and smoothed the planks with the adze. Presently Calypso reappeared with wimbles to bore holes through the newly made planks. He bored the holes, cutting each to fit with the other, then made dowels to join the joints, knowing that the wooden dowels would better suit his purpose than nails, swelling tightly one to the other when wet with seawater. Carefully he shaped the raft as would a shipwright, rounding the hull carefully to form a slip keel. Then he turned his attention to the deck and hatches, fitting each to the ribs at careful intervals before planing and attaching gunwales down the sides. He cut a long pine for a mast and spar and a rudder from an alder. He used willow wattlings from stem to stern to protect against heavy seas.

Meanwhile, Calypso had been busy at her cave, weaving a heavy cloth to make the sail, bringing it to him as he finished setting the mast. He attached the sail to the spar and, setting gables and hawsers, tacklings and frames, raised the sail on the fourth day and watched critically as a gentle wind filled the sail, tightening braces and halyards. Then he lowered the sail and moved the raft down to the bright-blue sea on rollers.

The next day, the fifth, the goddess bade him farewell, first bathing him and carefully dressing him in newly sewn clothes freshly washed in pine-scented water. Then she stored amphorae filled with wine and a clay stamnos filled with water. She placed with them a krater for him to mix his wine and water, then stored leather sacks filled with grain and dried meat around them to keep them from breaking in rough seas.

At last she was finished, and she commanded a warm and gentle breeze to rise and gently drive the vessel out and away from her island to where gentle swells rolled on the azure sea. She wept and her heart ached for her loss as she stared at the tiny dot on the sea until it disappeared, and she returned to her lonely cave and the ache of its emptiness.

A happy Odysseus spread his sail, stretching it tightly against the stanchions, carefully setting the tiller to gain the maximum speed from the winds. When night fell, he kept his eyes upon the Pleiades and the Great Bear, at times called the Waine, that moved warily around Orion the Hunter, for Calypso had told him to keep the ever-present Orion, who never drops into Ocean, on his left hand. He watched the slow-setting star called Boötes that some called the Wagoner, and always he thought about the end of his long journey.

And for seventeen days he followed the course given to him by the god- *277–303*
dess who loved him. And by the light of the eighteenth day, the shadowy mountains of the Phaeacian shore rose up out of the gray sea, and his heart leaped within him as he laid the tiller over hard to make for that land that lay like a shield over the dark seas.

But Poseidon, the earthquake lord, making his return from Ethiopia where he had visited for a celebration in his honor, saw Odysseus's tiny craft bobbing upon the low swells of his sea from the distant mountains of Solymi, and his heart burned with anger. He shook his head and howled, "Damn those fickle gods! I see now why they encouraged me to go to Ethiopia! Here is Odysseus nearing Phaeacia where his hopes of reaching home will be realized! Well, the gods may have changed their minds about this man's fate, but

I still mean to let him feel my anger and maybe feed my fishes before he reaches that haven."

He rose up in his wrath and gathered the clouds from land and plunged his horrible trident into the waves, stirring them angrily. He coaxed every storm possible from the gathering, brooding clouds and tossed them like a blanket over sea and land alike. Night fell, tumbling headlong down over the light and the winds clashed together, the East, the West, and the North winds came boiling down fast on its heels to roll a great wave in front of Odysseus's craft. Vainly, the mighty warrior tried to cling to the tiller bar, but the waves rose up and tore it from his grasp. His sail split, then shredded into tatters, and Odysseus clung desperately to the ropes, his knees trembling from the strain of staying with his craft as waves crashed over him.

304-331   "Fate!" he screamed into the blackness. "Fate! Why was I born a man to such miseries as these? Athene! You promised all too well the grief I would feel upon the broad back of the seas before I reached my native land! What black clouds Zeus has cast over me! How fierce the winds! And now I see the sea's bottom changing places with its top! Ah, how dreadful is the presence of our death realized! Twelve times blessed are those who sank beneath the Trojan army on the fields of Troy! If only I could have found my hour of death there instead of beneath these waves! If only I could have died the day a horde of bronze spears were cast at me over Achilles's corpse! Then would I have had the proper funeral and the games and honors that follow with it. But now, now! Ah, god! An ignoble death is mine!"

He seized the rudder and vainly tried to press his weight against the might of the sea. At that moment, a huge wave, a giant among the giants, rose in wrath from the depths of the sea and crashed down upon him, ripping the tiller from his hands and hurling him overboard. The warring winds curled around the mast of his tiny vessel and snapped it like a dried twig. Another huge wave rose and ripped the sail and half deck from the craft and carried it away.

And Odysseus sank beneath the sea, his muscled arms flailing against the strength of the waves, vainly striving against their might. His lungs burned and he pressed his lips hard together to keep them from opening and sucking in the dank seawater. The water dragged at his clothes given to him by the goddess Calypso and hindered him, keeping him from fighting his way up through the waves to air. But at last, when the wave relaxed to gather its strength for another try at him, he pulled his way up the watery ladder and drew a deep breath. He turned his head away from the rolling sea to spit out the briny water, then, exhausted, he remembered his craft and struck out for it, grasping the gunwales and pulling himself up and over the sides. He sprawled in the middle, clinging desperately with fingers and toes as the heavy seas tossed him from one wave to the other, playing him, taunting him, as the North Wind does when he drives down through the fall with heaps of thorn-fed grasshoppers, casting them here and there. Now Boreas played with his raft like a ball, throwing it to Notus, the South Wind,[9] who passed it to Eurus, the East Wind,[10] who threw it to the horrid Tenes.[11]

But from the the heights, one witnessed Odysseus's plight: Ino[12] of the *332-357* slim feet, Cadmus's [13] daughter, who once had a mortal woman's feelings before being taken into the marine godheads as Leucothea, the White Goddess. Her heart felt pity for Odysseus, and she rose from the waters like a cormorant and landed upon his raft beside him, saying, "Why, mortal, does Poseidon toy with you in this manner? No matter, tch. We won't let such a thing happen. Now, then, listen carefully to my words: Strip yourself naked—those clothes will only be your shroud if you don't—and leave your raft for these rude winds to toy with as they will. You must swim for your life to the Phaeacian shore where your glorious Fate will not pursue you with so much hate anymore. There, you will find deliverance. Now, do what I say! Wrap my favor, this ribbon, around your waist. Its eternal virtue will not let you perish. But listen carefully, now! Once you have safely reached the shore, untie the ribbon and throw it far back into the dark seas, turning your eyes away as you do so. Then do not look back upon the sea but go far inland before you rest."

As she spoke, she unwrapped the ribbon from her breasts and gave it to him. Then, turning again into a cormorant, she dove past him into the turbulent sea. Dark waters closed behind her white heels. Odysseus held the ribbon in his huge hand and sighed, sore and weary, groaning, "What to do? What to do? I'm afraid that this is yet another trick tossed to me by the fickle gods to tease me into thrusting myself into Poseidon's arms. Well, I'll not have it! No! I'll stay with these timbers until the waves break them apart, then I'll swim for Phaeacia's shore. There's nothing else for it! There's really no other logical course for me to take!"

Yet while Odysseus anguished over his decision, Poseidon raised a huge wave, a high and horrid sea, against him that seized his ship and raised it high in the air only to fling it down into the valley between it and its brother, smashing the timbers just as a fierce wind tosses dry chaff, scattering it in all directions. Odysseus seized one of the long timbers and swung his leg over it as if riding bareback on a running horse. He wrapped his sinewy thighs around it, holding it tightly as he stripped himself naked and wound the ribbon around his waist. Then, taking a deep breath, he dove into the seas and struck out boldly, swimming for the shore.

Poseidon watched him grimly from afar and now he shook his grizzled head, saying, "So much for you, mortal man! Swim, if you can, for that shore where live the people Zeus adores. Plow those seas with your puny arms, miserable man! I don't think you'll make much way!"

With that he whipped his long-maned horses toward his home at Aegas, his laughter trailing backward from him on Boreas's breath.

358-413 But Athene, the wise daughter of Zeus, had been waiting for Poseidon to vent his fury, and when his chariot's rail had disappeared, she set forth immediately to calm the winds. She pulled in the bleak North Wind and used his breath to flatten the waves in the path of Odysseus and ease his weary-armed way that he might be rescued from the wrath of the angry Furies and Death's grim jaw.

For two nights and days he wrestled with the sable seas. Often his heart suggested that he cease his attempts to make land and sink beneath the waves into the arms of Death. But grimly he fought off the sleepy suggestion and continued with his struggle against the seas. On the morning of the third day, when Dawn rose with her beautiful braids, the winds grew calm and the sky was clear. Not one breath stirred the placid sea, and Odysseus, keeping a sharp watch for land, caught a glimpse of the shore when a rolling wave lifted him high. Then he felt a glad relief such as children feel when their father rises from his sickbed after wrestling with a long illness and passes, by the gods' will, back into life. He caught a welcome glimpse of earth and trees and took new strength from this sight. Again he swam quickly on, eager to set foot on dry land.

As he neared the shore, he heard the thunder of the surf against the rocks and felt the shock of their fury as they lashed the hard shore. He raised his head again, but everything seemed gray, no cove for safe harbor, nothing but a rocky coast and jagged reefs. His heart stilled for a moment as he despaired, saying, "Misery, misery! Zeus raised my hopes by letting me see this shore after I won my way across these seas, yet I see no place against that rugged shore bristling with sharp flint where I might place my feet.

414-443 "What is left for me? A sharp reef ahead, a raging sea behind, a smooth cliff beyond the reef that offers no handhold, deep water offshore, no place where a man might set a weary foot and scramble inward. If I try to land there, an angry wave might crush me against the cliff. Yet if I try to swim farther down the coast hoping to find a harbor elsewhere, another squall might drag me back out to the sea or into the teeming deep where the great earthshaker might send a whale or horrid demon bred by Amphitrite[14] in her seas to seize me. I'm well aware now what the earthshaker wants with me. What do do? What to do?"

He swam idly against the land pull of the seas for a moment while he debated, but then a ragged wave rose beneath him and hurled him toward the cutting rocks looming out of the surf. His heart sank as he fought against the pull of the waves. Nearer and near came those flint-sharp rocks, but suddenly bright-eyed Athene whispered in his ear to swim no more and grab the first rock that came near him. Desperately, he reached out for a rock and clutched it, groaning with the effort. The sea slackened about him, and he took a deep breath, but then the water billowed back with such force that it tore him from his grip and cast him back out into the sea. The flesh flayed from his hands, and he rolled, tumbling helplessly in the sea surge, gravel and sharp stones lancing his flesh, and again Athene bent shapely lips to whisper into his ear.

He struggled again to the surface and turned his body to swim clear of the coast, watching for some other shelter to present itself. Then, suddenly, he came to where fair Callicoe's[15] flood had worn the rocks smooth and redeemed the land from the river's seaward roll.

He heard the singing of the river and knew that he was at the mouth, and *444-467* he opened his heart to the river god Callicoe and said, "King, I humbly request your aid as I try to slip past Poseidon's angry waves. Remember the words that Zeus bade all to follow whenever a man, despite his sins and erring ways, seeks their help. Let me swim to the sanctuary of your stream."

And although the words were silent and did not pass the lips of Odysseus, Callicoe heard him and reined in the horses of the river's current, smoothing the water in the swimmer's path. Painfully, wearily, Odysseus swam through the sudden stillness until his feet could touch the sandy bottom. Then his knees sagged and his hands fell loosely beside him. His flesh, bloated with brine, seemed purple with cold, and as he fell to his knees on the shore, seawater gushed from his mouth and nose. Dead weary, he lay limply on the shore until, remembering the goddess's words, he wearily untied her ribbon from around his waist and let it drop into the river where it floated out to the sea. Within moments, it returned to Ino's hands, and Odysseus rolled over to kiss the humble earth and pull himself painfully to his feet. He stumbled forward until bulrushes showed in his path and he collapsed gratefully within them.

He sighed and rolled over to look at the sky above the brown plumes of *468-495* the rushes, and said, "Ah, me! What strange things control my future now? Well, Zeus? What do you have in store for me now? If I stay here beside this river, the sea's chilly breath, bitter frost, and drenching dews dropping will bring my death. I'm too weak to travel farther inland. A cold wind could come up the river just before dawn and chill me then." He rolled over and looked up through the rushes toward the land. "But," he continued, "if I try to climb up this slope into those dark woods, the trees may well check the cold. I could lie in the undergrowth there and let my body repair itself through sleep. Yet there I might become prey for whatever beasts live on this isle. On the other hand, if I do not try to make the woods, I may anger Zeus. One is a fool if one angers both the sea god and the land god. Better to cast one's bones into the future than stay in the present."

He struggled to his feet and made his way up the slope, where he found two berry bushes growing between two olive trees. So thickly were they entwined that no damp wind could blow through them, nor could the sun's rays shine through them, or rain soak the ground beneath them. Odysseus crawled carefully beneath their branches. The ground was littered with brown leaves, and he scooped out a nest among them with his hands and rolled into it, covering himself with a blanket of leaves. Delighted with the sudden change in his fortunes, Odysseus sighed and closed his eyes, imagining himself lying on the hearth before a warm fire. And Athene gently pressed her fingers against his eyelids. And he slept.

Here ends the Fifth Book of Homer's Odyssey.

THE SIXTH BOOK

The Discovery of Nausicaa

❖ ❖ ❖ ❖ ❖ ❖ ❖ ❖ ❖ ❖ ❖

Nausicaa discovers Odysseus
And takes him to King Alcinous.

❖ ❖ ❖ ❖ ❖ ❖ ❖ ❖ ❖ ❖ ❖

And so weary Odysseus slept while Athene descended to the city   *1–27*
Of the Phaeacians whose ancestors once graced the lands
Of Hyperia and had been neighbors to the Cyclopes. Pity.
However, they could not defeat that monstrous band
That preyed heavily upon them until godlike Nausithous took
The Phaeacians away from the Cyclopes to Scheria
Where they laid out a new city as directed
Before building their homes and clean temples to the gods.
But Nausithous had long since moved to the Halls of Hades,
And now Alcinous, well loved among the gods,[1]
Ruled the Phaeacian land and kept order in the new city.

It was to Alcinous that Athene now traveled to seek supplies for the great-souled Odysseus to aid his return to neighboring Ithaca.

Athene slipped through the palace and went up to the bedchamber where the daughter of Alcinous, Nausicaa, tall and as beautiful as a goddess, slept peacefully behind a richly lacquered door. Silently as a puff of wind, Athene slipped in through the door to the virgin's bed near which lay two maids, each blessed with the figure and manners of the Graces, ready to do Nausicaa's bidding. But Athene passed quietly above them and leaned over Nausicaa and, taking the form of the daughter of the ship captain Dymas, a girl Nausicaa's age and one of her closest friends, complained to her, saying,

"Nausicaa! How did your mother give birth to such a lazy one as yourself?   *28–54*

Look at the way you have left your fine clothes scattered around the room. Tch, tch. For shame! And to think that your wedding day is nearing when you will need to have fine clothes to wear and provide for your wedding party! In the morning, call me and we shall go together to wash your clothes in the river. Now, don't dally, for your beauty grows daily and is often remarked upon by men to your father and mother. Now, when Day winks Night from her eyelids, rise and we'll go to the river and wash your wedding garments. Ask your father to give you mules and a coach to take your veils, girdles, mantles, the bright robes and rugs to the river. It would be better, as well, for you to ride than to walk and risk bruising your feet on the stony path, for it's a long way from the city to the bath fountains."

Athene smiled as she saw her words reflected in the beauty of the young girl's face and, leaving the bedside, rose up to Olympus where the gods have made their eternal homes, free from shaking winds, drenching rains, and freezing snows, set in serene skies where a sun-white radiance plays over all. There, the gods and goddesses spend their days in happy pleasure.

The next morning, when Dawn slipped into her throne in the sky, Nausicaa awoke in her filmy gown and yawned and stretched, her lovely breasts bouncing like ruby-tipped bubbles. Suddenly she remembered her dream and leaped from her bed and set out at once to find her beloved parents and tell them about the dream. She bathed quickly, using an arsenic mixture to clean her legs of hair, then slipped into a chiton, puddled her fingers with an aryballoess and dabbed the perfume behind her ears, and left, looking for her parents. She found her mother sitting beside the warm hearth with her maids-in-waiting, spinning sea-purple yarn. She caught her father just as he was leaving with his advisers to meet with his Senate, who had requested a conference.[2]

55–82   She rushed up to him, her breasts bouncing beautifully under their thin covering, her rosy nipples glowing like ripe plums. "Father!" she exclaimed, "I have had the most extraordinary dream! Would you please order a coach to carry me and the dirty clothes that I must clean to the washing pools? Surely it is only fitting and proper that you should have clean clothes upon your back when you sit in counsel to discuss the affairs of state. And," she continued, draping a white arm lovingly around his neck and breathing quietly in her ear, "you have five sons, two who have married and three bachelors who must have clean clothes when they go to dances to advance their, er, 'states' in marriage. Now, would it not be proper for me, their sister, to supply them with clean clothes to aid them in their suits?"

She was careful not to breathe a word about her own nuptials for fear that her father might think she had become too bold and wanton. Yet her father laughed gently and chucked her under the chin with a thick knuckle and said, "Little daughter! I can't deny you anything, you know that! You may have your mules and a fine, high coach well hooded to guard your fair skin from the hot sun to take you to the pools. We don't want you freckling, now. Go and dress yourself, er, more appropriately"—he cast a stern glance at his advisers who stared with appreciation at the nearly naked Nausicaa— "before you appear before our people. Mind, now! Sometimes you are too bold!"

Nausicaa smiled and kissed her father's cheek, then switched a saucy hip at his advisers before running off on dainty white feet to do her father's bidding. "Daughters," he mumbled, shaking his head. "Ah, me!" He looked sternly at his advisers, who hastily lifted their eyes from Nausicaa's switching backside to pretend fine contemplation of a mosaic mural over their heads.

Soon servants brought the coach and mules to the palace door while Nausicaa and her maids brought richly woven garments from her room and placed them inside the coach. Her mother brought a basket of food and a goatskin bottle of wine, rich with resin, to the wagon and stored it inside with a fine, golden alabastrum, a flask filled with rose-scented oil that the girls could rub into their skin to soften it after they rose pebble-fleshed from their cold baths.

Nausicaa thanked her mother and, while her maids stepped hastily into the coach, took the whip and reins and lashed the mules on their rumps until they stepped out smartly, their hooves clattering against the stones of the road leading down to the river.

Soon they arrived at the bend in the river where a deep pool had been *83–108* made. Here, the water ran across and through fine sand that kept the water pure the year round. A small spring bubbled up from beneath the pool and swirled vigorously enough to clean even the dirtiest of clothing.

The young maids unhitched the mules and tethered them on sweet grass near the river. Then they took the dirty clothing from the coach and steeped them in the sable brook. They soaped them vigorously, then stripped themselves naked and placed the clothes in the bubbling spring and danced upon them with their white feet, betting among themselves who would finish first with the cleanest clothes. Then, having rinsed the soap from the clothes, they spread them to dry over the hawthorn bushes beside the river and, giggling, entered the water to wash themselves. They emerged, dripping and clean, and worked the rose oil from the alabastrum into their rosy skin. When they had finished, they sat naked beside the river to enjoy their meal while the clothes dried.

And after the meal, ivory-wristed Nausicaa sang and kept time for her naked maids as they played wicker ball after carefully laying aside their shoulder-length ribbons. She sat herself comfortably on a tuft of sweet grass and watched the laughing maids as their white skin slowly turned gold under the rays of the sun. She looked like the chaste, arrow-loving queen, Artemis, gliding down from the mountains over Spartan Taygetus, or Eury-manthus whose wild heart loves the wild boar chase and hunting the swift-hooved deer. The Nymphs of the countryside (lovely bubble-breasted daughters of aegis-bearing Zeus) gladly joined with the Archeress in her sport, contending with each other to see to whom Leto's daughter would give preference to walk with her through the cool forests. As Artemis stood out from all the Nymphs, so did Nausicaa (whom no husband had ever tamed) stand out from her maids, rising above them all in flaming beauty.

109–135   Soon, however, it came time for them to make their way homeward. Nausicaa called to them to finish their game and yoke the mules and fold the now-dry clothes. But bright-eyed Athene had other plans and at that moment arranged for Odysseus to awaken and see this lovely-sighted maid Athene had decided would aid him by bringing him to the Phaeacian city and her father's court. So when the princess threw the ball toward one of her maids, the goddess touched the flying orb gently and directed it to land wide of its mark in the middle of swirling eddies that pulled it away from shore.

The maids shrieked with laughter at this and teased the blushing Nausicaa for her misaimed stroke. Their screams and chatter awakened Odysseus who sat up, startled, thinking, "And what type of people in what country have I come to this time? Are they civil? Hostile? Kindly and god-fearing?" He winced and vigorously dug a thick forefinger into his ears to ease their ringing. "What shrill echo is this? Nymphs sometimes cry like this from the tops of hills or in the springs by rivers, in marshes and grassy meadows and groves of oak. Perhaps I have come to a country where there are men like myself who can speak my language. Well, there's nothing for it but to go and see for myself what I have fallen into this time."

He rose and remembered his nakedness. He reached out a broad hand and snapped an olive branch from a tree and held it in front of his naked manhood. Then he slipped from the bushes, gliding like a lion upwind through heavy mist in search of oxen and sheep, his eyes burning like Hades's fires. Naked Odysseus came upon the maidens like an empty-bellied lion as they lounged, braiding their hair. Dry salt clung to him, his hair flew wildly around his face, his beard uncombed and tangled like a mat of vines. The girls screamed at his mad appearance and scattered in each direction among the sand spits.

136–161   But Alcinous's daughter Nausicaa stood fast as Athene slipped courage into her heart and boldness into her limbs. She faced him as he approached, slowly, wondering if he should throw himself to the ground and clasp her virgin knees. Her eyes watched him steadily, and he knew instinctively that this was not a woman to offend by grasping her knees. No, he decided, it would not do to be humble, to kneel and beg. Far better to stand his distance and courteously ask if he could have some cover for his nakedness and her good grace to guide him to a town. Carefully he chose his words before speaking.

"My princess, are you mortal or a godddess? If you are one of the gods who live in the wide-domed heavens, then I can only assume you are Artemis, the chaste daughter of Zeus. Your beauty and grace and stature remind me of her. If you are mortal, like me, well then, I can only say that your father and mother have been blessed three times over. How their hearts must swell with pride as you walk among their halls and join in the dances in their fine house. You are like the first trim of a willow tree! But this is nothing compared to how blessed the man is who might win you with his wedding gifts and take you across his threshold as his bride once you are yoked into marriage with him. I have never seen a man with so much spirit as I see in your eyes now. No, nor a woman to meet with your beauty. My eye is overjoyed with admiration.

"Only in sacred Delos have I seen something to compare and that was a 162–185 fresh palm tree that had newly leaped into the air from beside Apollo's altar. Ah, that was long ago, though, when I had a fine army at my back. I was amazed at the beauty of that sprig and now I see you and I feel struck dumb with the same beauty, and yet I fear to clasp your knees and beg for your help. A cruel calamity has overtaken me. This is the first day I have seen after spending nineteen on the sable seas, fighting to stay alive as heavy waves and stern storms tossed me up and down like a cork from the island shores of Ogygia. Now god has thrown me up on this shore for some reason or another. Who can know the wrinkled minds of the gods? To suffer more misery, I suppose. Although," he continued, dropping his voice, "I can think little else what they might want from me." He ruefully indicated his naked self. "I hope you take pity upon me, princess. As you see, my latest afflictions have left me, ah, as I was brought into this world. You are the first person I have seen and I know no one here. At least," he amended, "that I know of because I don't know where I am." He threw his arms wide automatically with an orator's gesture, and her eyes dropped down, widening at his man-hood suddenly exposed. He hastily dropped his arm to cover himself again. "Would you give me linen or woolen clothes to cover myself? And I'll call for the god's blessing to fall upon you and your house for your kindness and give you everything your heart could wish: a fine husband, a family, and a house of harmony, for there is nothing more desirable among two people than a peaceful life together, keeping a house as one mind and one heart. And I will ask the gods to wound your enemies and the enemies of your husband so that you may live in peace forever and that your fame resound from the far shores of the world."

186–214
Nausicaa smiled at him, a faint half flush appearing on her cheeks as she caught a glimpse of his maleness. She became aware of her own nakedness but suddenly didn't care and stood brazenly, her excited nakedness offered for his bold eyes.

"Stranger!" she said, her voice throaty. "Although you are poor and wretched, I can see that neither sloth nor folly are partners with you. Indeed, your broad brow and bright eyes suggest that you are no stranger to industry and wisdom—although your eyes do have a tendency to wander like all men's." Odysseus raised his eyes and smiled crookedly at her. "You appear new-baptized from the sea." She frowned prettily. "Perhaps Zeus has proclaimed this plight in you, and if this be the case, why, then there is nothing for you but patiently to endure until he tires of this game. But I can take you to my father's city and house to which you have been newly, ah, 'exposed' "—she grinned—"to which I can offer a humane hand to help you in your need. After all, what else could I do? We can't have you strutting naked through our fair cities. Although," she added, glancing at her maids peeking from bushes and around trees at them, "I dare say that quite a few of them would probably not take issue with your state. You appear to be fairly contrite about your condition and for that you should be granted your request. I will show you the way to our city and tell you the name of our people. This is the land of the Phaeacians and—since you seem so intent to learn my birth and wonder if I am mortal or godlike—I am of this earth and my father is Alcinous who rules this island."

She walked to her dress and shrugged into it, then crossed to the virgins hiding from them. She laughed. "Come out from your hiding. Why do you act so silly in front of a naked man? You have seen men like this before. Did you think he was one of the Cyclopes who used to prey upon our people? This is not a man who comes from the Underworld or the water world, and I don't think he wishes to ravish and rape you. On the contrary, I think he is truly manly, wise, and true in his dealings with people." She turned and looked back at Odysseus, her lips pursing thoughtfully. "Indeed, I think his soul is too rich to sink to such decadence that he would act lewd or take advantage of women, and I do not think he will try to take advantage of our people who are dear to the gods. He does appear to be pious. And what could he hope to gain? We are an island kingdom, you know. There is no place he can go without our knowing. No," she said decidedly, "he is simply a poor shipwrecked soul who needs our help and, according to the laws of hospitality given to us by Zeus, we must attend to his wants."

"Too bad," sighed one of the girls who, emboldened by her mistress's words, had stepped out from her post behind an oak to boldly eye the naked Odysseus. "This one looks like he could last a good dance or two."

"And," Nausicaa said sternly, eyeing the bold girl, "we must provide for him as we would all who are in need of a home. So, my maids, give the stranger some food and wine and see that he washes himself and give him scented oil to knead into his skin. Pick someplace where the wind will not chill him, for the waters are cold this time of day."

Slowly the maidens approached Odysseus, who waited patiently, smiling *215–238* gently at them to put them at ease. Timidly, one took him by the hand and led him to a small cove sheltered from the wind by a stand of oak trees and a dune that stood out like a humpback whale from the shore. Another followed and laid a tunic and cloak on the sand beside a gold flask filled with scented oil and told him to wash himself in the rippling water as Nausicaa had ordered.

One tried to enter the water to scrub the grime and rime from his body, but divine Odysseus refused her aid, saying, "Please, would all of you stand a short distance away that I might clean myself with fresh water of this sea-wrought brine and smooth clean oil into my shoulders? It has been a long time since I have known such comforts, and I do not wish to wash in the sight of fair maidens. I am afraid that I might blush to bare myself so to virgin eyes."

With great disappointment, they moved away to a discreet distance to allow Odysseus his privacy, for all had seen his broad shoulders and a glimpse of his great manhood when the leaves of the olive branch he held modestly before him shifted.

With handfuls of sand, Odysseus scrubbed his broad, solid shoulders and back, then used a bit of oil to clean his face and wash his wild, untamed hair free from the foam and seaweeds that had been knitted into the fair curls by angry waves. When he had cleaned himself, carefully scraping his skin with a curved stick, he kneaded the scented oil into his skin until it shone with a soft red-bronze glow. Then he dressed himself in the garments the virgin Nausicaa had ordered placed for him. And when he had dressed himself in the finery and walked over the sand hump to meet Nausicaa, Pallas Athene put a fire more than before into his sparkling eyes, and his freshly oiled locks gleamed and curled with a beauty to match hyacinth petals. His supple limbs and glowing flesh were as fine as any that could be made by a divine

workman, as fine as if Hephaestus and Athene had combined to create a soul
worthy enough to be lodged comfortably in such a house built by divine
craftsmen. No reproving thought could have changed a curling lock of that
mighty head, no art decreed by Apollo could match the grace that Athene
had wrought in him, and so beautiful was her sly work that all the maidens
felt their eyes ravished and longed to clasp his broad shoulders and wrap
their white thighs around his narrow waist. They watched discreetly from a
distance as he sat and ate and drank his fill from the simple fare they laid
before him.

239–268   Nausicaa drew respectfully off to allow him a comforting peace as he ate,
and said to her maidens, "Whist! you delicate creatures, I know this rare
man does not walk this earth against the will of some Olympian god! No,
not even jealous Hera has a hand against a man like this. A godhead has been
placed upon him and I hope that someday, whoever he is, my husband is as
likely blessed. Watch him carefully and serve him with great happiness and
cheer."

She said; they heard; they did. And gladly did they watch him for his
appearance was greatly pleasing to the eye—and memory, for all remem-
bered the sight of that naked man coming toward them. Famished, he fell
like a Harpy upon the simple meal laid out before him, his strong, white
teeth tearing the meat with a vengeance, and while he ate, Nausicaa of the
white arms, remembering her vow to help him reach the Phaeacian city, had
the mules yoked to her chariot and, seeing that Odysseus had eaten his fill,
said, "My guest, prepare yourself for town and my father's court where the
peers of the Phaeacian state will be meeting." She paused, frowning prettily.
"Now, listen carefully. While we are traveling through the countryside and
the fields where the farmers will be working, walk quickly with my maids
behind my chariot. I am sorry," she apologized, "that you cannot ride with
me to the city, but you will soon come to the city whose tall towers rise to the
heavens. There is an excellent harbor beside the towers where the curved
ships are drawn up to the highway, each in its own slip. Once we pass that,
we will come to the marketplace that lies in front of Poseidon's palace built
with quarried blocks of white marble deeply seated in the ground.

269–293   "Here, the sailors sit and tell their stories while they mend their sails and
polish their oars and tend to the rigging of the black ships, weaving cables
and smoothing masts." She smiled, looking at the scars on his forearms and
hands. "You will not find warriors there, for we are not conquerors with
bows and arrows but builders of cities and traders. We plow the sea with our
ships. But"—a light tinge of color touched her cheeks like peaches—"they
have a most saucy tongue, and if you were to ride through them with me in

my chariot, why, they would be bold with their speech." She dropped her voice, mimicking them. " 'Why, what's this? A handsome stranger riding with Nausicaa? Hm. I wonder where she found him? Aye, her future husband no doubt, fairly fashioned with those familiar clothes.' And amid their winks and leers, they would sneer and say, 'Aye, and no doubt it is with him that she has been gadding about in the bushes. Best this way, I suppose, that she should have some strange fellow—perhaps a god who dropped from the sky—instead of one of us Phaeacian fellows, for it's sure that she won't give any of us the time of day. (And praying hard to one godhead or the other she was, to get a wished-for husband like this one!)' " She took a deep breath, her white breasts rising prettily in the sun's light. "And that is how they will talk if you ride through their crowd beside me in the chariot. That foul-mouthed lot will put my home in disgrace with their wagging tongues, lancing my maidenhead with sly words of our rompings in the sweet grass. Such words would hurt my parents if I were accused in the open market of behaving like a married woman without the grace of nuptials. So please bear with my wishes and follow my words if you wish to enlist my father's help in completing your journey toward your home.

"Once we cross the marketplace, we will enter upon a path through a *294–326* pleasant wooded garden sacred to Athene. There is a spring in the middle that feeds the flowers and the olive trees and fig trees. This is where my father has his house—far enough from town to avoid the louts who laze about the marketplace yet near enough to be raised by shouts if the need arises. Sit and wait awhile in the marketplace, if you will, and let us go on ahead so that those there will not think that you are a part of my court. Then, when you believe a decent time has passed, follow my train to my father's house. Any infant can lead you there for it is well-known. Ask for the house where King Alcinous holds his court.

"When you have come to the courtyard, cross it and go into the first building, where you will come to a great hall. Cross it and go into the next room, where you will find my mother sitting in the firelight beside the glowing hearth, spinning her sea-purple yarn. She will sit with her chair braced against a pillar and her maids-in-waiting all around her. My father's dining throne is beside her and he will be there, drinking wine like a god, watching her while she spins her yarn.

"Now, this is most important: Go past my father and drop down and address my mother first if you wish to see your homeland." Nausicaa grinned, her nose crinkling prettily. "The way to my father's goodwill is through my mother's heart."

Nausicaa flashed a white smile and smartly laid her whip across the backs of her mules and trotted away from the shore where she and her maidens had frolicked. Her chariot wheels rattled over the stones. Yet she held the reins tightly, keeping the mules from running away with the yoke and leaving her maidens far behind. Odysseus followed behind the maidens, who cast quick glances back at his fine figure outlined by the sun as it sank into the waters. When they came to Athene's grove, Odysseus stepped away from the path and entered the cool shade of the trees. He dropped to his knees and prayed to the goddess, saying:

327-331 "Hear me, unconquered daughter of goat-kept Zeus, who bears the aegis. You turned a deaf ear to me when I was shipwrecked and Poseidon broke my raft with great glee and tossed my rock-torn body upon his watery bristles. Grant me the wisdom to deal with the Phaeacians in the right manner to obtain their pity and grace."

And Athene heard his plea but did not appear to him, as her father's surly brother, Poseidon, watched her suspiciously. Instead, she pretended indifference in order not to offend her uncle whose wrath still steamed against Odysseus and would remain so until the mighty warrior reached his own land.

Here ends the Sixth Book of Homer's Odyssey.

THE SEVENTH BOOK
The Palace of Alcinous

❖ ❖ ❖ ❖ ❖ ❖ ❖ ❖ ❖ ❖ ❖

Alcinous receives Odysseus and then
Extracts the tale of the roving band.

❖ ❖ ❖ ❖ ❖ ❖ ❖ ❖ ❖ ❖ ❖

And so Odysseus, the wise and god-observing man, prayed
While Nausicaa's mules brought her to town.
Her brothers flocked around her when she reined
In at the courtyard gate. She left the newly washed
Clothes for them to carry into the well-kept home.
She did not tarry but ran straight to her rooms
Where her maid, Eurymedusa, an old Aperaean woman
Who had stayed long with Nausicaa after being brought by the sea
To adorn the court of great Alcinous, could see that something
Had excited Nausicaa while she had been at the water.
Why, even her gown's hem had become frayed!

1–26

This was truly a wise woman, old Eurymedusa, and Alcinous, whose heaven-inspired words created laws for all the Phaeacians, who treated him like a god, valued her greatly and kept her, despite her age, as Nausicaa's maid so that she still oversaw the keeping of the maiden's rooms and carefully prepared her meals.

Then Odysseus rose from his prayers and made his way to the town. When he arrived, a mighty mist was cast about him by Athene to keep him from being jostled and jeered by one of the proud and haughty Phaeacians with a foul tongue. As he was about to enter the lovely town, bright-eyed Athene appeared before him as a young wench bearing a pitcher. She stood saucily in his path and asked him what he meant in that place.

"Daughter," replied Odysseus, "would you happen to know where Alci-nous, who rules this town, dwells? I am a poor, distressed stranger here and do not know to whom I should make this request."

27–58 She smiled and said, "Strange father, I know the way and will take you there. My father dwells near the house you seek. But be careful as you follow me and do not speak to or look at anyone along the way, for these are surly people who do not entertain strangers with kindness. They have not learned the manners by which to speak civilly to strangers, and they greet everyone suspiciously. They place their trust in their ships that top the watery towers of Poseidon like feathers and are as fast as a thought. Yes," she added as an afterthought, "and they make a jestingstock out of anyone they can. A rude bunch, they are, full of galling gabble and blistering blather."

And saying this, Pallas Athene ushered him through the town and Odysseus followed in the steps of the good goddess. The free-sailing men of Phaeacia could not see him, yet Odysseus passed well within their groups and by their houses, for the lovely tressed goddess kept a great darkness around him like a shadow through her divine spells that would not allow the townspeople to gape at him.

As they passed through the town, Odysseus took note of the huge harbor and the ships that lay on the beach or swung at anchor in the bay. The streets were wide and sunny, and rich stalls crowded the market surrounded by walls so large and wide with high ramparts so strongly built that any would-be raider would be wary of trying to breach them. And although he had eaten earlier, the rich smells of roasting lamb and goat heavily seasoned with rosemary made his mouth water.

Soon they reached the court and here Athene said, "Here we are. I have brought you to the house that you sought. Inside, you will find the king and princes, the favorites of Zeus, feasting cheerfully among themselves. Do not be afraid of them. The bolder a man is, the more he wins. And you," she said saucily with a wink, "appear to be as bold as a bull in a field of heifers in sea-son. Now, the first person you will meet is the queen. Her name is Arete and her ancestors were the same as Alcinous the king's.

59–88 "The first of that line was Nausithous, the son of Poseidon, the earth-shaker,[1] and Periboea, whose loveliness outshone all the other women of her time, the youngest daughter of Eurymedon[2]—who carried the imperial scepter of the vainly proud Giants and led that race to its destruction—where was I? Oh, yes. Nausithous had two sons, Rhexenor and Alcinous. Rhexenor, Arete's father—he had no male children, you know, which sug-gests to some that he was not well favored among the gods—anyway, to con-tinue the story, Rhexenor was slain in his palace by Apollo with his silver bow. A bad time, that, when great sickness ran through the town and the palace as well.

"He left one daughter, Arete, who was taken by Alcinous, her uncle, as his wife. 'Twas no obligation there, though. No, sir! He dotes well on her and gives her anything that her heart desires—fine clothes, rich jewels, good wine, fruits and nuts—anything. And because he loves her so well and his people love him so well, why then, they worship the very dust beneath her feet. She is named in all their prayers, and when she walks the streets, her radiance shines into every dark alley and corner. Yet she is also a very wise woman and many men come to her to settle their disputes. Now, if you can win her over to your cause—make friends with her, so to speak—then I can assure you that you will be able once again to return to your friends, your longing family, your fine home."

Having said this, Athene slipped through the mist and left the lovely land of Scheria to fly over the untamed sea to Marathon and ample-streeted Athens where she entered the house of Erechtheus that casts a thick shadow over the land around.

Odysseus approached the tall court of King Alcinous boldly, although his heart thumped and pounded with misgivings. He paused on the brazen threshold of that court before entering and glanced into the room. A strange light shone into that room as if the sun and moon had merged into one. On each side stood brightly polished bronze walls. The roof seemed sapphire, and silver pilasters had been hung with gates of gold set into the bronze threshold and topped by a silver lintel over which appeared a golden cornice. On each side stood hounds of gold and silver wrought by the skilled hands of Hephaestus, the lame god, to stand guard and keep death and age from invading the house.

Along the wall stood tall chairs richly carved from cedar and draped with 89–123 finely woven cloth. Here the Phaeacian princes sat and enjoyed food and wine in copious amounts. Statues of naked youths carved in gold stood on pedestals with burning torches held high over their heads to light the room at night.

Fifty women—saucy-breasted and beautiful—hustled and bustled around the palace, some grinding apple-golden grains³ in rich querns, some spinning spindles, and others working on looms weaving cloth, their hands fluttering like aspen leaves so fast did they work while soft olive oil dripped onto the cloth to bleach it. The Phaeacian sailors find their skill at building seacraft matched by their women—whose lusty humor can match theirs—at the loom.

Outside the courtyard and close upon the gate stood a fine orchard whose ten acres had been well planted with pomegranates, glossy-fruited apple trees, sweet figs, succulent pears, luxuriant olives. The fruit appeared constantly, despite the hardest winters and hottest summers. Sweet Zephyr breathed gently upon the orchard to make the trees and vines bear ripe fruits: pears after pears, apples after apples, grapes after grapes, figs after figs. Time never raped any dainty there.

Beside the orchard stood a rich vineyard where some grapes dried slowly in the sun while workers gathered others from deeply rooted vines or stepped patiently in the winepress upon others, their feet stained rich purple. Beyond the vineyard stood vegetable beds neatly laid while at either end stood two fountains that channeled water to all parts of the garden. A spring bubbled merrily, sending a channel of water to the people in the town and to the great house itself.

124–150 Odysseus stood patiently, his eyes drinking in the splendor of the court, and when he had admired it fully, he stepped briskly over the threshold and entered the palace, where he found the peers and captains of Phaeacia filling their cups with rich wine and offering it to sharp-eyed Hermes, the Giant-killer, to whom the last libation was poured before they stumbled off to bed. But these Odysseus passed, still wrapped in Athene's mist that protected him from wandering eyes so that he might reach Arete and Alcinous. There, he fell to his knees and clasped the beautiful queen around her knees and Athene gently pulled the mist cloak from his shoulders so that all might see him. The joking and jesting court slipped into silence and they stared in puzzlement, wondering a bit fearfully at the sudden godlike appearance of Odysseus while he spoke:

"Arete, daughter of the godlike Rhexenor,[4] I have come to ask help from you, your husband, and your guests. I ask the gods to grant them happy and full lives. May their fields be fertile and their houses rich with wealth and happiness. I ask if you would be so kind as to help me reach my homeland from whose shores I have been absent far too long."

151–178 Wisely, he held his tongue after delivering this short speech and went to sit down in the ashes by the hearth close beside the fire.[5] They stared in wonderment at him for a long time until finally the silence was broken by Echeneus, the Phaeacian elder much admired for his eloquent speech and the richness of his wisdom that he had obtained from his ancestors. He cleared his throat, peered closely at Odysseus, and said, "Ahem! Well, Alcinous! This seems most unlike you to allow your guest to sit in the ashes of your hearth while a richly adorned chair stands close by your hand"—and indeed it did—"that would be more suiting to this man. Have him sit there and command your heralds to mix more wine for us that we might drink to his health—after first, of course, offering the first sip or two to Zeus, the tosser of lightning bolts and patron of suppliants—and then command your women to bring a meal for him. I daresay that he looks as if he could use a bite or two."

Alcinous rose and seized Odysseus's hand and raised him from the ashes and brought him to a well-carved chair next to his throne, moving his son Laodamas (who glared darkly at the visitor) to make room for the wily seafarer. He snapped his fingers and directed a handmaiden to bring water in a golden pitcher and a silver basin. Odysseus held his hands over the basin and she slowly poured rose-scented water over them as he rinsed them carefully. Then a servant placed a small table in front of him set with bread and fresh goat cheese and slowly roasted meat. Odysseus took meat and wine and ate with great relish.

"Pontonous!" Alcinous ordered, raising his voice. "Mix a large bowl of _{179–205} wine and fill all the cups in the hall that we may pay proper rites to Zeus the lightener, who graciously helps all those who come to him with gracious requests."

Pontonous rose immediately to obey Alcinous's will, mixing a large bowl with wine rich with honey that made minds heady with pleasant thoughts. He filled a richly adorned pitcher and scurried around the room, filling all the cups generously. When all had spilled a few drops in remembrance and honor to Zeus and drunk their fill, Alcinous rose, saying:

"Hear me, wise counselors to the Phaeacians! Listen carefully to my words as I explain what I have on my mind." He paused until a respectful silence filled the room. "Now you have all eaten and eaten well"—a murmur of approval rose softly upon his words—"and now I charge you to return to your homes to spend the night in sweet sleep. Tomorrow we will summon the Senate and make our offerings to the gods and entertain our guest with a fitting feast. After we have eaten, we will discuss the necessary arrangements for his safe return to his homeland, however distant it lies. We will"—and here he turned to Odysseus, his black eyes brightly lit with solicitous care—"guard him safely against any attackers until he reaches his native shore. After that, he will have to leave his destiny in the hands of the Fates, who spun his life thread the moment he emerged from his mother's womb.

"But"—his brow furrowed with thought—"he may be one of the Immortals come to trick us with the laws of hospitality, although in the past they have always made themselves known when we offered a hundred cattle and other sumptuous sacrifices to them. Even when travelers encounter them in our lands, the Immortals do not cloak themselves in disguises, for we are as dear to them as the Cyclopes and the wild race of earthy Giants."

206–234 Odysseus listened to his words, then shrewdly answered, "Alcinous, put away any doubts that you might have. I am no god, but only a mortal of flesh and blood. I do not have the wit or stature to live in the heavens. But my sorrow-filled burden easily weighs as heavily as the most wretched of your subjects. In fact," he continued, warming to his task, "my tale would tear at your heartstrings far more than another's tale of woe. But"—he shook his head ruefully—"this is what the gods have dictated I bear. Let me enjoy the taste of your freely given food in peace, as it is well-known that the belly must not be knotted with grief while one eats. Although my heart is heavy, common sense says, 'Eat, man, and drink and live.' When the morrow comes, then please make the arrangements that will allow me once again to embrace my native earth and enjoy the warmth of my high-roofed house and the arms of my family. Then I shall be content to stay there and live until life seeps from my flesh."

All applauded his speech, and Eustathius, his eyes sparkling with tears from the eloquent rhetoric, said, "Since our guest has spoken his feelings and desires so eloquently, let us meet and send him on his way as we would be directed by Zeus, the lawgiver."

They drank a last draught of the wine, carefully spilling concilatory drops to Zeus, then departed, weaving their separate ways homeward, their minds delightfully befuddled from the honeyed wine. Odysseus watched the revelers depart in good humor, then sat silently, patiently waiting on his hosts, Alcinous and his queen, the all-loved Arete. The handmaids quietly cleared the tables of plates and goblets, tactfully leaving a golden pitcher of dark-red wine and clean cups behind. The silence grew deeper until at last white-armed Arete recognized the cut of his clothes, having woven the cloth and sewn them with the help of her maids.

235–265 "Dear sir," she said, clearing her throat, "first, let me ask what and where you came from, and then who graced you with the clothes that you are wearing? If I recall, I believe you said you only recently arrived on our shores after wandering long over the wine-dark seas."

The man of masquerades, shrewd Odysseus, the son of Laertes, smiled deeply within his beard and said, "My queen, to answer your questions opens deep wounds so sore they turn gangrenous with hurt the gods have sent my way. Yet I recognize your words and the need to understand behind them. I can tell you this: A long way across the sea lies an island called Ogygia where the daughter of Atlas, the beautiful Calypso, lives. She is a most ingenious woman, a grave goddess, who shuns the company of men and gods alike. Misfortune brought me to her island, where I lived with her as her, er, 'companion' "—he smiled faintly at the raised eyebrow of Alcinous—"after Zeus shattered the bow of my black ship with a fervent lightning stroke. Another severed my ship in the middle of that black sea, leaving my soldiers and me floundering helplessly against the tempest-tossed waves. I grabbed the keel and wrapped my arms around it, hugging it to my breast in a death grip while the seas tossed me from wave to wave like a wicker ball. For nine days, I floated on the white-capped crest of the waves until on the tenth, in the middle of the black night, the angry gods washed me up on the golden sands of Ogygia, where Calypso, the dreadful goddess with the beautiful hair,[6] lives. Yet she received me well, despite my unwilling invasion of her privacy, and for seven years fed and clothed me. She offered to make me deathless, to make me immortal and remain eternally young so that my powers would not desert me as I grew older. But not once did she weave her way to my heart with her magical eyes and red lips that tasted of sweet wine. For seven long years, I soaked every garment that she made for me with tears of longing for my own home, the arms of my wife.

"In the eighth year—whether it was her idea or an order given to her by Zeus I cannot tell—she gave way to my wishes and helped me to leave her magical isle. She helped to provision the many-jointed ship with wine (a most delicious blend), bread, and finely woven clothes. She conjured with the god of the winds to provide me with a harmless and sweet wind to aid my sailing, and those winds remained true, the sea swells gentle and rolling. And upon the eighteenth day, the dark hills of your earth thrust up from the horizon and my heart was much cheered. I did not know that this was only a teaser sent to me, for I had much suffering to undergo before I would be allowed to land upon your isle. Poseidon, the earthshaker, sent violent tempests to toss my vessel around like a fisherman's cork. Then bottomless seas rose up, billowing like huge clouds, to wreak better outrage against my poor ship until, at last, it ripped apart in pieces and the pieces were scattered by gusting winds. Grimly, I swam toward your shore, but time and time again the riptide pulled me back, dragging me to the depths of the seas, until at last, frustrated at my persistence, the waves rose and threw me upon the huge and craggy rocks that flayed the flesh from my mangled body. I tried to cross over the bar to land, but again the seas rose in fury and pulled me back from the land. I swam again until suddenly I came upon a river whose mouth provided rockfree access to your shore. The wind abated and I put in for the shore, swimming against the current between cliffs that provided a barrier to the winds.

"Gasping from my effort, I dragged myself upon the shore and crawled into a thicket. Divine night fell and I ruffled up fallen leaves and crept beneath them to sleep the sleep of the dead. I rested throughout the night

266–297

and to the meridian light, when I awakened and crept out from the thicket to explore my surroundings. It was then that I saw your daughter's maids playing delightfully upon the bank of the river. Like a goddess, your daughter shined upon them and to her I prayed. Through gracious and generous heart—as great as that of any deity—she took pity on me, showing a wisdom far beyond others of her youth, and gave me wine to drink (that makes the blood of humans grow warm) and food, and bathed my hurts in the river, and dressed me in the clothes that you see upon me now. This is the truth that I speak, although it is painful to do so."

298–326 Alcinous shook his head, saying, "My guest, thank you for your kind words about my daughter. And although you may think that her judgment was wise, it was faulty in one respect: She should have brought you home with her maidens instead of leaving you to follow after her. After all, this is within the laws of hospitality as she was the first person to whom you made your plea."

"No," Odysseus said, shaking his shaggy head. "Do not blame her for her actions. She is faultless in her behavior and acted in good faith. She told me to follow her maidens, but I knew that I was coming to the house of her father and did not wish to compromise her reputation by following too closely upon her heels lest others—such as those ragabouts loafing by the fountain in the marketplace—should make vile and lewd comments about her character. Indeed, I worried also that you might think badly of her behavior so I decided to not take chances with your daughter's well-being and trailed after her instead of following as she bade me." He shrugged. "Men are suspicious creatures, my king, especially in the guarding of our daughters' virtues."

Alcinous smiled gently and stroked his beard with the tips of his fingers. "My friend, please do not worry that I will punish my daughter for her behavior. You are right: It is good to be prudent and cautious when stepping into a lion's den and wise to treat men with great suspicion. It is always better to be reasonable than rash and cast caution to the winds. No, I think that you behaved in a most extraordinary manner and I thank you for thinking of my daughter's well-being more than your own needs. Indeed," he reflected, frowning gently, "I wish you, a man who thinks as I think, could marry my daughter and remain here in my court as my son-in-law. By the beards of Zeus and Poseidon and the wisdom of Athene, I wish this! Few men are here who would be wise enough or thoughtful enough to think of another before their own pleasures. I would even give you a house and riches beyond your dreams. That is, of course, if you were willing to stay here with us. But," he sighed, "there is not a single Phaeacian who will detain you from your journey, as that would violate those laws given to us by Zeus. So I shall set a day for your departure and we will work toward that. Tomorrow, if that suits you. And you can sleep while our men row you across the seas (if they are in calm temper) and take you to your own country, your own house, or anywhere you desire. Even if you desire to go to a place as remote as Euboea, which is at the end of the world, according to our sailors who took the golden-locked Rhadamanthys to visit Tityus, the son of Gaia, the earth mother. No sailors anywhere are as strong as the Phaeacians who whipped the water with their oars and bore our strong ships there and back in a day."

Odysseus sighed and ran his thick-knuckled hands through his hair, combing rats' nests out with this fingers. His heart swelled with gratitude and he raised his voice in prayer, saying, "Father Zeus, listen to what this generous man has offered and grant that Alcinous may accomplish his desire to have me brought to my lands. Allow his fame to live forever on this earth thanks to his generosity in bringing me to the land of my fathers." 327–347

And while they were speaking, white-armed Arete ordered her handmaidens to make a bed in the portico for Odysseus and cover it with purple blankets and warm covers. The handmaidens scurried to do her bidding, lighting their way with flickering torches carried by servants. When they had finished, they returned and, taking Odysseus by his hand, said, "Come, friend. Your bed is ready for your rest." Yawning, he allowed himself to be led into the portico of a loopholed tower, and there he fell upon the warm, wooden bed and slipped thankfully into the soft arms of Morpheus.[7] Alcinous rose with him and, taking Arete by the arm, retired for the night in his rooms at the back of the lofty palace where a bed and trundle bed had been prepared. There, she lay beside her lord and rested her reverend head upon his pillow.

Here ends the Seventh Book of Homer's Odyssey.

THE EIGHTH BOOK

The Songs of the Harper

❖ ❖ ❖ ❖ ❖ ❖ ❖ ❖ ❖ ❖ ❖

Presents are given by Alcinous
To the warrior Odysseus,
Who repays the kindness with a tale
Of his trials at sea while under sail.

❖ ❖ ❖ ❖ ❖ ❖ ❖ ❖ ❖ ❖ ❖

Now when rosy-fingered Dawn rose from her bed *1–29*
And stretched her fingers to touch the eyelids
Of sleeping Alcinous, the sacred prince rose and
Quickly dressed and went to search for Odysseus.
He found the ravager of cities sitting on a garden
Bench and, approaching, politely greeted him
Before conducting him to a building where
The Phaeacians held their shipping councils. There,
On well-polished marble thrones they sat while Pallas
Athene roamed the streets, in voice and feature the crier
Of the king, stopping passers-by and saying:

"Peers, Phaeacians, councilmen! Please hasten to the court where you will hear the stranger who has come among us after being lost at sea to plead for wise King Alcinous's aid. Indeed, he is surely more than man, for he has the bearing of an immortal god!" And she winked saucily at the women as she delivered the last and puffed her cheeks and blew noisily through pursed lips.[1]

Their curiosity tweaked by Athene's words, all made their way to the building. Soon, all the seats were taken and even the standing room at the back was filled by the throng crowding in behind the seats. Many eyes stared in admiration at Laertes's son, the men in envy, the women sighing as their breath caught in their breasts at the divine beauty that Athene had draped over his head and shoulders. He seemed taller and broader through the breast and over the shoulders, his bearing at once gracious and grave and reverend, which inspired the Phaeacian people with affection mixed with fear and respect. No one there had any doubt that he would be able to triumph in any test or trial the elders might wish to impose on him.

Alcinous waited patiently until the chamber had filled, then rose, draped his robe over his left arm, and spoke, saying, "Captains and lords, hear me as I place my hearty thoughts in words. This stranger"—he turned to indicate Odysseus sitting patiently behind him—"has come among us, finding his way to my court. I do not know whence he came—east or west, it doesn't matter—but he does desire to return to his native land.

30–56   "Now, he begs us to help him with his desire, and I say that, in accordance with our custom to aid those who come to us with a plea for help, we make immediate arrangements to outfit a ship to run down into the friendly seas for a voyage to his homeland. Nobody has ever come to my house with a complaint that I have not tried to help, and it is my desire that our generosity be continued in this matter. So come, then. Let us put a ship into the sacred seas and select fifty-two stalwart youths to ready her for sailing. As for the rest here, why, let us all return to my home and prepare a solemn feast for this occasion.[2]

"No, no"—he gestured disarmingly—"this is at my expense. I will provide for all. No one must refuse this request in honor of our guest. And," he added, raising his voice over the excited murmurs that followed his words, "summon our sacred singer, solemn Demodocus,[3] to whom the gods have given the gift of song that can excite the hearts of those who listen to his lilting words with delight."

He nodded politely as a joyous shout rang out from the rafters of the hall and led Odysseus from the building, followed by the scepter bearers and others in accordance with their rank. A herald scampered around and through them in search of the sacred singer while fifty-two young men with broad shoulders left to gather their oars and make their way to the chosen ship beside the untamed sea's shore. There, they ran the black-hulled ship out to sea, anchored it, then placed their oars with leather thongs in the oarlocks.

57–81   Meanwhile, the dry streets flowed with men who trooped up to the king's capacious court, clamoring excitedly among themselves about the godlike stature of the good king's visitor. The porticoes were choked with the mass of men who crowded in to take advantage of Alcinous's generosity. Their mouths watered hungrily as they smelled the roasting meat and then grew dry with thirst as they saw the many pitchers of honeyed wine, mixed with pure water from the fountain in the garden. They sighed with content and rubbed their hands, waiting for Alcinous to begin the feast. And a most magnificent feast it was, too, for the good king had slain twelve sheep, eight white-tusked boars, two crooked-haunched oxen and had them flayed and fat-rich roasts placed on a grid over glowing coals.

At last, at a gentle word from Alcinous, they all took seats and grabbed eagerly at the prepared meal. And while they ate and joked among the jocund company, the herald brought the blind singer among them and led him to a chair graced with silver studs and placed by Pontonous against a marble pillar where he rested in the middle of the feasters. The herald crossed to the pine peg where the well-tuned harp hung. He took it down and carried it reverently to the singer. A servant placed a small table at his hand and rested a bowl of wine upon it for him to drink at whim. The singer touched the strings of the harp, checking the song within it, and waited patiently, sipping the honeyed wine sparingly so the strength of the wine did not impair his song.

At last, the guests sat back from the table, sucking pieces of bread sopped in wine and olive oil, some worrying with thick forefingers at pieces of meat caught between molars, the fire of appetite quenched. The babble of talk lessened to a whispering stream and then a polite silence fell over the board, and all turned their attention to the singer waiting patiently. He smiled faintly as he felt the hand of the Muse, who took his sight for her gift of song, brush over his brow, and a great power coursed through his veins. His fingers touched the harp strings gently and a clear note as from a crystal bell rang through the great hall, thrilling all who heard it.

And then his voice lifted in melodic song and tales of glories sprang from his lips and all listeners applauded greatly as they recognized the story he had elected to sing about the great quarrel between Odysseus and Achilles,[4] the son of Thetis Silverheels. With great delight Agamemnon, he who slaughtered his daughter that the Greek ships might leave his tempest-tossed harbor for Troy, watched as the quarrel between Odysseus and Achilles grew hotter and hotter until cooler heads among the heroes at the sacred festival separated them when they threatened to come to blows. With great delight he watched, for he knew the prophecy of Phoebus Apollo that only after the noble ones had quarreled would the war come to an end. This was a prophecy made to Agamemnon when he crossed the sacred marble threshold of Apollo's temple in Pytho.

And so the poet sang of the argument between Odysseus and Achilles, *82–108* and as Odysseus heard his words, memory flooded back to him and he covered his head with the end of his purple cloak and cried silently as he was ashamed to allow the Phaeacians to see him weeping. And when the poet paused to sip delicately from the bowl of wine on the small table beside him, Odysseus wiped the tears from his eyes and reached for his golden goblet crowned with wine and raised it high, spilling a generous portion to the ground in sacrifice to the gods who had inspired the poet with a song so fit to do him honor and spread word of his wit worldwide.

When the poet began again—in accordance with the desires of all there— again Odysseus yielded to the soft passion that he cunningly hid from the sight of the others so that none, save Alcinous, could know his grief from the song of Demodocus. As the poet's sweet voice rose and fell in song, Alcinous heard the heavy sighs of Odysseus,[5] yet the good king held his tongue and let the singer play until at last he said to the sea-loving councilors:

"Princes and peers! We have eaten well and listened to the songs of Demodocus and heard his gentle fingers upon the harp strings. By now, our feast has settled, so let us take to the field and try our skills at various sports so that our good guest will be able to tell his countrymen and friends about our skills in boxing, wrestling, and jumping, and the swiftness of our runners."

He rose from his throne, and the others hastily pushed themselves up from their chairs to follow him from the portico. The herald hastened to take the singing harp from the hands of Demodocus and hang it back upon its wooden peg. Then he took the poet's hand and guided him out the same way to the games. A crowd followed in their wake, eager to see their heroes vie for honors in the games. Many fine young men came forward, eager to compete in their favorite sport.

109–139   Up rose Acroneus and Ocyalus, Elatreus, Prymneus and Anchialus, Nauteus, Eretmeus, Thoon,[6] Proreus, Ponteus and the strong Amphialus (who once threw a bull over a fence),[7] the son of Polyneus and grandson of Tecton. To challenge them came the great Euryalus, the son of Naubolidus, who once challenged Ares, the man-killing war god, the most handsome and strongest among the Phaeacians except for the champion, Laodamas. Along with him came Anabesineus, then the three sons of Alcinous—Laodamas, Halius, and Clytoneus, so godlike in grace that wishful sighs came from the women watching as the men stripped themselves naked to participate.[8]

The games began with a footrace. Together, they toed the mark, jostling each other with rude elbows as they sought with naked feet where the sand was firmest. At the start, all leaped forward, their heels kicking high behind them as they sped along the track. But Clytoneus shot ahead of all, and when he reached the turning post where the crowd had gathered, he had left the others as far behind as the length of a fallow field that could be plowed by a team of mules in a day. Wrestling followed the footrace, and here Euryalus threw all the would-be champions. Amphialus outjumped the field, and Elatreus hurled the hollow stone farther than anyone else. When it came time for the boxing, Laodamas, the king's fair son, had little trouble knocking all his opponents down.

He sauntered over to a water barrel, thrust his head inside, shaking it, then grabbed a goblet, drinking deeply. He winked saucily at a fair wench and was rewarded with a knowing smile and a promise from her pursed lips. He grinned and looked toward where Odysseus sat quietly beside Alcinous. He took another drink of wine, smacked his lips, then said, "Come, my friends! Let's see what skills this stranger, our guest, has." He squinted at Odysseus. "He looks strong enough to join us. I have a hunch he could show us a thing or two." A few snickers rose from those around him. "Take a gander at his calves, thighs, hands, and those broad shoulders that nature bestowed upon him."

"Ah, but he's old," another said, spitting a mouthful of wine onto the ground. He took another drink, gargled, then spat again and wiped his lips with the back of his hand. "There's enough frost in his hair to make him a councilor."

"I don't think it's age as much as he has been broken by hardships," Laodamas said. "There's nothing like the sea to break a man."

"Hm," Euryalus said. "I agree. Why don't you challenge him, Laodamas?"

Laodamas grinned and said, "Now, I know your thoughts, Euryalus. You'd like nothing better than to see me flat on my back, staring into the sun. Right? But"— he turned to look at Odysseus— "I don't think it will be this one who puts me there for you."

He hawked and spat, then swaggered forward and stopped in front of Odysseus. The man of many masquerades glanced up at him, a polite smile touching the corners of his lips. For a moment, Laodamas wavered in his intentions, then grinned and said insolently, "Come, father, try your hand with us.⁹ That is, if you are good at anything other than singing pretty songs for fair maidens? It is only right that you should join us, for every man wants his fame to spread, and what better way to spread it than with what he makes of himself with his hands and feet? Throw your cares away. We won't make you wait before your journey. Your ship has been readied and awaits only the turning of the tide to sail."

Odysseus leaned back, his thick-fingered hands resting upon his knees. He eyed the reckless youth thoughtfully for a moment, then said, "Laodamas, why are you mocking me? I have much on my mind and I have suffered much. Indeed," he added, "I am still suffering. I only wish to be taken home. That is all and that is why I am here in your assembly: to plead for help from your king and people."

140–168

Euryalus heard his words and laughed scornfully. He came forward and leaned into Odysseus's face. "Ah, but you are quite right not to join us in these games. It's our fault. We should never have taken you for a man of action. No"—he cast a quick glance over his shoulder at the others watching—"I can see now that you are much better suited for one who lazes aboard a ship—perhaps a prince of sailors, hm?" A snicker rose from the crowd behind him. "Yes, that's it. You are one of those who worry more about freight and cargo with an eye toward profit and gain—if the wind is right—than an athlete. No, it's sure you are no wrestler or fit for any noble contest."

A black cloud descended over the face of Odysseus, and a strange light began to flicker and glow in his eyes. "You are a man of words, that I give you," he said. "But it would be better for you if you knew the man you insulted before you let your lips flap ahead of your thoughts. You may be pretty of face, but no gods put pretty words in your mouth as they may in the mouths of plain men. Vanity, vanity! Tch. Tch."

169–194 He clicked his tongue against his front teeth. "No, far better if you had been plain of face with words that would delight crowds and woo women to your shoulder. Why, such a man would stand out in a crowd and draw admiring stares as he struts through the marketplace. Well," he sighed, "it's true as they say, I guess: Some men draw gifts from the gods but others gain nothing from their parents. Now you, sir, are obviously a distinguished man—one can see you use your head to keep your ears apart—but it's certain the gods shortchanged you on brains. You have a base and surly soul." He held up his hand as a hot retort sprang to the lips of Euryalus. "Spare us your posturing." He leaned forward, his eyes gripping and holding those of Euryalus. "Now, you have angered me with your pittling prattling like vain women pampering and primping before mirrors. I'm no beginner at these games of yours. When I had youth and strength of hand I was well regarded among others who were far better at the games than you. But"—he sighed and shook his head—"that was a while ago. I have suffered much and fought many wars with men and hostile seas, and those trials weigh heavily upon my shoulders. Yet, I'll give it try, for your words have stung like nettles upon my spirit, and there is nothing like an insolent goad from the lips of a vain and stupid youth to make one feel young again."

Odysseus rose, threw his robe over his shoulder, and seized the biggest stone on the ground, one that no Phaeacian had even tried. He dipped his shoulder, curled his arm around behind him, and unleashed a throw that sent the stone singing on its course. A wild scramble ensued as the stone soared close to the crowd, several falling flat on the ground as the stone passed over their heads and fell hard to the ground, easily surpassing all the marks of the others. Athene, pretending to be one of the seafarers, marked his pitch, then called out.

"Look, man! A blind beggar could find your peg with his hands without *195–223* fumbling over any of the others. Why, there ain't a man among that crowd of boys who could better this toss with a grapevine basket."

A roar of laughter arose from the crowd. The youths turned pink with embarrassment, and Odysseus threw back his shaggy head, shouting with laughter. He looked at the young men staring dumbfoundedly at his peg. He laughed again.

"Now, then, you young cockerels! Beat that toss—if you can. I'll send another along even farther. And now, whichever one of you wants a piece of this old man with frost in his hair and beard, come forth and try your hand. You've provoked me enough, by the gods! And now I'll see if there is sand or metal in your backbones! Come, now! Who will be the first to try this guest you tempted and taunted with such gross disgrace? Name your choice! I'll accommodate all: boxing, wrestling, whirlbat, footracing, what will it be? I exempt Laodamas from this challenge for his father is my host, and who would disgrace one's house by fighting or wrangling with a friend? Any who would do such a thing is unwise and a cur to bite the hand that feeds him. But as for the rest of you, why, I'm your man!

"I am familiar with any of what you call the manly sport. I am quite skilled with archery and I am among the first to fell enemies with a feathered shaft from a well-polished bow. Only one among all the Greeks could stand with me and my bow before the walls of Troy, and that was Philoctetes. Of all the others who still enjoy bread in their frail lives, none could surpass me! Although"—he amended—"I would not care to draw strings with Hercules or Eurytus of Oechalia[10] who challenged gods with their bows.

"Come to think of it"—he frowned—"his vanity with his bow brought *224–255* Eurytus to his untimely end when he challenged the incensed Apollo to a match. Hm. Yes, well. No bows offered? How about javelins, then? I'll hurl one as far as any man can shoot an arrow. No? Then how about a footrace? Some of you might beat me there, for I was knocked about by enough rough seas that my pins still haven't recovered and my knees are still a bit sore, but I'll have at you, if you wish."

Odysseus lifted his chin, sweeping all the youth with a challenging look, but all stood still and silent, staring at the broad-shouldered man of masquerades who stood bravely in front of them, throwing their taunts back to them. Finally, Alcinous cleared his throat and rose, speaking apologetically to soothe the ruffled feelings of Odysseus.

"My friend," he said, "you have spoken well and your generous tongue well delivers your, ah, skills to our youth. I can't blame you for this. It is only natural for a man to want to prove himself when rash youth challenges him. And our youth"—he stared sternly at them—"have been rash with their words addressed to you. But I hope, when you arrive at your home and are feasting with your wife and children, that you will not think badly of our people for the behavior of our youth. I hope that you tell your friends and family about our skills when talk should turn to the Phaeacians. Remember that Zeus has given us noble skills as well as others. Although we may not be as skilled with our fists and in wrestling, we are fleet of foot and first-rate seamen—which you will discover shortly, I assure you. No"—he looked out over the crowd watching and listening to his words—"we take great delight in other things: neighborly feasts, beautiful clothes, song and poetry, music, dancing, baths, and beds." A great giggling came from the audience at this. Alcinous turned a shade red and pretended not to notice.

"So," he said, "let us leave this athletic field, and you Phaeacians who bear laurel wreaths on your noble brows as champion dancers, show our guest your steps that he may be able to tell his countrymen that we are unmatched in all the world in dance, seamanship, footracing, and poetry and song. One of you call Demodocus to us with his soundful harp that he might play it for us. Oh, there you are," he said, spying Demodocus sitting at the edge of the crowd. "Well done! Someone bring him his harp. It's somewhere in my court."

256–284 Pontonous leaped forward to do the bidding of Alcinous while nine stewards rose to sweep the ground and prepare the surface for dancing. They cleared a wide ring among the crowd as Pontonous returned to reverently hand the singing harp to Demodocus. The poet rose and made his way to the center of the ground while a group of young men, chosen for their lightness of foot, gathered around him and began a divine dance, their naked heels kicking joyfully, their toes twinkling against the hard-packed earth. Odysseus watched the dance with great amazement, listening to the words Demodocus sang about the love of Ares and how he clasped the panting, brightly crowned Aphrodite in his muscular arms and how they secretly romped and rolled in naked joy in her husband Hephaestus's palace. But in a little while, the Sun, whose watchful eye gleams from the high heavens, spied upon the lawless joy of the sweating lovers and disclosed their lust to Hephaestus as he labored at his fire-blackened forge. Stung by the bitter news, he swept his anvil clean and bent to his task, shrewdly linking a net of chains, binding them with magic so that they could not be broken or undone by any save himself who knew the clever secret. When he had finished, he quietly carried the net to the room where his marriage bed stood. There, he carefully draped the bedposts and railings with the net and suspended it from the ceiling over the bed. Its filaments were as finely woven as if they came from a spider's loom, a masterpiece of cunning work that no man or god would be able to see. Then he pretended to leave for his favorite city, the well-built Lemnos, taking great pains that Aphrodite of the white thighs would know he would be gone.

Meanwhile, Ares of the golden reins, who kept an eagle eye upon the comings and goings of Hephaestus, waited impatiently for the master crafter to leave, then hastened to his house, came in through the door, his eyes falling on Aphrodite's white breasts and her barely hidden nipples swollen in lust like ripe purple plums. *285–316*

"Come," he panted, "let us go to bed and pleasure ourselves well while your husband's off somewhere in Lemnos playing games with his barbarous Sintian friends."

And Aphrodite shrugged her beautiful shoulders, and her diaphonous chiton fell in folds around her highly arched feet. Ares's breath caught in his throat as lust sang its way through his veins. He lifted her easily, feeling her breasts rub across his chest. Her lips clung eagerly to his, wild tongue probing deeply, as he carried her to the bed and tumbled with her onto its softness, her white thighs clasping hard around his lean waist. Immediately, the net fell down around them.

"What—what's this?" sputtered Ares as he tried to rise from Aphrodite's arms. But the netting held him tightly.

Aphrodite squirmed, trying to slide out from under his weight, but her thrashing arms and legs only tightened the net, and soon they were cocooned, their nakedness visible to all eyes. And then the great, lame god stepped into the doorway, his vengeful shadow falling across the lovers helplessly tied by their lust. His massive chest filled with air and his voice boomed across the heavens as he called for the gods to witness the adultery of the lovers.

"Father of the sky and all other deathless gods!" he cried. "Come all and see what a ridiculous object these two have made with their cruel adultery. Come and witness how, when I limped from my threshold, vain Ares came to my lusting wife, who yielded her charms to that lecher! See how the wanton lies, limbs sprawled, naked with desire! And all because he is fair of limb while I"—his brow darkened with fury—"I must limp like a hunchbacked dwarf through heaven's halls! Not my fault! Not my fault! I wish my parents had never given me life only to have it locked in this miserable form!"

He slammed his huge fists against his thick thighs and took a deep breath *317–340* to control his breathing. "Look at their shame! See how these two lie in each other's loving arms! Ah! My heart! My heart! A sword is driven through it! What? You want me to set you free? Never!" Spittle formed in the corners of his mouth. His eyes bulged wildly from their sockets. "Not until your father returns every one of the gifts I made for him as dowry for you, you brazen bitch! 'Tis certain I am that you were not a maiden when you crept between my sheets!"

The gods thronged to Hephaestus's house, slipping in to stand upon the highly polished bronze floor, elbowing each other out of the way. Earthshaking Poseidon bulled his way through the crowd to stare openmouthed at the bubbling bubbies of naked Aphrodite. Swift-running Hermes slipped in beside Apollo, lord of the harp and bow, and laughed with delight at the naked couple helplessly tied to each other. But no goddesses made their way into the bedroom, wisely keeping away lest their husbands wonder about their fidelity.

"Out of sight, out of mind," muttered one Nymph to another as they pretended to busy themselves at a loom. "But, hang it all, that Ares has quite a club upon him, I'm told!" And they giggled behind their hands and winked knowingly at each other.

"Hee, hee," laughed Hermes, pointing at the hapless pair. "Well, now! Looky there! The slow outgoes the swift. Lame Hephaestus, the slowest of the gods, has proved the swiftest in catching fast-running Ares in his race! The tortoise catches the hare! Cunning has proved far better than your twinkling heels, eh, Ares? And now justice will be done! Oh, yes! Now you'll pay the pretty penny for your adulterer's fine!" He dug his elbow slyly into Apollo's side and winked knowingly.

"Hm. Perhaps, Hermes," Apollo said. "But tell me"—he nodded toward the naked pair tied together—"would you be willing to pay the fine if you could exchange places with Ares and lie next to naked Aphrodite?"

341–367 Hermes took a long look at the golden-haired Aphrodite, at the lust shining from her purple eyes, and his flesh tingled from the sight. He sighed and ran his hand through his hair, rumpling his auburn locks. "Ah, me!" the Giant-killer said. "Lord Apollo, king of the archers, if only it were possible! Why, my arrow would fly as straight as Ares's and I know a trick or two that numbskull wouldn't think of! Even if three times the chains held me shamefully against that pink flesh and every light in heaven shined brightly upon our humping figures, yes, even then I would gladly sacrifice my body to those white thighs! Oh, yes!"

The gods roared with laughter and winked at each other. But Poseidon only chuckled, then begged the god of fire to free Ares from the net, saying,

"Let him go, Hephaestus! I promise you that he will make full payment to you for his adultery as required by our laws."

"Don't press me on this," Hephaestus snapped. "His deeds have caused me great pain. What paltry sum could he pay that would make that pain less? Eh? Your promises are only words. Air. What good are promises? They are worthless for the worthless. How could I wrap you in a net if somehow Ares manages to wiggle out of his bond after I free him from his chains?"

"Hephaestus," Poseidon said, shaking his shaggy head, "if Ares does not pay you what he owes, then I will pay you the fine myself. Free him."

"Well"—he cast a glowering glance on Ares—"put that way, how can I refuse? Ares, you can thank Poseidon for pulling your chestnuts out of the fire."

And the great god took the chains in each of his mighty hands and pulled them apart, freeing the pair from their shackles. They leaped up, their flesh rosy from embarrassment and the laughter of the gods, and fled, Ares to cold-blooded Thrace while laughter-loving Aphrodite fled to Paphos in Cyprus where stood her sacred sanctuary and altar fragrant with Arabian perfumes and bath filled with immortal balms to besmooth her skin. There, the Graces bathed her and anointed her with unguents to charm the gods before draping her with wondrous robes that would set beholders' hearts on fire.[11]

Odysseus applauded heartily as Demodocus finished his song, his gentle thumb striking a last note that hung in the air like crystal. 368–396

Alcinous ordered his sons, young Halius and divine Laodamas, to dance by themselves since no one had their skill in such competition. Demodocus accompanied them on the harp, strumming a lilting tune while the pair capered and twisted to the music. Polybus, a most cunning craftsman, had made a purple ball for them with which they played, one catching the ball and throwing it high toward the drifting clouds, the other leaping gracefully to catch it before his toes touched earth. Again and again they played their game, twisting and bending in time to the music, tossing the ball back and forth as they moved in their dance while the other youths formed a ring around them, beating time to the music with their hands.[12] At last, Odysseus turned to Alcinous and said, "Lord Alcinous, you said your dancers were the best in the world, and your claim has just been made good. I have never seen any who could dance as gracefully as these."

Alcinous grinned, his heart warmed by Odysseus's praise. "Well, my friends!" he called. "Our friend here has a most discerning eye and speaks knowingly upon this subject as well. It is only fitting that we should present him with many gifts, as is appropriate to one so gracious with his praise. Twelve princes among you rule equally—thirteen counting myself—and I say that each of us should present him fresh cloaks, tunics, and a golden talent. Now, while our celebrations continue, let us gather our gifts and bestow them upon him so that our guest may enter the feasting hall in a fine frame of mind. And you, Euryalus," he continued, turning to the blushing youth, "since you decided to bandy words with our guest, it is only fitting that you should make up for your flapping tongue with a generous heart."

397–421
        The princes sent their messengers away to gather the gifts Alcinous had ordered while Euryalus said, "My king, who commands all here, I give our guest this sword of red bronze with a silver massie handle and an ivory scabbard curiously carved with scenes that add terror to those who see it when worn." He handed the sword to Odysseus and said, "Honored guest, if my words have been offensive to you, let swift whirlwinds take them and ravish them from your thought and may the gods grant you safe passage to your homeland where you may see your loving wife and friends."[13]

        "My friend," Odysseus said, admiring the gift that Euryalus had laid in his hands, "may the gods bless and keep you. I hope you never come to miss this sword. Thank you for your kindness." He slipped the halter over his shoulder, and the sword swung to its place neatly at hand by his side.

        Twilight fell over the earth as the messengers returned from doing their lords' bidding. The gifts were taken into the feasting hall and heaped before the feet of queenly Arete.

422–447
        The feasters came in and took their places, and when all had settled themselves, Alcinous smiled at his wife and said, "My dear, have a trunk brought in that has been newly made from fresh cedar. Place in it a cloak and tunic of your own choosing, then heat a cauldron with water and see that our guest has been properly bathed and dressed. While this is being attended to, carefully pack these gifts in the trunk so that our guest will be able to enjoy the feast and listen to the poet's song. In token of my goodwill, I add this golden chalice to his gifts so that he will always remember me for the rest of his days when he sacrifices drink offerings to Zeus and his gods."

        White-armed Arete ordered her maids to heat water in a clean, three-legged cauldron for Odysseus's bath. They quickly filled the cauldron and placed it over the glowing embers to heat. Meanwhile, Arete brought a cedar chest from her chamber and placed the garments and the golden chalice in it, adding a purple cloak and tunic of her own choosing. Then she addressed Odysseus, saying, "Set the lid yourself, if you will, and tie the knot securely so that your gifts will not be disturbed during your sea voyage aboard the black ship while you sleep."

Noble Odysseus took her advice, fixing the lid at once and fastening it   *448–472*
tightly with a neat knot taught to him by Circe.[14] Then a handmaiden called
him to his bath and he lay back in its soothing warmth, reveling in the first
warm bath he had had since leaving the isle of Calypso.[15] When he stepped
from the bath, water streaming from him, the maids toweled him dry and
rubbed him with rose-scented oil until his flesh gleamed. Then they dressed
him in a purple-edged himation and led him to the feast where he joined the
men at wine.

As he entered the room, Nausicaa, her sovereign beauty softly glowing,
stood beside one of the columns that supported the massive roof, watching
Odysseus move with easy grace. She was filled with admiration and said,
"God save you, our guest! Be cheerful, and when you return to your lands,
remember me sometimes as the one to whom you owe your life."

Odysseus paused, his eyes holding Nausicaa's until she looked away,
blushing. "Nausicaa, flower of your father's garden, I swear to Zeus the
thunderer, husband to Hera, that on that desired day when I return to my
house that I will offer prayers to you as a goddess all the rest of my days. I
shall always remember that it was you and your kindness that saved me
when I was naked and destitute on the beach."[16]

He took a chair beside King Alcinous as servants bustled among the feast-
ers, bearing heavy trays laden with roasted meat and fruits and rich wine
carefully mixed in well-carved pitchers. Pontonous brought in the revered
Demodocus and led him to a special place against a lofty pillar. Odysseus
seized a knife and carved a huge slab of meat from the chin of a white-tusked
boar and held it, dripping with fat, aloft while he cried to a servant, "Here,
my good man! Take this to sweet-voiced Demodocus to eat. Tell him that I
salute him and honor him as all men should the bards and poets, for the
Muse loves that knowledge which is supreme in all men."

The servant took the portion from Odysseus and carried it to noble   *473–495*
Demodocus, who accepted it with pleasure. The feasters fell upon the ban-
quet spread out before them, and when they leaned back in their chairs,
thoroughly sated with food and wine, Odysseus cried out to the singer,
"Demodocus! I admire you among all the men here. Surely someone such as
Zeus's daughter, the Muse, or Apollo must have taught you your songs, for I
have never heard such a sweet voice in all my wanderings. It is quite remark-
able how well you sing the songs of the fate of the Greeks and their struggles
and sufferings. Why, if I didn't know better, I would say you must have been
with them on the plains of Troy, struggling beside them beneath those lofty
towers. But now, if you will, sing to us the song of the wooden horse built by
Epeius with the help of Athene and the strategy employed by the Greeks

there, which Odysseus used to be carried through the mighty gates into the citadel of Troy after he stuffed the hollowed horse with as many men as it could hold. Sing about the warriors who crept from the belly of that horse and sacked the town. Now, there is a story worthy to be told, and if you can tell it truly, then I will pronounce your fame to the world."

496–518
At Odysseus's words, Demodocus lifted his harp, resting it upon his thigh, touched his fingers lightly to the strings, and began to sing the invocation to the tale. He began where the Greeks had fired their huts and pretended to sail away in their ships, leaving a large wooden horse behind, the symbol of mighty Troy, in the marketplace. Concealed within the belly of the horse were Odysseus and his men, well chosen from the ranks of the Greeks, silently waiting for the Trojans to drag the symbol of their victory into the citadel.

Yet the Trojans argued among themselves, some fearing the gift of the Greeks while others, sickened of war, demanded that the trophy be hauled into the citadel and made the centerpiece for a feast of celebration. Three arguments were presented: Some of the warriors argued that the sides of the horse should be pierced with bronze spears to make sure that it was indeed hollow; others argued that it should be hauled to the sea cliffs and pushed over to plummet down and shatter upon the rocks; still others argued that it should be left to stand as an offering to the gods who had brought the terrible war to an end.

At last, the others gave in and the horse was hauled through the mighty gates to much joy and celebration as was destined by Fate that had decreed the Trojans would perish after the mighty wooden horse, filled with the mightiest of the Greek heroes, was brought into the city.

Demodocus continued to sing how the Greeks slipped from the belly of the horse and how they ravaged Troy, opening the mighty bronze-sheathed gates to let in the Greek army that had crept back under cover of night to wait patiently beneath the towering walls of Troy, and how the Greek warriors made the steep streets of the city run red with Trojan blood, leaving ruin in their wake. And then he sang about how Odysseus, with gallant Menelaus by his side, raced through the streets, his arms dripping gore like mighty Ares, until he came to the house of Eiphobos, where he fought the great Trojan prince with the help of Athene and slew him while the rest of Troy was being brought to its knees by the ravaging Greeks.

519–546
And while he sang, Odysseus's heart swelled with pride and then melted with grief, and hot tears ran down his cheeks as he remembered the old deaths and his own cruelty in the burning streets when he ruthlessly slaughtered the Trojans with his terrible sword. Tears flooded his eyes and fell to

the ground, and he wept as a woman weeps when she clasps her slain hus-
band or son to her breast on the battlefield and wails her loss to the heavens
while around her swords flash and crash upon bronze shields and she shrieks
her loss like a wind demon. Equally pitiful were the tears that welled up in
mighty Odysseus's eyes, and although he tried to hide them from the eyes of
others, Alcinous noticed his weeping and heard his sighs and groans and
spoke up, saying, "Hear me, my captains! And, Demodocus, stop playing
that mournful tune! Your song is not to everyone's liking here. Since the
divine Muse gave you your song, our guest has been seized with some secret
mourning. It may be that your song has brought back painful memories to
him. I don't know. But stop your song before our feast becomes maudlin and
tears flood this fine food. We must cheer our guest, not make him sad, for it
is in his honor that we are holding this banquet. We esteem him as dear as a
brother and would not see him cloaked with such misery. Thank you, my
friend."

He turned to Odysseus as Demodocus laid his hand upon the harp strings,   *547–576*
silencing them. "Now, my friend, I don't know what has caused you such
sadness, but I do think that you should speak about it and not bear it alone.
Now, don't by sly and pretend that it is nothing but meaningless words and a
mournful tune that have disturbed you. The sharper the knife, the cleaner
the cut, the less the pain. Truthfully, now, tell us your name and the names of
your parents, and the name of your country and friends. After all, we have
allowed you to be nameless among us long enough. No one comes into this
world without a name, and so it is only right—since our ships are to bear you
home—that we know what course must be steered and all that. You may
whisper it, if you will, for our ships are wisely built and know instinctively
where to go on their own when told. Hm. Yes. Well, they do! They know
every port, every city, every sea-lane, all fertile lands despite how well they
are hidden by mist and clouds and fog and rain.

"Now"—he shook his finger warningly—"I tell you about the warning
that I had from my father, Nausithous, who said that Poseidon had once
promised that he would someday wreck one of our fine, black-prowed ships
when she returned from taking one of our guests home, as is our habit, you
know, and when that happened, he would cause a wall of mountains to sur-
round our fair city. Well, that may be here or there, I don't know, prophecies
are legend, some say, while others claim them truth. It is up to him to decide
as he pleases.

"But as for now, tell us from where you came and what caused you to be   *577–586*
driven off your path to wander over the world. Where have you visited and
what have you seen? Did you meet hostile or hospitable towns? Why do you

weep so when you hear the tragic story of the Greeks and the fall of Troy? It is only a song that the gods have woven into the tapestry of man to make a history for future generations. Did you lose a kinsman by marriage at that battle? A worthy father-in-law or someone like a son to your heart? A friend, perhaps? A kindred spirit? For it is to a friend that a man is like a brother with an understanding heart that mourns the passing of such a one. Speak, if you will. Now is the time for your story; this is the place."

Here ends the Eighth Book of Homer's **Odyssey.**

THE NINTH BOOK
The Adventure with the Cyclops

❖ ❖ ❖ ❖ ❖ ❖ ❖ ❖ ❖ ❖ ❖

The Cicones and the Cyclops Polyphemus
Nearly put an end to great Odysseus.

❖ ❖ ❖ ❖ ❖ ❖ ❖ ❖ ❖ ❖ ❖

O*dysseus sighed and reached for his chalice.* 1-28
He drank deeply of the resin-rich wine. With his cloak
He wiped the tears from his eyes and looked around the palace
Before speaking. "Alcinous, mighty king, you misspoke
When you told your guests not to be happy." He looked
At the blind Demodocus. "This honey-tongued poet took
No liberties with his words. His song is sacred and sweet
And should be heard by all sitting here before bread and meat.
No." He shook his sable locks streaked with gray and
Again used his cloak to wipe his eyes. "This is civilized."
He touched his chalice. "Have the steward pass again
Among us and fill our cups with the flower of life.
Then I will let you know the cause for my sorrow.
What should I say first? Eh? How the gods tried
A thousand different ways to keep me from home?
Or perhaps it would be better if my name is known,
For that shall surely bind us in true friendship.

I am Odysseus, the son of Laertes." He paused to sip from his wine goblet while an excited buzz rose from the feasters who stared with renewed interest at the man sitting beside their king.

"Aye," one whispered, digging an elbow into the ribs of his neighbor. The other winced and glared back. "I knew there was something about him.

Remember? I told you when he tossed that stone over our heads that this wasn't any ordinary man the sea coughed up on our rocky shores. I did!" And he looked with satisfaction around the room at his neighbors.

"Ah, you speak with a sheep's pizzle, spraying your words hither and thither," his neighbor growled, rubbing his ribs. "It's easy for the priests to pronounce prophecies after the deed is done."

"Sh," another whispered, holding a dirty forefinger to his lips. "I want to hear this."

"Yes," Odysseus continued, "I am that one the whole world fears for his wise tricks. My fame reaches the heavens and"—he lowered his voice modestly—"my name slips occasionally from the lips of the gods and goddesses themselves. I dwell in Ithaca—whenever the gods let me, that is—that most renowned of island paradises of the earth. Ah, yes, I remember it well in my mind's inner eye—the golden sun shining upon Mount Neriton with oak and olive and fig trees covering its wide slope, the leaves quivering in the gentle breeze, white-fleeced sheep grazing in its green glades, goats bounding over the rocks higher up—and I remember well the islands clustered around it—Dulichium, Samos, and the wooded and fertile island of Zacynthus. But Ithaca lies the farthest away from the mainland, slanting to the west while the others face the dawn and the rising sun a bit to the north. Ithaca is a rough land, but strong men grow from its careful nurture. And I love it for all of that.

29-55   "Yes! Far better than even the home of the divine Calypso who kept me in her cavern home to satisfy her flaming breasts with plum-rich nipples and lusting loins and who desired to make me her lord and spouse.

"And Circe,[1] that witch-whore on the isle of Aeaea—kept locked there by the goddesses who tired of her seductive antics with their husbands (a right proper bed jumper she is, you know, well skilled in lovemaking and eager to test the stamina of any man) and banished her from lofty heavens to this mortal coil—aye, even she detained me to romp with her in her milk baths and bed, the sheets strewn with fresh lavender every night, by casting spells over me. Yet neither could own my soul or my love for all of their bribes and offers—yes, even immortality, the gift of the gods to a few mortals. This, too, I declined, preferring the sweetness of my own country's earth to the hallowed halls of heaven. Mark my words well: There is nothing grander than the land of our birth."

He sighed and stared deep into the distance of memory and the others stayed quiet, breathing shallowly in order not to disturb his thoughts for fear the story he was readying to tell would be lost.

"Ah, me!" he said at last. He smiled and combed his fingers through his

beard. "But this philosophy isn't what you want to hear at a feast. So let me
tell you about the plague-ridden voyage that Zeus sent me on when I tried to
return from Troy, my ships laden with treasure, much glory seated on my
shoulders like a gold-threaded mantle." He took a large swallow of wine and
swished it around in his mouth before swallowing it in stages. He sighed
deeply, the sound seeming to come from a dark place within him, silent and
as deep as a cavern. "But to begin. Well, then"—he paused, frowning, recol-
lecting—"we left Troy sacked and ruined, the once mighty towers ground to
dust, the male children dead—as many as we could find though I suspect a
few escaped as always happens in such things—and it was this that bothered
me the most. Now don't get me wrong, I can sympathize with killing the
men—who wants a revenge-minded warrior on his back trail?—but
Agamemnon had the babies and children taken to the highest ramparts and
thrown down to dash their brains out against the rocks at the base of those
mighty walls. The gods do not take well to the killing of children—remem-
ber the story of Hercules?[2]—where was I? Oh, yes.

"I commanded my ships to be outfitted, stocked with stores, sails repaired
and masts readied. Then we left Trojan shores, thinking that we would be
sailing for home. Foolish man that I was." He shook his head in despair. "I
should have known that the gods always take a dim view of those men who
are proudly content. Ill winds blew us from the Trojan shore to the coast of
the Cicones. There we found Ismarus, the city of the people. I suppose I
should have played a cautious role, but I was fresh from the Trojan victory,
and with my men I sacked the city and destroyed the race, slaughtering the
men and taking their wives and women as slaves. We plundered the city and
filled the square with the treasure taken. Each man claimed a share of it. It
was then that I had misgivings and ordered my men to leave with what we
had taken. But a troop of my men had discovered a warehouse of rich wine,
and they ignored me, slaughtering fatted sheep and sable bulls on the shore
while they filled cup after cup with the rich wine. They stripped the women
and had them as naked slaves. Debauchery, debauchery." He shook his
shaggy head. "Ah, me! While my men romped upon the shore with the
naked women, the Cicones who had escaped made their way inland to their
neighbors and begged for help. This was given cheerfully, for those who
dwell away from the sea in that cursed place are great warriors, well trained
in chariot fighting, and their foot soldiers are among the fiercest in the world.

"They fell upon us at dawn's early light, as thick and solid as the leaves *56–90*
and flowers that spring discovers when first light shines upon a winter-
sleeping world. And Zeus was terrible with his bitter fate that made us suffer
greatly. We ran for our ships, but they overtook us. A troop of their warriors

tried to cut us off from our ships, to fire them and cut off our escape. But we dug in grimly and fought hard against those fierce warriors who take joy in battle. Javelins flew like black clouds back and forth across the battlefield. Blows sounded and resounded upon heavy shields, and the battle din grew louder and louder with the cries of the men. I fancied I saw the great war god himself moving among us, his grim visage gaped wide with laughter as blood spattered his arms and chest.

"We fought through the early morning and held our ground as the sun climbed to its meridian height. But as Apollo dipped in his winged chariot to the horizon, the Cicones broke through the Greek ranks. They killed six of my bravest soldiers from each ship who guarded our rear while we boarded our ships to escape. We unfurled our sails and flew, leaving the dead on that shore. Yet I did hold the proper rites for their spirits. I would not let the curved prows of our ships carve a passage through the lead-gray sea until we had three times saluted their deaths so that the unhappy shades would not follow us.

"It was then that mighty Zeus, the cloud-gatherer, blackened the heavens with a storm. Thunder roared and lightning danced over the prow and mast and the seas rose up in mountains against us. Our ships bucked and rolled from one wave to the next. The wind tattered our sails, forcing us to furl them and man the oars. We rowed hard against that storm, our joints cracking and muscles straining against the pull of the sea as we rowed for land. At last we made it to a bay and laid up, watching the storm while Boreas ranted and raged against us. For two days and two nights, weary with exhaustion, we lay and waited with anxious hearts, fearing that the storm would come into the bay and dash our ships to kindling against the rocks. But on the third morning when golden-haired Dawn rose from her bed, we replaced the masts and set the remnants of our sails. We took our places in the ships, the pilot at the helm, and sailed from our safe harbor. We were well on the way to our homeland when we rounded the point off Malea and the North Wind made the sea rise against us and the current took hold of our rudders and pulled us out past Cythera.

"For nine days more we sailed with the adverse winds as they howled around our ears, driving us across teeming seas. On the tenth day, we reached the country where the blossom-fed Lotophagi live. I immediately ordered my men ashore to take fresh water while the rest of my crews cooked a meal beside the ships. After we had eaten and drunk our fill, I sent two of my strongest and best warriors and a herald inland to discover what sort of people ruled the land.

"They met the Lotophagi, who bore them no ill will and bade them to eat from their country's diet—a strange honeyed fruit that comes from the lotus plant. This diet takes all of man's cares from him, and our men lost any interest in returning to us with the news of their findings. Indeed, they were quite content to remain there and spend the rest of their lives in languorous content, eating that honeyed fruit throughout their remaining days.

"When I found them, they refused to leave with me, stating their wishes to remain with the Lotophagi and graze upon that divine and nectarous flower. They wept and fought when I ordered them to be seized and carried back to our hollow ships. I was forced to tie and bind them and place them beneath the hatches of our ships until they were no longer under the influence of the languid flower. I ordered the rest of my men to stay away from tasting the lotus too, lest they forget their duty and fall under the strange rapture that destroyed their memories of home. All came on board at once and took their places at the oars and rowed strongly, boldly beating the white surf with their blades to bring us away from that shore.

"And so we sailed away with sad hearts across the sea's smooth face, laboring against the tide across untried oceans. We came to an unknown land and, needing supplies, we warily put in to a sheltered cove on the leeside. We did not know at the time that this was the land of the outlawed Cyclopes, a race of proud-living loiterers that never sow the ground or place a plant in the earth or even use the plow to turn the rich black soil. Instead, they place their trust in god for all things great and small, and their unsown and unplowed earth yields every spring what other lands have: wheat and barley, vines bearing goodly grapes that can make delicious wines (if the louts ever learn that trick from wealth-giving Dionysus).[3] Zeus drenches the land in gentle showers to swell the grapes. But the Cyclopes are a lawless people who have no assemblies to make laws to govern the race, no legal codes, and are quite content to live in vaulted caves, each governing his own household by his own will, ignoring the decisions that his neighbors might make in regard to his women and children.

"Now, not far from the Cyclopes' country lies Lachaea, another little isle, *120–155* well stocked with wooded forests and wild goats that bound across the hills—a paradise undisturbed by the footsteps of man. Hunters do not visit the land, forcing their way through the verdant forests, tramping their way across the mountaintops. The land is not used for plowing or grazing by man, nor has it been sowed with seed. The Cyclopes do not visit the island, for they do not have ships like ours with their crimson prows nor shipwrights to build ships for them that they might sail to far-off cities and help to turn the island into a fine civilized land.

"Yet here grow sweet-grassed meadows with fresh streams flowing through them, fields with heavy crops wave their heads in gentle breezes, and vines flourish eternal green. There is a natural port there enclosed on either side where sea-weary ships might rest when the sea whitens with a rising gale. Alders form a shady cove at the far end for the sailors to rest away from the heat of the noonday sun next to a stream of fresh water that runs out of a cave. Here they may sleep and idle away their time while their ships are beached without need of anchor or hawser ropes to tie them to the thick trunks of black poplars.

"It was to this port that we came thanks to the graces of a sweet god who took pity on us, for it was a night that was so ghastly dark that the port was not visible to us. Clouds hid our ships and would not let the moon glimmer upon the dark waters to light our path. When day came, we reveled in the landscape and the unknown land before us. We walked with great delight around the land, roused by the woodland Nymphs, while the mountain goats bounded over the meadows. We immediately brought our bows and long spears from our ships and separated into three parties to hunt the goats that the god had sent to us. We had twelve ships, and each ship had nine fat goats allotted to it (with the exception of mine, which had ten) after we had finished the hunt.

"All that day until the setting of the sun we sat and feasted, sipping pleasant wine and eating rich meat dripping with fat. Our ships still carried amphorae of red wine in their cargo holds from when we ravaged the Cicones' sacred city. And so now we sat before a warm fire, contentedly sipping at our jars of wine while we looked across the bay at the Cyclopes' late-praised island, watching smoke rise from their cooking fires and listening to the bleating of their sheeps and goats. The sun set, and when night fell over the last of day's rosy robes, we sprawled contentedly upon the sand and slept, lulled to sleep by the low lapping of the sea on the shore.

"The next day when Morning appeared in her fresh robes, I called my mates to council and charged them to remain by the shore while I took a ship and crew to discover what sort of men lived on the island across from us. I was curious as to whether they were pious and hospitable or rude, disdaining the laws of hospitality, churlish and tyrannical in their behavior toward visitors.

156–219   "Having said this, I stepped aboard my black-keeled ship and ordered the men to row across the bay to the island. Their oars beat at the white beard of the Old Man of the Sea until we came up onto the nearest point of the island. We could see a cave close by the sea near a common road. Its entrance was thick with laurels hanging over it like a green curtain. Many flocks of sheep and goats nibbled fresh shoots of grass in a hall of torn-up stone shadowed by tall pines and high-branched oaks. Here was the den of a giant, monstrous and so quarrelsome that he lived a goodly distance from his brothers in lawless solitude. He fed all his flocks alone and was so crude and rude that he was unlike any man with whom I have broken bread in the past—much like a large hill overgrown with trees and brambles that forbids closeness.

"When we anchored in the island's bay, I ordered my loyal companions to stay aboard and guard the ship while I selected twelve of my best warriors to follow me and explore the island. I took along a goatskin flagon of wine, black and strong, that had been given to me by Maron, the son of Euanthes, who lived in Thracian Ismarus, a town that we raided. I had protected him and his wife and children in their house in the sacred wood of Apollo out of respect for his station as Apollo's priest, and in gratitude he gave me many fine presents—seven talents of fine gold, a massive silver bowl—but the greatest of his gifts were twelve great amphorae filled with rich, incorruptible, and divine wine that he had kept secret from all of his servants and underpriests and maids. So strong and wonderful was this wine that he poured a single cup into twenty of water and still the sacred odor breathed delicately around the bowl.

"I took a huge flagon of his wine along with a large knapsack of dried goat meat and headed inland. As soon as my foot touched the shore, however, a great foreboding came over me and I felt the presence of a barbarous being, strong and uncivilized and caring little for the rudiments of civilization.

"We climbed the steep slopes through the pine trees to the mouth of the cavern that gaped wide, but the owner of the cave was not at home; apparently he was tending his sheep in the wide vale to the west. We entered anyway and came up short, shocked at the enormous wealth we saw: shelves heaped with cheeses, sheds stuffed with lambs and goats and separated according to seasons and birth. Near them stood the troughs and pails he used for milking, some swimming with whey and ready for creaming in the evening, others scoured as bright as dew upon the hill.

"My companions begged my permission to take the kids, cheeses, and lambs aboard our ship and immediately sail away across the salty sea from the deathly place, but although I felt the wisdom of their advice, I was reluctant to steal away until I had met the owner of the cave and seen what guest gifts he would bestow upon me in accordance with the traditional rules of hospitality. I did not guess at what would be his rude behavior toward my men, but my men then grudgingly gave way and settled down to wait for the owner of the cave to appear.

"We lit a fire and burned a sacrifice, then helped ourselves to some of the cheeses from his laden shelves while we waited. At last, he came up the slope,

220–251

a huge man with one eye like a wheel, bearing a large pile of sere wood for his fire. He entered the cave and threw his burden down with a huge crash that frightened us so much that we withdrew into the deep recesses of the cave. He drove his fat flock into the cave—all whose bags hung heavy with milk—leaving the rams and male goats outside his lofty roof in· the walled courtyard. Then he lifted a huge rock—a slab so massive that twenty-two four-wheeled wagons could not have moved it— and jammed it into the entrance. He tugged at it for a moment, then, satisfied that it could not be easily moved, knelt and milked his ewes and braying goats, placing each next to her young as he finished. We watched as he dressed the milk up for cheese and pressed it into wicker cheese baskets, leaving the remainder in his pails for drinking when the thirst came upon him during his dinner.

252–280   "He turned to set his fire, and when the flames rose high, he spied us crouching in the depths of his cave. He rose to his full height and glared down at us, crying, 'Ho! Guests! What are you and where did you sail from across the seas? Are you traders looking for easy bargains or roaming the waves like pirates preying upon the unwary?'

"Fear filled our hearts at the sound of his thunderous voice. But I answered anyway, saying, 'We are Greeks who have lost our way. We were sailing for home after sacking Troy, but evil winds blew us off our course and unknown waves and rude seas—no doubt commanded by Zeus—tossed us up on your rocky shore. I am proud to say that we were among those who sailed with Agamemnon, Atreus's son, and sacked the topless towers of Ilium, destroying all its armies and bringing that great city to its knees. The stories of our deeds are well-known in the heavens and among other nations. Now we find ourselves at your knees, begging hospitality in the hopes that we might receive the gifts normally given to guests by hosts who follow the laws of hospitality as commanded by Zeus, the god of guests who are sacred to him.'

"But the monster laughed, the sound booming like fretful clouds, and he said, 'Fool! Who do you think you are to order me to follow the laws of Zeus? I don't care a fig for his so-called laws and even less for his presence. Ha! That goat-fed magus needs to keep his distance from my home! None of us Cyclopes worry much about Zeus and his magic aegis or those fawning weaklings who follow him! We are stronger than them.' He pawed at his chin with a massive hand, peering closely at me. 'Well, that's neither nuts nor berries! Tell me: Where have you anchored the good ship that brought you across the teeming waves to my shore? Eh? Up the coast or nearby? Careful, now! Don't lie! Zeus won't protect you here!'

281–313   "Now, I knew that his words were meant to frighten me and force me to betray the whereabouts of the rest of my men, but I had sailed enough in foreign ports to recognize the trickery of his words. I shook my head and said carelessly, 'Ah, well! 'Tis enough for you to know that Poseidon the earthshaker wrecked my ship upon the rocks of your shores, ripping her ribs out from the hull. But my friends and I managed to make it safely to shore.'

"He didn't answer my words but rushed in among us and seized two of my mates by their ankles, swung them high, and dashed their brains out against the rock-hard earth of the cavern floor as easily as if they had been puppies. Their brains splattered out and soaked into the earth. Then, like a lion among two lambs, he tore the flesh from the bodies and stuffed the raw meat and unclean guts into his mouth, wiping the dripping gore and blood from his thick lips with the back of his hand. He smacked his lips and rolled his eye merrily, murderously, at us, and we wept and raised our hands in prayer to Zeus at the horrid sight before us. He roared with laughter and rocked back on his heels at our pitiful prayers, belched, worried a piece of meat from a tooth with a dirty forefinger, then lifted a heavy bowl of unwatered milk and drained it. He belched again and laughed at our prayers, then yawned and stretched out over the floor among his flock. Soon snores rumbled throughout the cave, and I placed my hand upon the hilt of my sword, fury blazing through me, yet I kept myself from drawing my blade and running its keen edge around his neck and into his breast around the strings of his heart, carving his liver from his gullet, for I knew that none of us could move that huge rock that barred us from leaving that cave of death.

"And so I ground my teeth in fury and settled down to wait through the long night while the monster slept. When morning threw her sacred light across the skies, he rose, milked his goats and ewes and brought their young to them, then snatched two more of my men, dashed their brains from them, and ate them whole, washing the meaty mass down with fresh milk. Then, grinning and whistling through his crooked teeth, he set aside the rock and drove his flocks and herds from the cave, setting the rock back in the opening behind him before driving his flocks off toward the mountain pastures.

"Murder twisted its way through my heart and I gnashed my teeth as I   *314-346* schemed and prayed to Athene to grant me the wisdom I needed to escape that hellhole. And then the gray-eyed goddess heard my prayers, and an idea came to me as my eyes lit upon the monster's massive club lying carelessly to one side of the cave near his milk house, a huge club taken from an olive tree uprooted and stripped of its branches, so large that it could easily have fit one of our black-keeled ships of twenty oars as a mast.

"I took an ax and cut a fathom from its end and gave it to my men and commanded them to shave it smooth and then sharpen the end to a point.

Then I hardened that point in the monster's fire left glowing like the fires of the Underworld in the center of the cave until it rang like iron when thrummed with my sword. I hid the spar under a nasty dunghill, so thick and moist that it reeked everywhere. After this, I called my men to my side and had them cast lots to select those to help me bore out the eye of that cannibal, that man-eater, while he slept. Not surprisingly (for the gods look after those needs of man and assign them according to their ability), the lots fell to the four whom I would have chosen, could I have done so without misgivings.

"And so we waited and made our plans and brooded upon the ill will that had brought us to this cave of despair, watching the flickering flame throw shadows on the cave's wall that defied reality. Or were they reality? I no longer knew, for the horror into which we had come was so contemptible that I no longer realized what lay outside.

"In time came the evening, and with the evening came the Cyclops from the feast of his fat cattle. He drove all of them into the broad cave, leaving none, not one male, out in the broad yard walled by massive stones. I do not know if he was simply being cautious or if some god had warned him of danger, and a great wariness came over me as I suspected divine mischief interfering with my plans. But he ignored us as he lifted the great rock and rammed it into the opening of the cave. Then he sat down to methodically milk his ewes and the bleating goats, carefully placing the young ones next to their mothers when he had finished. After setting the milk, he seized two more of my soldiers, brained them, and ate them with great relish. He made to take a drink of milk to wash them down, and I stepped forward with my dark ivy-wood bowl filled with Maron's rich and heady wine undiluted.

347-372   " 'Here, Cyclops,' I cried. 'Take this cup of rich wine from my hands and use it to wash down the flesh you have gnawed from this man's bones. Then you shall see what riches lie within the hold of my ship. I brought this away as a sacred gift from a guest to a host in hopes that you would take ruth upon me and help me on my way home. But your rage is too terrible. How do you expect more men to visit such a man and inhuman creature such as yourself? Eh? Believe me, when this gets out among the stories of the world, men will steer a wide course away from your island. You will never taste the likes of this again. Mark my words!'

"He laughed and seized the bowl from my hand and, with vehement joy, drained it. His eyes widened at its rich taste and he smacked his lips and belched as a rosy warmth spread across his hairy cheeks. 'Good guest, pour me another cup of this warm drink and let me know your name. Quickly, now, so that I may award you with a gift'—here he laughed, the sound booming through the cave—'suitable to your pleasure. The gentle earth also awards us Cyclopes with generous wine from her plump grapes that grow in our rich soil thanks to the showers of Zeus. But this'—he paused to belch again—'ah, me! This rich wine that fell from the river is nectar and ambrosia! More!' he cried. 'More! There is not mortality in this drink!'

"I filled another bowl to brimming and handed it to him. He drained it greedily, then three more in rapid succession, and sighed and leaned back against his bed of animal skins, his senses covered with a dozy fume. I seized the moment and said, 'Cyclops! Remember your words and promise. As to my name, why, I am called No-Man by my parents and friends.'⁴

" 'No-Man,' he said, slurring the words. He yawned, his great maw belching forth foul odors, and smacked his lips contentedly. He scratched his oily locks with a dirty finger and laughed. 'No-Man! A rich name, indeed,' he said mockingly. 'Very well, No-Man, your reward: I'll eat you last after I have dined on your friends!'

Then the fumes of wine clouded his thoughts and his great head dropped on his breast and soon heavy snores rolled like sea waves through the cave. He belched and vomited, and gobbets of man flesh mingled with soured wine puked up from his gullet. _{373–405}

"I drew my sword and pricked the huge callus of his foot, but he did not move. I ran to the fire, whispering to my fellows to bring the club from the dungheap while I stirred the embers to a glowing red like a blacksmith's fire. We thrust the point into the bed of coals and watched it turn to a fiery glow, green as it was. Then we lifted the spar upon our shoulders and crept up onto the monster's bed. Carefully we aimed the glowing point, and then, as a shipwright directs his burning awl, we bore it into the monster's eye. The jelly burst as I turned the spar in my hands and leaned into it, boring deeper. Blood bubbled up and boiled around the burning point. His eyebrow curled back, singed from the heat, and his lid grew black from the burning. A great hiss sounded and steam rose from his socket, and his scream of pain echoed from the dark walls of the fire-lit cave.

" 'AHHH!' he cried, and flailing his huge paws scattered us from him. He seized the spar and jerked it from his socket and dashed it to the ground. He screamed again, his voice echoing like sharp thunder, and from his pitiful yell, others of his race bolted from their caves on that windy promontory and crowded around outside the entrance to his cave.

" 'What is it, Polyphemus!' one cried, hammering his huge paw on the rock jammed into the cave entrance. 'What hurts you? Why have your screams disturbed our sleep? Eh? What's wrong?'

" 'Ah, me!' he moaned. 'I am killed! I am killed!'

" 'Killed! Gods' blood! What are you talking about? Who has killed you?'

" 'No-Man has slain me! No-Man! In the hour of my sleep!'

" 'Ah,' they said disgustedly, 'he's drunk! Damn fool got into the wine again and now rolls upon his pallet a blind drunk! Are you listening to us, Polyphemus? If you were slain in your sleep as you say, then it came from almighty Zeus and there ain't nothing we can do to help you. Or want to,' one amended to a chorus of muttering agreements. 'Pray to your father, Poseidon, to help you. And stop shrieking as if the demons of the nights have come to you or the Furies tickle your dreams.'

"And so they left him, muttering to themselves about his drunkenness. A joyful fire filled my heart, my secret soul, and I took a savage pleasure in watching the monster roll and moan upon his pallet, his grimy hands clutching at the pain in his blackened and empty socket.

"He rolled from his bed, cursing and swearing, his great hands sweeping around him, trying to find me and my men, but we danced nimbly out of his way, keeping from him throughout the night. At last Dawn trickled golden fingers through the cracks into the cave, and his sheep and goats began bleating to be let out and his cattle lowed most pitfully. He groped his way to the great stone blocking the entrance to his cave and plucked it from the opening. He tossed it aside, then sat in the doorway, stretching out both arms to gather us if we tried to slip past him among the sheep.

"What a fool he must have thought I was to fall for such silliness. Quietly, I gathered the fattest and fleeciest rams of black wool. I yoked them together with willow strips taken from the monster's bed, three to a rank, and tied my followers beneath the belly of the middle one. For myself, I took the biggest, the sire of the flock, and curled myself into a ball beneath his belly, digging my hands and feet deep into the rich roll of fleece that hung from him. The ewes, their full bags sore from not being milked, bleated and brayed piteously, but the monster pushed them from his cave, carefully fingering them as they passed to see if we tried to slip past among them. But he never checked their bellies.

"The ram I had chosen lagged behind, and when it finally came to the opening, the monster stopped it, saying, 'Lazy beast! Why do you stay behind while the others bound outside and to the pastures? You have always been the first through my door so you could get the tenderest flowers for yourself. But maybe it is pity for my lost eye that keeps you back, eh? Ah! Perhaps your pensive pace is out of concern for your master's woe? Do you feel for your afflicted lord? Is it that which keeps you from bounding first to the pastures, first to the streams and rivers? You are reluctant to seek pleasure while I pain? Go now, though. I will suffer this pain as long as No-Man lives! Oh, that you could speak and tell me where he rests that I could grab him with my good hand and dash his brains out against the rocks! Alas! I cannot! I cannot!'

"And so he drove the ram out through the door as I clung to its belly. Outside, we quickly gathered the sheep and drove them before us down to the shore to my ship.

There, we told our story as we hastened to load the sheep aboard. Those *465-497* whom we had left behind broke down in tears at our tale of woe, at the loss of their shipmates, but they obeyed my commands and took the sheep aboard, securing them in the hold. Then we used our oars and pulled mightily away from that accursed shore. But as the savage coast fell behind us, I stayed the oars and cried out:

" 'Cyclops! You cur! You filthy beast! Know that it was no coward or slave whom you planned to keep for your last meal in your vile cave! I am he who brings down the vengeance of Zeus for breaking his laws! I am your judgment, the instrument of Zeus, the god who revenges by my hands'

"With a burning rage, the monster roared and seized a mighty pointed rock, shouldered it, then hurled its mass toward my voice. It flew high over our billowing sail and landed with a crash into the sea. A mighty flood rose up and threatened our helm. The sea shook and roared and crashed upon the shore behind us as my men frantically rowed to pull us free from its grip. A savage delight beat in my breast and I leaped to the mast and clambered up the rope, laughing and jeering at the blinded Polyphemus. My friends yelled and cautioned me to quiet, but my pride refused to listen to their warning words.

" 'Quiet, Odysseus!' they said. 'Why provoke that savage? That damned stone nearly drove us back to his land. He could still sink us with another if he gets our range!'

"But I ignored them and roared, 'Cyclops! If ever one asks how you came *498-525* to lose your wheel eye, tell them that it was taken by Odysseus, the son of Laertes, sacker of cities, king of Ithaca, who bore it out as easily as a shipwright would a stubborn knot in a plank.'

" 'Ahh!' screamed the monster. 'The ancient prophecies have come to haunt me![5] Eurymus's son Telemus warned me about the man who would take my sight. But I expected a powerful man with tremendous strength to bear that name, not a puny weakling who befuddled me with wine and took my light by trickery! Come back, Odysseus, that I might give you those friendly gifts you wanted from my hospitality! Come back that I may prevail upon my father, Poseidon, the great earthshaker, to draft you safely home! Perhaps he will heal me. Who knows? What? Afraid? Come back!'

" 'Would I could commend you to the god who would take both your life and soul from you and send those spoils of nature to burning hell. Cure you? Hah! Your father will never heal that orb I burnt from your socket!'

526–555 "And at this, the Cyclops raised his huge paws to the starry heavens and prayed, 'Hear me, Father Poseidon, whose sea-lands girdle the earth and who shakes his sapphire locks in its air. If I am indeed your son, grant my wish that Odysseus, the son of Laertes, the sacker of cities, the vain and proud man, will never see his home in Ithaca again. But if Fate deems it otherwise, let him return to his home in wretchedness, in poverty, a broken and defeated man who loses all in his journey. And let him find strife at his hearth and question in his own mind that which he once knew as home!'

"So Polyphemus prayed and the sable-locked god heard his prayers and whispered in his ear, and the Cyclops bent and picked up a rock twice the size of the one he had hurled before and wheeled it around his head with a mighty effort. He threw it high and far out to sea. It just missed our stern, and a mighty wave rose and drove us far away from the shore.

"I laughed with delight and swung from the mast to the deck and called to my men to row with a vengeance away from that cursed land. Soon we reached the other island where our crews kept a worried watch for our sail. We ran our ship up onto the beach and brought the sheep and goats we had taken from the cave from our hold and divided our spoil so that each would share properly. I was given the biggest ram, the one that had carried me to my freedom. Gratefully, I made him a sacrifice for me and all my men to cloud-compelling Zeus. I burned the thighs, but my sad hands received no grace from him who rules the black clouds, the son of Cronus, the lord of all. I suspect that he was already plotting the destruction of my ships and the slaying of those loyal to me.

556–566 "The rest of the day until sunset we sat and ate and drank deeply of wine. Then the sun dropped below the wine-dark sea and resigned us to night, and we slept beside our ships on the sandy shore. When morning came, fresh and rosy-fingered, I raised my men from their slumbers and we boarded our ships, lifted anchor, and rowed away from that place once again upon the aged sea, blind to the future before us, wary with our fears, happy to be alive, grieving for our dead with tears."

Here ends the Ninth Book of Homer's Odyssey.

THE TENTH BOOK

The Adventure with Circe

❖ ❖ ❖ ❖ ❖ ❖ ❖ ❖ ❖ ❖ ❖

Entertained by the wind god, Aeolus,
Presents are given to great Odysseus,
Who is again lost upon the sea
And comes to the island of Circe.

❖ ❖ ❖ ❖ ❖ ❖ ❖ ❖ ❖ ❖ ❖

1–30

Odysseus paused in his tale and drank a draught
From his cup of wine. With his palm he scrubbed
His beard. He sighed and burped, then gently farted.
He scratched his hairy chest and dropped his feet
On a stool in front of him and waggled his toes.
The foul odor of onions spread through the room.
He sighed, then launched again into his story.
The others leaned forward as he said, "We
Made our way to the island of Aeolus, the wind
King dear to the gods. It is a strange little isle,
Adrift upon the sea, surrounded by brazen walls
Above a sheer cliff. Twelve children he has at home,
Six daughters and six sons to be husbands to them.
Each day is a feast day, and the air is rich with
The smell of burning meat, and gentle winds sing
Their pleasure around the corners of his house."

Odysseus drank deeply from his cup of wine. He wiped his mouth and ran the palm of his hand down his beard, eyeing his audience from beneath heavy brows.[1] He sighed, and stretched back in his klismos,[2] dropping his heels on the small stool in front of him. He waggled his toes in his sandals, scratched his chest through his himation and burped gently.

"Ah, me!" he sighed. He shook his head. "Thistles and thorns! That's what we had fallen into, although we didn't know it at the time. So much the woe to us. Yes." He sat for a long moment, his chin on his chest, eyes brooding into the past. At last he raised his wine cup again, sipping. Then he smacked his lips and, gesturing airily, said:

"We unfurled our sail and turned the tiller over, following the ocean's current whenever we could. We could do little else, you know," he said—the others nodded sagely with him—and pulled a fold of his himation over his shoulder, setting it carefully. "We had no idea where we were. Should we row to the east? Or the west? North? South? No," he reflected, "not south. We had been there. That much we knew. So we followed the drift of the ocean, trusting ourselves to the whim of the gods.

"We came to Aeolia, that island that travels the ocean like flotsam, where Aeolus,[3] the son of Hippotas, makes his home. A wall of bronze"—he frowned—"no, that's not quite right, but I don't know what to call that strange metal—runs around it, and the seas move across rocks beaten smooth by the waves. Here, Aeolus lives with his honored wife and twelve children: six sons who are husbands to his six daughters. It is a hearty household, I can tell you! A marvelous feast is laid for them every day, and the house is always filled with the sweet smell of roasting meat and the banquet hall rings with merriment—fine stories and songs that set the toe a-tapping, I tell you. At night, there's no hanky-panky between them (as has become a popular fad in some houses where wives and husbands play couch games) and each son joins his own wife on his richly swaddled bed.

"We dropped anchor and made our way to the city where Aeolus's magnificent palace stands, high-roofed with ornate cupolas and curiously carved caryatids that hold the stoa's roof.[4] We were greeted magnanimously, and each was seated on a thronos and given choice cuts of meat to eat. For a month, Aeolus entertained us and entertained us well with lively dancing and singing. We told him the stories of our adventures, the war with Troy, the Greek fleet and how the heroes returned—insomuch as we knew what had happened to our friends and companions.

"At last, Aeolus asked politely how he could serve us, and I told him that we were tired of wandering hither and thither and hobnobbing with kings and queens and wanted only to make our way to Ithaca's shores. He leaned back in his golden chair, stroked his long beard, his bright eyes considering my request. Then he called for a hide that had been flayed from a nine-year-old ox. He formed a leather bag from this hide and, conjuring wisely, brought up all the ill winds that had blown us away from our homes for so long. Zeus had made him the steward of his winds, you see, so he had little trouble bringing them in (with the exception of Boreas, that Thracian devil who kicked and squalled something fierce, I tell you!) and curbing their rage—with the exception of the West Wind, dear Zephyr, who was commanded to blow us gently home. I bound the bag doubly tight with a glittering silver band so not a breath could escape from it and hung it up safely in my hollow ship where I could keep a wary eye upon it."

He paused, shaking his head mournfully. "But 'tis the folly of men to destroy the gifts of gods. And so it was with us. Senseless stupidity!" He grabbed his wine cup, drained it, and held it out to a servant who stepped forward hastily to fill it from a highly decorated olpe. "Where was I? Oh yes.

"For nine days and nights we sailed safely, and on the tenth we raised the shoreline of our country. We could even see people tending fires along the shore. And I"—he drummed his fists against his temples in frustration—"alas! I, thinking that we had safely made our way, gave up the tiller I had manned without a rest since leaving Aeolia and lay down for a little snooze. But then some rascal in my crew talked it up that I was smuggling home a great bag of gold and silver as a gift from Aeolus himself. 'Aye,' he sniffed, poking a grimy finger at the bag I had hung up where I could keep an eye on it. 'There 'tis and the proof is in it. Now, I ask you: What kind of captain do we have, asleeping on the foredecks and not making a mention of sharing the treasure among us? Eh? There he is, a valued man in every port and now he comes back home with his coffers full while we have only calluses and air in our hands. 'Tain't right, I'm saying. Fair's share among us all. Ain't a man among us not deserving of a little silver to grace his palm. We stood by him in briars and brambles and now look at 'im, sleeping as sweetly as a cozened babe and we still pull the oars for 'im. I say that we share this plunder of his'n. Only right, I says. Come! Let's see how much gold and silver this here bag holds!'

"And so saying, he took the bag down slyly and slipped his blade down the seam, opening it. The winds howled forth and leaped and danced upon the waves of the sea and bore our ship away from our homeland with a vengeance, tossing us from whitecap to whitecap like an empty wine jug. I heard the wailing of the winds and the cries of the men in my sleep and awoke, leaping to my feet. When I saw what they had done, why, I pulled my cloak over my head and sat down upon the deck, debating whether I wanted to continue on with the tauntings and teasings of the gods or just leap overboard and be done with everything. But little is to be done when the horse's gone, so I stayed myself and sat inside my cloak for a goodly time, letting the men stew in their own juices for a while.

"The winds blew us back to Aeolus and landed us there. I had little hope of gaining his friendship again—one doesn't misuse a gift, then beggar

31–62

himself by asking another of his host; bad manners, that—but we needed
water so I set the men to filling jugs and tubs and fixing a little meal for us.
Then I took a messenger with me and made my way with much misgiving
back to Aeolus's court. There I found him at his dinner (as I suspected; that
man's always eating) and I nodded at his servants and took a seat on the
threshold by the carved doorposts.

63–86　" 'Odysseus!' he said in amazement. He choked on a bit of meat and
coughed and hacked while his wife pounded him on the back. The meat
flew out and landed on the floor, and he gulped a cup of wine. He coughed
and ahemmed, then looked closely at me. 'Nope,' says he, 'it's not your shade,
is it? No shadow sitting there in your form. Ah, me! What brings you back
here? I thought we were rid of you when we gave you the winds as our guest
gift!' Then he frowned. 'What's this, then? Hm? What foul spirit brought
you back here?'

"Well, I tell you I was mighty shamed to have to confess the misdealings
of my men. But there was little else I could do, so I said, 'My ill-mannered
men have done me a bit of mischief. I admit part fault here for their senseless
stupidity by thinking we had come safely home when the shore of Ithaca
loomed across our prow and dropping down for a bit of sleep. Senseless stu-
pidity! And now, I can only ask if you would see your way to helping us
again?'

"I admit I did some fawning there, hoping that he would treat the whole
thing as a big joke. My messenger sat ruthfully beside me, not even daring to
raise his eyes to the room. But Aeolus didn't see things that way. His face
turned purple until I thought a piece of meat had lodged its way in his wind-
pipe again, then he thundered, 'Get off my island, you miscreant!'—he really
didn't use that word, but delicacy keeps me from saying otherwise, you
understand—'I don't know what god you angered, but I can see there's no
one in the whole world more damned than you! No one! And I'll be flogged
with oxtails if I'm going to sit here and entertain and gift a man who has
been marked by the blessed gods. No, sir! I can tell a sour apple when one
comes! You wouldn't be here if the gods didn't detest you! This shows your
ill favor among them! Go away! Now! Scat!'

"And so he drove us from the island." Odysseus paused to wipe a tear
from his eye for his tale, as the wine had made him maudlin. He coughed
and hacked, then took another sip of wine. "Ah, me!" he sighed. "Do you
know what it's like to be among the damned upon a hostile sea? The waves
broke against the prow of our ships, but we could take no comfort in their
passing although the sea miles fell behind us. Mad folly had lost us the slim
support we had, and although the sun shone upon that madcap sea, we could

take little heart from it as we traveled into the unknown for six days and six nights wandering aimlessly.

"On the seventh day we raised the lofty towers of Telepylus rising from the walls of the city of the Laestrygonians.[5] A strange place that"—he frowned, pulling at his beard—"for the meadows are grazed both night and day by herds and flocks, and shepherds and herdsmen exchange greetings as they pass each other when Dawn stretches her fingers over the land. The days and nights are of equal length, but the night herder draws double the wages of the day herder,[6] for he herds cattle instead of sheep. We did not have far to look before finding an excellent harbor surrounded by a ring of steep cliffs, the water calm and deep blue, an excellent anchorage and a sandy beach for drawing boats in close to shore.

87–119

"My captains brought their curved-prow ships in close together in that tranquil place. But a niggling thought tickled me and wouldn't let go—perhaps it was Athene, the wisdom goddess, herself warning me to lay off—and so I brought my black ship close by a rock at the end of one cliff point and tied on with a thick cable tow to the rock, ignoring the protests of my crew who saw clearly the deep blue calm of the harbor and their mates already shore bound. I ordered all to stand fast and scrambled up on the rock and from there climbed the cliff face to survey the land. Again, suspicion touched me, tantalizingly vague. I saw no fields being cultivated—indeed, I saw no evidence of any acreage having been worked by man or beast—with only a stream of dirty-gray smoke rising from a break in the earth like a ravine.

"I bit my lip, musing, maundering, then decided that I would send a small party inland to discover what manner of men lived there. I chose two who fought well together and a herald and sent them out. They climbed the rock beside me, muttering many dark words and glaring at me from frowning brows, but I ignored their suggestions that we row closer to the harbor and join the others. I pointed out a deep-rutted wagon path that was obviously used to bring down wood from the mountains to the city and sea and watched as they made their way down and around a bend, disappearing from view.

"I later discovered that they met a well-built girl, melon-breasted, her bubbies sliding sweatily under her chiton, the hem drawn to her shapely thighs. She eyed them boldly at their approach as she pulled water from the bubbling stream the townspeople called Artacie, which they kept free from animals. Now, you must remember that my men had been away from women for a goodly time, and such a winsome wench waggled their willies. After bantering words about a bit—and, I'm certain, making a few suggestions that did not go unrewarded with a flash of smile or two—they asked the name of the king and where they could find him.

" 'Well, sirs,' she said archly, 'I am the daughter of the one you seek—Antiphates, the Laestrygonian. That there'—she pointed to a high-roofed house standing a short distance away—'is where you could find him and my mother.' She eyed them saucily. 'And if you seek him there, you mayhap will find what it is you're looking for with your eyes bulging out that way.' She laughed as my men turned away and walked into the town to enter the palace she had indicated. They were met by a mountainous woman with breasts so large the movement of them rubbing together seemed to create a rumble from the earth. Her eyes were wild, her teeth the size of javelin heads, and a great fear came from the men as they looked at her thunderous thighs and imagined themselves locked between their deathly grip. She called for her husband, Antiphates, who entered the stoa, his brow furrowed, eyes snapping with impatience at being called from his meeting with his assembly. He grinned with relish as he saw my men waiting, and without any greeting or attempt at an amenity—most barbarous, that, I'm sure you will agree"—and heads nodded from Odysseus's rapt audience—"he snatched the smallest and gobbled him down—feet, guts, bones, and all—smacking his thick lips over the tasty morsel he had for his supper.

120–152   "For a moment my men couldn't believe what they had seen, then they drew swords and hacked their way out of the palace despite the alarm that monster of a wife raised, her thighs clapping like thunder as she ran after them, her breasts banging together like ships' hulls in a storm. They sprang away from her, however, and raced back down the path to the ships, while a mob of those hungry beasts howled at their heels. My men sprang aboard the ship and trembled as they told their tale. Meanwhile, the mob of giants raced to the shore and peeled flinty rocks from off the cliffs and bombarded our ships with them. Several shivered the ships and crushed men who vainly tried to raise the sails, smashing the oars of those who tried to row away from that deadly anchorage that had turned promised paradise into a hideous nightmare. Then the cannibals leaped aboard my ships and speared the men like fishes and carried them, crying and screaming, writhing from the pain of those blades in their guts, to a huge fire drawn up on the beach, where they thrust them, still alive, into the flames to singe them like slabs of meat for their foul feast.

"I drew my sword and slashed through the cable tow anchoring my dark-prowed ship to the rock and shouted to my men to man the oars and row as if the Furies chased them. Willingly the men bent to the task, and my ship flew lightly over the waves like a gull as they pulled us away from that frightful place to the safety of the open seas. I watched as my other captains tried vainly to bring their ships away from that stinking cesspool, but they had anchored too close together, and before they could navigate past each other, the flesh-eating monsters had them helpless. Not one escaped.

"With a heavy heart, I ordered the sail shaken out and raised and threw the tiller over, putting the land of the Laestrygonians behind us. We watched as that black land set deeper and deeper into the gray sea until at last it disappeared. Still, we could not shake the images of our friends, squirming like fishes on the ends of long lances, and the greasy black smoke of fires rolling up in ominous clouds toward the heavens."

Odysseus sat, sweating and dejected, his face drawn and brooding, deep pains of memory cutting into its bronzed flesh. His audience exchanged uneasy looks. A few pushed platters of meat away and buried their noses in cups of wine. Large june bugs slipped in from the twilight and slapped against the white walls, buzzing a deep dull drone as they moved sluggishly through the heat of the room. At last, Odysseus gave his beard a tug, wet his lips from his wine, and continued.

"We came at last to the island of Aeaea, where the fair-haired, dreadful, but eloquent witch-whore Circe reigned.[7] Ah, me! Had we only known! Yet, yet"—he smiled into his beard; his eyes took on the shining of fond memories—"there are always a bit of good times mixed in with the bad and so it was here. Circe, you may not know and if you do I apologize for taking your time, is the sister of Aeetes,[8] and both are the children of Helios of the Sun and Oceanus's daughter Perse.

"After we raised the island, we sailed around it, looking for a safe port and found one between tall cliffs that kept the pounding seas away in the most violent of storms. With the help of a god—I know not which one, but I suspect the hand of Hermes here[9]—we moored the ship and then collapsed upon the fine white sand of the beach. For two days and nights we lay there, our hearts destroyed with grief and trying to regain our strength from the ordeal we had just undergone.

"But on the third day, when fair Eos appeared in her saffron robes,[10] I rose and, taking my sword and lance, left the ship and moved inland, climbing for a vantage point where I could see if men had cultivated fields and still worked in them. I listened hard and carefully for men's voices but heard only the call of a cuckoo and the raucous cry of seagulls winging over my head. I strapped my lance and sword to my back and made my way up a rocky and perilous cliff, my heart hammering in my chest as I pulled my way up rock by rock, my toes scrambling wildly for purchase against the windswept face of that cliff.

"At last I reached the top and paused, panting, sweat streaming from me 153–182 in tiny rivulets. When my lungs stopped working like a blacksmith's bellows,

I stood and looked around the island. In the distance, I saw a stream of reddish-yellow smoke rising from where Circe's house lay in a thick grove of oak and pine trees. I debated if I should press on and investigate the place, then decided that it would be better if I were prudent and returned to my ship.[11] The sun was hot upon my pate and shoulders, and dust lay in a fine sift upon the leaves. I went down the cliff another way, finding my way along an old path that wound its way through the trees. Suddenly, a god sent a deer flushing across my path on his way to drink from the mountain meadows where he had been grazing. Quickly, I pinned his shoulder with my javelin. He grunted from the pain and fell to the dust, his hooves kicking his life from him. I pulled my javelin from his shoulder and laid it on the ground. Then I gutted him and, tying his feet together with creepers and willow shoots that I twisted into a rope, shouldered him, bringing him back to my ship. There, I threw him down in the sand and said, 'Now, my friends, we won't starve our way into the House of Hades. We at least will have a meal from this well-fed deer. As long as we have food and wine there is no reason for us to mope around here, wishing wishes about what could have been if we had not taken land up among those cannibals. But it's over and done with, and the berry doesn't grow again on the bush once it's picked. Let's spirit our blood, now, with a bit of drink and put away our hunger by roasting this fellow and eating him.'[12]

"And so my men fell to, digging a deep pit and lining it with stones. Afterward, they filled the pit with dry wood and built a roaring fire. We drank wine until the fire died down to flickering coals, then spitted the deer and set him turning over the fire, fat dripping from his flesh onto the glowing stones. My men made merry and we ate and feasted well into the night, telling stories and singing the old songs we sang when fear was unknown to us and we felt we had the world in our grasp.

183–213 "When Dawn again flickered her way over the horizon, I gathered my men around me, passing around a jug of wine for them to rinse their mouths with and to swallow to ease their pounding heads. When they had ceased their grumbling at being dragged from their sleep, I told them, 'Friends, we have to be reasonable now: We are lost. No two ways about it. We don't know east from west, where the sun rises and where darkness gathers. Face it: We can't do anything until we know where we are or at least have a good idea of this place. Now, yesterday when I climbed that cliff, I could see that we have landed upon an island. I could see little else because the middle of the island is covered with trees and brush. But I did see a bit of smoke rising from the center of the island and—'

"Well, that is as far as I got for a minute or two. My men could see where

I was going with my little speech, and they broke out in loud arguments, reminding me what Antiphates the Laestrygonian had done with their ship-mates and how that foul Cyclops had abraded their fellows between his massive jaws. When I refused to budge from my position as their captain, they broke into great lamentations, wailing and sobbing that I was bringing them all to some demon for lunch, but I waited them out, passing the jug around until it was empty.

" 'This is another fine mess you've gotten us into!' yelled Eurylochus.[13] He shook the jug and, finding it empty, handed it to Polites. 'These are wintry times and you are taunting the gods by tossing your men out into the heat of the day'—'Mixing metaphors,' I said mildly, and he glared at me—'and don't be giving me that. I *know* it's summer; it's always summer. But . . . ah'—he spat in disgust—'you do this all the time to confuse speakers. But it won't work now. No, sir! Why, I'm on to your tricks, Odysseus! Mind! Everything's as empty as that jug. Might as well break it and keep us from going crazy!'

"At which point Polites raised the jug over his head and dashed it to pieces against the rock. Eurylochus paused, his eyes opening wide in horror. He fell to his knees and picked up shards in his hand and sadly shook his head. 'Ah, Polites? It was only a metaphor.'

" 'Well,' sniffed Polites, 'keep your words together about what you mean and don't be scattering them over the land. Besides, Odysseus is right: We can't do anything until we know where we is—are,' he corrected. He glared at Eurylochus. 'And all your prattling and hand-wringing ain't going to change that.' He looked at me. 'Well?' he demanded. 'On with it, then. Who's going and who's staying?'

"I divided my crew into two parties, taking command of one myself and giving Eurylochus the other to placate him. Then we drew lots to see who would go and who would stay, and as the gods would have it, Eurylochus drew the traveling piece. His men shook their heads and, resigned to whatever lay ahead for them, all twenty-two of them followed him, weeping bitterly about their luck while we made ourselves comfortable to await their return.

"They made their way up and around the cliff and soon disappeared from 214–245 sight. Then, finding a path hammered hard by many feet, they followed its winding course into the center of the island and to where Circe's house stood, built of brightly polished stone. Hill wolves and lions prowled around the walls and lay before her gates, tails twitching from her magic spells.

My men shifted their spears and drew their swords, advancing warily upon them, but the wolves and lions rose and wagged their tails and fawned upon them, rising upon their hind legs to lick my men's faces with raspy tongues. My men moved quickly to the terrace and stood there, wondering at what they had just seen, when suddenly they heard Circe's voice crooning to them from the cold shadows as she worked at her loom, and all paused spellbound to listen to her lovely voice, rich and smooth as the voices of goddesses are.

"Polites, the man in the party I admired most for his good sense, finally said, 'Friends, someone inside there commends the place to me with her divine voice. Indeed, the whole place echoes with its lovely notes. Well, I don't know who the owner is, but I would wager it to be either a goddess or a woman.'

" 'Good thinking,' grunted Eurylochus. 'You have a keen grasp of the obvious, Polites.'

"Polites glared at him and called out. The voice stopped singing, and Circe came in answer to their bidding. She threw the well-polished cedar doors wide and invited them to enter. The sun touched her white dress, highlighting her breasts, and my men licked their woman-dry lips and crowded around—fools as they were to be thinking with their groins instead of their minds—and shoved their way through the door as Eurylochus tried to stop them.

" 'Here, now,' he said, pushing against them. 'Stay put! You don't know what waits in there for you!'

" 'Got a pretty good idea,' one of the men said, winking lewdly at Circe. 'A taste of those beauties would take a load of worry away, I tell you!'

" 'Give way,' another said, pushing him aside. 'Bastard's crazy as a loon and ain't no two ways about it! One look at her and one can see there's no place to be hiding a needle let alone a sword!'

" 'A woman's wiles are sharper than the finest sword,' Eurylochus said, panting from the effort of trying to push the men back. 'Words, my friends! Listen to her words first!'

"But they didn't listen and crowded in. She smiled that curved-lip smile of hers at Eurylochus, but he refused to budge. 'Work your pitfalls and ways upon them, if you will,' he told her. 'I'll stay out here and mind the sun.'

"She shrugged and closed the doors behind her, but Eurylochus made his way to a window and peeped in, spying on them to see what happened. She had my men enter the andron and take the couches covered with fine linen. The tables by the couches were set with warmed honey and delicate wine brought from Smyrna. Fresh goat cheese and ripe olives already pitted were placed in elegant bowls for them, and my men fell to eating and drinking greedily while wispy-clad women—more naked than clad, I tell you after having seen them myself—moved in to join them. But my men didn't know about the venom that witch-whore had mixed in with the resin-rich wine that made my men forget what they had come for, and all thoughts of their country vanished from their minds while they ate and drank and fondled a breast or thigh or two. Then, when they had finished, Circe rose and, touching each with a magic wand cut from a hazel tree, turned them into the pigs that they had made of themselves with their rude behavior. Swines' snouts, bodies, bristles, grunts, all transformed from their man shapes but keeping their man souls. Then she drove them with many proddings and prickings into the pigsties waiting for them and threw them oak mast and beechnuts and cornel berries to eat, forcing them to grovel like swine on earth in the foulest part, foraging around in their own urine and soupy shit.

"Eurylochus, seeing what had happened to the men, came running back 246–275 to the ship to report on the party's catastrophe. He was so worked up about what he had seen that he panted and puffed and wrung his hands in anguish until finally I gave him a cup of uncut wine to calm him. He coughed and sputtered, then glared at me and said, 'All right, Odysseus. You have what you wanted. We followed the path upward and down into the center of the island, making our way into the cool shade of the oak trees and pushing past the thorny brush. There we found a house of well-polished stone—parian marble, I think, though it could have been quarried elsewhere as white as it was.' 'On with it,' I growled. 'And there we heard the sweetest voice singing over a loom. We knocked at her bright gates, and she came to the door. Aye, a goddess she was! Had to be, what with those breasts and fine legs! She invited us in, and my men rushed like fools past me—although I tried to stop them, remembering what happened with the Cyclops and all—but they wouldn't listen—some were even downright rude, and I'll take my measure with those men if I ever see them again—but I refused to go in after them, suspecting a trap of some sort. It doesn't hurt to be too cautious, given the luck of our past doings, I tell you, right? Well, I can tell you that not a single man came out of there. Not a single man! I made my way to a window and peeked in, to watch how they behaved—no manners among those louts who have been away from women's company too long—and I can tell you I was most ashamed of them and what happened to them.'

"Then tears came to his eyes and he cried and wailed, beating his breast about the loss of his men. I took my silver-studded sword and slung it in its silver scabbard over my shoulder, then grabbed my bow and told Eurylochus to take me to the place he had been. He fell down on his knees and wrapped his arms around me, crying, 'No, no! Take pity! You have nothing to worry about, being the favorite of Zeus and all, but don't make me go back to that place! No telling what might happen to poor Eurylochus this time! I've pushed my luck far enough as it is. And I tell you that you're as dumb as an ox if you try to go back there to that magical place. As are any of the others who rashly follow you. No, it's all over. Best we make do with what we have and escape the destiny the others are suffering.'

" 'All right, Eurylochus,' I said. 'Stay here if you will and keep the ship safe. Eat and drink. But I have no choice. A leader must see to his men, you know. It's the nature of things to do so.'

276-305 "And so I turned and left the ship and sea, making my way along the sacred valleys all alone until I came at last to the house where that many-medicine-making dame lived—that witch-whore—and paused, considering my options. At this time, I sensed someone at my elbow and turned and saw a young man bearing a golden wand smiling at me. A handsome chap he was, too, I tell you," Odysseus added, looking up toward the heavens from beneath his beetled brows. He took his wine and spilled a few drops onto the floor and sipped in honor. "A young lad without the hint of a bristle on his chin. He took my hand and laughed and said, 'Now, my poor man! Where are you off to and what are you thinking about doing? Here you are, wandering like some poor benighted fool across unknown country all alone while your friends wallow in their own stink in Circe's sties. You think you can save them from themselves? And what do you carry with you to bribe that witch-whore to release them from the spell she worked over them? Hm? I don't think you'll come out the same way you go in if you try it without a bit of help.' He frowned, holding a finely formed finger to his lips. Then his face brightened. 'But, tell you what I'll do,' he says. 'I'll help you out of your trouble. Here'—he handed me a small plant he had grubbed from the earth—'take this. It will keep you safe from Circe's magic. Now let me tell you what to expect: First, she will work her black magic by preparing a sweet mixture from certain flowers by which she'll spice your bread. But it won't have any effect on you because this drug will keep it from enchanting you. Now, when she strikes you with her magic hazel wand, you pull that handsome sword of yours from its sheath and rush her as if you are going to stab her. Yes, do it! She will quail away from you in terror and then she will invite you into her bed. This is very important'—he waved his finger warningly—'you mustn't refuse her. She is a goddess for all her evil ways—although I'd be calling her a whore and a witch if I had my way—and you must do what she wants if you want favors in return. There's no other way you're going to make her set your men free from her spell. No one can alter what she has done but herself. Understand? Good. But when you climb into her bed with her and she is panting and puffing in rutting pleasure, before you, ah, satisfy her, you must make her promise by the gods' oath that she will not try any more of her tricks and ways with you. If you don't do this, once she has you naked and those winsome white legs wrapped around your waist, you will be helpless, and she will rob you of your courage and manhood.'

"And so he gave the plant to me. It was black-rooted with a white flower that the gods call moly[14]—a dangerous thing for mortal men to dig, but the gods can do anything they want. That's why they are gods, you know. Where was I? Oh, yes.

"Hermes flew away from me, his heels twinkling through the forest as he made his way back to Olympus. My heart filled with dark foreboding, I ate the plant—ach! I remember its bitter taste, a most vile thing—and made my way to the lovely goddess's palace and called out. She came immediately to my bidding and led me to a couch of a most curious frame and covered with a cloth so brightly woven that I felt as if I were sitting in a flame. She placed a footstool at my feet and then in a golden krater prepared a heady mixture that she poured into a gem-encrusted chalice that she handed to me. I drank it down, and no sooner had I placed the chalice back on the table than she drew her hazel wand and struck me on the shoulder, saying contemptuously, 'Out, away, and go and lie with your mates, the foul pigs that they are.' I immediately drew my sword and, placing it at her lovely white throat, backed her up against a pillar.   *306–335*

" 'What—what are you going to do?' she asked. 'And who are you? Where do you come from that you could escape my witchery? Who are your parents? Ah, but I have never known anyone able to drink that potion from this cup and resist the drug. Your heart must be strong indeed to escape that! You must be the mighty Odysseus, the man of masquerades, the man sly Hermes of the golden wand told me would land on my island in his black ship on his return from Troy. Now I remember,' she said slyly. Her hands moved upon my waist. 'And I also remember that I have heard about your powers in lovemaking.' Here her voice turned sultry and low. 'Put that sword up, Odysseus, and ready your other. Come with me to bed so that I may enjoy such a man as yourself and where we can prove that we believe in the love of each other.'

"I moved my sword, letting the point cut through her gown, which fell in a soft cloud around her white heels, and she stood naked in front of me. I felt my throat thicken with desire, but I remembered the words of Hermes and said, 'Circe, why do you ask me to be gentle with you after you have turned my friends into pigs? Although I know that your bed would be soft and I would be happy to lead a beast's life with you—soft, naked, stripped of garments, our flesh slapping against flesh—I know I would pay a heavy price to make love to you. No, I will never climb onto your bed until you promise, in   *336–370*

the sight of heaven—stop that!—you promise and swear—stop it, I say—
the great oath of the gods that you will not work any of your magic spells
against me.'

"She pouted, her lovely lips full and promising, but I drew back from her,
leaving her standing naked at the end of my sword, which was pressed
between her full breasts. Then she swore, and I tossed my sword aside and
swept her up in my arms and carried her to bed. And while we made love,
four handmaidens who served her, the daughters of silver fountains and
groves and trees and rivers that lead to the sea, moved throughout the palace,
placing fresh linen covers on couches and, over the linen, purple covers richly
embroidered in gold. They placed silver tables next to the couches and upon
the tables placed golden dishes. They mixed sweet wine with spices and
water and then built a huge fire under a bronze bathtub filled with water
and rose petals, adding cool water to it after it had boiled until it was com-
fortable to the touch.

"After making love with Circe, I stepped into the tub and felt all pain and
weariness slip from me as she scrubbed my hair and shoulders. Then she
rubbed me with rose-scented olive oil, clothed me in a purple-embroidered
tunic, and led me to a throne of massive silver and seated me. A footstool was
brought for my feet, and a maid brought water in a golden pitcher and
poured it over my hands into a silver basin that I might rinse them before
eating. Bread was placed on a table at my elbow along with choicely roasted
bits of meat and other tasties. But I could not eat and sat brooding, my mind
elsewhere.

371–402   "At last Circe said, 'Odysseus, why do you sit there like a dumb ox and not
enjoy yourself with the fine feast that has been laid out for you? Do you
think that I have another trap in mind for you? If so, don't worry; you heard
my oath and it was one that no god can break.'

" 'Circe,' I answered, 'how could any honorable man dare taste food or
wine before he sees his friends changed back from pigs to their former
selves? Now, if you really want me to enjoy myself with this fine food and
wine and, well, your lips—stop that, you insatiable woman!—you must
remove your spell from them.'

"At first she seemed ready to refuse me, but she could see that I was firm
with my words. Finally she rose and, taking her hazel wand with her, went
to the sty and drove my men out of the wallow. They grunted and nosed the
ground, searching for a stray acorn or such, while she moved among them,
smearing their bristles with an ointment. Then their bristles dropped from
their snouts and they emerged again as men, looking none the worse for
wear, younger in appearance than they had been before. They recognized me

and all rushed to me, seizing my hand and clapping me on the back, weeping tears of happiness at their release until the very walls echoed from their wails. At last, Circe came forward, saying, 'Odysseus, favorite of Zeus and Laertes's son, man of many masquerades, why don't you go back for the rest of your men and tell them to drag the ship up on the sands of my island where they might scrape her bottom and repitch her seams and joints before setting out again on the cold, gray sea? There is a cave there too that remains high and dry from all tides where they might store their tackle and wares. Then you can return here and bring your men with you.'

"My proud soul swelled at this, and I hurried to shore where my men waited for my return. I found them in tears, mourning as young heifers on a field of daisies when they are brought back from the pasture to their calves who frisk gladly around them, lowing again and again at their mothers' safe return. So did my men's tears turn to tears of joy when they spied me stepping down the path to them. 403–433

" 'Your return delights us!' they cried, waving their hands in joy. 'We feel as we would feel if we had just landed on our homeland! But come! Tell us what you discovered!'

" 'Well,' I said modestly, 'first let us draw the ship up onto dry land and stow our tackle and wares in a cave. Then, if you are all willing, follow me to the sacred halls of Circe where you will discover your comrades eating and drinking with great pleasure.'

"They all hastened to do my bidding save one—Eurylochus—who tried to check them, his voice surly with disbelief as he said, 'You sorry people! Why would you possibly want to court disaster by visiting Circe's house? Why, she'll turn you into lions, pigs, or wolves with her magic. And then we'll be forced to guard her house for her. Don't forget what the Cyclops did in his cave when our friends followed this fellow'—he looked rudely at me—'into that lair with his indiscretion.'

"I fingered my sword, thinking how his head would look hewn from his shoulders and lying upon the sandy beach at my feet, but Eurylochus was related to me by marriage and I had no design to dare the laws of Zeus by killing a relative without due cause. My men paused and looked at me. I laughed and said icily, 'Well, Eurylochus, if that is your wish, then you can remain here and stand watch over the ship.' 434–463

" 'Aye,' my men echoed. 'You do that while we follow Odysseus to Circe's sacred house.'

"And so we left, my men urging me to speed along the path as they thought about what awaited them at the end of the journey. I looked back and saw Eurylochus lagging behind but following dejectedly, more afraid of my words than of remaining, I think, for I'm certain he knew that his words had angered me.

"Meanwhile, Circe had had my other men bathed and their flesh smoothed with soothing oils. She dressed them in fine tunics and cloaks, and when we arrived they were dining on fine meats and dishes. But, I noticed, their manners had returned, and although gaiety and laughter rang throughout the hall, it was subdued and in good taste. When they saw the rest of the company behind me, they rose and shouted their welcome. Circe moved beside me and said, 'Now, no more crying and wailing, Odysseus, you wily man, you. I know the many woes you have suffered upon the seas and shores and how your men have been unjustly plagued simply because they have followed you faithfully. That is in the past. This is now. Here, eat the food and drink the wine and discover once again the man you were before you left Ithaca to begin your bitter wanderings. You've lived in grief much too long. Relax! Relax!'

464-492 "And so we did, through a whole year well into spring, for the meat was always finely cooked and the wine honey-sweet, and—I must confess here— Circe's bed was warm and filled constantly with the mysteries of lovemaking for me. In fact, so given was I, so entranced with her—perhaps I was under a certain spell that I had failed to guard against when I had her take her oath— that I forgot to mark the passing time until my men came to me and said, 'Come, Odysseus, wake up! Remember what we were about before we came here! Ithaca beckons, and although this is fine fare and a good place to rest, we want to return to Ithaca.'

"My heart swelled at their words, and suddenly I remembered my high-walled home and the people and my obligation. That night, when I returned to Circe's bed, I wrapped my arms around her waist and held her close and whispered into her pink, shell-like ear, 'Circe, remember your promise to me. Please help us to return to our home. I know what we have here and it is good. But when you are not in my arms, I remember my home, and my men ask me to take them to Ithaca. Release me from your lovely spell.'

"And the lovely goddess replied, 'Oh, Odysseus. If this is what you truly want, why then, you must leave my house. What we have is good and I shall miss it, but my place in your destiny is passed. However, you cannot reach your home until you complete yet another journey first—you must travel to the House of Hades and stern Persephone.[15] There you must find the blind prophet Teiresias the Theban[16] and beg of him the way to your island. He alone among the dead has managed to keep his wits after moving from the living plane to the land of the dead, thanks to a gift from Persephone. Mor-

tals lose much on that journey, I tell you, but not as much if they are allowed
to return to the living again. The others there are only wandering shades.'

"My heart fell as I listened to her words, and I rose and sat on the edge of   *493–522*
the bed, staring off into darkness, feeling sorrow well up inside of me. I felt
my soul fly from me, soaring around in the darkness as I wept and writhed at
her words. At last, I relaxed and looked at her, saying, 'Well, Circe, who will
pilot us on that journey, eh? It must be someone special, for no one has sailed
his black ship to the Land of Hades.[17] None who has returned, that is.'

"She kneeled upon the bed, placing her slim arms around my shoulders
and rubbing her naked breasts against my back. 'Odysseus, my man of mas-
querades, divine son of Laertes, don't be worrying about a guide to lead you.
Set your mast and raise your ship's white sails, then relax in peace. The fresh
breath of Boreas will take your ship across the spanless seas. You will see a lit-
tle shore where Persephone raised up a consecrated wood filled with tall firs
and willow trees and an apple orchard whose fruit falls before ripening. Cast
your anchor close to shore and go alone to the Halls of Hades where the
Pyriphlegethon, the River of Flaming Fire, and the River of Lamentation, a
branch of the Styx and Cocytus—two roaring rivers—meet and pour their
waters into Acheron. Here, dig a trench as long and wide as a man's forearm
and pour offerings to all the dead, first a mixture of milk and honey, then
sweet wine, and last water. Sprinkle white flour and then pray to the helpless
shades of the dead, promising them that when you return to Ithaca you will
sacrifice a virgin heifer in your palace and pile treasures of your most valued
goods upon the flames as well. Then, in secret rites, you will sacrifice to
Teiresias a coal-black ram.

" 'When you have finished your prayers to the dead, sacrifice a ram and a   *523–553*
black ewe, being certain to hold their heads toward dreadful Erebus while
you face the River of Ocean. The spirits of the dead and departed will answer
your prayers and come up from the lower reaches. Immediately order your
men to flay the sheep you have slaughtered and burn them in sacrifice, pray-
ing as they do so to Hades and severe Persephone. Then draw your sword
and stand firm, holding the blade over the trench you have dug, and do not
let any of the spirits come to drink of the blood until you have questioned
Teiresias. The prophet will come, my king, and he will tell you the route to
take and what dangers still lie before you across the raging seas.'

"After Circe had finished, Dawn lifted her fingers over the dark. Circe
rose from our bed and dressed me in my tunic and cloak, slipping over my
forehead a curious ornament that glittered like a flame. She slipped into a
long silver robe and veiled herself, fastening a golden belt around the robe. I

walked through Circe's house, rousing my men with a cheerful voice and telling them to rise and eat, then return to the ship and make ready to sail.

554-569 "My men leaped gallantly and thankfully to their feet and hurried off to the ship to do my bidding. But even here, on the lovely isle of Aeaea with Circe ever at my side and in my arms, I could not bring all away safely. Elpenor, the youngest of my party, not very good at weapons and a bit slow in the noodle, had gotten drunk a few days before and, longing for a breath of fresh air to clear the wine from his head, climbed up to sleep on Circe's roof. Hearing the bustle and rustle of my men, he leaped up and, forgetting that he was on the roof, ran to join the men as they swarmed through Circe's gate, and fell and broke his neck. His soul drifted down to Hades.

"When we all had gathered on the shore and the ship was made ready, I faced my men, saying, 'All of you may think that now we leave for Ithaca. But this is not so. None of us knows which way Ithaca lies. Circe, however, has given us a route that will take us first to the Halls of Hades and dreaded Persephone, where only the spirit of the Theban Teiresias can give us proper direction.'

"My heart ached at the sight of the crestfallen faces of my men, but their lamentations served nothing but to delay our departure. At last, however, we made our way onto the ship. There I halted and stared at a ram and black ewe tethered to our mast. Somehow, Circe had slipped unseen past us and given me a last gift. My throat filled with an ache for the love she had given me. I wondered how she had managed to pass unseen between us, but who can see a god or goddess who does not want to be seen?"

Here ends the Tenth Book of Homer's **Odyssey.**

THE ELEVENTH BOOK
The Visit to the Land of Hades

❖ ❖ ❖ ❖ ❖ ❖ ❖ ❖ ❖ ❖ ❖

Odysseus descends into the underworld of Hades
To consult with the great blind seer Teiresias.

❖ ❖ ❖ ❖ ❖ ❖ ❖ ❖ ❖ ❖ ❖

A*gain, Odysseus sipped from his goblet, swallowing*   *1–33*
The resin-rich wine. He sighed and waggled his toes.
Outside, others waited by the windows, seafaring men
They were and knew the daring of Odysseus, for they
Knew what it was like to be alone on the vast sea.
They could feel the same pain his grave words caused him.
They knew the high mountains he knew and the crystal
Streams that fountained there. They knew the Giants
Of the earth he had defied and the way sails billowed
In bellowing wind and the singing Nymphs that blew
Gentle breezes over wide Ocean's bourne. They listened
As he said, "And then we came again down to the sea,
Dragging the black ship to the godly water. There we set
The mast tightly stooped and brought sheep on board,
All the while blinking away salty tears that trickled
Through our rimed beards, as Circe sang mournfully
From a dark blue–prowed ship behind us. We set sail."

He shook his head and scrubbed his hands across his face. For a brief
moment, the others thought with a panic that he meant to tell no more, but
Odysseus was a craftsman at tale-telling and was simply working his audi-
ence's emotions.

"We pointed the blue prow toward the horizon and left the island. The helmsman kept the ship running taut as she sped across the waves till the sun set and all the sea roads fell under the dark shade of night.

"And so we made our way across the fathomless ocean to the end of the world where we found the land of the Cimmérians[1] whose home lives in eternal darkness, where the cheerful sun never shines when it mounts to the star-studded heavens. Here, night folds its waxen wings around melancholy people, and it was here that we drew our ship up on that gloomy shore. I took Perimedes and Eurylochus along with me to hold the black ram and ewe we had chosen for sacrifice, and we marched along the stony shore, searching for the cave described by Circe. At last we found it, and I drew my sword and carved a narrow pit a cubit on a side in front of it. I took honey mixed with wine and poured it into the pit, then crystal-clear water, and then the flour of wheat. I stepped next to the pit and raised my arms and began my prayers to the weak-necked dead, vowing that when I reached the shores of Ithaca I would sacrifice the best heifer from my herds and pile the pyre with the choicest treasures my house could offer. To Teiresias, I promised to sacrifice the finest coal-black sheep from my flocks.

34–64   "After I had finished my prayers and promises, I seized the ram and ewe and slit their throats, carefully holding them so the sable blood spilled over the offerings in the pit. Almost immediately a low keening built into a wail that raised the hackles on the back of my neck, and out of the dark depths of that infernal cave, like bees swarming, came the souls of the dead—beardless youths, wives, newlywed brides, old men and tender virgins, warriors and soldiers with horrible spear and sword wounds gaping wide and their armor drenched with dried blood—and as they crowded around the edge of the pit, their slack jaws opening thirstily, the sound rose to a horrid clamor. Blood drained from my cheeks and a greenish-yellow fear gripped my bowels. I drew my sword and set myself to guard the pit from them while I cried to my men to flay the sheep and put them into a fire while they prayed to mighty Hades and beautiful Persephone. And although my legs quivered and ached from the strength I summoned to stand my ground, I stayed, firmly holding the hilt of my sword until I could question blind Teiresias.[2]

"Then out of the shadowy recesses of the cave I saw the spirit of Elpenor make its way to me and remembered that his body still lay unburied in the bosom of Mother Earth. I tried to remind myself that we had not had the time to attend properly to his burial, but I knew that was a lie. Tears began to stream down my cheeks, matting my beard, and I called to him, saying, " 'How now, Elpenor! How did you arrive here before my swift ship?'

"He stared at me with a dog's eyes, and a deep groan rose from within him that tore chunks from my soul. 'Well, Odysseus'—the words spat at me from his tight lips—'and well might you ask how I came here, seeing as to how you left me lying in the dust without a proper farewell! I wouldn't have treated a dog in that manner! But neither sticks nor stones make a difference to that now! As to how I came here, why'—he sighed heavily—' 'twas the party that last night and the wrath of grapes that brought me here. You recall, I'm certain, those naked wenches dancing around us, rubbing themselves against our shoulders and keeping our cups filled with that nectar cursed Circe put out for us! Ah, me! I remember it well. Drunker than a spasmed cat I was. And hot from those wenches tiddling around us. I climbed up to the roof of Circe's house to catch the cool night air and fell asleep there. When I awakened, I forgot where I was and took a step and a tumble and broke my neck on the long ladderless fall! Then my soul took the long fall with the rest of these poor shades and, well, here I am!

" 'And now, you can make up for wronging me, Odysseus. When you leave here, you will stop again at the island of Circe. There, gather my body and burn it along with all the weapons I possess (unless my mates have gathered them to them, damn their wandering eyes and thieving hands) and place my ashes in a mound by the shore. Put my oar upon the mound that all who pass there might know that here lies a seafaring man! Now, do this, Odysseus, or I may bring down the gods' curse upon you!'[3]   65–96

" 'No need for idle threats, Elpenor,' I said. 'What do curses from the dead matter to me? Your fate has been made while mine lies before me somewhere upon the gray seas. But in the name of our former friendship, I'll bury you upon the chance return of my ship to Circe's isle.'

"And we sat opposite each other across that damned pit, my sword out over the pit to keep all from drinking, and played the remembering game, but there was little joy in our words. What can the living have in common with the dead when even memories are different and they know the truth of life?"

Again Odysseus paused to draw a draught from his goblet. He smacked his lips and stared off into the fire coming from the tripod lamp at his elbow as if seeing once again the flickering fires deep within the bowels of the earth in the House of Hades. He sighed and lifted his eyes once again to his audience, waiting silently upon him, and continued.

"Then came my dead mother's soul, Anticleia, the daughter of great Autolycus, and my eyes burned with tears as I remembered her standing upon the shores of Ithaca and waving farewell as we sailed for sacred Ilion. Painful fingers wrapped themselves around my heart and squeezed as she stood silently across from me, watching with burning eyes begging me to lift my sword and allow her to drink. Yet I stayed fast and would not allow her to approach the blood until Teiresias came forward, a gold scepter in his hand.

"He paused on the lip of the pit and stared sightlessly across until I thought that his dead eyes had found me and knew me well. Then he laughed and shook his massive head, saying, 'So, Odysseus, why do you come to this black place and the shadows living in it? Well, step back now from the pit that I might quench my thirst, and I will relate the truth of what Fate has in store for you.'

97-128 "I drew back, sheathing my silver-studded sword. He knelt and lowered his head and drank thirstily, then rose and wiped his blood-matted beard with his hand and said, 'By the gods, that was a worthy drink!' He smacked his lips. 'Now as to the pricking of your wishes, well, Lord Odysseus, you wish for a honey-sweet homecoming, but that is not to be. Poseidon is not finished with you yet, and I cannot see how you can escape the earthshaker's vengeance. Although'—he scratched his shaggy locks—'damn me if I know why he persists in this madness. Still, he carries his anger on his sleeve and I suspect that's because you blinded his son and'—he held up a hand as I tried to interrupt—'he will have his revenge for this upon you. You will reach home, but only after much suffering unless you can control the appetites of your men when your ship leaves the deep blue sea and comes upon the three-forked island of Thrinacia, where lie the pastures of Helios and his fine cattle. If, and I say *if*, you can escape that island without harming the cattle, why, then there is a *slim* chance that all of you may reach your home shores. Hurt those cattle and, well, I wouldn't want to row an oar in your boat, I can tell you that. Your ship and your company—every man-jack of them—will be destroyed. You will reach home in a foreign ship and there you will find trouble in your own house for you have inherited the wind, my friend, and now the wind will blow you upon your fated course. Oh, yes. You will find men eating your herds and your flocks and demanding that your wife choose one of them for a new husband. I feel your anger and that anger will blaze up and you will take a great revenge upon these men. After you have killed all of them—either with a sword or by trickery or both, that I cannot see—you must sail to a far land and there, taking your oar upon your shoulder, you must march inland until you find a people who know nothing about the sea and ask you why you carry a winnowing fan over your shoulder. These people never salt their food, and the crimson-painted ships[4] that are the glory of the Greeks are unknown to them.

129-157 " 'Here you will plant your oar and sacrifice to Poseidon a ram, a bull, and a breeding boar.[5] Then you will return home, and there you will offer a pious sacrifice of one hundred cattle to all the gods (with the appropriate prayers, of course, and the varying degrees, and so on) and spend the rest of your life on your native shores, eating succulent grapes and drinking rich wine and spending soft nights in the arms of your faithful wife. Death will be gentle to you and will come late to you, and when it does, you will be surrounded by your family and prosperous people.'

"A cold chill descended upon me and I felt the agony of defeat. Was this fatal fate predestined for me or pronounced by a spiteful god? I knew not which, but the words of Teiresias drew me down into the dark despair of that world, and I felt my soul hovering over the blood-drenched ditch between us. A great dizziness came upon me as if I stood on a high promontory and stared down at a bottomless abyss between my sandaled toes. I took a deep, shuddering breath and pointed to the shade of my mother sitting silently behind the learned seer.

" 'Teiresias,' I said 'undoubtedly your words have been decreed by the gods who have craftily spun the web that snares me in its deadly threads. There is nothing for that, I understand, but tell me why my mother's soul sits silently staring by the blood and does not acknowledge her own son with a word or glance. Is it because she does not recognize me? And if so, how may I alter the moment so that I can embrace her by words and looks?'

"Teiresias sighed, and his blind eyes stared knowingly into mine. He shook his great shaggy head and said, 'Ah, now, there's the rub, you see. Here we have a simple rule that binds all to Hades's hated house and that is simply that any spirit to whom you give leave to drink of the blood will speak to you and unfold the truth you wish to know. But any to whom you withhold the blood will withdraw and disappear again into the black deep.'

"And with that, the seer's spirit turned and descended once again into the black horror of the Halls of Hades. I held to his words and guarded the lip of the trench from the other spirits until my mother's patiently approached, then I withdrew my sword and allowed her to drink. When she lifted her head, blood dripping from her lips—oh, the horror! the horror!" And Odysseus bent his head and wiped streaming tears from his eyes with the corner of his cloak. Not a dry eye in the hall could be seen, and Alcinous reached out a gentle hand and soothingly patted the bronzed brawny shoulder. Odysseus grabbed his wine and drained it thirstily, then sighed and shook his head, saying, "You have no idea, my lords, the horror of seeing that blood-ringed mouth and knowing the fate that awaits us. How many times have we said in jest that we wanted to know what lies before us after we shuffle from our mortal ways to our immortal paths? But I tell you this: I have learned that it is the now that is important to the soul, not later. No, despite what our priests and philosophers maintain with their pithy prattlings, wasted moments here with disdainful dismissal of our days will be

regretted later. My mother recognized me at once and cried grievously at see-
ing me in that dark place.

" 'My son! How came you here to this deadly-darksome region? I don't
see death's languor in your eyes. This is no easy place for the mortal man to
find. Many mighty seas and horrible rivers—especially that of Oceanus—
separate it from the sun-stroked land. Have you made your way here from
Troy? Have you been wandering aimlessly all this time and never been to
Ithaca to see your wife in your palace?'

158–187   "A lump formed in my throat, making speech hard, but I swallowed past
it hurriedly for I didn't know how much time I would have with her in that
dreadful place before I would have to flee. 'Mother,' I said, 'I was forced to
come down to this Otherworld and consult with Teiresias to find the way
across the endless seas. I have not been near to Achaea, let alone set foot upon
the sunny beaches of Ithaca. I have been a wretched wanderer sailing from
land to land since the time I first sailed with Lord Agamemnon for Ilium,
the city of horses, to war upon the rapeful Trojans. But that is only weeds and
thistles, now; tell me how you came to be in this dreadful place? Did Artemis
the archeress kill you with her deadly darts?[6] And what can you tell me
about Father and my son? Is my kingdom still safely held by them, or has
some other man seized my lands and taken my bed? And . . . Penelope.
What can you tell me about her? How fares she? Well? Does she still rule
our lands? Or—tell me, Mother.'

" 'Sh. Sh. Ease your mind,' Mother said soothingly. I could almost feel her
gentle fingers stroking my brow. 'Of course your wife still holds your lands,
but her grip is slipping as the days and weeks and months pass.[7] She has
learned patience, spending much time at her loom and away from the people
so they will not see the daily tears in her eyes as she waits through the long
day for the sighting of your sails. Her grief is much, and her days have
become her darkness as well. Telemachus still holds on to your lands and
now takes your place at the banquets that justices are expected to give.[8]

188–217   " 'But as for your father, well, he no longer goes down into the city, elect-
ing to stay on his farm up in the hills despite all attempts to bring him back to
your house. He sleeps in a plain bed, and when the cold winds blow among
the mountain passes and across his pastures, he lies down in the ashes by the
fires as would a common worker. During the warm days of summer and mel-
low autumn he makes a bed of fragrant leaves in his vineyard and contents
himself there. And there he lies, his bones and joints aching and the misery of
age full upon him, praying to the gods to bring you back so he may see you
one more time before he shuffles off into the eternal darkness. That was my
dream, too, and it was not the keen-sighted Artemis who felled me with one

of her arrows or any of the black sicknesses that waste the body and send the soul out from it with horror and shame. No, my son, it was the eternal ache in my heart at your loss that finally broke it and ended my life bitterly.'

"At these words, I gave a strangled cry and leaped across the ditch to embrace her. But her shade slipped through my arms. Three times I tried to clasp her to my breast and three times she slipped away from me, leaving my heart aching.

" 'Mother!' I cried. 'Come back! Why do you go away from me? Why does Persephone, that grim queen, not give you form that our arms might hold each other one last time?'

" 'Alas, my son,' she moaned, 'that is not to be. Fate has decided that this is 218-247 to be and it is not the fault of Persephone. It is not she who mocks solid armies with an empty shade or suffers empty shades to invade flesh and bones, nor does she defraud the fire of man's flesh. No, she allows the soul to flit away like a sparrow on its own way. But enough of this. You must leave and leave quickly before you become a part of life in death. Go! Return home and tell your wife what you have learned about this place!'

"Then, as if sent by divine Persephone, a throng of women who had been the wives and daughters of the great, now leading their second lives, crowded around the black blood like bees swarming around flowers. I drew my long sword and held them back, allowing them to come one by one so that I could question them in turn.[9]

"The first was Tyro, the daughter of noble Salmoneus, who had married Cretheus, the son of Aeolus. Yet it was not the son of air she loved but the god of the River Enipeus, the prettiest river on all earth, that she desired. Often she walked alone among the willows and flowers that crowded its banks, rejoicing in the cool shade in the heat of the day. It was there that Poseidon discovered her and, taking on the shape of Enipeus, made love to her on the mouth of the eddying river. A dark, snaking wave rose up over them, hiding them as they lay together where his current falls into the sea. And there the earthshaker unclasped her virgin girdle, slipped her dress from her white shoulders, exposing her full, ruby-tipped breasts to the warm air, and made love to her long and hard until she fell into a deep slumber.

"And when she awakened, he took her by the hand, stroking the soft 248-272 mound with his fingers, and said, 'Woman! Rejoice in our bedding, for when the year has completed its run, you will give birth to two sons, for the matings of the gods are never barren. Raise them carefully, telling no one from whom they came. I am Poseidon, earthshaker, sealord.'

"Then he turned and plunged into the heaving sea, and when the year ran its course, she gave birth to great Pelias and Neleus who became powerful servants to Zeus, the thunderlord. Pelias lived in spacious Iolcus where he managed great herds of cattle while Neleus moved to sandy Pylos. Tyro's other sons were fathered by Cretheus: Aeson, Pheres, and Amythaon, who is quite adept at fighting from chariots and horses.

"Next came Antiope, the daughter of Asopus, who bedded in the arms of Zeus and gave birth to Amphion and Zethus, who founded the seven-gated city of Thebes, walling it round with towers that allowed the Thebans the strength to hold their city from sea pirates and armies.[10]

"Alcmene, the wife of Amphitryon, followed her. She too lay with Zeus to give birth to lion-hearted Hercules.[11] And then came Megara, Creon's daughter, who married Hercules.[12]

273–296   "Then came lovely Jocasta, the mother of Oedipus,[13] who in her ignorance of her son married him after he killed his father and took the throne at Thebes. But the gods soon made known his sin and brought a curse upon the lovely city: Oedipus was allowed to rule but suffered the pangs of remorse after Jocasta stretched her neck with a rope from the roof beam of their house. And so she was brought down to the House of Hades, leaving Oedipus to the vengeance of the Furies.

"And then came Chloris, the great beauty and the youngest daughter of Amphion, the son of Iasus, who ruled the great Minyaean Orchomenus. She married Neleus (who must have paid a bloody fortune for that beauty, I can tell you!) and brought to Pylos the glorious children Nestor and Periclymenus and Chromius. But of all her children, the most beautiful, Pero, was the wonder of the age. But Neleus refused to give her in marriage to the many suitors who flocked to Pylos like males after a bitch in heat until one of them could drive away the cattle of Iphiclus, the son of Phylacus. Now, this was no task for the fainthearted! No, the man who managed to drive away that broad-browed herd would be one well rewarded only after taking his life in his own hands. Now, along came a great and gifted seer, Melampus of the black foot, who volunteered for this venture.[14] But alas, cruel fate placed the prophet in chains as a prisoner until, after the hours ran through the days and a year had run its course, the seasons came again to spring. The mighty Iphiclus set him free for making the secrets of the gods known. Thus, Zeus's will was done."

Here Odysseus paused to drink deeply of the wine and puddle his fingers in a bowl of water in which delicate rose petals floated. He pressed the pads of his fingers to his eyes and patted droplets upon his cheek and beard. He drank again, then stretched his hands high overhead. His back popped and the great muscles relaxed. He sighed.

"Ah, well, but this rambling is tiresome, I know. Perhaps we should—"

"I pray you," Alcinous said quickly, "do not stop there but tell us what else you saw in that dreadful house."

Odysseus drew his shaggy brows down in a frown and pursed his lips, *297–324* shaking his head. "Well, my prince, there are always roses among the weeds if one is careful to search for them. I saw Leda, the wife of Tyndareus, to whom she bore the famous Castor, tamer of horses, and Polydeuces, the boxer never defeated, both of whom still roam the earth on alternate days, spending the others with their mother in the bowels of the earth.[15] To this day, each is honored as a god.

"And then my eyes fell upon Iphimedeia, who claimed to have been the lover of Poseidon (although that is a common claim among women, I have discovered in my wanderings, and I often wonder if this is true or simply a clever excuse for wives who have been caught on love-rumpled sheets— where was I? Oh, yes) and gave birth to those short-lived twins, god-opposed Otus and Ephialtes, the largest men raised on earth. (Well, save Orion, of course, but that's another story for another time.) When only nine years old they measured nine cubits across the shoulders and stood a full nine fathoms tall. And all here, I'm sure, are aware of their story—hm, no? Very well. In the rashness of youth, they bragged that they would war the very gods upon their own grounds atop lofty Olympus. Ah, the impetuousness of youth! They threatened to pile Mount Ossa upon Olympus and then wooded Pelion on top of that and so on to make a stairway to heaven.[16] And who knows? Perhaps if they had reached their prime before beginning, they might have achieved their end. Oh, don't look at me like that, prophet! Children are protected by Hera, but when stubborn pride masks common sense even among children, the gods punish them! Apollo it was this time, the son of Leto of the lovely braids, who punished the striplings by destroying them before wiry beards replaced the fuzz of their chins.[17]

"I also saw Phaedra[18] and Procris[19] there and the lovely Ariadne,[20] the daughter of evil Minos, whom Theseus tried to carry away from Crete to the noble soil of Athens. But he never gained her virgin flower, as Dionysus called in a favor from Artemis, who killed her in the seagirt island of Dia.

"She was followed by Maera there too and Clymene and much-loathed *325–351* Eriphyle,[21] who honored gold more than the life of her husband and convinced him to ignore the warnings of the gods and leave on a trip from which he would never return. Ah, but I could tell you hundreds of tales like these if I but had the time, but the ambrosian night would slip from us before I had finished all the stories of the great men's wives and daughters I saw while I lingered there before the House of Hades.

"But—" He yawned and stretched again, scrubbing his hands across his face. His eyes looked reddened and bleary in the flickering light from the lamp at his elbow. "But now I must go and sleep if I am to leave tomorrow for my homeland. And this I must do, for my journey is in the hands of the gods and I feel their urging upon me now."

He fell silent, and the whole hall, caught up by the spell of his words, remained quiet while shadows lengthened until at last Arete of the white arms broke the silence, saying, "Phaeacians, what do you think of this man, his bearing, his presence, his state of mind? I know that he is my guest, but all of you share that honor with me. Now, don't carelessly dismiss him without some reward for the stories he has told this night. I know that the gods have been kind to you all and that your homes are filled with riches. I suggest that you bestow some small token upon him."

The grave hero lord Echeneus, the oldest among all there, rose, his ancient joints creaking with the effort, and fixed the audience with a watery eye, saying, "Well, friends, our queen has spoken wisely. Her words don't miss the mark. We owe this good fellow a bit for his words, and I suggest that we all do what is right. But what to give him? Hm. Well," he turned to Alcinous, "let us let our king tell us what would be most appropriate."

Alcinous nodded and said, "Well, then, as the ruler of this nation and its sailors, I beg our guest to put aside his desires to return to his home for one more day until I have a chance to add my own poor offering to the gifts that you all are intending. In the meantime, we will make his trip home the priority of all the people's thinking. This I ask, and this I command as the prince of the land." He looked appreciatively at his guest.

352–382 Wise Odysseus, man of many masquerades, grinned in his beard and answered, "Alcinous, most duly glorified among us all. If you ask me to stay a bit longer, I will. Even if you ask me to stay a year—so long as you promise me a safe journey home. I couldn't linger here forever, you know, and I am most anxious to make my return. Methinks there is mischief afoot at my home that needs my attention. But it would be good to return with something to show for my long wanderings, and your splendid gifts would do nicely. At least I might receive a warmer welcome than if I returned with only the clothes upon my back. There are certain expectations that people make of their kings, you know, and people are no different in Ithaca than those in your kingdom."

Alcinous smiled and nodded in agreement. "You speak a good argument. At first I thought you might be one of those prollers or impostors who roam up and down the coast, putting in here and there, to spin their long yarns in the hopes of gaining a coin or two and some nights' lodgings from news-starved hosts, knowing full well that no one would be able to hold them accountable for their blanching tales. Yes, we've had a few of those rascals here." He looked around the room at a few knowing wags who exchanged glances. "But you move our eyes with form, our minds with matter, and our ears with the eloquence of your oration, and in your words I hear the music of truth in an ordered history that we have become a part of. Not even Demodocus"—he glanced as if in apology at the blind bard—"whose voice is admittedly sweeter than the rasp of your salt-strained throat, can sing to us all the Greek sorrows you have wept out in our presence here. But I do have one question to put to you."

He stroked his beard while gazing upon Odysseus with curious eyes. Odysseus gave a half smile and said, "Did I see any of the brave men who fell at Troy?"

Alcinous's mouth dropped open in amazement. "And now you read minds as well?" His eyes flickered out to his guests. "Surely this man has been touched by the hand of Apollo!"

"Athene," Odysseus corrected absently, drawing his brows together. "She is my constant companion."

"But you knew—"

Odysseus shrugged. "There is nothing to that, my lord. Of course, I knew what you wanted, for those heroes who were my friends before the walls of Ilium are the daydreams of youths who play their war games in the cool shade of vineyards and beneath the drooping branches of olive trees before the heat of midday. And men are not much more than little boys when it comes to that; but their games reek of blood and gore, and when the game is finished no one climbs from the earth to go home for dinner. Yet there is a reason for that: All men wish to be painted with glory if only briefly and at least once in their lives. All wish to live forever in the songs of poets and bards, but few are destined for that and fewer still accomplish it. But there is a time for long and wonderful tales and there is a time for sleep as well. However," he relented upon seeing the disappointment in Alcinous's face, "I cannot refuse to tell you a bit more. You will not take great joy in the telling, however, for the fate of those heroes was miserable indeed. Some fell in the war, others on the way home. Perhaps it is those you are more interested in, for the songs have already recorded the deeds and deaths of those who fell before the walls of Troy, but not much has been written about those who perished after Troy fell to our blades. And again, it was the will of a wicked woman that brought about their slaughter."

He paused, staring into the flames of the flickering lamp to gather his thoughts. "In the end, Persephone drove away the spirits of the women, and *383-413* approaching me out of the gloom came the ghost of Agamemnon, son of Atreus. His whole regal bearing seemed draped in sorrow, and around him gathered the souls of the damned who had died with him in the palace of Aegisthus. He bent his bearded face to the trench and drank the blood, and when he rose his eyes fell upon me and he uttered a loud cry and tears gushed from his eyes like fountains of water thrown up by newfound springs. He thrust out his hands, seeking to embrace me, but their old commands swept like shadows over me, for the legendary strength and vigor of those arms were no more.[22] I wept to see his weakness that death had given him and said, 'Oh, Agamemnon, king of men, what type of cruel death has brought you to this level? Did Poseidon raise fierce storms and tempestuous winds to sink your ships? Did a hostile tribe greet you in friendship only to fall upon you when your guard was down? Were you killed while trying to steal cattle and flocks or raid a city for riches and women?'

"And Agamemnon fixed me with his soulful eyes and said, 'Nimble-witted Odysseus, by none of these did I die but by the hand of Aegisthus and my murderous wife. Upon my homecoming, I was invited to a banquet at his house, and there, along with my faithful comrades, I was butchered like a swine led to the slaughterhouse. A most pitiful end. You may have witnessed many deaths of men in lone combat and duels, Odysseus, but you have never witnessed the horror that felled me.

414-443   " 'We were left lying in the feasting hall on tables and chairs and couches, our blood mingling with the spilled wine, washing the floor in a sea of red.

" 'But the most terrible of all was the cry I heard from Cassandra, Priam's daughter, murdered by my treacherous wife, that whore Clytemnestra. I threw up my hands, trying to help her, but another sword stroke felled me, and that bitch laughed to see me lying there, taunting me with her naked body, her breasts and white belly splattered with my blood, while my soul seeped from me and began its journey to Hades. She refused even to shut my eyes or close my mouth with her hands.' And he shook his great head, tears dripping from his eyes. 'Ah, Odysseus. There is nothing more shameful than a woman who can kill her husband who married her while a maid and brought her to a house such as mine to give her children and servants and hope that my love would find a place in her heart. But now she must wear the brand of her evil deed, and her name will be forever linked with infamy. Yes, not only herself but all women will have to bear such villainy for all eternity.'[23]

" 'Alas!' I cried. 'Why does Zeus so despise the House of Atreus that he would work his hatred among the sons of Atreus through their women? Because of Helen's lust hundreds of good men went to their deaths, and now—ah, but it pains me to speak even now about it—your own wife, Clytemnestra, birthed a plan that brought you to the House of Hades.

" 'A wise observance,' said he. 'And take heed from your own words for your own advice, Odysseus. Faithful Penelope waits, but don't trust her too far. And don't tell her all that you have upon your mind lest she find an opportunity to use it against you. Oh, I expect you, like all husbands, will tell a bit of your plans and triumphs, but keep most to yourself and do not let it out. The husband who lets his wife know all is a willing fly in the widow's web.[24] Oh, now, lose that skeptic frown, Odysseus. I'm not saying that your wife will murder you. Penelope is far too loyal with her thoughts and ways. And I remember how she was a young bride who had just delivered a son and held him nursing at her breast as we left for the war. I imagine by now that he has taken a seat in the council at your house. And I envy you, for you will see your son again and he will finally kiss your cheeks. That is the way things should be! That is what my wife refused me. I did not even have the satisfaction of seeing my own son during my brief homecoming before she killed me. Ah, me! But that is the past and we cannot step in the same place twice in a moving stream. Now listen to me: Do not take a ship directly into harbor. Anchor off and away from knowing eyes that you may creep upon your own homecoming and see how the sail sets in your own house. Be secretive. Disguise yourself. Women cannot be trusted, and until you see how she remembers you, do not even trust faithful Penelope. Remember Clytemnestra and how she greeted her lord so the same fate may not befall you. But tell me: Have you heard anything about my son? Does he still live in Orchomenus or Pylos? Perhaps he has moved to the plains of Sparta to hunt with his uncle Menelaus? I have not seen Orestes[25] in this hellhole yet, so I can only presume that he must still wander among the living?'

" 'Alas, but I cannot give you any news. I have no idea if he lives or if he is dead. There is no sense in giving you empty words. I am sorry,' I said.

"So we stood, telling each other stories and exchanging words, but there was no happiness in our words for tears rolled down our cheeks. What should have been happiness became sadness and what was sadness became happiness and so we passed the time in sorrow until the shades of Achilles and Patroclus[26] and Antilochus and Ajax came forward. Achilles recognized me immediately and said mournfully, 'Odysseus, Zeus's favorite! What brings you to these lower depths? Why would you come here to the regions where the dead live mindlessly?'

" 'Achilles, the strongest of the Greek warriors, I came to consult with Teiresias for virtuous advice on how to return home, for we have most certainly lost our way and cannot make our way back to rugged Ithaca without his guidance. Indeed, by my reckoning, I have not even come close to Achaea in my wanderings. Misfortune and the gods' mischief have kept me roaming the seas all these years. I envy you, Achilles. You are the most fortunate among all that I have known. In the old days you were honored more than any other man, and I see that even now, down here among the legions of the dead, you exercise great power as well. So why do you speak so melancholically about your own death?'

"Bitter laughter echoed hollowly from him, and his eyes burned sadly. 'Ah, do not speak lightly of death, Odysseus, and do not rub salt into the wound of my own. Note this: I would rather be the most common slave in the fields for some landless peasant than rule these lifeless dead as their king. No wonder Hades wears such a gloomy look. There is nothing to them but hollow moanings and aimless ramblings. But enough of this melancholy. Give me word about that son of mine. Tell me: Did he follow me to Troy and take a hand in tumbling those topless towers? Do the Myrmidons hold him in such esteem as they did, or is he sneered at in Hellas and Phthie now that age may have twisted his bones and withered his flesh? (For such is the way of mortals that the heroes of today become the forgotten of tomorrow.) I fear for him since I no longer walk in the sunlight to protect him as I once did whole armies, yes, even to laying low the champion of the enemy upon the fields of Troy. Ah, tell me that this isn't so, for if I could return to my father's court—even if only for a brief moment—those men who demean him would cringe before my unconquerable hands.'

504-535 " 'Well spoken, Achilles,' I said carefully. 'But I can tell you nothing about what lies in Hellas and Phthie. As to your Neoptolemus, well, I can tell you a bit since I brought him from Scyros in my own ship to join the Greek army. We spent many a night there as did you and I, talking in front of the city of Troy, making our plans. He was like you in that regard, always speaking first and to the point. Tactless, perhaps, but among such ramblings and pontificating the lack of tact can be refreshing at times. Nestor and I were the only two to convince him that certain ideas he had were contrary to our plans. On the battlefield, he never lagged behind the ranks or hid in crowds. His spirit led him to run far ahead of the others. He killed many men, Achilles, so many I cannot give you their names. I do, however, remember one—the mighty Euryplus, Telyphus's son, fell to his sword after that handsome lad tried to burn our ships. God's balls, but I never saw a better-looking man than that one, Achilles! He wore many favors from many mistresses. More than any other with the possible exception of Memnon.[27]

" 'Well I remember when all of us took our places in the wooden horse Epeius built. It was my job to throw open the door when I judged the time to be right for us to descend and destroy the city. Many of the Greeks who stayed with me in the belly of that horse wiped tears and tried to keep their legs from trembling, but not your son. Not once did a tear fall across his cheek. No, quite the opposite. Contrary that he was, he kept urging me to throw back the door and let him jump out of the horse. He kept fidgeting so much with that ivory-handled sword and his great bronze spear that I had to warn him sternly more than once to keep quiet or all would be lost. When I did open the trapdoor, he was among the first to slide down to the ground. He killed many that day, including Priam, slaughtering that man at the foot of Zeus's own altar, and gathered his share of the spoils and his special prize[28] and left sound in limb in his own ship. I was truly amazed, for in close battle, Ares never fights but rages and does not watch where his sword lands.'

"At this, the soul of swift-footed Achilles sped down the asphodel 536-565
meadow, shouting in glee at the news of his son. But then the mourning souls of the others pressed around me, each demanding news that mattered to him. Only Ajax, the son of Telamon, stood proudly apart from the others, and I could see on his face that he still bitterly resented losing Achilles's armor when it was awarded to me, by the Trojan captives and Athene, who judged us both, instead of him.[29] I called to him and asked him why he was so troubled.

" 'Ajax, you wear our glories full upon your broad shoulders. Have you forgotten that in death? Do you still blame me for losing the arms of Achilles? Those were cursed by the gods, I tell you, for we lost much of our strength when your towering frame was laid low by the gods. We still mourn your death as one of the best among us with the same honor that we mourn Achilles, Peleus's son. If you must blame someone, then blame Zeus, who hated the Greek army. It was he who brought you low. Now, come closer and hear what I have to say. Put a bridle on your anger and pride for a moment!'

"But he ignored me and went away to join the rest of the souls of the dead in Erebus, the River of the Dead. I regret that he was so moved by his anger that he could not make his peace with me. Perhaps I should have asked him again to come and speak with me, but I was pressed hard at the time by the souls of others.

"I saw Minos, the famous son of Zeus, with his golden scepter held fast in 566-594
his immortal hand, delivering judgment upon the dead before allowing them to pass further into the House of Hades. I saw Orion, the giant hunter, driving a throng of savage beasts across the field of asphodel. He held a club of solid and indestructible bronze in one huge hand.

"And there was the son of Gaia, the earth mother, Tityus, stretched full upon the ground for six hundred cubits with two vultures on either side pecking at his liver, jabbing their ripping beaks full into his body, tearing huge chunks of flesh from him as punishment for his daring assault on Leto when she made her way across Panopeus toward Delphi.[30]

"I also saw Tantalus in deep torment as he stood in a pool of sweet water that nearly reached his chin. Above him hung clusters of pears and pomegranates and apples and sweet figs and plump olives. When he bent his head to try and reach the water to slake his terrible thirst, the water receded from him, and when he tried to reach high to pluck the fruit, the wind would toss the branches of their trees high away from him toward the shadowy clouds.

595–625   "And Sisyphus,[31] he who had twice tricked Death, sweat gushing from every pore, trying to push a great boulder up a hill only to have it slip from his grasp as he neared the top and roll back again onto the plain from where he had started. Sweating, straining, again and again he tried to push that boulder up the hill and again and again it slipped from him and rolled back down.

"Next I saw the mighty Hercules—or rather, his shadow, for his form lives high among the deathless gods along with lovely-ankled Hebe, his wife, the daughter of Zeus and golden-sandaled Hera—and from the dead surrounding him rose a loud noise like ruffled wings from birds scattering in terror. Dark terror clung to him, for he looked as black as the night, and in one hand he held a bow with an arrow nocked as his mighty head bent left and right as if looking for a target to shoot. Terrible as well was the mighty belt around his chest, gold-embossed with horrifying lions with massive manes, bears, boars, duels and battles, massacres and murders. I pray to the gods that whoever made that baldric never be allowed to make another one. He saw me and knew me straightaway and he wept and spoke and his words flew on wings to me, saying, 'Son of Laertes, man of masquerades, oh, unhappy man! You bear a destiny like mine, and I can see in your soul the sadness of it and feel it as I felt it when I lived under the sun. Although I was Zeus's son, many troubles came my way. Countless battles I fought! Countless labors did I perform for a master far beneath my rank to atone for my sin. Once, that miscreant sent me down here to fetch the Hound of Hades— a task he thought to be the most dangerous of all—yet I brought it back from this place thanks to the help of Hermes and Athene, the gray-eyed goddess.'

626–640   "Well he might have said more, but Hercules disappeared into the mists rising around him. I lingered long, hoping to hear more from the lips of that giant among men, but he did not return. I waited long for more of the dead heroes from the past stories and songs of poets—Theseus and Perithous, I hoped for—and I would have seen them, too, but suddenly a large crowd of lost souls, whole tribes of dead, came up and gathered around me. Tens of thousands, all making an eerie clamor that rose the hackles on the back of my neck. I felt the blood leave my face and my legs begin to shake, and suddenly I feared that dreaded Persephone would send up from Hades's Halls the Gorgon's head,[32] that grim monster, and I hurried away to my ship. Scrambling aboard, I ordered my men to loosen the hawsers and push off and away from that cursed land. And so we sailed down the River of Ocean, helped along first by our oars, then a fair wind sent by a friendly god."

Odysseus sat back and shadowed his eyes with a hand. Silently Alcinous handed him a large cup of wine and the hero took it gratefully, lifting it and draining it in one long draught. He ran his tongue over his lips and looked up from beneath lowered brows and smiled sadly. "Ah, but give me a minute or two to catch my breath, and I'll tell you more."

Here ends the Eleventh Book of Homer's Odyssey.

THE TWELFTH BOOK

The Great Perils of the Sea

❖ ❖ ❖ ❖ ❖ ❖ ❖ ❖ ❖ ❖ ❖

The adventures with the Sirens and Scylla
And Charybdis bring Odysseus to Ogygia.

❖ ❖ ❖ ❖ ❖ ❖ ❖ ❖ ❖ ❖ ❖

*O*dysseus paused and stretched his knotted frame.　　　　1–32
His joints popped. He sipped his wine and blearily
Looked around the room. A serving wench came
Forward with a bowl of water and silently
Held the bronze bowl in front of him. He puddled
His fingers in the sweet, rose-petaled
Water and flicked the drops against his face.
He sighed deeply and tilted his head to press
His finger pads against his eyes. He moaned
Softly to himself, and the others heard him groan
With sadness. He drew a deep breath and said:

"Ah, me!" he sighed. "It's a terrible thing to have the truth shown to a man
who has lived by his wits for so long. And that was not the end of our trou-
bles, either, as the gods were not finished casting lots concerning our fate.
Damn poor game, that is, when man isn't given a fling of the cup for himself,
but man isn't, and it is up to us to make the best of whatever comes our way."
He paused. "The trouble is that man will make the best of it, and the gods
will deliberately push another block in his way, forcing him down another
path. There's the rub of the whole thing, I tell you! The gods become like lit-
tle children playing with frogs in a puddle, poking us one way or the other,
meddling in our affairs, yet when we try to meddle in theirs we get slapped
arse over pins for our trouble. Where's the fairness in that, I ask you?"

Alcinous moved uneasily on his throne and glanced around the room at the wary frowns of Odysseus's audience. He pulled at his finely combed beard and said, "As you say, my good man, the gods are fickle and perhaps vain, but it is not to us humans to point out their failings to them. That is why they are immortal and we mortal. And," he added tactfully, "as such we must take great care not to offend them. As you say, they can be . . . vindictive, shall we say, when they wish, and punishment whether deserved or not is still punishment. Better simply to trek the path they want, don't you think?"

Odysseus took a long draught from his cup, sighed and belched, then shook his shaggy head. "Yes, that is without a doubt the most prudent way. But what sort of man is he who does such a thing? If man is given the earth to walk, then why did the gods put the stars over his head for him to ponder? And why do we have monsters to fight? And pirates and thieves? No, it is a puzzle that we are supposed to figure out, I believe, and these are the choices we have: to live our lives as men or slaves. But"—he wagged his head— "there comes a time when man must rest and when man has done all that he can with the gods' whimsical ways. And so we turned our black-prowed ship toward our homeland. Or," he continued after a moment's hesitation, "toward what we hoped would be our homeland.

"And so we sailed down the flowing waters of Ocean's River to the wide-open sea, making our way to the island of Aeaea where Eos has her palace and comes out to dance in dawn's light from the rising sun. We drew our ship up to the golden sands and climbed wearily upon the shore. Tired and bone-weary from rowing, we fell asleep on the warm sands, waiting for the golden light of dawn.

"When the white-and-red-fingered lady spread her saffron flame and touched the mountains with gentle fingers, we awoke and I sent a party away to Circe's house to fetch Elpenor's body. While they were gone, the rest of us built a respectable pyre upon the sands, trimming trees from the forest, pausing now and then to wipe the streaming tears from our eyes as we remembered brave Elpenor's ways. There, upon the boldest point, we honored our dead comrade—although I can tell you there was a certain pungent ripeness to his body as the gods had not seen fit to treat him as they did Hector when Achilles left his body upon the dung heap before giving it over to Priam for proper rites—by piling his armor around him before setting a torch to it all. When the corpse was burnt, we raised a funeral mound over him and hauled a stone over it for a proper monument, planting his oar— which he had curiously carved to his own liking—upon it.

"When we had finished, Circe came, bringing her handmaidens with her and bread and red wine and roasted goat. She fixed the feast beside a gentle brook where a cool breeze cooled our sweating brow and said, 'Ah, what men are these who dare to descend alive into Hades's dismal mansion? You have ensured yourselves of a double death, you know. But that's nettles and thorns in the past now! Come, eat! Enjoy yourselves, for I fear tomorrow you shall have to be on your way again. This time, I will give you the route to travel over the seas and'—here she paused to wrinkle her fine brow and tease my beard with her dainty fingers—'give you a bit of advice how to avoid the woeful ends that may arise from your willful actions. But I know that you are men and will make your own way despite my advice. Think about it! That's all I can say! Think before you act rashly!'

"Well, we weren't that difficult to persuade as we had just heard the worst that man can hear—the truth—so we listened with all thoughts to be wise to her directions while we sat and feasted on rich meat and mellow wine. When the fingers of darkness streaked across the sky, my men settled into sleep by the ships, but Circe took me by the hand and led me to a secret grotto.[1] There, she dropped her gown, and I stood bewitched by the loveliness of her ruby-tipped breasts, her shapely legs. We swam naked together in the soft waters of the grotto, and then she lay beside me and begged me to tell her about our adventures.

"And when I finished, she lay silently, toying with the hair on my chest, and said, 'You have been sorely tested, but the worst is yet to come. First, you will come to the Sirens[2] whose bewitching song is the wrack and ruin of many a man. Whoever hears that song most dear to him will so despise his homeland, his wife and children, that he will stay and listen to their sensuous charm. And so he will not know the loving arms of his wife again or be greeted by the bright faces of his little children. He will join the Sirens who charm him with their high and clear song and sit in the meadow with them amid the piles of bleached bones, some still bearing the tattered skins of the men who came before him. But there is a way past them, my love. Soften some beeswax and plug the ears of your men and yourself so that you cannot hear the pounding of the surf and row past that cursed island. But you won't do that, will you? Not the brave Odysseus who challenges the gods whenever he can! So have your men bind you hand and foot with the strongest cords they can find to the sturdy mast of your ship and tell them not to free you despite your orders until you are four leagues past the island. When you try to free yourself, they are to wrap more and more ropes around you and fairly cocoon you, if they must, despite your struggles and shouts. That way, you will be able to enjoy the Sirens' song and live.

" 'Now, after you have safely passed that island, there are two routes still

33–62

open to you. Here, I cannot make a choice for you—as a mortal, that is what you must determine for yourself. Life is full of choices, and although you may think the gods meddle too much in your life, there are still some things that we cannot alter. But that is milk and gall now! You are impatient, I know. That is the case with the mortals who are in a hurry to get on with their lives.

" 'You have two routes open to you. One will carry you to two steep rocks that rise above the roaring black sea. The gods call them the Rovers, for they come together like hands clapping whenever anything tries to pass through them. No bird passes safely through them—no, not even the divine doves that Zeus loves so greatly and who bring the ambrosia to him. Blue-eyed Amphitrite[3] plays her playful games by slapping the rocks together whenever the doves deign to pass between them, and Zeus has to add still another to the dove flock after one falls to the rape of those rocks[4] to keep the holy number.

63-93   " 'Any ship that tries to slip between these black rocks comes to ruin, simple wreckage floating upon the scumlike foam of the sea. Any sailors who dare the tossing waves perish there, for the seas retain a whirling fire[5] that singes their flesh. Only one ship has survived this ordeal and that is the famed *Argo*,[6] but even she would have perished upon those granite faces had Hera not lent Jason a helping hand. (There are those who think that she and Jason had a fling or two, but that's only a spring fable that arises now and then among us like sap in a tree.)

" 'Now one of these two black rocks raises its pointed peak toward the heavens. Black clouds constantly cluster around its peak both summer and fall when the harvest is gleaned. Never does clear weather show. The sides are smooth and slick as ice and no man could scale it even had he twenty hands and feet to help him find a purchase. Yet halfway up there is a mist-ridden, gloom-draped cave facing the setting sun toward Erebus. No bowman could shoot a shaft into its depths, and it is from here that bawling Scylla[7] with her lionlike caterwauling and her belt of barking dog heads constantly baying for food comes to seize her prey. A loathsome creature! No god can look upon her with other than contempt. Twelve foul feet she has and six necks, and her six heads each have three sets of gnashing teeth stained with black death. She stays deep in the black depths of her cave and lunges forth only when dolphins or whales or any of Amphitrite's pets swim by in the roaring seas to seize them for food. No ship sails by without losing a man to each of those heads.

94-123   " 'The second rock lies lower than the first and a good man with a bow could hit one from the other. There, on the lesser rock, grows a huge fig tree[8] with dense foliage, and below this tree is dreaded Charybdis[9] who three times a day drinks deeply of the seawater, then vomits it back up again. Any ship passing within her grasp is doomed. Not even Poseidon could save you from her greedy lips—and we all know that isn't likely, given your feud with him, eh? No, best to row close to Scylla and give up six than to doom all.'

" 'Ah, yes,' I said. 'But surely there is some way that I can steer away from Charybdis and still escape Scylla.'

"Circe rose indignantly, swinging her legs around to sit cross-legged, her plum-tipped breasts heaving indignantly. "Fool! Have you not yet learned man's limitations? You have brought this upon yourself with your constant spoiling for a fight. Now accept it! Either sacrifice six or all. The choice is yours. Defeat Scylla? Impossible! She is immortal. Terror, blind terror! Fierce and impossible to fight for a mortal out of favor with the gods! Best you realize your limitations, Odysseus, and leave off tilting against the gods. You waste time putting on your armor to fight her and she'll grab six more of your men. The best thing for you to do is to row as fast as you can past her cave and beg Cratais, Scylla's mother, the bitch who brought her into this world, to keep her satisfied with only six.'

" 'Ah, now,' I said soothingly. I cupped one of those plum-tipped pome- *124-156* granates with my hand, watching her eyes turn smoky. Then she slapped my hand away, saying, 'Enough of this. For now,' she relented. 'Don't look back and dwell on what has happened. You come next to the island of Thrinacia where Helios, the sun god, keeps his prized cattle and sheep. There are seven herds of cattle with fifty head in each—these are holy numbers that never increase or decrease—and they are guarded by the shepherds Phaethusa and Lampetie, braided-haired Nymphs, the children of Helios and Neaera, who put them on that island to watch over their father's flocks and herds. You must leave them alone if you want to reach Ithaca unharmed. But if you harm one of those crooked-horn beasts, you'll bring about the destruction of your ship and crew. Then, when you arrive at home, you will be the most wretched of all men for having lost all of your companions.' "

Odysseus sighed again and shook his head. "But man seldom believes words that he doesn't want to hear. When Circe finished we cocked a bit there—ah, that wanton wench!—until Dawn mounted her golden throne and played lovely rosy fingers over the sky. Then Circe left me and I returned to my ship and told my mates to make ready for leaving. They rose, rinsing the night from their mouths with gulps of wine, and we rowed away. Circe sent silver winds to fill our sail and so we left that milk-and-honeyed land.

"But her words lay heavily upon me, and after the last tree dipped over the horizon, I called the men together and told them what she had said. After all, what could I do? It wasn't seemly for me alone to have the goddess's knowledge; all should know what risks lay ahead of us. So I told them of her warning about the Sirens and their divine song and how we had to give a wide berth to their flowery meadow surrounded by the bones of the unwary sailors who came too close to their shores. 'But,' I added, 'their song will reach out across the waves to your ears anyway. So what you must do is bind me tightly to the mast, and when I struggle and cry out to be freed, wrap even more rope around me. Plug your own ears with beeswax so that you cannot hear a single word or note from those vagrant lips.'

157–188   "By now I could see that we were fast approaching that land. The wind dropped and an opiate stillness stretched over the waves, leaving them in languorous slumber, and a breathless calm dropped over us. The air felt heavy and ponderous. I ordered the sail to be dropped and the men to ready their oars while I took a clump of beeswax and cut tiny pieces from it with my sword. I kneaded each piece frantically, warming it between my palms, and walked among the men, stopping up their ears with plugs. The men bound me hand and foot to the mast, then took up their oars, flailing hard against that lead-gray water.

"Slowly we moved away from the surf's pull, then, as the men caught the rhythm, we gathered speed. We rounded the point of land and the Sirens became aware that a ship was nearing their shore and burst into a high and clear song, singing:

'Ah, there you are, man of masquerades!
Come! Many men have visited us and stayed
Here on our verdant shores. Beach your ship
And listen to the songs from our lips
That you most want to hear. No man sails
Past this point without hearing the tales
He most wants to hear. We know how
Armies fought at Troy and how men plow
The fruitful earth. Our songs will delight
All and leave the listener with greater sight
Than he had before. So pause and pay
Attention to our words. Hear what we say!'

189–217   "And I listened to the sweet song that the Sirens sang and my heart filled with an ache to hear everything they had to offer (for that is the secret of the Sirens' song, you see: what each man wants most to hear) and I strained at the ropes holding me tightly to the mast and begged the men to free me. But they ignored my words, and then I remembered that if they couldn't hear the

Sirens' song they couldn't hear my words and so I waggled my eyebrows and tried to tell them that way to free me. But they rowed on steadily, chopping at the seas with their heavy oars. Perimedes and Eurylochus saw my struggles and leaped up and wrapped more rope around me until I was fairly cocooned with the heavy strands. And then, thankfully, we had rowed past the Sirens' call and I slumped wearily against the ropes. Seeing this, my men cautiously removed the waxen plugs from their ears and then hurried to free me from the ropes.

"I fell to the deck of the ship and lay there exhausted while they poured a cup of wine for me and bade me to drink. I shook my head and rose, looking wearily seaward, and suddenly I realized the danger that lay ahead. A plume of spume rose skyward and I heard the crash and roar of a raging surf, the thunder of breakers banging against rocks. Terrified, my men dropped their oars to gawk at the horrible sight. I roared at them to man their oars, drawing my sword and beating them back to their rowing benches with the flat of the blade. Then I relented and said, 'Men, we've been in worse fixes. Remember the Cyclops and how the goddess gave me the wisdom to work our way out of that fix? Well, this is no different! Soon it'll all be behind us and we can have a good laugh at our fears. But you have to do exactly as I say! Pick up your oars and bring up the count. Pull hard against the sea, men! Helmsman, steer wide of that foaming water and hug that high cliff to the east!'

"To my shame I did not mention the horror that awaited them above that 218–250 high cliff. And how could I? Had I mentioned Scylla and what would happen to six of them, why, they all would have stopped rowing and tried to save themselves and damn all in the bargain. So I kept my own counsel, and while they rowed hard against the pull of the sea, I ignored Circe's irksome words and dressed quickly in my armor and took two lances with me to the prow of the ship where I took my stand, hoping that I would catch the first view of Scylla's horrible chops and maybe beat off disaster for my crew. But although I racked those rocks until my eyes burned, I could not catch hide nor hair of her. My men began to wail in terror as we sailed up those straits. Charybdis roared on one side, sucking down salt water like a drunkard on rare wine and vomiting it back up along with sizzling fire from the seabed. When her maw gaped wide, I could see the swarthy sands of the seabeds lying naked beneath us and felt my legs tremble. I glanced at the terror-stricken faces of my men, and as I did, Scylla darted from her foul lair and snatched six men out of our keel. I saw them fly skyward, writhing in her terrible jaws, screaming with pain as her teeth flayed the flesh from their backs, crying "Odysseus!" in their agony.[10] Yet there was nothing that I could do to end their agony or to help them, and I was forced to watch helplessly as they held out their hands beseechingly to me in their desperation."

Odysseus fell silent, shuddering from the memory of his men being eaten by the dread monster. His audience looked uneasily around the room into the hidden shadows away from the flickering lamp and waited for him to continue. He sighed and glanced toward the sky outside the room. He shook his head.

251–279 "There is not much left to tell, and there is no reason for dwelling on what remains longer than what is needed. We left those blood-drenched rocks and soon reached the sunny isle of Thrinacia where the sun god kept his herds of cattle and flocks of sheep. From far out to sea we could hear the lowing of the cows and the bleating of the sheep. I recalled the words of Teiresias and Circe who had warned us to avoid landing on these sun-drenched shores. I glanced at my men and read the longing in their gray faces to put the thoughts of what had happened at those black rocks behind them and bask in the sun upon those sylvan shores. With a heavy heart I said, 'My friends, I have hard news to tell you. Circe and Teiresias both warned me against putting in at that island where the sun god dwells, for that is where the greatest peril waits for the unwary. We have just come through a terrible time, and it would be best for us not to tempt the Fates by paying no heed to the warnings that have been given to us. I suggest that we man the oars and row past this forbidden place.'

"But my men would have none of my words, and Eurylochus gave vent to their anger by saying, 'Odysseus, you have a bronze heart with a strength and nerves that remain unflagging despite all that we have just been through. But we are not like that. We are not made of iron, and we need the rest that we could receive by stopping on that island to soothe our jangled nerves. How could you dare to refuse us this? Night falls fast and yet you want us to put this island behind us and sail on over the foggy sea without stopping to cook a warm supper to lift our spirits. Have you forgotten how the night winds came up when we were near our homeland and blew us off course? What safe harbor could we possibly find in the dark if the wicked West Wind should suddenly rise against us? I say that we put in and enjoy ourselves this evening and in the morning we venture out upon the open sea with full bellies and well rested.'

280–311 "The others greeted Eurylochus's speech with glad hands, and I felt the ominous hand of some dark god upon my shoulders. Yet there was nothing that I could do except chance mutiny by demanding that the men follow my orders and sail away from the beckoning shores of the island of the sun god.

Yet I tried again to warn him, saying, 'Eurylochus, you are forcing my hand. Very well. I'll agree to stopping over under one condition: Every one of you must solemnly promise that you will not touch a single animal on that island. The cattle and the sheep that you are hearing belong to the sun god and are precious to him. To slay them would be a wanton and reckless act that will bring about our doom. We may land there, but we must eat only that food Circe gave us. Now swear!'

"And so they swore, each and every one of them. But it was still with a heavy heart that I had the ship brought around and anchored in a sheltered cove near a fresh river. Scarcely had our sail been dropped than the men left with the food, prepared by Circe for our trip, for the sunny shore. There they ate, and after having eaten, they remembered the six Scylla stole from our ship and they wept from the memories they had of them until sleep overtook them and they fell, exhausted, to the sands.

"During the third watch that night, the stars began to stoop, Zeus   *312–339* unleashed his thunderbolts, and the clouds gathered grimly overhead. Then the gale hit, drenching us with its violence, and through the remainder of the night, we kept watch lest our ship be dashed away from its anchor and wrecked upon the rocks. When Eos finally stretched her rose fingers over the land, we dragged the ship up on land and into a hollow cave used by the Nymphs for their strange dances. I gathered my men around me and again warned them not to touch the sun god's cattle or sheep else we be doomed for our irreverence. Again they agreed, and for a month we languished there as the South Wind wailed around us. As long as our bread and red wine lasted, the men were content to wait out the gale raging around us and whipping the sea into gray mountains that would have wrecked us had we been caught in it. But then the food ran out and then the wine, and the men took to the waters and the bushes with barbed hooks for fish and nets and spears for game. I felt the gloom of their spirits and went inland until I found a secluded spot away from all, and there I washed my hands and made my offerings to the gods and prayed that the gods would take pity upon us and allow us to leave in peace. A soothing sleep came over me, and I lay down under the shelter of a fig tree and fell fast asleep.

"While I slept, Eurylochus gathered my men around him and said,   *340–368* 'Friends, all forms of death are abominable to men, but the worst of them all is to die with empty bellies and dry throats. Now, we can see the fat cattle and sheep around us and have only Odysseus's word that they belong to the sun god. But what if he is wrong? Eh? What then? Why, we will have sat on this miserable island for a month or two—the last with empty bellies—while relief was only a spear-cast away. Now, I say let's round them up, all these cattle and sheep, and offer them to the gods all, and just in case these are the cattle of the sun god, why, let's promise Helios that if we should reach Ithaca safely we will build him a temple in thanks for the food that he has provided. That should soothe his ruffled feelings, I would think. But if he is too angry to take our trade in part, why then, I'd sooner drown in the seas than waste away from hunger. What do you say?'

"Alas, his words were to their liking, and while I slept, the men rounded up the cattle and the sheep and made their prayers to the gods, using fresh leaves they stripped from a tall oak tree and pure water from a nearby stream since they had already eaten all the barley and drunk nearly all the wine. Then they slit the throats of the cattle and flayed them and wrapped the pieces in folds of fat. They spitted the flesh and roasted them over open fires and feasted heartily.

369–390   "It was during their feasting that I awakened with a feeling of dread and hurried back to my ship. I discovered what they had done in my absence, and I cried out in horror to the gods, 'Great Zeus and gods! What cruelty is this you have brought by lulling me to sleep and, while my guard was down, letting my men commit this crime against you?'

"But my words arrived too late to do any good. Fast-footed Lampetie of the golden robes flew to Helios to report what my men had done. Enraged, he cried out to the Immortals, 'Ah, Zeus and blessed brothers! Help me gain revenge upon these followers of Odysseus, the man of masquerades, those impious men who have drained the lifeblood from my cattle! If I am not repaid for this insult I will join Hades in his grim palace and shine among the dead and let the living wither and die!'

" 'Helios,' Zeus answered, 'revenge shall be yours. My red-hot bolts will strike their ship on the wine-dark sea and send it burning with my fire into the briny deep.' "

Odysseus paused, looking around at the doubtful faces of his audience and laughed. "Yes, I know your thoughts. How did I, a mere mortal, know what transpired among the gods in the heavens? You forget that I was for seven years a love captive of Calypso upon her lovely isle, and many times she told me of the comings and goings among the gods at this time. She learned this when Hermes brought the news to her on his vain attempts at seducing her. But even then, when I came down to the seas again and found my men lolling around on the sands with filled bellies, I knew then that there would be no forgiveness. No, not with dead cattle lying around.

391–421   "And then the gods sent portents of the doom that was waiting for us. The hides began to crawl about and the meat roasting upon the spits bellowed with anguish so we heard the death cries constantly about us. Yet my men did not repent but laughed at what they saw and heard and for six days they feasted well.

"On the seventh day, though, Zeus's fury lifted, and we quickly dragged our ship down to the sea and set out away from that accursed place, rowing strongly to drive the thought of our sin away from us. But we found nothing ahead of us except open sky and sea. And then Zeus sent a gray cloud to hang somberly over us, darkening the seas with its ominous shadow. A howling wind came up out of nowhere and the seas rose up in fury, driving us before it in a series of squalls that snapped our cables and tore our sail. The mast snapped in half like a twig and struck the helmsman, killing him instantly. A wave washed over the stern and lifted him away, and then the dreaded bolt of Zeus struck the ship and everywhere was the smell of brimstone. Wave after wave crashed over us, washing the men one by one overboard.

"And then there was none.

"Except me.

"I dashed from one end of the ship to another, trying to avoid the waves searching me out with foamy fingers. Then one mighty wave ripped the sides away from the keel and tore the rest of the mast out of its seat. A leather-braided rope fell across the mast, and I used it to lash the mast and keel remains together and draped myself over them as the winds whipped me furiously through the gray waves.

"The South Wind took over from the West Wind and, helpless, I held on 422-449 grimly as I watched in horror the retracing of my route back to Charybdis. All through that night I drifted closer and closer to those black rocks, and when gray light seeped through dense night, I found myself back at Scylla's rock. Charybdis opened her mouth and began guzzling seawater like a drunkard lying beneath a tun. My rude timbers were seized and sent spinning around the edge of her gaping maw. In desperation I looked up and saw the leafy foliage of the fig tree hanging over Charybdis's mouth. I made a frantic grasp and twined my fingers among the green leaves and hauled myself up and away from the greedy lips of Charybdis and watched as the keel and mast of what had been my ship were sucked down to the seabed. I clung grimly to the fig tree and waited until Charybdis vomited up my mast and keel. Then I dropped back upon them and paddled rapidly with my hands to put distance between us before the greedy slut drank again.

"For nine days I drifted until on the tenth the gods washed me up on the 450-453 golden sands of Ogygia, the home of Calypso. There she discovered me half drowned upon her beach. But why go through all this again? This was the beginning of my story and now you have heard the rest. It is senseless to retell it and to do so would serve no purpose. As to the ending, why, the ending has yet to be written."

Here ends the Twelfth Book of Homer's Odyssey.

THE THIRTEENTH BOOK

Athene Advises Odysseus

❖ ❖ ❖ ❖ ❖ ❖ ❖ ❖ ❖ ❖

Odysseus is set ashore at Ithaca and
Is transformed into a beggar man.

❖ ❖ ❖ ❖ ❖ ❖ ❖ ❖ ❖ ❖

And so his tale ended, yet no one stirred or sighed *1–28*
In the shadowy hall where all sat lost in the tale
Still before them like the words above Apollo's gateway.[1]
Dark circles appeared under Odysseus's hollowed eyes.
A lone tear coursed down his leathery cheek.
In the light, Odysseus, the man of masquerades, suddenly
Appeared old. Alcinous frowned as someone hawked and spat.
Another blew his nose like a honking goose. Silence grew.
At last Alcinous cleared his throat, saying, "Odysseus, I know
The gods are staying silent, but I feel they are now content.
I do not think that you will be discontent with their will.
You'll be returned to your town and to the famed House of Laertes."

He turned to face his guests and said, "Well, friends, this is my wish. You have sat many times in my house, listening to the songs of the praise-singer, drinking my wine. The gifts that have been gathered for our guest—the clothing, the gold trinkets, other worthy gifts—have all been carefully packed and made ready for travel. I suggest, in addition, that we give him a large tripod and cauldron."[2] He cleared his throat, looking apologetic. "And since we cannot be expected to bear this expense by ourselves, I think it only fitting that we take up a special collection from the people to reimburse us for our generosity."

His words pleased all, and after a bit of idle chitchat, all rose and went home, weaving through the early dawn to their beds. When Eos touched the sky with her rosy fingers, servants bearing bronze gifts bustled back and forth between houses and the dock where the ship waited to take Odysseus back to his home in Ithaca. Long-suffering Penelope was remembered by one with a cleverly worked enameled toilet box, the top intricately decorated with a representation of Aphrodite. Even the great Alcinous walked the deck of the vessel, supervising the storing of the great gifts so that they would not hinder any of the crew manning the oars.

At last they finished readying the ship and returned to the palace of Alcinous, where the great king had a huge ox brought forth, perfect in all ways without a blemish to be seen on the brown hide, and slew him to appease black cloud–gathering Zeus to ensure safe travel. They burnt the thighs wrapped in thick fatty folds and settled down joking and laughing among themselves while divine Demodocus sang songs of praise and trickery and idle tunes and tats to notes plucked on his harp to the amusement of all. Children joined them too for this feast, the boys cockfighting like banty roosters while girls and women played knucklebones.

29-52   A young girl, lightly dressed to show her fine thighs and bubbling breasts, danced a twelve-hoop dance to a paean played to Pan[3] on a syrinx.[4] Tumblers flipped and flopped around the floor.

Yet Odysseus remained solemn, turning his face toward the rising sun blazing high in the sky and sending sunlight shafts into the shadowed room, waiting impatiently for the sun to dip below the sea's horizon. Like the weary plowman who toils a full day in the fields with twin brown oxen pulling the plow through deep furrows, he waited for sunset. And when the final rays swept redly over the sky, he begged the oar-loving Phaeacians and Alcinous to make their final farewells.

"Alcinous, renowned prince, I beg you to pledge your final drinks and see me safely on the seas. Farewell to you all! I thank you for your gifts and for making my fondest wishes come true! May the gods bless your every wish for granting me safe escort home. May you all bring happiness to your wives"—suggestive laughter followed his words as the women blushed and cast saucy winks at the men—"and may the gods bring prosperity to you and your children and keep you safe from harm."

Odysseus's speech brought glad shouts from the party, whose members nodded knowingly at the wisdom and generosity of his words. They called out to mighty Alcinous that they had wabbled and wagged enough and it was time for the guest to be on his way. Alcinous raised his hands, calling for quiet, and when the hum had died down called to his servant.

"Pontonous, mix a bowl of deep-red wine and set a cup before all in the hall that we may make a drink offering to Zeus, the weather watcher, before sending Odysseus back to his birthland."

And Pontonous obediently walked to the black amphorae where the resiny wine was kept and carefully mixed the mellow wine in a deep bowl. He carried cups to each of the guests, who drank the health of Odysseus to the gods of the far-flung heavens. Then bold Odysseus, the man of masquerades, rose and put his two-handled cup in Arete's hands and said, "My queen, I give you fortune for all and may your life be filled with happiness until man's lot falls to you in old age and death takes you from us." He turned back to the guests. "And so I take my leave from all here. May your homes be filled with happiness and may great joy find its way to your people and Alcinous, your king!"

And folding his robe around him, Odysseus stepped across the room and over the threshold. Alcinous ordered a servant to follow him and take him down to the bold ship waiting by the seashore. Arete blinked back tears and sent her handmaidens after him with an embroidered box, a clean cloak of finest wool, and bread and red wine to hold him on his journey.

When they came to the hollow-keeled ship, the young lords silently took his baggage and stowed it, then spread a rug and blanket over the polished deck for Odysseus to sleep unsullied sleep while they rowed him over sylvan seas. He climbed aboard and lay down while the rowers took their places. No sooner had they dipped their shiny blades into the sea than his eyes closed in sweet repose and he fell dreamless into the little death.

And like bold stallions drawing a prize chariot over green fields, so swung the ship onto a dead course for the rocky shore of Ithaca, and the wine-dark sea streamed back from her bold prow. Speedily she drew up to slide the waves faster than a falcon flies to fasten on its prey, bearing a man wise as the gods are wise, who wound his way over harsh seas and suffered fallen spirits but now slept peacefully on the ship's deck.

When bright Morning Star sparkled from the heavens, they drew near to Ithaca and to the cove named after Phorcys, the aged sea god who makes his home where two points of land stoop steeply to the sea and protect vessels from heavy swells of the open sea. A fully foliaged olive tree grows next to a dry cave sacred to the Naiads.[5] Bees hummed around the entrance and darted among two-handled cups and basins and shuttles and looms all carved from stone where the Nymphs wove sea-purple mantles amid bubbling springs and tiny pools of crystal water. The cave has two entrances— one facing north for men to use, the other facing south for the gods and forbidden to men. Here, the Phaeacians beached their ship and gently lifted the slumbering Odysseus and his bed from the deck and carried him into the cave and placed him upon the sandy floor. Next they removed all his treasures, prompted by gentle Athene, and stacked them carefully beside the great olive tree well away from the path so a casual passer-by would not be tempted to rob him. Then they silently boarded their vessel and pulled away onto the open sea.

119–143   But now Poseidon, the vengeful lord of earthquakes who still smarted from Odysseus's tricks, asked Zeus his intentions. "Well, brother, you've cast me upon the nettles for certain, now. The Immortals surely have lost respect for me since these Phaeacians—I know they are favorites of yours and my lineage as well—have given Odysseus a leg up on his journey home. I said Odysseus would suffer much for the slights he gave me before he reached his home. But I kept a final ban from his return at your request, er, command," he hastily amended as Zeus's brow pulled down in a frown. "Now these Phaeacians bring him home in one of their best ships and leave him asleep like a babe on Ithaca. They have given him gifts so his return would not be empty. Great gifts, I might add. Far greater than anything he would have brought home from tower-toppled Troy."

"Tch. Tch. Really? Hm. Your words are a bit trivial for your standing, mighty earthshaker. I would have thought someone like you would be above petty peevishness. You whine and whimper like a pouting child puling over a parent's scolding. The gods don't disrespect you. That's a figment of your imagination, of your want. That would be a serious matter indeed. But to wail about prideful men whose vanity lets them treat you with disrespect is beneath you, I would say. After all, you have eternity to play with them and punish them as you wish."

144–169   "Black cloud gatherer, I know what I can do, but will you allow me to do my will? I have great respect for your, ah, anger and would like to keep out of its way. Sometimes you forget yourself and lash out heedlessly"—he gulped as Zeus's eyes glinted dangerously—"but then your reasons are not always clear to the lesser gods and so, well, ahem. I propose to wreck that damned ship as it comes out of the misty seas. That should teach the Phaeacians once and for all to stop treating travelers in the manner in which they greeted Odysseus. I also want to ring their city with high mountains and block them from the sea. That is, if this meets with your approval?"

Zeus sighed and rubbed a heavy hand across his wide brow. "Brother, I think it would be best if you simply turned the ship into stone as it nears the city so that all watching its approach will know they have found disfavor among the gods. But I see no reason to ring the city with mountains."

"But—"

"There is such a thing as going too far, dear brother," Zeus said quietly. "I have spoken. That is enough."

Poseidon wisely held his tongue and backed away from the throne of Zeus. He made his way to Scherie, the Phaeacians' home, and there he waited, seething with rage, until the ship came close to land. Then he rose in wrath from the seas and slapped his mighty hand upon the ship, turning her into stone and driving the roots deep into the seabed.

"There! Take that! You, you malaperts!" he crowed. Then he dusted his hands and went away in triumph.

"What's this? What's this?" the watching Phaeacians cried. "Who did this monstrous thing to our ship? Only a few minutes ago she was making her way to dock." They turned, pulling their hair and muttering to each other until Alcinous finally remembered his father's words.

"Ah, me!" he cried. "It all comes back to me now." The people turned and 170–196 looked in puzzlement at him. "My father warned me that Poseidon hated our custom of giving safe passage and conduct to any who asked for it. He said that one day we would irritate the cranky god one too many times and he would wreck our best ship as it sailed on his frothy sea. Well, the time has come! He also said that Poseidon would ring our city with mountains and cut us off from the sea. That hasn't happened yet, but I think it prudent that we give up our kindly ways and try to appease the piqued Poseidon by sacrificing twelve prized bulls to him.[6] Perhaps he'll take pity on us and refrain from the second part of that prophecy."

The people at once moved to prepare the bulls for the sacrifice to the god of the waves, gathering around the altar and beseeching Poseidon to leave their city alone.[7]

And now brave Odysseus woke from his sound sleep, stretching his sleep-knotted frame until his joints creaked and popped. He glanced around curiously, wondering where he was, for he had been away so long that he no longer recognized the place where he had played as a child and come as an adult. Besides, Athene drew a gray mist around him to disguise the man of masquerades and tell him about the wooers and the woes that had befallen his country and palace. Until he fully understood what was going on, it was best for Odysseus to remain disguised before his wife and friends and the townspeople until he had repaid the wooers for their rude actions and arrogant ways. So now all looked strange to Odysseus as he contemplated the bays and beetling rocks and leafy trees. He sighed and climbed to his feet, shaking his head and feeling great bitterness toward the men he thought had wronged him at the last.

197–224   "What now?" he cried out in dismay. "What more are you going to do to me? Now where have you dropped me? Who lives in this place? Savages or civilized people?" But no answer came down from the heavens to him. He looked around him and said, "Well, until I see what the lay of the land is, I need to find a place to store these fine gifts. I guess it would have been better if I had stayed with Alcinous and his people. Then I could have found another prince who would have brought me home instead of stranding me in this place. Hm. But where should I put these gifts where they won't be discovered by some stranger idling by? How could those lordly people have done this to me? They promised me sunny Ithaca and now I'm in this gloomy place. Broken promises are punished by Zeus and I hope his heavy hand falls fully upon them. Hm. Perhaps I'd better count my gifts and make certain that a sticky-fingered member of that crew didn't short me when they put me here."

He carefully counted the fine tripod and cauldron that had been given to him by Alcinous and the woven mantles and cloths and golden trinkets, but all was there. He shook his head, trying to puzzle out the way of things, and walked down to the sea. He stood staring out at the lead-gray water, trying to figure out what had fallen over him when Athene, disguised as a shepherd, walked up to him. A fine cloak had been thrown over one shoulder, and upon her glistening feet she wore carefully worked sandals. She carried a javelin in her hand.

225–255   When Odysseus saw her, he walked up to her at once, saying, "Good morrow, friend! You are the first I've seen since I've come to this place. Don't ask me about that, I pray you. But please tell me the nature of things around here so I may judge for myself what I have fallen into. Where am I? Who lives here? Is this an island or part of the mainland? In short, what?"

The gleaming-eyed goddess smiled and said, "Well, you surely must be the simplest of men if you can't figure out for yourself where you have come. Everyone from the crack of dawn to the sun setting knows this land. You can't drive horses over its rugged mountains and crags, but it isn't a rocky poor place either. Grain grows well here. And good wine comes from the vineyards growing upon the mountain slopes. Rain falls freely and the dew is always fresh and heavy on the lush grassy pastures for the goats and cattle. The mountains are heavily forested with fine timber and the water is always pure. Ithaca is well-known from Greece to Troy."

And Odysseus's heart leaped up at the words of the aegis-bearing daughter of Zeus. He looked at her closely and bit his lip to keep from saying the words he most wanted to say.

"Oh, that place," he said carelessly. "Why, of course I have heard of Ithaca *256–286* in the spacious land of, er, Crete. In fact, I have journeyed here, bringing half my fortune with me. I left the other half with my children," he added carelessly. "You see, I have been"—his mind raced—"exiled. Yes, that's it. Exiled. I slew Orsilochus, the son of Idomeneus, who was the fastest runner in all of Crete. That crook tried to weasel me out of the booty I brought back from Troy, which was rightfully mine for the agonies I suffered there in that long war. I had refused to serve under his father in the army there, you see, and Orsilochus decided that he would take a share of my booty for that. Well, I waited for him beside a road one dark night and when he came along— zip!—I slipped the head of my bronze spear between his ribs. No one saw me, but I decided that it would be best if I left. I found a Phoenician ship with an honest crew and, for a share of my booty, they took me aboard. I told them to let me off in Pylos or Elis where the Epeians rule, but apparently the wind grew too strong and drove them off their course. I know, now, that they had no reason to cheat me. We made this harbor through a long night's rowing, I tell you! By the time we came into this sheltered cove, why, we were all faint from hunger. We tumbled out of the ship and stretched out on this sand to sleep a bit. I guess I was more tired than the others, for I didn't hear them bring my belongings out of the ship, but, well, here they are and all. I guess they left to continue on to their fine city of Sidon. I can't blame them really for leaving me and my troubles behind. After all, sailors are a suspicious lot and probably thought the trouble they were going through was brought upon them by me."

He cleared his throat and blinked at the shepherd. Athene laughed loudly *287–314* and reached out a slim white hand, drawing it across his brow. He blinked again, and now a shapely woman stood before him, tall and beautiful. He swallowed as she spoke, and her words flitted on owl's wings to him.

"Ah, Odysseus! My man of masquerades! Even a god would have to be a fancy trickster to get the better of you in quick words. You always were a deceiver, clever with your thievish tales. I wondered if you would pass up your trickery when you came to your own country. I see you haven't. Well, enough said. On to other matters. There's no sense in trying to worm your way past me. I know your reasoning and cunning ways. Yet I am amazed that you didn't recognize me through my disguise, since you have adopted many for yourself on a moment's notice. A thief can always recognize another thief, and a magician knows the tricks of other magicians. So I thought you would know me, for none among the gods has my wiles and ways. Yet you do not recognize Athene. Tch. Tch. And here I went to so many pains to stand beside you and guard you throughout all your adventures. I am the one who touched Alcinous with a gentle hand and told him to take care of you. And now I'm here to help you out once more. Listen to me carefully, now: You must hide your gifts that the nobles gave you. Many trials lie ahead of you before you can call yourself safe at home. Be patient, now. You've been away a long time. A few more days won't make any difference to you. Don't tell a single person—man, woman, or child—who you are. They will treat you with contempt, for that is the way that they have fallen to in your absence, and heap many indignities upon you. Bear them patiently and wait until the time is right before making yourself known."

"Well, my goddess, it's pretty hard for a mortal man to recognize you however expert he may be," Odysseus said after clearing his throat. "But then, mortals are not privy to the ways of the gods unless the gods want them to be. That is why they are gods and mortals are mortals. I knew you were with me in Troy and guarded my back a time or two in battle.

315-345   "But after we sacked Troy and I carried my spoils aboard my ship and we set sail for home after a god scattered our fleet over the broad sea, I do not remember you being around me. Nor do I remember you stepping in to save me during the troubles that followed. Uh-uh. It seems to me that I was forced to wander around the world, trying to find my way home until the gods tired of playing cat-and-mouse with me. I suspect that day was in the land of milk and honey owned by the Phaeacians when you gave me comfort and guided me to their city. Now I beg you, in the name of your father—I find it hard to believe that I am in sunny Ithaca with this mist and fog roiling around me—tell me: Am I really home?"

Athene's eyes flashed. "Well, that shows how your mind works: always suspicious, aren't you, Odysseus? That's why I love you, I suppose. I always admire a man with nimble wits who keeps his calm and resolve around him. Any other man would have turned and run away from me after I told him he had arrived home, but not you. Yet I know you wish deeply to see your wife and son. Cautious Odysseus! You have learned much, I see! Even now you are careful to ask of news and doings around and about. So I warn you: Be patient; first make certain that your wife waits for you. Incidentally, I can tell you that she ignores everything and contents herself to remain at home, sorrow filled, waiting patiently through the long days and nights.

"Now, I knew you would get back home despite losing all your men. I know you think that I should have helped you over the times and trials you have faced, but you must understand that I couldn't go against the wishes of my uncle, Poseidon. Besides, you sorely tried him when you blinded his son.

He has hated you since then. Now I see you are still unconvinced about where you are. Well"—she gestured around her—"this is where Phorcys lives and that olive tree is the long-leafed tree you used to play upon as a child. Over there"—she pointed—"is the Naiads' cave where you made, er, 'sacrifices' to the Nymphs—and you can stop your grinning, for I know what those sacrifices were!" The remembering smile slipped hastily from Odysseus's lips. "Behind you are the tree-covered slopes of Mount Neriton. Convinced, now?"

With a sweep of her hand, the goddess dispelled the mist, and the sunny *346–372* land sprang into view. Tears of joy leaped into the eyes of Odysseus, and he dropped to his knees and joyfully kissed the fertile soil of his homeland. He raised his hands and looked toward the cave, saying, "Ah, you daughters of Zeus, you Nymphs of the Spring! I thought I would never see you again. I promise that I will give you gifts if"—he arched a quizzical brow at Athene—"this daughter of Zeus will allow me to see my son grown."

"Don't worry about that," Athene said. "But first things first. Right now you must hide your treasures in a corner of this sacred cave where no one will come upon them. Then we'll make plans for the future. Come on. I'll give you a hand."

Together they gathered the gifts and carried them into the gloomy recesses of the cave to stow the gold, the well-beaten bronze, and the fine fabrics. Then Athene gathered a huge stone and blocked the entrance to the cave.

"There," she said with satisfaction. "That takes care of that, I would say. Now on to other things."

They sat on a grassy sward at the trunk of the olive tree and leaned back to contemplate what method they would use to rid the home of Odysseus of the unwelcome suitors. Sparrows and wrens sang cheerfully from the long-leaved branches of the tree. Butterflies danced across the grass in front of them. A gentle wind blew in from the sea.

At last Athene broke the silence, saying, "Odysseus, man of masquerades *373–401* and Zeus's favorite, son of Laertes, you need to think how those shameless suitors have arrogantly taken over your palace for the past three years, trying to convince patient Penelope to abandon her vows to you and wed one of their scurvy lot. They've given her many gifts as a way of bribery. Now, it is true that she has not withdrawn all hope from them, but that is just a bit of politicking to keep your son safe from harm."

"Egods, but I would have fallen to the same miserable end as Agamemnon if I had rushed unthinking to my home. Thanks to you, I waited to see which way the wind blew. I remember how you always stood beside me and gave me sound advice in Troy. Now, my bright-eyed beauty, help me again, if you will. Why, I'm willing to go alone against even three hundred would-be wooers with you beside me. Now what am I going to do with these beetle-headed, flap-eared whoresons?"

"Oh, Odysseus, you do have a way with words!" Athene laughed. "Yes, I will help you when the time is right. These would-be suitors will soon find their blood staining your fine floor, don't you worry about that. But first, a bit of ground checking. Now, I propose to alter your appearance so none will see you. Your fine skin must wither a bit and I will gray your dark-brown curls into a tangled mop. We'll drape a deceiving cloak over your broad shoulders and stain it with dung so all will look at it with loathing. Let's take the twinkle from your eyes as well, for one look into them and the person will know you for the rogue you are.

402–428   "Now, this I will do for you. Afterward, you must go to the swineherd you left to care for your pigs. This man is as loyal to you as he ever was. He is completely devoted to your son and wife. You'll find him by the Raven's Rock[8] where he watches the pigs as they feast upon the fallen acorns there by Arethusa's spring. Stay with him and listen to what he has to say before you go anywhere else. Meanwhile, I'll go to Sparta, the city of fine women—get that look out of your eye; you're home now!—and fetch your son Telemachus back home. He traveled there to question Menelaus about any news he might have heard about you."

"Hm." Odysseys scratched his chin through his beard. "But knowing everything as you do, wise woman, did you not tell him yourself that I was safe? Did you want him to wander the rude seas in misery while unworthy men eat him out of house and home?"

"Don't worry yourself about that," Athene answered. "I've been with him as much as I have been with you. He needed to have a bit of fame for himself so he could be worthy of you. He's quite safe, I tell you. Even now he sits in Menelaus's palace with all the comforts while men wait in a black ship to kill him before he reaches home. But I don't think they'll succeed in that." She closed an eye in a saucy wink, and Odysseus laughed gleefully. "No, long before he dies the earth will have crusted over those suitors. I promise you this."

429–440   And with that, Athene rose, placing her hands on her hips and pursing her lovely lips as she contemplated Odysseus. Then she nodded and reached out and touched him gently upon the forehead with one shapely finger. His smooth skin withered over his supple limbs and a gray sheen fell over his dark-brown hair. An old man's rheum gathered in his once twinkling eyes and his clothing altered into a shabby cloak and tunic grimy with ancient smoke and grease. Over his back she draped a moth-eaten ancient stag skin.

Then she handed him a staff well polished as if from many miles of travel and a shabby sack to hang from his shoulder.

And then they parted, Athene dancing her way on nimble feet to sacred Sparta to fetch Odysseus's son while Odysseus hobbled on rheumatic feet along the path leading to the Raven's Rock.

Here ends the Thirteenth Book of Homer's Odyssey.

THE FOURTEENTH BOOK
The Visit to the Swine-keeper

❖ ❖ ❖ ❖ ❖ ❖ ❖ ❖ ❖ ❖ ❖

Odysseus goes to Eumaeus, the master of the swine,
And tells a made-up story about his time.
He discovers the worst of the wooers
And lays a plan to kill the suitors.

❖ ❖ ❖ ❖ ❖ ❖ ❖ ❖ ❖ ❖ ❖

*T*he length of Helios's rays scorched the path as the son
Of Laertes climbed the stony way. Ancient odors rose
From his clothes. The sun grew more intense, seeming
To bake his bones. He paused, wiping the sweat from
His brow as he stared up through the woods, a scowl
Crossing his face. How far to the swineherd's hut?
He couldn't remember. The path seemed longer, but that,
He knew, was the fault of time. Eumaeus would still be there.[1]
Of that, Odysseus was certain. Unless, of course, his bones
Had been bleached white by this blasted sun.

He discovered Eumaeus resting from the heat in the shadows of the cottage porch he had built with stones by himself, without the help of his mistress or old Laertes. Wild pear grew on top and grapevines crawled the sides, leaving the interior cool in summer heat and warm in winter cold. A fence of black oak wrapped around his house and the twelve pens where he kept his herds, fifty sows in each. The boars slept in random patches they had rooted out of the ground around the pens. There were considerably fewer boars than sows, for the boars fought constantly among themselves whenever one of the sows came into season, slashing at each other with their razor tusks. They were also the first chosen by the noblemen courting Penelope, who raided the swineherd's place for fatted hogs for their many feasts and banquets. Three hundred and sixty of them lay in the cool earth, all guarded by four mastiffs as savage as wild beasts who answered only to Eumaeus.[2]

As Odysseus approached, the swineherd sat cobbling sandals for his feet from a piece of well-tanned oxhide. Three servants had moved the sows to their pastures while a fourth had taken a sow to the city in answer to demands from the suitors who planned a feast that day. The mastiffs lay around his feet, massive heads resting on huge forepaws. Suddenly their heads rose and a low rumble issued from their throats as Odysseus, disguised as the meanest beggar, hove into view, using his staff to pry himself up the rocky path leading to the leafy arbor.

30–57   They leaped to their feet, hackles bristling, bounding down to the gate in the black oak fence, guarding the way from passage. Odysseus immediately dropped his staff and held his hands palm out down at his side. He squatted on his heels, facing them as they crept nearer.

"Here, then!" Eumaeus shouted, hastily dropping the leather from his walnut-stained fingers. He picked up a handful of stones and pelted the dogs with them. "Away, now! Mind your manners, you whelps of Hades!"

The dogs dodged the stones and moved on stiff legs away from the gate, growls still bubbling up from their massive throats. Eumaeus shook his head, moving through the gate. He took Odysseus by the arm, lifting him gently to his feet. He bent and picked up the staff and pressed it back in Odysseus's hand.

"Whew! That was a narrow one, uncle!" he said. "Those brutes would have ripped you slats to strips in another minute and you would have lashed me bloodily with your tongue for my lack of hospitality. I don't need any more grief from the gods! I have enough, sitting here and mourning for my master's return! Egods, I wish he'd come back. Why, just today I had to send another sow down for those thieving sons to stuff down their gullets! More than likely their owner himself is starving and wandering around like a mismatched wastrel in some strange town or land, looking for a good hand to lift him up! But"—he sighed, shaking his head—"that's neither here nor there now. Come on, old man! Let's go up to my home and you can give me the news over a loaf of fresh bread, some olives, and good clean wine!"

The good man led the beggar to his leafy arbor and placed him on a well-carved chair he had covered with a wild goat's shaggy skin in the coolest shade. Odysseus smiled thankfully at his greeting and said, "May Zeus and all the immortal gods lay their good fingers upon your shoulders for your kindness!"

Eumaeus grinned and ran gnarled fingers through his tangled beard. He ducked his head in embarrassment. "Well, now, it isn't much I'm doing for you, but you are welcome to what I have! I can see from your sorry state that you have fallen upon hard times! Aye, make no bones about that and it is no need for embarrassment on your part. No, sir! Why, even my master might be wandering about in shabby robes himself and I would hope that someone would treat him as well as he could in that place!

"You'd receive no less from me if you came naked and covered with dung! After all, the poor strangers and beggars all come from Zeus hisself, and anything a person like me can do is welcome and warranted, I should say. Well, enough said!" He glanced over his holdings and shook his head. "But, now, if my master was around, he would have seen that my home was not as shabby as this and would have given me more to greet you with than I have—a kinder master could not have been given to a man like me by Zeus—and I suspect if he were alive and around he would have taken you— as he always did all strangers who wandered into his lands—to his home down in the city for a better bite than I can give you. But I fear he's dead and gone now! And all because of that bitch Helen who couldn't keep her ankles crossed at the sight of a curly-headed man! Better for all if she'd been sworn to Aphrodite by her father instead of married to that Menelaus. Aye, women are the curse of men, that's for certain![3] But," he hastened to add, spreading his hands, "that is my own feelings since my master was taken with Agamemnon's army to mighty-towered Troy in Ilium, the land of the horses, to fight on account of her! Ah, well!" He grabbed the hem of his tunic and hitched it under his belt, then stepped over the narrow railing into one of the pens and grabbed two piglets by their hind legs, holding them kicking and squealing as he carried them to the slaughtering pen. There he cut their throats quickly and efficiently, then singed them, quartered them, and skewered the meat. He roasted them, then brought the smoking meat to the table, dropping it on platters. He sprinkled it with white barley, then took common cups from a shelf and filled them with fresh wine. He beamed as he placed the wine in front of Odysseus.

"Now, stranger," he said, "have a bite of suckling. 'Tis ill enough fare what with those suitors constantly taking the fatted pigs for their own gluttony. Patience, I tells myself, patience! The gods punish wicked acts, and their time is coming. But," he amended, "it wouldn't be hurting my feelings any if the gods would speed matters up a bit instead of taking their own sweet time about it all. Even a slap or two from Zeus's mighty hand would be welcome among the pious men still hereabouts, I tell you! I don't know why Zeus allows this. Why, even pirates tread warily on the decks of their ships after raiding a wealthy coast waiting to see if Zeus is going to thunder about their heads a bit. I guess some rumor about my master's death has brought these wastrels to his door. Otherwise, I should think they'd take a more prudent attitude around here instead of strutting like black-combed roosters in a white-hen yard. Never seen people waste so much! Slaughtering animals left and right and half the time not leaving enough to sacrifice for a pigeon let alone Zeus and his Immortals. And drink? Why, they swill enough wine to drain a year's blood from the vineyards. Half the time they don't even bother to prepare it, just tip the flagon and drink it raw in their drunkenness.[4]

"Well you might ask why these rogues come to his place now. It isn't my mistress's beauty only that brings them—although there's many who still sigh when she walks about near them, I tell you—but my master was a very wealthy man. Not a lord on all of fertile Ithaca—or elsewhere, for that matter—could claim to be richer! Ten, twenty of them would need to pool their wealth to be his equal. And his holdings stretched over to the mainland as well. Why, over there twelve herds of cattle and as many sheep and pigs are all tended by his herdsmen. Here on Ithaca he has eleven herds of goats up and down the coast and back in the mountains. And"—his face grew red with anger—"yet every day each herdsman has to cull out a fatted member to send down for those dilly-dalliers dawdling around his house. Bunch of ne'er-do-wells if I've ever seen one, and I've seen dozens over the past year or so sniffing like randy rakehells around the queen's doorstep."

He smacked his hand hard against the tabletop, fuming, his dark eyes sparking with anger. Odysseus watched carefully while he ate the suckling and drank the wine, relishing his first taste of food from Ithaca. His stomach tightened at mention of the wooers, and he drank deeply of the wine to wash the foul taste of their name from his tongue. Then he finished eating and wiped his mouth with the back of his hand. He filled his cup brimming with wine and handed it to Eumaeus. The herdsman took it with pleasure and drained it at one sip. He belched and smacked his lips and slumped back, sighing.

113–142   "Now, good friend, tell me who was the lord rich enough to pay your bondage price and powerful enough to draw praise from you?" Odysseus asked, drawing his fingers through the tangles of his beard. "If I understand you rightly he was killed at Troy while following Agamemnon? Perhaps I know him. Or met him, at least. Chances are slim that I would know him, but then again I have roamed over much of this world, and if I didn't run into him at Troy, well, perhaps elsewhere."

Eumaeus sighed and said, "Good uncle, I hope you're not looking to make your fortune by making news of Odysseus for his wife and son. If that is what brought you to Ithaca, why then, forget your plans. You'll receive no credit there. Oh, many have come claiming news of Odysseus in order to gain a bite to eat and some clean clothes or perhaps even a few small coins for their troubles. Many a traveler has gone through those doors with his lies and been properly met by the queen who cries heavily at any story she hears. That's the ways and means of it all, you know: Women stay at home and weep while their husbands go off adventuring. Why, I daresay you look clever enough to be able to lie convincingly enough to draw a day or two lodging at the house of Odysseus—if one would give you a fine tunic or cloak for your troubles.

"But"—he sighed again and rubbed the callused heel of his hands against his eyes—"as for my master, why, he's long been fodder for the dogs and carrion birds. Or maybe the fishes of the sea have feasted on him and now his bones lie heaped upon strange sands. That's how he ended his days. I'm as certain of it as the path of the sun from east to west. And his death has brought only grief to his friends—if they're still alive," he added, muttering more to himself than his guest. "I tell you that I'll never find one like him again. More friend than master, he was. No, not even if I go back to my parents' home."

"Good friend," Odysseus said, "I know you won't believe me, but Odysseus will return to Ithaca. Of that I am as certain as the breaking of the sea on land. When, I do not know. But he will come during the dark night between the waning of the old moon and the waxing of the new. He will be more terrible than the Furies as he punishes those who have dishonored his fair wife and son. I will swear to this by any of the gods on Olympus, including that gray-eyed lovely of Zeus himself.[5] When he returns—and only then—will I claim my reward, and you yourself may hang my new cloak over my shoulders. Until that time comes, why, I will accept nothing. Although, as you can see," he added wryly, "I am as poor as a field mouse in a drought-ridden land."[6]

Eumaeus, the watcher of the roads, vigorously rubbed his head with callused fingers. "Well, these are good thoughts well-spoken, my friend! But they are only the wishes and dreams of one who can only wish and dream. I'm afraid that Odysseus will not be coming home again. So drink your wine in peace and let us turn to other matters to talk about. My heart is too sorry to take much talk about what may or may not have happened to Odysseus in his wanderings. I sat here many a day and sleepless night looking down that road, hoping against hope that my master would step up its rocky way. But the gods didn't answer my prayers. Fickle ones, they are! Forget your oath. I'll not hold you to it. And if I'm wrong and Odysseus wanders up that path to my house, why, that'll be an end to my worrisome ways. I hope he does. For the sake of Telemachus and Penelope and ancient King Laertes, I hope he does.

"Ah, there's another worry for me, you see: Telemachus, Odysseus's son. Here I had high hopes for that lad as I watched him grow from a twig to a

143–173

174–202

young sapling. But then some god robbed him of his wits and sent him off to that sand heap Pylos on a whimsy. Now those scum-sucking pigs lolling around his mother's palace have plotted against him. Even now they lie in ambush, waiting for his return along the watery ways. Yes, they aren't content with the absence of Odysseus—they wish to end Arceisius's line forever. Probably strike the name of Odysseus from every tablet and stone once they kill his son too. Well—" He paused to reach for a cup of wine, draining it. "Ah, that's better! Wine drives away man's worries and I have enough of them for a whole jug to myself! Drink up, my friend! There's nothing to it but to leave Odysseus to his fate. Would be that we could help him, but we can't and so there's a sad end to it! It's in Zeus's hand now.

"So tell me about your own troubles, now, my friend. You've heard enough about mine to nod yourself to sleep on. I want to know everything. Who are you and where do you come from? I know you didn't walk across the seabed from the mainland, so what ship brought you to our rocky shores? Who landed you here and what did they claim to be? Merchants? Pirates? Give me your story."

And Odysseus, the man of masquerades, slipped into his storyteller guise and said, "Well, as long as the food and wine last,[7] I imagine I can hold your ear. Perhaps even for an entire year without beginning to touch on the prickles and thorns of my life, thanks to the gods' fickle pleasures.

"Crete is my homeland where my father, a rich landowner, lives. I have many half brothers and all were raised in the house as his lawful sons from the same mother. My mother was, er, a concubine, shall we say, that he bought from either a seagoing pirate or a merchant. (I'm rather vague on this, you understand, as my mother was reluctant to explain.)

203–233 "But my father—Castor, the son of Hylax—raised me as an equal to my half brothers. My countrymen honored him greatly as one whom the gods had smiled upon and gifted with a fine home and lands and a good family, and I enjoyed his company until death-dealing Fate hauled him away in her chariot to Hades's Halls. My fortunes took a hard fall at that, I tell you. Why, those arrogant brothers of mine showed their true colors by casting lots and dividing his estate according to the fall of the dice. The lion's share went to them, I tell you, while I was given the chaff and the husks of what remained—a few drachmas and the poorest of his houses. Yet 'twas enough for one wily with his ways, and I soon won a wife whose father was a rich landowner. No mean task that, and not one for the fainthearted, I tell you! But now"—he sighed—"now, all is gone. Yet I think enough remains of the stubblefield that you can tell the richness of the wheat and rye harvest.

"Only black clouds hovered over my head as evil days came my way.

Devious Zeus devised evils for me! But I did have my glory days! Ah, yes! Ares and Athene rode beside me on their dappled ponies, I tell you! Yes, it is true! They gave me the skill to select the strongest men to sit in ambush with me against our enemies, and when those men came between us, I leaped out bravely to fall upon them and drive my black-bladed lance deep into their gullets. I could have sat quietly at home on my arse and passed my days with cups of watered wine, but I chose war to advance my fortunes. I cared little for domestic chores—tilling the land or the house or even my children. Instead, I had a passion for many-oared ships and the clash of arms and men. A polished javelin drew my admiration more than my wife's shapely leg. That which men fear, I loved; that which men love, I loathed." He shrugged. "Well, that's the difference the gods placed between men, I suppose. Each must chose his own way of living and advancing his fortunes. And who knows their reasoning? Can't say as to how I would fault them for all of that; it would be a shabby existence if we were all the same. But where was I? Hm. Ah.

"By the time the Greek forces reached the plain of Troy I had increased my command ninefold, and I had led a fleet of fast-sailing ships on several raids before we made that journey. I had my pick of booty, and when we cast lots for the leftovers, why, I won even more. (The gods, you know, favor daring men.) My house became rich, and my countrymen honored me and feared me. So much so that when Zeus the thunderer devised that dreadful brain-splattering, windpipe-splitting vulture feast that cut men off at the knees, the Cretans begged me to join with Idomeneus and lead our armies to Ilium.

"And for nine years we forayed at Troy, winning land and grimly giving 234-262 it back to the Trojan forces until the land turned black with blood. At last we sacked Priam's fair city—the tenth year, that was—and gladly made for home. By then even I longed for my homeland, my spirit for war long sated by that bloodletting. But now the gods decided to toy with me, and our fleet was scattered by a vengeful god—one, I would wager, who favored Troy. But this is only speculation, you understand.

"As for me, why, Zeus's fertile brain hatched more mischief, and when I finally made it to my home, I had only a month to take pleasure in my house and lands and family. For some reason—I know not why—a great yearning came over me to see Egypt. And so I gathered nine black-prowed ships and a hearty crew for each. For six days we feasted on bulls and sheep I provided, and on the seventh—this is a lucky number, you understand—left for the delta. Ah, that was a fair sailing with a good North Wind that cooled our brows and filled our sails. Like sailing downstream on a lazy, hot day. All of our ships arrived safely without a plank damaged, the crew hale and hearty.

On the fifth day, we anchored in the Nile and I posted guards and sent out scouts to determine what was in front of us. But they disobeyed me—too used to remembering their old ways at Troy, I suspect—and when they came upon peaceful farmers, they went marauding, plundering the fields and fine homes, taking the women and children captive, killing the men.

263–296

"The farmers fled to the city, and when Dawn rose over that broad plain, it was filled with flashing bronze and clashing arms, infantry and men in war chariots. And then Zeus struck hard against my party, driving panic into them, making their legs quiver and their bowels run loose as fear filled their frames. We were surrounded by the Egyptians, and then they fell upon us like hawks upon rabbits. Sharp shafts and spears felled many, and then they rode riven-sharp through my army, killing many and carrying off others to serve their days as slaves.

"But then Zeus sent an idea leaping into my mind—though I'd rather he'd have let me die on that field instead of foisting the miseries upon me that he did—and I ripped my helmet from my head and threw my great shield away. I dropped my lance as I ran toward the king's chariot and clutched his knees and kissed them. He took pity on me and lifted me up into his chariot and took me, weeping salty tears, to his house. And that was no mean feat, I tell you, for there was many in that angry crowd who wanted to kill me, to lance my innards with their ash spears. But the king kept them at bay and honored Zeus, the protector of strangers, by invoking his rules of hospitality.

"For seven years I stayed in that country, and slowly the Egyptians came to like me. My fortunes grew, but on the eighth, this rascal Phoenician—a more thieving rogue I've never encountered—came and talked me into returning to his homeland with him where he had lands and houses. I stayed with him for a full year until the months and days and seasons came and went and then sailed with him to Libya when he guiled me with the promise of a heavy cargo. After I boarded the ship, I learned of his real plan, which was to sell me into slavery there.

297–324

"We left with a good stiff wind behind us. The ship sailed south of Crete, and here it was that Zeus brought wrack and ruin upon them. We passed my homeland, and after we were in the middle of the boundless sea, he placed a dark cloud over our ship. The sea grew black and the waves rose. Then Zeus threw his thunder over us and our ship shuddered from a bolt of lightning. Burning brimstone broke from the masthead and fire streaked down the gunwales. Another bolt blew the men from the ship and they floated around the black hull like seagulls upon the white-capped waves. No generous homecoming feast for them! I found myself floundering in that black water,

but then Zeus placed the mast of the ship between my arms and I wrapped
my arms and legs around that splintered wood and rode it determinedly
through the boiling waves while the cursed winds pulled at me, trying to
yank me from my makeshift raft.

"I drifted helplessly upon those seas for nine long days and then, on the
dark tenth night, a roller washed me up on the shores of Thesprotia, where
the king, Pheidon, took me in after his son found me exhausted upon that
shore and, taking me by the hand, lifted me up and took me to his house.
There I was given a fine cloak and tunic to wear.

"It was here that I heard about your Odysseus. Pheidon told me how he
had feasted Odysseus and showed me the bronze and gold and finely
wrought iron that Odysseus had gathered in his wanderings that he, Phei-
don, was keeping for Odysseus until his return. There was enough to last
heirs through ten generations!

"As for Odysseus, well, he had gone to Dodona,[8] where he might hear   *325-356*
from Zeus through the holy, heavily leaved oak tree sacred to that god how
he should safely approach his own Ithaca after being absent for so many
years. Should he go openly, boldly sailing into Ithaca's deep harbor? Or
should he disguise himself and see how the land lay before making himself
known? That was a strong conundrum for any man. Pheidon told me that a
ship stood by with a hearty crew to carry Odysseus home after he had gained
Zeus's advice, but I left before him when a Thesprotian merchant ship,
bound for the grain-filled isle of Dulichium, made ready for sailing. Pheidon
cautioned the crew and the captain to treat me well upon the voyage and
leave me safely at the home of the Dulichium king, Acastus.

"But we were no sooner out of sight of land when the crew hatched their
own evil scheme to sell me into slavery. They stripped me of cloak and tunic
and left me with the filthy rags you see around me now. When we arrived in
Ithaca, they lashed me to the benches, twisting the tarred rope tightly about
me. They cast many raw-butted jokes at me as they left me aboard and went
onto the rocky beaches for supper. But while they were enjoying themselves,
a god—I know not who—quietly undid the knots holding me. I tied my rags
around my head and slipped down into the water with a well-polished load-
ing plank and made my way through the sea to land. I found a thicket filled
with scented flowers—do you know it?—and hid there while they shouted
and cursed during their search for me. At last they gave up and climbed back
on their ship and left. I tell you that it was the gods who kept me hidden
from their eyes and it was the gods who led me here to the house of one who
understands such things. So I must be a man whose road still stretches out
before him."

357–382   And now, swineherd Eumaeus, you answered this story with "Ah, pitiful stranger![9] Your trials and tribulations torture my soul! But one thing bothers me: your tale of Odysseus. I think you've tripped over your own tongue with that one! Now, why would you want to fill my ears with this airy nothing? I know the grim reality of my lord's disappearance and how the gods all hated him. Why, had they not hated him so much they might have let him die with honor on the plains of Troy and there his friends and admirers would have heaped a huge burial mound over him and honored him with great games. But instead a foul wind blew him away to where only the gods know. And so I keep away from the doings of the town and the House of Odysseus. I stay here alone with my pigs unless lovely Penelope sends for me when a stranger comes with news. Others come then and beggar the man with the same tiresome questions, pining away for their long-lost king. But I have lost interest in all of that nonsense now. I can even mark the day when a scoundrel from Aetolia lied with a story that gave me great hope.

"It seems this fellow had killed a man who had strong and rich friends who pursued him all over the world until he finally tripped his way up the path leading to my door. I practice the rules of hospitality—as you well know, sitting here and enjoying my wine and olives—and it was him— damn his lying hide!—who told me that he had noticed Odysseus with Idomeneus in Crete when Odysseus put in to repair his ships that had been damaged in a gale. This slippery and subtle scapegrace said Odysseus would sail here by summer with all of his treasure—by fall at the latest—but he didn't."

383–408   Eumaeus drew a deep breath, and his eyes flinted with anger. "And now you come here with your tales. Well, you are welcome—since the gods have seen fit to bring you here—but don't be bandying about my ears with your tall tales. They won't make you any the more welcome at my table. I do this because I fear Zeus, the patron of strangers, and pity you."

A common man might have been chastened by those remarks but not cunning Odysseus, who pressed his case, saying, "Well, now, it is certainly a suspicious nature you have about you, my friend. All brambles and briars, you ask me. Apparently not even my oath will convince you of my truth. But let us make this bargain—and the gods can witness both—if your master makes a gladsome homecoming at his palace, you will give me a fine cloak and tunic to wear and mark my passage to Dulichium where my heart beckons. But if your lord does not come when I say he will, then you can tell your men to throw me over the cliff onto the jagged rocks as a message to future beggars not to tell lies. What say you? Shall we have this?"

"Aye, yes!" cried the glorious swineherd. "That would win me fame and fortune in this world if I killed you after wining and dining you and playing host to you in my house. I'm certain that I could go to Zeus and plead my case after a stunt like that! But enough of this airy nattering! It's suppertime, and as soon as my men return we shall prepare a tasty meal in the house."

At that moment they heard the steps of the herdsmen upon the path and soon they hove into view, driving the pigs before them to their sleeping sites. The grunts and grumbles of the contented sows filled the twilight, and Eumaeus called out, saying, "Here now! Bring the best hog among the lot so we can slaughter it to entertain this guest from abroad. It's time that we enjoy ourselves after our wretched work with the white-tusked boars while others take advantage of our labors to feast upon them." 409–439

Eumaeus rose and, taking up his broad-bladed ax, moved out to the woodpile and began splitting kindling while his men brought in a fat five-year-old pig and held it fast beside the flickering flames of the hearth. The good and virtuous man remembered the Immortals and pulled a tuft of hair from the white-toothed victim and tossed it onto the fire as an offering, praying to the all-seeing masters that they might relent and let Odysseus come home. Then he spat on his hands and, taking a firm grip on a solid piece of oak, swung it hard against the boar's head. The pig grunted, its legs splaying out as it fell to the floor with a *thud!* dazed. A man passed a sharp knife under its snout, slitting its throat, then they slaughtered him and singed his bristles. Quickly they butchered him, and the swineherd laid the joints, covered with rich fat over the thighbones, upon the fire and sprinkled them with finely ground barley meal. They spitted the rest of the meat and roasted it carefully, then divided the portions evenly into seven parts (for Eumaeus was always a fair-minded person) and laid one portion aside with prayers for the Nymphs and the quick-witted god Hermes, the son of Maia. The rest he gave to his men, but to Odysseus, as the stranger among them, he honored with the choicest cut—the hog's chine.

Odysseus's heart grew warm at this gesture, and he said, "Eumaeus, may Zeus look as kindly upon you as I do for giving the best of this feast to a man like me." 440–465

And you, kind-hearted Eumaeus, said gruffly, "Eat, eat! Don't stand on ceremony around here. The gods give and the gods take away and it's best not to leave much lying about without putting a mouth to it."

He paused to make a burnt offering to the Immortals, then poured sparkling wine well mixed for Odysseus, sacker of cities, man of many masquerades, and placed the cup in his hand before sitting down to his own meal. Mesaulius served the bread.[10] He was a servant Eumaeus had purchsed from the Taphians without help from his mistress or old Laertes. All ate fully until they had satisfied their hunger. Then Mesaulius cleared the table while the others prepared themselves for bed.

Night came swiftly over the mountains, and along on its heels came foul weather. The moon disappeared behind heavy clouds, and then rain poured down from Zeus the cloud bringer and a West Wind blew hard against the sides of Eumaeus's house, finding its way in through cracks and creases. Odysseus shivered and decided to test the swineherd to see if the man would give up his cloak for his guest.

"Well, friends, listen to a bit of boasting from me. Maybe I can entertain you with a bit of a story. Put it down to the wine if you don't believe me— after all, wine makes men do crazy things; the strongest become silly and giggle like women while others dance and still others unleash their tongue and give words better left unsaid—but since I've opened the door for the cat I might as well let it play.

466–496
"If only I had the youth and strength I had when I was a young warrior at Troy. One night, Odysseus and Menelaus decided to set an ambush for some prowling Trojans lurking around the camp. They asked me to come along as another leader, and so I went with them. But when we made our way unseen to the glowering walls of that tall-towered city, we lay down in the middle of a marsh in a thick stand of swamp grass. The cruel North Wind fell upon us as we lay shivering there in our armor, and then snow began to fall, thick as hoarfrost, and bitter cold racked our very bones. Ice formed like a thick coat upon our shields. I shivered more than most because being a vain youth and sure in my own strength, I had left my cloak back in camp.

"When the third watch came around and the star change had made itself known, I nudged Odysseus with my elbow, saying, 'This cold locks my bol- locks tight like a gelded horse! I think I shall die soon because I have no cloak to keep that icy breath off my flesh! The gods have tricked me into leaving my cloak back in camp and now I see no way out of this. Tomorrow you will find a frozen log here where once lay a man.'

497–528
"Now I could see this was working on Odysseus as he turned and mulled it over in his mind. Then, 'Quiet!' says he. 'Don't let any of the others hear you jabbering and your teeth chattering.' He lifted his head and whistled softly, calling to the others, 'Friends, wake up! I just had a dream from the gods while I dozed here. We have come too far from the ships and now I must send a message back to Agamemnon to bring others to join us here.' Thoas, the son of Andraemon,[11] ever one to curry favor with vainglorious actions, leaped to his feet without another word, threw off his purple cloak and dashed down toward the ships. I took his cloak and snuggled warmly in it with a grateful sigh until Dawn warmed us with her rosy heat. Ah, me!"

He shook his shaggy head. "If only I was young and stronghearted as I was then! And if only some herdsman here would loan his heavy cloak to me instead of letting my wretched rags serve me ill tonight."

And you, Eumaeus, replied, "A fair story that, my friend! And not a word poorly spoken! We catch your drift—although we would be poor listeners not to take the hints you have dropped—and I have a cloak here for you to wear through the night. Tomorrow, however," he added hastily, shaking a thick forefinger, "you will have to wear your own rags. We aren't rich men here; each man has his own cloak to wear and little else. But"—his eyes gleamed with amusement—"when Odysseus comes before the waning of the moon"—he grinned as he threw Odysseus's words back to him—"I'm certain as the stars that he will give you a rich cloak and send you on your way to where you will."

He rose and prepared a pallet next to the fire for Odysseus, laying down a thick covering of sheep and goatskins. Odysseus dropped down gratefully upon the bed and rolled up warmly, his backside to the fire. Eumaeus dropped a thick cloak over him—the one he kept as a spare against the hard rains that might soak his other one. And there Odysseus rested as snug as a bug.

Next to him lay the other younkers while Eumaeus readied himself to   *529–533* spend the night outside next to his pigs where he could guard them against wolves or men. Odysseus watched with a glad heart, thankful to the gods who had given him such a man to guard his goods while his master was absent. Eumaeus wrapped himself in a thick cloak and the fleecy hide of a great goat. He draped his sword over his shoulder and took his sharp javelin and stepped out to spend the night beside his pigs in a hollow rock that sheltered him from the cold North Wind.

Here ends the Fourteenth Book of Homer's Odyssey.

THE FIFTEENTH BOOK

Advice to Telemachus

❖ ❖ ❖ ❖ ❖ ❖ ❖ ❖ ❖ ❖ ❖

Athene tells Odysseus's son, Telemachus,
To return home, where he goes to Eumaeus.

❖ ❖ ❖ ❖ ❖ ❖ ❖ ❖ ❖ ❖ ❖

And while Odysseus slept contentedly beside the warm fire 1–29
In the hut of Eumaeus, Pallas Athene made her way rapidly
Over Sparta's plain to prod Telemachus, the long-suffering
Son of Odysseus, into returning home. With Peisistratus,
Nestor's son, Telemachus sat in the portico of Menelaus.
Bees buzzed sleepily to and fro around their heads in
The sweetly scented air, looping lazily from the wine-cupped
Flowers drooping in the dustless room. Telemachus slumped
Drowsily beneath the heat-wrapped vines, for he had stayed
Awake through the long, starlit night, pondering the news
He had heard about his father, the raider of cities, the man
Of masquerades who dared to play games with the wily gods.

Peisistratus snored gently in his bed while Telemachus lay naked upon his
own bed, tenacious thoughts tumbling through his mind, his soul worrying
itself about the fate of his father.

Suddenly gray-eyed Athene stood beside him, her lovely form outlined
beneath her purple-edged white chiton. He shook his head, wondering if a
hidden dream had made its way into the room. She spoke, saying,
"Telemachus, you've wandered long enough from your home. Do you wish
to follow that closely in your father's footsteps? Enough, I say. You have left
your possessions, your land, and now men loaf rudely around your palace,
eating you out of house and home. If this happens, why, then you have

wasted your time on this journey for there will be nothing left for you to return to—or for your father to come home to, for that matter. Now rise and bid Menelaus of the loud war cry to let you return to your homeland at once. That is," she added harshly, "if you wish to find your faith-worthy mother still in Odysseus's palace. It seems her good father and brothers are pressing the suit of Eurymachus who continues to offer more and more gifts. The palace portico is fairly packed with his gifts and promises. And"—she paused delicately for a moment—"you know the fickle state of a woman. She could well carry off some of your own possessions if she goes to another's house. And her widow's bed has been empty and cold for a long time. A woman's patience does have its limits, you know. She may easily forget the dead husband she once loved or the children she bore him. A woman does like to take a few riches to her husband's house.

30–55   "I would suggest that you find a handmaiden you trust—at least the most worthy—and appoint her to care for everything you hold most dear until the gods reveal your bride's name to you."

Telemachus sat up quickly and fumbled for his tunic and sandals.

"One more thing," Athene continued. "Along the straits that separate the rugged coast of dusty Samos from Ithaca the best (perhaps an oxymoron, that) of the suitors lie secretly, waiting to pounce upon you when you pass and slay you before you can reach home. I don't think they will succeed—the earth will close over those who desire your fortune—but"—her brow furrowed—"it would be well to steer a course clear of that Samos shore and sail through the night instead of laying up somewhere. I suggest you land at the nearest point in Ithaca and send the ship on ahead to the harbor. You must, dear boy, visit the swineherd who cares for your pigs before you do anything else. He's a kind man who cares deeply for you. Sleep there and send him off to Penelope and let her know that you have arrived safely back from Pylos."

Telemachus blinked and looked around the dark room, looking for the goddess, but she had disappeared, leaving for lofty Olympus after delivering her warning to the young man. Telemachus turned and nudged Nestor's son from his sweet sleep, saying, "Up sleepyhead! Get up, Peisistratus. Yoke the swift-footed horses to our chariot and let's be on our way."

Peisistratus muttered crossly and rolled away. Telemachus nudged him harder with his foot. Peisistratus groaned and opened a bleary eye. "Telemachus, despite what you want to do we can't ride through black night. Dawn's not far off. Wait until then. Besides, I'm certain Menelaus will want to say good-bye and won't be sending us off without a few presents. And it's his right to do so. After all, a guest always remembers the kindly host. Would you deprive him of that right?"

He smacked his lips and rolled away from Telemachus's anxious foot. The   *56–83*
son of Odysseus watched impatiently for Dawn to mount her golden throne.
When her fingers peeked redly over the horizon, Menelaus of the loud war
cry rose from the side of sweet-haired Helen and came to the youths. As soon
as Telemachus saw him, he turned and kicked Peisistratus awake and
slipped into his shimmering tunic, draped a great mantle over his shoulders,
and went to meet his host.

"Menelaus, son of Atreus, great leader and friend, the gods' favorite, I beg
you to allow me to return to my country. I long to see my own house and
land."

Menelaus of the wild war cry smiled and said, "Well, Telemachus, I won't
keep you here if you desire so much to return to your homeland. Why, that
wouldn't be right for any host to so deprive his guest. A host must not be too
kind or not kind enough. It's a delicate rail to tread. Moderation: that's the
key, I say. One mustn't speed a guest away or jealously keep him from what
he sees as his own duties. I say treat a man well while he's in your house, but
then let him go when he wants to.

"Now then"—he rubbed his hands together—"I don't want you rushing
off into the morning with an empty chariot. Let me have an hour or two to
pack some fine gifts in your chariot. And," he added, "let me have the
women ready a meal from my rich larder for you in the hall. It's a grand
thing to travel wide and far in the world but only after you have a good meal
in your belly," he cautioned. "Especially if you plan on swinging through
Hellas and Argo on your way. Now, if you want to do that," he said, warm-
ing to his task, "why, then, I'll yoke my own horses to my chariot and guide
you on the way through those cities. Eh? What?" He nudged Telemachus
with his elbow and winked at Peisistratus. "What say you to that? Why, I
don't think anyone there will send us away empty-handed. At the least we'll
gain a brass tripod or perhaps a cauldron, a pair of mules—a gold cup?"

He clapped his hands together as the thought of the trip pleased him and   *84–113*
raised a shaggy eyebrow at the youth. Telemachus smiled and gently shook
his head.

"You are too kind, my friend. But I am most anxious to return home. I've
been away far too long as it is, and I'm afraid someone may do a bit of mis-
chief in my absence. After all, there's no one to guard my home, you see.
Although I do want to continue searching for my godlike father, I really
can't afford to lose any valuable heirlooms from my house as well. You
understand, I'm certain."

Menelaus tried to hide his disappointment and nodded and left immedi-
ately to tell his wife and handmaidens to ready a meal in the large hall from

his stores for the youths. At that moment, Eteoneus, Boethus's son, who'd risen from his bed nearby, came in, yawning and stretching. Menelaus ordered him to kindle the fire and roast the meat laid by for the morning meal. He rushed to do Menelaus's bidding while the great lord of the wild war cries took Helen and Megapenthes down to his storeroom fragrant with the scent of cedar. There he selected a two-handled cup and told Megapenthes to find a silver mixing bowl to match it. Helen dropped down on her knees beside one of the cedar chests that held elaborately woven robes and removed one that glittered like a star in the pale morning light. Then, together, they returned to the great hall where they found Telemachus waiting, impatient to be off.

"Now, Telemachus, I certainly hope that Zeus, the thundering husband of Hera, will keep you safe on your journey and make your homecoming all that you most desire. That is possible, you know," he said sagely. "Gods can do wonderful things when they want to. But anger them—" He shook his head. "Enough of that. Here. These are the best and most beautiful treasures my palace holds. This silver bowl with its gold rim made by Hephaestus"— he paused and indicated it in Megapenthes's hands—"was given to me by Phaedimus, the king of Sidon, when I stayed with him on my journey home. It's only fitting that I should give it to you on your journey to your home."

114–144   He handed the two-handled cup to Telemachus, then stepped aside while Megapenthes handed over the silver bowl. Then Helen stepped forward, the robe she had chosen draped over her arm, and said:

"Dear lad, I also have a present for you. This is a keepsake from Helen, made by herself for your bride to wear when your wedding day comes. Until then, I suggest you leave it in your mother's care—that would be only appropriate, you know—and"—she hesitated, then her lovely face shone—"may the gods let you reach your native land safely and may you find joy upon your return."

And with that, she handed the robe to Telemachus. He took it and folded it reverently over his arm. Peisistratus looked at the gifts with great wonder, then took them from Telemachus and safely stored them in their chariot. Auburn-haired Menelaus waited until the gifts had been placed, then took the men back into the house and led them to the table that had been set for them. A servant materialized beside them and spilled water from a golden olpe into a silver basin that they might wash their hands. Another servant place a small polished table beside them while yet another brought bread and fresh-roasted meat to place upon the table. Eteoneus stepped forward to carve and serve the meat while Megapenthes poured out freshly mixed wine.

145–168   The youths ate with great relish, and after they had satisfied their hunger and thirst, Telemachus and Nestor's noble son stepped outside and quickly yoked their prancing horses to their painted chariot. They stepped into the chariot and drove out the gateway, the horses' hooves thundering upon the pavement of the courtyard past the colonnade to where Menelaus stood with a golden cup filled with honeyed wine in his hand. He raised the cup to them.

"Farewell, young friends. And give my best to King Nestor, the good shepherd of his people. When we warred together at Troy, he was like a father to me."

And wise Telemachus responded, "Menelaus, favorite of Zeus, I promise you that I will personally give him that message. I hope that I might find Odysseus at home when I arrive there that I might tell him about your great kindness and how you have treated us so hospitably and bade us good-bye with rich gifts."

At that moment an eagle flew by carrying a great white goose in its talons that he'd snatched from the courtyard. A crowd of men and women chased him, screeching shrilly, but the eagle ignored them and turned right across the path of the horses. Everyone smiled at this omen. Nestor's son spoke first, saying, "Wise Menelaus, tell us what you think. Was this omen heaven-sent for you or the two of us?"

The man of Ares pondered deeply for a moment, but it was long-robed *169–197* Helen who said, "I can explain this omen. As this eagle came from the mountains where he was born and where his brood waits for his return from snaring our white goose, then so will Odysseus return after his weary wanderings and take revenge upon the evil suitors. That is," she added, "if he hasn't already returned."

The face of Telemachus brightened at her words, and he gathered the reins in his hand and said, "May Zeus give you all that your heart desires and may he act upon your words. And if this comes to pass, when I reach home I shall lift my prayers to you as a goddess."

And so saying, he laid the lash along the backs of the horses, and the chariot thundered away from the home of Menelaus, through the city, and across the great plain, the horses straining at their yoke, eager to put the miles behind their flying hooves.

Darkness fell over the earth as the sun dipped beneath the horizon. Soon they reached Pherae and drove straight up the road to the house of Diocles, the son of Ortilochus, the son of Alpheus.[1] Diocles gladly made them welcome for the night, but when Dawn's fingers touched the night sky, they rose, harnessed their horses once again, and before Helios appeared in his chariot, they thundered down the echoing portico and through the gates, driving hard for the high citadel of Pylos.

While they rode the road along the high cliffs, Telemachus turned to the son of Nestor and shouted above the crashing waves, "Peisistratus, will you do something for me? As our fathers' friendship has formed a lasting fellowship between us—after all, we are the same age and this journey has brought us even closer together, fondly so—I know your father would be eager to serve once again as my host with a great feast. But time is pressing, now, I fear, so I ask if you would not take me past my ship but put me down there. I fear your father's hospitality would keep me prisoner for many days more if I returned to his house. I must return home as quickly as possible."

198–226 Peisistratus frowned as he mulled the words of Telemachus, wondering how he could possibly go against what his father would wish. At last he nodded and, turning the horses hard, drove down to where Telemachus's ship sat on the seashore. He reined in at the ship's side and, leaving the panting horses to rest, took Menelaus's fine presents of clothing and gold and silver and stowed them in the ship's stern. Then he turned to Telemachus and said with winged words,

"Leave at once, now. Order your men on board and set sail before I reach home and break the news of your leaving to my father. I know him well, and if he should think there is a chance to keep you as a guest, he will rush to the sea himself to see that you don't leave. You will have to stay then, for he will not return to the house with empty hands. In either case, I'll have to face his wrath for not coming back with you and I might as well face it with you safely away on the sea."

With that, Peisistratus left him and slowly drove his bright-maned horses back to Pylos, dawdling as much as possible to give Telemachus the time to get under sail. The stalwart son of Odysseus wasted no time as he called to his crew, "Men! Stow that tackle aboard the black ship and raise sail! It is time we put an end to our trip!"

Eagerly his men raced to fulfill his orders. They leaped aboard the ship and made their way to their oars, stretching the long blades out to touch the sea. Telemachus was just finishing his prayers and sacrifices to Athene along the shore when a stranger appeared beside the ship.

227–250 He was a seer descended from Melampus, who once lived in Pylos, the mother of flocks, a rich man with his own house and well-known among peopled Pylos.[2] The time came, however, when he was forced to flee the proudest of all living men, great Neleus, who seized the lands and houses of Melampus and kept them for one full year while Melampus languished in the cells of Phylacus, suffering great tortures for his brother's love of Pero, Neleus's daughter, a madness the avenging Furies, wreckers of houses, cast upon him. This came about after Melampus tried to drive home the great cattle herd that was to be the bride price for his brother's happiness and was captured. He escaped, however, and drove the lowing herd back to Pylos where he gained his revenge upon Neleus for the injustices of seizing his lands and houses and brought fair Pero back to Bias's house. He left for Argos, the land of great horses, where he set his home and ruled over many people. There he built a magnificent palace and raised two strong sons, Antiphates and Mantius. Antiphates sired bold Oicles, and Oicles sired the great leader Amphiaraus, well loved by aegis-bearing Zeus and Apollo, who blessed him and marked him with great favor.

Amphiaraus never gained the silver-locked years but died at Thebes, the victim of a woman's greed, leaving two sons, Alcmaeon and Amphilochus.[3] He had a brother, too, Mantius, the father of Cleitus—ah, a handsome youth, he, captured by Dawn of the Golden Throne, who carried him away to live among the Immortals themselves—and Polypheides, who became the most famous prophet of all after the death of his father, thanks to Apollo. He migrated to Hyperesia, where he made his home. It was his son Theoclymenus who appeared before Telemachus, while the son of Odysseus made his prayers and offerings beside his black ship, and said, 251–275

"My friend, since I have found you making sacrifice in this place, I assume you are a reverent person and will tell me the truth. Who are you? Where is your home? What is your town and people?"

Telemachus paused and eyed the man and said, "Stranger, 'tis an honest person who would give you an honest answer. Ithaca is my home, the land of Odysseus, my father—or was, if ever he existed—who I fear has come to an unhappy end somewhere. That is why I have sojourned here with my ship and crew—to find what has happened to my long-lost sire."

"Hm," the noble Theoclymenus said. He cupped his hand around his chin and drew it hard down his beard, stroking it. His bright eyes looked shrewdly at the grandson of Laertes and said, "Well, like you, my friend, I have been forced to flee my homeland, after killing a countryman who had, alas, too many brothers and kinsmen on the horse plains of Argos. Only a foolish man would stay there under those circumstances, and my father sired no stupid children. I confess I ran away to avoid black death, and now my destiny is to become a wanderer upon this earth. (Interesting that, because a man can't piss in the same mud puddle twice, you know—this is metaphysical speculation only, although the time isn't right for its contemplation. Ahem!) Hm. Yes. What? Oh, yes. I think, however, that one of his brothers—or maybe it was a cousin, doesn't matter—saw me in Pylos and even now may be following me. I beg sanctuary from you. Take me on board, if you would, and don't let them kill me."

276–303 "Come aboard," the gracious Telemachus said. "I grant you what you wish—as I must under the laws of hospitality—and will greet you more pleasurably with my hospitality in Ithaca."

He reached out and took Theoclymenus's great bronze spear and laid it upon the curved ship's deck. Then he stepped to the stern and, motioning Theoclymenus to take the seat beside him, ordered the crew to cast away the hawsers and rig the sail. They dropped the fir mast in its socket and tied it off stoutly to the gunwales with twisted oxhide halyards. Athene caused a fair wind to fill the sail as the men dropped to their oars and began pulling steadily, moving the great ship out through the rolling combers onto the great sea. The boat surged ahead, sailing fast past Crouni and lovely streamed Chalcis, the sea hissing away from the curved prow of the ship.

They sailed through the day, and when the sea road grew dark with night, they drove on, making for Pheae as the good Zeus-given wind blew them steadily on their course. They passed Elis where the Epeians rule, and Telemachus took a sighting and set his course for the Pointed Isles, pondering his fate.

304–335 Meanwhile Odysseus and the honest swineherd sat with the farmhands, eating their supper. After they had eaten and drunk, Odysseus belched and studied the swineherd, wondering just how courteous a man his servant was. Would the noble swineherd bid Odysseus to stay at the farm or send him away to the city to beg for a crust of bread and cup of soured wine from a city dweller?

"Well, that was well-done, my friends," Odysseus said. He wiped his hands on his stomach, looked from beneath bushy brows at Eumaeus, and said, "I shall leave in the morning and go into the city to beg for bread. I don't want to overstay my welcome, you see. It's a bit much to have a guest eating your fare in uncertain times like this what with Odysseus away and all. But give me a bit of advice and a guide to show me the way, if you will. Once I'm in the city, why, I'm certain I will find someone to take me in— although I probably will have to wander around a bit to find a generous soul in that place—fallen upon hard times, I think it has. I'll settle for water and a crust or two of bread. 'Twill be enough. Beggars can't be choosers, you know!" He scratched his chin thoughtfully beneath his beard, frowning. "Of course, I would like to go to the palace where I can tell all-wise Penelope the news I carry in my noodle. I wouldn't mind mingling a bit with those high-handed suitors you mentioned, either. They seem to have a lot of everything and should be willing to spare a bit of something for the poor soul who has fallen upon hard ways. I'm even willing to work at whatever chore they set me to earn an honest meal, if it comes to that. After all—and listen carefully to my words here—Hermes, the messenger god, grants grace and dignity to all common labor. And I'm a jack-of-all-trades! You won't find a man who can lay as good a fire, split as many dry logs, carve a joint—aye, or cook it for that matter—and mix wine as well as I. Whatever a humble soul like me can do by way of serving his betters, why, I can rise to the occasion!"

And you, Eumaeus, why, your very nostrils twitched with indignation. "What, now," you said. "No, I don't think this will do. What put this idea into your head? Are you challenging the gods or stupidly looking for your own death? That's what'll happen if you go in among that swarm of pit vipers sucking out the lifeblood of Odysseus's home. Their evil ways reach as high as the heavens, and I can tell you that those who serve them are not hard workers but soft and simpering men without an oiled hair out of place or a stray whisker hanging from their handsome cheeks. They are well-dressed men in mantles and tunics to match their masters. These are the types who wait on those polished tables groaning under their load of bread and meat and wine. You'd be better served staying here among the honest folk. We may not be as fancy as those there, but nobody here will say you're unwelcome, and the meat's good and honest fare. When Telemachus comes, he'll dress you finely and send you on to wherever you want."

"Ah, Eumaeus," the patient Odysseus said, his eyes misting a bit at the good swineherd's honesty. "I daresay you will find Father Zeus smiling fondly upon you for all of that. It's good to feel free from the pain and misery of wandering hither and thither, hurrying and scurrying, trying to keep warm out of the cold rain and mist. That has to be the worst fate to befall a man— to be homeless and forced to roam. But since you press me to stay, stay I will. Tell me, however, how fares the noble Odysseus's mother and father. If I remember rightly, they were far to getting on when he left to go a-sailing. Do they still enjoy the sun's warmth? Or have they journeyed to Hades's Halls?"[4]

"Alas," the swineherd said, leaning back and rocking on his stool while he clutched his knees, "I can tell you that old Laertes still stands beneath the sky, but he's unhappy in his lot. Each day he prays that Zeus will let him die and release his spirit from his aged flesh. He grieves daily for his lost son and for the wise and gentle lady he married who has gone on before him—that was a heavy blow for the old man to endure, I tell you! She took to yearning to see her glorious son so much that she'd forget to eat or drink. Brought her to her grave, I think. I hope none that I love in this room or Ithaca comes to an end like that! But while she lived, I always asked about her. She was like a mother to me, you see. Raised me together with her youngest daughter, Ctymene. We were brought together and treated as equals, we were!"[5]

336-365

366–394 "However, youth is fleeting, and when we reached our majority, they married her off to someone in Samos—and a price he paid for her, I tell you! I was given a fine cloak and tunic by her mother and stout sandals for my feet and sent out to work the fields. But she never forgot me and, I think, kept a tender spot in her heart for me. Ah, but I have missed her kindness!" He paused to wipe a tear from his eye with his horny thumb. "The gods have blessed my work for I bring in enough to eat and drink and give to those less fortunate than I. But"—his face clouded—"nary a gentle word comes from the lips of Penelope or a kind deed from that house since these dungheels have come. And the servants feel this, too, as they can't speak to our mistress's face and get the news or a bit of meat and drink to bring back to the farm. Such things warm a servant's heart, you know. Makes him feel welcome."

"This is a bit of a surprise to me," Odysseus answered. "From what I understand and all, why, you must have been a little lad when you were taken from your parents and home. What happened? How did this come about? Was the city sacked where your parents lived? A band of raiders come upon you while you tended sheep and steal you away by ship to the palace here where they ransomed you?"

Eumaeus hawked and spat and cleared his throat. "Well, my friend. My story is something else and a tale you might enjoy. Sit back. Have a cup of wine against the long night. There's no need for an early bed, but if one here desires a bit of sleep—although too much sleep dulls the wits, you know— then he can go and have a lie-down.

395–422 "But," he warned, "when Dawn comes, so does breakfast, and they will have to go out to mind our master's pigs. Now, as to the two of us"—he paused to fill their cups with wine—"why, we can share our unhappy memories drinking and eating in this hut and delight each other with our yarns. A man who has suffered much, as you have, can forget his bitter trials by hearing about the times of others. So, let me begin.

"There is an isle—maybe you've heard about it? Syria? North of Ortygia where the Sun makes his turnings for the solstice—that is not very well populated although the land is filled with rich grass for cattle and sheep and the ground is fertile with deep black earth to feed fine crops of grapes and grain. Famine is a stranger there, as are plagues and other illnesses, and the men and women grow old in their homes, with their tranquil ways, until silver-bowed Apollo or Artemis slays them in their sleep with kind arrows. Two cities lie at each end of the island, and my godlike father, Ctesius, the son of Ormenus, ruled over both.

"One day the Phoenicians came to the island—good sailors, perhaps, but greedier souls I have never seen—with their ship's hold filled with trinkets and baubles for trading. Now, in my father's house was a handsome woman, tall and too clever with her hands, who came from their race. She was fond of men—aye, goodly fond—and few were ever turned from her bed. When she went to wash the clothes near where they had moored their ship, one of the Phoenicians found her, and the two of them took to tumbling on the grassy banks there.

"Afterward, when they lay perspiring in the noon heat, he began to ques- *423–456* tion her and she answered freely, for there's nothing like a few caresses and a bit of pleasuring to lead a woman astray, you know. She told him about my father and even pointed out the high roof of his house peeking over the cedars and said, 'I'm from Sidon, the land of bronze and able craftsmen. There lives my father Arybas, a wealthy man who lost his daughter to Taphian pirates who found me as I came home from the fields and stole me. They brought me here and sold me for a handsome price.'

" 'Now, how,' the pirate said, caressing her heavy thigh, 'would you like to see your father and mother again, your old house in your own land, eh, my beauty? I know them well, and they still live, pining away for their lovely daughter.'

" 'Ah, yes,' she sighed. 'If only that would be possible. I don't suppose you and your friends would take me safely there?'

"As you can imagine they all swore, for the others had seen her skills and charms and willingly took solemn oaths to do their part. But this woman was a wily wench, for she told them, 'Let this be a secret, now! None of you must say a word or even nod to me in the street when you see me or ask for a drink of water from my hands at the well. All here know me, and several of the women would like nothing better than to take tales to my master who would bind me in chains, hands and feet—now there is something for you—and kill you all if he should suspect you. Remember your oaths, now, and finish your trading quickly. When your ship is stowed and buckled well, send word to me then and only then at the great house. I'll come and bring what gold I can lay my hands upon. And,' she continued with relish, 'there's a bit of something else there too. I am also the nurse in that house to his son, a spritely boy who is quite clever with his ways and likes to follow me around. Now, I'm quite willing to throw him in the pot—metaphorically speaking, you understand—as well if you should take me. He'd fetch a handsome for- tune at whatever other port you should put into on your way home.'

"And having said this, she dressed, gathered the wash, and left for my *457–488* father's fine home.

"The traders were in no hurry, however, and stayed with us for an entire year, making their barters and wheeling and dealing until they had acquired

a vast store of goods that fairly strained the hold of their ship. At last, how-
ever, the hollow ship was filled and they were ready to leave, and they sent
word to this woman by way of a cunning rascal who brought a long necklace
of gold and amber beads to the house to trade. While my mother and her
handmaidens were haggling over the price, the rascal gave the eye to my
nurse and slipped away back to his ship. My nurse took me by the hand and
held a finger to her lips. I thought it was a new game that we were playing
and followed her willingly as we left my mother's room. We stopped in the
outer hall where she found the golden cups and plates set on tables that had
been used by my father's councilors where they had been feasting. She
quickly hid three goblets in her bosom—aye, her bubbies were big enough
for that, I tell you!—and ran with me to the ship.

"The sun had begun to set as we ran down the backstreets to the harbor
where the Phoenicians waited impatiently beside their fast ship. As soon as
we came into view, they grabbed us and hustled us aboard and pushed out
into the sea.

"For six days and nights we sailed on calm seas, but on the seventh, Artemis
the archeress laced an arrow into the woman's heart and she dove headfirst
like an albatross after prey down into the hold, where she landed with a thud
that nigh shook the ship from timber to timber. They threw her overboard as
a meal for the seals and fishes, and I was left to my own miserable ends.
Eventually they landed here, on Ithaca, and kindly Laertes took pity upon
my wretched state and parted with a bit of his wealth to buy me."

"Ah, Eumaeus," Odysseus said, shaking his head. He took a deep gulp of
wine. "Your miserable story has touched me deeply."

489–514 He thumped his fist gently against his chest. "But you mustn't feel too
badly about your state, you know. Zeus has treated you fairly well, allowing
you to live in the generous house of one who always made certain that you
had plenty of food and drink to keep you. I, on the other hand, have reached
this place only after having tramped through many backstreets, puddling my
feet in gutters to cool them, in many cities in many lands."

They lifted their wine cups and sipped and visited a bit more as the bugs
bounced around the walls of the hut, smacking against the light reflected
there. Soon they tumbled off to their beds, but not for long before Dawn
flowered.

Meanwhile, Telemachus had been sailing closer and closer in the dark to
Ithaca, and now his crew struck their sail and downed the mast. They rowed
cautiously until they reached their anchorage, where they threw over the
anchor stones and made fast the hawsers and jumped out and prepared a
meal on the beach, mixing sparkling wine to soothe their tired throats. After

they had eaten, clever Telemachus spoke and gave them instructions, saying, "Men, row this ship around the island to the city while I come overland. I must visit the estate and pay my respects to the herdsmen who have been minding my cattle in my absence. This evening, after my inspection, I will come and set a great feast for you with fresh meat and sweet wine for having voyaged with me."

"And what about me, dear child?" asked Theoclymenus, his godlike passenger. "Which way should I go? Which house should I seek among the chiefs of this rugged Ithaca? Or should I go straight to your mother's house and advise her on the safe return of her son?"

Careful Telemachus shook his head. "If things were different, my friend, I would certainly invite you to my house where you would receive a proper warming. But this is the time for prudent men to be wary, for this has been a winter of discontent for all at my house.

"My mother stays as far away as she can from visitors and seldom appears ⁵¹⁵⁻⁵⁴¹ in the great hall where her would-be suitors lounge and loaf their days away. Instead, she stays upstairs in her room and works away the time at her loom. However, there is a man you might attend—Eurymachus, the son of wise Polybus regarded as a god by the people. He is the noblest of the suitors and the most eager to win her hand and seize the rights and powers of Odysseus. But far-seeing Zeus, who dwells on lofty Olympus, knows if judgment day will lower its doom-filled hour upon his neck before weddings are planned!"

At that moment a hawk, Apollo's winged herald, flew away to his right, holding a dove in its claws. It plucked the feathers and strewed them down to earth between Telemachus and the black prow of his ship. Theoclymenus took Telemachus by the elbow and drew him aside, whispering in a low voice, "Telemachus, this bird was sent here by a god. As soon as I saw it, I knew it for an omen. There will be no house in Ithaca as strong as yours. You will rule forever."

"I hope you are right, my friend," Telemachus said. "If you are, after this is over you will receive so many gifts that any man who sees you will say you've been blessed with good fortune."

Then Telemachus turned to Peiraeus, his faithful friend, and said, "Peiraeus, son of Clytius, among all my friends who followed me on this goose chase to Pylos, you have never questioned any of my whims or ways. Will you take this man as a guest in your own house until I return?"

"Of course I will, Telemachus," said the great spearman. "And there's no ⁵⁴²⁻⁵⁵⁷ reason to be in a hurry about it, either. He's welcome as long as he wishes to stay. And the stories we will tell—he won't find my hospitality lacking in any way, I promise you."

Peiraeus turned and reboarded the ship and ordered the men to cast away. The others quickly seated themselves at the oars, and as they made ready to pull strongly away from the cove, Telemachus tied his elegant sandals around his shapely feet and, picking up his great bronze-headed spear from the deck, jumped lightly to the shore as the men made away according to his orders. He turned and set out, walking with rapid steps along the steep path that led inland to where his large herd of pigs was kept by Eumaeus, he of the loyal heart, the most faithful servant of his master.

Here ends the Fifteenth Book of Homer's Odyssey.

THE SIXTEENTH BOOK
The Discovery of Odysseus

❖ ❖ ❖ ❖ ❖ ❖ ❖ ❖ ❖ ❖ ❖

Telemachus sends Eumaeus to tell Penelope
That he has arrived home in Ithaca safely.
Then the youth Telemachus
Discovers the beggar is Odysseus.

❖ ❖ ❖ ❖ ❖ ❖ ❖ ❖ ❖ ❖ ❖

A rooster crowed the night away as Telemachus climbed
The stony path leading to the hut of Eumaeus.
A calf bawled for its mother, and Odysseus rose
To help the loyal swineherd blow the fire awake.
Dawn's rosy fingers played golden harmony with morning
While the men prepared their breakfast in the thin
Light, paying little heed to the barnyard din.
The dogs recognized the step of Telemachus and barked
A welcome greeting. Inside, Odysseus noticed their tail-wagging
And turned quickly to the swineherd, saying:

1–29

"My friend, one of your men must be returning—or else it is a close friend of
yours, for your dogs are fawning about like puppies instead of giving their
watchdog bark. And I can hear his footsteps—"

He stopped as Telemachus appeared in the doorway, eyeing the youth
with puzzlement. Eumaeus leaped to his feet in amazement, the bowls in
which he had been busily mixing water and wine spilling from his grasp.
They shattered on the floor, wine splattering over his feet, but he paid no
heed to the broken shards and rushed to meet his youthful master. He
seized the youth's head between callused hands and kissed his forehead, his
shining eyes, and both hands, tears welling from his own eyes, greeting
Telemachus as would a father his son who had been absent ten years and
just returned from a distant land—his only son, more dear than gold,

265

whose long absence from his father's house had caused his father more grief than one could bear—and now the faithful swineherd threw his arm around the shoulders of Telemachus and clasped him tightly, holding him as one would hold a loved one who had just returned from death's embrace.

"You're back! At last! Telemachus, sweet light for these sore eyes!" he said through his tears. He stepped back to study the youth and grabbed a rag from the table, blowing his nose. "And here I was thinking that you would never bless my eyes after you sailed to sandy Pylos. Come in, come in, don't stand there as if you've never been in this house before, although you are no frequent visitor to farms and herds—you prefer the town and city, but that could change. I still have hopes. Come in! You're no stranger to my table! Let me feast my eyes upon you for a moment, you wanderer! We herdsmen don't see enough of you. I think you take a perverse joy in watching the antics of your mother's suitors, that malicious rabble."

30–59   Telemachus laughed, delighted at his greeting, and said, "Well said, old friend. In fact I came here because I wanted to see you and hear from an honest man how my mother has fared in my absence. Is she still at home, or has she married another man and left Odysseus's bed empty with dusty spiderwebs hanging from its posts?"

Eumaeus scrubbed his hands vigorously through his head. "Well, she's still at home," he said cautiously. He hawked and spat through the doorway behind the youth. "But I wouldn't give that for how long. Her nights are dreary and the days are long and she spends most of the hours weeping them away. A woman can shed only so many tears before the well runs dry."

As he spoke, he took the long bronze spear from the hand of Telemachus and stood it in a corner. Telemachus stepped over the stone threshold, and Odysseus rose from his seat at the table, offering it to the youth. But Telemachus refused it, holding him with a gesture.

"No, no. There's no reason to get up, my good man. There's another stool somewhere around here on this farm that will serve me as well and a man here who will fetch it for me. Perhaps the milking stool?" He turned, raising his eyebrow at Eumaeus.

Odysseus nodded and returned to his seat while Eumaeus heaped green brushwood beside the table and draped a fresh sheepskin over it. Telemachus sat and Eumaeus scurried around the room, placing a platter of cold meat left over from their supper the day before in front of them. He placed baskets heaped with fresh-baked bread and hurried to mix honeyed wine in a wooden bowl carved with ivy designs. Then he took his own seat facing the divine Odysseus and beamed his pleasure.

"Eat, eat!" he said, shaking his hands at the pair. They helped themselves to the good food in front of them, and after they had filled themselves, Telemachus wiped his mouth on the back of his hand and looked curiously at Odysseus.

"So, old friend," he said to Eumaeus. "Where did your guest come from? I know he came with some ship's crew, but who were they and who did they claim to be? (For I know there's a big difference between the lip and the truth.) I presume that he didn't walk to Ithaca."

And you,[1] Eumaeus, answered, "My son, I'll tell you what I know. This man claims to have been well born in Crete and that a god has spun his fate by forcing him to become a tramp, wandering from city to city, begging for bread. Just now he has managed to escape from a Thesprotian ship and found his way up that rocky path to my house. He's decided to cast himself upon your good graces." Eumaeus shrugged. "Do with him as you will." 60–92

"I see," Telemachus said, frowning. "This is a bit of a problem, my friend. You see, I really can't receive a stranger in my house. In the first place, I am very young and lack the strength to fight with one who might wish to argue with me. And my mother is torn between staying at home and caring for me out of respect for her husband's bed and public opinion or eloping with one of the suitors who is the best among that rabble and offers her the most gifts to be her new mate. And there is the question of the people who have been sitting the rail, reluctant to jump one way or the other but who tend to play it safe and look the other way at the atrocities these suitors heap upon my house." He sighed and studied Odysseus opposite him. Then he shook his head again, saying, "But since he has come to you seeking refuge, I will give him a good cloak and tunic and a good sharp two-edged sword to protect himself with and stout sandals for his feet. I'll arrange for him to be taken wherever he might wish to go as well. But I ask that you keep him here at the farm with you and I shall send all these things to you here. I'll also send food that he won't be a burden to you and your men, but it would not be wise to bring him down to the palace and those suitors there. They are reckless and in their boredom might do him violence and bring the wrath of Zeus down upon my house. Of course I would try and stop that, but it is very hard for one man to deal with so many, however strong and gifted he is with a sword. One man is only one man, and a crowd is many."

Bright Odysseus replied, "I hope, young friend, that you will let me speak freely here as it is the well-being of myself that seems to concern you. I have listened to your good servant here and to yourself about these reckless men who boldly take advantage of a poor woman's house when her husband is absent and, frankly, I am outraged. My blood fairly boils at the indignations 93–123 they have heaped upon you. Beggarman I may be, but there is a man beneath these rags, and clothes do not make a noble soul. The conduct of these wanton suitors that you fine people have been forced to endure is outrageous. But tell me: Have you stood idly by and watched these atrocities being practiced, or have the local people—who should have remained loyal to your father—been turned into your enemies by some wrathful god? On the other hand, perhaps you have been cast adrift in the open sea by your brothers who normally would stand beside you in an argument no matter how many others stand against you. Ah, if only I had the strength of youth back in these old muscles and bones! It's a shame that youth is wasted upon the young. If I were noble Odysseus's son or even Odysseus himself—there's still hope despite what this noble man"—he indicated Eumaeus—"might say—why, then you could strike my head from my shoulders if I wouldn't fall upon those rascals like an evil shade from Hades's Halls when I entered the palace of Odysseus, the son of Laertes. Even if I were forced to fight alone against all of their numbers, why, I would sooner go down with my sword well bloodied in my hand in my own house than stand by and watch how these would-be nobles behave in that noble house—violating the laws of hospitality Zeus handed down to us, dragging helpless maids onto whatever couch is available, wine running like a river down their gullets, gorging themselves on the fattest of animals. Disgraceful, I tell you."

"Hm. Yes. Well, stranger, I'll tell you what you want to know," Telemachus said. "Basically the Ithacans are good people. They do not join with the suitors but neither do they help me to rid the house of them. I suppose I can't blame them for not standing by me as brothers-in-arms. Fact is, I'm alone. For as long as I can remember, Zeus has made our family stand alone. One son, that's the rule. Arceisius had only Laertes and Laertes had only Odysseus who had only me before he left his home—and little joy he had in fatherhood for I was only a babe when he was forced away. That's why so many enemies crowd our house now. His reputation held the suitors away for a long time, but memories fade with time, and I haven't earned a reputation strong enough to keep them away. Perhaps if my father could have taught me what fathers teach their sons things would have been different.

124-151 "But there's no sense crying over spilt wine. As it is, all the island lords—the rulers of Dulichium, Samos, and the wooded isle of Zacynthus, and the nobles here on rocky Ithaca—court my mother and arrogantly ravage my house. My mother cannot bring herself to reject all of them or accept one of them although I know she hates the idea of remarrying. Soon, however, they will bring poverty upon my house and destroy me with their wanton wants. But"—he shook his head and spread his hands in dismay—"what can I do?

This is all in the laps of the gods. But enough of this whining and playing 'if only.' " He turned to Eumaeus. "Old friend, would you travel this rocky path to my house and tell wise Penelope that I have returned safely from Pylos? I'll stay here and wait until you come back. But please be certain that you tell her personally that I have returned and let no other person hear your words." He smiled wryly. "I have a hunch that there are many in that house who plot a bit of mischief for me."

And you, swineherd Eumaeus, said, "Yes. Of course. I understand. Don't worry about me. I'll be as close with my news as the meat in a walnut shell. You won't find me bandying words in the marketplace! But"—he leaned closer—"tell me, lad, should I make one trip out of it all and tell Laertes the news as well? That poor man could stand a bit of good news, and despite his daily grief for Odysseus, he has for the most part kept an eye on the farm and helped us out here and there with our chores. Ever since you sailed away for Pylos, however, he hasn't been down here for a bite to eat or a cup of wine to drink or taken much interest in what work we do. Not even a bit of chatter in the evening. He just sits there and moans and groans in his misery while his flesh withers away from his bones!"

"No, that wouldn't be wise at the moment," Telemachus said thoughtfully. "I feel sorry for the old man, but I think we should leave him alone for now. If wishes were horses, why, then I would wish the gods to have my father return. But we can't have what we want, only what the gods will give us. So deliver your message and come straight back here without seeking Laertes on his farm. Tell my mother to send her housekeeper to him secretly with the news of my return."

Eumaeus frowned but nodded his agreement and bent and picked up his _152–177_ sandals, quickly tying them on his feet. He slung a wineskin over his shoulder and picked up his staff and hurried down the path toward the town. Athene watched him leave as she approached the farmhouse, and when she stepped inside the gate, she took on the form of a lovely woman, tall and skilled in beautiful handiwork. She stood in the shade of the arbor and smiled at Odysseus. But Telemachus did not see her for it is not given to everyone to see the gods all the time even though they may be standing right at a person's shoulder. Only Odysseus and the dogs saw her, and the dogs ran whimpering from her to hide on the other side of the farm. Athene raised her eyebrows and Odysseus coughed and excused himself from Telemachus, saying that he had to water the vines. He left the hut and went to stand beside her.

"Odysseus, man of many masquerades, son of Laertes, now is the time to let Telemachus know who you are so that the two of you can plot the downfall and death of the suitors. After that, make your way to the town. I won't be far behind you for I too am eager for the fight."

She touched him with her golden wand, transforming him instantly from the beggarman forced to live in burdocks and brambles who had stood before her, eyes red-rimmed and bloodshot, rags fluttering like swallows in the breeze. First she placed a well-washed cloak and tunic over his broad shoulders and chest, then took away age, turning the sallow of his cheeks a healthy tan, filling his jaw, his beard blue-black upon his chin. Then she disappeared, and Odysseus turned and reentered the hut. His son's eyes rose in astonishment at the change in Odysseus, and immediately he shielded his eyes with his hand in case the man who left had returned as a god.

178–206   "Stranger," he said, "I don't know what you are but I know you are different from what you were before you left. Your clothes are different and your skin isn't the same either. Surely you must be a god, one of the lofty Olympus dwellers. Be kind and we'll offer rich sacrifices to you and golden gifts as well."

"I'm no god," Odysseus said kindly. He laughed. "Why do you think I'm one of the Immortals? I am, however, the one you have mourned for so long—your father. I am the one who has brought so much sorrow and persecution upon you."

And then tears fell from his eyes, soaking his beard, and he bent and kissed his son. Telemachus drew back in amazement, staring the him, saying, "No, you're not Odysseus. Not my father! A demon is what you are! A trickster playing a monstrous game with me to make me grieve even more! No mortal man would do what you have done, sitting here all the time and pretending to be a stranger while his son grieved for him. I know that gods can make a young man old and an old man young—after all, they're gods— and the proof of this is here before me. Only a minute ago you were an ancient man with bones creaking and popping when he moved and now you stand godlike before me. Trickery's afoot here, I say! Trickery!"

Odysseus smiled gently and said, "Telemachus, there's no mystery here. No other Odysseus will be coming. I am the one who has been wandering all these many years and who has finally returned after twenty years to his own country. As far as these changes that have you worried, you see the work of Athene, who can make a person look as she pleases.

207–238   "It was her magic, not mine, that made me look first like a beggar and next as you see me. This is an easy matter for the gods in heaven who can glorify a mortal man or debase him."

He sat down, and Telemachus threw his arms around his father's neck and wept salty tears, soaking his father's tunic. His father clasped his rough arms around him and held him close. Together they wailed for the twenty years they had lost, their cries scaling up to the heavens as loudly as the hunting cry of a hawk. For a long time they hawked and snuffled together and would have cried on through sunset if Telemachus had not suddenly pushed himself away and, wiping his eyes, said, "But tell me, dear father, how did you at last come to Ithaca? What ship brought you? I know that you did not walk across the teeming seas."

Then Odysseus, who had borne all the barren sea could bring, said, "My son, I'll tell you everything in time. But as to how I arrived here, why, it was the good Phaeacians, those renowned sailors, who brought me here. They are a kindly people, willing to help any man who comes to them with a reasonable request and asks for passage home. I slept deeply while they brought me on one of their fastest ships to Ithaca's shore along with marvelous gifts of bronze and gold and finely woven clothes, all of which I hid with the help of the gods in a cave not far from here. I came here at Athene's prompting so that together we could plot our revenge upon those scheming scavengers! Now, sit here beside me and tell me how many of them I will find in my house when I return. Name them, so I will be able to know whom I face. Then I will decide how best to handle them. We may need help."

"Father," Telemachus said cautiously, "I'm well aware of your great reputation as a fearless man in combat. But the odds against two men doing what you plan are overwhelming. There aren't just ten men wooing your wife's hand or even twice that number. Scores of men have come lately to haunt our doorstep. Why, fifty-two men with armor came from Dulichium alone. From Samos twenty-four have arrived and twenty would-be noblemen from Zacynthus. A dozen from Ithaca have made their intentions known along with Medon the herald and a master harper. Even two servants have pressed their suits! If we try to beard that lion in its den, why, I'm afraid that you and I will be the meal. We would pay in salty blood for the vengeance you would wreak upon them. I suggest that you try and figure a way of bringing others to help our cause." *239–267*

"Now listen carefully," Odysseus, the man of masquerades, said. "We have a stronger ally than any of those so-called fighting men could put together. Athene will be beside us. Who could ask for a better ally than her? Father Zeus may help as well. Do you think that would be enough, or should I rack my brains for more?"

"They would be two great allies, that's for certain," cautious Telemachus said. "They may sit in the clouds and look out over the world, but they rule that world as well and the men and the gods in it."

"Justly so," Odysseus said, satisfied. "It won't be long before the two of *268–301* them stand at our right and left hands in the battle that will be coming. Of that I am certain. And then Ares's fury will rage fully! But it isn't quite time for that yet. We must see what else can be done. The gods are willing to help those who help themselves, you know, so let us see what we can do to lessen the odds a wee bit. You go back home at first light and mingle with those worldly princes. Later, the swineherd will take me down by the left trail to the house. I will be disguised as an old beggar on his last legs. They may poke fun at me and ridicule me, but you are to ignore whatever they say or do. Understand? Hold your anger if they insult me in your house. Oh, it probably would be all right if you would plead with them to take mercy upon an old man. Now that I think on it, that would help put their minds at ease, you begging for a beggar. They would think less of you, and when a person thinks less of you than you are, why, then you have the upper hand. They won't listen to you—arrogant men usually don't—but we know one thing that they don't: Their judgment day is near at hand.

"Now, here is one more thing." His eyes grew distant and narrowed and tiny lights danced and darted in their depths. "When clever Athene whispers to me, I will give you a nod. It won't be much, so be looking for it at all times. As soon as you see my signal, carefully gather up the weapons lying around the hall and lock them away—all of them, now!—and if the suitors suddenly miss them and ask you about them, say simply that you thought you would move them out of the smoke because they were no longer the bright arms that Odysseus had left in the hall. Claim that the smoke and heat had damaged them and that you had simply put them away until they could be repaired. If they press you further, say that Zeus came to you and suggested that you lock them away as the suitors have been drinking much wine lately and have begun quarreling among themselves and you did not wish to leave weapons out where they might seize them and disgrace their position in the house as suitors for your mother's hand. After all, the wise man knows that tempered iron brings man's savage blood to the surface. But leave two strong swords and spears nearby for our own use where we can lay hand upon them easily after Pallas Athene and Zeus the wise befuddle the wits of our young princes.

302–332   "Now, one last piece of advice. If you are my son and my blood sings in your veins, be certain that no one hears that Odysseus has returned. This is very important. Tell no one! Not Laertes, not the swineherd, not the servants, no, not even Penelope herself lest she let word slip unguarded from her lips. You and I will have to judge which of the women we can trust and sound out the one or two servingmen who remain loyal and respect us and those who think of you as only a bothersome boy."

Telemachus drew himself up and Odysseus could see the iron running through him, and his heart swelled with pride as his son spoke, saying, "Father, rest assured that you will soon see that your blood runs thickly through my veins. I am not a mooncalf or chucklehead who plods through the day with straw in his hair. But I really don't see the need to go checking the field hands or the servants at this point. There's no profit there for us! I say you'll waste our time if you persist in checking out all the servingmen, the herdsmen, the field men, to see who remains loyal to us. Meanwhile, those wastrels will be eating up our flocks and herds and drinking up our wine, leaving us with nothing to show after this is over. The maids, yes, I think that would be helpful for us to know which of the girls remain true to our house and which prefer the company of the suitors. But to go around to the farms, no, I don't see that as being useful. Save it for later—if Zeus of the thunderbolt has indeed bent your ear."

And so father and son bent heads together over the table and talked about their plans while the good ship that had brought Telemachus from Pylos cleared the rugged outcrop and made its way slowly into the deep dark harbor of Ithaca. The sailors hauled her up onto the dark land and beached her carefully, then took out the oars and folded sail for their eager squires to carry to the house of Clytius along with the valuable gifts that had been bestowed upon Telemachus by his hosts. First, however, they sent a runner to tell Penelope that Telemachus had returned safely from his wanderings but had gone out into the country after ordering them to sail around to the city. They did this so that the good queen would not be alarmed at seeing the black-prowed ship hove to in Ithaca's harbor without her son.

Now, as it happened, this runner met the swineherd as he approached the palace, and the runner stood among the handmaidens and delivered his message, "My queen, I am happy to report that your son is safely returned." The swineherd, however, waited until he could catch Penelope alone and whisper the full message Telemachus had given him in her ear and, having faithfully delivered what he had been instructed, hurried away, shaking the dust of the town from his sandals as he made his way back to his pigs.

The news came as a shock to the suitors who heard the message, and gloom fell like a dark shade over their spirits as they made their way out of the great hall into the high-walled courtyard where they held their meeting in front of the gates. Eurymachus, the son of Polybus, spoke first, saying, "My friends, that insolent pup Telemachus has made the round-trip to Pylos and back although we said that he would be food for the fishes by now.

333–359

There's nothing to it but to find the best ship on the island and send it out to those who wait on the island to ambush him and tell them that Odysseus's whelp has managed to sneak past them and return safely. Some god must have been standing by his shoulder, that's all I can say."

360–391   They left for the beach to select their ship, but Amphinomus saw the black cutter making its way into the harbor and pointed and laughed, saying, "Well, there's no need to be sending a message now. Maybe Telemachus's ship was a bit too fast for theirs or maybe they just got tired of playing the fox's game and decided to come back. At any rate, there they are." He laughed again as if the whole thing was a great jest that had been played on all, drawing several black looks and dark mutterings from the other suitors, which made him laugh all the harder.

"By Hermes's balls, my friends, but you take things too seriously! Are we any the worse off now than we were when Telemachus strutted like a barn-yard rooster among us, cocking and crowing and throwing up his spurs in useless challenge? Annoying, yes, but come now: Is he any better off than he was, or are we any the worse?"

The suitors ignored him and made their way down to the beach to help draw the ship up. Proud squires were already carrying off the armor when they arrived, and together the suitors withdrew to the assembly ground, allowing no others to sit with them, no seers or aged men, no young women with gladsome thighs to draw their attention away from what needed to be discussed. It was then that Antinous, the son of Eupeithes, spoke to them, his black brow furrowed angrily.

"By the black god!" he swore, ripping out an oath. "I don't know how that Telemachus managed to weasel his way past us. There must be one god or the other standing at his shoulder for him to pull this one off! We kept a watchman on the lofty cliff throughout the day and night, watching for his sail. We never even slept on shore—although that would have been a lot more pleasurable than that hard deck, I tell you. As soon as the evening star twinkled over the waters, we all went aboard and sailed out onto the dappled sea in hopes of catching him as he came by. And while we were doing all of that some god crept him home. Hang it!

"But," he continued, drawing a deep breath to calm himself, "enough of that. No sense complaining the light's out when the lamp's dry. Still, we must not let him gain a hold over us. We need to put him deep into the ground as soon as possible because all that we have tried will not bear fruit as long as he lives. He's no dummy, you understand. He's a schemer, and I think Hermes whispers trickery into his ear now and then to give him an edge over us. We can't be resting on our heels now with people's favor. He might have learned something to turn them against us, and then our suits will be finished!

"Now, before he has a chance to call a grand assembly, I suggest we figure a way to get rid of him. It'll be one angry man who rises up in that gathering to denounce us, I tell you! He'll let them know how we had planned his journey to Hades's Halls and how he made fools of us. They may not believe him fully, but the idea of the grand joke that was played on us will be enough to earn their laughter. Then it's a short step to exile for us, my friends. We must keep him from this, and I say we try to catch him in the country or the town or on the road to the town—who knows where that rake is?—and make him"—he waffled his fingers daintily in the air—"quietly disappear. Eh? Then we can seize his lands and goods and share his wealth equally among us. I daresay there's not a one of us who couldn't use a coin or two in his pot after this long wait we've had. Of course, we'd give the palace to his mother and"—he smiled wolfishly—"the man she weds. So all won't be a total loss. But"—he shrugged—"if you don't like this plan, why, then, come up with one of your own. Know this, though: We let that boy have his patrimony and there'll be no more good roasted mutton for us to fill our bellies with. I say we have waited long enough. Let each of us gather the best of our goods and present them to the queen and demand that she make her choice straightaway. We've waited long enough in this tiresome game!"

They all stared thoughtfully at each other at the end of his speech, then 392–417 Amphinomus, the son of Lord Nisus and grandson of Aretias,[2] stirred and stepped up to speak. The others gave him room; despite his jesting, they found him to be a pleasant companion from the fields and pastures of Dulichium. Penelope was especially fond of his idle chat, as he was a principled man and did not constantly pressure her to marry him.

"Friends," he said, "you can leave me out of this plotting. It simply won't do to kill Telemachus, I say. I should have stepped up and tried to stop you the first time, and I didn't, much to my regret. It's a terrible deed to kill a king's son. If anything will bring down the wrath of the gods it's to do that without their kindly permission, and I don't see that coming from any of them soon, let alone Zeus the thunderer. Now, if Zeus lends his approval to this, why then, I will lop off the head of Telemachus myself. But I don't think he will, and if he says no, then I advise all of you to hold your hands and bite your tongues. Leave it in the hands of the gods, I say."

They all agreed to this and turned and made their way back to the house of Odysseus. There, they entered and took their seats on polished chairs, awaiting what would come.

Meanwhile, a sudden thought came to Penelope that she should face the suitors in all of their insolent pride, for rumors had whispered their way to her shell-like ears about the death threat that had been levied against her son in the great hall. Medon, the herald, had carried the news quietly to her. Now, with her handmaidens in her wake, the angry Penelope stormed through the palace to the great hall where the suitors sat. They looked up in amazement as the angry queen suddenly appeared beside a pillar that held the roof, and holding a shining shawl in front of her face, she turned on Antinous, lashing him with her tongue.

418-443 "Arrogant and evil man!" she said, loathing dripping from her words like the Gorgon's blood. "Your manners and way of speech are among the most eloquent on all of Ithaca, but you are a slimy fraud, an arrant braggart spilling soothing words to seduce young women. You make much of the rights of hospitality that Zeus has created, but there are the rights of hosts too. Do you think that he guards only you with his words? You would knit death's veil for Telemachus and think that Zeus doesn't know your plotting, your knavery? Before the gods there can be no sanction whereby one conspires to kill another in the peace of a house. Did you not know that this great house once sheltered your father when he fled here seeking sanctuary when his own realm came up in arms against him and we granted that sanctuary to him? Yes, it's true, you wanton womanizer! Your father was little better than the Taphian pirates he had joined to raid the Thesprotians who were at peace with us. If the people could have, they would have killed him and put an end to your line, swallowing up all his goods and gold and dividing his lands among those who were strong enough to hold it. And they were like ravenous dogs scenting a defenseless deer as they chased him. Why, they would have cut his heart out of his breast and butchered all his flocks and herds to eat! But Odysseus held them back, stayed their rage. And now you would plot against his son in his own house? You prey upon his good name and his goodwill and refuse to pay for that which you arrogantly take under the guise of hospitality. And you bring me grief. Tell your comrades it's time to stop their conniving ways, stop their plottings and schemings. And as for you, you—"

Words seemed to fail her and she stood fuming while the suitors watched, awed. At last Eurymachus, the son of Polybus, spoke. "Penelope, wise daughter of Icarius, put your fears to rest. Push these ugly thoughts out of your mind. The man doesn't exist who would dare to lay a hand, nay a finger, upon brave Telemachus while I live and draw breath and walk this earth! Yes, I will use my eyes to keep your son safe and swear that the first man who dares to lay a finger against your son, why, I'll draw his black blood with my spear and leave him gasping on the ground, writhing in agony!

"Didn't Odysseus, the sacker of cities, dandle me on his knees when I was *444-467* young and push roasted meat into my mouth and lift red wine for me to taste? That alone makes Telemachus my dearest friend on this earth, and I promise you that he need not tremble in fear for his life while I still stand on this good earth. No, by the gods! No suitor's hand will touch him. Of course, I can't promise what heaven will deliver—no man controls death, only the means of it."

But in his black heart he continued to plot the death of Telemachus while his lips still smiled beguilingly at the queen. Penelope drew away from the great hall and made her way to her room where she wept for her missing husband until gray-eyed Athene took pity upon her and cast the veil of sweet sleep over her eyes.

That same evening the swineherd made his way back to Odysseus and his son. He discovered they had killed a shoat and were even then preparing it for supper. Athene had touched Odysseus, the son of Laertes, with her golden wand and turned him back into an old man, disguising him once again as the beggar. His tattered rags flapped in the breeze like a swallow's wings once again, and his hands were old and gnarly, his eyes rheumy with age. She did this to keep the swineherd from rushing out into the country-side and spilling the news of Odysseus's return to Penelope before his senses sorted the grain from the chaff.

Telemachus heard the gladsome barking of the dogs and turned to greet Eumaeus as he came up the path. "Eumaeus, so you've returned, have you? Well, then, what word runs rampant in the city? Have those suitors who sat in ambush for me returned in their black ship yet? Or do they still drift on the lapping sea, waiting for me to come innocently by?"

Then you, swineherd Eumaeus, said, "I was not so inclined to pander about the market like a fishmonger looking for tales and tattles to tell. Instead, I followed my heart, which was to deliver the message as truly as you set it to me and return as rapidly as possible.

"I did, however, meet a herald from your crew, a messenger they sent out *468-481* as soon as they arrived in Ithaca's deep port to tell your mother the gladsome news. And—this I saw with these own two eyes above the city as I made my way along the rocky north path—a ship put into harbor with the gunwales fairly bristling with spears like sheaves of grain. I think those were the men who lay waiting for you—but who knows? I could be wrong."

And Telemachus turned and smiled knowingly at his father, avoiding the swineherd's eyes. When the meal was finished and each man had contented his belly with good meat and wine, they took themselves to bed and so to sleep.

Here ends the Sixteenth Book of Homer's Odyssey.

THE SEVENTEENTH BOOK
Telemachus Visits with Penelope

❖ ❖ ❖ ❖ ❖ ❖ ❖ ❖ ❖ ❖ ❖

Telemachus tells his mother, Penelope,
What he learned across the wine-dark sea.

❖ ❖ ❖ ❖ ❖ ❖ ❖ ❖ ❖ ❖ ❖

When youthful Dawn rose and stretched her fingers   1–28
Across the sky, Telemachus leaped from his bed.
He dressed quickly, refusing to linger in the hut.
He tied his rawhide sandals, and from beside the door
He took his spear and hefted it to find its balance.
He felt the excitement of returning home fluttering
In his stomach as he turned to the swineherd, saying:

"Now, friend, I'm off to town to see Mother. I expect she'll never stop crying bitter tears until I make my appearance and she can see for herself that I'm all right. After I'm gone, I want you to take this poor stranger to the city where he can beg for a crust and a cup of water. I can't be bothered with that at this moment. My heart is too heavy. And if he thinks that I have insulted him with this brevity, why then, so much the worse for him. I'm plain-spoken; here's an end to it."

"Friend," Odysseus, the man of masquerades, put in, "I too am eager to be off. I don't wish to insult any here, but a town is a better place for a person to beg his bread and I am not yet so old that I must lay up and mumble my yeses to a master's beck and call. Off with you, lad! There's no hard feeling here on my part. I like plain speaking myself at times—although a beggar can rarely afford such luxury—and as soon as I've had a bit of the fire to warm my bones and the sun upon my shoulders to take away the night's knots, why, my new friend here can lead me down the right path to the town." He fumbled with his rags and said ruefully, "The truth of the matter is that these thin old rags may well be my death on a frosty morning. Well, I'll warm on the walk. It's quite a ways to the town, if I hear you right."

29–56   And so Telemachus left with rapid strides, bouncing with the vigor of youth down the rocky slope away from the swineherd's house, his mind mulling vengeance on the suitors waiting at the end of his path. When he made his way to his stately home he leaned his spear against a lofty pillar and boldly crossed the stone threshold, his eyes flickering around to see who lounged about the porch of stone.

The first to spy him was the nurse Eurycleia, who had begun the day by covering the chairs in the great room with soft fleeces. Tears sprang to her eyes and she lifted herself up with a great cracking and popping of her knees and ran to him, clutching his tunic with her thick-knuckled hands. Other maidservants of the old soldier Odysseus heard her crying and ran into the room and clustered around the brave son, showering him with kisses on his head and shoulders.

Penelope heard the commotion and ran down from her lofty room where she rested like wise Artemis or golden Aphrodite, paused, the back of her hand covering her mouth briefly in shock, then stumbled into the room and threw her arms around the fine neck of her son, hot tears gushing forth as she kissed his forehead and fine eyes. She cried out, "Ah, you're back! You're back, Telemachus! Sweeter than sunlight! I thought you would never again bless my sight when I heard that you had sailed a night ship for Pylos—and without my blessings! But come, now! Tell me! Did you find your father? Did you see him?"

Tactful Telemachus avoided her questions, protesting, "Ah, Mother! Not now! Not now! My heart still aches and you would make me weep even more with your questions. I nearly died at sea, you know." She weaved back, her fine eyebrows frowning. He shook his head. "I will tell you all later. Meanwhile, go back upstairs with your ladies. After you have bathed and changed your dress and made your morning prayers, we'll talk. Be certain that you make a goodly offering to Zeus, who may lend a hand to our revenge here in this house and promise us a day of reckoning. Meanwhile, I'll go have a word with those in the courtyard. I sent a guest who came back with me ahead with Peiraeus to take home and treat respectfully until I arrive. I had best check on him as well."

57–84   Protests leaped to her tongue, but Penelope held them back and left silently to do her son's bidding. As she bathed and made ready to wear fresh clothes, she vowed solemnly to offer hecatombs in sacred fire to Zeus if he would only grant their house a day of reckoning.

Telemachus shrugged his way free from the handmaidens' greeting and strode out of the hall to the courtyard, pausing to collect his spear from where he had leaned it against the great pillar. Athene slipped down to walk beside him, touching him softly to endow him with goodly grace. All eyes turned to him, burning with admiration as he came up to the suitors and stopped in front of them, grounding the haft of his spear close beside his leg. His eyes burned as he stared at the highborn suitors gathered around him, friendly words fresh on their lips to put him at ease despite the deadly plotting that turned their hearts black. He glared at them and they stopped, shuffling nervously, then a thin smile touched his lips and he walked past them to a seat beside Mentor, who sat next to the old friends of his father, Antiphus and Halitherses.[1] He leaned his spear against an olive tree and made himself comfortable beside them. They greeted him warmly and plied him with questions about his travels.

Peiraeus spied him and made his way through the throng, bringing with him the guest, Theoclymenus, whom he had escorted through the twisting town streets. He paused uncertainly as he saw Telemachus busily chatting with the others, but Telemachus caught sight of him and leaped to his feet to greet him. Peiraeus smiled and said jokingly, "Ah, now, my friend Telemachus! You must send some handmaidens—and make them beautiful, if you will— to my house to fetch the gifts that Menelaus sent home with you."

Telemachus cast a quick eye around to see if anyone had heard the words of Peiraeus, then leaned forward, cautiously lowering his voice, saying "No, Peiraeus, if you don't mind, keep them a bit longer for me. None of us can see how this affair is going to end, but I feel that it is coming to a head quickly! One of these suitors may draw his sword and kill me as I walk unaware in my palace. Then they will split my estate among themselves, and if that happens, then I want you to have what we brought back. But when that hour comes and the gods are willing for me to send them to their own bloody doom, why, then you may bring them to my house and the two of us will rejoice in our good fortunes!"

Peiraeus paused and looked around at the suitors watching them suspi- *85–115* ciously and slowly nodded. He reached out and clasped Telemachus by the hand and patted him roughly on the shoulder. Then he stepped aside as Telemachus took his travel-worn guest, the long-suffering stranger who had sailed across the treacherous sea with him, into the house to make him welcome as he had promised back in sandy Pylos.

They draped their cloaks over chairbacks in the hall as they passed into the room where stood great polished tubs. There they dropped their tunics upon settles and bathed. Afterward, handmaidens rubbed them with rose-scented oil and gave them clean tunics and draped cloaks over their shoulders as they left the baths. They took their seats upon chairs and a servant laved their hands with fresh water from a golden jug poured in a silver basin. Another drew up a polished table while yet another placed a platter of bread with fresh goat cheese and black olives on it. Penelope sat opposite them by a pillar in the hall and spun soft threads of wool on her distaff and watched fondly while the young men ate with great relish.

After they had finished, she spoke. "Telemachus, I believe it is time for me to return to my room and lie down on my bed—the bed of sorrows that has become well watered with my tears ever since Odysseus put out to sea to join the sons of Atreus on their way to Ilium. I have been waiting patiently for you to tell me what you discovered while on your journey. Can you not tell me now before the suitors fill our house? What news have you about your father's return?"

Telemachus pursed his lips and leaned back against his chair. He passed his hand over his eyes, shading them from her. "Very well, Mother," he said. "You have asked a second time what news I have. You have earned the truth. We left, as you know, for Pylos, and there we visited Nestor, the lord and guardian of that sandy country, the shepherd of his people. I was received with honor in his great house—just as a father would greet a long-lost son who had finally returned to his house.

116–147 "When I questioned him about Odysseus, he said that he had not heard one way or the other whether Odysseus lived or had gone to Hades's Halls. He then loaned a great chariot to me and sent me overland to the son of Atreus, Menelaus. I saw Helen of Argos there—the one whose face launched a thousand ships and for whose sake the Greeks and Trojans suffered much. Menelaus of the great war cry asked me my errand in the land of Sparta, and after I told him what I sought, he shouted, 'Intolerable! Disgraceful! So a spawn of jackals wishes to creep into a brave man's bed when he's not around to challenge them, eh? Fawns in a lion's den! It's as if a doe had placed her little unweaned fawns there while she grazed in a grassy glen. The lion returns to his lair and the fawns meet their grisly fate, the lord dealing out wretched doom with a bloody hand! These suitors will suffer a like fate at the hands of Odysseus! Mark my words! Much has yet to come to pass. Why, once I was in Lesbos and saw him stand up to Philomeleides[2] and throw him with such force the ground fair trembled and a cloud of dust rose to the tops of the houses! I would give a golden bowl cunningly wrought to see that Odysseus meet with those suitors slinking around his house! By the gods, that would be a sight! It would be a quick answer to their wedding hopes and a lot of empty brides' beds from the future, I tell you! But, alas! I have no answer for you either, and I won't deceive you by making up some tale to set your heart at ease. I did hear from the Old Man of the Sea who said that he had seen the mighty Odysseus on an island in the Nymph Calypso's castle where she keeps him captive, for he hasn't a ship or crew to man it if he did have one to sail home with."

Telemachus spread his hands and sighed deeply. "And that is all that I *148-176* have heard," he said quietly. "I left the famous warrior Menelaus, and the immortal gods gave me a favorable wind that drew me swiftly to beloved Ithaca."

Penelope sat in deep silence for a long while after hearing Telemachus's words. Then she sighed heavily, and Theoclymenus, whose ears share the gods' voices, felt her aching heart and took pity upon her.

"Fair lady," he said, "Menelaus knows only what he learned in his own wanderings. You have been kind to me, and the hearth and fine table you have shared with me moves me to speak. Don't despair! I swear by Zeus and the other gods on lofty Olympus that even as I stand here in your hall, Odysseus has already landed upon the shores of Ithaca and makes his way to this house. He comes slowly, learning what he can about what evil has befallen his home in his absence. I know there is a great darkness within him that will bring a black hour indeed upon those carrion who lurk by his door, hoping to pick up a scrap from a brave man's meal. I saw all of this in an omen while on board the ship and read it to Telemachus even as we sailed!³

Penelope heaved another sigh and clasped her hands together, praying. "Would that this is true! Stranger, I thank you for your kindness, and if this comes true you'll see my kindness in so many gifts that anyone who meets you will say you are blessed."

Meanwhile, outside Odysseus's home the suitors amused themselves by swaggering back and forth in their games, primping and posturing as they threw the discus and javelin, marking their distances with taunting jests. As the dinner hour came near and a flock of sheep was driven in to be slaughtered for the meal, Medon, the herald they had taken into their gathering, came out to announce the setting of the table.

"Now that you sports have had your fun and games, come in for supper. There's much more to a well-done roast than the throw of a discus."

The suitors laughed and dropped their games and entered the stately *177-210* palace where they carelessly tossed their cloaks on chairs. They drew their knives and, as had come to be their ritual, fell with relish upon the helpless animals that had been brought in for slaughter. Great rams and fat goats, pigs, and a cow all fell to their slashing and stabbing. Blood flooded thickly

over the floor as the animals cried in fear and the suitors laughed and
shouted with glee at the sight of the animals' dying.

And as this cruel game was being played out to its full, Odysseus and the
loyal swineherd made ready to leave the farm. Eumaeus spoke as he noticed
his companion's impatience. "My friend, I know you have high hopes of
reaching the town today and making your way about it—that's what my
master said you would want and I'll do his bidding. But I would rather have
you stay here and guard the farm with me than go into that pesthole! Still, I
respect my master's wishes. I don't want him to have cause to rebuke me
later, as that is a bad thing when a master has to scold his servant for not
doing his wishes. So it's best that we be on our way. The better part of the day
has already passed and I'm afraid you'll find things a bit chilly in the evening."

"I agree," Odysseus said. "By all means, let's be off. You lead the way. But
if you have a staff about that's doing no one any good, I would have one to
lean upon if the path is as steep and slippery as you say."

He flung his well-patched bag over his shoulder, holding it against his side
with its well-worn rope, and took the stick Eumaeus found for him. Then
the two set out, leaving the boys and dogs to guard the place as they made
their way down the path toward the city. Eumaeus went slowly to allow his
lord to hobble along with the staff like the very old beggar he was pretending
to be.

They came to the city and made their way to a springhouse where clear
water bubbled gently from deep within the earth. Here the people drew
their water. It was an old springhouse that had been built by Ithacus, Neri-
tus, and Polyctor.[4] A stand of black poplars grew around it on the humid
ground. A cool stream streaked down, ice-cold in crystal clear runnels from
a high rock, and over the spring stood an ancient altar, well covered with
lichens, erected to the Nymphs. Here travelers paused to refresh themselves
and make their offerings.

211–238 It was here that Melanthius, the son of Dolius, made his way, driving a
small herd of goats before him with the help of two goatherds for the suitors'
table. He spied Odysseus and the swineherd and shouted and taunted them,
heaping vulgar abuse upon their shoulders. Odysseus tried to hold his anger,
but as the young man spoke, he felt the red madness coming upon him.

"And here comes one pigmonger leading another," Melanthius said con-
temptuously. "Tell me, you scurvy swine swivver, where do you take this
dirty old pig, this scum-sucking plate-licking beggar? Why, he's just the type
to rub his back against the doorposts of his betters, whining for whatever
garbage would be better served to the hogs. He's the type to ask for scraps
rather than swords or cauldrons, that's for certain![5] Hand him over to me

and I'll put him to good use looking after the folds and mucking out the stalls and such. He'd make a better fodder carrier for the kids and such and might put some muscle on him. Better that than plying his dodges in towns, I'm sure. Though, now that I take a better look at this scurvy knave, I can see that honest work on the farm is the last thing he wants. He'd rather fill his hoggish belly begging than that. Look here, you go to noble Odysseus's hall, and footstools and pots and jugs will fly about your noodle. Your backside and ribs will take a hiding for certain!"

He laughed and swaggered past them and then, like a sotted soaker, tried to plant a heavy kick on Odysseus's hip and push him off into the ditch beside the trail. Odysseus, however, stood his ground and seethed, wondering if he should whirl his stick around his head and beat the life out of the young fool or simply lift him above his head and break him against the stony ground. The swineherder, however, made the decision, looking Melanthius full in the face and raising his arms in fervent prayer.

"Nymphs of the fountain, daughters of Zeus, if Odysseus ever honored *239–263* you with a burnt offering of a thighbone heavy with fat—a ram's or even a kid's—hear me now and grant my wish that he be brought back to his home to rid you, Melanthius, of your swaggering ways that you have picked up from your betters by loafing around them like a dog looking for a scrap from his master's table. All wine and wind, that's what you are. And if the Nymphs do grant this wish it will be all the better—poor shepherds ruin the flocks!"

"What's this? What's this?" Melanthius snarled, whirling upon the honorable swine-keeper. "A mongrel snapping at the heels of his betters! One of these days I'll take him on a black slave ship over the seas and trade him for a few coins or a herd. I'll get a pretty profit from him." He stared at Eumaeus with loathing. "And may Apollo use his silver bow well upon Telemachus and put an arrow in his ribs where it will do the most good this very day. Or may those suitors crush him." He laughed. "There's no future for him now that his father is surely lost at sea."

He spat and hurried away from the pair and made his way to the home of Odysseus, where he entered and took a seat across from Eurymachus whom he fawned upon. Servants plopped meat down in front of him and dropped bread beside his plate as they hustled to serve the suitors.

Reaching the gate to the house, Odysseus and the swineherd paused as sweet notes filtered out on the night air to them. Phemius was tuning his hollow harp, setting himself for song.

Odysseus caught Eumaeus by the arm and held him back from entering, *264–292* saying, "My friend, this must surely be the home of Odysseus. Why, there's no other hall like it! Look how one chamber grows out of another tightly around the courtyard. The coping is a fine piece of work and those doors folding back upon themselves as they are—why, there's no one could storm a palace like this!" He cocked his head and listened for a moment, then smiled and said, "And judging from the sounds I'd wager there's good company for dinner. My nose tells me that a rich roast has been prepared and music ready to lay by. Harping and feasting! Ah, the gods were good to man when they made those!"

"You have a keen grasp of the obvious, my friend," Eumaeus said sourly. "But think, now, before you step across that threshold. How should we proceed from this point? Will you leave me here and enter first to face the suitors, or should I go in and see how the land lies? But if I go first, don't dawdle long out here or they may take it in their minds to drive you away with a club or lance. Think a bit on this, I say, before you act."

"Just what I was pondering," the patient Odysseus said. "So. Let's see. Suppose you go in first while I step about and put my wits in order. Don't worry about them throwing anything at me. Occupational hazard, you know. I'm quite good at dodging stones and bones when they come my way. I've lived a life on enough waves and battlefields not to mind a bruise now and then. Ah, well, there's no matter! A man's belly drives him on, you know. A terrible thing that! Causes a man no account of trouble. Even to fitting out great ships with good stout planks and fighting men to man them to ride the barren seas! And why? Hunger, my good man! Hunger! The wolf's hunger to feast upon his enemies!"

293–320 At the sound of his voice, an old dog lying beside the gate lifted his head, pricking his ears. Argus, he was, trained from a puppy by Odysseus to be the king of hunters. But his master left before they could hunt the mountains and crags together. Young men took him out hunting when he reached his prime, and none was swifter along the track of wild goats and deer and hares. But now, his master long gone, he lay unwanted, kicked and cast aside upon a pile of mule and cattle dung heaped outside the door by the servants to be hauled away to enrich the wide fields. Flies buzzed around him and fleas bit him, causing his skin to tremble. But when he heard his long-lost master's voice, his tail wagged feebly, then his ears dropped and he tried to crawl to the side of Odysseus. But he was too weak. Odysseus turned away, wiping a salty tear from his cheek, making sure that Eumaeus did not notice, and said, "It's a wonder to me that they would treat a dog like this. From the looks of him he was a fine hunter in his day. First to the kill, I'd say. I doubt if any could have matched his speed when he was young."

And you, Eumaeus, spoke saying, "His master was a great hunter, but alas, he died abroad. A pity. This old dog had a form that would be pleasing to you when Odysseus left him for Troy. None was as swift and strong as he was. He never shrank from a quarry and chased the game deep into the dark woods. No other dog could match his skill! And now he lies here with death nearby. The slave women ignore him—you know how servants are when the master's away! They have little desire to do their duties then. Zeus makes a man a slave and takes away part of the man."

And Eumaeus left Odysseus standing there and entered the courtyard, *321–347* crossing into the men's hall[6] where the suitors shouted and feasted. At that instant, death and darkness came on Argus, who had waited twenty long years to gain one last glimpse of his master before he died.

Telemachus caught sight of the gray swineherd as he entered the courtyard and beckoned for him to join him at the table. Eumaeus glanced around and, noticing a stool sitting ready for the meat carver to carve the suitors' meat, picked it up and carried it to Telemachus's table. He dropped the stool opposite Telemachus and sat. A servant silently placed a portion of the meat beside him along with a basket of fresh-baked bread.

At this moment, Odysseus shuffled through the door, bent like a mendicant, humped over his stick like a bundle of rags. He paused, blinking owlishly in the bright firelight of the room, then took a seat beside the ash wood sill with his back against a pillar of cypress that formed the doorjamb laid true by the carpenter years before with a plumb line. Telemachus saw Odysseus and reached into the basket of bread beside him and removed a whole loaf, split it lengthwise, and piled it high with meat. He handed it to the swineherd and ordered him to take it to the beggar at the door.

"Here, my friend. Take this to the stranger over there. Tell him that he may go among the suitors on his own and beg all he wants. But hanging back from the whim of his betters is no way of putting bread and meat into a poor man's belly," he said.

Eumaeus nodded and rose and carried the bread and meat to Odysseus, *348–375* saying, "Stranger, my master bids you to feast on this before you make the rounds among those present begging for something. He says to warn you that a beggar who sits shyly away from his betters is a beggar destined to be hungry." He leaned down and said quietly to Odysseus, "Frankly, my friend, I'd put a great distance between this house and the filthy vermin here, if I were you. No good will be coming of trying them for a few coins. Mark my words! These are wintry times, indeed!"

Odysseus took the bread and meat from his hands and said, "Thank your master for his kind generosity. Zeus will smile favorably upon him for this, I'm certain! And thank you for your words. But it is an even hungrier beggar who steps away from the possibility of a few coins. Gods help those who help themselves!"

Eumaeus shook his head as Odysseus took the bread and meat and placed it on his bag—a lowly table, indeed!—and fell to it, eating ravenously like a wolf who has just plucked a sheep from the fold. While he ate, he listened to the harper, who sang a sweet song, and finished his meal as the harper finished his song. Immediately the room broke out in raucous talk, the suitors bragging about their games and boldly breasted bawds who had spread their legs for them on their couches.

Unseen by all, Athene appeared beside Odysseus and whispered to the son of Laertes, "Yes, yes. Now that you have filled your belly it's time to try the suitors. You may get a few scraps from some, but it's good to learn who has a few good streaks left in him and who are nothing but arrogant fools. This is good to know, but it still won't excuse a person from death! Go! Make your rounds like a good beggar should."

And Odysseus rose and hobbled painfully around the room, going from left to right, stretching out his hand like a well-practiced beggar. Some expressed surprise that such a pauper pleaded pitiously before them and placed a bit of bread in his palm, asking each other where such an almsman could come from in rich Ithaca, for by now all were well acquainted with the beggars of Odysseus's homeland. Then Odysseus came to Melanthius who recognized him from the road and rose, saying mockingly, "Suitors of Ithaca's noble queen!" He had to call twice before he could make himself heard above the din. "Hear me! I can tell you a bit about this stranger in our midst. I found him on the road with the swineherd, who was leading him down to our fair town. I don't know who or what he is, but he is a creature of disgust, that's for certain. I wonder what he's doing in our midst?"

376–400 At once Antinous flashed hard on Eumaeus. "Now if this isn't just like our famous breeder of pigs! Well, what have you to say for yourself, pig farmer? There are enough vagabonds around eating your master's food that we don't need any more. Aren't we plagued enough by beggars and rats and other vermin that you should bring yet another to annoy our senses?" He pinched his nose with thumb and forefinger and shook his head. "*Whew!* The stench is enough to put a man off his appetite. Bad enough that these fellows come among us, but it wouldn't hurt if they'd dip themselves in the river a time or two first. *Phaugh!*" Mocking laughter rolled from the suitors as they lolled back to watch Antinous play his game. "I say give the lout a swift kick in the arse and send him on his way."

Eumaeus's eyes glittered angrily, but he swallowed and said, "Not very nobly spoken for such a noble man, Antinous. Or wisely spoken, for that matter," he added under his breath, ignoring the sudden glare from Antinous. He met Antinous's stare fearlessly. "Now who in his right mind would bring in a stranger wandering the countryside unless he were a famous artisan, a worker of fine metals, a harper whose melodious voice would make the rafters sing, or one who could work for the town, repairing the walls and ditches and such? Perhaps he's a prophet or a physician? A carpenter whose skill at woodcarving is yet to be tested? All of these would be welcomed here without question. But a beggar, well, the poor are always among us and who can tell them not to eat when food is available to them? As for you, you leader of these pussle-gutted wastrels, you have been the hardest upon the servants of this house—and me. But I've taken your pissy sneers simply because Penelope, the tender mistress of his hall, and godlike Telemachus are alive—"

"Ah, enough, now!" wise Telemachus said, pressing the arm of Eumaeus hard. "Don't bandy words with Antinous. He uses his tongue as a lash, a goad, to raise the blood in a prudent person." He leaned back in his chair and fixed Antinous with steely eyes. "Antinous," he purred, "I appreciate your looking out after my well-being and all. But don't tell me to order strangers from my own hall. By the gods' graces, that won't do at all. I'm not niggardly, and a hungry man is always welcome at my table. Remember that there but for the grace of the gods go you!" Nervous titters followed his words, then silence as all watched Antinous's face turn red with anger. "Why don't you give him something yourself and earn a bit of favor from the gods? Lord knows that you could use a few good marks next to your name. Go ahead. It's my food, but I don't begrudge you sharing with others. And I know my mother wouldn't be offended either or any of our servants at your—charity." He drew out the last word with great irony. "But," he sighed, "I can see that no such gesture is within you. You'd rather eat everything yourself like a proper pig than to give a single crust away! Quite a belly god you've become!"

A deathlike silence came over the hall, then Antinous, barely able to   *401–426* restrain his anger, clapped his hands mockingly and said, "Well-spoken, Telemachus! I sense a bit of temper behind your words. I'll follow your advice, and if all others treat him here as I do, why, then I'm certain the man will take to his heels and we won't see him again for three months!"

He reached down and seized the footstool upon which his shining feet had rested and brandished it threateningly. The others, however, had heard enough from Telemachus's words and dropped a crust or piece of meat in

Odysseus's bag. He took the bag in his hands and shuffled back toward his place by the threshold. At first it looked as if he would not have to pay for causing Antinous embarrassment, but he paused beside Antinous.

"Ah, my friend. Give me a token for my troubles. You don't seem to be a lowly man among all the Greeks here. Fact is, you look rather kingly, if one were to ask me. Few don't, of course, because many think a man's words are reflected by his appearance, but that is the thought of fools. Many a wise man dresses poorly, for ideas and words are not riches that fill a man's belly. Come now! There's no reason that you shouldn't better the gifts of the others here. I'll sing your praises, wherever my wanderings take me, for a bit of your generosity. If you look carefully upon me you might see a bit of a reflection of yourself too. There was a time when I had a fortune and I shared it well among others and gave to the homeless such as I am now when they came to the door of my rich house. I didn't care about who he was or what he needed. I gave him what I could to help his lot in the world.

"But"—and here he sighed—"Zeus didn't look favorably on me. Don't know what it was I did to make the son of Cronus mad at me, but there was something there. He wrecked my life by sending me off to Egypt as one with a company of picaroons—I should have known better, but hindsight is always the ruler of foresight and wishes don't bring the wheat in from the field or separate the grain from the chaff or—where was I? Oh, yes.

427–455   "Well, we anchored our curved ships in the Nile and I ordered my men to guard them well while I sent lookouts high upon the heights to see the lay of the land. But these greedy rovers ran off to plunder the rich farms they saw and carry away the wives and children. News of what was happening in the countryside ran on the heels of the wind to the city, and by dawn, why, the plain was filled with flashing bronze and chariots and the sound of swords banging against shields. That was when Zeus shot fear among the hearts of my men and they turned and fled. Not one was willing to stand his ground to face that army. Why, there was disgrace on every side, and then that army fell upon us like wolves on a fold. They cut through our forces and slaughtered my men left and right. The survivors they carried off as slaves. As for me," he sighed, "well, they handed me over to a trader who happened to be visiting their shores. Dmetor, son of Iasus, who rules Cyprus by force. I came from there as the beggar you see before you now."[7]

456–480   "Will you listen to this rascal?" Antinous demanded, raising his hand to indicate Odysseus. "Surely we have irritated the gods. Otherwise why would one send this pest to plague our feast with his fish story? Get away from my table! Go on! Stand out there in the middle of the room or you'll find a harsher Egypt or Cyprus here than you ever did there! I have never seen such a pattering pest! These men here are willing to give you food that isn't theirs, but that's easy to do when you don't have a stake in it yourself!"

Wise Odysseus drew back, saying, "Tch. Tch. A pity your manners don't match your good looks. So you wouldn't give a pinch of salt from your table to your servant, eh? Yet you sit at another man's table and won't take a pinch of his bread to give to me even though he gave you permission to do so freely. There's no heart in you, man! Nothing but flint!"

A black look flared from Antinous's eyes as anger came over him. His nostrils widened and he said, "A fancy speech deserves a proper reward! I'll see that you don't leave this hall without a bit for your pains." He grabbed his stool and threw it hard at Odysseus. It struck him on the heavy muscle under the right shoulder, but Odysseus failed to flinch and stood his ground like a rock. He shook his head silently, keeping his bloody thoughts to himself, and made his way back to the threshold. He squatted on his heels there and dropped his bulging bag on the floor in front of him, then looked around slowly at the suitors.

"One more word only, you lordly suitors of an illustrious queen! A blow given to a man trying to take another's cattle or white sheep is to be expected, and there's no dishonor in that. But this hit from Antinous was given only because I was hungry. Yes, I was punished because my wretched belly was empty and forced me to beg for a morsel from him. Very well. Then hear my words: If there are gods and goddesses who watch over beggars and send avenging Furies to aid them, then I pray that Antinous die before his wedding day."

"Enough, stranger," Antinous, the son of Eupeithes, said through thin lips. "Your lip has drawn the blow, not your hunger. Eat what you have or I'll have you dragged through the house by arm or leg until your skin hangs in ribbons from you."

But the rest of the suitors stirred uneasily at his words and someone spoke $_{481-504}$ from the crowd, saying, "You've behaved badly, Antinous. Why would you strike a vagrant like that? He can't help being homeless any more than you can help how you were born. You know guests are under the protection of Zeus and woe be to you if this stranger should turn out to be a god from lofty Olympus. You know they do occasionally disguise themselves and wander around from town to town to see what we mortals are doing and watch how others are treated."

But Antinous ignored him and the rest of the suitors who turned away to talk quietly among themselves. Telemachus held his anger at the blow struck on his father, remembering what wise Odysseus had warned him about earlier in the day. But when good Queen Penelope heard how Antinous had struck the stranger (for such acts spread like wildfire among the servants in all proper homes), she cried out in anger: "May the great god Apollo send an arrow to strike him as he struck that man!"

"Ah, my queen," her housekeeper, Eurynome, said, shaking her head. "If the gods were good and gracious there wouldn't be a man-jack a-one of them alive tomorrow."

"Hm," Penelope said, tapping her fingertips upon her dressing table. "You have a point there. I hate all those blackguards but most especially Antinous who seems like a black wind from Hades's Halls.[8] There was no reason for him to treat that stranger, who came to our hall for a bite to eat, by throwing a stool at him. The rest of the suitors were generous and filled his bag overflowing with tidbits, but Antinous, no."

505–530 While Penelope spoke, Odysseus contented himself by the door, eating his fill of the scraps that had been placed in his bag by the suitors. After thinking for a moment upon her words, Penelope sent for the swineherd, and after he appeared before her, she commanded him, saying, "Go, Eumaeus, and ask the stranger to come before me that I may question him about the rumors he may have heard about Odysseus."

And you, Eumaeus, shook your head, answering, "My lady, if these snot-nosed whippersnappers would cease their yowlings and listen to the man I daresay they could learn a thing or two. But they babble endlessly about nonsense. This man has tales that could charm your heart. I had him as a guest for three days and nights in my hut. He came straight from a ship to me, you know, so I've had time to listen to his tales. Even then, I didn't have enough time to hear his full story. And he held *me* spellbound, as surely as a bard singing a tale of glory. You know how that goes when the story is so good you find yourself in it? Well, that's the way this clever fellow weaves his words. He does claim an old acquaintance with Odysseus—mind you, I'm not saying it's true or no," he cautioned, "but it's there on his lips, nevertheless. He claims to come from Crete, the land of Minos. And from there he came, like a rolling stone gathering no moss, to our own beach after being blown helter-skelter by the foul winds of life. He claims that Odysseus is near home— somewhere around rich Thesprotian country—and on his way with great riches."

531–559 "Then," said thoughtful Penelope, "we should listen to what he has to say. Go and fetch him so that he can tell me his story. Don't bring any of the others. They can sit outside or in the hall below drinking themselves senseless with the wine. They seem carefree enough, and why not? They aren't home eating and drinking their own stores but content themselves by gorging themselves here at my expense. They slaughter our cattle and sheep and pigs and guzzle our good dark wine without giving a thought to how much of our rich stores they are squandering. Ah, if only Odysseus would return to purge his house of this blight! He and his son would make short work of those down below, I tell you!"

As she finished, a loud sneeze came from the hall below—*AHHHH-HHH-ker-CHAWWWWWW!*—startling Penelope, who quickly laughed as it echoed through the halls. She looked up at Eumaeus, smiling. "Well, then. Why do you dawdle so? Go and fetch the stranger. As you heard, Telemachus's thunderous sneeze has blessed my request. May death come as sudden upon the suitors. One more thing," she added as Eumaeus turned to go. He stopped and looked back at her. "If I see this man is a truth-teller, then I will promise him a new warm cloak and tunic. You might make mention of this to him."

Eumaeus nodded and left, making his way back to the hall where he made his way to the beggar by the door and said, "Old man, wise Penelope, the mother of good Telemachus, wants a word with you. Now, she has suffered much and wants more news about her husband. Be good to her but be truthful. If she senses the truth behind your words she'll give you a tunic and a good warm cloak to help you through our frosty nights. And that you need more than anything else at this point. You've filled your stomach here, and you can fill it again in town where someone may give you food. More so if you're decently clad, I should think. So let your words be true to her."

"Eumaeus," the suffering Odysseus said, "that would be easily done, for 560–586 the two of us have suffered roughly the same fate. I only wish I could go at once to her but—" he paused to stare around him at the suitors. "I fear this hot-tempered lot are a bit mercurial for me to take such a liberty. To appear before the queen now would draw their anger down upon me. Why, just a short time ago that fellow there"—he pointed at Antinous—"dealt me a painful blow without warning and I have done nothing to him. So who would lift a hand, a finger, to help me? Telemachus? Perhaps. But anyone else? I don't think so. So please ask the queen to be patient until sundown and these fellows are a bit more into their cups and then she can question me all she wants about her husband's homecoming. Ask her, though, if she'll have a stool placed by the fire for me. These rags"—he glanced down ruefully—"are poor cover against the night's cold hours, as you so aptly point out."

Obediently the swineherd returned to Penelope to tell her what Odysseus had said. As soon as he crossed the threshold to her room, Penelope saw he was alone and said, "What's this? You haven't brought him? Why, old friend? Is he a bit shy? I can't believe that a beggar would also be a hangdog! How does such a person get by?"

"He has his reasons, my queen," the blunt-spoken swineherd said. "And to my way of thinking they're good ones. There's no reason to tempt a bit of tomfoolery from those drunken sots downstairs by letting them see him come up here to your rooms when many of them haven't made the trip. He asks only that you wait until sundown and then he will come to you. That would be better for you too because the two of you can sit and have your bit of talk in private without the ears of others horning in upon your business."

"I can see that man is no fool," the good Penelope replied. "There's a strong head upon those aged shoulders, I'm thinking. In all the world I don't think there's a more brutal or evil gathering than that lot downstairs. Very well. We'll wait on the beggar's pleasure."[9]

587–606 Eumaeus nodded and returned to the hall, making his way to the table of Telemachus. He glanced around to make certain that they weren't overheard, then lowered his head and whispered to the strong youth, "My prince, I must return to look after the pigs and farm. After all, that's what's keeping us from poverty now. You'll have to keep a good watch on everything here. Watch your back! There's none here that you can trust. These Greeks harbor evil thoughts, and I don't trust a one of them to have a true word on his lips! Beware the one who pretends to be your friend and trust no one who seems to offer you a gift! And may Zeus destroy them before they destroy us!"

"Well-spoken, uncle," Telemachus said. "Eat, then return to the farm and set everything right. But come back by dawn and bring a few pigs for slaughtering. It would be good to have you at my back again. Meanwhile, I'll keep close eye on the happenings here—the good gods willing."

And the swineherd sat again at the polished table and ate his fill. Then he rose and left the hall. Behind him, he heard the sounds of singing and dancing and carousing as he climbed the rocky path in darkness to his farm.

Here ends the Seventeenth Book of Homer's Odyssey.

THE EIGHTEENTH BOOK

The Return of Odysseus

❖ ❖ ❖ ❖ ❖ ❖ ❖ ❖ ❖ ❖

Odysseus fights with the blubbering bully, Irus
And admonishes the suitor Amphinomus.
From the suitors Penelope receives
Those gifts meant to deceive.

❖ ❖ ❖ ❖ ❖ ❖ ❖ ❖ ❖ ❖

*A*nd now a common tramp known to everyone came   *1–27*
To Ithaca. A true scavenger, he was notorious for his greed,
One who always left the table swag-bellied after feeding
And drinking the day to night. His mother had named him
Arnaeus, but all others had nicknamed him Irus,¹ for he would
Run any errand that didn't tire him much. But that errand
Had to be finished before supper. He was a big and bulky man,
A bully, which is often the case with men who see the weakness
Of others as the source of their fun. When he saw Odysseus
In his disguise, he puffed his suety cheeks, growling at him:

"So, old man, you'd block the way of your betters, eh? This is my area for begging, fellow. Clear out or else get hauled out by the ankles. Look around at your betters. There won't be any help from them. Can't you see them tipping me the wink to haul you away and be done with you? Move your arse, now, or you and I will come to quick blows!"

Odysseus gave him a black look, eyeing his girth carefully and noticing the blubber hanging from his bulk. "What's the matter with you?" he asked. "I'm not troubling you here. This doorway is big enough for both of us and the house is rich enough to keep the two of us from starving. I won't begrudge you whatever you can con from the others. So why should you mind what others give to me? You're a tramp like me, and both of us depend upon the graciousness of whatever gods look over beggars for whatever we can get. Now, mind your manners and think twice before you push your luck any further. Rouse me again, and as old as I am, why, I'll douse your lips and nose and crack a rib or two for your troubles. My own life would be a bit more peaceable for all of that for I wouldn't have to put up with your flapping lips any more in the house of Laertes's son."

"Well, I'll be damned!" Irus the beggar swore. He glanced around at the others grinning at the parley by the door and, taking heart, said, "Would you listen to how this clucking, oven-tending hag speaks! Why, you'd think he was a pig in his own sty, now, wouldn't you? Take care, old man, or I'll put both my fists in your chops and smash what few teeth are left in your gums out onto the ground like a sow caught in the turnips![2] So, it's fisticuffs you want, eh? Well, tuck up your rags, then, and show these good gentlemen how handy you are with your fists! A lot of frost hangs in your beard, you old fart! Do you think you can fare well against a younger man?"[3]

28-53   They held their rough talk on the doorsill of wide, smooth ash while the suitors broke into waves of laughter. "Look here," Antinous crowed. "What a farce the gods have provided us for a bit of entertainment tonight! Irus and the stranger challenging each other to a fight! Well, let's see what they can do, eh? Should provide a bit of sport for us!"

And they all laughed again and crowded around the pair, egging Irus on against the ragged beggar who stood eyeing him carefully. Antinous said, "Well, now, listen carefully, you two! There's a goat's paunch cooking on the fire with good blood pudding. A fine fare for the man who wins! We had planned that for our own taste tonight, but hang it! I'll give it to the one who puts the other down for the count! Now, what say you? Whoever proves the better man can take the lion's share of the pudding and join us regularly at evening supper. And we'll sweeten the bargain by throwing out any other tramp who comes to the doorway."

The other suitors clamored their agreement, and Odysseus pulled his hand through his beard and said thoughtfully, "Well, I can see that the odds are stacking against me already." He sighed heavily and shrugged his shoulders. "I don't see how an old man like me can stand against a young stump like this. I suppose I'm in for a thrashing, but I'm willing to take the blows for the chance to keep my empty belly filled. I can't be any the worse off than I am now. And as the gods say, help yourself and we'll help you. Who knows what might happen? But," he continued, "for the sake of a fair shake, I ask your oath that none of you will step forward to give this lout a helping hand. And if you agree to this, why, then I'm game for him!"

54-79   They all laughed and hooted and shouted their promise to the rafters, and after the oath had been taken by all, the great Telemachus pronounced his solemn vow, saying, "Well, old man, if you have the nerve to go through with this, you won't have to worry about one of these putting in his hand against you. If he does, he'll have to face all the rest. I am the host here, and Antinous and Eurymachus will hold with me on this."[4]

All of the suitors shouted again their agreement and made a rough circle around the beggars. Odysseus shrugged and leaned his stick against the jamb and pulled up his rags to tuck them in the twine serving as a belt. The laughter chilled somewhat as they all caught sight of his massive thighs, and when he lowered the rags from his shoulders, they all fell silent at the sight of the ropy muscles along his chest and his brawny biceps. Athene stood silently beside him, lending him power and bulk, and the suitors backed away, watching with narrowed eyes, muttering among themselves, "This doesn't bode well for Irus—Aye, I think he'll be un-Irused—Look at those shoulders! Who'd think the old man would have a set like that upon him!—Well, it's trouble Irus was looking for and it's trouble he found, I'm thinking!"

And Irus felt a thread of fear snake its way down to his huge belly as he heard the mutterings and natterings from among the suitors. For a moment, his flesh quivered and he took a half step back, but the servants quickly came up behind him and pulled up his clothes, tucking them in the rope wrapped around his girth and pushed him to the front. His thick lips blubbered and Antinous spoke harshly.

"You sack of guts! Better you were never born if you stand there shaking before a man as old as this one! Why, you've got years and weight on him, man! He's an old man, broken by all the hardships he's faced in his long life! Now, get in there and beat him to a frazzle, or by the gods I'll have you hauled away in a black ship and taken to the mainland where King Echetus[5] skins all who come his way like a butcher a cow's hide. He'll cut off your nose and your ears and pull your pizzle and pouch out by the roots and feed them raw to his hunting hounds." *80–108*

When he heard Antinous's words, great Irus trembled more. But those behind him continued to push his fat bulk forward until at last he found himself in the ring opposite great Odysseus. He raised his fists and squared away, staring at the old man in front of him. Odysseus eyed him calmly and debated whether to drop him like a poleaxed heifer to the floor with one blow or simply to tap him soundly enough to put him asleep. He decided on the latter to keep the Greeks from suspecting something was afoot. He put his hands up, and when Irus made a ponderous swing at his right shoulder, Odysseus stepped in with a clubbing right below Irus's ear that crossed the great ox's eyes and smashed the bones. Blood gushed a crimson flood from his mouth and the fat man swayed, groaned, then toppled to fall with a crash to the floor that rattled the cups on the tables. He groveled and bleated like a sheep, thrashing with his hands and legs, trying to get away.

The noble suitors whooped with laughter and swung their arms, imitating Odysseus's blow. Odysseus bent and seized Irus by his ankle and dragged him over the threshold and out into the courtyard and pulled him across the courtyard, his head bouncing like a wicker ball against the stones. He dropped him next to the wall and propped his begging stick in his hand and said, "Here, now! Here's a post for you to guard and a stick to keep away the hogs and dogs. I advise you to forget your swaggering among the rest of the beggars who tramp up to the door. The next man to whack your jaw might not be as easy on you."

109–136

He slung the strap of his worn swag over his shoulder and made his way back to the threshold where he once again took his seat. The laughing suitors came back in, some pausing to drop a coin or two upon him saying, "May Zeus and all the other Immortals fill your bag and grant you your deepest wish for this night's sport![6]—Good riddance to that guzzling gasbag! We'll pack him away to the mainland soon enough!—Aye, Echetus the Skinner will soon have his way with him."

Odysseys took grim cheer at their words. Antinous brought him a large goat paunch stuffed with blood and fat and onions and spices. Amphinomus selected two large loaves from a basket of bread and put them down beside him. He poured a golden cup full of rich, dark wine and raised it, saying, "Although your sorrows hang heavily upon your shoulders now, may your days promise brighter ahead. To your health, my ancient friend!" And he drank deeply, smacking his lips over the wine.

"Ah, Amphinomus," Odysseus said, "you seem a sensible lad—much like your good father Nisus of Dulichium"[7]—he caught himself and continued smoothly—"whose reputation as a good and honest and rich man has come to my ears during my wanderings. So you are his son. Well, you seem to be wise enough, so here's a bit of advice to you: No creature is as frail and fragile as man. As long as the gods smile graciously upon him, he is happy and doesn't give a thought to chance misfortune.

137–164

"Yet that too can fall upon him when he leasts expects it, and no matter how brave he is or how strong his knees are at standing against it, when the blessed gods decide his lot is cast, it's cast! The only thing he can do is to endure and not rant and rail at being one of fortune's minions! Whatever we see ourselves as can change at the whim of the gods. Zeus gives us a life day by day and what we make of it is only a whisper in the wind. I too was once blessed by the gods' kiss, but I became a looter and raider and stained my hand with lawlessness. I trusted that my father and brothers would stand by me, but no man can trust any other man to be with him forever through thick and thin. Now, what I see happening here is a bunch of young men set on a disgraceful path, wasting riches and abusing the hospitality of the wife of a strong man who is not far from hearth and home. So I say that I hope some god takes pity on you and leads you away from here and back to your own home so that you will not fall to the husband's anger when he returns. And that anger will be great, I assure you. I don't think any who stay beneath this roof to woo his wife will come out of this without bloodstains."

Having said this, Odysseus took the honeyed wine, poured a large draught, and drank deeply. Then he thrust the cup back into the young man's hands. Amphinomus looked at him strangely for a long moment, a black cloud descending over his gaiety, then he turned and made his way back to his place at the table. But Odysseus's words were not enough to save him from his fate as he too had been numbered by gray-eyed Athene for the hand of Telemachus whose lance would pierce the breast of Amphinomus who took his seat now at the table.

At this moment, Athene slipped a thought through the shell-like ears of wise Penelope to make an appearance among the suitors and try and convince them to honor her wishes, her house, and leave. But this was all a ploy by the great goddess who meant to rile the blood of the suitors again with Penelope's beauty.

The queen laughed shakily and said, "Eurynome, I have a sudden desire to go to the suitors—as much as I hate them—and speak with my son and warn him not to stay too long in their company. A man is known by the company he keeps, and I would hate him to take on any of their evil ways." _{165–191}

"This is a good idea, child," Eurynome said. "You should do just such a thing. But first, wash yourself and pinch your cheeks a bit to bring a healthy blush to them—you look so pale!—and bathe your eyes to take the redness of your weeping away. Always crying and sighing! I'd think you had enough of that by now. Your son's full-grown and it's always been your fondest prayer that you see him grown and with a beard. Well, it isn't much of a one, but there it is about his chin now!"

"I know you love me, Eurynome, and you mean only what you think is best for me, but don't try and make me seem beautiful by washing myself and anointing myself and blushing my cheeks. Since the day that my lord left in his hollow ship the gods have taken away all beauty that I once had. Now go and bring Autonoe and Hippodameia to me. I'll not face that bunch of roustabouts alone; it wouldn't be seemly."[8]

The old woman left to find the handmaidens that her mistress had requested. Bright-eyed Athene took the opportunity to send sweet sleep upon her eyes and Penelope stretched out on her couch and within moments slept quietly. While she slept, Athene busied herself preparing Penelope with the immortal gifts of the gods to make the Greeks marvel at her great beauty.

192–222   First she bathed her cheeks with the balm of Aphrodite—that which the great goddess uses when she dances the seductive dance of the Graces—which made her seem taller and well figured, her skin like carved and polished ivory. And then Athene disappeared as the handmaidens, bare-armed and chattering, came in and awoke the queen from her sweet sleep. She yawned and rubbed the palms of her hands against her cheeks, saying, "My! What a wonderful nap I had, free of worries! If only lovely Artemis would give me as gentle a death as this little one and save me from spending the rest of my days languishing in agony for my dear husband, the finest in all Greece!"

She rose and left her room still glowing from the goddess's presence and made her way downstairs. Her two handmaidens trailed her, still talking excitedly about seeing the suitors in the hall. As she neared the hall, Penelope pulled a fold of her mantle over her face, veiling it, took a deep breath, then stepped around a pillar and stood in full view of the boistering blackguards.

For a moment no one noticed her, then suddenly the noise stopped in the room as quickly as a sharp knife cuts a lanyard, and the suitors turned to stare at her, their knees suddenly turning to water. Desire made their hearts faint and not a manjack there didn't make a hundred promises to his favorite god if the god would only help him bed her. The fire fanned her fine form and seemed to grow bright in the room. She was modestly attired but such was the gift of the gray-eyed goddess that she appeared naked, and suddenly the room thickened with lust. The great queen noticed the sudden tension in the room but ignored the suitors and turned calmly to her son and said, "Telemachus, what is the matter with you? You are of age now, and a foreigner would know you for royalty by one look at you. But have you no more common sense than to keep company with this lot?

223–254   "And how dare you allow a stranger to be so abused in our house? I heard about the boxing match. For shame! You should not have allowed that to take place. Guests are not to be treated so shabbily. What if our guest had suffered harm from what I'm sure you thought to be a prank? You would have been blamed and disgraced."

Telemachus looked levelly at her and said, "I don't resent your anger in this matter, Mother. Yes, I was wrong to allow that to happen. I can only say that I'm still learning what is right and wrong. But"—he paused to indicate the others—"I cannot always behave in a sensible fashion when I must take into account these who surround me. There's no one here to back me against these loutish loafers. I can tell you, however, that this fight did not go as the suitors intended; the stranger was far stronger than Irus and left him wobble-legged as a drunk sprawled by the outer gate. Oh, if only father Zeus, Athene, and Apollo would come down and help, I would love to leave these men beaten, their heads lolling like lushes on their shoulders and their limbs as weak as an empty wineskin—pig drunk and broken men!"

As they spoke quietly, the suitors grew bolder, and now Eurymachus stepped forward, brushing past Telemachus to purr, "Ah, Penelope, beautiful daughter of Icarius, if all the Greeks in Ionian Argos could only feast their eyes upon you, your great hall would be filled to bulging with scores more suitors for your delicate hand. There are no other women to match you in loveliness of face and, uh, form"—he tore his eyes from her breast and added hastily—"and wisdom."

Penelope gave him a tolerant smile and said, "Finely spoken, Eurymachus, but the gods robbed me of beauty and grace and form when Odysseus sailed away with the ships bound for Ilium.

"Now if he were to return, why, then my good name would be even more 255–284 graced, my fame renowned. But," she sighed, "grief has fallen heavily upon me—years of pain. Perhaps—is it possible?—I could forget then the day that he left this island, taking my right hand and wrist in his and saying, 'My wife, not all the Greeks will return from Troy. They say the Trojans are equal fighters with good lances and fine bowmen and horsemen and charioteers—those can turn the battle tide at any given moment. I cannot promise that I will return home to Ithaca or' "—her voice caught for a moment— " 'fall upon Trojan soil. That is in the hands of the gods, and who knows their fickle ways and will? You must attend to our house and lands in my absence. My father and mother will help the best that they can in my absence. But when you see a beard on our son's cheek' "—the eyes of the suitors clicked like agates toward Telemachus—" 'then you may marry whom you will and leave this house.' "

She took a deep breath and stared around the room. "What he said has come true. The night approaches when I must make a bitter choice and accept a marriage I do not want. And that will be the end of my happiness, thanks to Zeus who will have destroyed my life.

"But until that choice is made, I am still mistress here!" She squared her shoulders and stared loathingly at all. "I do not understand this new way of courting, these new manners that seem to have replaced the traditional way of courting a rich man's daughter who comes from a good family. Such suitors would not plant themselves in the house of the lady and feast on her cattle and sheep and drink her wine by the tun! No! They would have brought their own cattle and sheep and prepared banquets for the lady's friends and given her rich gifts. None would have dared to live at her expense. And what sort of man is he who would say that he was being supported by a woman?"

Odysseus stuffed the end of his ragged tunic in his mouth to keep from laughing aloud at her words, noting with satisfaction how she made it impossible for the suitors not to give her rich gifts with her bewitching words, even though her heart had set its trek on a different road.

285–311   The suitors looked sheepishly at each other until Antinous, the son of Eupeithes, answered her. "Well-spoken, deep-minded daughter of Icarius. And there is no reason for you to turn away any gift that any here is willing to give you. But as for leaving this house"—he shook his head—"no, I think not. All of us will stay here until you agree to marry the best man among us."

The others agreed, and a sudden squalor erupted among them as each one called for his squire and sent him running to fetch a gift for the lovely Penelope. Antinous arrogantly called his squire to him and whispered in his ear. He scampered off only to appear shortly with a long robe, finely embroidered and fastened with twelve golden brooches, their pins neatly fitted into a sheath. The squire of Eurymachus brought a long golden chain cunningly worked around amber. Eurydamas's squire brought back a pair of earrings with three pips in pomegranate clusters. Polyctor's son Peisander's squire appeared with a necklace of fair jewels, and so it went with each of the squires there presenting Penelope with the choicest of his treasures. Penelope watched their offerings pile high before her as offerings to a goddess, then she turned and slowly mounted the steps to her room, her handmaidens coming behind her, well laden with the suitors' offerings, their eyes wide at the riches they carried.

And now the suitors turned to singing and dancing, the music from the harp a haunting sound in the night. Three torch fires were placed high in sconces on the wall and as the suitors danced, strange shadows formed on the wall, fluid and flickering. Braziers were heaped with fresh-split kindling and the room grew heady with the scent of resin from pine knots that attending maids added to the fire. That's when long-suffering Odysseus finally spoke.

312–340   "You housemaids of Odysseus would be better off to go to where your mistress sits spinning wool and charm her with your chatter while you card the wool with your fingers. I'll sit here and feed the flames for these men as long as they want to drink and dance 'til dawn. I'm not easily tired."

The women giggled at his words and some eyed him boldly, remembering suddenly his thick thighs and brawny chest when his rags had been tucked up and down in readiness for his bout. Their cheeks burned and lights danced in their eyes, but pretty-cheeked Melantho,⁹ who had been Penelope's favorite as a child and grew up spoiled and petulant, laughed contemptuously at him, for despite all that her mistress had done for her—children's tops and spools, fine clothes and perfumes—she felt nothing for Penelope. Lately she had been rutting like a rabbit with Eurymachus in the grape arbor, behind columns and in sheltered nooks and crannies of the palace. And now she sniffed and looked haughtily at Odysseus.

"Why, you punch-drunk old jack-pudding! Are you still here? You must be puddle-brained if you haven't crept off to the smithy to bed down there or a doss-house where they aren't particular about who brings crabs and ticks in with them. Instead you babble here pretending to be an equal with your betters. You may have thumped the beggar Irus, but there are others here who will rattle your brains with hefty fists for your troubles and kick you arse over pate out the gate."

"Why, you Cyprian hussy!" quick-witted Odysseus said blackly. "Mind that cullion-kissing lip of yours or I'll fetch Telemachus and watch him hack off your bubbies and butt!"

The women drew a sharp breath at his words and scuttled sideways like crabs away from him, their knees rattling like rat bones with fear, for they had no doubt he meant his words. Odysseus watched them scurry away into the darkness, then took his place by the burning braziers and slowly fed them pine knots to keep the light flickering in the great hall. But his thoughts were not on his work as he busily schemed, racking his brain and plotting plans that would soon be fulfilled.

Athene, meanwhile, simmered angrily at the catcalls and caustic words flung at Odysseus and opened his ears that he would hear everything so the words would sear his heart and feed his angers as he fed the flames. Eurymachus wiped the sweat off his brow and glanced over at Odysseus standing patiently by the cressets and said, "My friends! Something just occurred to me." The others paused in their merrymaking for Eurymachus had devised grand pranks in the past. "This man is a godsend to this grand place. Why, his noggin gleams like a polished knob. Not a single hair curls from that shining pate!"

Laughter broke out and Eurymachus strutted forward to stand before Odysseus. "So how would you like to work for me, stranger? Eh? I have some stones to be set in walls and some timber that needs cutting and trimming on a farm on the other side of Ithaca. You would eat daily and well and

341–369

I'd give you a set of clothes and sturdy sandals for your feet. But"—he turned and walked away, gesturing to his fellows—"on second thought, I can see that you'd not callus your mitts as you'd find it easier to fill your greedy gut grubbing and groveling around the town!"

The suitors bent over in laughter, and quick-witted Odysseus waited until the laughter and catcalls quieted, then said, "It might be interesting, Eurymachus, for the two of us to labor in the fields when spring comes and there is hay to lay by. Why, I would play that game with you, a curved scythe in my hand, another in yours, and a great field of fresh grass to winnow.

370–398   "Or maybe we could team sleek-hided oxen to a plow and see who could plow the straightest furrow the longest? Or maybe you'd prefer a contest of arms? Perhaps all-seeing Zeus can find a war someplace and give me a shield and a couple of spears and a bronze-plated pate cap to snug my temples. You'd find me in the front ranks, then, and there'd be no more quips about my belly. But no, that wouldn't suit you, would it, you blustering bullyboy? A blatherskite like you has no belly for the sound and fury of men. No, you'd rather sit with a wineskin and taunt those few who seem undistinguished to your dull wit. If Odysseus returned now, you'd soon find that wide doorway too narrow for your fat buttocks to bounce through."

Anger boiled over in Eurymachus, and his piggish eyes turned red as his cheeks burned brightly. He drew himself up like a puffed frog and said, "You slippery pig mucker, I'll scramble your brains for that! How dare you flap your insolent tongue in this company! Has wine muddled your wits? Maybe the beating you gave Irus makes you think you are better than the whoreson you are?" He spied and seized a stool and waved it threateningly, but Odysseus ducked behind the knees of Amphinomus of Dulichium as Eurymachus flung it.[10] The stool struck the wine steward on the right hand, knocking the jug to the floor where it broke in pieces, the dark red wine puddling across the floor. The man fell backward in the dust, crying and groaning.

399–426   The shadowy hall broke into a great clamor as the suitors yelled curses at Odysseus. "What's this?" one bawled loudly. "Better for this braggart to have come to dust before he came to us! Then we'd have some peace among us instead of this bedlam and bickering over beggars. 'Tis enough to put a man off his feed, thanks to his mischief-making!"

"Silence!" great Telemachus roared. His voice cut harshly through the din, and they all paused to stare wonderingly at the youth who dared to speak so commandingly. "What's rattled your brains? I think you've gorged too much meat and swilled too much wine. Some god has his spurs in your sides, that's for certain! Now the feast is over and it was a good feast as feasts go. I suggest you trundle off to bed with your bawds, but"—he spread his hands— "I'm not pushing you out, you understand. Just a kindly suggestion."

They bit their lips and stared through wine-soaked eyes at the youth who suddenly seemed to have the nerve to address them so. At last, Amphinomus, the son of noble Nisus, grandson of Aretias, spoke. "There's truth to his words, and no carping criticism of this stranger needs to be said further. Enough, I say. Leave well enough alone and let's spill a libation for offerings to the gods and make our way to home and bed. We'll leave this visitor in Telemachus's hall where he can sit by the ashes beneath Odysseus's roof. After all, it is his house to which the stranger has come."

All agreed with his words, and Mulius, one of Amphinomus's squires, 427-429 hastened to mix a bowl of rich wine and serve them. They sprinkled a few drops to the gods and drank deep the mellow wine and stumbled out the door into the night for their homes.

Here ends the Eighteenth Book of Homer's Odyssey.

THE NINETEENTH BOOK
The Discovery of the Nurse

✧ ✧ ✧ ✧ ✧ ✧ ✧ ✧ ✧ ✧ ✧

Telemachus removes the weapons from the great hall,
While the old nurse discovers the secret and all.

✧ ✧ ✧ ✧ ✧ ✧ ✧ ✧ ✧ ✧ ✧

And so the great Odysseus studied the coals of the fire and   *1–27*
Wished for aid from Athene. He tried to dream himself into
The swirling heat as if he could once again visit with the blind
Seer who had warned him against what he would find
Upon his return home. He sighed, feeling the quiet of
The great hall bearing down hard upon his shoulders.
He wished the suitors buried, but the ways and means
Of sending them down that dark road to Hades escaped him.
Telemachus cleared his throat and his father looked up and
Bade the son to draw near. He smiled gently at his son as he said:

"Telemachus, all the arms, weapons and spears, must be put out of sight.
The suitors, I'm certain, will notice their absence—all it takes is one—and
you'll have to come up with some plausible excuse such as, 'I stored them
away from the smoke. They have become fouled with soot and grime since
Odysseus left for Troy and I thought it best to put them away until I have
the time to clean them. Besides, since you all were so in your cups last night,
I thought it better to keep the weapons from being so easy to hand. A force
exists in iron that draws a man to it and changes him from gentleman to
savage."

Telemachus nodded and summoned Eurycleia to him and said, "Nurse, I
want you to shut the women in their rooms while I place my father's glorious
arms back in the inner rooms. They have become fouled with smoke and

grime since he left and I think it best if we get them out of sight and where they cannot be destroyed by the fire."

"A good idea," his good nurse said. Then she shook her head. "I wish, however, that you would care equally for everything in the house and not just the arms of your father. You're old enough to start taking an interest in other things than galavanting around the world like your hapless father. But tell me, who'll light the way for you while you carry them?"

Telemachus shrugged and gestured carelessly toward his father. "I'll have this stranger carry the torch. We've fed him well and although he journeyed far to reach our house there's nothing to keep him from a bit of work to earn his keep."

28-56   The nurse eyed Odysseus, then turned and locked all the doors leading away from the great hall. Telemachus and his father sprang to work and gathered massive shields, helmets, and sharp lances. Pallas Athene went in front of them, carrying high a golden lamp that beamed light into every dusty corner they passed. Telemachus exclaimed, "Father! Look! Some god has certainly come to help us. The high pine ceiling beams, the polished wall and massive pillars reflect a red flame."

"Sh," Odysseus said. "The walls also have ears. Keep your thoughts to yourself and don't ask questions, for questions challenge the gods and it's best that some things be accepted for what they are.[1] The gods work this way. They live above the stars and shine through all darkness. Now go to bed and leave me here to see what your mother and her maids think. I'm certain your mother will want to know everything. And maybe I'll take a bit of time to prick the maids a little more as well. They could stand to come down a peg or two, I think."

Telemachus went across the hall and courtyard to the tower room where he always slept and settled down to wait for divine Dawn to touch his room with tender fingers. Odysseus took a deep breath and slumped down once again before the fire in the great hall, plotting the destruction of the suitors with Athene's help.

57-87   Shortly Penelope came down from her chamber. She glowed like Artemis or golden Aphrodite, and her handmaidens hastened to set a chair close by the fire for her. The chair was heavily inlaid with old ivory and silver and showed the cunning work of the great Icmalius whose work was highly sought by the nobles. He had carefully built a footstool that could be folded out from the frame, and over this the ladies laid a soft fleece for Penelope's feet. While Penelope settled herself, the handmaidens and servants materialized and began busily to clear away the remains of the feast, mopping up spilled wine, sweeping the floor with brooms made of rushes, stacking the greasy platters the arrogant men had gorged themselves from. Others raked the ashes and cinders from the braziers and cressets onto the floor and swept the ashes across the floor to scrub it clean while still others carefully laid fresh wood for new fires for light and warmth.

Melantho saw him sitting by the fire and, remembering his earlier words to her, said savagely, "Still here, you worthless rascal! I suppose you'll plague us throughout the night demanding this and demanding that as if you were a welcome guest in this house. Why don't you stop poking your nose in the house corners? I know about men like you—always sneaking around, ogling the women like a lecher, trying to catch them at their baths. Be gone, and be grateful for the meal you've grubbed, or we'll put a torch to your backside and drive you from this house!"

Odysseus, the man of masquerades, whirled upon her, a black thunder-cloud descending over his noble brow, and said, "What's biting your backside, woman? Why do you hate me so? Is it because I am dirty and wear ragged clothing that hasn't seen a wash in a while? Is it because I am a beggar? The gods don't smile equally upon everyone, you know. That's the fate of vagabonds and beggars and other homeless. I once lived in a house as rich as this, and in my house all were welcome. I treated wanderers as I treated the wealthy. No one could count my slaves and I had all the blessings of the gods. But Zeus took care of that by sending me out as a beggar. I'd suggest that you put a lock on your lip and learn to hold your lickerish tongue or you may find you no longer hold your fine position over all the other maids in this house. Your mistress may send you away, or Odysseus may return. Don't laugh, woman! There's still that possibility, and it is a foolish person indeed who tempts the gods suchly. Don't forget that Odysseus has a son too who, by Apollo's good graces, will not tolerate such behavior in this house."

Penelope heard Odysseus's rebuke and whirled upon the maid, saying, ^{88–116} "Arrogant slut! Yes, don't give me that look! I know of your hanky-panky, your indiscretions in the nooks of the house. You'll be properly rewarded for that, I assure you! You heard me say that I wished to visit with this man here to see what he had heard about my husband. You had no right to use those words on him." She turned to Eurynome, her eyes glittering with anger. "Bring a chair with a pad on it for this man to sit on so we may visit in comfort. There is much I want to ask him."

Eurynome scurried away before she drew a tongue-lashing from the queen since Penelope was obviously in the mood to flay the flesh from the backs of lazy servants with her serpent tongue. She returned with a well-polished chair and padded it quickly with a fold of fleece. Odysseus sat and

Penelope said, "Well, stranger, I must ask you first who you are and where do you come from?"

"My lady,"[2] Odysseus said, evading the question for the moment, "no mortal women on this rich earth could fault or flaw you. Your fame and patient waiting have reached to the heavens as certainly as would the good name of a righteous king ruling a mighty country. Such a king is well rewarded by the gods who allow the dark soil of his land to yield rich crops of wheat and barley and the trees to bow their boughs, heavy with fruit, to the picker. His flocks are always fertile and the seas around his land heavy with fish. Prosperity graces his people because of his good government.

117–148   "So I say that now we are together, ask me what is in your heart, not about my ancestry or my country. That tale tires my heart and to recall the past causes me great sorrow. My sobbing and wailing in this house will suit no purpose and might cause you or your servant to lose patience with me and think that I am little better than those who have left your house and have befuddled my mind with good wine that has made me maudlin."

Penelope sighed and said, "Stranger—and I've said this often—my face and form have flown on the wind. When the Greeks left for Troy and took Odysseus with them, I began to wither with waiting. But if he returned and once again began to care for me, well, perhaps then my fame would grow and become widespread. But now I grieve for the sorrows the gods have heaped upon me. I am a most miserable one for all of the chieftains of dusty Dulichium, Samos, woody Zacynthus—yes, even here in my own country there are many who force their unwelcome selves upon my house. So if it seems that I do not trust you, do not take it personally. I have learned to become suspicious of all strangers who come to my door willing to trade news of Odysseus for a bite to eat and then stay. So I have become a recluse and neglect my duties as a hostess and ignore messengers. I spend my days thinking about Odysseus while my suitors press me to name a wedding day. They have forced me to become a trickster and weave schemes to deceive them. At first, I set up a great loom in my room and began weaving a web of long and fine threads. I said, 'Young men, now that my lord is dead'—I have had to pretend this, you see—'I cannot marry until I have finished weaving this shroud for the great Laertes. I would not want to be accused of being hard-hearted by not having prepared a good covering for him when Death calls him to its dark doors. That would be scandalous among my country-women here.'

149–176   "And they agreed. So by day I wove and at night I unraveled a bit by torchlight to slow the work down. And when they asked impatiently why it was taking me so long, I said that I had to pause frequently when tears filled my eyes for my work was doubly sad for both Laertes and his son. This lasted three years. When the fourth slipped into seasons, some of the shameless bitches who served me betrayed my plot and my suitors caught me as I was unraveling my cloth."

She sighed and tears sprang to her eyes, glinting like rare jewels in the firelight. "Well, the cloth is finished now, and I must choose from among them. Even my parents will not help me, and my son despairs at the drain upon his wealth. But"—she wiped her eyes and smiled—"that is enough of my sorrows and woes. Tell me about your land and family for I can sense that you were not born of stone or trees or sprang from the ground like the old fables say."

The man of masquerades shook his head, saying, "Cherished wife of Laertes's son, Odysseus, why do you keep nagging me with questions about my ancestry? I told you that telling this tale would only make my sorrows heavier. But nevertheless, since you have asked again, I will tell you.

"Far out in the wine-dark sea there is a land called Crete. It's a lovely island, richly wooded and peopled. Ninety cities lie within its seagirt boundaries and the people speak many different languages.

"Some Greeks live there: Cretans, who are proud of their native ways— *177–204* wealthy men, those; Cydonians; three clans of Dorians; and lastly the noble Pelasgians. But the greatest of those cities is Cnossus, once ruled by mighty Minos who personally spoke every nine years with the great Zeus. He fathered my father, the great Deucalion who sired me and my brother, Idomeneus. After Idomeneus went off adventuring to Troy with his great hawk-beaked ships, it fell to me, Aethon, to host Odysseus and exchange gifts with him when he came to our shores. It seems a gale had blown him far off course at Cape Malea when he was on his way to the topless towered city. He managed to avoid the tempest's path and dropped anchor in the harbor at Amnisus, where Eileithyia's[3] cavern stands, a most difficult harbor to make.

"He came to town and I led him to my house and offered him every care and kindness that I could. I gave his crew barley meal and dark wine and a couple of bulls to sacrifice to the gods. They stayed with me for twelve days while Boreas blew a gale around the island. On the thirteenth day, the wind stopped and they put out to sea."

He lied so convincingly that great tears welled and flowed down Pene- *205–237* lope's fair cheeks like runnels from snowcapped mountains when the West Wind melts them and the East Wind thaws them. But although Odysseus felt his heart ache at her sorrow, his eyes, as hard as horn, stayed dry beneath their lids. After Penelope managed to bring herself under control, she wiped her eyes and said, "Well said, stranger. But now let us see to the truth behind your words, shall we? You claim that you entertained my husband. Very well. Describe his clothes, if you will, and how he looked and the men who were with him."

"My lady," Odysseus said again, "this is a difficult thing to remember after so many years—how many, let's see?—twenty?—that sounds right—but as I remember him he wore a thick, double-folded purple cloak with a golden brooch and the pins set in sheaths. I think there was the picture of a hound holding a stag in its forepaws and ripping out its neck with its great teeth while the stag's hooves pawed the air in vain. His tunic glowed like the skin of a dried onion, thin and fragile, and shined like the sun. All of the women in my house were fascinated by it and kept fingering its texture.

238–263   "I don't know if this is what Odysseus was in the habit of wearing at home or whether someone he visited before me gave them to him—he had friends everywhere, you understand—but this is what he wore when he visited me. I gave him a bronze sword and another purple cloak double-folded and a fringed tunic. Oh, yes. He had a squire with him, a little older than himself, as I recall. Round in the shoulders, he was, and dark-faced with long curly hair. I think he was called Eurybates. At any rate, Odysseus thought more of him than any of the others in his crew."

These words made Penelope weep again, this time harder, the tears falling and soaking her dress, for she knew that the story she had heard was true. She forced herself to stop crying and said, "I felt pity for you before, stranger, but now, because of your truth, you shall be an honored guest in this house. I gave Odysseus those clothes you just described. I took them with my own hands from the storeroom and I pinned that brooch upon his shoulder when he was leaving. But"—tears welled again in her eyes—"I will never see him again in these halls. That was indeed an evil day when he left for an evil city."

264–293   "Weeping wastes the mind, my lady," Odysseus said quietly. "It is time to stop wringing your heart, crying for that which you cannot control. I don't blame you for doing this, mind you—any woman would weep when she loses the husband—especially if he is a man like Odysseus, who some say is like to the gods—but it is true what I'm about to tell you. Odysseus lives not far away in green Thesprotia. He has a huge fortune that he has gained through his victories during his wanderings, but he has lost his great hollow ship and the men who sailed it. He lost his company in the wine-dark sea off the coast of Thrinacia. His men had slaughtered the sacred herds of Helios and for their sin were drowned in a roaring tempest that Poseidon threw up against him with the blessing of Zeus. He alone survived that gale, clinging to the shattered keel of his ship until he was thrown up on the coast of the Phaeacians who live closely in accordance to the ways of the gods.[4] There he was received graciously by those who were willing to return him to his homeland. But Odysseus decided that he had more fortune to earn while wandering through many lands. No other person can match his cunning. I was told this by Pheidon, the Thesprotian king, as he poured libations and drank offerings to the gods. He swore that Odysseus had gone to Dodona to discover the will of Zeus from the great oak tree there that is sacred to the god. Pheidon said that he kept a ship and crew standing by for when Odysseus decided it was time for him to return home and that I would sail with him. But, eager to be away, I left first on a ship bound for the grain island of Dulichium.

"I have seen the huge store of treasure that Odysseus has earned. It is such that it will keep a house through the tenth generation. And he will bring that treasure to Ithaca when it is time for him to return. So, dear lady, dry your tears. Odysseus will soon sail home either openly or secretly. I swear this to you and may Zeus be the first witness to my oath. I swear again by the great open hearth of Odysseus. He will return within the year.[5]

294-324

Penelope sighed and said, "What you say may prove true, my friend. I certainly hope so. And if it does, why, then you shall receive great friendship from me that wherever you go people will call you truly a blessed man. But I do not think Odysseus will come home nor do I think you will sail from here. Forgive my black humor, but we no longer have leaders like Odysseus—if ever there was such a man, so long has he been gone that he seems more myth than man now—who were magnaminous hosts and would greet guests and send them on their way when they wished. Now this house has fallen upon hard times, indeed."

She sighed again and gestured to her handmaidens. "But we still can observe some of the amenities. Come, my maids, wash this stranger's feet[6] and make his bed good and tight with soft blankets and fleece to keep him warm against the cold night. When Dawn spreads her fingers through the house, then bathe him and rub him with scented oil so that he may be refreshed when he takes his breakfast with Telemachus in the great hall. Should any of those men—you know the ones I speak of—stress this man's soul, remember that they are vain and arrogant men and their boasting words are only air with no feats behind them."

She smiled charmingly at Odysseus. "Otherwise, my friend, how would you be able to discover my intelligence and kindness that you say surpass the rest of any other worldly woman if I were to let you go about this hall with

325-357

your bums peeking through those rags? It is a poor hostess indeed who lets a man sit down ragged and dirty to meals in her house. Man's life is short enough that he doesn't need discomfort when hospitality is near at hand. A man who treats others harshly gets willed a harsh death by the world while the kindness a man does lives long after he is dust. His name is spoken reverently far and wide while the other's name dies on the wind."

The man of masquerades shook his head and said, "My lady, I have lived too long on hard decks and ground since I left Crete's snowcapped peaks that a comfortable bed means an uncomfortable night for me. So, with your permission, I will just lie here by the fire as I have many another sleepless night and wait for Dawn to shine forth from her bright throne. And the thought of having my feet washed by one of these outspoken wenches is not pleasing to me. No, leave me in peace unless there is an old and faithful servant in this house whose soul has suffered like yours and mine. That woman may touch my feet, no other."

"Very well," wise Penelope said. "These are strange words indeed and strangely satisfying to me. Many strangers have come through that door over these past many years but none has pleased me more than you. You are a kind and thoughtful man and now I tell you that among my servants there is such a woman as you requested: a kind, thoughtful woman who is old and wise. She was the nurse of unlucky Odysseus and raised him lovingly from the moment he was born. She is rather frail, but she will wash your feet."

358–385 She raised her voice and called, "Come, Eurycleia! Wash the feet of this man—bathe your master, I almost said, for he is of the same age as Odysseus and his hands and feet are seamed like his would be. Hardship ages a man greatly."

The old nurse hid her face with her hands at hearing Penelope's sad words. Warm tears slid between gnarled fingers. "Oh, my child! I wish there was something I could do to ease your pain. I can see how the smallest thing makes the pain of your loss grow greater. What manner of gods are these such as Zeus who has refused the many burnt thighbones you have offered to him and kept Odysseus away from you? Why has he refused your prayers that you reach a comfortable age and raise a fine son? Other women less deserving have welcomed their husbands home, but not you. Not you." She sighed. "Well, stranger, do not think badly of my queen. She cannot control the wayward words vain women speak. Perhaps some woman in a far-off land mocks my lord as much as these strumpets mock you. I don't blame you for wanting to keep away from their whorish hands even if it means no bath for you. But I will do what my queen asks. So, let me serve my lady by serving you. Many men have come here over the years but"—she frowned thoughtfully—"I can say that none bears more resemblance to Odysseus than you."

Odysseus smiled and said, "Strangely enough, old woman, others have said that too when our paths have crossed."

The old woman brought the burnished basin she used for washing strangers' feet and poured in fresh cold water, then slowly added warm that had steeped in rose petals. Odysseus suddenly swung away in his seat by the fire to face the dark, a premonition gripping his heart, for he suddenly remembered the old scar he had from a wound made by a boar's white tusk. He had been visiting Parnassus and Autolycus and his sons, his mother's father. He was the greatest thief and maker of cunning oaths among all the mortals, thanks to a great gift from Hermes who had taken a liking to the old scoundrel. Often Autolycus had roasted the thighs of goats and lambs to Hermes as a friend.

It was Autolycus who had been visiting Ithaca when his daughter gave birth to her great son, and when the baby was placed in his lap, Eurycleia said, "Autolycus, here is the grandson you have longed for. Now it is up to you to name him."

And Autolycus lifted the baby, studying him closely, and said, "I will give him the name that you, my daughter and son-in-law, must use for him from this day forward. I have angered many on my trips across this earth and so I call this child Odysseus, the son of wrath and pain. When he has grown, let him come to Parnassus where I keep my riches, and I will send him back fine gifts to set him right in this world."

And so it was that Odysseus visited the home of his grandfather, and Autolycus and his sons greeted him with open arms and great gifts and his grandmother, Amphithee, hugged and kissed him. They butchered a fatted five-year-old ox and slaughtered it, flaying the meat into roasting slabs for long skewers. They feasted that day until the sun swept low over the horizon and then slept contentedly through the night. When young Dawn touched their eyelids, they were up and off hunting and climbed the rugged peak Parnasso, entering the deep and cool forest at high noon when Helios pounded the valley floor with heat. The hounds quested ahead, trying for a worthy scent, and then bayed strongly. Odysseus and Autolycus followed them and soon came upon a great boar lying hidden in a heavy thicket against the sun's heat and the wind, shadowed away from needling sunlight. Rain never poured through that thick canopy of leaves. Odysseus brandished his long lance, anchoring it firmly against his thigh as the boar, suddenly aware of their approach, burst out from his den, his back erect and bristling, tiny eyes burning redly.

446-475   Odysseus set himself to take the boar's charge on the lance, but the boar danced nimbly aside and swept his tusk along Odysseus's ankle, ripping the flesh to the bone. Odysseus struck then, driving the bright head of his lance deep through the boar's right shoulder. The beast squealed with pain and fell back into the dust. His hooves scrambled wildly in the dust for a moment, then lay still.

Autolycus's sons quickly bound Odysseus's ankle, stemming the flow of bright blood, and hurried back to the house where they healed Odysseus and heaped fine gifts on him before sending him back to his own Ithaca. He told his mother and father the tale of his great adventure and how he had been wounded.

And now the old woman took the same foot and her fingers touched the grooved scar along his ankle. Astonished, she dropped his foot. It struck the basin with a loud ring. The basin tilted and water sprayed out over the floor as she stared at the great scar, tears streaming down from her rheumy eyes. She lifted her hand and took Odysseus's chin and stared deeply into his eyes, saying, "I knew it! I knew it! You are Odysseus! I didn't know that until my hands touched the very flesh of your feet."

476-502   Her eyes flickered toward Penelope, but the look was lost upon the queen whose mind was elsewhere, distracted by Athene who wisely knew that the nurse would recognize the great scar on Odysseus's ankle. Odysseus grabbed the back of his nurse's neck and pulled her close, whispering urgently, "Sh. Would you ruin me now? You suckled me at your own breast and now that I have at last returned after twenty years' wandering you have found me out. But be quiet. Sh, now! I warn you and I mean it! Otherwise I will kill you, nurse or not, when it comes time for those vain hussies to die!"

Eurycleia kept her wits and patted his hand reassuringly. "Hush, child! How you talk! You know that I don't have a feeble spirit although my body is old. There's not a whip made that could pull this out of me. I'll be as silent as stone. And I will help you. When the gods deliver those suitors"—she nearly spat with contempt—"into your hands, why, then I shall winnow out the women who have been disloyal for you!"

"No need for that," Odysseus said urgently, quietly. "I haven't been an idle toad sitting by the threshold. I've seen those who favor the suitors and those who sneak off behind pillars and into shadows to let the suitors fondle them. Now keep your knowledge secret until the gods say it is time."

503-530   The old woman nodded and patted his hands and rose and picked up the basin and left the hall to replenish it with water. She returned and scrubbed his feet clean and rubbed them well with scented olive oil. Then Odysseus drew his stool closer to the fire to warm himself, carefully covering the scar with his rags as Penelope approached.

"Stranger," she said, "there is one small thing I have to ask before we retire for the night. Some may sleep sweetly, but"—she sighed and shook her head—"such a thing heaven refuses to grant me. I wander through the day with my heart aching while I watch the women work. That helps sometimes, and I can forget for a moment my grief, but when night comes and my bed is empty, I feel the loss and sorrow deeply and my thoughts become bitter. Think how Pandareus's daughter, the nightingale, trills her lonely song in the long quiet hours of the night for Itylus, the son she loved and killed accidentally. There she sits in her orchard, unhappy night after night, forever singing his name. I think then, wondering if I should stay beside my son and guard the hall, my maids, forever honoring my lord's bed, or would it be better if I were to take a suitor for a new husband, the one most noble with his gifts? When my son was young, he stoutly argued that I remain faithful. But now he is grown and his words have changed and he sings a different song, urging me to take another husband.

"I had a dream, stranger, and wonder if you could interpret it for me. Twenty fat geese feed on grain at the water's edge. I am happy to see them for they are quite beautiful. But then a huge mountain eagle soars silently out of the sky, his cruel crooked beak breaking their necks, throwing their bodies hither and thither aimlessly. He soars away, back into the bright sky, and I feel a scream welling from my throat. I cry, and all around me softly braided Greek women gather and mourn with me because an eagle has slain my geese.

"Then the eagle drops down from the sky and perches upon a heavy cross- 531–558 beam. He opens his beak and speaks in mortal words, saying, 'Daughter of far-famed Icarius, do not mistake this for a dream, but reality. The geese are your suitors and I am your husband now returned from my many wanderings to strike the suitors with dark death.' And then I awakened, and freed from heavy sleep, I glanced anxiously around and there were my geese still feeding happily beside the waters just as they have always done."

"That is easy, my lady. There is only one way to interpret this dream. Odysseus has shown you that death will come to the suitors. No one will escape the terrible vengeance he will take upon them. That is their destiny," the man of masquerades said.

Penelope shook her head and said, "Spoken well, dear guest. But dreams 559–587 are awkward and sly things that bump strangely in the night. Not all that men see in them comes true—fact is, more often than not they are only delusions. They come to man through one of two gates: the gate of horn or the gate of ivory. Those that come through the ivory gate are wily wants that delude the dreamer for they are built only upon air. Those that come through the gate of polished horn, however, are hard and true. I do not think my dream came through the gate of horn. If it had, my son and I would feel happiness in what it suggested." She paused and stared distantly into the dark beyond the fire. "I hate the day that will come, my friend, that will drive me from this house. Today I must test those suitors and so I will set the twelve axheads that Odysseus used to place like wedges for a ship's keel. He would stand a goodly distance from them and shoot an arrow through them all and strike a mark at the other end.[7] Whoever can string the bow of Odysseus and can send an arrow through those twelve axheads is the man I will marry and with whom I will leave this lovely house that is so full of good things and fond memories of the time when Odysseus was here."

Odysseus remained quiet for a while, then said softly, "My queen, do not delay this contest. Let it take place tomorrow, for I have a feeling that mighty Odysseus will be here long before those louts manage to string the bow with their fumbling hands, let alone shoot the arrow through the iron axheads."

588–604   "Ah, stranger, thank you for those thoughts. Would you sit beside me through the rest of the night here in this hall? Sleep will not close my eyes tonight." Then she sighed and shook her head. "But I suppose that is unwise, for the gods have dictated that man must sleep. So instead I shall go to my bed of sorrows and wait for Dawn. I curse the day that Odysseus sailed away to that evil city whose name I will no longer pronounce. I will lie down, however, and perhaps sleep will come to me. You may rest within this hall, if you will, on either a bed of your own choosing or have my maids prepare one for you."

And so Penelope bade the stranger a good night and climbed the stairs to her room. And there she wept for Odysseus until Athene took pity and gently closed her eyes in sweet sleep.

Here ends the Nineteenth Book of Homer's Odyssey.

THE TWENTIETH BOOK
Advice from a Goddess

❖ ❖ ❖ ❖ ❖ ❖ ❖ ❖ ❖ ❖ ❖

Odysseus consults Athene on how to gain
Control of his home once again.

❖ ❖ ❖ ❖ ❖ ❖ ❖ ❖ ❖ ❖ ❖

Wearily Odysseus made his bed outside where apricots and   *1–29*
Dates flowered sweetly. First, he carefully laid a newly flayed
Oxhide upon the ground. Upon that he piled fleece from
When the Greeks butchered his sheep. He lay upon his bed,
And Eurycleia threw a heavy robe over him to cover him
From the night chill that could bring ague to man's bones.
Yet the man of masquerades could not sleep, his mind
Twisting and turning with thought about destroying his enemies.
The heavy dew was sinking and the smell of apricots and
Dates in the air swelled like a blanket of perfume over him.
A nightingale called, and a covey of women, filled with ribald
Thoughts, slipped out of the house. They giggled as they made
Their way toward the suitors' beds. Anger filled Odysseus and
He wanted to leap into their midst and kill them all, but
The time was not right—yet—but that time would come and
Then his wrath would be bloody. Odysseus muttered darkly:

"Still. Be still. Quiet, now. Remember the greater shame when the Cyclops
ate your men. You found patience then that allowed you to get clear of that
cave instead of dying inside it. You can use your cunning here as well."

But although he convinced himself to continue lying before the fire,
ignoring the giggling women, he rolled from side to side like a cook turning
a bloody and fat sausage on the fire, rolling it left and right to keep it from

burning. And so Odysseus tossed and turned, searching for a means to defeat the suitors.

30–57 Suddenly Athene appeared beside him in the form of a lovely mortal woman. She said, "What, again, Odysseus? Why are you still sleepless? True, you are among the most sorrowful of men, but you are home and you have seen your wife and son, a son that most men hope for."

"True," Odysseus said. "But, my goddess, I still have to lash these dogs out of my house. Or kill them. But how can I do that? They are always together and there is force in numbers. And, I'd wager, more on the way. Even if I killed all of them, where could I go to escape blood revenge?"

The gray-eyed goddess smiled and shook her head. "Ah, what faith you have, Odysseus. Have you forgotten that I will be with you at your side when the time comes? With me by your side, it does not matter how great the odds. Fifty men could swing singing swords, trying to slay you, yet you will still drive off their sheep and cattle. Now put our mind at rest and go to sleep. Long nights weary the flesh. All these trials will soon be behind you."

She passed her fingers across his eyes and they closed in sleep. She smiled down at him for a moment, then returned to Olympus. But while Odysseus slept peacefully, his faithful wife suddenly awoke and sat up straight in bed, tears flowing from her beautiful eyes.

58–87 She wept for a long time, then, weary of weeping, rose and prayed before Artemis, saying, "Great Artemis, daughter of Zeus, use an arrow wisely and end my life before this hour passes. Or send a great wind to snatch me up and carry me on a foggy path to where Ocean begins and drop me there as were the daughters of Pandareus after the gods killed their parents and left them orphans before fair Aphrodite fed them on cheese and sweet honey and Hera graced them with beauty and wit that surpassed all other women. I know you gifted them with regal bearing while Athene gave them cunning in weaving. When Aphrodite asked mighty Zeus to give them a good marriage, he sent the winds to carry them away to the Furies. So may the gods of Olympus grace me—or kill me. This I ask, great Artemis. Then I might see the shade of Odysseus in the rotting Underworld. Evil can be endured during the day only if sleep reigns over us at night. But I do not sleep dreamless sleep and my dreams are as terrible as my days. I just dreamed that a man like Odysseus lay beside me, and it was so real that I thought it wasn't a dream. This is unbearable!"

88–111 But the goddess did not answer her, and as she spoke, golden Dawn peeped over the horizon and shafted her fingers into the corners of the room. Odysseus awakened and heard his wife's lament, and in his mind's eye he saw himself climbing the steps to comfort her. He sighed and rose, took the blanket and folded it and placed it on the chair, then bundled the fleece and rolled it into the oxhide and stored it in a nook by the door. He drew a deep breath and walked to a secluded part of the courtyard beneath a flowering almond tree and raised his hands to Zeus, crying, "Father, I have waited long for this day and been tried hard by the gods. If I at last have found favor with you, give me two signs. Let one who awakens now inside the hall speak prophecy while out here beneath the canopy of the heavens, send me another sign."

Far above, Zeus the cloud-gatherer heard it and caused a deep rumble in the clear sky. Close upon that came words from a serving woman who toiled in a nearby shed where the hand mills ground grist. Twelve slept there after having ground the grain and barley meal. One awoke, an old and frail woman, slow with her movements, who rose creaking from her bed and hobbled to the door to peer up at the sky.

"Ah, Zeus! Now that was a mighty bang indeed to come out of the sky *112–138* and not a cloud in sight. I feel you've nodded to someone who has offered a prayer to you. Well, here's another from an old woman. Let this be the last day we grind grain for those filthy suitors in the hall. I've ground enough grain in the past few weeks to make my heart thump. Let them feast no more, I says!"

The servant's prayer touched the heart of Odysseus and made him a happy man. A sense of crushing revenge came over him.[1]

Meanwhile, others rose and came down to light the fire in the great hearth and busy themselves preparing the morning meal. Great Telemachus rose as clear-eyed as a god and dressed himself quickly in a tunic, belting his sword at his side. He disdained his usual sandals and instead tied a pair of rawhide sandals, sure of footing, around his feet. He gathered his bronze-headed lance and came down to stand on the doorsill. He called to Eurycleia.

"Nurse, dear, did you attend well to our guest with food and bedding? Or did he make do? It would be just like my mother to spend her time on lesser men and send off the best."

"Don't blame your mother without cause!" snapped Eurycleia. "The good man sat and drank as long as he wanted and when she offered food to him he refused it, saying he had no appetite.

"When he yawned and said he would like to sleep, she ordered her maids *139–169* to make him a bed, but he would have none of it. The poor fellow has slept on stony ground so long that he couldn't sleep on a well-made bed. He made do with a few sheepskins and an oxhide for a ground cover. I placed a blanket over him myself, howsomever, against the chill of the night. And a good thing, too. My bones fair ache from the night's chill!"

Telemachus smiled and whistled up two hunting dogs and set out from the hall, making his way to the assembly place to join his friends. Meanwhile, Eurycleia, the daughter of Ops, Peisenor's son, clapped her hands and gave her orders to the slow-moving maids who appeared, swollen-eyed and sated.

"To work! To work!" she said crossly. "Sweep out the hall and sprinkle it down with water to settle the dust. I want purple pillows placed on those chairs. You and you"—she pointed to two who showed the effects of their carousing—"take care of that while the rest of you scrub down the tables and scour the plates and two-handled cups[2] and fetch clean water to mix wine. The suitors will come early today; this is a sacred day."

"What's this?" one asked. "What sacred day?"

"Fish heads and tails! You'll be told in time," she said. "Now, to work! And be quick about it or I'll have the master lay a belt across your bold buttocks."

The women grumbled among themselves but hurried to do her bidding. Twenty left to draw water from the well while the rest cleaned inside. Then the sturdy men came in and split the logs and kindling for the fire. The swineherd trailed up behind the women as they returned from the well, driving three fatted hogs in front of him. He shooed the beasts into a corner of the yard where they rooted contentedly, then he crossed to Odysseus.

"Well, my friend! Did you sleep well? Are they treating you any better than before, or are you still getting pig slops?"

170–196 "Good morning, Eumaeus," Odysseus answered. "The gods will soon pay these scoundrels for their insults and poor manners. Not a spark of shame shows among them! I hope the gods are quick against this obscene scheming of theirs in the House of Odysseus!"

While they visited, Melanthius the goatherd drove in the goats he'd picked from his flocks to serve the suitors for their feast. He saw Odysseus and Eumaeus standing apart and, after tying his goats under the echoing portico, swaggered over to them saying, "Still here, beggar? I suppose you think that you'll spend the day skulking around your betters and upsetting the running of this house. A plague upon you." He waved a fist in Odysseus's direction. " 'Fore the day is out you'll have a good taste of my fists instead of a meal. You want a meal, go bother another house with your whining and moaning."

Odysseus shook his head and ignored him, although his heart seethed with rage at the insult of the rash youth. Melanthius grinned and spat in the dust, then turned and swaggered back toward the hall.

Philoetius, the cattle foreman, came next, bringing an ox and fat goats for the suitors. A ferry had just brought these over from the mainland along with more travelers. He tied the beasts under the portico, noticed Eumaeus, and walked over, wiping the sweat from his brow with his broad hand.

"Hello, who's this?" he asked. He frowned as he squinted at Odysseus. "He seems down on his luck but he carries himself like a king. But that means nothing! Kings and commoners all have misery in their lives a time or two."

He put forth his hand. "But you have my welcome, sir. And may the gods *197–227* grant you good graces from this day forward. I can see you have been down a bit on your luck. That Zeus!" He shook his head. "Cruelest of gods, he is, although he claims to befriend all of us! He doesn't seem to mind a bit dabbling in the mischief and miseries he tosses our way. Yet he did give us life. I'll give him that much." He peered closely again at Odysseus, appraising him. "You know, but for those rags, you could be my master Odysseus. Don't laugh, Eumaeus! Why, when I saw this good fellow here, sweat broke out on my forehead and tricked into my eyes. Odysseus could be just like this fellow here—forced to wear rags and beg his way across the earth—if he still lives and can bask in the sunlight that is free for kings and commoners alike!"

He took a cup of water from a serving maid and drank thirstily. "Ah! That's better. But if Odysseus has gone to the Halls of Hades, then I mourn my dear lord for it was he who put me in charge of the cattle on the mainland. And I've kept his trust and done well by him. Those herds are countless by now, but"—he stepped closer and lowered his voice—"don't be gadding that about among the worthless cuttles here! They order me to bring in my choicest just as if they owned the house and there was to be no end to the feasting. They don't care one whit"—he snapped his fingers—"for my lord's son or fear a god's wrath. Like vultures they are, carrion birds, eager to divide up what they haven't earned now that the king is gone. And that worries me, you see. For as long as the king's son lives, why, they don't dare take the cattle somewhere else. I'd have left long ago, but I won't leave that boy alone to deal with those suitors. I keep hoping Odysseus, my sad lord, will return and rid his house of this vermin!"

Odysseus felt touched by the cowherd's words and said, "Well spoken, my *228–254* friend. I can see that you are a thoughtful and honorable man who looks well after his lord's property. So I'll make you a promise on the beard of Zeus himself that your master will soon return to this hospitable hearth and then you will see a great and terrible slaughter of these suitors, for Odysseus can be the nightmare to end all nightmares when he is pressed!"

"I hope, stranger, that your words aren't woven on the wind! The sooner the better, I says! And if he comes"—he whacked the ground hard with his staff—"why, I'll show you what a pair of sturdy hands can do. I'll addle a few pates, I tell you!"

While they spoke and shared their thoughts, the suitors bent heads together, devising a plot for the murder of Telemachus. Suddenly a bird of omen flew high above them, an eagle clutching a dove in its talons. Amphinomus rose immediately and said bluntly, "My friends, any plot to kill Telemachus won't succeed at this time. Leave it to later. Meanwhile, let's turn to feasting."

They glanced up at the bird, then shrugged and rose, following him to noble Odysseus's palace. When they arrived, they tossed their cloaks carelessly on the tables and chairs and, taking great knives, moved eagerly out to slaughter the animals that had been left for them. They roasted the portions and served them to each other and mixed wine in bowls that had been laid out for them. The swineherd stayed his tongue and helped, placing a cup near each man while Philoetius brought around fresh-baked bread in clean baskets. Melanthius brought pitchers filled with wine and all settled to eat greedily what had been laid before them.

255–282 Telemachus cleverly placed a battered stool for Odysseus beside the stone threshold next to a small table. He brought sweetbreads to him and poured a large portion of little-watered wine in a golden chalice for him, saying, "Make your place here and eat and drink with our friends. No one will cuff you or insult you here. Harsh words belong in a tavern, not here in the House of Odysseus, which I have inherited. And you"—he turned to the suitors, staring warningly at them—"put a leash on your tongues and leave the good man alone. We have no need of brawls or bandying words today."

They paused with meat and cups halfway to their lips, staring in amazement at him. Antinous laughed and said carelessly, "Well, my friends! I suppose we must put up with the words of Telemachus. If Zeus hadn't sent that bird of omen, why, we would have stilled his shrill voice by now."

He stared mockingly at Telemachus, but the youth ignored him and went on about his business.

While they ate, servants were bringing the beasts chosen for sacrifice into town as offerings to the gods. The Ithacans slowly congregated in the grove of Apollo,[3] but the suitors ignored what was going on outside the palace walls, contenting themselves with feasting. Servants made certain that Odysseus received his share of the well-roasted meat the moment it came off the spits and was carved.

283–307 But Athene made certain that the jackals gathered around his table did not leave off the harsh words. She made certain that the anger in Odysseus's heart grew greater and greater. Ctesippus, a Samos man arrogant with his father's riches, stared with piggish eyes at Odysseus, then turned and said loudly, "Hear me, you hearty boasters! Our newly arrived friend has been equally served with us. There's nothing wrong with that, you understand. Why, isn't that what hospitality is, after all? So it would be improper, to my way of thinking, for us to turn a cold shoulder to whatever tramp turns up as Telemachus's guest. He must have prizes, you know, something that he can give to, oh, say a serving wench or bath man, or"—he shrugged—"whomever he wished to grace. So here is an offering for him."

With that he pawed into a bowl, seized a cow's foot, and hurled it at Odysseus. But Odysseus rolled his head away and the missile flew harmlessly away from him. He smiled crookedly at Ctesippus, but the smile did not touch his eyes and a strange chill seemed to come into the room. Telemachus rose immediately, his eyes flashing angrily as he turned toward Ctesippus.

"You are a very lucky man, Ctesippus. Had that struck my guest I would have spitted you on my spear and your father would have a grand funeral instead of a wedding to prepare for.

"Hear me again, dolts! I will not have anyone disgraced in my house. I know right from wrong now—that's something that raises the man from idle youth—and although I have to put up with this slaughter of my sheep and the wine and bread eaten because I can't face all of you at once, I will not tolerate any more of these malicious and wicked acts. If you decide that you would rather murder me with bronze, far the better than for me to be dishonored by allowing my guest to be insulted in this manner and my servingwomen dragged through these halls. I've had enough of your boldness." 308–340

All fell silent and stared at Telemachus. Then Agelaus, the son of Damastor, spoke. "He makes sense, my friends. Anyone here would not answer that with a bit of bickering, I would say. Enough of this bandying the stranger. Leave him alone and the servants. But"—he turned to Telemachus—"I would offer a bit of counsel to you and your good mother. We do not fault you for hoping that your brave father would return home. But he hasn't and there's the nut of it all. It is time for you to sit beside your mother and help her choose the best man to wed in Odysseus's place. Then he would help to maintain peace in these hallowed halls."

Telemachus stopped his quick tongue and said, "May Zeus and my father's suffering lend truth to these words, Agelaus. I will not stand in the way of my mother's marriage any longer. In fact, I advise her to wed whomever she chooses.

"And when she does, I'll give her many fine presents when she leaves this 341–368 house. But I will not drive her from this house and heap shame upon my name. Gods save me from that."

Pallas Athene moved quickly among the men, causing them to laugh at what they thought a grand joke and the vain words of a youth. Then she moved again, and suddenly the strain of their laughter caused blood to fleck the meat they ate and their eyes shed tears as their spirits suddenly thought terrible thoughts. Theoclymenus the prophet noted this and said, "What's this? Why this unhappiness, men? What horror has suddenly descended upon you? What pit have you gazed too long into? Why, a shroud of darkness seems to have wrapped itself around your faces. Phantoms crowd the colonnades and court and I sense spirits rushing toward the Halls of Hades. The sun has suddenly blotted out and now a foul mist creeps from the earth to wrap itself around you."

Again they laughed delightedly, pounding the table with their fists. But one failed to see the humor. Eurymachus rose and shouted, "It seems this man has lost his mind. Quick! To the assembly place with him for he thinks day has become night."

"Eurymachus," Theoclymenus said hollowly, his words echoing like from a sepulcher, "I don't need you to help me find my way in dark or light. I have my own eyes and ears and two sound feet. My mind is sound as well and not weak. But I will not stay any longer in this place. I see quite clearly enough that a great evil will soon overtake you and none here will escape or stop it. All who are free with their insults in Odysseus's great halls will suffer for your brutal acts and reckless plots."

369–394 And with that he rose and strode purposefully from the hall and went down the trail to the house of Peiraeus who greeted him warmly. But all the suitors, after exchanging laughing glances, baited Telemachus about his choice of friends among his guests.

"Telemachus," cried one young man, sneering at Odysseus's son, "I don't think I have ever seen one as unfortunate as you with his choice of guests. First you drag in this grubby tramp, a man who scrounges bread and wine and is unfit for work or war, just taking up space on this earth. Then you have another who wishes to play prophet. If you take my advice you'll bundle them onto a ship and sell them both in Sicily for a coin or two."

The other suitors shouted, echoing his words, but Telemachus ignored them and settled himself, watching his father with both eyes, ready for the moment when Odysseus struck the suitors.

Penelope had had her chair placed where she heard every word spoken in the hall while they had laughingly prepared their feast by butchering the beasts for their midday meal. But their supper would be bitter as gall with the help of a gray-eyed goddess and a man whose anger would finally bubble over, and a terrible destroyer would fall over all.

Here ends the Twentieth Book of Homer's **Odyssey.**

THE TWENTY-FIRST BOOK

The Test of the Bow

❖ ❖ ❖ ❖ ❖ ❖ ❖ ❖ ❖ ❖ ❖

The challenge of Odysseus's bow,
The failure of the suitors, a great blow.

❖ ❖ ❖ ❖ ❖ ❖ ❖ ❖ ❖ ❖ ❖

P*enelope stared out the window at the gray mist swirling*
Languidly and heard gray-eyed Athene's voice whispering
That it was time to test the suitors. She stirred herself and,
Calling her handmaidens, took a great ivory-handled bronzed key
To look in a far-off room of the palace where others went not.
There she stared upon the riches of the room and to where
The great recurved bow of Odysseus hung with the gray-fletched
Arrows in a quiver Iphitus[1] had made out of leather in Sparta.
She stood, tears streaming softly down her cheeks at the memory.

1–28

He had met Iphitus at the house of wise Ortilochus in Messenia. Odysseus had traveled there to collect a debt after three hundred Messenes had raided the shores of Ithaca and stolen three hundred sheep and the shepherds to handle them. Young though he was, Laertes and the council had chosen Odysseus for this. He was joined by Iphitus who had lost a dozen mares to the raiders along with their mule foals they had been nursing when stolen. (These horses led to Iphitus's death when Hercules, the lion-hearted son of Zeus, slew him after the madness slipped upon him and drove him into the mighty labors as penance. Hercules, a vain and cruel-hearted man, killed Iphitus in his own house despite the hospitality rules given to man by the gods—feasting him, then killing him and keeping the large hooved mares in his own stables.)

While searching for the mares, Iphitus met Odysseus and gave him the *29–55*
mighty bow that Eurytus had carried until his death. Odysseus gave his new

329

friend a sturdy spear and sharp sword.² But they never shared a meal as host and guest for Hercules cut short the life of Iphitus before those amenities could be carried out. Odysseus had left the bow behind on his journey to the shores of Ilium as a memory of his beloved friend. Only in Ithaca would Odysseus use that bow.

And now the great queen reached the storeroom and stepped on the oaken sill carefully laid by the carpenter long ago who had planed and laid true the board before he carved the jambs and set them in place and hung the well-polished and oiled doors upon them. Penelope quickly freed the key from its thong and fitted it to the lock and shot the bolts. As a bull bellows in a grassy meadow, the great doors flew open before her and she stepped into the room where the great cedar chests held Odysseus's clothes. She marched across the pegged floor to the wall where the bow hung and took it down in the oiled case in which it was kept. Then grief overcame her and she sat on a chest and laid the bow across her lap and wept hot tears as she drew the bow, long and gleaming, from its case.

56–87 Then she wiped her tears and, resolute, stood and carried the supple bow in her hands with the quiver full of its death-dealing darts over her shoulder back to the great hall where the suitors feasted. Behind her came her hand-maidens bearing the great axheads in baskets.

She paused behind a pillar and adjusted a shimmering veil over her beautiful face and took a deep breath. Then, summoning her handmaidens, she stepped out from behind the pillar and faced the suitors in the great hall.

Immediately a hush fell over the room as all looked up at the strange sight of Penelope with the great bow of destruction in her hands. She looked with loathing around the hall until her eyes lit upon the beggar, and then they softened. But then she remembered her purpose and a hard light shone from her eyes as she spoke.

"Listen well, proud suitors, for this is the time you have waited long for and ate and drank in endless feasts and harassed the house of one who is not here to defend it. Your excuse was that you wanted to wed me and bed me. So now, you wanters, stand and come forth and try to win your prize. Here is Odysseus's mighty bow. Whoever can string this bow and send an arrow through twelve axheads to its mark may claim me and I shall follow him wherever he wishes. I will leave this house where I was bride and wife and will remember it only in my dreams."

She turned to Eumaeus and ordered, "Carry the bow to them and set the axheads in a true row."

Tears streaming from his eyes, the swineherd took the bow from her white hands and carried it across the room to the suitors and laid it at their feet. A strange coughing sob came from the cowherd who watched from across the room. Antinous turned scornfully on them, heaping great abuse upon their heads as he spat, saying, "You sniveling boors who see only the hind end of an ox plowing a furrow, why shed tears and upset your mistress with your whining and bawling like milk-faced brats?

88–119

"She's suffered enough what with her husband gone. Sit down, I say, and eat in silence or leave this hall and whine among the dogs in the stables. Leave the bow where it is. From the looks of it, I don't think stringing it will be that simple. I saw Odysseus once—though I was only a child—and there isn't a man here who can equal him."

But a secret desire lurked in Antinous's black heart that he would be the one to string the great bow and shoot the arrow to its mark through the iron axheads. He would be the first to taste an arrow from the hands of the great Odysseus he insulted and encouraged the others to follow his lead.

And now Telemachus spoke up, saying, "Ah, me! Zeus has muddled my wits, addled my brains! Mother dear says wisely that she will marry the one who can win this test and leave the house, and—curse me for my weakness!— I am glad of it. So stand, you would-be suitors, and try your hands. Your prize awaits over there—a worthy prize unlike any in all Greece. Not even sandy Pylos or Argos or Mycenae, not even in the dark mainland or this island of Ithaca will you find such a one as she. But you all know this well enough so there's no reason for me to sing my mother's praises like a pimp in a tavern. Enough delays and excuses have been made. Now, string that bow and show us what you are made of. By the gods, I wouldn't mind having a try at it myself, and if I succeeded, why, I wouldn't sob and beat my breast if she left the house for another. At least I would have tried my strength at my father's arms."

And saying this, he flung the crimson cloak from his shoulders and took his sword and carved a long trench in the dirt and set the axheads in a line, stamping the dirt down upon them to plant them securely.

120–147

He had never done this before, but the men took him for an old hand at it and admired his ease and skill in aligning them with a taut cord through the sockets. Then he took the great bow and stood by the threshold. Three times he tried to bend it and three times it quivered in his hands and stoutly stood unstrung. The fourth time he nearly had it, straining with all his muscles, when Odysseus shook his head silently.[3]

Ruefully Telemachus let off his attempt and exclaimed, "By the gods! Am I forever to walk in my father's shadow? Maybe it's my youth and I still lack the courage to face one who would quarrel with me. I don't know. It's up to you men who have the power." He shook his head. "I am finished."

He placed the bow on the ground and leaned it against the massy-timbered door with the arrow against the horn of the bow. He returned, shaking his head, discouraged, to his seat. All remained silent, having watched the youth straining against the massive bow. At last Antinous laughed and shouted, "The speech of a youth! Always offering excuses! What, Telemachus, did you think to break our hearts with the song of your weakness? Your mother didn't bring you into this world to string bows and shoot arrows. Perhaps a harp will be more to your liking. Enough nonsense. Let's do it in order. Left to right from where they dip the wine."

Leodes, the son of Oinops, who used to find visions in fire smoke for them[4] and kept his chair well away from the loutish manners of the others, preferring to sit near the wine bowl instead of bellying up to the table with the others, rose reluctantly and took the bow. But his thin and delicate hands could not bend the bow and he returned it silently to its place.

148–176   "My friends," he said softly, "I cannot bend this bow. It is one that will break the heart and spirit of any strong man who is not worthy of bending it. It is a sad state that we will have to leave without one of us winning the fair lady Penelope. But so it goes. Are there other takers here willing to challenge the gods and Odysseus? If so, take up the bow and have your try. Then leave with me for another court and take your gifts with you to win another daughter elsewhere."

Antinous laughed scornfully, mocking him as he made his way back to his chair. "Nonsense," he snorted. "Words like that cause my blood to boil. You can't string the bow because you're too weak. The gods have nothing to do with it. 'It is one that will break the heart and spirit of any strong man who is not worthy of bending it.' Stuff and nonsense, I tell you! It is only a scrap of wood and that's the nose and tail of it. There are men here who can bend that bow and will." He called aloud to the goatherd Melanthius. "Stir your bones, Melanthius, and kindle a fire in the hall. Bring a large bench and cover it with a sheepskin and a large round of tallow from the storehouse. We will heat and grease that chunk of wood and make it limber before we try it further."

177–208   Melanthius eagerly rushed to do Antinous's bidding. He threw fresh kindling on the glowing coals and placed a bench near the fire while it flickered and laid a sheepskin over the bench. Then he hurried to fetch the rind of tallow. The young suitors warmed the bow and greased it heavily with hot tallow, but none could bend the bow and string it. Antinous and Eurymachus held back, however, each waiting to see if the others could bend the bow and weaken it or loosen it by their efforts.

While the suitors were busy trying to string the bow, Odysseus motioned to the cowherd and swineherd, and together they slipped out of the house. He stopped them under a spreading almond tree and said, "My friends, I wonder if I should speak out and voice my mind or keep silent? Hm. No, I think I should speak. Let us suppose that Odysseus suddenly appeared. Would you fight with him? Or would you join with the others in there"—he tossed his head in the direction of the great hall—"and help them steal this great house and lands?"

The cowherd shook his fists in the air and danced angrily. "Let him come! Let the master come, I says. I'm aching to step in and bash one of those louts in there with a good fist to his jaw. Ah, would great father Zeus grant me this!" He shook his fist under the nose of Odysseus. "The master come back and let me at them and then you can judge for yourself what sort of man I am!"

"Aye, I'm of the same mind, I tell you," Eumaeus said fervently and added a quick prayer to the heavens that Odysseus would drop from the sky and together they could drive the filthy lot from his house.

"Very well," Odysseus said. He drew himself up and a light seemed to 209–238 shine from him. "Then, here I am. Yes, my friends. I am Odysseus, home again at last after twenty years of suffering and wandering. And what do I find? The two of you alone still waiting for me, glad to see my return. I have not heard a single other person offer a prayer for my return. So now I'll tell you what is in store. If Zeus helps me regain my lot, I'll arrange marriages for each of you and give you cattle to begin your own herds. I'll build houses next to mine, and from the day of my triumph you will be regarded as friends and brothers of Telemachus. But first the proof, for anyone can say he is Odysseus, but only the real Odysseus has this—the wound I received from the great boar's tusk when I went hunting with Autolycus's sons on Parnassus."

With that he drew up the trail of his rags and showed the long scar, white against the bronze of his leg. They examined the scar carefully, then, tears flowing heavily from their eyes, they embraced him. He kissed each man's head and hands, then stopped them.

"Enough of this," he said roughly. "Someone from the hall might see us and think to tell the others what he has seen. Now, follow me and return to the hall, each of you, but go separately. Wait for my signal. You'll know it. After each of the suitors has a try with that bow, I will ask permission to set my hand to it. 'By Hades's Halls,' they'll swear. 'Give the beggar a bout with the bow? Next thing he'll be claiming to be among our brethren.' But you must not listen to them, Eumaeus. You must take the quiver and bow and put it in my hands and demand that I be given a chance. Then"—he looked at both—"while I work the bow, you must push the ladies out of the hall and lock the doors and warn them not to come into the room despite what shouting and moaning they might hear and keep on with their weaving or whatever womanly task they set their hands to. Philoetius, you must run and bolt and bar the outer gate. Lock it and throw the crossbar over the clasps and lash it firmly so that it cannot be thrown back easily by anyone."[5]

239–264   They agreed to do his bidding and Odysseus left them and went back into the great hall and quietly took his seat once again by the threshold. No one had noticed his absence, being intent instead on warming and greasing the great bow. The two servants wandered casually in and took their places as Odysseus had told them.

By now Eurymachus had taken the bow and was turning it slowly near the heat of the glowing fire, warming it and rubbing tallow along its great length. Then he placed the tip against his foot and tried to draw it down for the woven cord. Sweat stood out on his brow and his face grew red with his efforts, but he could not bend it. At last he groaned from the depths of his proud heart and raged, "Blast this damn thing! This is a black day when we are humiliated by such a thing as this. There are plenty of other women in Ithaca and other towns. But how will we fare there when the story of our failure here leaks out? We will be seen as children when we are measured with Odysseus. We cannot even string his great bow let alone hope to hold his house. The shame of it!"

But Antinous sneered at his words. "Ah, Eurymachus. Forget this paltry thing. This is a holy day, a feast day, not one to be whining and whimpering over a bowstring. I say that we forget the test and return to our feasting. Leave the axes where they've been planted—they won't grow there," he added as a feeble joke, but no one laughed. "No one will be coming to Odysseus's hall today or tonight. They'll all be off lifting their cups and wenching their way around the town. We'll feast and drink rich wine and burn thighbones tomorrow from the fat goats Melanthius has brought down to Apollo the archer while we try the bow and make that shot. Though," he added, critically eyeing the setting axes, "that is a tough shot to make."

265–294   All quickly agreed to this for all wanted to forget the trial and put it behind them with a cup or two of rich wine. Their squires came and sprinkled water over their hands while others scurried around filling wine cups. Heavy joints dripping fat made the rounds, and each man spilled a few drops of red wine as an offering to the gods before drinking his full. Odysseus waited patiently through all of this, and when they had all mellowed from the wine, he said, "Listen to me, you suitors for the great queen's hand. I am moved to speak and I direct this to Eurymachus and Antinous especially. Put the bow aside as he advised. Perhaps Apollo will grant you strength tomorrow to bend the bow and make the shot. Who knows? Meanwhile, let me have the bow. I would like to see if I still have any strength in these hands, or if my wastrel life has robbed me of the power I once had."

They stared open-mouthed at the brazen words of the beggar, then their faces purpled with rage and fear that he might bend the bow. Antinous turned furiously to him and said, "Why, you arrogant beggar! Have you taken leave of your senses? You have been coddled and pampered at this table despite being a tramp and now you think that you have the same rights as gentlemen? I think you have drunk too much of that mellow wine to suit you! Wine brings down the boldest of men who swig it instead of sipping it moderately. That's something you learn when you are a gentleman.

"Remember the story of Eurytion the Centaur?[6] How during his visit to   295–325 Lapithae in Peirithous's hall he ruined himself by gulping cup after cup of wine? It drove him crazy, it did, and he went wild for rape and the other guests leaped upon him and dragged him from the house and cropped his nose and ears to remind him to mind his manners at future feasts. And that was the beginning of the war between Centaurs and men. All because one got drunk when he should have remained sober. Wars are started through one man's intolerance, you know. Take heed! You string this bow and you'll come to a similar grief. We'll pack you away in a black slave ship to the skinner of men Echetus. And there you'll not escape. Do you want to risk that fate? I think not. So sit there and quietly drink your wine and stay out of the business of gentlemen before you are tossed out upon your ears for your trouble."

And now bold Penelope broke in on the give-and-take and said, "Antinous, you are being extremely rude again to Telemachus's guest. Look at the stranger and see him for what he is. Even if he should bend the bow, do you really think he has any desire to carry me off to his palace and make me his wife? I don't think so. Your argument is only a lot of mumbo-jumbo, airless words meaning nothing. Go back to your feast and stop spoiling everyone's dinner with your senseless argument."

"That's not it at all, wise Penelope," Eurymachus, Polybus's son, said testily. "We are quite aware that this man will not win your hand. The point is that we don't want the commonfolk to say, 'A sad lot those suitors! Why, not one of them could do a beggar's job! Whatever made them think they could earn a fine man's wife! And here comes a casual tramp who strings the bow and sends an arrow through the axheads like a woman stringing a needle.'

326-352 "And that is what we will have to put up with. Why, we would be disgraced! Our reputations muddied!"

"Reputation? What reputation, Eurymachus?" Penelope retorted sternly. "A man who is part of a group that has behaved like all of you have over the years, desecrating a good man's house and name while eating up his cattle and drinking his wine and abusing his servants, has no good name to protect. Why, whatever reputation you all had has blown on the wind. You've already shamed yourselves deeply enough. What's another matter to you now when you won't be able to hold your head in polite company anywhere in the world? Now, this stranger seems to be a big man and well built and claims noble blood although he seems to have fallen on evil ways. That's no disgrace; most of you are nearly there now yourselves. So. This is what I say: Give him the bow and see what happens. If he succeeds I promise—and this is not idle chitchat, I assure you by Apollo's graces—I will give him a good tunic and fine cloak and a lance for keeping dogs or men such as yourselves at bay. I will also give him fine and sturdy sandals for his feet and a good sword to drape over his shoulder. And," she added, "I will place him on a ship to wherever he wishes to go."

"As for the bow, Mother," Telemachus said before any of the others could answer, "no one here has more right than I to allow any Greek to try his hand at it. That goes without saying for anyone in Ithaca or the isles off Elis where great horses graze. None here can take that away from me. It is mine by right. If I choose to give it to the stranger to try his hand, why, then I will. Now go to your quarters and take up your work on your loom and spindle and let the servants do theirs as well. This is a question for men to settle, and most of all me, for I am the master here. Not you, Antinous. Nor you, Eurymachus."

353-375 Amazed, Penelope opened her mouth to respond to her son, then shut it and rose obediently, quietly, and left, climbing the stairs to her room, followed by her servants. There she wept again for Odysseus until Athene took pity upon her and again caused sweet sleep to slip over her eyes.

While all eyes followed Penelope up the stairs, however, the swineherd took the moment to collect the bow and quiver and started to take it to Odysseus. One of the suitors saw this and bawled, "What's this? What do you think you're doing, you insolent pig swiver? You mucker? Gods' balls! If Apollo hears this, why, may his dogs rip you to pieces and scatter them among your pigs away from all of us."

Eumaeus meekly laid the bow on the floor as angry cries echoed around the great hall, but Telemachus's voice roared loud and menacing above them. "Bring the bow, old man! You can't obey everyone, that's for certain, but I warn you that I am more powerful than any here in this regard. Disobey me and I'll dust your hide with a stout stick! If I had numbers on my side, I'd send these louts packing, I assure you, instead of being forced to sit here and listen to their outlandish plots and pricklings!"

The others roared with laughter at this and the swineherd chose that *376–400* moment to collect the bow and quiver and carry it to Odysseus. He placed it in his lord's hands, then turned to Eurycleia and said, "Eurycleia, you're a wise woman, that's saying a lot! Telemachus has made orders for you to get the women out of here and lock them away in their own quarters. And keep them there," he cautioned, shaking a bony finger under her nose, "despite what you might hear from this room."

Eurycleia hurried to do his bidding while Philoetius slipped out quietly and barred the great gate as he had been ordered. He dropped the bar into its brackets and lashed it firmly with a hawser woven from papyrus reeds that was lying forgotten after being carelessly tossed behind a column. Then he went back and took his seat again, his eyes fixed steadily on Odysseus.

Now Odysseus had his bow in his hands and he twisted and turned it, carefully inspecting to see if worms had eaten their way through the great horn. The suitors watched him, amused, and one fellow piped up, "Look at the expert. Why, one would think he was a connoisseur of bows. I'll bet he has one just like it at home or else intends to carve one like it for himself."

Another laughed and said, "I'll expect he has as much luck doing that as *401–428* he does stringing it."

And so they babbled among themselves while the man of masquerades finished his inspection. Then as a minstrel skilled at the harp tunes the strings easily with the pegs,[7] he effortlessly bent the bow under and over his leg and pushed the twisted cord over the tip of the bow and plucked the cord. A high, clear note sang a swallow's song in the room and all fell still in wonder. Color faded from their cheeks, and then a loud thunderclap from Zeus boomed and echoed ominously through the house and Odysseus's heart leaped in gratitude at the sign.

He took an arrow from the table where the suitors had carelessly dropped it during their attempts to string the bow and nocked it. He drew back the string and, without rising from his stool, sent the shaft whistling through the axheads. When the arrow buried itself in its mark at the other end of the hall, Odysseus turned to Telemachus and said, "You see, the stranger has not disgraced you in your own hall. I did not miss the mark and did not strain to string this bow. The taunts these wastrels heaped upon me did not take away my strength. And now it is time to feed these scoundrels their long-awaited supper and then we can pass on to the music and dancing, what?"

429-434   He nodded grimly, and Telemachus leaped to his feet and slipped his sharp sword over his head and, seizing his lance, took his place near the chair at his father's side. Light glittered horribly from his weapons.

Here ends the Twenty-first Book of Homer's Odyssey.

THE TWENTY-SECOND BOOK

The Bloody Hall

❖ ❖ ❖ ❖ ❖ ❖ ❖ ❖ ❖ ❖ ❖

The justice of Odysseus is fast and swift
And the souls of the suitors are set adrift.

❖ ❖ ❖ ❖ ❖ ❖ ❖ ❖ ❖ ❖ ❖

*O*dysseus shrugged off the rags that hid his warrior's body   *1–29*
From the others and leaped to stand on the great threshold.
His bid to reclaim Penelope, his lands, and his house had begun.
Flickering lights glinted from his heavy muscles. A glow lifted
Upward from his face. He dumped the quiver of swift shafts
At his feet. A shiver raced through the suitors at his grim smile.
"That game is over, lads," he said. "Now, for another mark I've had
Yet to hit—which, with Apollo's help and Zeus's will, I shall!"

He nocked a bitter arrow and drew it back to his ear, aiming at Antinous just
as he reached to take his two-handled gold cup. The wine was at his lips
when the shaft sliced through his throat to the feathers.[1] He had no notion of
death. Who would have in that room and among familiar company? Who
would have imagined that a single foe would have lurked in that festive
group and dared black revenge upon such a man, the best of all there? The
cup dropped from his nerveless fingers, clattering to the floor as black blood
burst in brilliant runnels from his nostrils like artesian water from twin
pipes. His feet kicked hard at leaving life and upended his table, knocking
the bread crusts and meat scraps to the floor where they mingled in the
welling pool of blood.

The suitors leaped to their feet to stare in horror at the throat-pinned
Antinous lying lifeless in his own blood. An uproar of curses cried out in
madness, and frustration filled the air as they looked wildly about the walls,

searching for weapons, but Telemachus had wisely followed his father's advice and moved the weapons from the walls to a storage room far away in the palace. Not a shield was to be seen; not a spear; no sword was at hand. They yelled in outrage at Odysseus, heaping abuse at him as one would throw rotten fruit.

"If you wanted to kill yourself, stranger, this is a sure way of doing it," one cried. "You have killed the noblest of all here. Vultures will soon feast upon your liver!"

30–58   "An accident," another spat, looking at Antinous. He shook his head. "You should have taken more care, stranger."

Still they could not believe that the shaft sang true for Antinous's throat. And now the master trickster Odysseus stared blackly at them and said, "Dogs! You played your mewling games confident that I would never return from Troy. Yet here I stand. You sacked my house, raped my maids, and tried to bed my wife in secret. All this though I still lived and without fearing the gods who loathe injustice! Now all of you are carrion feast! I can smell your blood!"

Death's pale fingers touched the brow of all there and blood drained from their heads as they looked at the promise of the great abyss in Odysseus's eyes. Death cleaved their tongues to the roofs of their mouths, all except Eurymachus, who spoke.

"You say you are Odysseus. Perhaps you are." He shrugged. "But who's to say? You've been gone a long time. Yes, perhaps we have behaved badly in this house and violated the limits of hospitality with your fields and animals. But the man who is responsible for this lies dead at your feet already. Antinous is the man who whipped us on to feast and eat what we would. Marriage was not foremost on his mind but the power that would come from such a marriage. Power made him plot against your son, Telemachus. And now he has his portion of the estate in death—the ground that he lies upon. There's no reason to kill the rest of us. We are your own people. And we are quite willing to pay you for all that we have eaten and drunk over the years. Twenty oxen each will we add to your fields and a heaping treasure of gold and bronze that will grow into a mountain until your heart softens. We do not blame you for being angry, for your madness."

59–85   But the stern mask about Odysseus's face did not relax and his eyes narrowed with anger as he said, "Eurymachus, your life would still be forfeit even if you shower me with all the riches that you have inherited and everything that you have earned. No, not even that will keep my hand from plucking this bowstring. But you have a choice, as do all of you—fight me or die where you stand. Of course," he shrugged—"you may try and run from your death, but I do not think that any of you will leave this room alive. All will make that steep descent to the Halls of Hades. And, Eurymachus"—his lips parted in a thin smile—"I have been there. I have seen what you will see. I have looked into that abyss."

Their hearts leaped fearfully at his words and their knees trembled. A bladder loosened itself. Again Eurymachus spoke, saying, "Ah, my friends! This man is mad! He will not put his bow aside. He'll shoot his shafts from that door until he kills all of us! Madness, I tell you! Stark madness! Well, you forced your way into this house, now fight your way out of it! Draw your swords, you who still carry them. Lift up the tables for a shield! Rush him! He can't kill all of us at once, I say! If we can drive him from that doorway and escape to the town, we will find fellows there to put him to his heels! And then he will have shot his last shaft."

He put movement to his words, reaching beneath his cloak and pulling out his razor-sharp sword, and shouting a hoarse war cry, launched himself at Odysseus. But the man of masquerades plucked the string almost carelessly and a shaft appeared like magic in his breast, the feathers quivering at the nipple as the barbed end buried itself in his liver. His sword dropped from nerveless fingers and clattered on the ground. He shuddered, blood gushed from his mouth, staining his tunic, and he fell across the table, his body bending in agony against the pain erupting from his breast, his food and two-handled cup falling to the floor. His forehead struck hard against the floor and his feet twisted in pain as a gray mist rapidly turning black closed over his eyes.

Amphinomus came hard upon his heels straight toward Odysseus, his *86–111* sword raised high to slash him from the door. But he had forgotten the brave man's son, and Telemachus struck him from behind with his great lance, stabbing midway between his shoulders with such force that the bronze point came out his breast. He too crashed forward and struck the ground with his forehead. Telemachus leaped away, leaving his lance buried in Amphinomus's body, afraid that if he paused to drag it out another suitor would rush him as he bent over the corpse. He ran to his father's side and said, "I will fetch a shield for you and spears and a helmet for your noble head. I'll bring back armor and swords for myself and Eumaeus and the cowherd. We stand a better chance armed."

"Be quick," his father said, grinning Death's grin. "I still have arrows, but when they are gone I will be quickly driven from this doorway."[2]

Telemachus did not hesitate on hearing his father's words but sped straightaway to the storeroom where he had placed weapons. He picked up four shields and four bronze helmets with thick horsehair plumes. He grabbed eight spears and ran back to his father's side.

112–140 He dropped his load at his father's feet and quickly readied himself for battle. The swineherd and cowherd followed him, then all took their place beside Odysseus as he made the bowstring sing a high clear continuous note. Shaft after deadly shaft darted from his quick hands. The suitors tried vainly to dodge them, but they bumped and crowded each other and the shafts found their murderous marks. The bodies began to pile up, and then the last arrow strummed from the great bow and Odysseus propped the bow against the doorjamb, slipped a four-plied hide shield over his arm, clamped a helmet on his head, and picked up two spears with gleaming bronze points.

A postern door stood inside the wall, raised by a beam from the floor, that led from the great hall to an outside hallway.[3] Usually it was locked, and Odysseus directed the swineherd to stand next to this side door for which there was only one approach. Agelaus saw the possible escape and shouted, "Friends, one man must reach that door and alert the people in the town about the murder in here! Then we would see the last of these attacks!"

But the goatherd Melanthius shook his head, shouting, "Ah, impossible, my lord! The entryway is too narrow. One good man can hold all of us away from that portal. No, I must go inside to the storeroom where the arms are kept. I'm certain I know where that whelp Telemachus hid them! Inside, not outside! That's our hope!"

141–169 Dodging and darting, Melanthius ran away from the great hall, making his way deeper into the palace where he found the great storerooms of Odysseus. He quickly gathered a dozen shields and spears and horsehair-plumed helmets and ran back to the hall, where he handed them to the suitors. When Odysseus saw the suitors armed and the numbers facing him, his heart lurched, and for the first time his knees quaked as he realized how perilous the situation had become. He shouted at his son, "Telemachus! One of the women in this house has betrayed us. Either that or Melanthius."

Telemachus answered, "My fault! I left the door open to the storeroom. It seems they are smarter than I thought. Even now Eumaeus is trying to seal that door and find out if it is a woman who opened it or Melanthius. I would wager he is the one, though, not a woman."

Even as they spoke, Melanthius was trying to return to the storeroom for more weapons. But now the worthy swineherd saw him and said, "Wise Odysseus, Melanthius has again left the hall. What should I do? I'll try and stop him, but should I kill him or bring him back here to the hall for you to sentence him for his foul antics against your house?"

170–199 "Telemachus and I will keep these arrogant louts here! Take the cowherd with you and the two of you tie and truss him to a board and throw a twisted rope high over the roof beams and pull him to the sky where he can swing and suffer longer."

The pair hurried away and found Melanthius busily selecting weapons in the storeroom. He didn't see them, and when he came out of the room, carrying a fine helmet and an old shield heavy with mildew and rust that Laertes had carried when a boy, the two men seized him, dragged him by the hair down the hall to a pillar where they tied harsh knots around him and hoisted him high to the rafters. That was when you, Eumaeus, mocked him as he swung like a bag of manure high overhead.

"Watch well, Melanthius, from your soft bed. From there you won't miss Dawn's light when she climbs from Ocean's stream to mount her golden throne. Keep a sharp eye for the hour when you must drive the goats for the suitors' feast."

And they left the hapless Melanthius swinging there as they slammed the 200–225 great door shut behind them and gathered their shields and spears and returned to their master, Odysseus.

And at last the four of them faced together the armed group of suitors who grimly challenged them from across the hall. It was then that Athene came down, disguised in voice and form as Mentor, and when Odysseus saw her he shouted with joy, "Mentor, old friend! It is good of you to join us. Remember all that I did for you in the past! Now is the time to repay that!"

But beneath the disguise she wore, he recognized the gray-eyed goddess Athene who had been by his side for so many years. The suitors, however, saw only what they wanted to see and greeted her with great hoots of laughter. Agelaus, the son of Damastor, spoke first, saying, "Don't let those sweet words sway you to his side, Mentor! Once we have killed the father and the son, then we shall kill you as well. You may want to help him, but your head will pay for your stupid actions. And when our swords have drunk your blood, then we shall add your house and lands to those of Odysseus and divide them among us. No son of yours will inherit your house, and your daughters and wife will not be able to show their faces in the streets of Ithaca again!"

The words angered Athene, and her great wrath rose as she faced 226–252 Odysseus and spoke scathingly to him, saying, "What is this, Odysseus? Where is that great spirit that once caused men to quake and fear at the very mention of your name? Where is your vaunted power, eh? The great hand that slew hundreds? I don't see the man who fought nine long years on the plains of Troy for Helen's white arms. It was your wisdom that burnt Priam's city and now you stand on your doorsill and curse your luck not to be stronger than you were? You wanted your house and lands back. Well, here they are for the taking. You fought long for others, now fight for yourself. I'll stand by you. Watch and learn how Mentor, the son of Alcimus, repays your kindness."

But she was not yet ready to grant Odysseus the victory he wanted. Instead, she chose to test him and his son further. She changed into a swallow and flew high to perch on the smoke-blackened main beam that ran the length of the hall.

And now the suitors gathered behind Agelaus, son of Damastor; Eurony-mus; Amphimedon; Demoptolemus; Peisander, son of Polyctor; and nimble Polybus, the best of the suitors still alive. Agelaus shouted to them, "My friends! This man's hands are tired. You heard Mentor—that braggart—but see how the old man ran away and now those four stand alone at the door. Don't throw your spears at once. Six throw first and hope that Zeus will guide at least one of them to its mark. Then all of us can claim the prize we wanted and will not be afraid of the three remaining."

253–281   Six threw their spears with all their strength, but Athene caused each to miss its mark. One struck the great doorpost, another the door, a third and a fourth of the ash-wood shafts clattered their bronze points against the wall. Odysseus laughed, feeling the wildness come back into him. He spoke to his companions, saying, "Take aim, men! Select your targets well and throw your darts into them before they add our death to their deeds."

Four sharp lances laced their way toward the suitors. Odysseus's spear struck Demoptolemus while Telemachus's spear struck Euryades in the waist. The wily youth closed quickly and drove his spear the rest of the way through Evenor's son and he crashed face-first to the ground. Eumaeus slew Elatus while Peisander fell to the cowherd. Odysseus and his followers swiftly moved forward, seizing weapons from the fallen men.

Again six suitors threw with all their force but Athene made the volley miss and one man struck the doorpost of the great hall while another's spear sank into the solid oak door. A third struck the wall, but Amphimedon's managed to slice above Telemachus's wrist. A long spear from Ctesippus's frantic throw scratched Eumaeus's shoulder.

282–311   Again Odysseus's men hurled their spears and Eurydamas fell to Odysseus, raider of cities, sacker of Troy, while Amphimedon fell to Telemachus's toss, and Polybus to the swineherd. Ctesippus blubbered and blurted his fears, then bled when Philoetius spitted him in the breast. "How, now, you foul-mouthed simpering son of bragging Polytherses! Your fat-tongued folly and flimflam ways are gone forever, eh? Remember the cow's hoof you flung at Odysseus when he begged in the hall? Here's your pay-

ment for those fine ways!" The great master of the black herds laughed with
satisfaction as Ctesippus cried and fouled himself as he died.

Odysseus lunged in under the shield of Agelaus and, taking a short hold
on his spear, struck him hard in the belly, gutting him. Telemachus gutted
Leocritus whose head smacked the ground. Then from her perch high above
the killing ground, Athene took out the aegis and held it high above their
heads, and the horrible sight sent fear streaking through the suitors' hearts
and they dashed around the hall like dragonflies hazing above sweet grass,
bawling for a way from the war, running here and there like a herd of cattle
when a gadfly has stung their rumps. The others swooped down around
them like vultures from the high mountaintops upon darting desperate birds
dancing through the air, knowing there is no escape. They bunched together
in one corner and, half crazed with fear, launched their weapons without
aiming at the four brave men standing alone against their numbers. And
Odysseus and his men fell upon them, hacking at them as they had hacked at
the animals led in to slaughter for their feasts. Horrible screams echoed from
the stones in the hall and the ground streamed with blood.

Leodes ran forward, blubbering and wailing, and fell to the ground
and grasped Odysseus tightly around his knees, begging, "Mercy, mighty
Odysseus! I'm at your knees, begging. Begging! Pity! Pity! I swear I have
done no wrong to any woman in your house and even tried to stop the others
when they wooed and wained their wanton ways. But they wouldn't listen
to me. No! Not me! I was their priest! That's all! I should not die as they did!
I did only good deeds!"

But the man of masquerades scowled heavily at him and said, "If you
were their prophet, then your prattling prayers pleaded with the gods to
keep me from returning to these halls. False prophet! You would have my
wife choose you and bear your sniveling brats. For that, I kill you!"

And he gathered the great sword of Agelaus from his death-gripped
hand, and with one mighty swing severed Leodes's head from his shoulders.
Bright blood fountained into the air and his head bounced in the dust like a
large hailstone before his lips stopped protesting.

And now Phemius, the son of Terpius, who unwilling sang many songs in
the hall, hoped to escape the black death creeping toward him from across
the room. He stood close beside the postern door, harp in hand, unsure what
to do. Should he run from the hall and seek sanctuary by the altar of Zeus in
the courtyard where Laertes and Odysseus had sacrificed many fat oxen and
burned many fat-covered thighs? Or should he follow Leodes's lead and fall
to Odysseus's knees and beg for his life? On instinct, he laid the hollow harp

312–341

on the ground between the mixing bowl and silver-studded chair where
Penelope sat and fell beseechingly to Odysseus's knees.

342-368   "I beg you, mighty Odysseus! Pity me. Kill a bard whose music reaches
the ears of the gods and men and you'll feel only regret. I have been taught by
no one; my songs come from the gods themselves. I can verse and sing as well
in your company as any. Telemachus will tell you that I never sang for my
own will or for the love of the suitors at their feasts but that they forced me
with their strength to make merry!"

Telemachus heard his plea over the din of the battle and called to his
father, saying, "Spare that one! He's innocent! And our herald Medon who
cared for me as a boy! By the great balls, where is that man? Has Philoetius
killed him already? Or Eumaeus? Did he fall when you stormed through
the hall on your first rush?"

At his words Medon popped out from where he'd been hiding under a
chair after draping a freshly slaughtered ox's hide over his head. He threw it
off and dropped to Telemachus's knees, clasping them tightly.

"That's right, my boy! Spare the old man. Tell your father to leave off
cleaving me with his great sword. It's by accident only that I'm still in this
hall and I'm not certain he'll still recognize me in his bloody fury!"

369-394   Odysseus heard his plea and smiled through his blood-drenched beard,
saying, "Take heart, good man. Your plea hasn't fallen on deaf ears and I
have heard my son's words as well. I'll spare your life so you will know and
tell others that a good heart will triumph often over evil. But make your way
outside away from this blood—you and the singer, too—before you get
caught up in my killing rage. I still have work to do here!"

The two men scampered from the hall like hares with swift hounds on
their trail. They took seats beside the great altar of mighty Zeus and watched
fearfully from their perch for they sensed Death's hand still hovering over
the palace of Odysseus.

Now Odysseus's eye ranged around the house, looking for those hiding to
escape his wrath. But he found the suitors lying in heaps in their own blood
like fish dragged from heavy nets upon the sands. He moved among them,
nudging them with his bloody spear point until, satisfied that none lived, he
placed the butt of the spear against the ground and said to Telemachus, "Call
Eurycleia here so that I can tell her what I want done."

395-421   Telemachus, heavily spattered with blood and gore, nodded and banged
the haft of his sword hard against the door to the women's hall and shouted,
"Eurycleia! Get up, old woman! Stir your bones out into the hall! You are in
charge of the women servants and your master wishes to speak to you!"

Immediately Eurycleia threw the door open, for she had been listening hard behind it to the shouts and screams and pleas for mercy. And now she came behind Telemachus, nearly stepping on his heels, as they made their way to the great hall where mighty Odysseus stood bloody and victorious among the heaps of dead men. He looked like a lion who has just feasted on the belly of a bullock, blood and gore dripping from his shoulders and breasts. But when Eurycleia saw the dead men heaped upon the floor and the great sea of blood, she started to cry out in triumph. But Odysseus sternly rebuked her, saying, "Hold your tongue, old woman! Gloat quietly. There's no triumph here. Only dead men who died because of their arrogant pride and evil ways. They fell to the gods and their own carelessness. But now tell me which of the women have been loyal and which have been bedded with these men and wished me dead."

"By the great gods," Eurycleia breathed, studying the dead men. Reluc-   422–452
tantly she jerked her eyes away from them and looked at her master with shining eyes. "Yes, I'll give you that! Fifty women we took in and fed and clothed and taught them how to serve and card wool and weave wool, cautioning them to remain chaste in their ways. Only twelve of them slept with the enemy and made themselves popular with their wanton ways so they felt they could snap their fingers and send the rest of us running at their whims. Some even defied Penelope openly like the brazen whores they are! Telemachus could not stop that because his mother forbade him from ordering them from the house, but now, now"—she took a deep breath—"now it's time for me to climb the stairs and tell the queen that the king has returned. She still sleeps deeply from where some god has sent her."

"Not yet," Odysseus said sternly. "Instead, bring those women you have mentioned to me."

The old woman hastened along the hall to bring the women to her master. Odysseus turned to Telemachus and the two faithful herders who had sided with him and said, "Start hauling the dead out of here. Have those women help you. They were familiar with the bodies when they were alive, now let them handle them dead. Then make them wash and sponge the blood from the chairs and tables in this house, and once they have finished with that, take them outside between the tower and the wall by the stables and use the suitors' long sharp swords and slash those sluts until they no longer remember practicing Aphrodite's sweet art under the rutting suitors on their couches."

Down the hall came the women, crying fearfully and begging for their lives. They came into the great room and saw the heaping dead. Some vomited, but all quickly bent to the task given them by Telemachus and the

453–478 herders and dragged the men out by their heels, laying them in the court-yard, one body propped against another.

When they had finished, they gathered the water and washed and sponged the blood from the chairs and tables while Telemachus and the herders took hoes and scraped the floor clean of blood and gore, but they made the wanton women carry the muck from the house.

And when the great room was once again clean, Odysseus's faithful drew their swords and forced the women out of the house to the place Odysseus had assigned them. They cried and they begged, but Telemachus said, "Sluts and trulls, I wouldn't give a fig for you who mocked us and spread your legs for the suitors' rutting pleasure."

But he would not let the others touch the women with their swords. Instead, he took a long rope that had seen service on one of the great sailing ships and tied one end to a pillar and threw the other over a beam. Then he passed a noose around their necks and raised them until their toes did not touch the ground. He left them there, dancing and dangling, caught as certainly as thrushes in a snare set in a thicket. And then their feet ceased to twitch and jump.

Then they went into the great house and brought Melanthius from his perch and drove him out of the hall into the courtyard and next to the stable where the dung heap lay. They took a sharp knife and cut off his nose and ears, ignoring his shrill cries of pain and pleadings for mercy. His bowels loosened and a horrible stench rose from him and he screamed in a high thin voice like a woman as they grabbed his genitals and sliced them away and tossed them, a raw meal, to the dogs. Then a great fury fell upon them and they hacked off his hands and feet and left him bleeding on the dung heap as
479–501 they returned to the house to clean themselves.

And finally, the bloodletting was over.

Odysseus turned to Eurycleia and said, "Nurse, bring brimstone and a brazier and burn a fire to clean my hall. Then fetch my queen, Penelope, and her maids, and all of the servants who have remained faithful to me in my long absence to the great hall."

"Yes, that I will," Eurycleia said. She touched gnarled fingers gently, fondly, to his cheek and said, "But first let me bring you a fresh tunic and cloak so that you will not frighten them by standing in your hall in your blood-soaked rags."

"First build the fire," Odysseus commanded.

And Eurycleia rushed to do his bidding, bringing brimstone and a brazier to purify the hall, the house, and the great courtyard. Then she rushed to spread the news, and the maidservants flocked out of their rooms to embrace him and weep and kiss his head and shoulders and his hands. And sweet tears came to his eyes and a lump to his throat as he remembered every one of them.

Here ends the Twenty-second Book of Homer's Odyssey.

THE TWENTY-THIRD BOOK
The Secret of the Bed

❖ ❖ ❖ ❖ ❖ ❖ ❖ ❖ ❖ ❖ ❖

Odysseus reveals his identity to Penelope,
And tells his adventures briefly.
Then he goes to his father, Laertes,
To set the old man's mind at ease.

❖ ❖ ❖ ❖ ❖ ❖ ❖ ❖ ❖ ❖ ❖

Cackling like an egg-laying hen with pleasure, the old nurse stalked
Stiffly up the stairs, her feet slapping hard against the stone steps.
She ignored the pain in her joints that cracked and popped.
"Told you he would return," she muttered smugly. Scurrying
Down the long hall to her mistress's bedroom, she cried, "Doom
Has fallen upon the suitors! Awake, Penelope! Awake! We must
Prepare a wake! Come and see with your own eyes
What you have longed for these many years! Odysseus is here!
Too bad for those arrogant thieves who made his house a brothel
And dared to raise their hands against his noble son.
Ignoring the gods' warning brought their deaths—so I'm told!"

She grabbed Penelope's shoulders, bouncing her upon her bed until her silver-gold tresses flounced. "Odysseus has returned! Yes, I say, returned! And he has killed those arrogant louts who have tried to take you by wedded vow to bed all these years and cleaned his house out as a wasp does its nest. All those braggers who defied Telemachus and plagued this house: gone!"

Penelope stared at her in wonder, then sighed and said, "Dear nurse. Calm yourself. Some god has driven you mad or else you've been tippling too much in the wine. All of that can rob the wise of their wits and give the fool wisdom. Stop mocking me while I grieve for my husband. Why wake me with wild words when I slept sweet sleep, the sweetest I have slept since

Odysseus left for that damnable city? Now leave me alone. Return to your own room. If another had awakened me like this with her babbling blather, I would have slapped her cheeks and sent her packing to her room in tears. Your age saves you from that, at least."

But faithful Eurycleia ignored the anger in Penelope's eyes and stood her ground as stalwart as Telemachus and the herders had stood beside their master in the fearful battle in the great hall. "I don't mock you, dear child. It's the truth! By the great gods! Yes! Odysseus has returned. He was the stranger that they all taunted in the hall. Telemachus has apparently known for quite some time now but kept his father's presence a secret until they could make their plans to rid this palace of that vermin who lolled around the place, gorging and lapping up wine like a thirsty dog water!"

32–66   Penelope's heart thudded in her breast and she rose quickly from her bed and burst into tears, hugging the old nurse fiercely. "How—that is, why—Tell me how he managed this great feat! Home in secret, you say? Then he killed all of them single-handedly? All of them? The whole crowd?"

Eurycleia hugged her mistress back and said, "Well, I didn't see it, you know—I only heard the screams and groans of the dying. We—the women, all of us—hid huddled behind the doors, terrified about what was happening! You should have heard it! The clamor, the clanging, the din! I stayed in my room until your son came and pounded on the door and called me out into the hall in bidding to his father. It was there I saw your husband, standing like a terrible and vengeful god, blood and gore dripping from him, the bodies of those vain men lying about him in heaps. Your heart would have leaped to see him! Like a lion, he was. At once he burnt brimstone in the hall to purify it and ordered me to fetch you. So come, come! Stop your dawdling, now. The two of you can once again be happy now that he has returned to his hearth and found his son and wreaked his revenge upon those suitors—every one of them—who wronged you and him."

"Don't laugh and carry on so," prudent Penelope cautioned. "No one here more than I would welcome him, you know that. But"—she shook her head and despair again came to her eyes—"no, it's not possible. No. Some god has killed the suitors. That I don't doubt. It's been long overdue and the gods have finally sent a vengeful demon to weed them from here. But Odysseus? No. He's long dead in some distant land far from Ithaca."

67–94   "Stuff and nonsense," Eurycleia said impatiently, tugging at her arm. "How can you let your teeth chatter such nonsense. You've grieved so long you know nothing but grief. How can you say that Odysseus can never return? Are you the gods that you have that distant vision? I tell you he is here, at home, standing before his own hearth! But," she said, leaning closer, "there is one more thing that makes me know it is Odysseus. Remember that scar the long-toothed boar gave him long ago? The one that curled up his leg? No other man has that scar and I saw it on Odysseus when I washed his feet. I wanted to tell you then, but he refused to let me speak. Yes, he is a smart fellow," she said with great relish. "Another would have sent me scampering up here to you and doomed himself in the bargain. But not that one! So lay your grief aside, my lady. It's an overused mantle you've worn long enough. Come on with me. If I'm lying to you, why then, you can have me killed for my troubles and babbling lips."

But Penelope demurred, still shaking her head. "Ah, this is still a hard thing to believe. Who can read the countless ways of the gods? But if what you say is true, why, then let us hurry to my son so I can see the slaughtered suitors for myself and the man who killed them—whether it is Odysseus or not."

As she spoke she left her upper rooms and hurried down through the long corridors to the great hall, her mind working with indecision. What should she do? Should she run to her husband and kiss his hands? Or should she stand aloof and question him? She stepped across the threshold into the great room and saw him standing against the far wall. She felt weak in her knees and immediately dropped onto a seat beside the fire, staring at the man who leaned against a pillar across the room, eyes downcast, waiting for her to speak. For a long time she sat still, studying him silently, wondering—yes, it looked like him, but rags and blood still covered him, and could that man beneath that gore be the husband she waited for?

Telemachus's voice broke in on her thoughts, rebuking her. "Mother, how 95-122 can you remain so hard-hearted? Have you lost the love you claimed so long for my father? Why don't you cross to his side and speak to him? Ask him questions? What type of woman are you that would stay silent like this after years of weeping for a husband who has just returned home after roaming for twenty years hither and thither like a feather upon the wind? I guess your heart really is made of stone."

Wise Penelope shook her head in wonder, saying, "Shock, child, shock. I'm numb to my toes. I can't think of a single thing to say to him. I can't even look into his face. But"—she paused, studying him hard—"if this is really Odysseus, why, we shall know soon enough for there are things between us that no one else could ever know."

Odysseus smiled patiently at her, then turned to his son, saying, "Telemachus, leave us alone. Your mother must decide for herself if I am Odysseus or another stranger beneath this dirt and blood that cake me now. I don't blame her for doubting me. But we have other matters that we must take care of now. When a man kills another—even if that man has no friends at all to exact blood vengeance for him—the killer must go into exile and abandon his family and lands. But we have not killed one man; we have slain many of Ithaca's finest here. I don't say they weren't deserving to go knocking at Death's door, but we have to consider what to do now."

"That's up to you, father," Telemachus said shrewdly. "I've heard the stories about your trickery, your wisdom. No one living has more cunning, the bards say. So the three of us will do what you decide and give you what strength we still have among us."

Odysseus smiled at his son and said, "All right. Here's what I think best. First, clean yourselves and dress yourselves in fresh tunics. Tell the women to dress in their best and the singer to take up his harp and pluck and sing happy songs so those who chance along the road outside will think that a wedding feast is on and about this house. Such a party will keep neighbors guessing as well and keep them away from learning about the suitors' death until we leave for my well-wooded farm. There we will see what Olympus has in store for us. That will give me a little time to think."

They hurried to carry out his orders. The men filled tubs and doused themselves in them and put on fresh tunics the women laid out for them. The women decked themselves with the loveliest jewelry and dabbed perfume on themselves, and then the harper, remembering how Odysseus had spared him, took up his harp and strummed it vigorously, breaking out into gay songs that moved all those there to stamp their feet and dance and make merry until the manor hall echoed with their gaiety so that anyone passing on the road outside would nod to his fellowman and say, "It's taken time, but the queen has at last given in and married one of those upstarts! Sluttish vixen! Should have waited, I tell you! Nothing good will come of this, mark my words!"

But no one guessed the truth that the suitors lay in a rotting heap and that Odysseus, the man of masquerades, had come home at last and even now was being bathed and scraped and rubbed with rich oil by Eurynome and dressed in a beautiful tunic and rich purple cloak with gold threads spun through it. Then Athene made a soft glow form over him, straightened him and made his shoulders square and brushed his locks to curl and hang from his head like hyacinth petals in bloom. She worked carefully, as carefully as Hephaestus with the secrets of his art to inlay silver with delicate filigrees of gold. He stepped out of the bathing room looking every inch the god and went across the room to sit beside his patient wife. He stared at her wonderingly for a long moment, then smiled gently.

"You are a strange woman, Penelope. The gods have made you hard. Oth-

erwise, how could you sit there calmly staring at me. No other woman would
be this way after her husband has spent the last twenty years trying to find
his way home."

"And you are a strange man," she answered quickly. "Don't misunder-
stand what you think you see. I don't scorn you, nor does pride keep me
away. I remember quite well how you—he—looked when he left that day
aboard a ship bound for Troy. But—" She turned to Eurycleia and said,
"Enough of this for now. Eurycleia, have the great bed moved out of the bed-
room my husband built before he left and cover it with warm fleece and
blankets and rugs."

Odysseus's eyes flashed at this and he stood up, looking down at her, anger *179–207*
spilling from him as greatly as the anger that ravaged the great hall earlier.
"What's this? By the gods, woman, you've goaded me strongly, now! Who
has moved my bed? What man dared? No one had the art for that—unless a
god whispered secretly into his ear. No mortal could move that bed with a
rock and lever unless he knew the secret that we kept between us and built
into that bed. I built that bed around an old olive tree that had grown fully. I
lined the plot with stones and erected the wall and roof and set the door-
jambs solidly in their frame. Then I cut off the silver leaves and branches of
that olive tree and hewed and shaped that stump, rounding it smoothly with
my adze, planing it true to a line to be a bedpost. I built the bed around that
stump while its roots stood fast in the ground, lining it with an inlay of gold
and silver and ivory and stretching a web of crimson oxhide thongs between
it and the other bedposts. That is its secret, my lady, and no one could have
known that if you had not told him. And to move it, he would have had to
cut the stump itself!"

At this, Penelope felt her heart leap in her chest and her knees trembled *208–233*
violently as she realized that it was indeed Odysseus who stood before her.
No other man could have known that secret about the bedpost, and bursting
into tears, she leaped up and wrapped her arms around Odysseus, crying
greatly, "Do not be angry with me, Odysseus! You always understood more
than any man. It is the gods who have brought our great unhappiness upon
us and who couldn't bear to see us so happy with each other and share the
years across to the threshold of old age. Do not be hurt that I didn't make you
feel more welcome before this moment for I have always feared a fraud
would come claiming to be Odysseus and the great gods would not give me
the wisdom to see beneath his masquerade. And so I kept myself aloof from
all, fearing impostors more than anything. I wonder if Helen of Argos,
Zeus's daughter, would have slept in Paris's arms had she known the great
war that would be waged to bring her back to her country. A god drove her

to adultery, leaving her blood cool toward war and the coming insanity. The years! The years! The loneliness! Ah! What could I do? The secret of the bed I kept all these years and no other set of eyes has ever seen it except for Actoris, the maid my father gave me as a gift when I first came with you to this house. She has been the keeper of the bedchamber all these years and only she has seen that bed. My darling, you are my Odysseus!"

And great tears flooded Odysseus's eyes as he wrapped his huge arms around her and held her to him as would a sailor who wrapped his arms around a spar and held tightly in a tempest-tossed sea until he spied warm earth on the horizon.

234-264   Many men would have gone down before Poseidon's buffeting, and so he held Penelope while she cried with joy, her white arms wrapped around her husband's sturdy neck. Dawn would have touched them with her rosy fingers had not Athene slowed the night and held Dawn down beneath Ocean's distant reach and kept the goddess from harnessing her noble steeds, Lampus and Phaethon, the colts who draw Day's chariot.

At last Odysseus said, "My dear, I fear we have not come yet to the end of your trials and troubles. I have one last adventure that I must see to. This was given to me by the great seer Teiresias in the House of Hades when I went down there to find a way home. But for now, let us go to bed, dear wife, and at last enjoy each other's arms."

"The bed is yours whenever you are ready for it," she said, caressing his face. "But tell me: What is this great trial that you must face? I will learn it soon enough, why not now?"

265-294   The man of masquerades stared fondly at her and said, "Strange that you press me so. Well, no harm in it, I suppose. Teiresias said that I was to take an oar upon my shoulder and make my way inland from town to town until finally I arrive at a place where no man has ever seen the wide wine-dark sea or tasted salted meat, and all are strangers to bold craft that slip delicately over the water. A man will look at the oar over my shoulder and ask, 'Why do you carry a winnowing fan over your shoulder, sir?' And at that spot I must plant the oar and make burnt offerings to Poseidon of a ram, a bull, and a great boar. Then I may return home and offer full hecatombs to the gods. And then, dear wife, I shall know peace and we will live the rest of our lives together until Death comes in old age to take us gently away from the sea. I will die, he said, peacefully, surrounded by those who love me."

"If the gods grant us peace in our age, then all the trials will end in peace," Penelope said.

While they spoke, Eurynome and Eurycleia worked by torchlight to put fresh bedding on the great bed, and when their work was done, the nurse returned to her own room and bed while Eurynome lighted the happy couple to the readied bed.

And they lay down together, and Telemachus hushed the dancers and 295–322 singer and caused the great hall to go dark. The swineherd took himself to bed as did the cowherd, and the entire palace fell into a quiet sleep that it had not known for twenty years.[1]

And after they enjoyed making love, Odysseus and Penelope lay quietly in each other's arms in the bed and the noble queen told her husband all that she had been forced to endure in her home during his absence, watching the suitors as they slowly and arrogantly took control over her home and tried to force her into the marriage bed. She told about the great numbers of sheep and cattle they had slaughtered wastefully for their feasts and of all the wine they had drunk. And Odysseus told her about the great adventures and the trials that he had been put through and she listened wide-eyed to his stories until everything was finished.

He began by telling her about the Cicones and his visit to the land of the lotus-eaters. He told her about the Cyclops and how that fellow ate heartily of his men (she shuddered greatly here) and how Odysseus had made him pay for his arrogant flaunting of the laws of hospitality. He told her about Aeolus who had been friendly to him and how the gale rose up to keep him from reaching home. He told her how he came to Telepylus where the Laestrygonians smashed his ships in the bay and ate his companions.

He spoke of Circe and her magic and wizardry and of his voyage to the 323–351 dark Underworld and the House of Death where he met the great Theban seer Teiresias. He told her about the great shades of his dead companions that he saw there, his mother too, and he told Penelope about the Sirens and their song and the Wandering Rocks, of dreaded Charybdis's pool and the monster Scylla. He told how he was disobeyed by his men who slaughtered the cattle of Lord Helios and how Zeus thundered from his heavenly tower and sundered his ship with a lightning bolt. He told how he was greeted by Calypso on the isle of Ogygia and how she pampered him and offered him immortality (and Penelope hugged him when he told how he had refused her for his wife's love) and how she had helped him to leave on a raft and of his arriving in Scherie where the Phaeacians honored him and brought him home in a ship filled with treasures and gifts. And then sleep suddenly fell upon the great Odysseus and he breathed gently, contentedly, relaxing fully for the first time in years and banishing his cares to the dark of the night.

Meanwhile, Athene watched as he made love to his wife, and when he at last fell asleep, she moved quietly among them, satisfying herself that all was right once more in Odysseus's world before she stirred Dawn from her bed to stretch her soft fingers into Odysseus's bedchamber.

352–372   Then the great warrior rose from his bed and said to Penelope, "My wife, we have endured much. More than other mortals have or will. Of this I'm certain. Long have I yearned to return to Ithaca only to be kept away tantalizingly by Zeus. Now we have finally returned to our bed together. I must leave again, my love. I leave everything in your care and I will replenish our herds and stock by raiding the shores where the suitors lived before coming to Ithaca. The people of Ithaca too, however, must help replenish our wealth for they could have stopped this—and should have—before it got so far out of hand. Today I must go to our wooded farm and visit the orchards and see my father, Laertes, who has suffered much in my absence. I ask you to be wise once again, my dear, and take your ladies to the tower room where you waited for me and again wait there quietly. Word will spread quickly today how I killed all the suitors in my house, and I must deal with that."

And with that, Odysseus fixed his great armor around him and placed his sword belt carefully over his shoulders. Then he awakened the herdsmen and Telemachus and ordered them to arm themselves. They dressed quickly in their war gear and followed Odysseus, the man of masquerades, raider of cities, sacker of Troy, out the gate and along the rocky path leading through the town of the mountains and valley of the farm.

Now daylight was full, but Athene cloaked them in darkness.

Here ends the Twenty-third Book of Homer's Odyssey.

THE TWENTY-FOURTH BOOK
The End of the Adventure

❖ ❖ ❖ ❖ ❖ ❖ ❖ ❖ ❖ ❖ ❖

Now we see the burial of the suitors,
And the relations of the wooers
Plot to destroy the warrior Odysseus,
But are defeated by Odysseus, Telemachus,
And Laertes and the servants, and then
Athene draws the great adventure to an end.

❖ ❖ ❖ ❖ ❖ ❖ ❖ ❖ ❖ ❖ ❖

And now patient Hermes Cyllene led the dark souls
Of the suitors from the door of the palace of Odysseus. 1–31
With his wonderful wand of gold that weaves deep sleep
Upon man or awakens him, Hermes directed them
First left and then right as they followed him,
Squeaking like blind bats in a high-ceilinged cavern
After one slips and falls. They treaded closely upon his heels
As he led the way down the dark and dank paths,
Over gray bays and snowy peaks, past rosy Dawn's door
And the gates of the Sun. Here, some souls dwelled
Upon the large Plain of Asphodel. They met Achilles's ghost
And Patroclus and Antilochus too, then moody Aias,
Most noble after Achilles in strength and beauty.
Here, the newly dead crowded together, whispering
Their fears while the soul of Agamemnon, suffering
Forever black pain, stood nearby with those soldiers
Slaughtered with him in treacherous Aegisthus's hall.

Achilles's shade greeted him.

"So here you are, Agamemnon. You know we were certain—when we smelled roses and saw the sun daily—that Zeus walked steadily beside you, his hand upon your shoulder, all the days and weeks and months and years that we fought on the plains of Troy. You seemed more kingly than the rest of us. You had more ships, the largest army. Yet you still met fellow Death in the prime of your life. But it was a pitable death, dying in your lady's chamber like that, locked between her white legs—or was it in your bath? I forget. Doesn't matter—while her lover stabs you in the back. Far better for you if you had died with us at Troy while leading us and received that honorable death. Why, we would have built a great funeral mound for you and had the greatest funeral games. Tch. Tch. A shame." He shook his head.

32–59   "You were fortunate for all of that, I suppose," the soul of Agamemnon said sorrowfully. "When you fell there was a great battle over your corpse with Trojans and Greeks fighting fiercely back and forth, each trying to claim the body as a trophy. Many fell around you. By Hades's glower, but the halls below here seem filled with them! Yet you lay in the dust like all the others before you for a whole day as we fought to bring your body back from the field for proper burial. We succeeded only thanks to a storm Zeus called up for us. We carried you away from that battlefield to the ships and there we bathed your handsome flesh with warm water and spread scented oils over you. The Greeks wept wildly and cut their hair in mourning. When your mother heard our wailing she knew life had fled from your body and she rose up from the sea waves with her Nymphs and gave an eerie wail that swept across the deep. So unearthly was it that all the Greeks would have run in panic back to the ships save for wise Nestor, whose words proved proof in the past, who stopped them, shouting, 'Wait! Hold your pattering feet! This is the mother of great Achilles who has risen from the sea to mourn the death of her son!'

60–87   "And the Greeks stopped their panic flight and stood away, watching warily as the daughters of the Old Man of the Sea crowded around you, wailing and wrapping your body in an ambrosial shroud. The nine Muses came and sang a sweet antiphony in high keening voices as they lamented your passing. For seventeen days and nights you were mourned by mortals and Immortals alike before we consigned you to the flames after slaughtering many fat sheep and curved-horned cattle around you. The Nymphs dressed you and bathed you with honey and rich oils, and while you turned to ash, the Greek heroes, dressed in their best armor, passed solemnly by your pyre. After Hephaestus's flames finished, we gathered your white bones and steeped them in unmixed wine, rich and heady—one sip would make a man drunk for the day—and oil. Your mother brought Dionysus's gift, a double-handled urn made of hammered gold by Hephaestus, richly engraved, and in this we placed your bones, Achilles, and the bones of your friend Patroclus, Menoetius's son, who died before you. Above all this we built a funeral mound next to the bones of Antilochus, the one you loved second only to

Patroclus. This we did on the Hellespont where it forks out over the waters so that the great mound can be seen by sailors seeking a mark to steer by.

"And then we turned to the funeral games, and never were such prizes offered for the contests.

"The great gods gave your mother great gifts that she placed in the mid- 88–117 dle of the field for the champions. You have seen many of these games, Achilles—you have even been the cause of many—but never have you seen the treasures silver-slippered Thetis gave. Your name will live forever, Achilles. But that's what you wanted, isn't it? Didn't you choose the short life with great honor instead of long and melancholy when the gods gave you a choice?" He shook his head. "But what for me? Nothing. And it was I that ended the war only to return home to the miserable end Zeus planned at the hands of that miserable whore my wife! Ah, me," he sighed. "A death's a death for all of that, I suppose. Still, the manner of going is something to soothe the soul afterward. A little something to remember."

And so the banter went as Hermes guided the suitors' shades toward them. They paused as they looked on in wonder, then Agamemnon recognized Amphimedon, the son of Melaneus, his friend. He frowned, puzzled, and said, "Well, Amphimedon, what strange ruin brings you to this gloomy place? Eh?" He glanced back at his companions and shook his head. "Why, all of your companions are of the same age! One would think the best and the brightest of a city had been emptied deliberately by someone. Did Poseidon destroy you with a raging tempest? Were you slain raiding a distant coast? Or trying to take a city? Perhaps," he added, remembering Troy, "it was a woman? What's the matter? No words? Have you forgotten me? Oh, thinly lies man's memory after one is dust! I once came to your house on noble Ithaca along with my brother, Menelaus, to persuade Odysseus to sail away with our army. Don't you remember how hard we reasoned with that great sacker of cities to get him to join us? Why, it took us over a month sailing east, west, north, and south with our words before we could bring him on board!"[1]

"I remember you, Agamemnon, the greatest of commanders," Amphime- 118–146 don's soul said sadly. "And as for our sudden manner of death, well, it was a sorry state of affairs. Those sorry gods—" He broke off as Hermes's face lowered in a black frown. "That is," he added hastily, "it was the fault of Odysseus's wife. Yes, that's it. After he had been gone for years on end, we became suitors for his wife. A fickle woman, she was, leading us on. Neither saying yes nor no to our proposals for marriage. Now, an honorable woman would have said flatly no and sent us on our way from the beginning. But she was a will-o'-the-wisp flitting here and there, first flirting with one, then the

other. And so we stayed, waiting for her to make up her mind as she pos-
tured and preened. Then she came up with a trick to keep us there, saying
that she would make her choice after she finished weaving a shroud for
Laertes. She set up a huge loom in her room and told us, 'My lords'—she
simpered, you understand?—'now that my lord is dead'—and we took great
heart at that for at last she admitted that Odysseus had to be dead; after all,
why would a man stay away so long from a woman like that?—'now that my
lord is dead,' she said, 'let me finish my weaving before I choose the next to
marry. 'Tis a shroud I weave for Lord Laertes for when Death's cold hand
closes his throat. It wouldn't be seemly if I didn't do this, and I don't want the
women of Ithaca to think the less of me because I hadn't prepared for old
Laertes's going.' Now we were only men, you understand, and those words
touched our manly hearts. Who among us wouldn't want to be laid out right
and proper when he died? So for three years we bided our time, waiting for
her to finish that damnable shroud. But then one of her maids tumbled the
secret to one of us after a bit of tickle.

"That night we waited until she retired, then slipped in and caught her
unraveling the work she wove during the day. We could have forced her to
live up to her words then, but being honorable men, we made her finish the
damnable work willy-nilly, and that was our undoing, you see. On the day
she finished and washed that shroud, why, we were laying for her to make
her choice. But then one of those evil gods"—he cast a quick look at frown-
ing Hermes—"arranged for Odysseus to land somewhere on Ithaca. He put
up in a swineherd's hut—appropriate, if you ask me!—and then Telemachus
returned from sandy Pylos where he had gone to find what he could about
his father and he ended up in the same place. Wild accident? I don't think so,
but what do mortals know? There the two of them plotted our murder. Yes,
I said murder. And then they came down to the town. Not together, you
understand; Telemachus came first to set the stage. Then the swineherd
brought Odysseus, that man of masquerades, disguised as a pitiful beggar all
in rags to the manor house. A good disguise, I'll give the man that! No one
saw through those rags to the man beneath. So we teased him about his tat-
tered state and took a few potshots at him—all in fun, you understand—and
he sat there and bore it, patient as stone. But Zeus muttered matterings to
Telemachus and that night the boy took all the arms and locked them away
in the storeroom deep in the house somewhere, leaving us with only what we
had about us. That was when the master trickster worked his cunning. He
told his wife to prepare a test of the bow—you frown; well, you plant these
twelve axheads all in a line like saplings and then you try to shoot an arrow
through the haft holes—but none of us could even string the damn bow of

Odysseus let alone shoot an arrow with it. We protested when they gave the bow to Odysseus to try, for none of us wanted to risk being shamed by a hobbling beggar. But Telemachus said he should have a go with the thing. And he did.

"He strung it and shot an arrow through those axes as simple as a seam- 178-206 stress threading a needle. Then he leaped up with murder glaring from his eyes and took a stand on the threshold. He dumped the arrows out of their quiver at his feet and put a dart right through Antinous's throat. And that was the beginning of the slaughter. He shafted us, one by one. A massacre! Men lay groaning out their life here and there on the blood-slippery floor. Then when his arrows were gone, he and his son and the cowherd and swineherd charged through us, hacking us, and we fell like wheat to the scythe. The only way that could have happened was if some malignant god worked his magic alongside of them. Our screams filled the hall and the floor puddled with blood.

"And that, brave Agamemnon, is how we came to be destroyed. Even now our bodies still lie in a heap outside Odysseus's hall like slabs of meat freshly butchered. No one knows about our dying and so none of our families or friends have come to wash us and lay us out right and proper. All we are is dead. No honor there!"

Agamemnon's shade clapped his hands gleefully and said, "Shrewdly done, mighty Odysseus, son of Laertes! The gods smiled well upon you when you chose that woman for a wife! That is a woman, by the gods, to keep her virtue with trickery like that. And who here wouldn't have loved to have a wife like that to keep her husband's memory faithfully with all the youths buzzing around her like bees around a honey hive? That story will not fade for years and I daresay even the gods will make a song about patient Penelope. A far sight from my Clytemnestra, the daughter of Tyndareus, who spread her legs for another before my sails were out of sight, plotting to kill me at the first chance. That song will not be an honorable one. Why, that woman destroyed not only her reputation but that of all women as well!"

These were the words that they bandied back and forth, each jockeying to tell his story in the land of Hades under the rim of the world.

Meanwhile Odysseus and his men had reached the fertile fields of Laertes 207-236 that he had slowly taken from the wilderness long ago, building a good home with huts around it for his field hands to rest and eat. He kept one old woman from Sicily to care for him in his dotage in his house, refusing to go anywhere but his farm.

When they arrived at the edge of the first of his fields, Odysseus halted the others and took off his armor. He handed it to one of the others, then told his son, "Go into the main house and slaughter the best pig you can find and roast it well. I'll try to find my father. I wonder if he'll remember me after twenty years. It seems few do."

He left them and moved away toward the thick vineyard standing a short distance from the house. As he made his way along the rows, he found no trace of Dolius or his sons or any of the workers. They had all gone to bring stones back from a quarry to build a wall for the vineyard. He found his father busily hoeing weeds from around a young apricot tree. He wore a patched and soiled tunic ragged along the hem and oxhide leggings tied around his legs to keep them from the thorns. He wore gloves and a cowl of goatskin to shade his pate. Odysseus paused by a tall pear tree, a lump coming into his throat as he watched the wasted figure, racked by years of grief, bending slowly with the hoe, scraping the earth. He wondered if he should run forward and hug and kiss his father and tell his tale or first question him and test him. He heeled the tears from his eyes as he decided he'd better find out his father's thinking before anything.

237–267 And so he sauntered toward the old man and stood by his shoulder as his father patiently worked the earth.

"Old man," the man of masquerades said, "it's a good eye the orchard keeper you work for has. Everything is well tended. Why, there's not a fig tree, vine, olive or pear tree that doesn't show careful pruning and trimming. But—and I hope you don't take offense at my words—you don't seem to care as much for yourself as you do these trees. A bit shabby you are in those old clothes with your hair and beard still night-knotted. Yet I don't think you are a slave. No"—he frowned, pretending to study the old man—"I see a certain nobility in your bearing that makes me think that you must be kingly when you are bathed properly and eating well by a warm fire. But tell me: Who owns this orchard? A fellow I met down the road a bit told me that this is Ithaca, but I think he was a sail shy on the ship, for when I asked about my friend who lives here, he couldn't be bothered to say if my friend lived or had traveled to Hades's Halls."

Laertes kept hoeing steadily as Odysseus spoke, not showing if he had heard one word from the trickster or not. "Well, let me tell you about him. Perhaps you may have heard of him?

268–298 "A while back this stranger came to my house—doesn't matter where— and had the best humor I have ever seen about him. Made us all laugh, you know? He claimed he was an Ithacan and that Laertes was his father. Well, I took him in and bathed him and made him welcome and gave him many presents worthy of such a man—seven bars of scaled gold, a silver wine bowl with flowers engraved around it, twelve light cloaks for summer travel, twelve rugs, robes and tunics—and his choice of four women to serve him. Well-trained ones, if you catch my drift?"

Laertes paused in his hoeing and, leaning on the handle, looked up at Odysseus, tears streaming through the deep seams of his leathery cheeks. "Well, sir, you have come to the right place if you're seeking Ithaca. But it has fallen upon evil times. Evil men hold the reins of the power here now. All those gifts you gave were given in vain. Sorry to have to tell you this, but there it is. If you could find that man here in Ithaca, rest assured that you would be made equally as welcome as you made him with your hospitality. But tell me: How long ago was this that that man—my son—visited you? That is, if he ever even existed. He's been gone so long that one could almost claim that he was a figment of the imagination, and maybe he was. I suppose he has become food for fishes by now. Or maybe eaten by wild beasts or lying forgotten on foreign soil with no one to properly wrap his body or his wife, Penelope, to close his eyes.

"But"— he blew his nose with his fingers—"tell me about yourself, if you would. Where do you come from? What's your family? Who are you?" 299-324

"Well, uncle, I come from Alybas.[2] I live there and my father is Apheidas, Polypemon's son. I am called Eperitus. My ship is anchored in a barren cove far from the town. I came here by accident from Sicania after a foul wind drove me off my course. So I thought I would look up my friend when I discovered the name of this island. How long has it been? Let's see, must be almost four years—no, make that five—since Odysseus said his good-byes and left my country. The omens were good when he left, for a flock of sparrows flew on his starboard side as he pulled away from shore. We planned to meet again and exchange gifts."

Pain flickered over his father's face. Laertes bent and picked up a handful of dust and sprinkled it over his head. He moaned, and his anguish lanced its way to Odysseus's heart. His nostrils prickled and suddenly Odysseus knew he couldn't watch his father's agony anymore. He stepped forward, threw his arms around the old man, and kissed him.

"Stop it, Father," he said over a lump in his throat. "I am Odysseus. I have been gone twenty years and now at last I have returned."

Laertes stared in wonder at the man holding him, seeing the silver in his 325-353
beard and hair. He shook his head and tried to push away, but Odysseus held him firmly.

"Yes, I am Odysseus," he said. "Now hold your tears. No more grieving. I bring good news for you. The suitors are dead. I killed every damn one of them. All of their crimes and bitter insults and arrogant ways have been stopped."

Laertes shook his head. "Ah, stranger! Many claim to be Odysseus, but there is only one. Give me some proof you are who you claim."

"The scar. Remember the scar from the great white tusk of the boar that lanced me in Parnassus? You and Mother had sent me there to claim the gifts my grandfather, Autolycus, had promised when he visited us the day I was born. I can also tell you all the trees you gave me on this acreage when I trotted after you, stepping on your heels and badgering your years with countless questions while you named them for me one by one. There were thirteen pear trees, ten apple, and forty fig trees. You promised to plant fifty vines for me too and each would bear purple fruit that would hang in the sultry summer days, the gods willing."[3]

A strange clicking came from Laertes's throat and black misery fell over him as he heard Odysseus's words. Tiny dots appeared before his eyes and he swayed and would have fallen if Odysseus hadn't stretched out his hands and caught him by the shoulders.

"Zeus!" he cried. He drew a deep, shuddering breath that whistled through his ancient lungs. "If those savage louts have been at last cleared from the house and paid the penance for their pompous pride, then I know you still reign on mighty Olympus. But now"—he shook his head woefully—"now another great blackness comes to my heart. All of them had family, and I fear even as we speak messengers make their way through every city, town, and village in Cephallenia,[4] spreading the word of their deaths."

354–383 "Put your mind at ease," Odysseus said. "Come, let the moment rest for a while. Let's go to the farmhouse by the orchard. I sent Telemachus there with the cowherd and swineherd to ready a meal for us. See? The sun is already at its meridian high."

And so they turned and made their way slowly down the rows of the vineyard to the house where Telemachus and the herdsmen were already serving the meat they had roasted and mixing amber wine in a krater. The Sicilian woman bathed Laertes and anointed and dressed him, combing the tangles from his hair and his beard while the others finished readying the meal. Platters of meat were laid out for them along with bowls of ripe olives and chunks of fresh goat cheese and baskets of bread. Laertes paused on the threshold to the room and Athene came down and filled his spare form once more, and he straightened his shoulders and his chest filled out against his tunic. His son looked wonderingly at the great light shining around the noble head of Laertes.

"Surely one of the gods has blessed you, Father!" he exclaimed. "You are—magnificent!"

"Harrumph!" Laertes coughed, a light red touching his weathered cheeks. "By Zeus and Athene and Apollo, I wish your words were true and that I was as I was when I led the Cephallenians. I remember when I took the walled city of Nericus on the point. Ah, me! If only I could have had that youth back and stood with you last night against the suitors. I would have crumbled many a knee and left them writhing in their blood in that hall, I promise you! That would have made your heart sing with joy, I'm certain!"

And while the father and son spoke, the herdsmen drew the chairs back *384-411* from the table and soon all were seated with bread in their hands. They spoke lightly, enjoying their meal, when a shadow suddenly filled the doorway. They looked up to see old Dolius and his sons standing there, sweat staining their tunics, their faces flushed from the sun and showing the weariness from hauling the great stones to make the wall. The old Sicilian woman, their mother, had called her husband and sons back to the house to care for them—especially Dolius, who was well on in years.

They stared in amazement at the men eating, instantly recognizing Odysseus. At last Odysseus said, "Well, old man, are you going to stand their gaping or are you going to come and join us for lunch? All of you close your mouths before flies get in and drive you crazy. We've been waiting for you and finally started just this minute for we were fair famished."

Dolius shook himself and ran up, seizing Odysseus's hand with his great horny hand and kissed his wrist. "Master!" he cried. "You've returned. Finally! We thought you had fallen somewhere, but the gods have led you back to us. Welcome, welcome, welcome! May your health be strong! But tell me: Does Penelope know you are on the island? Have you sent a messenger to her? If not—" He turned, indicating his sons still standing in the doorway.[5]

"She knows, old man," Odysseus said gruffly, his heart glad with his reception. "Don't concern yourself with that. Sit! Sit!" He pushed a stool and Dolius sat down as his sons flocked around Odysseus, clasping his hand and slapping his shoulder, welcoming him back to Ithaca. Then they all took their seats beside their father. And all ate hungrily and listened while Odysseus spoke.

But news ran throughout the town on fast heels about the suitors' bloody *412-439* death in the great hall of Odysseus. A crowd gathered at the House of Odysseus to stare at the bodies heaped outside in the courtyard. A great wailing rose as they recognized sons and friends, and slowly they claimed the bodies of those they knew and carried them away to be buried. Those who came from other islands and the mainland were loaded upon ships and sent back in the care of the crews. When they had finished and left the bodies to

be tended, they met again at the assembly and Eupeithes rose, tears stream-
ing from his face, to address them. Grief placed painful lines over his face,
for his son Antinous had been the first to fall from Odysseus's bow.

"My friends"—he choked and drew a deep breath—"this is terrible. Ter-
rible. What sort of man is this Odysseus who led the finest of our spearmen
away to war and returned alone after losing all of his ships and all of his men?
And now he has killed the best of the Cephallenians! Enough! Vengeance, I
say! Quickly, now, before he escapes to sandy Pylos or hides at Elis under the
sacred rule of the Epeian law.[6] Why, if he escapes, we will be disgraced for-
ever! We will not be able to hold our heads up high anywhere and people
will point fingers at us and snicker as we pass and say, 'There they go, all who
were afraid to revenge their people Odysseus slew!' I would rather die than
be forced to listen to flapping lips like those! I say we hunt the rascal down
and deal with him!"

440-469   All those there were moved to tears by his words and nodded and snuffled
and mumbled words against Odysseus. But then Medon and the bard from
Odysseus's hall appeared after awakening and seeing the crowd gathered.
Medon heard the words of Eupeithes as he neared, and he seethed with rage
at the plotting of Antinous's father. The fruit doesn't fall far from the tree, he
thought, then he spread his arms and said loudly, "Friends, Greeks, Itha-
cans! Listen well to my words! This was not done without the say-so from
the great gods. Why, when the slaughter was high I saw a divine Immortal
standing beside Odysseus. It looked like Mentor, who led Odysseus in his
work and swept the suitors down the hall where they died like cattle in a
holding pen. And I saw how this Immortal struck terror in the hearts of the
suitors and how they blubbered and bawled and begged for mercy before
they fell in heaps before the flashing sword of Odysseus."

The blood drained from the faces of the assembly and their bowels grew
loose with fear. Then the old hero Halitherses, Mastor's son, the only one
who could glimpse the future and reckon it with the past, stood creakingly
and said, "Well, Ithacans! It's your own stupidity that has led to this! Yes,
your fault! You wouldn't listen to my words to Mentor when we tried to tell
you to hold your sons back and teach them a few manners before they boldly
went to the House of Odysseus. Fools, all of them! Rank stupidity, and I see
that it still stinks here! Why, your sons don't deserve a fig's blessing for what
they did! They didn't die like heroes. Instead they were only sniveling brats
whose fathers pampered them too much and didn't flog their backsides a
time or two when it would have made a difference. Well, you reaped what
you sowed. You wouldn't teach your sons good manners, and now their bad
manners have brought them low. What did you expect? They insulted a

great queen, stole a great man's flocks and his wine and insulted his house and his servants. Did you think when he returned he wouldn't punish them for that? Gods' balls! Let it rest. Enough has been done. You push this any further and you'll only meet a bloody end yourselves. Leave it lie. They have paid the price and that's the end of it."

He stumped back to the shade of the great olive tree, thumping his staff upon the ground. Some stood silently, looking with shamed eyes at each other, but many leaped to their feet, shouting hotly at his words, supporting Eupeithes, the faulty persuader. They swore at the old man, then ran to arm themselves and meet outside the town.

"Madcaps, all of them," Halitherses muttered. "It's a poor orchard-keeper who can't spot rotten fruit."

Eupeithes took command of them outside, his mind seeing his paunchy figure bravely leading his army to avenge his son. But his folly made him blind to his own end, which was to join his son in bloody death.

Athene saw the banging and clattering of swords on shields and approached *470–495* her father grimly. "Well, Father dear, what is your pleasure this time? See the fools frolicking frantically below? What should we do with them? Let them have their war and blood or settle it peacefully?"

Zeus yawned and shook his head. "Well, Daughter, why come to me with your formal petition? This is your run of things. Didn't you ask for Odysseus to have blood vengeance when he returned home? And didn't I tell you to decide for yourself? Well, you're the bee in the hive now. As for me, I see only one right way to do it up good and proper and that's to let Odysseus's honor be fully satisfied. A man's half honor is no honor. If it was me, I'd see that they all swear to uphold him as their king and rightful ruler forever and then wipe their minds clean of all hate and memory of the slaughter of their sons and brothers and friends. Put everything as nearly as possible as it was before all this rigmarole. Right now all you have is a bunch of ragtags playing at war, and nothing good will come of that, I'm thinking. But you decide."

Athene, who had already readied herself for action, took heart with his words and sped down the slopes of Olympus, launching herself toward Laertes's farm. There she found them sitting back after enjoying their meal.

"Well," Odysseus said, yawning and stretching. Idly he took a straw and picked at his teeth. "Would one of you step down the path a yard or two and see if you can see the vengeful-minded ones coming?"

One of Dolius's sons leaped up and went to the threshold. He shaded his eyes with his hand and saw Eupeithes leading the Ithacans near the edge of the field. He called over his shoulder to Odysseus, "They're here! Make ready!"

496-522   Odysseus and the others leaped up and hurriedly dressed themselves in their armor. Laertes and Dolius, rime-headed though they were, joined Dolius's six sons and Telemachus and the two herdsmen, arming themselves in gleaming bronze as well. Then, with Odysseus leading, his grim face setting itself in its war mask, they opened the gate and stepped out to meet the Ithacans bent on revenge.

    And now Athene once again drew on Mentor's appearance and voice and came to stand beside them. Odysseus's face brightened at seeing her, and he turned to Telemachus, saying, "Son, you are soon to battle with armed and ready men. This is not the same as those suitors. I'm counting on you to live up to your good name that has come down from many warriors over the ages. There have been no piddling heroes in our line."

    "I won't be disgracing your house, Father," Telemachus said grimly. "You can count on that."[7]

    Laertes's heart soared when he heard the exchange between father and son, and he exclaimed, "By the gods, but this is a day to warm the old cockles! Son and grandson fighting side by side, each testing the other's courage! Enough to make the old blood sing, it is!"

    And then Athene of the flashing eyes stepped close to him and said, "Laertes, Arceisius's son, my dearest friend, say a quick prayer to the goddess of the gray eyes and Father Zeus, then poise your spear and make your toss."

523-548   A surge of raw power flashed through him and he felt his blood sing a familiar song half forgotten over the years. He raised his long spear, offered quick prayers, and threw. The spear struck Eupeithes on the bronze cheekplate of his helmet and pierced through to his brainpan. He dropped like a stone to the ground, dust rising in clouds from the force of his body.

    Odysseus sounded his war cry and, his son at his side, fell upon the front ranks with his terrible sword lifted high. Hearts quaked and legs trembled as the swords slashed down and double-pointed spears stabbed toward them. Many would have died that day had not Athene raised a cry that halted everyone.

    "Enough!" she shouted. "Stop this shameless skirmish at once! No more blood is to be spilled!"

    Their faces paled before the sight of the bright-eyed daughter and her flashing eyes. Their hands opened nervelessly and weapons clattered to the ground to lie in the dust. Then they turned on their heels and, bleating like sheep, ran lickety-split back for the city as if the hounds of Hades were snapping at their heels.

    Odysseus unleashed his mighty war cry once again and gathered himself to pounce upon their rear ranks, but Zeus dropped a smoking thunderbolt at his feet, stopping him in his tracks. He staggered back from the burning brimstone, tears streaking down his eyes, his sense momentarily rattled.

"By the gods," he muttered thickly. "That was a close one."

And then Athene spoke, her words working through his anger. "Odysseus, favorite of Zeus, hold your sword. Call off your men before you anger the cloud-gatherer."

And Odysseus obeyed, his heart leaping with pleasure.

And Athene, still disguised as Mentor, brought peace between both parties, who swore to the terms as outlined by Zeus, the aegis-bearer.

Here ends the Twenty-fourth Book of Homer's Odyssey.

Envoi
   The song of Homer is done
   With the return of Laertes's son.
   Yet, the sea's tides still call
   Softly to Odysseus and fall
   Softly upon the rocky shore
   Of Ithaca, and we know more
   Songs have yet to be told
   About the wine-dark sea and bold
   Odysseus and his vast
   Wanderings in the past
   Among enchanted isles and on rolling seas.

R.L.E.

TRANSLATOR'S NOTE

Of course, the story of Odysseus does not end here with the bed test of Penelope and the final fight with the families of the suitors who sought revenge for the bloody deaths of their kinsmen. Strange as it may seem, the families of those seeking to force Penelope to choose a new husband saw nothing wrong with the suitors' abuse of the laws of hospitality as laid down by Zeus. Indeed, throughout *The Odyssey* the families supported the men who wanted to be Penelope's husband. Penelope was old enough to be the mother of most of the suitors, but she was still a beautiful and desirable woman. More important, she was queen of Ithaca, and the man she married would become its king.

After Zeus threw his famous thunderbolt to stop Odysseus from his wholesale slaughter of the suitors' families, peace followed. But this did not put an end to the adventures of Odysseus, according to a number of non-Homeric tales. They describe prophecies by the seers Odysseus visited while trying to make his way home after the Trojan War. Homer, however, foresaw a quiet life in Ithaca and a peaceful end for Odysseus.

In Homer's *Odyssey,* the blind seer, Teiresias, told Odysseus to go to the mainland and walk inland, carrying his oar upon his shoulder, until he met someone who asked why he was carrying a winnowing fan.[1] There he would place the oar into the ground and sacrifice a ram, a bull, and a breeding boar to Poseidon. This, according to Teiresias, would reconcile him finally to the god of the sea. After this, he would be allowed to return to Penelope in Ithaca, where he would live to a ripe old age until a gentle death would come to him out of the sea. Although Odysseus was a great warrior, he was not to undergo a "war death," as did Achilles; instead, he was going to be honored by being allowed to shuffle peacefully off this world and into the next.

Centuries later, a minor legend was sometimes attached to this account. It relates that the oar Odysseus planted far inland took root and grew into a tree (either oak or ash), and around that "miracle" was built a city that eventually became Ophir, the legendary city of Solomon and the site of his mines.

But there are many tales about the later adventures of Odysseus. According to one of these non-Homeric tales, Odysseus went to Thesprotia and married Queen Callidice while Penelope still lived (a bit of bigamy, to be certain) and led the Thesprotians against the Brygi, who were being supported in the battle by Ares, the god of war. In this story, Odysseus lost the battle and was succeeded as king by the son he had with Callidice, Polypoetes, who was named after the Thessalian who was the eldest son of Pirithous and Hippodamia and who, along with Leonteus, grandson of Caeneus, led a contingent of forty ships to the Trojan War.

In still another story, Odysseus was slain by Telegonus, his son by Circe, who had sent Telegonus to find his father. Telegonus led a raid on Ithaca and, not knowing the name of the man he was fighting, struck him with a spear tipped with a stingray, thus bringing him death out of the sea in accordance with the prophecy of Teiresias. After Penelope learned the identity of Telegonus and his connection with her husband, she went with Telegonus to Circe's island, Aeaea, and buried Odysseus there in a secret ceremony.[2] A further account of this has Penelope marrying Telegonus, while her son, Telemachus, marries Circe.

Another tradition has it that the suitors' families were finally able to gain revenge on Odysseus by bringing him to justice, and that Neoptolemus, who was selected as the judge, ruled in their favor and condemned Odysseus to exile. This apparently happened after Odysseus discovered that Penelope had not been faithful to him during his wanderings and he sent her back to her father, Icarius. This was not a fair judgment. Neoptolemus had his eye on the island of Cephallenia that was under Ithacan rule at the time, and by condemning its king to a life of exile, Neoptolemus was able to extort Cephallenia from the Ithacans by way of reparations for the rash and murderous deeds of Odysseus. Following his exile, Odysseus apparently went to the island of Aetolia and married one of Thoas's daughters, who bore him a son, Leontophonus. Here Odysseus lazed away the rest of his life in idyllic splendor, finally realizing peace. This legend brings an end to the story of a man who was named Odysseus by his grandfather, Autolycus, a famous thief and trickster who had collected many enemies during his lifetime. Odysseus means "victim of enmity" or "victim of hate" and apparently comes from the Greek word *odyssesthai,* "to hate," which would put a neat, literary turn to the end of the story.

Dante, however, places Odysseus (Ulysses in his poem) in one of the lower circles of Hell in the *Inferno,* XXVI. This seems strange for a man whom the Greeks considered a hero, but Dante saw Ulysses/Odysseus as a flawed individual, very human, who used his trickery and wisdom for his own benefit rather than that of others. Additionally, the fact that Odysseus was quite willing to sacrifice his men to attain a greater end did not sit well with the Christian views of Dante, who was trying to establish a meaning or direction for himself and Christianity by showing the world God's divine plan. Consequently, Ulysses/Odysseus, having not been baptized, is considered a heathen and not able to enter heaven. Unlike Vergil, Dante's guide, Odysseus was "unrepentant" and therefore was punished for the life that he had led. This idea is a bit Calvinistic and seems somewhat hypocritical: Vergil is rewarded for using his intelligence in the manner of his time for his own benefit (and the glory of Rome) while Odysseus is punished by Dante for using his intelligence in the manner of his time. It appears that Dante was willing to place the traditions and values of one civilization on another and judge its people by the former's merits.

Inevitably, readers question the validity of *The Odyssey* as a historical document. It certainly allows us to analyze institutions and the character of Greek people in antiquity—their values and traditions, their hatreds and prejudices—but the jury is still out regarding the historical accuracy of Homer's story. Of course, we have to remember that Homer's *Iliad* likewise was thought to be only a story founded on one man's great literary imagination until the German archaeologist Heinrich Schliemann determined from his excavations at Troy (modern Hissarlik) in the 1870s that Homer's story was based on fact and that the Trojan War had occurred. He documented his findings in *Ilios: The City* and *Country of the Trojans* and other books. A vivid account of the "discovery" of Troy and an attempt to verify Schliemann's claims appears in Michael Wood's *In Search of the Trojan War,* but readers are cautioned that the flamboyant Schliemann was given to leaping to conclusions from a small evidence of possibility. For more exact research, readers should consult the works of Wilhelm Dörpfeld, Sir Arthur Evans, and C. W. Blegen.

Several accounts of Troy's existence, however, were published, or at least indicated, by authors prior to Schliemann, including Lord Byron, who spent seventeen days anchored off the shore of where tradition located the Plains of Troy.[3] Byron claimed that he had an intense sense of the past while he walked the same land where the feet of Odysseus, Agamemnon, Hector, and Achilles once trod. We can see a bit of this in his *Don Juan,* canto IV, 77:

High barrows without marble or a name,
A vast, untilled and mountain-skirted plain,
And Ida in the distance, still the same,
And old Scamander (if 'tis he) remain:
The situation seems still formed for fame—
A hundred thousand men might fight again
With ease; but where I sought for Ilion's walls,
The quiet sheep feeds, and the tortoise crawls.

Surprisingly, Schliemann ascertained that Troy did exist and was in what was then a pasture at the same spot where Byron claimed he felt the intrusion of Troy and its heroes upon his spirit more than half a century earlier. In a letter, Byron wrote, "It is one thing to read the *Iliad* with Mount Ida above you, yet another to trim your taper over it in a snug library—this I *know*." In *Don Juan,* Byron sums up his feelings about Troy and the dispute raging even then among scholars:

> . . . I've stood upon Achilles' tomb,
> And heard Troy doubted; time will doubt of Rome.

From the comparative historical and anthropological evidence suggesting that Troy does exist and the studies that reveal the life of what is now called the Mycenaean Period (c. 1400–900 B.C.)—the forms of government and religion, the behavior of the people, the environment—we can draw a few conclusions. First, there probably was a king of Ithaca named Odysseus who was a great warrior. But as to the tales of his adventures, we can assume only that they are a product of literary minds. Whether this was the sole work of Homer is immaterial except to a few purists. The world of fantasy that the storyteller gave us is undoubtedly created from tales of heroes in other cultures as well. In fact, the tales seem to have been carried from one part of the world to another by travelers and traders for so many years that it is impossible to trace their beginnings. We must remember also that Homer placed the account of Odysseus's journey in the mouth of Odysseus himself, forcing us to decide the character of Odysseus. Do we believe the story of the Cyclops, of the Sirens (these appear in an older story about Jason and his search for the Golden Fleece), the Laestrygonians, and others? Probably not. But they are the type of story that a man would tell if he was searching for an excuse for not having gone home directly after a war. In a world where accounts of the meddling of gods and goddesses in the affairs of man were famous and believed (even if tongue in cheek), who would dare commit sacrilege by doubting a man who claimed that he had been made a victim by the gods?

The value of Homer's *Odyssey* is, therefore, as a mirror to the past in which we can ascertain what type of people lived during this time and, by seeing what our cultural ancestors were like, we can understand a bit more about our own place in the world today. Did *The Odyssey* actually happen? Perhaps, perhaps not. The answer is immaterial. The story is all that matters.

APPENDIX A

The Gods

The Greeks thought that their most important gods dwelled on top of Mount Olympus, with the minor gods scattered here and there in places that had special meaning to them. These twelve who lived on Olympus were:

ZEUS, the thunder god, the most powerful of all. He and his brothers Poseidon and Hades cast lots for the universe. Poseidon took the sea, Hades the Underworld, and Zeus the heavens. As the Lord of the Sky, Zeus ruled over all. His breastplate was the aegis, terrible to behold; his bird was the eagle, and his tree the oak.

HERA, his wife, the goddess who was raised by the Titans Oceanus and Tethys. She protected marriage, and married women were her particular care. She was not an attractive goddess, as she was snappish and bitter, almost like a fishwife on occasion. She never forgot an insult real or imagined and punished ruthlessly those she believed to be wrong, whether they were or not. She did not listen to reason. The only story in which she appears in a good light is that of Jason and the Golden Fleece.

POSEIDON, the god of the waves, was second only to Zeus. His wife was Amphitrite. Although he had a palace beneath the sea, more often than not he could be found hobnobbing with the gods on Olympus. He was also called earthshaker, for he caused earthquakes by thrusting his trident into the earth.

ATHENE, the daughter of Zeus alone. No mother bore her, for she sprang full-grown from the head of Zeus when he complained of a headache and commanded Hephaestus to cut his head open with an ax. She was a fierce battle goddess, but there was a feminine side to her as well—she taught the women of the earth handicrafts and the men how to plant. She was the chief of the virgin goddesses and in poetry was the goddess of wisdom, reason, and purity. Athens was her special city, her tree the olive, and her bird the owl.

APOLLO, the son of Zeus and Leto, was born on Delos. He was associated with poetry, and as a master musician he entertained the gods by playing on his golden lyre (harp). He was the the archer god, who slayed with a silver bow but also healed. He was the god of light and truth, and his Oracle at Delphi was one of the most powerful for it had the gift of prophecy as well. His tree was the laurel, his bird the crow.

ARTEMIS, also called Cynthia from her birthplace, Mount Cynthus. She was the twin sister of Apollo and one of the three virgin goddesses (along with Athene and Vesta). She loved the wilderness and all wild things. She was the chief hunter for the gods—an odd thing for a woman to be. She protected young people, although some stories about her contradict this role; for example, Artemis demanded that a virgin be sacrificed to her before she would let the Greek ships sail for Troy. When women died painlessly, they were said to have been slain by Artemis with her silver arrows. She was also connected with the moon, often being referred to as Phoebe and Selene. In later poetry, she appeared as a tripartite god: Selene, the moon; Artemis, the earth hunter; Hecate, a goddess of the Underworld. Her tree was the cypress, her animal the deer.

APHRODITE, the goddess of love and beauty who could steal the wits from the wisest. In *The Iliad,* she appeared as the daughter of Zeus and Dione, but later poems and legends had her stepping from the foam of the sea (caused by the testicles of Ouranus after Cronus castrated him and flung them into the sea) onto either Cyprus or Cythera; both islands were sacred to her. When she was seen in a lustful manner, she was often referred to as Cyprian; when in a manner associated with love, Cytherian. She had a deadly side to her, too, and often exercised a destructive power over man. Surprisingly, she was married to the ugliest of gods, the blacksmith Hephaestus. Her tree was the myrtle; her bird was the dove, although the sparrow and swan are often associated with her as well.

HERMES, the son of Zeus and Maia, a daughter of Atlas, was the messenger god. He was graceful and always in motion. He wore a low-crowned hat (sometimes referred to as a helmet) and winged sandals. His magic wand was the caduceus. The shrewdest and most cunning of all the gods and also the most mischievous, he was the god of commerce and the marketplace and the protector of traders. Hermes also was the guide who led souls to the Underworld.

DEMETER, the goddess of corn (an all-inclusive term for small grains), a daughter of Cronus and Rhea. She was generally considered an earth goddess, but a clear distinction was made between her and Gaia (Gaea), who was the earth mother. She was one of the most beautiful of goddesses and associated with the harvest. She was the mother of Persephone, and when Hades abducted Persephone, Demeter went into mourning and allowed nothing to grow on earth until Zeus stepped in and arranged for Persephone to spend six months of the year with her mother and six months of the year with Hades in the Underworld. This explains the two basic seasons of earth: summer (when Persephone is with her mother) and winter (when she is with Hades). A great temple was erected to Demeter at Eleusis, a little town near

Athens, but the type of worship there remains a mystery (Eleusinian Mysteries), providing grounds for scholarly speculation. Cicero wrote that "Nothing is higher than these mysteries. They have sweetened our characters and softened our customs; they have made us pass from the condition of savages to true humanity. They have not only shown us the way to live joyfully, but they have taught us how to die with a better hope."

DIONYSUS, the god of the vine, was the son of Zeus and the Theban princess Semele. His city was Thebes, and he was the only god whose parents were not both divine. Semele was desired by Zeus, who told her she could have anything if she would sleep with him. She took him at his word (an oath sworn on the River Styx was a promise that no god can break) and slept with him. Hera found out about Zeus's indiscretion and, since she couldn't punish him directly, she punished Semele (as she did other women Zeus slept with) by making her wish to see Zeus in all his glory. Zeus knew what would happen—Semele would be burnt to a crisp by his thunderbolts—and tried to talk her out of it. But Semele reminded him of his oath and he sadly appeared to her in all his glory, and she flamed into ashes. Before she was consumed by the terrible fire, however, he snatched the baby from her womb, sliced open his thigh, and put the baby there to mature. When Dionysus was born, Hermes carried the infant to the Nymphs of Nysa (the Greek Garden of Eden, a valley that is the most fruitful and beautiful on earth, which no one has seen and whose location no one knows). Dionysus taught man how to culture the vine by cutting it back at the end of the growing season so that it would grow more fruitful at the next season.

HEPHAESTUS, the god of the forge, was the son of Zeus and Hera. Sometimes his birth is attributed to Hera alone, who is said in a few stories to have borne him out of vindictiveness when Zeus bore Athene. He was the only ugly one among the gods, and he was lame. One story has him being born deformed, while another attributes his lameness to a temper tantrum by Zeus who picked Hephaestus up and threw him from the heavens to earth, where his hip shattered when he struck. Appalled at what he had done, Zeus gave him Aphrodite as his wife when Athene refused him. He was the most cunning workman in metal among all the gods. He was usually a kind and peace-loving god, and when children were formally admitted to the city, the god of the ceremony was Hephaestus.

ARES, the god of war, was the son of Zeus and Hera. He was the most detestable of the Greek gods and hated by Zeus. He was not as brave as one would expect, being the god of war and all, but was a brutal coward whose temper tantrums were legion. A train of attendants followed him around, including his sister Eris (discord) and Strife (her son). Enyo, the goddess of war and terror, trembling, and panic, also attended Ares on the battlefields. He was not worshiped in any city but was said to come from Thrace, whose people were known for their rudeness and cruelty. His tree is sometimes the elm, his bird is the vulture, and the much-maligned dog is said to be his animal.

Some believe that Hestia was part of the canonical twelve at one point and was later replaced by Dionysus. Hestia was Zeus's sister but has no distinct personality that is seen in her own legends. She was the goddess of the hearth (although this is sometimes attributed to Hera) and the symbol of the home around which newborn children must be carried. Every meal began with a prayer and offering to her, and each city had a public hearth sacred to her where the fire was never allowed to go out. If a colony was to be founded, burning coals from her fire were carried to the hearth in the new city to kindle the fire.

Strangely, Hades was not included in the hierarchy of twelve. This might be partly because he lived in the Underworld and partly because he was so feared that none cared to worship him, for that would be worshiping death. He was one of the original children of Cronus and Rhea along with Hera, Hestia, Demeter, Poseidon, and Zeus. Few cults worshiped him and few statues were erected to him. Hades does not appear often in myth, with the exception of his rape of Persephone, yet the Greeks were constantly aware of him. As a people who were more concerned with life than death, the Greeks did not include him in their hierarchy, but they recognized that Hades was a god who had to be tolerated.

Other important gods were Asclepius, Cabeiri, Charites, Cybele, Eileithyia, Enyalios, Eros, Hecate, Helios, Leto, Leucothea, the Muses, Pan, Thetis, the Titans, and various sea gods such as Glaucus, Nereus, Pontus, and Proteus.

APPENDIX B

The Action of *The Odyssey*

The Odyssey seems to take place in the thirteenth century B.C. There are problems with dating it more precisely than that, but the period toward the end of the Mycenean age is generally accepted for the action of the poem.

The action of *The Odyssey* takes place over forty days. Their breakdown is as follows:

Day 1: The assembly of the gods. Athene visits Telemachus in Ithaca. (The First Book)

Day 2: The assembly of the Ithacans. Telemachus prepares for his journey and sails away during the night. (The Second Book)

Day 3: Telemachus arrives at Pylos and hears Nestor's story. (The Third Book)

Day 4: Telemachus leaves Pylos for Menelaus's palace. (The Third Book)

Day 5: Telemachus journeys to Sparta and is received at Menelaus's palace. (The Third Book)

Day 6: Telemachus stays at Sparta and hears Menelaus's story. In Ithaca, the suitors discover that Telemachus is missing and plan to ambush and kill him. Penelope has a dream and the conspirators set out. (The Fourth Book)

Day 7: The second assembly of the gods. Hermes is sent to tell Calypso that she must release Odysseus. (The Fifth Book)

Days 8–11: Odysseus builds a raft. (The Fifth Book)

Days 12–28: Odysseus sails safely across the seas. (The Fifth Book)

Day 29: Poseidon wrecks Odysseus's raft. (The Fifth Book)

Days 30–31: Odysseus drifts on a spar until he reaches land. (The Fifth Book)

Day 32: Athene sends Nausicaa to wash her clothes near where Odysseus is sleeping. They meet. Odysseus is received at Alcinous's palace. (The Sixth and Seventh Books)

Day 33: Alcinous entertains Odysseus with feasting, singing, dancing, and games. In the evening, Odysseus recites his adventures. (The Eighth through Thirteenth Books)

Day 34: Odysseus sails from Phaeacia and arrives in Ithaca. (The Thirteenth Book)

Day 35: Odysseus stays with the swineherd. (The Thirteenth and Fourteenth Books)

DAY 36: Telemachus reaches Pylos, sails home. Odysseus stays with the swineherd. (The Fifteenth Book)

DAY 37: Telemachus evades the ambush, lands on Ithaca, joins Odysseus and the swineherd. (The Fifteenth and Sixteenth Books)

DAY 38: Odysseus goes home disguised as a beggar. He comes among the suitors. He fights a rival beggar, talks with Penelope, and is recognized by Eurycleia. (The Sixteenth through Nineteenth Books)

DAY 39: The contest with the bow. The killing of the suitors. Penelope accepts Odysseus into her bed. (The Twentieth through Twenty-third Books)

DAY 40: The souls of the suitors go to the House of Hades. Odysseus visits his father. Athene makes peace between Odysseus and the kinsmen of the suitors. (The Twenty-fourth Book)

APPENDIX C

GREEK TEXTS AND ENGLISH TRANSLATIONS

Many difficulties appear when scholars and translators try to work with ancient Greek. The original texts include words and phrases so obscure that there is no agreement on their meaning. In this translation, I have tried to give a modern version of Homer's *Odyssey,* working Greek idioms and epithets into modern usage. I have no doubt that some will object that I have intruded too much on the original. Yet we do not have any idea what constituted the original text. What we have today is the result of scholars piecing together fragments of text from many places and over many centuries.

When the English archaeologist Arthur Evans excavated the palace of Minos at Cnossus on Crete starting in 1900, he discovered clay tablets apparently written by palace scribes. The tablets were written between 2200 and 1500 B.C. in three different scripts. The first used Minoan hieroglyphics; despite several symbols that appear to have been borrowed from Egyptian hieroglyphics, no one has yet deciphered this script. The second script, known as Minoan Linear A, also remains undeciphered. Those tablets bearing Linear B script, however, have been translated by scholars, thanks to Michael Ventris, who figured out how to decipher them in 1952. At first he suspicioned that Linear B was Etruscan, but as he continued to work on the tablets, he concluded that Linear B was an early form of Greek. This conclusion was confirmed by Carl Blegen as a result of his excavation of the Mycenean palace at Pylos, the legendary home of Nestor.

Linear B was the script used in the Greek world at the time of the events in *The Iliad* and *The Odyssey,* but so far no tablet mentions Odysseus or any other characters or events in Homer's epics. There are, however, intriguing similarities between the famous catalogue of ships in the Second Book of *The Iliad* and catalogues found on the Linear B tablets.

Homer's *Odyssey* is usually dated from the latter half of the eighth century B.C. and about twenty-five years after his *Iliad*. Written in a complex dactylic hexameter with twelve to seventeen syllables in a line, *The Odyssey* has about 12,000 lines and is divided into twenty-four books. (*The Iliad* is longer by a third, consisting of 15,600 lines, but it too is divided into twenty-four books.) The repetition of formulaic epithets has caused debate over the years, especially certain adjectival phrases that some scholars have insisted were intrusions in the text. In the disputes that followed, some wanted to delete these "corruptions" from the standard text, but Milman Parry, a noted scholar of oral literature, aptly demonstrated that such repetitions were not the fault of copyists but rather followed the common practice of bards reciting their tales before an audience. Whether Homer belongs to the category of bards is immaterial; he could simply have been patterning his verse on the literary technique of his day, one that had been established by unlettered bards.

Homer could even have been involved in transcribing his epics, as the alphabet of classical Greek was coming into use about the time he was com-posing his works. Scholars are divided on whether Homer set down his epics in written form, but a majority believes that Homer's versions were probably bardic and were known only as oral literature. This raises the question of how Homer could have composed such a long poem and retained it in mem-ory. As far back as 1795, the German scholar Friedrich August Wolf sug-gested that Homer could not have composed the thousands of verses of *The Odyssey* in his head and that instead several bards must have memorized and recited shorter poems, loosely linked together by the epic's general plot and theme.

We have only the vaguest ideas as to the nature of the text before 300 B.C. A story of questionable authenticity relates that Peisistratus, a sixth-century B.C. tyrant in Athens, decided that the sequence of events was out of order, and he devised a new pattern and ordered his version to be recited at the Panathenaic festival. True or not, the text does show a distinct Athenian ele-ment in some episodes, indicating that Athens had a part in its transmission. Indeed, a case could be made for all of today's texts finding their provenance in an Athenian recension.

From commentaries by Didymus Chalcenterus about 20 B.C. and by Eustathius, the bishop of Thessalonica, about A.D. 1170, we learn that *The Odyssey* existed during the Hellenistic period and early Christian era in the vulgate or common text, in regional or city texts, and in special texts edited by scholars.

The text we use today most likely derives from a "standard edition" put together by three Greek scholars—Zenodotus, Aristophanes of Byzantium (not the playwright), and Aristarchus, who worked at the great library at Alexandria in the third and second centuries B.C. This text would have been written on papyrus rolls, and if the rolls were too large, they would break when unrolled. Scholars surmise that twenty-four papyrus rolls were needed for Homer's long epics, and that is why both *The Iliad* and *The Odyssey* are divided into twenty-four books.

Many fragments of *The Odyssey* written on papyrus have been discovered in Egypt, some with long passages of verse. The earliest of these papyri date from 3 B.C. The oldest complete manuscript is the Laurentianus (Laurentian Library, Florence) from either the tenth or eleventh century A.D. The first *printed* edition of Homer's Greek text appeared in Florence in 1488 and was prepared by Demetrius Chalcondylas, an immigrant scholar from Crete. In making this translation, I followed *Ομηρου Οδυσσεια* (*The Odyssey of Homer*) edited with general and grammatical introduction, commentary, and indexes by W. B. Stanford, Litt. D., volumes I and II, 2d edition (New York: St. Martin's Press, 1967). All line references are to the Greek text of this edition.

SOME NOTABLE TRANSLATIONS

George Chapman (c. 1615), John Ogilby (1669), Alexander Pope (1725–26), William Cowper (1791), William Sotheby (1834), Philip Stanhope Worsley (1861), Samuel Henry Butcher and Andrew Lang (1879), William Morris (1887), Samuel Butler (1900), A. T. Murray (1919), H. B. Cotterill (1924), W. Marris (1925), John William Mackail (1932), T. E. Shaw (aka Lawrence) (1932), W. H. D. Rouse (1937), E. V. Rieu (1946), Robert Fitzgerald (1961), Richmond Lattimore (1965–67), and Robert Fagles (1996).

NOTES

INTRODUCTION

1. Cassandra (Alexandra) was the daughter of Priam and Hecuba, and a great beauty. One day Apollo spied her, fell in love, and tried to bed her, but she refused him unless he would give her the gift of prophecy. Blinded by desire, he agreed, but when he tried to press his suit, she again refused him, knowing that a gift bestowed by the gods could not be taken back. Angered at her trickery, Apollo decreed that she could keep the gift of prophecy but no one would ever believe her. And no one did, perhaps because just before Cassandra uttered a prophecy, she would go into an ecstatic trance that caused people to think her mad. Throughout the ten years of war, Cassandra rightly foretold important events, including the fall of Troy. Brought to Mycenae by Agamemnon as a war trophy, she was murdered by Clytemnestra.

THE FIRST BOOK: THE COUNCIL OF THE GODS

1. The most important Muse considered here is Calliope, the Muse of epic poetry. The Muses, the daughters of Zeus and the Titaness Mnemosyne (whose name means "memory"), were the goddesses of the fine arts, music, and literature, and later of history, philosophy, and astronomy. The ancient poets believed that they received their inspiration from the Muses, and always invoked them for the wisdom to sing well. Originally, there were three: Melete ("practice"), Mneme ("memory"), and Aoede ("song"). Later, the number was increased to twelve by adding Calliope ("fair of voice," who watched over epic poetry), Clio ("renowned," whose interest was history), Euterpe ("gladness," who liked flute players), Terpsichore ("joy in dance," who governed lyric poetry and dance), Erato ("lovely," the one who watched over lyric poetry and songs), Melpomene ("singing," who was the Muse of tragedy), Thalia ("abundance," who governed comedy), Polymnia ("many songs," the Muse of mime), and Urania ("heavenly," whose domain was astronomy).

2. Hyperion was the Titan associated with radiance and matchless beauty and splendor. With Thea, he fathered Helios (sun), Selene (moon), and Eos (dawn).

The Titans had been created through the lust of Ouranus (Heavens) for Gaia (also Gaea, Mother Earth). Ouranus was a cruel lover, and his first children, the Cyclopes, he loathed and imprisoned in Tartarus. The Titans were created with his second rape of Gaia and kept out of his way. When he raped Gaia a third time, she gave birth to the Hecatoncheires (hundred-armed) Cottus, Briareos, and Gyes. They possessed fifty heads and a hundred arms each. Ouranus was so disgusted with them that he tried to push them back into Gaia's womb. For this last act of cruelty, Gaia persuaded Cronus, the last Titan to be born, to castrate his father. With her help, he fashioned a sickle, and when Ouranus came to rape her again, Cronus hid until Ouranus was locked in an embrace with Gaia, then slipped from hiding and, with one sweep of the sickle, castrated his father. Ouranus fled back to the heavens, where he remained docile. Cronus threw his father's testicles into the sea, where they floated upon a bed of foam until they bumped up against the island of Cyprus. There, Aphrodite stepped ashore.

3. The name of Odysseus is highly reflective of the man himself. The word *odysseus* could easily be translated as "trouble" or "the man who finds trouble." This could suggest a man who arrogantly challenges the world and is prone to finding trouble. One could make a case too that his name suggests "excessive suffering," as in line 62 of the original text where Zeus says that excessive suffering comes from the act of folly. Athene replies to this by asking, "Why do you odysseus [trouble] him so?" Zeus is hard put to answer and really avoids the question by admitting that Odysseus is the wisest of men. We can only assume that Zeus allows Poseidon to "trouble"

Odysseus to make Odysseus even wiser, helping him to establish his identity by exploring his own existence, which will emphasize its meaning.

The poetic similes attached to his name to describe his character are often difficult to translate. I prefer using "the man of masquerades" to suggest his trickery. Although this epithet is not literally correct in some instances, I believe it is thematically accurate.

4. The story of Agamemnon and his wife, Clytemnestra, is a complicated and tragic one. When Agamemnon had assembled the Greek army at Aulis in Boeotia to sail for Troy, the fleet could not sail because the wind was blowing landward. When Agamemnon asked why the wind was against them, the prophet Calchas answered that Poseidon and Artemis were angry because the Greeks had neglected to make a proper sacrifice to the sea god and to perform a duty to Artemis. The sacrifice for Poseidon was a bull, and that omission was easily remedied. Artemis, however, demanded the life of Agamemnon's daughter Iphigenia. Agamemnon decided to deceive his wife by sending a message that he had arranged a marriage between Iphigenia and Achilles. When Clytemnestra and Iphigenia arrived for the wedding, Agamemnon had his daughter seized and sacrificed. (This story does not appear in *The Iliad,* where Agamemnon offers all three of his daughters to Achilles years later, after the Greeks have arrived on the plains of Troy.) Clytemnestra never forgave Agamemnon for the death of Iphigenia, and while he was away at war, she began seducing men in order to find one who would help her take revenge on her husband. All accounts treat Clytemnestra as a beauty (see Euripides, Stesichorus, Lucretius, and the epic *Cypria*), but also a nymphomaniac. She eventually found Aegisthus, the captain of the guards and brother of Tantalus, who had been her first husband before Agamemnon slew him. Aegisthus became enamored of her skill in lovemaking and agreed to help her. When Agamemnon returned to Mycenae, he took his wife to bed after the homecoming feast, and while they were making love, Clytemnestra locked her long white legs around him and held him tight while Aegisthus stabbed Agamemnon to death. Clytemnestra and Aegisthus were slain later by Orestes, the son of Agamemnon and Clytemnestra.

5. Cronus was the Titan who castrated his father Ouranus (Sky) with the help of his mother Gaia (Earth) and seized control of the cosmos. Afraid that a son of his would duplicate his feat, Cronus swallowed his children when Rhea, his wife and his sister, gave birth. These were Hestia, Demeter, Hera, Hades, and Poseidon. When Zeus was born, Rhea gave Cronus a stone wrapped in swaddling clothes. Cronus swallowed the stone, believing that it was the baby. Zeus was secretly raised by the Nymphs of Mount Ida in Crete. They hid him in his cradle high in a grove of oak trees and fed him with the milk of the goat Amalthea (hence the epic epithet attached to his name as "goat-raised"). When he reached his majority, Zeus became Cronus's cupbearer. He married his aunt, Metis (Thought), and persuaded her to prepare a purgative for Cronus. Zeus disguised the potion in a cup of wine, and when Cronus drank it, he vomited up his children. A war broke out in the heavens between the Titans and the Olympians and was eventually won by Zeus, who exiled Cronus to Tartarus.

Gaia prophesied to Zeus that if Metis bore him a daughter, she would become his equal in wisdom and would bear a son mightier than he. Zeus tricked Metis when he discovered that she was pregnant into shape-shifting into a fly and swallowed her. The child (Athene) was brought forth full grown from Zeus's head one day when he complained of a headache and had one of his sons, Hephaestus, take an ax and cut open his head. Zeus retained the wisdom of Metis, however, and this kept him from being overthrown.

6. Calypso, the daughter of the Titan Atlas, lived on the mythical island Ogygia. She was beautiful and a bit of a sorceress and fell in love with Odysseus. According to some accounts, she bore him a son. Traditionally, she is seen as a counterpart to Circe—that is, love as opposed to lust.

7. Atlas ("he who carries or endures") was the son of Iapetus and Clymene, two Titans. Originally he was thought to be the guardian of the seven pillars of heaven but in later legends was punished for taking the side of the Titans against Zeus and his Olympians in the battle of the cosmos by being forced to hold the heavens on his shoulders.

8. Penelope was the daughter of the Spartan king Icarius and his wife, the Nymph Periboea. Her name is traditionally associated with marital fidelity and patience and is sometimes defined as "she who waits." Although most scholars today associate the etymology of her name with "weaving," the word is sometimes translated as "to duck," which suggests the ability to cleverly avoid difficulties. Since Penelope keeps the suitors at bay several years with her tapestry trick, the latter interpretation seems correct in this instance. One legend, however, associates Penelope with the ducks of the farmyard. Nauplius, angry because Odysseus killed his son Palamedes, told Penelope that Odysseus was dead. Penelope tried to drown herself but was saved by ducks. Odysseus had killed Palamedes because Palamedes had been the messenger sent by Agamemnon to remind Odysseus of his oath of obligation. When Odysseus tried to pretend he was insane and, consequently, could not serve in Agamemnon's army, Palamedes saw through his deception and forced him to go with the army. When the Greek army reached Troy, Odysseus hid a large quantity of gold in the tent of Palamedes and forged a letter from Priam, king of Troy, to Palamedes in which Priam promised Palamedes the gold for betraying the Greek camp. The letter was "intercepted" by a Phrygian slave and given to Agamemnon, who ordered a search of Palamedes's tent. The gold was found, and Palamedes was stoned to death for treason.

9. Telemachus, the son of Odysseus and Penelope, develops throughout the story from a youth into a self-confident and resourceful man. His name refers to "distant war," which foreshadows his involvement in the slaying of the suitors after his father's return.

10. Telemachus's leaving is paralleled in many works, such as James Joyce's *Ulysses* when Stephen Dedalus leaves the Martello Tower after, he feels, being forced out by Haines and Buck Mulligan. In the last word of Joyce's opening chapter, Dedalus sees Mulligan as a "usurper" in the same manner that Telemachus sees the would-be wooers as trying to usurp his father's throne. In this manner, Mulligan, as the leader of the "usurpers" of the Martello Tower, parallels Antinous, the leader of the wooers. Needless to say, the Martello Tower becomes a parallel for Ithaca as well. Special attention must be given to Stephen's Greek surname, which is the object of ridicule by Mulligan in much the same manner that Antinous ridicules Telemachus's manner of speaking.

11. Telemachus's generous actions as a host simply obey the laws of hospitality as laid down by Zeus. A host gave shelter and gifts to his guest(s), for he could never be certain if the guest was mortal or a god testing his goodwill toward his fellow man. Breaking the laws of hospitality was unthinkable and usually brought about severe punishment from the gods.

12. A problem exists here. Ilus is seen as the son of Mermerus, who is sometimes described as a Centaur—half man, half horse—and at other times as one of the sons of Jason and Medea. The latter is probably the true story, as Ilus is credited with having great wisdom in the art of wizardry. He is not to be confused with the son of Tros and Callirrhoe, a daughter of the River Scamander, who founded Troy (Ilium).

13. Eos is the goddess of Dawn, the daughter of the Titan Hyperion and the Titaness Theia and sister of Helios (Sun) and Selene (Moon). Her first husband was Astraeus ("starry"), to whom she bore the winds, the stars, and Eosphorus the Morning Star. Her chariot is pulled by two horses, Phaethon ("shining") and Lampus ("bright"). After Astraeus, she falls in love with a number of young mortals, but all her affairs end unhappily thanks to Aphrodite, who was annoyed at her interest in Ares.

THE SECOND BOOK: THE COUNCIL OF THE ITHACAN ELDERS

1. Tantalus was the son of Zeus and the Titaness Pluto, whose name means wealth. One of the richest of all, he married Dione, the daughter of Atlas. The gods allowed Tantalus to eat at their table, thus making him immortal, but he offended them when he invited them to dine with him, for he killed his son Pelops and cooked his flesh in a stew that he served them. Still, it wasn't

until Tantalus stole nectar and ambrosia from the gods' own table that they punished him by sending him to Tartarus and chaining him in a pool of water where tree branches heavy with fruit hung over him. Tantalus could not bend his head low enough to get a drink of water, nor could he reach high enough to grasp the fruit. In addition, the gods suspended a large stone on a thread over his head so that he lived in constant terror of being crushed.

2. Antiphus had sailed to Troy with Odysseus in one of the "hollow ships," which are vessels carrying little or no cargo. He was the last of Odysseus's men to be eaten by the Cyclops Polyphemus.

3. Homer never explains why no one in Ithaca knows the fate of Odysseus when Aegyptius knows of his son's death. This appears to be an inconsistency in the Greek text.

4. Themis was a Titaness, the daughter of Uranus and Gaia, whose name is associated with "justice" and "order." She was the second Titaness that Zeus took to bed after Metis. She presented the Hours and the Fates as offspring from that union. Her original husband, however, was Iapetus, to whom she bore Prometheus. He gained much of her wisdom and the gift of prophecy from her. Themis succeeded Gaia as the keeper of the Oracle of Delphi and gave Deucalion and Pyrrha the knowledge they needed to repopulate the earth after the great flood. She eventually gave the Oracle to Apollo after he returned from being purified for slaying Python.

5. Only the man who held the speaker's rod had the right to speak at any one time in a formal assembly. This rule kept the proceedings orderly.

6. Penelope's name can be translated as "to duck." Homer and his audience would have been familiar with farm animals and have seen ducks make quick and clever maneuvers. Ducks also stay close to the nest while drakes, whether the wandering Odysseus or the suitors, tend to stray. Subtle allusions and puns were expected of poet-singers, and those who could elaborate them were greatly admired.

7. The father usually arranged the marriage of his daughter to the man he considered to be most suitable or who could provide the best life for his daughter. Consequently, a woman's marriage was often conducted on a type of bartering system with the father trying to marry his daughter off as inexpensively as possible. Of course, in the better houses, the size of the dowry was a matter of social standing as well. In some instances, the father would place limitations or rules on the intended husband; in others, if the daughter was sought after by many (as in the case of Helen), then the would-be groom would offer presents to the father. In the case of Penelope, her father, Icarius, a Spartan king, was unwilling to lose her. When Tyndareus (another king of Sparta— Sparta was ruled by two kings, one in peace, another in war), who was the father of Clytemnestra and Helen, persuaded Icarius to marry Penelope to Odysseus, Icarius tried to convince Odysseus to stay and live in Sparta. Odysseus refused, and when the couple departed for Ithaca, Icarius rode after them and argued so hard with Odysseus that at last Odysseus told Penelope to choose between him and her father. She veiled her head and remained silent, electing Odysseus.

8. The women mentioned here were forced to live by their wits after having affairs with the gods. In the case of Alcmene, her lover was Zeus, to whom she bore Hercules. Tyro had an affair with Poseidon and bore him two children, Pelias and Neleus. Alcmene was the victim of Hera's wrath for having had the affair with Zeus, while Tyro's stepmother, Sidero, treated her with extreme cruelty. Mycene was the daughter of the river god Imachus. She was an Achaean beauty after whom Agamemnon's capitol had been named. She was the mother of all-seeing Argus.

9. Antinous's argument here is highly illogical but colorful and crafty. (His name could be translated as "deceitful one.") Although he is violating the laws of hospitality by taking advantage of them, he places the blame on Penelope for not having made a choice earlier. He also reminds the assembly that although Telemachus might wish to get rid of the suitors, he still has not reached

his majority, and although Telemachus would like to think of himself as the master of the house, he is not.

10. Telemachus's answer to Antinous's charges is logical and shows a maturity far beyond what one would expect from a youth. The name Telemachus traditionally means "penetrating," which suggests his ability to see to the truth of the man.

11. This is out of character for Eurymachus, who is generally seen as being the most polite and best mannered of Penelope's suitors. This speech implies that even Eurymachus, known for his levelheadedness, was tired of Penelope's game and thought it was time for a choice to be made.

12. Nestor was a highly respected statesman who was much older than the other commanders in the army of Agamemnon. He was considered to be a wise man, although some of his advice was ill founded. He did, however, become suspicious of the other leaders in the Greek army and left the Trojan shore early, thus escaping the great storm that Athene used to destroy the ships of those whose conduct was questionable.

Menelaus was the brother of Agamemnon and the husband of Helen, whose abduction by Paris brought about the Trojan War. Actually, Helen eloped with Paris when Menelaus went to a funeral, leaving the two together in his palace at Sparta. Helen, considered to be the most beautiful woman in the world, was Aphrodite's reward to Paris for selecting her as the most beautiful in a contest with Athene and Hera.

13. This cooking is being done in a sort of outer courtyard or enclosure. Here there would be stables, barns, and storehouses, and a huge altar in the center dedicated to the god or goddess the owner considered to be his patron or patroness, who governed his business or livelihood. Hera and Athene were the usual two represented by this altar, but Zeus, Apollo, and Demeter were also honored.

14. Amphorae were oval jars with a narrow neck and two handles. Often highly decorated, they were used for storing wine and other liquids. Their thick walls helped to keep the wine cool.

THE THIRD BOOK: A VISIT TO THE LORD OF THE PYLOS

1. Nestor, the Greek soldier and rhetorician who helps to keep administrative order during the Trojan War, was known as an expert horseman. He is paralleled in Joyce's *Ulysses* by Mr. Deasy, the headmaster to whom Stephen Dedalus must report and who gives him sage advice. Like his counterpart, Deasy brings order to the hockey field, the modern "battleground," as Nestor does on his battleground at Troy. Nestor, in Homer's *Iliad,* is often satirized for his ponderous way of speaking, a habit that is seen here when Nestor relates his wanderings to Telemachus. Nestor's skill as a charioteer is mirrored in Deasy's horse-racing mementos as well.

2. The aegis was a shield or breastplate, and Athene's bore the image of Medusa, which frightened away all who looked at it. Medusa was one of the Gorgons, three daughters of Phorcys and Ceto, and the only Gorgon who was mortal. Her name means "ruler" or "queen." Poseidon made love to Medusa, who was extremely beautiful, in Athene's temple, upsetting the goddess. Later on, Medea boasted about her beauty, claiming that she excelled Athene. In revenge, Athene turned Medusa's hair into snakes, making her so repulsive that a single look at her would turn a person to stone. Perseus killed Medusa when she was pregnant, and the blood from her wound gave birth to Chrysaor and Pegasus. After Perseus decapitated Medusa, he gave her head to Athene, who placed it in the center of her aegis.

3. Ajax the Greater (also Aias) was second only to Achilles as a warrior. He spoke little and slowly, but he had great courage. Taller than the other warriors, Ajax carried a shield so large

that no other man could carry it alone. His feats were magnificent, and he was considered to have a good heart, willing to help others.

4. The friendship between Achilles and Patroclus has been hotly debated; some view it as a homosexual relationship, while others consider it a paradigm of male friendship. Aeschylus, Plato, and some other Greek writers maintained that the two were lovers, but Homer's text is not explicit on this point.

When Achilles withdrew his forces from the Greek army in anger at Agamemnon for taking the slave woman Briseis from him to show his power as the king of kings, the Trojan forces began to overrun the Greeks. Led by Hector, the Trojans managed to beat the Greeks back to where the ships were pulled up on dry land and were in the process of setting fire to them. Had the Trojans managed to burn the ships, they would have cut off the Greeks from the supplies needed to feed their army and eventually would have managed to bring the war to an end by starving them out. In desperation, Agamemnon went to Achilles and tried to bribe him to bring his Myrmidons back into the fight, since the Myrmidons were the fiercest warriors that the Greeks had. But the Myrmidons would not fight unless they were led by Achilles. Agamemnon offered Achilles the slave girl back, but Achilles refused because he knew that what Agamemnon had once taken he could take again after Achilles had saved the Greeks. Agamemnon offered him gold, but Achilles did not need any more gold than he already had. Then Agamemnon offered him any of his own three daughters as a bride, but Achilles refused this gift as well. Some scholars believe that Achilles did this because he and Patroclus were lovers, while others say that this merely shows that Achilles was still sulking over Agamemnon's insult.

Patroclus, however, could see the need for Achilles's and his men among the Greek forces, and since Achilles still refused to rejoin the battle, Patroclus asked Achilles to lend him his armor so that, in disguise, he could lead the Myrmidons into battle. Reluctantly, Achilles agreed, warning Patroclus not to do more than defend the ships from being burnt. But when Patroclus, wearing Achilles's distinctive armor, came into battle, the Trojan army retreated in mass confusion, and Patroclus, feeling powerful, pursued them. He eventually came face-to-face with Hector, the Trojan champion, who killed him, stripped the armor from his body, and took it to Troy, where he set it up as an offering to the gods. When the body of Patroclus was brought to Achilles's tent, the great warrior wept bitter tears and begged his mother, Thetis Silverheels, to get new armor for him from Hephaestus, the smithy god. Thetis tried to warn him that if he continued in this war, he would be killed, but Achilles ignored her warning and begged again for the armor. Sadly, Thetis, who had dipped Achilles in the River Styx at his birth to make him immortal but who had forgotten to let the waters cover the heel by which she held him, went to Zeus, who owed her a favor for releasing him from a trap set by Hephaestus and Hera, and begged him for the armor. Zeus ordered the blacksmith to make the armor. The most important piece was the shield, which has become highly symbolic as an archetype in literature. (See, for example, W. H. Auden's poem, "The Shield of Achilles.") Achilles returned to the battle and eventually drove the Trojans back into their city. He killed Hector and continued to defile the body until Thetis told him to give the body to Priam and the Trojans for a proper burial. Achilles held elaborate funeral games in honor of Patroclus and awarded great prizes to the winners.

Later, Achilles was killed when Apollo guided a black arrow from the bow of Paris that struck the hero in his heel. He threw up his arms in distress, the reins he was holding went around his neck, and he fell from his chariot and his neck was broken. His body was rescued by Ajax. The Greeks honored him greatly in ceremony for seventeen days. When Thetis and the Nereids came and sang a dirge in his honor, the entire Greek army fled in terror to the ships. The Muses also joined the lamentation. On the eighteenth day, Achilles was cremated and his ashes placed in a golden urn made by Hephaestus and then in a tomb by the sea where his bones were mixed with those of Patroclus.

5. Antilochus was the eldest son of Nestor and one of the suitors for Helen. He was a close friend of Achilles and brought him the news when Patroclus was killed. He was not of sterling

character, however, and during the funeral games for Patroclus, he cheated in the chariot race. He was killed by Memnon while defending his father, who was helpless when Paris shot and killed his horse. Antilochus was buried in the grave along with Patroclus and Achilles, although not with equal pomp and circumstance.

6. Atreus was a cruel and wicked man. He promised Artemis the finest lamb born in his flocks, and the goddess sent him a lamb with golden fleece to test him. Atreus did sacrifice the lamb, but he locked the golden fleece into a treasure chest and hid it away. His wife, Aerope, however, had fallen in love with Thyestes, his brother, and secretly gave him the golden fleece. Thyestes used the golden fleece to gain the throne by trickery, but then was deprived of the throne by Zeus, who took a dim view of his adultery with Aerope. Atreus held a banquet for his brother in a gesture of good-will, then killed the three sons of Thyestes (after they had sought sanctuary at the altar of Zeus) and served them up as a delicate dish to his brother. When Thyestes had finished eating, Atreus showed him the hands and feet of his dead children. Thyestes asked the Oracle at Delphi for help, and the Oracle told him to have a child by his own daughter Pelopia. He disguised himself as an intruder and raped her, but she found his sword and hid it. Later, when Atreus was wandering, he came across Pelopia at the court of King Thesprotus and fell in love with her even though she was pregnant. He asked for her hand, and Thesprotus agreed without telling him that she was his niece. When her baby was born, she named him Aegisthus and abandoned him. Atreus, however, heard about the child, who was found by a goatherder, and had the child brought up at court. When Aegisthus reached his majority, he was given the sword of Thyestes. Atreus sent Agamemnon and Menelaus off to find Thyestes and place him in prison, where Aegisthus visited him. Thyestes recognized the sword and asked where Aegisthus got it. Aegisthus said his mother had given it to him. Thyestes asked to see Pelopia and told her about the incest. Pelopia killed herself with the sword. Aegisthus took the bloody sword to Atreus and claimed he had killed Thyestes with it. Atreus prepared an offering of thanksgiving to the gods for this, and as he stood by the altar on the seashore, Aegisthus stabbed him to avenge his father's imprisonment and dishonor. The curse of Thyestes continued when Clytemnestra took Aegisthus as her lover and convinced him to kill Agamemnon on the latter's return from Troy. Aegisthus was then slain by Agamemnon's son, Orestes.

7. The Greeks believed that physiognomy was a key to character. A wide brow was the mark of intelligence.

8. This Aias (Ajax) is not to be confused with Ajax the Greater (see note 3, page 391), although both fought on the side of the Greeks during the Trojan War. This Aias was a suitor for Helen, but he was not a valiant or honorable man as was the other Ajax. This Aias was small and a good sprinter and excellent spear thrower, but he was arrogant and conceited, and the gods hated him greatly, especially Athene. At the funeral games for Patroclus, he insulted Idomeneus in the chariot race. He made Athene so mad that when it came time for the footrace, Athene made him slip in a pile of manure, thus allowing Odysseus to win. He cursed her for his failure to win the race and thus earned even more anger. After the sacking of Troy, he pulled Cassandra away from Athene's statue, where she had gone to seek sanctuary, to rape her. He pulled down the statue and turned it to face the sky so that Athene would not see him during his defiling of Cassandra. The other Greeks wanted to kill him for this, but he wrapped his arms around the statue of Athene and claimed sanctuary, thus saving himself. Later, when the Greeks were sailing home, Athene asked Zeus to help her gain revenge upon Aias. Zeus blew up a huge storm, which wrecked the ships off Cape Caphereus in southern Euboea. Athene threw a thunderbolt at the ship of Aias, but Aias managed to swim to a rock (later called Gyrae) and pull himself up, shouting defiance at the gods and boasting that they could not kill him. Thereupon Poseidon split the rock with his trident to punish Aias for his arrogance and pulled him down beneath the waves, drowning him. According to tradition, the body of Aias was recovered and buried by Thetis on Myconos, but Athene still was not satisfied with her revenge. She demanded that his homeland, Locris, send two virgins every year to serve in Athene's temple at Troy. If the girls

were seen arriving at the temple, the inhabitants of Troy would kill them. According to history, the Locrians kept this practice going for a thousand years.

9. After Aias raped Cassandra, she was taken from him and given to Agamemnon as a war trophy. She bore him two sons, Teledamus and Pelops. Agamemnon took the Trojan princess home despite her prophecy of what would happen to them when they arrived at Mycenae.

10. Diomedes, a great warrior and one of the sons of the Seven against Thebes ("epigoni" or "second generation"), was a favorite of Athene during the Trojan War. As king of Argos, he had been a suitor for the hand of Helen and brought eighty ships to the Greek cause. His feats in *The Iliad* are second to none. He killed the Trojan prince Pandarus, wounded Aeneas, and drove Ares from the field after wounding him and wounded Aphrodite as well after the two gods tried to help the Trojans. He was a close friend and companion of Odysseus and helped him steal the Palladium, Athene's sacred image, from the citadel of Troy after Helenus prophesied that the side that possessed it would win the war. He was one of the few Greeks allowed to return home safely after the war, but there Aphrodite had caused his wife, Aegialia, to betray her husband by taking Cometes as a lover. Since Diomedes was related to the royal house of the Argives by marriage only, he was forced to flee and take refuge at the altar of Hera, who helped him escape from Sthenelus, the father of Cometes. Hera, the guardian of the family, later punished Aegialia and the others for betraying Diomedes, but meanwhile Diomedes had sailed to Italy, where he remarried and lived happily after several other adventures. Upon his death, he received divine honors.

11. The Myrmidons were the best warriors in the Greek army and were led by Achilles until his death.

12. Philoctetes was the only one who dared to light the fire when Hercules lay in agony upon the funeral pyre. For this favor, Hercules gave Philoctetes his marvelous bow and arrows. Philoctetes later became one of Helen's suitors. On the way to the Trojan War, a sacrifice had to be made to Apollo on the island of Chryse. Philoctetes led his troops there, but was bitten by a snake while offering the sacrifice. The snake was sent by Hera to bite Philoctetes for helping Hercules, whom the goddess hated. Philoctetes's pain was so great that he cried out curses that frightened the Greeks and the stench of his festering wound was so offensive that none would come near the man. Odysseus suggested that the famed archer be marooned on the island of Lemnos while the rest of the fleet continued on to Troy. Alone on the island, Philoctetes kept himself alive with his bow and arrows that never missed their target. Yet his wound failed to heal. After ten years had passed, Odysseus captured the Trojan prophet Helenus, who told him that the Greeks would never defeat Troy until Philoctetes was brought back to the army. Odysseus knew that Philoctetes would not agree to rejoin the Greek forces if he asked the archer, so he arranged for Achilles's son, Neoptolemus, to offer Philoctetes safe passage back to Greece. Philoctetes was so grateful that he gave the bow of Hercules to the youth, who then refused to return it unless the archer rejoined the Greeks. Philoctetes agreed and fought at Troy, where he was cured of his wound by either Machaon or Podalirius. It was Philoctetes who killed Paris with a poisoned arrow. Two stories exist about the end of Philoctetes: In one, he returns home safely and lives out his life in peace; in the other, his ship is driven off course by Zeus's storm and lands in southern Italy, where he establishes Crimissa and builds a shrine to Apollo in which he places Hercules's bow. Sophocles and, many centuries later, André Gide wrote plays about Philoctetes.

13. One of Helen's many suitors, Idomeneus was much older than the others. He was the leader of the Cretan forces in the Trojan War and was one of the Greeks inside the Wooden Horse. In one legend Idomeneus promises Poseidon to sacrifice the first living creature he sees if he escapes the storm and returns safely to Crete—and that person turns out to be his son. The sacrifice of his son, however, turns everyone against Idomeneus, and he is driven away to Italy, where he

founds a city on the Sallentine Plain. Greek legend says that because Idomeneus was a compulsive liar (a curse placed on him by Medea after Idomeneus judged Thetis to be more beautiful), all Cretans to this day have the reputation of being liars.

14. The Furies were female spirits who were born from the blood of Ouranus that fell upon Gaia after he was castrated by Cronus. The Furies (Alecto, Megaera, and Tisiphone: "unceasing," "grudging," and "avenger of murder," respectively) stand for righting all wrongs.

15. Orestes was the son of Agamemnon who avenged his father's murder by killing his mother, Clytemnestra, and her lover, Aegisthus.

16. Phaestus was a Cretan, a son of Talos. Talos was a Giant and the last survivor of the bronze race. He had only one vein in his entire body that ran from his head to his foot, and in place of human blood, he had ichor or "gods' blood" in that vein, which was sealed at the bottom by either a flap of membrane or a nail. His job was to run around Crete three times a day and keep the invaders away either by sinking their ships with huge rocks or burning them by turning himself into a red-hot mass. He was killed by Medea, who sang spells to put him asleep when the Argonauts wanted to land on the island and then pulled the nail from his foot (or sliced open the membrane) so that he bled to death. His body sank into the waves and curled around the island in the shape of a reef. A city in Crete was named in the honor of Phaestus.

17. According to one story, Telemachus was so taken with the charms of Polycaste that after his father's return to Ithaca, Telemachus returned to Pylos and married her. We know very little, however, about Nestor's seven sons and two daughters.

THE FOURTH BOOK: A VISIT TO MENELAUS AND HELEN

1. Megapenthes was a bastard son of Menelaus from a favorite slave woman. He was well loved by Menelaus, who preferred him over his other children. He was given a daughter of Alector for his bride, and after the death of Menelaus, he drove Helen from Sparta. Megapenthes was not named the king of Sparta, however, that position going to Orestes, the nephew of Menelaus, the closest legitimate heir.

2. Hermione, the daughter of Menelaus and Helen, was abandoned by her mother when the child was only nine, when Helen ran off to Troy with Paris. Several accounts of her life exist, but the most probable is that Menelaus had her married to Neoptolemus, Achilles's son, after his return from Troy. She tried to kill Andromache, the Trojan concubine of Neoptolemus, because she believed her husband's lover was a witch who had made her barren. Her husband's grandfather stopped Hermione from killing Andromache, and she fled to Sparta to seek refuge with Orestes, who killed Neoptolemus at Delphi after Neoptolemus went there to ask Apollo to intercede on his behalf for recompense for the death of Achilles. After slaying Neoptolemus, Orestes married Hermione, and they had a son, Tisamenus. Her beauty was legendary and, according to some poets, rivaled Aphrodite's. Surprisingly, Aphrodite apparently never sought revenge for this slight, although she did on other mortals whose beauty challenged hers.

3. An andron was a dining room or a banquet room. Here guests sat on couches, each with his own table, while slaves served them. Hetaerae—unmarried women trained to entertain men with music and conversation or with other, more sensual arts—often joined them. They might play cottabos, a game in which one player flicked the dregs of his winecup at another.

4. A himation was a large, rectangular piece of cloth that was wrapped around the body and draped over one shoulder, usually the left.

5. A krater was a large jar in which wine and water were mixed with certain spices.

6. A thronos was a special chair carved out of stone, usually marble, and meant for an important official or a god. It was an honor to be offered a seat in a thronos, even though it was extraordinarily uncomfortable.

7. Hephaestus was the smith god or metalworker. According to one legend, he was produced by Hera without a father; others claim him to be the son of Zeus. He was ugly and lame and was originally thrown out of heaven and into the ocean. Thetis and Eurynome, the Oceanids, found him bawling and abandoned and secretly brought him up for nine years in their cave. There, he learned the secrets of metalworking. Several stories exist concerning his revenge on his mother: One is that he made a magnificent throne out of gold, but when Hera sat in it, she was imprisoned and none could release her until Dionysus made Hephaestus drunk and stole the key from him. Another legend has it that Hephaestus fashioned magnificent sandals for all the gods that lent them grace while on their feet, but Hera's sandals were fashioned out of adamantine, and when she put them on, she fell flat on her face. He was constantly ridiculed by the rest of the gods, but Zeus gave him Aphrodite as his wife. This, however, did not bring him happiness, as Aphrodite committed adultery with Ares and others. Although his life was bitter, the other gods often came to him for favors when they needed something crafted. He created new armor for Achilles at the request of Thetis, who had been Hephaestus's nurse, and armor for Aeneas at the request of Aphrodite.

8. Young men wore a short cloak called a chlamys, which was sometimes draped over the himation. An older man as important as Odysseus, however, would not have worn a chlamys, as that attire was informal.

9. Sicily was the Greeks' source of amber, which they used for decoration and jewelry. Homer never mentions amber in *The Iliad*.

10. Helen's handmaiden Alcippe may have been named after an earlier Alcippe, the daughter of Ares and Aglaurus, who was raped at Athens by Halirrhothius. Ares killed Halirrhothius for his crime and was brought to trial by Poseidon on the charge of murder. The trial took place at the place of the rape, Areopagus, or "Ares's Hill," which eventually became the seat of the highest court of Athens. This was the first murder trial, according to Greek myth, and Ares was acquited by a jury of other Olympian gods.

11. This Polybus was possibly the king of Corinth who adopted Oedipus when as a foundling he was brought to the royal palace by a shepherd.

12. It is important to remember that when Paris took Helen back to Troy, the couple raided the treasure storeroom and took much of Menelaus's wealth. This explains, in part, why so much mention is made of the wealth Menelaus gathered on his trip back home after the Trojan War.

13. It is Menelaus's promise to build a palace and city in the name of Odysseus that shows the extent of the relationship between the heroes and the gods. Upon his death, Menelaus is made immortal and taken to the Elysian Fields in the company of Helen. Menelaus always thought about the good of the people, which is indicated in *The Iliad* when he tries to mediate between the Trojans and the Greeks for Paris having violated the laws of hospitality by taking Helen from her husband's house and fleeing to Troy. Menelaus tried to settle the dispute with a duel, and just when he was about to kill Paris, Aphrodite spirited the Trojan prince away to Helen's bedroom in Troy. He was not faultless, however, as he neglected to offer sacrifices to the gods who had supported Troy in the ten-year battle, and they punished him by destroying all but five of his fifty ships when he tried to sail back home after the war. The accounts of his goodness are many: He refused to slay Helen after the war; he saved Orestes after the youth had slain Aegisthus and Clytemnestra for killing Agamemnon by persuading the people to commute the sentence to a year's exile; and he assisted Telemachus. Of all the heroes involved in the Trojan War, Menelaus is one who is apparently admired by all the gods, even if somewhat reluctantly by some.

14. Paeon was the god of healing who cured Hades when he was defending the entrance to the Underworld from Hercules and was wounded by one of that man's arrows. Hades went to Olympus to be cured, and Zeus entrusted his brother to the care of Paeon, who spread ointments on the wound and healed it instantly. Paeon also apparently healed Ares after the god of war was wounded by Diomedes in battle.

15. The truthfulness of this account is questionable, for Helen also tried to betray the Greeks when they were inside the Wooden Horse. She imitated the wives of all the Greeks inside the horse and called out to them, trying to get them to answer. She is a highly controversial figure in Greek legends. Even her birth has more than one story: One claims that she was the daughter of Zeus and Leda; the other, that she was the daughter of Zeus and Nemesis. At one time, she professed to love Paris, and later she claimed to hate him.

16. A modern parallel: In 1848, when a group of university students in Padua rebelled against Austrian rule, eight young men hid from the police for a week in Donatello's gigantic wooden horse.

17. Proteus was one of the ancient sea gods who is sometimes described as a son of Poseidon but is probably older. He was responsible for herding seals and other creatures of the sea for Poseidon. Proteus could change form, not only to that of an animal but also to elements such as fire and water. He also had the gift of prophecy, although he was reluctant to use it; he invariably told the truth, which no one believed anyway. In one story, after Paris steals Helen, they sail to Egypt where Proteus, angry at Paris for breaking the laws of hospitality, places Helen under his protection and forces Paris from his shores. Paris returns to Troy alone (or sometimes with a phantom or doppelgänger of Helen). When the Greeks arrive, they refuse to believe that Helen is not in the city. Only after the city has been sacked does Menelaus realize that the story of Helen being held safely by Proteus is true. However, this is a story from Euripides's *Helen* and not the account of Homer. In Joyce's *Ulysses,* Stephen Dedalus is forced to undergo many changes that parallel the shape-shifting of Proteus.

18. We can only assume that Eidothea betrayed her father because she was in love with Menelaus.

19. Rhadamanthys was a judge of the dead. He was either a son of Zeus and Europa and a brother of Minos and Sarpedon or else a son of Phaestus, son of Talos. One account has him ruling Crete before Minos and giving that island an excellent code of laws that the Spartans later copied. He was driven out of Crete by Minos when he and Sarpedon quarreled with Minos over a handsome youth. After his death he was made a judge of the Underworld and sometimes was described as the king of Elysium, where the blessed shades pass their time. Homer contends that Rhadamanthys did not act as a judge of the deeds men had performed before their deaths but arbitrated between quarrels the shades had.

20. Zephyr, the god of the West Wind, was a son of Astraeus and Eos. He fell in love with Hyacinth, but when that youth favored Apollo over him, Zephyr caused a disc thrown by Apollo to veer off course and kill the youth. Zephyr was the father of Apollo's immortal horses, Xanthus and Balius, having slept with their mother, a harpy, while she was in the form of a filly and grazing in sweet grass meadows beside the ocean. The West Wind was considered to be the most favorable, in contrast to the North Wind, Boreas. Zephyr's wife is sometimes thought to be Iris, the goddess of the rainbow.

21. Dolius was an old servant who remained constantly faithful to Odysseus. Six of his sons followed their father in support of Odysseus, but the seventh, Melanthius, and a daughter Melantho, supported the suitors for Penelope's hand and were subsequently killed. Dolius and his six sons supported Odysseus in the final battle when Ithacans led by Eupeithes, the father

of Antinous, the leader of the suitors, tried to wrest the throne from Odysseus in a war of vengeance for the killing of his son. Eupeithes was slain by Laertes, the father of Odysseus.

THE FIFTH BOOK: THE LOVING NYMPH AND THE OPEN SEA

1. Tithonus was the son of Laomedon, king of Troy, and the Nymph Strymo. He was an extremely handsome youth, and when Eos (Dawn) first saw him, she fell in love with him and brought him to her palace by the stream of Ocean in Ethiopia. They had two children, Memnon and Emathion. Emathion became a king of Arabia and tried to prevent Hercules from stealing the golden apples of the Hesperides and was subsequently killed by him. Memnon took a force of Ethiopians to Troy and died while fighting the Greeks.

2. A daughter of the Titan Atlas, Calypso made her home on the mythical island of Ogygia. Her love for Odysseus is considered to be "mortal," and, consequently, she is forced to give him up. Sometimes the love of Calypso is contrasted with the love of Circe, with the latter considered "lust" while the former is considered "complete love." The reason for this is that Calypso gives up Odysseus after he refuses her gift of immortality because she realizes that she can never take the place of Penelope in his heart. Circe, on the other hand, simply wants Odysseus for selfish reasons and because she cannot have him.

3. Hermes is the messenger god, who guides shades to the House of Hades. He is seen also as the protector of travelers and patron of thieves and merchants. He is the son of Zeus and Maia, a daughter of Atlas. He is seen as a young man with a wide-brimmed hat, winged sandals, and carrying a caduceus (a herald's staff with two serpents entwined upon it). As a child, Hermes was highly precocious. He made the first lyre out of a tortoiseshell and stole fifty cows from the herd of Apollo. But when Apollo came to punish the child, Hermes was sleeping innocently in his cradle and claimed not even to know the meaning of the word *cow*. While Apollo was protesting this to Zeus, Hermes stole Apollo's quiver and bow off his back. Eventually, Hermes atoned for his theft of Apollo's cows and gave him the lyre that he had made. Later, when he returned the bow and quiver, Apollo was amused, and the two became fast friends. Many stories exist concerning Hermes's trickery, including how he disguised himself as Ares, the son of Hera, and took Ares's place at Hera's nipple, thereby making her his foster mother and keeping her from punishing him as she frequently did the children of Zeus by other women. He arranged the beauty contest among Hera, Athene, and Aphrodite and helped Odysseus out of several difficulties. He had several love affairs, including one with Aphrodite. He was helped in this love affair by Zeus, who sent his eagle to steal one of the golden sandals belonging to Aphrodite while she was bathing after having spurned Hermes. Zeus gave the sandal to Hermes, who offered to return it to Aphrodite only after she slept with him—which she did. Zeus's favor was given as thanks for Hermes having helped Zeus in his love affair with Io by helping her escape from Argus of the many eyes, whom he killed, thus earning his other name Argeiphontes.

4. The aegis was the breastplate or, sometimes, the shield of Zeus and was awful to behold. According to some accounts, it was a goatskin bag converted into a shield. The goatskin came from the goat Amalthea, who had been the nurse of Zeus. Enemies who glimpsed Zeus's aegis were seized by terror and fled.

5. Orion ("urine") was the son of Hyrieus, who, unable to have children, asked Zeus, Hermes, and Poseidon to help him. They told him to fetch the hide of a bull he had sacrificed to them, urinate on it, and bury it. Nine months later, a boy grew from that place, and Hyrieus named him Orion. He turned into a giant hunter, so tall that he could walk on the seabed and still keep his head and shoulders above water. He had a number of mistresses, including Side ("pomegranate"), who boasted she was more beautiful than Hera and was sent to Hades as punishment. He fell in love with Eos (Dawn) while he was hunting with Artemis. Artemis became jealous of this, and when he was hunting on the island of Delos (the birthplace of Artemis), she killed him with her

arrows. Other stories of his death exist, with Artemis at the center of each of them. Afterward, however, the goddess was sorry for what she had done and placed him in the sky as a constellation.

6. Demeter is the earth goddess (not to be confused with Gaia the earth mother) and patroness of fertility and goddess to the Eleusinian Mysteries. She was one of the six children of Cronus and Rhea.

7. While attending the wedding of Cadmus and Harmonia, Demeter met and fell in love with Iasion, a mortal. While making love in a freshly plowed field, they were discovered by Zeus, who killed Iasion with a thunderbolt. She gave birth to two sons from this union, Plutus ("wealth") and Philomelus ("lover of song"). The Eleusinian Mysteries may have come from this, a reenactment, perhaps, by her mortal handmaidens that led to a "secret" religion that spread across the world. Thomas Tryon used this story as the basis for his novel *Harvest Home.*

8. In Hesiod's *The Works and Days,* we note that when the sailor-farmer had dry-docked his boat for the winter, he then began his fieldwork. This would have been in or about November. According to Hesiod, the farmer was told by Zeus that if he wished to be successful, he had to plow, seed, and harvest his fields in the nude. After harvesting, the ground was to be plowed again in the spring and tilled again in the summer.

9. Although usually personified as warm and gentle, Notus brought the autumn storms that frequently destroyed crops and fields.

10. Eurus is usually seen as blustery and wet, and symbolizes a boasting person who cannot live up to his or her words.

11. Tenes was the son of Cycnus, the king of Colonae near Troy, and Proclea. He claimed Apollo as his father, and when his mother died, he was forced to live with and do the bidding of a wicked stepmother named Philonome, who later tried to seduce him. When he refused her advances, she complained to his father that he had tried to rape her. After a flute player named Eumolpus supported her story in exchange for the privilege of sharing her bed, Tenes and his sister were placed in a chest and thrown out to sea. There they floated to Leucophrys, where the people named Tenes their king. Cycnus later discovered his wife and the flute player in bed and learned that Philonome had lied about Tenes. He punished her by burying her alive and stoning Eumolpus to death. He sailed to Tenedos to make peace with his son, but as the ship tried to dock, Tenes cut the hawser with an ax, casting his father adrift as his father had him so many years before. This is where the Greek expression "axe of Tenes," describing a rash deed, originates.

12. Ino was the daughter of Cadmus and Harmonia. Zeus fathered Dionysus with Ino's sister Semele, which angered Hera. Since Hera could not punish Zeus directly for his affairs, she exacted retribution from his lovers or the children who resulted from those unions. She suggested that Semele ask to see Zeus in "all his glory," that is, with his thunderbolts. She did so—and was immediately burnt to a crisp. Dionysus was still at risk, so Ino disguised him by dressing him in girls' clothing. Hera discovered this ruse and drove Ino and her husband, Athamas, insane. In their madness, they killed their children: Learchus was killed by Athamas with arrows, and Melicertes was killed by Ino either by boiling him alive or by jumping from a cliff into the sea with him in her arms. Afterward, Ino was transformed into the sea goddess Leucothea ("white goddess"), who, aided by Melicertes (sometimes called Palaemon), helped sailors in trouble.

13. Cadmus was the founder of Thebes who fought and killed a terrible dragon. Athene helped him to build the city by telling him to take the dragon's teeth and sow them in the earth. He did this, and armed men sprang up from the earth. He threw a stone in the middle of them, and they turned upon each other in anger and fought until all but five were killed. These five (called "Spartoi" or "Sown Men") helped him build Thebes. He supposedly introduced the Greek

alphabet. He was married to Harmonia, the daughter of Ares and Aphrodite. Oedipus was a great-great-grandson of Cadmus.

14. Amphitrite was a sea goddess, the daughter of Nereus and Doris (a daughter of Oceanus). One day Poseidon saw her dancing on Naxos and fell in love with her. He tried to catch her, but she fled to Atlas for protection. Poseidon sent out dolphins to search for her. They discovered her and pleaded with her to marry Poseidon. At last she gave in and married the god of the sea. They had many children, among them Triton, Rhode, and Benthesicyme. As a gesture of his love, Poseidon placed the constellation of the Dolphin in the sky.

15. Callicoe is the name of the river god.

THE SIXTH BOOK: THE DISCOVERY OF NAUSICAA

1. In a work where much is made of harsh and, in some cases, murderous kings, Alcinous seems decidedly out of place. He is kind and so well loved among the gods (most of them, at any rate) that his gardens bloom in every season and guests entertained in his home come away refreshed and relaxed. One could make a case for the palace and gardens of Alcinous as symbolic of the Garden of Eden or even an earthly paradise reminiscent of Olympus itself. The reason the gods like Alcinous is that he pays diligent attention to each and every one of them and honors the laws of Zeus to the letter. The one god who does not care for Alcinous is Poseidon, who, we must remember, does not like Odysseus. Despite his warnings, Alcinous is gracious to Odysseus and helps him on his way home. But as Alcinous's ship returns after leaving Odysseus in Ithaca, Poseidon turns it into a rock and blocks the Phaeacians' harbor with a mountain, which is detrimental to a nation that makes its living with sea trade. Years before, when Jason and Medea were fleeing Colchis, the Argonauts took shelter in the Phaeacian harbor as well. When Alcinous decreed that Medea must be returned to her father if she was still a virgin, Jason and Medea hastily consummated their marriage in a cave, thus allowing Alcinous to give them shelter without disobeying the laws of Zeus.

2. King Alcinous wisely listened to his counselors before making decisions. This distinguished him from some of the other tyrannical rulers who are encountered in Greek literature. In the classical period, most Greek city-states had governments democratically elected by the citizens (which excluded all women, foreigners, slaves, and freed slaves). During the time of Odysseus, however, kings ruled. Because he is listening to his "Senate," we can assume that Alcinous was ahead of his time and listened to his archons, or chief counselors.

THE SEVENTH BOOK: THE PALACE OF ALCINOUS

1. Trying to keep the lineage straight can be very difficult. For example, Poseidon was also the father of the Cyclops Polyphemus, which made Polyphemus a half-brother to Nausithous, and uncle to King Alcinous, and a great-uncle to Nausicaa.

2. Eurymedon was the leader of the Giants, created when the blood from Ouranus's genitals fell upon Gaia following his castration by Cronus, in a war against the Olympians after Zeus defeated the Titans and imprisoned them in Tartarus. This war, called the Gigantomachia, was one of the most severe wars that the Olympians would fight, since the Giants were immune from death at the hands of the gods but not from a mortal hero. Consequently, Zeus prepared for this by siring Hercules. Gaia, who did not want the Titans imprisoned and so pushed the Giants into the fight against the Olympians, created an herb that rendered the Giants invincible at the hands of mortals. Zeus, however, forbade the Sun and Moon and Dawn to make their regular appearances until he could find the herb and destroy it. The last battle, an armageddon, took place at Phlegra ("the Burning Lands"), and the giants, led by Eurymedon and the Giants' champions, Alcyoneus and

Porphyrion, fell upon the gods by throwing huge boulders and mountain peaks. Their clubs were oak trees ripped from the earth and stripped of their branches. Hercules used his poisoned arrows (made so from the venom of the Hydra's blood) to shoot the Giants, then dragged them away from their homeland so that they would die (they could not die within the boundaries of their homeland). Porphyrion grabbed Hera and was trying to rape her when Zeus stunned him with a thunderbolt, allowing Hercules time to kill him too. (Surprisingly, Hera still bore a grudge against Hercules even after this.) Each Giant was subsequently finished off with Hercules's arrows after the various gods stunned them in individual combat. (Athene, for example, fought Pallas, eventually flaying him and covering her breastplate with his skin that had the texture of leather. Poseidon buried Polybotes by tossing the island Cos on top of him. Hermes defeated Hippolytus, and Artemis shot Gration with her arrows while Dionysus brought down Eurytus with his staff.)

We find a reference for a race of Giants in Genesis 6:4 as well: "There were giants in the earth in those days . . ." The Giants are the Nephilim in Greek texts.

3. The Greek word *kôrn* is usually applied to small grains as a sort of generic term. From the adjectives used, I assume that the poet is probably using an analogy for wheat. The grain that we know as corn did not appear in Europe until the end of the fifteenth century, when it was brought back by explorers from the New World.

4. Rhexenor is Alcinous's brother and the elder son of Nausithous. Arete, his daughter, married her uncle, Alcinous. Although "excellence" would be a possible definition of Arete's name, "compassion" is far more applicable here.

5. Anyone who sat in the ashes by the hearth was seeking help from the owner of the house. Symbolically, by sitting here, Odysseus is acknowledging that he has no resources and, therefore, is entitled, under the laws of hospitality, to help from Alcinous.

6. Odysseus's description of Calypso here as "dreadful goddess" must suggest that she is dreadful in that she kept him from returning home as long as she did, not that she is malicious or wrathful. Love, Odysseus seems to be suggesting, is not only a blessing for man but also a curse, for man is not quite sure how to handle its power. C. S. Lewis approached this mystery in *The Four Loves* and *The Allegory of Love*.

7. Morpheus was the son of Hypnos ("sleep") and was generally seen as a dream god. His name is taken from *morphe* ("form") and suggests "one who transforms or shape-shifts." As we do not know for certain if Odysseus was dreaming here, Hypnos would probably be more apt.

THE EIGHTH BOOK: THE SONGS OF THE HARPER

1. Athene is probably trying to enlist the women in the cause of Odysseus as well. Although women had no say in political gatherings, some did have influence with their husbands and fathers. This description of Odysseus differs from one we have from another writer, who describes him as "bandy-legged, long-armed, with a sloped forehead, and very hirsute."

2. There were two distinct classes being referred to by Alcinous. One class would be given food that they would cook themselves in an outer courtyard, while the upper class would enjoy the privileges of court and have their cooking done by servants and slaves.

3. Like the legendary Homer, Demodocus was blind. This suggested to the Greeks that Demodocus was capable of looking into things with an "inner eye" that made him closer to the gods than those who possessed all their senses. The deprivation of one sense was thought to force the others, including a "sixth sense," to become more "sensitized."

4. We have no account of this quarrel from any other Greek poet. This, of course, does not mean that there was not one, simply that the only mention of a quarrel between Odysseus and Achilles is recorded here by Homer.

5. One definition of the name Alcinous is "sharp-witted," which suggests his compassion and ability to see the pain that Odysseus suffers on hearing the bard's song.

6. Thoon was apparently named after one of the Giants who, along with his brother Agrius, was killed by the Fates in the terrible battle between the Olympians and the Giants. To name a child after an enemy of the Olympians seems a bit daring, in a way defying the gods. Homer, however, may have been using this as a poet's trick, a form of foreshadowing, if you will, to inform his listeners that these youths will be very rude to Odysseus.

7. This seems to be a reference to either Poseidon or Theseus, who also, according to one story, lifted a calf from one side of a fence to the other so that it might take full advantage of grazing (the grass is always greener).

8. Little is known about the individuals Homer mentions other than the brief description he himself gives. We assume that they were the best warriors that Alcinous had, or at least the most promising ones, to have been included by Homer here. Perhaps they were men to whom Homer felt he owed an obligation and so he made them a part of his song, relegating them to minor mention but making them famous nonetheless simply because of their place in his story.

9. The use of "father" here is intended as an insult, although at times the usage would be a compliment, connoting wisdom and deference. Here it is used to mean "useless man."

10. Eurytus was the king of Oechalia (perhaps Thessaly), who once held an archery competition with his daughter Iole as a prize to anyone who could beat him or his son Iphitus. Hercules answered the challenge and won, but Eurytus withheld his daughter because Hercules had already killed his children that he had had with Megara. Hercules left, reportedly taking with him some of Eurytus's prize mares. Eurytus then challenged Apollo to an archery contest, and Apollo slew him for his affront to the god. His great bow was inherited by his son Iphitus, who left in search of the mares that had disappeared from his father's stable. On his journey, he stopped off in Sparta, and there he met Odysseus who was contending for the hand of Penelope. One story says that he gave his great bow to Odysseus who used it to win the hand of Penelope by shooting an arrow through twelve axheads and striking the mark at the other end. The bow was so powerful that only Odysseus could string it. When he left for Troy, Odysseus left the bow behind. Iphitus went on to Tiryns, where he was greeted formally by Hercules but was later killed when he tried to bring the mares back to his home. Another version has Hercules killing Iphitus when he went to Tiryns to ask Hercules to help him find the thief who had stolen the prize mares. Hercules thought Iphitus was accusing him and killed him; he later murdered Eurytus and took Iole as his concubine. Deianira, the wife of Hercules, sent him a cloak dipped in Nessus's blood. (Nessus was a Centaur who had tried to rape Deianira. As Nessus was dying from an arrow shot by Hercules, he told Deianira to dip her cloak in his blood and use it as a love amulet when her husband seemed to fall out of love with her.) The cloak caused Hercules so much pain that he built a pyre, climbed upon it, and had himself burned to death.

11. This story earned Plato's disapproval in Book III of his *Republic,* and he called for abandoning the study of Homer on the grounds that Homer was irreverent and by telling such stories about the gods was encouraging the youth of Athens to behave likewise. The gods, to paraphrase Plato, should be held above reproach and used as examples to govern man's behavior. The Greeks, however, saw the gods as extensions (but on a grander plane) of themselves, privy to the same frailties as the humans: love, hate, anger, jealousy, pride, etc. Thus, the statuary of their

gods resembled the most beautiful among themselves. Stories about the gods explained not only the unexplainable forces of nature and the mysticisms of man, but by explaining the gods, the Greeks explained themselves as well. Plato took exception to this and in Books II and III of *The Republic* called for the destruction of the works of Homer and Hesiod (at least the *Theogony,* where Hesiod explains the dethroning of Ouranus) and others who treated the gods in what he determined to be a disdainful and harmful manner.

12. Homer's description of young men performing an athletic dance reminds us that the Greeks valued not only feats of arms, but the fine arts as well. Sparta, of course, was a war-favoring state, but Athens, whose concept of democracy and arts still governs us somewhat today, favored the fine arts—poetry, music, dancing, sculpture, etc. Although such a description might seem out of place in an adventure story, it does illustrate the multifaceted lives the Greeks led.

13. This was a great gift to an individual such as Odysseus; by giving it, Euryalus recognized his greatness not only as a warrior but as one who could appreciate the finer things in life as well. The sword, an instrument of war, seldom becomes a symbol of art as this one does.

14. As Circe held Odysseus captive through her love sorcery, so did Molly Bloom hold her lover captive in Joyce's *Ulysses*.

15. Calypso kept Odysseus a love captive for seven years just as Leopold Bloom was held a prisoner of his wife, Molly. Odysseus, however, was not as willing a captive as Leopold. Additionally, we see Molly as being a dual image of Calypso and the witch-whore Circe.

16. This speech by Odysseus reemphasizes the emergence theme of *The Odyssey*—that Odysseus cannot return home until he can admit his own shortcomings and realize that his pride is his downfall. By being cast naked and weaponless upon the Phaeacian shore, he emerges from the sea as newborn, ready to assume his "new life." Of course, we realize that Odysseus has not lost any of his old skills—he is still strong and crafty—but he has gained the knowledge of his own weakness, his pride. This is, in a way, a needed purification ceremony prior to his apotheosis.

THE NINTH BOOK: THE ADVENTURE WITH THE CYCLOPS

1. Circe's name means "hawk." She was the daughter of Helios and Perse, an Oceanid. She was a powerful witch whom the gods kept on the island of Aeaea (presumably Cape Circaeum on the west coast of Italy) because she had a strange habit of changing her lovers into animals that symbolized what they had been in human form—or at least what Circe saw them as. When Odysseus came to her island, she could not change him into an animal because Hermes had given him the herb moly to counter her spell-casting. According to one story, Odysseus had three sons with Circe: Telegonus, Agrius, and Latinus. One day when Circe longed for Odysseus and desired him to return, she sent Telegonus after him, but on his arrival in Ithaca, Telegonus accidentally killed Odysseus. When he returned to Aeaea with the body of Odysseus, he took along Telemachus and Penelope. Circe made the pair immortal and married Telemachus, while Telegonus married Penelope.

Jason and Medea came to Circe's island to be purified for the murder of Apsyrtus, the younger brother of Medea. Jason and Medea took him as a hostage when they fled her father's court: When her father nearly caught up with their ship, Medea killed her brother and dismembered his body, casting the pieces overboard, so that they could escape while her father stopped to pick them up. When Circe discovered why they had come to the island, she refused to complete the purification process and drove them away even though Medea was her niece.

2. Here, Odysseus is drawing a parallel between Hercules and Agamemnon. Agamemnon's bloody end to the Trojan War and the slaying of children, the slaying of innocence, is suggested as one reason for his own death. Hercules was driven mad by Hera, who was jealous of Zeus's

affair with Hercules's mother, Alcmene. While mad, Hercules took his bow and shot his three sons along with his wife, Megara, who tried to protect one son with her body. As penance, he was ordered to perform Twelve Labors for Eurystheus: killing the Nemean lion; killing the Lernaean Hydra; catching the Erymanthian boar; catching the Cerynean hind; driving off the Stymphalian birds; cleaning the Stables of Augeas; capturing the Cretan bull; capturing the mares of Diomedes; stealing the girdle of Queen Hippolyte; killing the cattle of Geryon; stealing the golden apples of the Hesperides; and capturing Cerberus.

3. Dionysus gave the vine to man and taught him how to make wine from the grapes. One day while he was out walking, a group of women who had been drinking his wine spied him and made a rush for him. Each woman wanted him for her lover, and in the process of tugging at him, they managed to tear him to pieces. Aghast at what they had done, they threw the pieces of Dionysus's body into the river where they floated down to the sea and came together with Dionysus emerging whole again. This legend explains the necessity of cutting back the vine to the earth after the harvest so that it will emerge healthy and hearty again at the start of the next growing season.

4. The name Odysseus gives Polyphemus here is a fine example of his trickery. The Greek for "no one" or "no man" is *me tis,* but if the two words are combined into one, then it becomes *metis* and means "a schemer, one who is resourceful."
    Metis was the daughter of the Titans Oceanus and Tethys. She was the first goddess with whom Zeus had an affair. He convinced her to give his father the purgative that forced Cronus to vomit up Zeus's brothers and sisters and give him the numbers he needed to fight the Titans for control of the heavens. Gaia, however, prophesied that if Metis bore Zeus a daughter, she would be his equal in wisdom and would bear a son who would be far stronger than Zeus and eventually would overthrow him in much the same way that he overthrew his father. When Metis became pregnant, Zeus tricked her and swallowed her whole. She still bore him the child, which came full grown from his head: Athene. The powers of Metis stayed with Zeus, however, and the wisdom she gave him kept him from being overthrown.

5. Before being blinded by Odysseus, Polyphemus had a tragic, but comical, love affair with the Nymph Galatea. He ignored a warning from the prophet Telemus, that if he persisted in this affair, he would be blinded by a man named Odysseus (Greek meaning: "a man of vengeful anger"). Polyphemus ignored the warning, declaring that he had already lost his heart.

THE TENTH BOOK: THE ADVENTURE WITH CIRCE

1. The reader must remember that this is Odysseus's version of events and decide if his account can be trusted. As Odysseus traditionally personifies the master trickster, his narration must be taken with a grain of salt. In *The Inferno,* Dante encounters Odysseus (Ulysses) in the Eighth Chasm (Canto XXVI) and discovers that he must suffer the flames there for his part in the treachery of the wooden horse and for inducing Achilles to sail for Troy, leaving behind Deidamia, daughter of Lycomedes, king of Scyros, at whose court Thetis had left her son Achilles in female disguise to prevent him from sailing to Troy and his death. Deidamia, who bore Achilles a son, died of grief at Achilles's leaving. In addition, the Palladium, a statue of Pallas, was stolen by Odysseus because the fortunes of Troy depended on its safety within the walls of the city.

2. A klismos is a carefully built chair with a curved back and legs. The seat is plaited leather, and sometimes a cushion is placed on top—especially if the guest is considered an important person. Most people would sit on stools called diphros, which were usually padded.

3. Aeolus was the son of Hippotas and king of the floating island of Aeolia (perhaps north of Sicily). He was a mortal who supposedly invented the use of sails and won the favor of Zeus, who gave him control of the winds. He kept the winds in a cave on his island and released them upon his or the gods' whim. He lived a remarkably free life with his wife, Cyane, the daughter of

Liparus, who was the original king of Aeolia. Together they had six sons and six daughters who married each other. The four chief winds were Boreas, the North Wind; Zephyr, the West Wind; Notus, the South Wind; and Eurus, the East Wind. One legend has it that Aeolus gave the bag of winds to Odysseus after Athene promised Aeolus one of her Nymphs or handmaidens as a concubine if he would help Odysseus. Another legend has it that it was Artemis who bribed Aeolus with a handmaiden or Nymph as a favor to Athene, who was under close and suspicious observation at the time by Poseidon.

4. A caryatid is a column carved in the shape of a woman. A stoa is a roofed porch with a front colonnade.

5. The Laestrygonians were Giants and cannibals. The Laestrygonians lived in a city called Telepylus, founded by Lamus, a son of Poseidon. The country had a peaceful harbor that deluded sailors into landing there. The daughter of the Laestrygonian chief, Antiphates, led the forward party of Odysseus to her father, who ate one. Little credence is given to accounts that Odysseus learned about the cannibalistic nature of the Laestrygonians during a feast when Antiphates asked if he liked the meat he was eating. Odysseus replied that it was very tasty, and Antiphates laughed and said that he was eating one of his own men. This legend appears to have been added to the Odyssean story from the legend of Tantalus. Some scholars place the land of the Laestrygonians in one of the small islands near Sardinia.

6. Odysseus has posed a strange situation. The Laestrygonian land had days and nights of equal length—or else, extremely short days and nights (the Greek text has it both ways). Apparently some of the animals—cattle, goats, and sheep—thrive at night while others content themselves during the day. The suggestion is that this is a magical or strange place where the ordinary habits of a human world do not hold sway. The passage, at least in its intent, is a bit vague: ἐγγὺς γὰρ νυκτός τε καὶ ἤματός εἰδι κέλευθοι.

7. The figure of Circe in legend is very controversial. Some modern scholars suggest that she symbolizes all that is in man's vision of the so-called perfect woman: one who is a mother to him, a wife to him, a prostitute for him, and possessing great magic that he must harness—but once he has won her over to him, that magic is used only for his betterment. This literary figure can be summed up by the term "witch-whore," as it appears that Circe's magic is linked directly to the sexual act from which she gathers her power. Traditionally she symbolizes lust. The literal meaning of her name ("hawk") suggests a predator who preys upon men.

8. Aeetes, the brother of Circe, was the son of Helios and the Oceanid Perse. He was the father of Medea and the king of Colchis on the southeastern edge of the Black Sea. Colchis was an extremely barbarous and cruel place in Greek myth, and Aeetes was well made to be its ruler. His wife was Asterodea, a Caucasian Nymph, with whom he had a daughter, Chalciope. He was also married to Idyia ("all-knowing"), who the mother of Medea and Apsyrtus. Aeetes welcomed Phrixus, who came to Aeetes on the back of the golden ram as he fled Athamas. Chalciope was given to Phrixus in marriage by Aeetes, who nailed the Golden Fleece from the ram to an olive tree in the grove of Ares. After this, Aeetes learned from an oracle that one of the Greek race would kill him and, fearing his son-in-law, had Phrixus put to death. When Jason came, Aeetes feared that Jason was the man of the oracle and so imposed seemingly impossible labors on him before he would give Jason the Golden Fleece. After Jason completed the labors, Aeetes broke his promise, fearing that he would die if the fleece left his land. Medea, however, had fallen in love with the handsome Jason and helped him steal the fleece and fled with him. Aeetes came after them, but Medea killed her brother, Apsyrtus, chopped him into pieces, and dribbled the pieces overboard, forcing her father to halt his ship and pick up the pieces of his son for a proper burial. Aeetes was eventually defeated by his brother, Perses, king of the Tauri, but when Medea returned after her betrayal by Jason, she restored him to his throne. When he was eventually killed, Medea's son Medus succeeded him to the throne.

9. Odysseus was right to suspect that Hermes was the god who might have guided the ship into the harbor. Hermes, we remember, is the patron of travelers.

10. Eos is the goddess of Dawn and the daughter of the Titan Hyperion and Titaness Theia. She was the mother of the winds, the stars, and Eosphorus, the Morning Star. Along with her brother Helios, she drove a chariot with a pair of silver horses through the sky. The horses were named Phaethon ("shining") and Lampos ("bright"). She was fated to fall in love with many mortals, most affairs ending in unhappiness, as Aphrodite bore her a grudge for having flirted with Ares. Homer uses several epithets to describe Eos, such as "rosy-fingered," "early-rising," and "saffron-robed." The best-known story about her concerns her desire for the mortal Tithonus. She begged Zeus to grant Tithonus immortality but forgot to ask that he retain eternal youth as well. When Zeus granted her wish, Tithonus aged endlessly until he was dried up like a cicada and even chirruped like one. Eos locked him in his bedroom to keep him from escaping. Together they had the children Memnon and Emathion, who were, respectively, the kings of Ethiopia and Arabia. She also abducted Cephalus when she saw him hunting in Attica early one morning. He continued to long for his wife, Procris, but Eos refused to release him. They had a son, Phaethon. Eos was also the lover of the gigantic hunter Orion and took him to Delos, thus offending the virgin Artemis who considered Delos sacred and not to be defiled by lovers. Artemis put Orion to death. Although Dawn is beautiful to behold, as the stories suggest, there is a lot of deadliness to her that should make us wary of how day is to be lived.

11. This retreat causes some scholars to argue that Odysseus is not the great warrior we would like to believe but often "hedges his bets" by sending others out to discover danger before he reacts to it. The same argument is made about the Scylla and Charybdis episode, when Odysseus arms himself and takes his position at the prow of the ship. Some argue that Odysseus, well acquainted with war and tactics, knew that the point man is always allowed safe passage, as those lying in wait want to catch the rest of the warriors by surprise. The suggestion is that Odysseus is not a hero, because he is quite willing to sacrifice others so that he may come unscathed through danger.

12. Here we can see that Odysseus is offering this counsel to his men in order to lift their spirits, which were surely flagging after the encounters with Antiphates and Polyphemus. Odysseus needs to do this before he sends out a scouting party to investigate the island, knowing full well that they will remember what happened to the last party he sent out to reconnoiter. This shows him as a master trickster and does little to raise our admiration for him as a hero, for he is manipulating his men in the hopes that he will be able to use them after they have been sated with food and wine.

13. Eurylochus was the husband of Odysseus's sister and one of the nobles from Samos. His friendship with Odysseus is questionable. Although he appears to be loyal to Odysseus, he does not return to Circe's palace to help Odysseus free his men (the party that Eurylochus led) from Circe's spell, and, he later goes against the orders of Odysseus and persuades the rest of the crew to slaughter the sacred cattle of Helios, the sun god. Some scholars suggest that Eurylochus is jealous of Odysseus.

14. Moly is considered by most to be a mythical plant, although I believe this to be mandrake, in America called duck's foot, ground lemon, hog apple, Indian apple, mayapple, raccoon berry, or wild lemon, and in Europe mandragora or Satan's apple. It is a perennial plant that forms dense copses in open woodlands. It is dark brown and fibrous, and has a jointed rootstock that produces a simple, round stem that forks at the top into two petioles, each supporting a large, round, five-to-nine-lobed yellow-green leaf. A solitary waxy-white or cream-colored flower grows on a short peduncle from the fork in the stem. The root of the European version often resembles a human figure. In ancient times it was used as an anesthetic for surgery, and the fresh root is strongly emetic and purgative. It is highly poisonous and must be handled and prepared with

great care by someone who has been trained in its use. I have drawn my conclusion regarding the identification of this plant from Odysseus's further explanation that this plant is dangerous for man to dig although gods can handle it with ease. George Chapman's note reads: *"Credo in hoc vasto mundi ambitu extare res innumeras mirandae facultatis: adeo, ut ne quidem ista quae ad transformanda corpora pertinet, iure e mundo eximi possit."* As mandrake was also used by wizards in the Middle Ages to help with some of their most difficult spells, it seems logical that this might be the plant Hermes hands to Odysseus. As a further note, in the legend of Merlin, the secrets of the mandrake root are part of the knowledge that Merlin gives to Nimue (Viviane), who demanded magical secrets from him in exchange for her charms.

15. Persephone was the daughter of Zeus and Demeter, the earth goddess, who was one of the original six Olympians born to Rhea and Ouranus (the others were Zeus, Poseidon, Hades, Hera, and Hestia). Persephone was originally a goddess of grain. The Greeks associated the growing of grains with the eternal return—plants die, then are reborn again in the spring. Consequently, the seeds were buried in the dark during the summer months before the autumnal sowing occurred. The return to life after burial is symbolized in the myth of Persephone and her abduction by Hades and her return to the upper world. This story gave way to the ritual of the Eleusinian Mysteries, as those who worshiped Persephone and Demeter in this fashion would also, according to ancient belief, be given the chance to return to life after death. The exact ritual of the Eleusinian Mysteries was carefully guarded by women who were the prime worshipers at these rites and has been lost over the centuries. One story has it that a young, handsome, and virile male would be selected as a type of harvest lord by the priestesses and for either three, five, or seven years (the figure is vague) would be worshiped and given everything he wanted. On the eve of the most holy of days, he disappeared in the mass celebration that traditionally was held in an oak grove. What happened is anyone's guess.

Persephone was extremely beautiful, and her mother loved her dearly. To protect her from the lascivious advances of the male gods on Olympus, Demeter kept her on Sicily. There Persephone occupied her time by wandering through the woods near Henna along with the Ocean Nymphs. One day, however, when she was picking flowers (Zeus had placed a large dark-blue narcissus in her path to tempt her as a favor to his brother Hades, who wanted her for his wife), there was a great rumbling from deep within the ground. The ground gaped wide and flames licked out (one explanation for Mt. Etna), and Hades rode out from the Underworld in his chariot drawn by two dark-blue horses. Although Persephone screamed and fought, he was too strong for her and carried her off into the Underworld to become his queen. The Nymph Cyane saw this and protested in vain, and her grief melted into water. When Demeter discovered what had happened to her daughter, she approached Zeus and asked for Persephone's return. Zeus said that she would be returned to Demeter only if Persephone had not eaten anything in the Underworld during her captivity. Unfortunately, Persephone had eaten eight pomegranate seeds (which explains why it is the seed of the pomegranate that is edible and not the meat, unlike most fruits, and why the seeds appear like rubies), and so she could not return to the upper world. Demeter went into mourning, and the entire earth underwent mourning with her. All animals, including man, were doomed to die as the earth no longer bore fruit to help sustain life. In desperation, Zeus interceded and proclaimed that Persephone would spend six months in the Underworld with Hades and six months on earth with Demeter. This corresponds with the growing seasons: For six months the earth is without fruit (winter) while for six months it bears fruit (summer).

16. Teiresias was the son of Everes, a Theban nobleman descended from Udaeus. Two legends explain how he came by his blindness. One regards his mother, Chariclo, who was allegedly Athene's favorite and bathed with her every day at a certain spring. One day, Teiresias spied Athene naked and, overcome by her loveliness, ran to her to hold her in his arms. Athene covered his eyes with her hands and blinded him. Chariclo wailed about her son's loss of sight and, taking pity upon her, Athene now placed her hands upon Teiresias's ears, and when she took them away, he could understand the speech of the birds. She then gave him a cornel-wood staff that would guide him as easily as if he could see and endowed him with a life of seven generations and the gift of prophecy.

The other legend has it that Teiresias saw two snakes copulating on Mount Cyllene in Arcadia. He grabbed a stick and killed the female. Instantly he was transformed into a woman and remained a woman for seven years until he came upon another pair of snakes copulating. Again he struck the pair, this time killing the male. Instantly he was transformed back into a man. One day Zeus and Hera were arguing over who had the greatest pleasure from sexual intercourse. They asked Teiresias to solve the problem, for he had lived as both male and female and known love in both guises. When Teiresias declared that a woman's pleasure was nine times greater, Hera became enraged (because Zeus now knew her secret) and struck him blind. Zeus could not undo his wife's act (the gods do have certain limitations, such as not being able to take back promises) but he compensated Teiresias by giving him the gift of prophecy based on his ability to understand the speech of birds. Teiresias had a special grove near Thebes where he lived, served by a young boy. Teiresias reportedly died after drinking water from the spring of Telphusa at Haliartus and was buried there.

17. The Land of Hades was created after the Olympians defeated the Titans for control of the cosmos.

THE ELEVENTH BOOK: THE VISIT TO THE LAND OF HADES

1. The Cimmérians belong partly to legend and partly to history. That the Cimmérians did exist we find in Herodotus, where they are driven from their home (the biblical Gomer) north of the Black Sea sometime in the eighth or seventh century B.C. by nomadic Scythian tribes. Around the middle of the seventh century, they overrun Midas's kingdom at Phrygia (Midas takes poison to avoid being captured by them) and attack Lydia and kill King Gyges. They also capture the capital of Sardis with the exception of the citadel, which they could not breach. Two Greek poets, Callinus and Archilochus, explain how the Ionians lived in terror of the Cimmérians. The plague ultimately destroyed their power and they retreated to the east.

Homer, however, insists that they are a wonderful people who live on the edge of the world where Ocean begins. Their land is shrouded in perpetual mist and darkness. Homer could be suggesting Ireland, as the early Irish legends suggest a land of mist and darkness, and the Tuatha Dé Danaan (people of the goddess Dana [or Danu]) may have gone to Ireland from northern Greece. The Tuatha Dé Danaan were the Otherworld (Underworld) people. The story of the Tuatha Dé Danaan is found in Ireland's mythological cycle and in the *Lebor Gabála (Book of Invasions)*. Dana [Danu] is sometimes linked to Athene, although she is also linked with Danaë, the mother of Perseus (the father was Zeus).

2. We must point out here that the ancient Greeks' version of life after death differed starkly from the Judeo-Christian concept of peace and serenity or the milk and honey of some theologians. To those Greeks, the life they lived in the known world was far better than the stark and bleak life they expected after death. Some of the "mysteries" did, however, differ from this, promising a great afterlife in exchange for obedience in this life.

3. Death was the last journey a Greek had to take, which was to the land of Hades. After death, the body was laid out, usually on soft wool, and an obol (a coin valued at one-sixth of a drachma) was placed in his mouth for expenses (mainly to pay Charon to ferry him over the river). A honey cake was laid with him as an offering to the Underworld gods along with a flask of scented oil that was placed by his head. The body was then placed on a bier and carried on the shoulders of friends to the place of burning. Professional mourners and flute players followed. The body was then burned to free the spirit, and the ashes were placed in an urn with some of the dead man's possessions for his use in the spirit world. After this, there would be a funeral feast and games in which magnificent awards were given to the victors. The most famous funeral is probably the one Achilles gave for his friend, Patroclus. In this instance, a huge pyre was built and the Myrmidons (Achilles's men) armed themselves and rode in the procession in their chariots. Patroclus's friends cut off their hair and placed it upon the body. Then sheep and oxen were sacrificed and the corpse was wrapped from head to foot in the fat taken

from their bodies and placed on the pyre with the flayed bodies of the animals around it. Huge two-handled jars of honey and wine were added, and four strong horses and two house dogs were killed and placed beside him. Then twelve Trojan youths who had been captured by Achilles were brought up to the pyre and killed and their bodies piled on top of all the rest. The pyre was lit and burned throughout the night. In the morning, Achilles told the Greeks to quench the fire with wine and then to gather up the bones of Patroclus, wrap them in a double fold of fat, and place them in a golden urn. Since Achilles knew that he too would die (this had been foretold by his immortal mother Thetis Silverheels), he ordered that his body would likewise be treated and added to the same urn so that he and Patroclus would sleep together in eternity. After this, a decent barrow would be raised and the urn placed in that. Then Achilles held the funeral games and awarded prizes. For the fastest chariot racer, he gave a woman skilled in sewing and an eared tripod so huge that it could hold twenty-two measures. Second prize was a six-year-old unbroken mare; third prize was a cauldron untouched by fire; fourth prize was two talents of gold; fifth prize was a two-handled urn that had been untouched by fire. The winner of the boxing match earned a strong mule; the loser received a two-handled cup. The wrestling winner earned a great tripod for standing on the fire and, curiously, the second prize was a woman who was skilled in many crafts. (The wrestlers were Aias and Odysseus, and as neither could gain an advantage, they were told to take equal prizes, but we do not know who got the woman, who was valued at four oxen.) Winners of footraces were given silver mixing bowls from Sidon, an ox, and a half talent of gold.

4. Confusion exists among scholars about the various references to the ships of Odysseus. Sometimes his ships are referred to as black or crimson or a mixture of the two colors. One suggestion is that the ships might be black with the prow painted crimson, which would be a frightening combination to see coming at one while sailing upon the seas. More than likely, however, a black ship suggests "doom bringing" while crimson refers to the warriors it carries.

5. One legend has it that the city of Ophir was built on the site where Odysseus planted his oar, which flowered into a Judas tree. This was the famous Ophir that supposedly held the secret to Solomon's mines.

6. Artemis was one of the twelve great Olympian deities. She was the goddess of hunting and archery and, paradoxically, the protector of wild animals and children. According to legend, she roamed the high mountain country with her bands of Nymphs and took harsh vengeance upon any who tried to impede her progress. She is characterized by a deliberately chosen and rigidly maintained virginity and punishes those who violate or wish to violate that state. She insisted that all her attendants likewise maintain their virginity and defended that concept among the mortals. Her vengeance on those who lost their virginity was harsh and sometimes vicious. For example, when Zeus raped Callisto, Artemis changed Callisto into a bear and drove her away from the goddess's side because Callisto was no longer a virgin. To this extent, the idea behind the cult of the Virgin Mary probably has its beginnings here. Strangely enough, however, Artemis does not seem to be an "original" virgin goddess but seems to have come from an earth mother and thus is commonly associated with the many-breasted goddess of Ephesus. She was the bringer of fertility and protector of the newly born. Artemis was the daughter of Leto and twin sister of Apollo, either born with him on Delos or just before him on Ortygia. Consequently, she is referred to as Delia and Cynthia. Hera was jealous of her and in *The Iliad* takes great pleasure in insulting Artemis by spilling her arrows and boxing her ears. Along with her brother, however, Artemis avenges the Giant Tityus's attempted rape of Leto by slaying him and consigning him to eternal punishment in Tartarus. Since she brings death primarily to women, she is associated with the witch goddess Hecate, who is sometimes called Artemis of the Crossroads. One legend has Artemis falling in love with Orion. Apollo, jealous of her love for the hunter, saw Orion swimming far out in the sea one day when he and Artemis were hunting on Crete. Apollo challenged Artemis to try and hit the distant object with an arrow. Artemis casually unleashed an arrow, then watched in horror as it killed Orion. The most vicious story associated with her concerns Actaeon, who came upon her bathing one day while he was hunting.

Afraid that he would boast that he had seen her naked, she turned him into a stag, and he was devoured by his own dogs.

We can find similar stories in other cultures. For example, in the Ulster Cycle, Fergus Mac Róich, one of Maeve's many lovers, was bathing one day in a lake when Maeve's husband, finally fed up with Fergus, either slew him or had him slain in the same manner that Artemis slew Orion, except a spear was used. According to one story, Ailill challenged an expert spear caster to hit the distant mark while Fergus was swimming, or swimming and making love with Maeve in the middle of a lake. The cast was on the mark and Fergus was slain. Fergus was so insatiable that it took seven women a night to satisfy him, while Maeve needed thirty men a night to satisfy her. In both legends, we see punishment for adultery and illicit love and the concept of the male as a sacrifice for a woman's love, along the same lines as the ancient mysteries associated with Demeter whereby a harvest lord was chosen to reign for seven years, at the end of which he reportedly was sacrificed.

7. The answering of Odysseus's questions in reverse order is called by the ancients Homeric last-first. In poetic form, this gives a certain unity to a poem that would otherwise become a simple narrative.

8. This is another dimension of Odysseus's importance to Ithaca in that he was not only a king of the island but one of those who dispensed justice as well.

9. Here Odysseus lists many of the women he saw in the land of Hades. All of these women were celebrated beauties of their time and became the paramours of the gods. Each of them was the mother of a great hero. Tyro, for example, gave birth to Pelias and Neleus, who were fathered by Poseidon. When Tyro's stepmother, Sidero, discovered that Tyro was pregnant, Sidero refused to believe that the father was Poseidon and treated her cruelly throughout the pregnancy. After Pelias reached majority, he supplanted Aeson as heir to the kingdom of Iolcus and killed Sidero for her cruelty to his mother. Tyro's husband was her uncle, Cretheus.

10. The twins Amphion and Zethus were reared by shepherds in the mountains after their mother, Antiope, was thrown in prison in Cadmeia. Amphion became adept at music and Zethus at war. Amphion set up an altar to Hermes, who presented him with a lyre. Amphion married Niobe, the daughter of Tantalus. After he and his brother were full grown, Antiope escaped from prison whereupon Amphion and Zethus attacked Thebes and killed Lycus who was acting as regent for Laius. They tied his wife Dirce to the horns of a bull (the fate she planned for Antiope) and became kings of Thebes. Amphion played the lyre with such magic that the stones floated into place of their own accord. Because the lyre had seven strings, seven gates were established to the city. They then named the city Thebes after Zethus's wife Thebe. But they did not live happily ever after. Indeed, the entire story is drenched in blood. Niobe boasted that her twelve children were better than the children of Leto, who had only Apollo and Artemis. Apollo took vengeance upon her by killing her sons while Artemis killed her daughters. Niobe returned to Lydia where she was turned into a pillar of stone (possibly an archetype for the story of Lot's wife being turned into a pillar of salt). Amphion tried to kill Apollo and was slain in an attack upon Apollo's temple. Zethus died of grief over his only son who died in childhood.

11. Alcmene was pregnant with twins, Hercules (also called Heracles or Herakles, which means "Hera's glory") sired by Zeus, and Iphiclus sired by Amphitryon. When the time came for the twins to be born, Zeus boasted to the gods that a mortal ruler who would descend from his loins was shortly to be born. Hera overheard this boast and knew that Zeus intended Alcmene's son to be the ruler of her native land. She sent Ilithyia, the goddess of childbirth, to delay the birth of Hercules until Eurystheus was born to Nicippe and her husband, Sthenelus, as Eurystheus was descended from Perseus and would, therefore, fulfill Zeus's prophecy. One must remember that once a god makes a pronouncement, he or she cannot take it back.

12. Megara gave two children to Hercules, but Hera, angry about Zeus's dalliance with Antiope, drove Hercules mad, and in his madness, he slew his children and killed Megara when she tried to intercede. When the madness was lifted from Hercules and he saw what he had done, he was going to kill himself but was saved from this ignominy by his friend Theseus. Instead, he was sent to Eurystheus for penance. Eurystheus hated Hercules, for being everything that Eurystheus was not. Consequently, Eurystheus devised twelve "impossible" labors, hoping that Hercules would be killed.

13. Jocasta, called Epicaste by Homer, was married to Laius, king of Thebes. When she gave birth to their son Oedipus, Laius consulted an oracle. Told that the son would kill the father, Laius commanded that the baby be taken out and left on the sides of the mountains for the wolves to devour. Laius drove an awl through the heels of the infant (hence the name Oedipus, meaning "swollen foot" or "pierced heel") and abandoned the baby on the slopes of Mount Cithaeron. But the Theban shepherd who was to leave Oedipus there took pity on the baby and carried him over the mountain to Corinth and its king Polybus, who was childless. Polybus adopted the child and raised him as his own. One day while at a banquet, a drunk taunted Oedipus about his being a bastard. Oedipus went to Delphi to consult the Oracle and learned that he was destined to kill his father and marry his mother. Since he still believed that he was the natural son of Polybus and Merope, he refused to return to Corinth and instead wandered to Boeotia. At a crossroads, a chariot driver ordered him to give way, and when Oedipus refused, the driver ran the chariot over his foot and struck him a blow. Enraged, Oedipus killed the driver and the rest of the party, except one servant who ran away. Oedipus continued on his journey and came at last to Thebes. The city was in great distress since their king had been killed while on his way to Delphi to consult the Oracle about the Sphinx, a deadly monster who was eating the citizens of Thebes when they ventured out upon the highway and couldn't answer her riddle: "What walks on four legs in the morning, two legs at noon, and three legs at night?" Creon, the regent of Thebes, offered the throne and the hand of the queen Jocasta to the person who could rid Thebes of the dreaded Sphinx. Oedipus took the challenge and correctly answered the Sphinx's riddle (man) and killed the Sphinx. He then married Jocasta, thus completing the oracle at his birth. Jocasta gave him four children, two sons and two daughters, according to the tragedies by Sophocles. In Homer's version, Jocasta became aware that she had married her son and hanged herself. Oedipus continued to rule for many years. Pausanias, a geography writer, suggests that Oedipus remarried a woman named Eurygania, the daughter of Hyperphas, and it was she who bore him his two sons. Homer does not mention any daughters. After many years, a plague struck Thebes, and the blind prophet Teiresias told Oedipus that he was the cause of it for having killed his father and married his mother, but Oedipus did not believe him. At the same time, Polybus died in Corinth, and the Corinthians sent word to Oedipus that they wished him to be the new king. He told the messenger that he was afraid to do so for an oracle had told him he would marry his mother, Merope. The messenger, who was the shepherd who had saved Oedipus, told him that he was not Merope's son. Thereupon, Oedipus realized the terrible truth. Oedipus blinded himself (according to Sophocles, with the pins of the brooches he took from Jocasta who had hanged herself at this time) and was banished from Thebes by Creon in accordance with the oracle. In another version, Oedipus quarrels with Eteocles and Polyneices, his sons, because they had served him a meal on Laius's plate (which he thought to be a curse) and had also given him the second-best portion of meat. Creon cast him out for cursing his children. The curse held, and Eteocles and Polyneices eventually destroyed each other. Oedipus went to Colonus after being banished by Creon. Later Creon learned that wherever Oedipus was buried, that city would be safe from a conquering army and tried to bring him back. Theseus, however, protected Oedipus, and in gratitude, Oedipus blessed Attica, the land that had given him refuge. Theseus had Oedipus secretly buried to keep his body safe. One other story is that Oedipus was buried by the Thebans outside their city at Ceus. But a plague afflicted the city, and his bones were secretly moved to Eteonus, where they were buried in the Grove of Demeter. The people there complained about his burial and sought to move him once again, but after consulting the Delphic Oracle, they were told to leave him in peace as he was now a guest of Demeter.

14. Melampus, whose name means "black-footed," founded a great family of prophets. He was the son of Amythaon and Idomene of Thessaly and was brought up along with his brother Bias in Pylos. Once when he accompanied the king Polyphantes on a saunter into the countryside, a serpent bit one of the king's slaves and the king killed it. Melampus discovered the nest of the serpent with its young in an oak tree and secretly took them to raise after piously cremating the body of their parent. The young snakes rewarded him by licking his ears when he was asleep so that when he awoke, he knew the languages of the animals and birds. Later he helped found the cult of Apollo, and the god gave him the gift of prophecy. When Bias fell in love with Pero, Melampus volunteered to try and drive off the cattle of Iphiclus, the son of Phylacus (a condition imposed by Neleus for the hand of Pero) so Bias could marry her. However, a wild hound raised the alarm, and the herdsmen captured him and placed him in prison. One day, Melampus over-heard the woodworms in his cell say that they would finish devouring the main beam over his cell that night, and Melampus persuaded the jailer to move him to another cell. When the roof collapsed that night, Phylacus heard about the seer and had him brought to his chambers where he consulted him about the impotence of Iphiclus. Melampus offered to solve the problem in exchange for the cattle, and he sacrificed two bulls and invited the birds to feast upon them. The last bird to arrive was an old vulture who remembered that Phylacus had unthinkingly fright-ened his son one day after castrating rams, holding the bloody knife in his hand. When the boy screamed in fright, Phylacus buried the knife in a sacred oak tree and went to the boy, forgetting about the knife. Melampus led the king to the tree where the knife was found inside the bark that had grown over it. He took the knife from the tree and scraped some of the rust from the blade into a cup of wine each day for ten days, giving the wine to Iphiclus to drink. After ten days, Iphiclus was cured of his impotence and sired two sons, Podarces and Protesilaus. Melam-pus was given the cattle as a reward and drove them back to Pylos. He also healed the daughters of Proetus and other women from madness caused by their rejection of the rites of Dionysus, by driving the frenzied women into the Temple of Artemis at Arcadia. For a reward, Proetus gave him and his brother Bias (Pero had died by now) two of his daughters to wed. Melampus had three sons—Abas, Mantius, and Antiphates (the grandfather of Amphiaraus)—and became king of Argos. Bias and Pero had a son Talaus while Bias's second wife, Iphianassa, gave him Anaxibia who eventually married Pelias, king of Iolcus.

15. Leda was not only the mother of Castor and Polydeuces but also of Helen (the wife of Menelaus, the woman responsible for the Trojan War—"Was this the face that launched a thou-sand ships, And burnt the topless towers of Ilium?" Marlowe, *Doctor Faustus*—when she deserted her husband and eloped with Paris) and Clytemnestra (the wife of Menelaus's brother Agamemnon who went to whoring to find a man willing to kill her husband). According to some legends, Polydeuces was Helen's twin by Zeus and Castor their half brother, sired the same night by Tyndareus. Another story, however, has Helen being born from an egg as Zeus made love to her mother while in the form of a swan. See "Leda and the Swan" by William Butler Yeats.

16. This tale of constructing a route to the heavens is similar to the story of the Tower of Babel in Genesis 11:4–9. Some scholars think that Homer's account is older than the account in Gene-sis. These are the same scholars who liken the Flood of Gilgamesh to Noah's flood, which pre-dates that Genesis account by a number of years, suggesting that the book of Genesis was a compilation of existing legends of the time altered to serve the purpose of the authors.

17. The two Giants were called the Aloadae or "sons of Aloeus." Iphimedeia fell in love with Poseidon and sat by the seashore, allowing his waves to wash over her lap. She conceived Otus and Ephialtes, who grew so quickly that they were fifty-four feet tall by the time they were nine years old. Their first exploit was to capture the war god, Ares, and imprison him in a bronze jar when he killed Adonis after Aphrodite had given him into the protection of the boys. Ares stayed in the jar for thirteen months until the lads' stepmother, Eriboea, told Hermes where he could find Ares. By the time Hermes rescued him, Ares was near death. The boys then fell in

love with Artemis and Hera and decided to capture them for their concubines or wives (accounts are vague on this point, but chances are it was the former for the young boys were arrogant enough not to care for the conventions of the time) by piling various mountains on top of Mount Olympus until they could reach the heavens. Apollo and Artemis killed them either by shooting them with arrows or by Artemis sending a deer between them and each twin throwing a spear at it, which missed the deer and killed the other. Their deaths occurred in Naxos, but tradition has their bodies being moved to Anthedon in Boeotia and buried there. Sometimes they are connected with the cult of the Muses and the founding of the city of Ascra, where they were worshiped as gods. They were punished in Tartarus for their arrogance in trying to topple the gods by being bound with writhing snakes back to back against a great column and bitten constantly, the burning poison racing through their bodies both day and night.

18. Phaedra was the daughter of Minos and Pasiphaë and was given by her brother Deucalion to Theseus as a wife after Theseus's attempt to carry off Ariadne failed. Phaedra later fell in love with Hippolytus, Theseus's son by an earlier marriage to Hippolyta, the Amazon queen. When she tried to climb naked into his bed one night, Hippolytus drove her away. Miffed, she told Theseus that Hippolytus had tried to seduce her. She then hanged herself, and Hippolytus, cursed by Theseus, died soon after. She bore Theseus two sons, Demophon and Acamas.

19. Procris was the daughter of Erechtheus, the king of Athens. The story of her love for Cephalus is told by Ovid in *Metamorphoses,* which may be a composite version of two earlier stories. When Cephalus married Procris, he vowed eternal faithfulness. But one day when he left Procris's bed early to go hunting, his good looks attracted the attention of Eos, the Dawn goddess, who had him abducted, much against his will, for he did love Procris deeply. Some stories claim that Cephalus slept with Eos and was the father of Phaëthon and remained with her for eight years. When he returned to Procris, he became jealous and wondered if she had been true to him. With the help of Eos, he disguised himself as a stranger and tried to bribe Procris to be his mistress. Finally, after much persuasion, she reluctantly agreed to his proposal. He then revealed himself to her. Horrified by the trick, she fled and shunned the company of men, living in the mountains and becoming a follower of Artemis. Eventually Cephalus found her and begged her to return to him. She took great revenge upon him, however, but Ovid does not specify exactly what it was. Another story has Cephalus and Procris returning to each other, whereupon Procris gave Cephalus the magic spear Laelaps, a gift from Artemis. One day, Procris heard Cephalus calling for "Aura," and mistaking his call for a Nymph (the word means "breeze" and Cephalus was asking for a breeze to cool his overheated body), she crept forward, trying to catch her husband in adultery. Alarmed by the rustling of the bushes and thinking a wild animal was stalking him, Cephalus cast Laelaps into the bushes. The spear struck Procris, mortally wounding her. As she lay dying in his arms, she begged him not to marry Aura, and Cephalus, understanding everything at last, including the jealousy of Eos, told Procris the whole story. Cephalus was put on trial by the Athenian court and exiled. He went to Cephallenia, where he became its king and eventually married Clymene. Their son was Iphiclus.

20. Ariadne was the daughter of Minos of Crete. When Theseus went to Crete to kill the Minotaur, Ariadne fell in love with him and gave him a sword and a ball of thread with which he could find his way out of the Labyrinth in which he had to go to kill the monster. Theseus promised to marry her after killing the Minotaur, and they sailed away from Crete. On the way, Theseus stopped at the island of Dia (Naxos) and left Ariadne there. She was rescued by the god Dionysus, who married her. One island tradition has it that Theseus abandoned her while she was pregnant and that after her death in childbirth, Dionysus placed her wedding garland in the sky as the constellation Corona Borealis.

21. Eriphyle was the daughter of Talaus and Lysimache. When Polyneices was beginning his war against Thebes to recapture the throne, she was asked by her brother Adrastus, the king of Athens, to convince her husband Amphiaraus, a prophet, to go with them on the expedition.

Although Amphiaraus knew through his powers that if he joined with the forces of Adrastus he would die, he told his wife to make a choice: their happiness together or a long separation. Polyneices bribed Eriphyle with the necklace of his ancestress Harmonia, the wife of Cadmus, to tell her husband to join the expedition. Amphiaraus had forbidden his wife to accept any gifts from Polyneices and knew when she told him to go that she had disobeyed him. He made his children swear to avenge him, and he left. He was killed in the battle for Thebes. Alcmaeon avenged his father by leading a force to conquer Thebes. When he returned from the war, he killed Eriphyle. Her avenging Furies drove him mad, however, and he could have no rest until he had found a land that had not seen the sun at the time of his mother's death. He finally found such a place at the mouth of the River Achelous, and his madness was lifted.

22. Much has been related about the appearance of Agamemnon here and what it symbolizes. The story of Agamemnon's death reveals the depths to which a woman will go to seek revenge on those she feels have wronged her. Or does it portray a woman seeking greater and greater power? The debate continues.

The last words of Agamemnon, ὤμοι, πέπληγμαι καιρίαν πληγὴν ἔσω" (I am struck by a mortal blow within my own house), have been used as an epigraph by many, most notably T. S. Eliot in "Sweeney Among the Nightingales."

23. This is similar to the story of Eve and her betrayal of God in the Garden of Eden. The concept of betrayal of one's god here is important. In ancient Greece, the husband was seen as the lord or god of the household and all were servants to him. His own wife owed him the greatest allegiance, and to plot to bring about his downfall and then to carry it out is betrayal of the strongest sort. Thus, Agamemnon's pronouncement here concerning "all women" is similar to God's pronouncement upon Eve: ". . . I will greatly multiply thy sorrow and thy conception; in sorrow thou shalt bring forth children; and thy desire shall be to thy husband, and he shall rule over thee" (Genesis 3:16).

24. The reference is to the black widow spider who eats her husband after he impregnates her.

25. Orestes was still a youth when his father was killed by his mother and Aegisthus. To save his life, his sister Electra took him to Phocis, where King Strophius, an old friend of Agamemnon's, raised him with his own son, Pylades. (In Aeschylus's *Agamemnon,* however, Clytemnestra tells how Strophius sent for Orestes before the murder of Agamemnon to keep him safe during an uprising.) The two boys formed a lasting friendship and accompanied each other in the terrible affairs that were to come. Nine years after his father's death, Orestes goes to the Oracle at Delphi and asks what he should do about his father's murder. The Oracle tells him to kill Clytemnestra and her lover. With Pylades, Orestes makes a secret voyage to Mycenae, where he finds Electra (according to Euripides, Aegisthus had married her to a peasant in order to degrade her) and tells her what he has learned from the Delphic Oracle. Electra immediately agrees to help him, and he kills both Aegisthus and Clytemnestra. (See *The Libation Bearers* by Aeschylus, *Electra* by Sophocles, and *Electra* by Euripides.)

Homer, who knew the story, applauded Orestes and said that the youth did not suffer any evil consequence for his deed, since he was acting as an instrument of the Furies, who punish great sinners. Other stories say Orestes was first driven mad for slaying his mother (parricide must be punished, regardless of the reason for it) and later brought to trial before the Areopagus, a court of Athenian elders founded by the gods. At the trial, Orestes was represented by Apollo, and the Furies were the prosecutors. When the votes of the jury were counted, half had voted for acquittal but the other half found him guilty. Athene, who was the president of the court, broke the tie in favor of Orestes, stating that a father was more important than a mother and therefore revenge in the father's name took precedence over punishment for slaying one's mother. Orestes died from the bite of a viper when he was very old and was buried at Tegea in Arcadia. Years later, guided by the Delphic Oracle, a Spartan located Orestes's bones beneath a blacksmith's forge and moved them to Sparta. The transplanting of Orestes's bones brought luck to the Spartans and they never lost a war with Tegea. Several places had shrines built to commemorate Orestes's cure from madness. The shrine at Megalopolis was supposedly located on the site where Orestes, driven mad by the Furies, had bitten off one of his fingers and the Furies, sated by that self-sacrifice, made him sane again.

26. In the oldest tale regarding the invulnerability of Achilles, his mother, Thetis, was preparing him to be immortal by anointing him with ambrosia during the day and burying him in the embers of a fire at night. His father, Peleus, discovered her doing this. Angry at his interference, Thetis left her husband and her son, returning to the sea whence she came. Much better known is the tale in which Thetis dips Achilles in the River Styx while holding him by his heel. Achilles's real "heel," however, was his arrogance and pride. He is also petulant and cruel, though everyone admired his prowess as a warrior. Patroclus, on the other hand, was considered kindhearted and willing to do anything for a friend or ally.

27. Memnon was the son of Eos and Tithonus. His brother was Emathion, and both were black-skinned because of their mother's association with the Sun (Helios). Each day, they accompanied Helios's chariot across the sky and went to the hottest part of the world. Memnon became king of Ethiopia and Emathion king of Egypt. In the tenth year of the Trojan War, Memnon led his forces there to help his uncle Priam. Wearing armor made by Hephaestus, he killed Antilochus, the son of Nestor and Achilles's friend. Finally, Memnon and Achilles came face-to-face and fought hard against each other while their mothers pleaded with Zeus to save both. Memnon, however, fell, and Eos asked Zeus to show him special honor. Some myths claim that Zeus made him immortal, others that the smoke from Memnon's funeral pyre turned into two groups of birds that circled above his pyre, fighting each other until all were killed and they fell into the fire as an offering to the hero's spirit. Each year thereafter, the birds would appear and fall dead after fighting on the hero's tomb.

28. Neoptolemus's special prize was the widow of Hector, Andromache, and her brother Helenus.

29. Ajax (Aias), the son of Telamon (sometimes called Ajax the Greater), was second only to Achilles among the warriors in feats of strength. It was Ajax who rescued the bodies of Patroclus and Achilles when both were killed in battle, and on this basis he laid claim to the latter's armor. After Helenus, the Trojan captive, awarded it to Odysseus, Ajax went on a drinking binge. That night, in his drunkenness, he thought he saw Trojans creeping up on the Greek camp. He sounded the alarm and went out among them, slaughtering them left and right with his great sword, only to discover that he was slaughtering sheep instead. Ashamed at what he had done, he killed himself. Where his blood fell, the hyacinth sprang up with its petals marked in the shape of *AI*, the first two letters of his name and the Greek word meaning "alas!" Despite the refusal of Agamemnon and Menelaus to allow his body to be buried, Odysseus arranged for his funeral. In another legend, however, he is murdered by Odysseus so that Odysseus would be awarded Achilles's armor. Still another says that he was killed by Paris with an arrow, and another claims that he was buried alive by the Trojans who threw clay on him because Hercules had made him invulnerable by wrapping him in a lion skin when he was a baby.

30. Tityus was a Giant, the son of Gaia, who lived on the island of Euboea. One day, Hera teased him into trying to rape Leto while she was crossing the fields of Panopeus on her way to Delphi. Artemis (or maybe Apollo) shot him, and Zeus nailed him with a thunderbolt. He was taken to Tartarus where he was bound to the ground over a couple of acres, and a pair of vultures were sent daily to peck at his liver, which grew back again at night. The ancients considered the liver to be the seat of sexual desire.

31. Sisyphus was a cunning and crafty man who proved that Autolycus had stolen his cattle because he had secretly filed a series of grooves in their hooves. According to some legends, to get back at Autolycus, he seduced his daughter Anticlea so that he, instead of Laertes, was really the father of Odysseus. Sisyphus founded Ephyra and held the Isthmian Games in honor of

Melicertes whose body he had found and buried there. One day, he stumbled upon Zeus as he was carrying off Aegina, the river Nymph and daughter of Asopus and Metope. Zeus took her to the island of Oenome, where he raped her. Asopus, who was trying to find her, asked Sisyphus if he knew where Zeus had taken his daughter. Sisyphus promised to tell him in exchange for a spring of fresh water. This made Zeus furious, and he sent Thanatos (Death) to take Sisyphus to the House of Hades. Sisyphus, however, tricked Thanatos and bound him and threw him into a prison. The mortals ceased to die, and the gods sent Ares to release Thanatos after killing Sisyphus. Sisyphus, however, had left instructions with his wife Merope not to bury him or make any of the customary offerings. Hades became angry at the lack of the proper ceremonies and allowed Sisyphus to return to the mortal world in order to punish Merope and make her bury his body. Upon returning to Corinth, however, Sisyphus simply resumed his life. For thumbing his nose at death and the great god Hades, Zeus sent Sisyphus to Tartarus where he was to push a stone up a hill. If he could reach the top, he would be set free, but each time he neared the top, the stone slipped from his hands and rolled back to the plain, forcing Sisyphus to begin over and over again throughout eternity.

32. Odysseus is referring to Medusa ("queen") who was the daughter of Phorcys and Ceto. Her sisters were Stheno ("strength") and Euryale ("wide-jumping"). Their other sisters were the Graiae and Echidna. All were immortal with the exception of Medusa. Medusa was extremely beautiful and vain. She was also the lover of Poseidon, who once made love to her in a temple consecrated to Athene. When Athene complained about this, Medusa taunted the goddess, claiming that Poseidon obviously had found her far more beautiful than Athene, whereupon the goddess, in fury, made her beauty so extreme that it became ugly and repugnant to man. Snakes replaced her flowing black locks, and a single look from her eyes could turn men to stone. She was eventually killed by Perseus, who cut off her head. The blood that dripped from her head fell upon the ground and gave birth to Chrysaor and Pegasus. According to one legend, Asclepius, the god of healing, managed to get some of Medusa's blood, which he used on his patients. One vein produced blood that healed people and revived the dead, while another was extremely lethal. (See the myth by Apollodorus.) When Perseus, wearing Hermes's winged sandals, flew by Atlas, the Titan begged Perseus to allow him to look at the head. Perseus agreed, and Atlas turned to stone (the Atlas Mountains in northern Africa). Eventually Perseus gave Medusa's head to Athene, who placed it in the center of her breastplate (the aegis). Another legend has it that the goddess buried the head under a stone in the market of Athens and gave a lock of its hair to Tegea to protect it in war.

THE TWELFTH BOOK: THE GREAT PERILS OF THE SEA

1. This scene of Circe and Odysseus frolicking on the beach is paralleled in Odysseus's recollections of his time with Calypso. This famous and familiar image has appeared countless times since in such works as James Jones's *From Here to Eternity* and James Joyce's *Ulysses*. The suggestion is that the sea is a cleansing agent, washing away the sin and bestowing a blessing on what might otherwise be seen as adultery. The gods take a dim view of adultery despite their own notorious couplings and exchanges of partners. Yet there are times when such couplings are blessed by the gods, even if only in a temporal mode.

2. The Sirens were birdlike women similar to the Harpies. We do not know how many there were; accounts differ from two, to three, to four. If two Sirens are mentioned, their names are given as Himeropa ("soft-voiced") and Thelxiepeia ("beguiling speech"); if three, their names are Leucosia ("white"), Ligeia ("sharp" or "shrill"), and Parthenope ("maidenlike"); if four, Thelxiepeia, Aglaopheme ("beautiful speech"), Peisinoe ("persuasive"), and Molpe ("song"). They were the daughters of a Muse and Phorcys or Achelous, a river god. Their home was reportedly Anthemoessa, a flower-filled island near the straits where Scylla and Charybdis lived. The Sirens sang so sweetly that a sailor was enraptured by their songs and stayed to listen to them until he died. The ground around them was filled with white bones. Another legend

has their songs being different for each sailor, singing of that which each person most desired, and so ships were turned toward their island only to wreck against the rocks, the sailors drowning in the raging seas. According to prophecy, if a ship managed to sail past the island without turning in to land, the Sirens would jump into the sea and drown. Little credence is given to this, however, as there are two accounts of ships making their way safely past the Sirens: Orpheus drowned out their music with his in the *Argo* while Odysseus escaped after following the advice of Circe.

3. Amphitrite, the queen of the sea as Hera is queen of the heavens, was the daughter of Nereus and Doris (one of Oceanus's daughters) and became the desire of Poseidon after he saw her dancing naked on the island of Naxos. She fled to Atlas for protection, but Poseidon sent out searchers for her. The dolphins found her and pleaded Poseidon's love to her so successfully that she married him. Poseidon placed the Dolphin constellation in the sky in gratitude. Her many children include Triton, Rhode, and Benthesicyme.

4. Some scholars think the doves (πέλειαι τοήοωνεζ) represent the Pleiades, or Seven Stars. The twenty-third book of *The Iliad* describes Greeks using a dove (πθλειαν τοήοωυα) as a target during an archery contest as shooting at the Pleiades, and Athenaeus suggests their perpetual number is seven. But other sources say that the doves of Zeus numbered only six. According to a footnote to George Chapman's *Odyssey,* the *Chronicle Amphipolites* suggests that it is odd to identify the single dove allowed to pass through the Roving Rocks in the Argonaut story with the doves of Zeus because the latter always flew in a group. Academics disagree as to why Zeus continues to replenish the number instead of halting their destruction. Perhaps the act of replenishing represents reincarnation or the continuing of life in a chaotic universe constantly seeking order.

5. This may be a reference to St. Elmo's fire, a luminous charge of electricity that extends into the atmosphere from some high point at sea or on land. In *Moby-Dick,* Captain Ahab uses the phenomenon to unite the crew in a solemn bond to destroy the white whale. Cowboys also see small balls of electricity that bounce between the horns of cattle and cause a stampede. Consequently, such a fire has come to symbolize cataclysmic catastrophe.

6. The *Argo* was the famous ship that carried Jason and his band of heroes in their search for the Golden Fleece. The best account of this is in Apollonius Rhodius's *Argonautica,* although accounts appear in Pindar's work as well. Jason's father Aeson, the rightful king of Thessaly, had his throne usurped by his half-brother Pelias. Aeson sent Jason to the Centaur Chiron to be raised as he was afraid that Pelias would kill the child. Pelias was warned by prophecy that he would be killed by a descendant of Aeolus who would come to him wearing only one sandal. When Jason became a man, he went to Iolcus to claim his throne. When he arrived, Pelias was making a sacrifice to Poseidon, his father. Hera, who had a grudge against Pelias, tested Jason by disguising herself as an old woman and asking Jason to carry her across a river. Jason did so, losing a sandal in the act. When he arrived at Ioclus, he went to the marketplace to search for Pelias. Pelias discovered him sans sandal and told him he could have the throne if he gathered the Golden Fleece—the wool of the ram on which Phrixus escaped the murderous plotting of his stepmother Ino. When Phrixus arrived in Colchis, at the far end of the Black Sea, he had sacrificed the ram and hung the fleece in the Grove of Ares, where it was guarded by a huge serpent. Jason, with the help of Hera, put together a band of heroes that included Hercules and Orpheus, Zetes and Calais (the winged sons of Boreas), Peleus, Telamon, Castor and Polydeuces, Idas, Lynceus, Tiphys the helmsman, Argus (the shipbuilder), Admetus, Augeas, and Periclymenus. The ship sailed away with fifty-six men rowing while Orpheus sang a song to calm the sea and Tiphys steered. The ship was protected by Apollo and Athene. The Argonauts (as the heroes were called) had many adventures before gaining the Golden Fleece.

    a. Lemnos, where Aphrodite had caused the women to smell horrible. Their husbands had deserted them, and the women, in revenge, murdered them. When the Argonauts arrived, Aphrodite removed the horrible stench and the Argonauts stayed there a year, living with the women. Their offspring repeopled the island.

b. Arctonnesus (Bear Island) where the earth Giants Gegeneis, each with six arms, attacked the ship while the crew was visiting the Doliones. Hercules killed the Giants and left them piled on the beach.

c. A storm blew them back to the island, and this time they were attacked by the Doliones, who were beaten by the Argonauts. The Dolionite king Cyzicus was slain and his wife Clite hanged herself from grief.

d. At Bithynia, Hercules broke his oar and the ship put in so that he could carve a new one. While he was working on his oar, Hylas, the young man Hercules loved, went wandering across the island. He came to a well, and the Nymphs so loved his beauty that they pulled him into the well. When the Argonauts were ready to leave, Hylas couldn't be found and Hercules went to search for him. The Argonauts left Hercules there on the island and continued their voyage.

e. At Bebryces, King Amycus, who challenged all visitors to a boxing match and then killed them, dared the Argonauts to send their champion against him. Polydeuces took the challenge and crushed Amycus's skull with a blow behind the ear.

f. At Salmydessus, the capital of Thynia in Thrace, Phineus, who was a prophet in addition to being king, was besieged by the Harpies for having betrayed Zeus's secret plan for the human race. He had been blinded, and the Harpies constantly took his food from his table and covered him with their droppings. He received the Argonauts and read the future for them, then asked their help. Calais and Zetes drove the Harpies away.

g. The Wandering Rocks (Roving Rocks, Clashing Rocks) was the next challenge for the Argonauts. Euphemus, a son of Poseidon who could run across the sea without getting his feet wet, released a dove that flew between the two rocks. When the rocks came together, they caught just the tip of the dove's tail. As they were drawing apart, Jason sent the ship on ahead, sailing between them, barely making it when the rocks came together again, crushing only an oar. (*Homo supra humanam naturam erigitur, et in Deum transit. Plat.*)

h. At the Isle of Ares, they were met by a flock of birds who shot steel feathers at the crew. The Argonauts covered their heads with their shields and clashed their swords against the shields, frightening the birds away.

i. At Aea, Jason went to the royal palace. Medea, King Aeetes's second daughter and a witch, saw Jason there and fell in love with him. She helped Jason gather the Golden Fleece and left with him. Aeetes took a ship to try and catch them, but Medea killed her brother, Apsyrtus, and cut up his body into tiny pieces, dropping them over the side of the *Argo*. Aeetes had to halt his ship in order to collect the pieces of his son, and the *Argo* got away.

j. The ship put in at Aeaea, Circe's island. Circe was horrified to hear what Medea had done and sent them away. The *Argo* went southward, past Scylla and Charybdis, the Sirens, again through the Roving Rocks, until it reached Scheria, the island of the Phaeacians. There they found a fleet of ships waiting to take Medea back. Arete, the wife of Alcinous the king, had persuaded her husband to give up Medea only if the marriage to Jason had not been consummated. It hadn't, but Arete arranged for the consummation to take place that night in a cave, and Medea was kept from having to return to face her father's wrath.

k. At Libya, the ship came into a huge storm that carried it inland and dumped it in the desert. The crew was dying of thirst when three Nymphs dressed in goatskins told Jason how to save his crew. Peleus interpreted the oracle by identifying the mother of the Nymphs as the *Argo* herself. The heroes lifted the *Argo* up and carried it nine days to Lake Tritonis, near the garden of the Hesperides. There they discovered the spring created by Hercules and slaked their thirst. Unable to find a way out of the lake back into the sea, they offered a sacrifice to Triton, who pushed the *Argo* down the river to the sea. There Talos, the bronze man who guarded Crete, hurled rocks at the ship, trying to sink it. Medea put a spell on him that caused the nail that held the blood in his one vein to come out of his ankle, and he bled to death. The ship escaped again.

l. A deep darkness falls over the ship until Jason prays to Apollo who lights the way with a flaming arrow. By its light, they see the island Anaphe ("revelation") where they land and make a proper offering. Apollo brings back the light, and they sail on to Iolcus where Jason gives the fleece to Pelias. But he does not take the throne there and deserts Medea, who slays their children and escapes the guards on the back of a dragon.

The *Argo* finally ends up at Corinth, where it is beached. One day, Jason is sitting under the prow of the ship, remembering the past glories of his sailing, when the heavy timber falls away from the rotting hulk and kills him. The gods then raise the ship into the sky and make it a constellation.

7. Scylla was a sea monster who lived in the Straits of Messina. Homer's description of her reminds one of a lamprey eel in that she keeps half of her body inside her cave and lashes out to seize whatever prey comes near her. Her teeth are almost exactly like those of the lamprey as well. Scylla's parentage is highly disputed, although she appears to have descended from Phorcys and Cratais and, at one time, was exceptionally beautiful. She spent her days frolicking in the sea and rejected all lovers who tried to seduce her. One day, the sea god Glaucus chanced to see her and fell in love with her, but she repulsed all his advances. Finally he went to Circe for a love potion, but the witch-whore fell in love with Glaucus herself and turned Scylla into the six-headed monster with twelve feet. Around her waist was a belt of dogs' heads that bayed and cried for food. She was immortal, and the only way to beat her was with the help of her mother, Cratais. When Aeneas passes her way, he discovers she has been turned into a rock, but by whom is open to conjecture. Perhaps Perseus allowed her to see the Gorgon's head, for a legend about Perseus states that he fought a battle with certain "women from the sea." The changing of Scylla into stone might have been in that myth.

8. The fig tree is a symbol that appears throughout literature in various forms. We encounter it in Genesis when Adam and Eve sew fig leaves together to hide their nakedness, again when a hungry Jesus approaches a fig tree only to discover that it is not bearing fruit and curses it (suggesting the "man" who acts rashly), and parallels of that in Luke 13, Jeremiah 8, and Matthew 21. Figs are mentioned constantly as the basis of food in many texts, but there is a deeper meaning. As the fig tree with its fruit was a necessity for life and sustained life by giving its fruit to man, so does this fig tree save Odysseus's life. Odysseus, clinging to its branches when the wreckage of his ship is sucked away from him beneath Charybdis, receives the fruit of life as a gift from the tree whose roots are firmly embedded in the earth. Circe's warning here foreshadows the eventual need of Odysseus to cling to the earth for his salvation. There is no reason for that fig tree to be in the story other than for the hero to cling to in time of need. We note as well that Circe does not tell Odysseus that the fig tree is going to be extremely important to him but rather simply leaves that information to him to use as he desires during his adventure. We must remember that throughout *The Odyssey* the adventure itself demands the presence of mind of its hero. Consequently, although Circe might dangle bits of information in front of Odysseus, it is up to Odysseus to make the most of what she has given him. To fully understand the importance of this simple symbol, one must also consider the position of land in *The Odyssey*. In his essay "Valeurs religieuses et mythiques de la terre et du sacrifice dans l' *Odyssée*," Pierre Vidal-Naquet suggests that one needs to use Hesiod's *Theogony* and *Works and Days* in order to cast light upon Homer's obscure references. To Hesiod, man is a cultivator of the land. Therefore, Odysseus's roaming is a rejection of the land and, consequently, a rejection of the gods for which he must be taught the value of land as a gift from the gods to man. In short, only by coming to desire his homeland more than his nomadic existence does Odysseus reconcile himself to the gods. It is this association among agriculture, family life, and the origin of civilization implied by Hesiod that Odysseus is missing and must discover during his wanderings. Note that when Odysseus arrives at last upon Ithaca his first action is to "joyfully . . . kiss the fertile soil . . ." (XIII.354), which is not the act of a man merely returning to his native land but one who has finally come to realize the value of his homeland, the land itself. "The movement of the *Odyssey* is essentially inwards, homewards, towards normality," writes W. B. Stanford in *The Ulysses Theme* (1954). This means that Odysseus has finally accepted the human condition. This particular fig tree, therefore, despite its innocent appearance, is extremely important to the change in Odysseus.

9. Charybdis is a mythical whirlpool that allegedly existed at the north end of the Straits of Messina off the coast of Sicily. Charybdis is seen as a female monster (father: Poseidon; mother: Gaia) who sucked seawater in three times a day and spat it out. Any ship passing her way was destroyed.

10. Compare this terrifying image of Scylla with Dante's first sight of Lucifer (*Inferno*, XXXIV), chomping with relish on three sinners, one in each of his mouths:

> The Emperor of the dolorous realm stood
> From midbreast forth from the ice;
> And I am closer in size
> To a giant than giants to his arm.
> Note how great this whole must be
> When compared to each part of him
> Who is in the frozen sea.
> If once he was beautiful as he
> Is now ugly when he struck defiantly
> Against his Maker, then one is certain
> That all evil must stem from him.
> Oh! But what a marvel it seemed
> To me when I then deemed
> The three faces on his head!
> The one in front fiery red
> Joined by two above the middle
> Of his shoulder and crested together:
> The right between yellow and white
> While the other seeming to those
> From where the Nile descends.
> Under these issued forth mighty wings
> Larger than sea-sails. Plumeless
> They were, bearing bat-like texture,
> And three winds blew forth
> From his angry flapping that froze
> All of Cocytus while he wept
> Bloody tears from each of six eyes,
> That gushed down the three chins
> In bloody foam. He chomped with relish
> Upon a sinner in each mouth,
> Keeping each in torment.
> The one in front suffered nothing
> Compared to the stripping
> Of his skin in the back.

As the description in my translation here suggests, Scylla is similar to Lucifer. The monster's lower half is kept locked in her cave, just as Lucifer's lower half is locked in the frozen lake. The jaws of each flay men's skin from them, baring their souls.

According to the philosopher's discussion with Glaucon in Book X of Plato's *Republic,* the heart of the human soul is love of wisdom. And one of the reasons that Odysseus manages to reach home while his companions perish is that he has wisdom.

THE THIRTEENTH BOOK: ATHENE ADVISES ODYSSEUS

1. Apollo had the words "Know Thyself" chiseled deep into the granite span above the entrance to his temple. The adventures that Odysseus has just related have led the seafaring men in his audience to examine themselves and compare their experiences with his.

2. A tripod and cauldron appear to be rather odd gifts to give to Odysseus since gold ornaments and trinkets and such have already been awarded. But the tripod and cauldron had a more important symbolic value. They represented life and solidarity. The tripod represents the three stages of life—youth, manhood, age—anchored to the earth. The cauldron represents the heav-

ens. Together as a unit, meant for use in the home, they represented the fulfillment of life that is found in the family. Formal tripods and cauldrons were often placed in the center of the room where guests were received and entertained.

3. Pan was the god of the country and protected flocks from harm. He wandered through the forests and led the Nymphs in many dances. If you heard his pipes, there was no telling what might happen, but there would be an adventure, of that you could be certain. He was the son of Hermes and either Callisto or Penelope (not the wife of Odysseus but probably the daughter of Dryops) or a she-goat. According to legend, when his mother saw what she had produced, she left him in disgust, and he was raised by the Nymphs. He had the legs of a goat and little horns on his head. Hermes, however, was very proud of him and presented him to the gods on Olympus. As a rustic god, he was extremely lustful and constantly chased the Nymphs to seduce them. He invented the pipes on one of his amorous adventures while chasing the Nymph Syrinx. When she reached the River Ladon, the river was in full flood and she could not cross it. In desperation she asked the Nymphs to make her into a bed of reeds, which they did. Pan made the pipes from these reeds. He was also in love with Selene the moon goddess and lured her into the woods by offering her a beautiful garment made of white fleece. He was, however, not always a genial god and often went into fits of rage—especially if his sleep was disturbed. Our word *panic* comes from his name. One of the Homeric Hymns, given below in my translation, is dedicated to Pan:

> Muse, make a song of Hermes's son
> Who, with two goat feet and two horns
> Loves the sweet songs singing up and down
> The forest-filled valleys where he wanders wild
> With sensuous Nymphs who dance lightly
> Over the rocks, calling aloud, Pan! Pan!
> As they seek the pasture god, the master of hills,
> The dancer on dazzling mountain peaks
> And along winding paths and in forest glades,
> Making his way through thick bushy tangles
> And along the banks of sylvan rivers
> And steep cliffs haunted in sunlight to where
> Shepherds perch watching their flocks.
> Echo grumbles from the mountain glens
> At his words wafting among saffron stems
> And larkspur blossoms, softly saying, Pan! Pan!
> He drives wild animals from the slopes
> And in the evening cries out his loneliness
> As he moves away from the hunt and plays
> Low music on reed pipes, deep and sweet.
> No bird sings as lovely as the great god Pan.
> No bird's voice is as honey-sweet or tearful.
> When he plays, clear-toned mountain Nymphs
> Sing with him, lifting their voices like trickling water
> And dance dense dances daringly beside black fountains.
> Echo moans an answer from the high hilltops
> While the god stabs staccato hooves sinuously
> In answer while a blood-red lynx skin hangs
> Carelessly over one shoulder. There his heart dances
> To the music while his feet play among crocus and hyacinth
> And Nymphs fall to make careless love in the grass.
> Once a lustful Hermes found Dryops's daughter and he
> Brought a happy marriage to his home. There she bore
> Him the peculiar son, goat footed and twin horned,

Whose laugh tickled the fancy and frighted the nurse
Who left the dear infant, bony-faced and fine-bearded,
And Hermes took the baby in his own two hands,
Nestling him in the crook of his elbow, taking vast
Pleasure in the child's rattle noise, and wrapped
The babe in tightly folded rabbit skins as he laid
The babe before the feet of Zeus and the Immortals.
Proudly he showed off his young hero, and the deathless
Mood lifted from the halls of Olympus. Dionysus gave
A happy shout and cried out his name to all: Pan! Pan!
He shouted and the newly christened god lifted
His voice, singing and bringing pleasure, saying,
I shall honor you always with my song.

4. A syrinx was a panpipe made of graduated reeds fastened together with wax and cords.

5. The Naiads were Nymphs who were water goddesses of a very seductive nature and amorous disposition. Nymphs in general were usually associated with some form of nature and thought to be associated with free love. Hence our term *nymphomaniac,* which is a bit of misnomer since the word *nymph* suggests a free-loving female spirit. It was not meant to be a derogatory term, however, as it is currently used, but rather, among the Greeks, who considered lovemaking a natural act, a compliment to a beautiful woman.

6. It was Poseidon who gave bulls to man. A great sport was held in Crete where a youth would face a charging bull, grasp the horns, and vault over the bull's back.

7. In the harbor at Corfu there is the Rock of Odysseus, which looks like a ship at anchor. This is proof, the locals claim, that Corcyra, or Corfu, was Phaeacia in Homer's *Odyssey.*

8. The raven is a bird of ill fortune that appears in many mythologies. In Norse legend, Odin has a pair of ravens that speak to him and offer him advice as they perch on or near his shoulders. In Irish myth, Badb, the goddess of battle who is regarded as one of a triune—Badb, Macha (Nemain), and the Mórrígán—is married to Net, a shadowy god of war. She often appears on the battlefield disguised as a crow or raven. When the mortally wounded Cúchulainn ties himself to a standing stone so he can face his enemies on his feet with his last breath, no one dares to approach him until Badb, disguised as a raven, lands on his shoulder and plucks out an eye to tell them that the hero is indeed dead. The use of a raven here is a portent of what is about to happen to Penelope's suitors.

THE FOURTEENTH BOOK: THE VISIT TO THE SWINE-KEEPER

1. It is appropriate that the one person Odysseus can trust at this time is the swineherd or pigkeeper. Scholars have mixed feelings about this. Some hold that the swineherd would be a lowly individual, which indicates that Odysseus must begin rebuilding his place in Ithacan society "from the ground up." Others point out that to be entrusted with animals was a sign of respect because at this time a person's wealth was based on the number of animals he possessed. This can be seen in Hellenic times during the festivals of Lemmas and Dionysus, when playwrights competed with their yearly offerings for the grand prize, which was usually a goat. Drama of this type was referred to as "tragoida" or "goat-song" and became the basis for our word *tragedy,* which Aristotle in his *Poetics* refers to as "high drama," while comedy becomes "low drama" as it is coarse and fit for the common folk. According to Aristotle's definition of drama, only the nobility could suffer a tragedy as only the nobility had room to "fall." Apparently Aristotle thought the common people had already fallen and were, therefore, unable to have tragedy occur in their lives. Nevertheless, Eumaeus is the only person whom Odysseus can trust at this time, and that is because the swineherd has lived away from the corrupting influences of the

palace where the wooers are content to keep themselves. We also see this as the finding of truth in pastoral places while evil or "badness" lives in urban areas.

In Greek, the swineherd here is called *dion* "noble." Eumaeus, however, is not just any swineherd but is the son of a nobleman and has been made a slave, as we will discover later in *The Odyssey*. He is, however, a proud man who plays well the role that fate has thrust upon him. Like the energetic servant in Matthew 25:14–30, Eumaeus has worked hard to increase his master's lot.

2. These dogs were probably the Molossian breed from Epirus.

3. The misogyny being voiced by Eumaeus here is typical of the period. Greek men were highly suspicious of women and considered them a "beautiful evil both wild and untamed, essential to the continuation of the human race" (Hesiod, *Theogony*, 585). Women have a dual role—basically reproductive and pleasurable or serviceable—but are considered physically and mentally inferior to men. Even in the Spartan Constitution, women were required to go through the same rigorous training as men but more to strengthen their bodies for childbearing. The fear of their power of sexuality and seduction was such that men were taught that women had to be tamed, instructed, and watched carefully that they did not gain too much power and weaken man's position in the world. In classical Greece, a woman's name was not given in public unless she was dead or a prostitute. Some exceptions were made, but these were few. Although prostitution was subdivided into sacred and secular classes, Eumaeus is not referring to Helen here in either category but rather as a whore. Had Eumaeus intended something different, he would have used the term ἀποσίωσαμένη, indicating a woman who was practicing prostitution in service of the goddess Mylitta (the Greek transcription for the Assyrian goddess Mullissu) or Aphrodite as a religious obligation. Eumaeus blames not only Helen for taking away his master; his hatred has now extended to all women as well. In contradiction of these views, he also bewails the fact that he doesn't have a wife/woman to help him and to perform womanly duties for him. This self-contradiction shows the complex nature of Eumaeus's character.

We can see this illogical thinking reflected by Aristophanes in *Thesmophoriazusae* (v. 789) when he has the question raised in the parabasis, "If we are an evil, why do they marry us?"

4. The Greeks considered it boorish to drink wine that had not been diluted with water.

5. Odysseus is referring to Athene. We must remember, especially at this point, that Athene is watching over and protecting Odysseus. Athene, the goddess of wisdom, is often referred to as *glaukōpis* or "bright-eyed." The suggestion here is that she is capable not only of seeing things others cannot but understanding the meaning of what she sees as well.

6. Odysseus is making more than a simple comparison here. He refers also to the fact that Ithaca, deprived of her king, has fallen upon hard times. He also is prophesying his own later return since, technically, he cannot return in his god-given disguise. Odysseus the person is present; Odysseus the avenger and king is still absent.

7. "As long as the food and wine last" would by implication have been a strong oath in Homer's time. Swearing by food and wine would acknowledge the divine powers of Demeter and Dionysus—indeed a strong oath. This is difficult to understand, but that is the nature of trying to explain idioms or formulaic oaths. How would we, for example, explain "That's the way the cookie crumbles"?

8. Dodona was the site of the sacred oak grove where the ancient oracle of Zeus was located. Legend has it that Zeus communicated his wishes and desires to the oracle through the rustling leaves of the oak trees.

9. This point-of-view switiching by Homer seems awkward to modern sensibilities, but it is an old convention. It occurs in *The Odyssey* only with Eumaeus, while in *The Iliad* it occurs with five

different individuals: Patroclus, eight times; Menelaus, seven times; Phoebus, twice; Melanippus and Achilles, each once. In *The Odyssey,* Eumaeus is addressed fourteen times directly and once indirectly in the Greek edition. W. B. Stanford suggests that the relative frequency of the apostrophes in *The Iliad* might indicate that they were still a popular convention of storytelling at that time, but by the time *The Odyssey* was written, they had become a bit outdated, surviving only in the case of the swineherd. Stanford rejects the idea that this particular apostrophe is a mark of honor or of the poet's special affection for Eumaeus.

In Henry Hayman's three-volume commentary on *The Odyssey* (London, 1866–82), he suggests that this apostrophe might be "a vestige of a primitive balladsinger's phrase," a plausible explanation since a poet-singer was required to have his narrator apostrophize one or more figures in his work.

10. Mesaulius is an obscure person in the poem. Apparently he was simply a servant, but why a specific name would be attached to such a person is unknown. In other places in the poem some minor characters are identified. One speculation is that Homer might have been using one of his host's names as a point of honor in his narrative, but this is only a theory and is not given much academic credence.

11. Thoas was the son of Andraemon and Gorge. He led a contingent of forty ships to the Trojan War. One tradition has it that Odysseus discovered that Penelope had been unfaithful to him during his absence and sent her home to her father after he had massacred the suitors. He was driven out of Ithaca by Neoptolemus who was called upon to arbitrate between Odysseus and the families of the suitors that Odysseus had killed. Neoptolemus, however, had his eye on the land of Cephallenia that Odysseus owned and so ruled against him. Odysseus went to Aetolia where he married one of Thoas's daughters, and they had a son they named Leontophonus. This is a hotly debated issue, especially between the traditionalists and the revisionists.

THE FIFTEENTH BOOK: ADVICE TO TELEMACHUS

1. Diocles was the son of Ortilochus, the son of Alpheus. This is one of Homer's obscure references. One classical reference to Alpheus is that it is a river in Elis that flows past Olympia. Alpheus was a son of Oceanus and Tethys. The story connected with this river is that the Nymph Arethusa once bathed in the river, and Alpheus, noticing her nakedness, fell in love with her. He turned himself into a hunter and chased her as she fled across the sea to Sicily. There she took refuge on a small island, Ortygia, near Syracuse. Artemis, taking pity on her, changed her into a spring, but Alpheus still refused to be stopped. He ordered his waters to flow under the sea as far as Sicily where they merged with Arethusa's waters. Another story reveals that Alpheus fell in love with Artemis while she was bathing and chased her. Artemis ordered her Nymphs to cover their faces with mud as did she, and when Alpheus could not tell them apart, they drove him away with their mocking. The waters of Alpheus were also those waters that Hercules diverted to clean the stables of Augeas.

All of this appears to have little to do with *The Odyssey* unless Homer was using it as a metaphysical allusion whose purpose has escaped modern scholars. One could suggest a foreshadowing with the story of Alpheus's vain pursuit of Arethusa and the suitors' vain pursuit of Penelope, but this is so vague as to be almost worthless. One other possibility is that Homer intended to show that a close link between man and the gods was commonplace in these times or that to claim such a link was a common practice.

2. The background to this story can be found in the Eleventh Book. Melampus (see note 14, page 412) was the ancestor of the Melampodids, Greece's most renowned family of seers.

3. See note 21, page 413, on Amphiaraus. It was Eriphyle, bribed by Polyneices with the necklace and wedding dress of Harmonia, who convinced her husband, Amphiaraus, to go on the expedition of the Seven Against Thebes. Amphiaraus knew the expedition was doomed, but

went anyway, after telling his sons to avenge him on their mother and the Thebans. He horrified Athene by eating the brains of Melanippus when Athene, who was in love with Tydeus, was bringing ambrosia to make the dying Tydeus immortal. The story is that Melanippus and Tydeus fought a duel and Tydeus was fatally wounded. Amphiaraus placed the severed head of Melanippus into the hands of the dying Tydeus and ate Melanippus's brains. Athene was revolted and turned away, leaving Tydeus to die instead of granting him immortality.

4. This is the same sort of testing that Odysseus used when he told the story about the cloak in the Fourteenth Book. In the Greek, the same line that describes the type of testing forms the introduction to both speeches: κέκλυθι νῦν, Εὔμαιε, καὶ ἄλλοι πάντεζ ἑταιροι (XIV:462, XV:307). This suggests a formality of a testing pattern.

5. We do not know much about Odysseus's sister, Ctymene, other than what is recorded by Eumaeus here. This is one of the mysteries of Homer's *Odyssey*. We can only assume that she had a happy life after being married, as her husband, Eurylochus, allegedly paid a very handsome bride-price for her. Had the situation been otherwise, Eumaeus would have told Odysseus how unhappy his sister had become, even as he has been unhappy in the absence of Odysseus. The fact that he did not would suggest that Ctymene was happy in her life and home. That Eumaeus and Ctymene were raised as equals suggests as well that Eumaeus's life as a swineherd is not without honor and that he is not "low-born" or treated as such.

THE SIXTEENTH BOOK: THE DISCOVERY OF ODYSSEUS

1. Homer again apostrophizes Eumaeus, switching the point of view.

2. Amphinomus is the least offensive of all of the suitors for Penelope's hand. His father Nisus and grandfather Aretias are mysterious figures. Amphinomus is the friendliest suitor, but he stays too long among them and meets the same fate despite his generous heart.

THE SEVENTEENTH BOOK: TELEMACHUS VISITS WITH PENELOPE

1. Halitherses was the son of Mastor. He favored Odysseus and viewed the suitors with great contempt. He was quite skilled in prophecy and predicted Odysseus's return. After Odysseus killed the suitors, it was Halitherses who tried to prevent their kinsmen from attacking Odysseus in revenge. He is one of the few individuals who were staunchly faithful to the House of Odysseus and disdained all attempts by the suitors to win them over to their side.

2. Philomeleides was a champion wrestler and one of the minor kings of one of the islands in the Aegean Sea. He was known for his strength and cunning and for being a bit of a bully as well. The parallel being drawn here between Philomeleides and the suitors is a remarkable piece of foreshadowing.

3. Theoclymenus refers to the hawk that flew away to the right of Telemachus, holding a dove in its talons. The right side was considered highly favorable to the Greeks. The hawk is symbolic of Odysseus, and the dove symbolizes the unwary suitors. That the dove is in the talons of the hawk represents that the suitors will be coming to a grisly death very soon. This is emphasized by the feathers falling on the earth between Telemachus and the ship. The ship symbolizes the possibility of escape, but that the feathers fell to the earth indicates that not one of the suitors will escape the wrath of Odysseus.

4. These three were the founders of Ithaca. Since the springhouse is old and has been used to draw good, clean water and was built by the founders of Ithaca, then we can see that this was, indeed, a very special place. Clean water was valued by the Greeks and that this has remained so for so long has earned it a special place in Homer's recitation.

5. Swords and cauldrons were the traditional gifts that a respected guest could request and have granted to him by his host. Speaking like this to a stranger was the rankest insult and smacks of high arrogance, for Melanthius does not know if the stranger he addresses is really a beggar or a god disguised as a beggar to test the mortals. Melanthius (his name means "black") has sided with the suitors, much to his father's chagrin, for Dolius was one of Odysseus's faithful servants. Both Melanthius and his sister Melantho were highly insolent to Odysseus, and Melanthius suffered greatly at the hands of Eumaeus and Philoetius.

6. The megaron or "men's hall" was usually on the north side of the courtyard. Here is where meat would be grilled and feasting done.

7. This speech should be compared with the one that Odysseus gave earlier to Eumaeus when the swineherd asked him about himself. We can see how the wily Odysseus is a true master of masquerades by the way he can create different personae for himself as the situation warrants. We must remember that stories of this sort reflect the glory of the man himself. It may seem odd, however, that a beggar would react to Antinous so strongly and assertively. After all, isn't a beggar supposed to be humble and know his place in the scheme of things? The answer, however, lies in the warnings repeatedly given to Antinous that he needs to treat the stranger with respect, as all strangers, not just those who smell right or look right, are under the gods' protection. That Antinous ignores this is a mark of the man's own arrogance and self-confidence in that he obviously fears little from the gods. We are aware, of course, that Odysseus's very name is associated with the ambiguous practices of trickery and his descent from the well-known trickster Autolycus. For those who are interested in exploring this theme further, I recommend the article "*Kleos* and Its Ironies in the *Odyssey*" by Charles Segal in *L'Antiquité classique* 52:22–47.

8. There is a difficulty in trying to personify evil in the Greek world, as there was no devil in ancient religions. There were, however, dark and dangerous sides to all the gods, who had the ability to destroy life even though they could not give it. Athene and Hera are excellent examples here with their hatred of Troy. Apollo, the god of healing, often sends plagues to man. Artemis destroys the children of Niobe. Athene confuses Hector by pretending to side with him in his fight with Achilles, while Aphrodite, the goddess of love, cruelly destroys Hippolytus when he does not yield to her demands. We can see this paradox even extending to Zeus who "plans evil things."

9. We can see that Penelope is now beginning to search for ways to rid her house of the suitors. Earlier, although she expressed displeasure at them being there, she was still playing the part of the patient hostess. Now, however, she can see that her patience has only lent strength to the unruly mob that has become so strong that they can laugh at anyone who tells them to leave. Although she certainly wants to hear about the whereabouts of her husband, she also is willing to grant a personal audience to a beggar—practically unheard of.

THE EIGHTEENTH BOOK: THE RETURN OF ODYSSEUS

1. Iris was the female messenger of the gods in *The Iliad*. Here the suitors are making a play on the name and suggesting that there is something less than masculine about Arnaeus. His own name, Arnaeus, is either a play on his begging profession or a suggestion that he has a sheeplike nature.

2. On Cyprus, anyone who caught a pig damaging his crops was entitled to pull out its teeth.

3. Although this is a comical episode, we note that Odysseus must fight to maintain his place in his own house.

4. There is a bit of irony here in that Telemachus claims the backing of the two men who, more than any of the others, have been plotting his own death. This fight should not have been allowed by Telemachus—as his mother will sharply remind him. He had no right to expose the

stranger to possible harm. That is not the function of a host. We know, however, that Telemachus is in on the rather grim joke in that it is his father, not the beggar, who will emerge victorious here and give the lout a sound thrashing in the process. Still, we must be aware that Telemachus is not behaving as a worthy host in this scene.

5. Echetus, the king of Epirus, epitomized cruelty. He even blinded his own daughter and placed her in a dungeon to grind grain. What Antinous describes as a possibility for Irus is almost exactly what happens to Melanthius at the end of the Twenty-second Book.

6. The suitors unknowingly wish for their own destruction here, for to call upon Zeus to grant Odysseus his heart's wishes is to wish for their own death. This is emphasized when Odysseus "took grim cheer at their words."

7. This is a bit of carelessness on the part of Odysseus. He almost gives himself away here. No beggar could have known the lineage of Amphinomus or the reputation of his father Nisus. But he recovers nicely in midsentence and tries to warn the nobleman. This is, of course, a warning of words only, for Athene has already marked every suitor for death in the great hall. Still, it is a good gesture on the part of Odysseus and makes him seem less like a bloodthirsty avenger at the moment than he is to become.

8. This is a strange passage and a bit of a departure by Homer, for there is no reason for Penelope to break tradition and appear in the great hall unless she is curious about the stranger. We know that she is not descending solely to warn Telemachus about the company he keeps, as Athene is sending her down to fan the flames of desire among the suitors and to highlight her beauty in the eyes of her husband and son who will see her beauty in the reactions of the suitors when they see her. This sudden appearance, however, is not without parallel in other works. Esther appears suddenly among her enemies (Esther 5). Although Penelope laughs almost in embarrassment at her nurse's suggestion that she dress herself becomingly—almost as if she is eager to attract a husband, and perhaps she unconsciously is: her own—we wonder just what is it that Penelope might be embarrassed about.

A couple of other oddities exist here. One is the choice of handmaidens Penelope takes with her as she goes down to meet the men: Autonoe and Hippodameia. Why these names were chosen for these characters is a mystery, for they do not post favorably at all with Penelope.

One Autonoe was the wife of Aristaeus and the mother of Actaeon and Macris. She was one of the daughters of Cadmus of Thebes and Harmonia who refused to accept Zeus's choice of her sister Semele as the mother of his child. Dionysus punished her and her sisters by sending a bacchic frenzy upon them under which they murdered Pentheus, the son of Agave. After Artemis killed Actaeon, she went to live near Megara at a village called Ereneia.

One Hippodameia was the daughter of Oenomaus, the king of Pisa. An oracle warned him that his son-in-law would cause his death and he made a condition of Hippodameia's marriage that her suitor should carry her off in a chariot. Oenomaus dressed himself in full armor and attempted to kill the suitors along the road to the Isthmus of Corinth. After he had killed numerous suitors in this fashion, Pelops bribed Myrtilus, his charioteer, to replace the pin in his chariot with a dummy made of wax. When Oenomaus's chariot broke apart, he was either killed in the crash or stunned by the crash and killed by Pelops. Hippodameia bore Pelops several sons including Atreus, Thyestes, and Pittheus. She hated her husband's bastard Chrysippus and persuaded her sons to kill him. When Pelops heard about Hippodameia's part in the crime, she either hanged herself or fled to Midea, which Atreus and Thyestes were, by then, ruling.

The curiosity here is why, knowing this, did Homer give these two handmaidens these names?

9. Melantho is the sister of Melanthius. Both are children of Dolius. While Melantho is the mistress of Eurymachus, Melanthius enjoys his patronage. Even though Eurymachus spends many nights in her bed, Melantho is jealous of his pursuit of Penelope. This may be the reason that

Melantho does not support the queen, who had taken good care of her when she was a child. In addition, the response here to Odysseus is indicative of how far the women of his house have degenerated in his absence. Sleeping with the suitors and joining them in their debaucheries is tantamount to treason to the House of Odysseus.

10. The name Eurymachus could be translated as "bluster-battle."

THE NINETEENTH BOOK: THE DISCOVERY OF THE NURSE

1. This is a strange bit of advice for Odysseus to be giving as he has spent his entire life challenging the gods. We must remember that this is one of the reasons that Odysseus was forced to wander for so long: His pride gave him an arrogance that displeased the gods.

2. The Greek word *gyne* used here can be interpreted as either "wife" or "lady." This is Odysseus's way of avoiding lying to Penelope, although when she continues to press him he is forced to repeat his story. Some scholars ask why Odysseus doesn't make a clean breast of things now. Doesn't he trust Penelope? Others claim that this is a testing of Penelope and Odysseus's willingness once again to win her in contest with the other suitors. It is this latter, I think, that makes more sense: Odysseus has been away so long that he feels he must again win her as he did before. Obviously, of course, Odysseus is planning on ridding his house of the suitors, but we have to remember that he cannot simply come in and start slaughtering the suitors left and right. There are far too many of them for him to accomplish this by himself (Telemachus has yet to be tried in combat) and he is not yet certain who remains loyal to him. Additionally, he cannot violate the laws of hospitality until Zeus gives him permission to do so, and so far Zeus has withheld his hand from Odysseus. We have the assurances of Athene, of course, that Zeus will support this effort by Odysseus, but timing is everything and Odysseus has learned by now not to place demands on the gods.

3. Eileithyia is the goddess of childbirth and associated with Crete since a clay tablet found at Cnossus was discovered with her name on it. Sometimes the goddess is seen as a compilation of herself, Hera, and Artemis, but at any rate, we know from stories that she was controlled by Hera, who twice prevented her from allowing mortals to give childbirth. Once when Apollo and Artemis were being born she tried to prevent Leto from giving birth to them, but Eileithyia went to Leto after being bribed by other goddesses with a gold necklace. Hera prevented the birth of Hercules for a number of days by having Eileithyia sit outside Alcemene's room with her legs, arms, and fingers crossed.

4. It is interesting that Odysseus gives an abbreviated version of his wanderings, tactfully leaving out his associations with Circe and Calypso. Such an omission could suggest that Odysseus is still unsure how Penelope would react to the news that he had dallied with these goddesses while she waited for years in a lonely bed. This could also be seen as a weakness in Odysseus, in that he doesn't give Penelope credit for knowing that man is a frail thing in the hands of the gods. Perhaps Homer decided that he had related this story enough through the course of his epic poem that he didn't need to tell his audience again of Odysseus's travels and associations with the gods and goddesses. Still, it is a weak point in the poem and needs to be dealt with.

5. The home and hearth were sacred to the family-oriented Greeks. Such an oath is terrible to violate, so the truth of it was pretty well assured. Such was the strength and unity of the family that the harshest horror was the violation of it, such as the slaying of one's son and feeding his flesh to guests as Tantalus did with his son Pelops, serving him in a stew to a feast of the gods.

6. This amenity calls to mind the washing of Christ's feet by Magdalene and indicates that this must have been an ancient custom that lasted through centuries.

7. This test has been the subject of long debate among scholars. Some insist that this was not the true test of Odysseus, for the archer would have to lie on the ground to place the arrow through

the holes where the haft would fit. They insist that the arrow was shot through rings that were used to hang the axes as ornaments on the wall, but this seems highly unlikely. Others claim that the axes were planted on a beam and the beam set on a table. This seems to be correct, because when Odysseus makes his shot, he is seated on a stool.

THE TWENTIETH BOOK: ADVICE FROM A GODDESS

1. This "crushing" adjective is a deliberate play on Homer's words when juxtaposed with grinding and mill stones. Odysseus is the mill stone that will grind the suitors down to dust. The use must be deliberate, as a "crushing revenge" is an awkward phrase to be used in this context.

2. A two-handled cup was used by a host to show that he did not plan mischief by drinking with one hand and stabbing with the other.

3. This festival in the Apollo grove likely was one of the *apellai* or annual gatherings of the region that celebrated the youths' coming of age. This also could have occurred at the Daphnephoria or the celebration of the purifying bay, which was brought by Apollo to Delphi. This is a distinct possibility and would fit in neatly with Telemachus's coming of age as well.

THE TWENTY-FIRST BOOK: THE TEST OF THE BOW

1. Iphitus, the son of Eurytus, the king of Oechalia (Thessaly?), was eventually slain by Hercules during the siege of madness that Hera placed upon him. Hercules had claimed Iole in an archery contest and was accused of stealing some of Eurytus's mares. Iphitus took Hercules's part against his father and went on a search for the mares. He met Odysseus in Messenia and they became fast friends. When they parted, he gave Odysseus his father's bow. Eurytus had withheld Iole from Hercules, as he had killed Eurytus's other children by Megara. Eurytus was famous for his skill with the bow and was eventually killed after he challenged Apollo to a match. His great bow he had inherited from his father. In another version, Iphitus went to Hercules to seek his help in recovering the mares that had been chosen, and he was killed by Hercules in his madness. Hercules then returned the body to Eurytus and killed Eurytus and took Iole back home with him. Eurytus's wife sent him a cloak dipped in the Centaur's blood, which eventually brought about his death.

2. This was obviously meant to be a great friendship, as the two have, figuratively, exchanged arms. This was one of the greatest marks of friendship that could be given between two men at this time.

3. As pointed out in note 7, page 428, the setting of the axheads in this manner makes no sense, since it would have been impossible to sight an arrow through the heads. More than likely they were placed on a beam and the beam on a table. That Telemachus and the others cannot string the bow is not surprising, as they did not know the trick: plant the recurve around the calf of the leg, the bell around the thigh, and, using the leg for leverage, pull the tip forward to slide the string across the nocks. That none of the suitors could figure this out shows their ignorance as well.

4. Leodes was a prophet who could read the signs in the smoke rising toward the sky from offerings to the gods.

5. Odysseus wants the door locked not only to keep all of the suitors in while he slaughters them but also to keep reinforcements out if someone happens to hear the great commotion and screaming coming from the hall. Wisely, Odysseus is isolating the suitors from the outside world.

6. Eurytion was a Centaur who began a riot at the feast celebrating the wedding of Peirithous and Hippodamia. He tried to rape Mnesimache, the daughter of King Dexamenus of Olenus, and was slain by Hercules, who was also a member of the wedding feast.

7. The early lyres or harps did not use pegs but instead had leather straps that were twisted to tune the strings.

THE TWENTY-SECOND BOOK: THE BLOODY HALL

1. It seems strange that after all the trouble and misery Antinous brought to the House of Odysseus he would be treated in such a manner as this, but it appears that Homer felt a certain compassion for Antinous's death.

2. At this point Odysseus is still unsure how many people in Ithaca will support him. It is necessary, therefore, that he kill all of the suitors so none can escape into the town and bring back others to help them kill Odysseus and those who are willing to help him.

3. This is a strange description that seems out of place here. Most of the palaces or great houses of the time had similar designs, and such a passageway does not seem to exist in the ruins that archaeologists have examined. This suggests that Homer is taking poetic license with the description of the palace.

THE TWENTY-THIRD BOOK: THE SECRET OF THE BED

1. Claudio Monteverdi's opera, *Il Ritorno d'Ulisse in Patria* (1640), which dramatizes Odysseus's journey from Phaeacia back to Ithaca, ends at this point, with Penelope and Odysseus reunited. Many scholars claim this is the true end of Homer's *Odyssey* and that the remainder was added by later poets. Others disagree, saying that many major themes of *The Odyssey* are satisfactorily brought to a conclusion in what remains and that the writing is typical of Homer.

THE TWENTY-FOURTH BOOK: THE END OF THE ADVENTURE

1. A later epic poem, the *Cypia,* informs us that Odysseus, loathe to leave his wife and newborn son, pretended to be mad in order to remain at home while others of the Greek expedition sailed for Troy. When Palamedes came to get Odysseus, Odysseus had an ox and an ass harnessed to a plow and sowed salt in the furrows. Palamedes suspected Odysseus of trickery and placed Telemachus, then a babe, in the path of the plow. When Odysseus turned the plow aside rather than plow through his son, his plot was exposed. Joyce remarked that once Odysseus was at war, however, he became a *jusqu' auboutist.*

2. The words Odysseus uses here are puns. *Alybas* = a passage for rovers; *Apheidas* = stalwart man; *Polypemon* = all sorrowful; *Eperitus* = one who argues (actually a takeoff on his own name); *Sicania* = perhaps Sicily.

3. This memory is forty-five years old and shows that Laertes had always carefully tended the farm where Odysseus has found him now.

4. Cephallenia is the largest of the western Greek islands and is located between Leucas and Zacynthus west of the entrance to the Corinthian Gulf. It was apparently inhabited as early as the neolithic period, and even today has many Mycenaean tombs that have been preserved. Tradition holds that it avoided the destructions of the Bronze Age and apparently was the most important part of Odysseus's realm, according to the discovery of a large tholos near Poros. In historical times it was a tetrapolis that contained Samos, Pale, Crane, and Proni (near modern Sami, Lixouri, Argostoli, and Poros).

5. This is a strange welcome, coming from Dolius, for Odysseus killed his son the goatherd and arranged for the death of his daughter as one who had betrayed Penelope. Of course, Odysseus is clever not to come straight out and tell Dolius that he has killed his son and daughter, but rea-

son tells us that Dolius knew well how wicked his other two children were. This increases the pathos of the two men meeting.

6. Elis was a Greek state in the northwest Peloponnese where Olympia is situated. (It is not to be confused with Olympus, the highest mountain in Greece overlooking the Vale of Tempe. Olympus is where the twelve gods had their houses built by Hephaestus.) Olympia was the main sanctuary of Zeus on the north bank of the Alpheus River. This is where the festival of Zeus was held in ancient times, including the Olympian (Olympic) games. The territory was in dispute by Elis and Pisa, and after Elis eventually absorbed Pisa, the word *Pisa* was sometimes used in poetry to denote Olympia. This was a holy site, and the Greeks believed that before Zeus took control of the heavens, the area was controlled by Gaia, Cronus, and Eileithyia. The burial mound of Pelops is supposed to be located here. Since this place was sacred to Zeus, one could supposedly receive sanctuary here.

The assembly here mirrors the assembly that Telemachus calls at the beginning of *The Odyssey,* thus bringing the story full circle.

The fact that Eupeithes stands to speak in the assembly is indicative of the way his son spoke in the various assemblies in the suitors' meetings. Here we can see a good example of the man's cowardice as he pictures Odysseus fleeing from Ithacan justice. He continually incites the Ithacans to a sense of revenge against Odysseus instead of seeking it himself as he should have under the concept of the blood feud.

7. After Odysseus returns home, Telemachus is banished when an oracle foretells that Telemachus will kill his father. In one account, after Odysseus is killed by Circe's son Telegonus, Telemachus returns to Ithaca where he buries Odysseus. He eventually marries Circe, and the witch makes him immortal and gives him a son, Latinus. In another account, Telemachus marries Nestor's daughter Polycaste, who bathed him at Pylos; in a third account, he marries Nausicaa, the daughter of Alcinous, king of the Phaeacians, who helped Odysseus on his final journey home.

TRANSLATOR'S NOTE

1. A winnowing shovel, or fan, as it is sometimes called, is used to separate the chaff from the grain either by tossing the grain into the air and allowing the wind to separate the grain from the chaff and dirt, or by fanning a thin layer to bring the grain topmost. Odysseus had to do penance by traveling many miles from the sea until he met someone who did not recognize that what he carried was an oar. Thus, the god of the sea came to be worshiped in a strange and new land, expanding his influence.

2. This secret burial rite appears in quite a few legends. We do not know where Arthur was finally laid to rest (that is, we do not know where Avalon was) or where Arturis, the Welsh general who appears to have been the prototype for Arthur, was secretly interred by his knights after his death in battle. Likewise, we do not know where the great Irish hero Cúchulainn, Roland, John the Baptist, or even Peter was buried. The burial of Odysseus could be the archetype for these later stories.

3. In April 1810 Byron had been sailing at the invitation of Captain Walter Bathurst, aboard the frigate *Salsette* (bound for Constantinople from Smyrna). On the fourteenth they anchored off Cape Janissary, or Sigium, which is only a few nautical miles from the Hellespont. Detained for two weeks by uncommon winds and needing a pilot to guide them through the strait, they had ample time to explore "the ringing plains of Troy." In his diary, Byron recorded: "I have stood upon that plain *daily* . . . and if any thing diminished my pleasure it was that the blackguard Bryant had impugned its veracity. . . . But I still venerated the grand original as the truth of *history* (in the material *facts*) and of *place.* Otherwise, it would have given me no delight." Byron was referring to Jacob Bryant, who insisted vehemently that not only did the Trojan War not take place but also that Troy itself had never existed. Bryant's argument, however, was based not

on facts but on carping criticism of Homer's incorrect details of ships and the environment. This was an extreme case of what we today would call being anal retentive.

While the *Salsette* was anchored near Troy, Byron emulated Leander and swam the Hellespont, which although only four miles wide, has extremely cold water and a strong current. It was not the most difficult of Byron's swimming feats; he also swam the Tagus at Lisbon. The romance of this swim, however, made it far more important than any other.